European Politics
in Transition

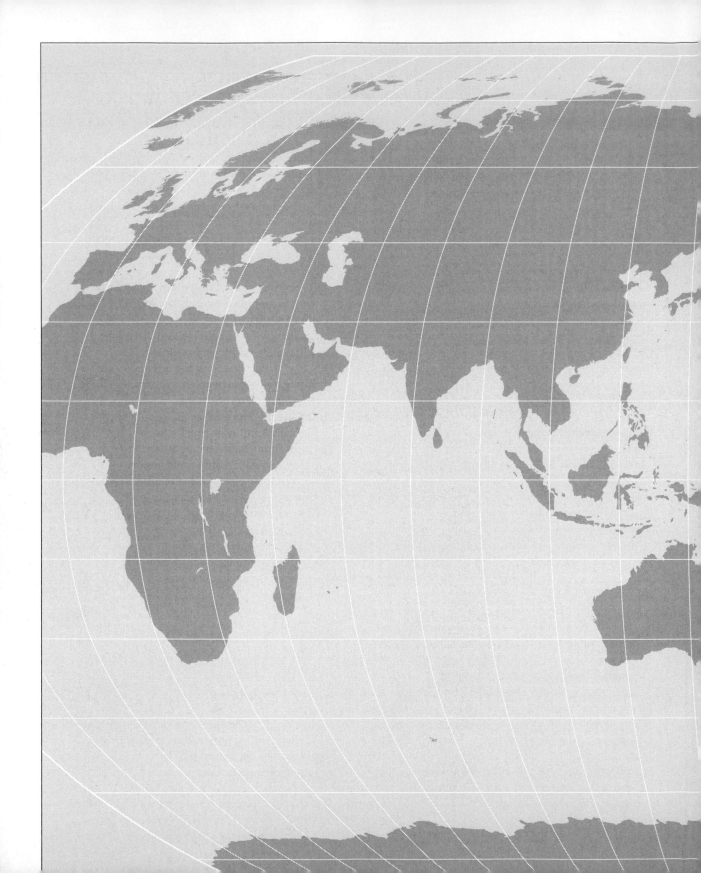

European Politics in Transition

Sixth Edition

Mark Kesselman
Columbia University

Joel Krieger
Wellesley College

Christopher S. Allen
University of Georgia

Joan DeBardeleben
Carleton University

Stephen Hellman
York University

David Ost
Hobart and William Smith Colleges

George Ross
Brandeis University

Houghton Mifflin Company
Boston   New York

MK–for Rasil and Romen Basu
JK–for Lyn and Patrick Dougherty

Publisher: Suzanne Jeans
Senior Sponsoring Editor: Traci Mueller
Marketing Manager: Edwin Hill
Discipline Product Manager: Lynn Baldridge
Senior Development Editor: Jeffrey Greene
Associate Project Editor: Susan Miscio
Senior Media Producer: Lisa Ciccolo
Senior Content Manager: Janet Edmonds
Art and Design Manager: Jill Haber
Cover Design Director: Tony Saizon
Senior Photo Editor: Jennifer Meyer Dare
Senior Composition Buyer: Chuck Dutton
New Title Project Manager: Susan Peltier
Editorial Assistant: Evangeline Bermas
Marketing Assistant: Samantha Abrams

Cover photo: © Getty Images Taxi/Benelux Press

Printed in the U.S.A.
Library of Congress Control Number: 2007932848

ISBN-13: 978-0-618-87078-3
ISBN-10: 0-618-87078-4

3456789-VHO-11 10 09 08

BRIEF CONTENTS

CONTENTS

Whenever we plan a new edition of *European Politics in Transition*, we consider whether to retitle the book to better reflect the current state of European politics. However, as the Conclusion to this edition makes clear, never since the book was first published in 1987 has "transition" been a more timely and appropriate way to characterize the study of European politics.

From the founding of the European Economic Community (EEC) in 1958 by six prosperous West European countries to a mélange of twenty-seven diverse polities tilting east and heading south today, Europe has been transformed. And the end is still not in sight, as illustrated by the persistent debates over the content of a treaty modifying and "constitutionalizing" European Union (EU) governance; the thorny issue of Turkey's application for membership in the EU; and sharp domestic debates over economic reforms, the integration of immigrants, and how to take advantage of the opportunities offered by the global economy without taking heavy political losses at home. As we noted in the preface to the last edition of *European Politics in Transition*—and the point remains as pertinent as ever—Europe remains a moving target. The institutional, cultural, constitutional, and geographical dimensions of the continent—and the Union—remain in flux, and dramatically so. Who knows what other changes instructors and students of European politics will have to absorb in the coming months and years?

This context of fast-paced and in some cases historic change has inspired the work of all the contributors to the sixth edition of *European Politics in Transition*. Like any text in comparative politics, *European Politics in Transition* looks to bring politics alive for students and provide the wherewithal for instructors to come to terms with the protean patterns of continuity as well as change in the institutions and processes of government within—and across—the countries that make up our case studies.

New to This Edition

This edition of *European Politics in Transition* reflects several significant developments:

- We analyze more fully the consequences of globalization.
- We analyze in detail the tortured progress of constitution-making in the EU, including the French and Dutch no votes in the 2005 referendums, the subsequent two-year stalemate in strengthening the EU, and the attempt to rebuild momentum to reform EU governance in 2007.
- We analyze the implications of the substantial enlargement of the EU from the perspective of the fifteen members of the EU in the West as well as from the perspective of the newer members to the East.
- We highlight even more than in past editions the centrality of the EU for the domestic politics of our country studies. The country treatments include a subsection on the EU, thus providing clear comparative analysis of the interplay of domestic and European politics and policies. We identify the EU as the last historical juncture in the first chapter of each country section; in the second chapter, we provide a subsection on European integration; the third chapter emphasizes the European dimensions of governance and policymaking; and the fifth chapter includes the challenges of European integration.
- The section on the EU is the penultimate section (Part 8) of the book and follows the country studies. The reason is certainly not that the EU has become less important in European politics. However, the major focus of *European Politics in Transition* is on the domestic politics of European countries. The present structure of the book more accurately conveys its central message: that understanding European politics requires in-depth study of the domestic politics of individual European states.

- We consider the continuing repercussions of September 11—as well as the war in Iraq and its aftermath—on European countries' relations with the United States.
- We highlight issues involving immigration and the challenges posed by growing ethnic and religious diversity.
- In response to requests from colleagues, we have added a country section on Russia to this edition, written by Joan DeBardeleben. We agree with instructors who assign *European Politics in Transition* that studying Russian politics is essential to gaining an adequate and up-to-date understanding of European politics.
- We include a Conclusion for this edition. The Conclusion analyzes key elements of the transition occurring in European politics. It identifies three key issues at the core of the transition: the scope and meaning of European identity, the adoption in most European countries of variants of Third Way economic policy, and persistent questions about the extent and meaning of democracy in Europe. The Conclusion is intended to make it easier for students to engage in comparative analysis and to provide clear and important lessons they can take away from their initial study of European politics—and consider further as new developments in Europe capture their interest.
- In response to colleagues' recommendations, we have significantly shortened the length of country sections. Moreover, despite the addition of Russia and the Conclusion, overall this edition is shorter than earlier editions. We achieved this sleight of hand by trimming considerable detail from country analyses. We believe the result does not detract from accomplishing—indeed, it may facilitate the achievement of—the double-edged goal of *European Politics in Transition*: to help students grasp the broad political features shared by most European countries as well as the importance of each country's specific historical, socio-economic, and institutional trajectory.

Themes and Organization

Despite the many changes we have enumerated, when it comes to the organization and design of the text, there is far more continuity than change. As in recent editions of *European Politics in Transition*, we organize our treatment within the same framework for analyzing continuity and change that is used in *Introduction to Comparative Politics* (Houghton Mifflin, fourth edition, 2007), an introductory comparative text that we co-edit with William Joseph. A distinctive feature of both books is our application of four comparative themes to frame the analysis and presentation of each country study. We explain the themes in the Introduction, which provides a general framework for the rest of the text. The Introduction also presents an intriguing puzzle for each theme to stimulate student reactions and encourage students to extract a variety of "solutions" as they work through the country studies. These themes focus attention on the continuities and contrasts described in the text:

- **A World of States** highlights the importance of state formation and the changing dynamics of interstate relations, transnational processes, and globalization for understanding domestic political developments.
- **Governing the Economy** analyzes state strategies for promoting economic competitiveness and stresses the effects of globalization on domestic policies and political outcomes.
- **The Democratic Idea** examines the challenges posed by citizens' demands for greater control and participation in governance and highlights the gaps everywhere between theory and practice.
- **The Politics of Collective Identities** considers the political consequences of race, ethnicity, gender, religion, and nationality, the problems of social exclusion, and the challenges of governance.

Instructors who have previously used *European Politics in Transition* will find that this edition both reflects the approach we have developed in earlier editions and involves a root-and-branch updating and refinement of our coverage to reflect the epochal developments and new scholarship of the past few years. As always, the contributors and editors have done everything we can to provide timely, engaging, and authoritative analysis of European politics and EU developments as they unfold, and to locate these developments within firm institutional and historical contexts.

Website

A new feature accompanying this edition is a website. For instructors, all the maps and figures in the text are available in PowerPoint format for easy presentation in class. For students, there are ACE questions for practice tests and web links for additional information.

Acknowledgments

We have been fortunate to receive excellent advice from many colleagues, including:

Peggy Hahn, University of Michigan – Flint
Kerstin Hamann, University of Central Florida
Paulette Kurzer, University of Arizona
Jonathan Laurence, Boston College
Boyka Stefanova, The University of Texas at San Antonio

We are grateful to the superb staff at Houghton Mifflin Company, including Traci Mueller, Jeff Greene, and Susan Miscio, as well as to Leslie Kauffman of Litten Editing and Publishing Services, Inc., and Alison Fields of Books By Design.

M. K.
J. K.

European Politics
in Transition

PART 1

Introduction

Mark Kesselman
Joel Krieger

"It was the best of times; it was the worst of times." We borrow the famous opening line of Charles Dickens's *A Tale of Two Cities,* set in London and Paris during the French Revolution in the late eighteenth century, to describe the tumultuous character of the current transition in European politics. As it was when Dickens wrote, Europe is apparently at the close of one era and the beginning of another.

Let's begin with the positive. Europe has been among the wealthiest regions in the world for centuries and is home to more than its fair share of great powers: France, Britain, and Russia are three of only five permanent veto-wielding members of the United Nations Security Council and are joined by Germany, Italy, and the European Union representative in comprising six out of eight members of the inner circle of great power politics referred to as the Group of 8 (or G8). European states provide their citizens with extensive assistance to counteract life's hazards, including nearly free medical care, extensive unemployment insurance, decent (and in some cases generous) pensions, paid maternity (and in some cases paternity) leave, low-cost university education for those who pass stiff high school graduation exams, and on and on.

During the glory years following World War II, Europe seemed to have it all. It had found the secret of combining both economic growth and efficiency along with social equity (provided by the extensive social provisions just described). Moreover, European countries had developed a unique international organization to advance regional cooperation and cohesion. First known as the European Economic Community, it was established in 1957, not long after World War II, in reaction to the horrific violence and destruction of that war (the second world war in less than three decades). Its aim was to promote economic cooperation and peace among its members as a way to prevent another cycle of interstate violence on the European continent. Its success in fostering cooperation has been so complete that it would be nearly impossible to imagine a war between EU member states.

The EU initially included only six member states of continental Western Europe who joined together on a quite narrow basis: EU member states agreed to reduce tariffs on imports of raw materials, notably coal and iron, from other EU member states. From 1957

until 1995, the organization grew from six to fifteen members; it changed its name in 1994 to the European Union. The difference in designation reflected the fact that the EU has substantially broadened and deepened the scope of its activities to the extent that the cooperation among member states was so extensive that it amounted to "pooled sovereignty" in which EU institutions trumped national governments in an increasing range of policy areas. And it continued to grow. By 2007 the EU included twenty-seven countries, with more on the waiting list and eager to join. Among the international organizations in the world today, such as the United Nations, the International Monetary Fund, and the World Trade Organization, the EU ranks as the one with the broadest regulatory scope and most extensive powers over the citizens, organizations, and member states.

Despite the problems that challenge European countries as well as the EU, from the outside the grass looks very green. Policymakers in Africa, Latin America, and Asia look with considerable admiration (if not envy) at Europe's geopolitical power, stability, democracy, and economic competitiveness—and the institutional capacity of the EU to advance Europe as a powerful and highly cohesive regional bloc. Regional trade associations in other parts of the world are a pale shadow of the EU.

In addition, after a decade or more of economic doldrums—slow growth, high inflation, and high unemployment—the core European economies are on the upswing. Newspapers are full of exuberant reports about a "perfect economic recovery" in the euro zone[1] (the geographic and economic region that consists of the thirteen EU member states that use the euro as their currency). Similarly, in the fall of 2007, despite some concern about increasing inflation, most observers emphasized a new economic miracle in Europe led by a resurgent Germany.[2] In Europe it was the best of times—or was it?

As usual, there was another side to the story—one that painted a more somber picture of developments in the countries of Europe and in the EU, itself. If it can be said that countries and entire regions, like people, have moods, then we can say that the member countries of the EU are grumpy. On the occasion of the fiftieth anniversary of the signing of the Treaty of Rome in March 2007 the British news weekly, the

Economist, captured the mood when it labeled its commentary on this historic milestone, "Europe's mid-life crisis."[3]

Despite the recent economic upswing, concerns remain about sluggish growth and high unemployment. In addition, Europeans feel an economic and political malaise. They are uncertain about the role of Europe in a world that is still dominated by the United States, with India and China the rising stars on the horizon. They are intent on making the most of global economic competition, but reluctant to swallow the bitter medicine that may be required. They face pressure to roll back welfare state provisions for pensions, housing, education, health care, and unemployment that benefit the vast majority of Europeans in one way or another and are far more generous than in the United States—but whose hefty cost contributes to budget deficits. As European countries struggle to revitalize their economies, they probably cannot avoid making painful changes in labor markets that enable companies and managers to lay off workers, and create more part-time and short-term employment with lower pay and fewer benefits.

It is hard enough for the leaders of national governments to push such unpopular changes through legislatures and get their citizens to accept them without getting thrown out of office. But politics is even tougher in Europe, because it is played out at both the national and the EU level. Hence, politics is a two-level game. The term *multilevel governance* (MLG) has come into widespread use to describe this phenomenon of overlapping jurisdiction and pooled sovereignty between the member states of the EU and the EU itself. The EU has been a great success—but Europeans are more preoccupied with—and grumpy about—what seems like an endless series of stalemates over institutional reform of the EU. They are uneasy about the very rapid and unsettling enlargement of the EU to include more and more countries with no clear end point in sight. They mistrust the EU for its distant bureaucracy and endless red tape, and relatively few Europeans give it passing marks for openness or democracy or decision making. They blame the EU for forcing painful political choices, such as cuts in social programs mentioned above.

Moreover, the EU's fiftieth anniversary occurred in a Europe that had been fundamentally altered by 9/11/01, as well as terrorist attacks within Europe itself. On 3/11/04, terrorists bombed rail lines in Madrid, Spain, during the morning rush hour, killing nearly two hundred commuters. On 7/7/05, British Muslims set off bombs in the British transport system that killed fifty-two commuters. These attacks, along with more generalized anti-immigrant sentiments, have fed xenophobia directed at Muslims, another troubling fact of life in Europe. And, to contribute even further to the somber atmosphere surrounding the EU's fiftieth anniversary, it occurred just when there was a revival of tensions between Russia and the United States, following many years of relative harmony between the two countries after the crumbling of the Soviet Union. Indeed, Europe was an unwilling participant in what has been described as tendencies toward a new cold war. These developments help explain why the fiftieth anniversary of the EU did not produce spontaneous celebrations but rather a sense of collective disillusionment.

Once this celebration that wasn't had passed, big questions were left on the table. Does Europe comprise, as it has for centuries, discrete sovereign states, animated by national identities and interests? Or have the processes of European integration that were inaugurated more than a half-century ago produced a European Union that is a genuinely transnational polity? Each proposition captures important truths about contemporary Europe. Considered side by side, they identify the current transition in European politics, which is marked by the challenges of overlapping jurisdictions, multilevel governance, and the shifting boundaries of Europe.

When Bulgaria and Romania, the newest entrants to the EU, acceded to membership in 2007, what had begun as an exclusive club of six of the most prosperous core countries of Western Europe had morphed into an association of twenty-seven (including ten East-Central European countries from the former Soviet bloc). Moreover, the EU's agenda had spilled over from the original aim of promoting economic cooperation to including everything from foreign affairs to climate change.

The transformations in membership and agenda of the EU are only one piece of a larger transformation of Europe. The revolutions of 1989 in Eastern and Central Europe marked the disintegration of much of the communist world. When the Berlin Wall, which divided East and West in both physical and symbolic terms, was dismantled brick by brick in November 1989, the architecture of Europe was forever altered. Within a year, Germany was unified after nearly a half-century of cold war division, and by the end of 1991 the Soviet Union had splintered into fifteen troubled republics. The destruction of the wall, resulting from the pent-up pressures for change originating in the East, opened the floodgates between East and West Berlin, East and West Germany, and Eastern and Western Europe. The result was a massive movement of ideas, commodities, capital, technology, and people. Immediately, the people of East-Central Europe faced rapid and often disorienting dual transitions—to market economies and to democratic polities. These transitions, swiftly followed by the accession to EU membership of many of the former communist states in East and Central Europe—literally unthinkable until the 1990s—are fundamentally redefining the political geography and the identity of Europe. EU Europe has been extended to Finland and Sweden in the north, to Spain, Malta, and Cyprus in the south, and to Romania and Bulgaria to the east.

Despite its sequence of enlargements, the EU does not include a number of states in Europe, including some that had previously been part of the Soviet empire. Two states should be singled out for particular notice. One is the biggest and most powerful state of them all: Russia, which straddles Europe and Asia. Because cold war divisions have not entirely disappeared and because of Russia's renewed nationalism and great power ambitions under Putin's leadership, there is no imminent prospect that Russia will seek membership in the EU. The second state is Turkey, which also straddles Europe and Asia.

In contrast to Russia, Turkey has ardently pursued the dream of joining the EU. However, until 2004, it had consistently been turned away. The stated reason is that Turkey is not a sufficiently authentic democracy to qualify for membership in an organization that puts a premium on democratic governance. But this is not the only reason why there has been persistent reluctance to admit Turkey to the EU. A more troublesome reason is that Turkey would be the first predominantly non-Christian country to join; indeed, although it is a very secular country, nearly all of Turkey's almost 70 million people are Muslim. In

2004, the EU Commission agreed to open negotiations with Turkey over Turkey's joining the EU, but significant stumbling blocks cloud the prospects of Turkish accession. These include civil liberties and freedom of expression, minority rights for Kurds, and the highly fraught issue of relations between Cyprus and Turkey. Negotiations were suspended in 2006, then resumed in March 2007—and even if they continue, these negotiations are expected to take ten to fifteen years. The Turkish case has significant ramifications for the meaning of Europe as well as for Turkey's future. Thus, despite the enormous changes that have occurred toward enlarging and integrating member states in the EU, Europe remains an unfinished story in key respects.

Although much remains unresolved, one thing is clear and helps define the project of this text: the wall dividing Europe has come down in intellectual terms, and the patterns of development and questions we ask about East and West are more similar than they were before. Without neglecting the distinctive historical and institutional legacies of the nations of East-Central Europe, we can now—perhaps for the first time since the early twentieth century—consider some critical common themes. We can study the political causes and consequences of changes in economic performance, and we can investigate in each country the growing demands for political participation by those who do not consider themselves adequately represented through the formal channels of government. We can consider the ebb and flow of xenophobic and hypernationalistic movements. And we can study the complex interplay of international and domestic politics within a context of increasing global interdependence, European integration, and the shadow of terrorism after 9/11, 3/11, and 7/7.

In fact, we have just sketched out the four key themes that frame our discussion of European politics in transition, at the level of each country we analyze and at the level of the EU: the interaction of states within the international order; the role of states in economic management; the challenges resulting from demands for more participation, transparency, and accountability facing the transitional democracies of East-Central Europe, the durable democracies of Western Europe, and the EU itself; and the political impact of diverse sources of social identity and group attachments.

What Makes Europe . . . Europe?

This book is about the politics of Europe, a politics shaped by specific country-by-country histories as well as regional histories, cultures, political systems, and institutional genealogies. The countries of EU Europe share important similarities in levels of development and long-standing democratic traditions with the United States and other capitalist democracies, such as Canada, Japan, and Australia. Yet there is both a quite distinctive European model of political governance and social policy, and significant country-by-country variations. Similarly, the countries of East-Central Europe share some common experiences and challenges with transitional democracies in other parts of the world, such as Argentina or Nigeria, but the challenges they face are compounded by their need to develop democracy and the market economy at the same time. Few other transitional democracies in regions outside East-Central Europe have to confront a nearly half-century legacy of coercive state-directed economic management imposed by the Soviet Union. Moreover, the postsocialist pathways that these countries follow are highly influenced by specific national trajectories.[4]

European Politics in Transition investigates both the whole and the parts: European politics at a critical juncture in the geographical and political-institutional integration of the region and the different ways that specific countries address common challenges such as competitiveness and economic integration, democratization, social diversity, EU membership or exclusion, terrorism, and relations with the superpower across the Atlantic Ocean. Before undertaking the systematic study of European politics, we need to clarify some important issues concerning the meaning and practice of democracy, the organization of the economy, and the cultural context.

What Is the Meaning—or, Rather, Meanings—of Democracy?

All the countries analyzed in this book pride themselves on having democratic political institutions. But, as with many other important concepts, debate over the meaning of *democracy* is contentious. The wide popularity of the term conceals some important ambiguities,

and we can identify contending positions on many key issues regarding the very definition. Should democracy be defined solely on the basis of the procedures used to select top governmental officeholders? That is, for a political system to qualify as democratic, is it sufficient that occupants of the highest offices of the state be selected on the basis of free, fair elections in which opposing parties are allowed to organize to present candidates and all citizens are entitled to cast a vote for a contending party? Or must there be respect for citizens' civil liberties (including rights of free expression, dissent, and privacy), regardless of what a democratically elected government might desire? What is the relationship between religious practice and the exercise of political power? To what extent must all citizens be guaranteed certain minimum economic and social rights and resources in a democratic regime, as distinct from political and civil rights (such as the right to vote and criticize the government)? To put this another way, what is the relationship between democracy defined in purely procedural terms and democracy defined as a system that provides an adequate level of resources and promotes a high and a reasonable degree of equality of outcomes?

Despite intense debates about the meaning(s) of democracy, a rough consensus has emerged among practitioners and students of comparative politics, or "comparativists," about the minimum required for a regime to qualify as democratic. Generally, the following conditions must obtain:

- Selection to the highest public offices is on the basis of free and fair elections. For an election to qualify as fair, votes must be counted accurately, with the winning candidate(s) selected according to preexisting rules that determine the kind of plurality or majority required to gain electoral victory.
- All citizens possess civil and political rights—the right to participate and vote in elections periodically held to select key state officeholders—and civil liberties—the rights of free assembly, conscience, privacy, and expression, including the right to criticize the government.
- Political parties are free to organize, present candidates for public office, and compete in elections.
- The opposition party or parties—those who are not represented in government—enjoy adequate rights

of contestation—that is, the right to organize and to criticize the incumbent government.

- The elected government develops policy according to specified procedures that provide for due process and the accountability of elected executives (at the next election, through judicial action, and, in parliamentary systems, to parliament).
- The political system contains a judiciary with powers independent of the executive and legislature, charged with protecting citizens' civil rights and liberties from violation by government and other citizens, as well as with ensuring that governmental officials respect constitutionally specified procedures.

Although these six points make a useful checklist of the essential elements of a democracy, several qualifications should be added. First, this definition does not claim that electoral outcomes are always (or even often) rational, equitable, or wise. Democracy specifies a set of procedures for making decisions, but it does not guarantee the wisdom of the outcome. Indeed, as we discuss below, in the fourth qualification to the checklist, we believe that political outcomes in all democracies, in respect to both elections to office and the decisions of officeholders, are systematically and importantly influenced by economic inequalities that limit the ideal of "one person, one vote."

Second, no government has ever fully lived up to democratic standards. All democratic governments at various points in their histories have violated them to a greater or lesser extent. For example, Britain retained a system of plural votes for certain citizens until after World War II; French women did not gain the right to vote until 1945.

Third, the way that the constituent elements of democracy on the checklist are interpreted and implemented is often debatable and sometimes becomes a contentious political issue. For example, in the 1990s, and again in 2004, there was intense controversy in France about whether Muslim girls should be permitted to wear a headscarf, which signifies adherence to Islam, to public school. On the one hand, many public officials and citizens wanted to prohibit girls from wearing the scarf on the grounds that France is a secular state and that prominently displaying the scarf constitutes proselytizing in public schools and symbolizes girls' subordinate status. On the other hand, defenders

of the practice argued that Muslim girls were simply exercising their fundamental right of self-expression.

Fourth, economic inequalities stack the political deck. Wealthy citizens, powerful interest groups, and business firms can use their substantial resources to increase their chances of winning an election or influencing public policy. This creates a tension in all democracies, to a greater or lesser degree, between the formal political procedures (such as voting), in which all are equal, and the actual situation, in which the affluent are, in George Orwell's famous phrase from the satirical novel *Animal Farm,* "more equal" than others because of their ability to have greater political influence.

The tension between citizens' economic inequalities and their equal right to participate in the choice of elected officials and governmental policies—that is, the tension between "one person, one vote" and "one euro, one vote"—is found in all European democracies and is typically a source of intense political division. Opposing political coalitions advocate very different governmental policies that reflect the interests of their distinctive socioeconomic constituencies. Three key areas of policy difference involve the following issues:

- *The distribution of tax burdens.* Although all governments levy taxes on citizens and businesses to support government activities, who pays how much is often a source of intense political debate.
- *Governmental economic priorities.* Should economic policy be directed above all toward restraining inflation (a particular concern for the affluent or elderly, since inflation threatens to reduce the value of their assets and savings) or toward reducing unemployment (which traditionally has harmed working people the most)?
- *The extent of governmental spending for social programs.* How much can and should be spent on the public provision of job training, unemployment compensation, old-age pensions, assistance to the needy, and other programs that are part of what is commonly called the welfare state?

Finally, although all democracies share the six key elements outlined above, democracies vary widely in their political institutions. A common classification of democracies is based on differing relationships between the executive and the legislature. In presidential systems, such as in the United States, the chief executive (the president) and the national legislature are chosen in separate elections, and there is a sharp separation of powers between the executive branch and the legislature. Americans might be surprised to learn that this system is not the most prevalent form of democratic regime. Most of the world's democracies (including Britain, Germany, and Italy) have parliamentary regimes. In a parliamentary system, executive and legislative powers are fused rather than separated: the chief executive (whether called prime minister, chancellor, or president) and the cabinet are chosen from the legislature and generally are the leaders of the dominant party in parliament.

The formal and informal rules of the game for reaching and exercising power are very different in presidential and parliamentary systems. In presidential systems, members of the legislature jealously preserve their autonomy. Because the legislature is elected separately from the president, it is constitutionally authorized to set its own agenda, initiate policy proposals, and defy presidential directives. Presidents may deploy powerful resources in order to persuade the legislature to go along, but even when the same party controls both the presidency and the legislature, the key word is *persuade*.

In parliamentary systems, the legislature may serve as a forum for dramatic policy debate, but it represents neither an independent source of policy initiatives nor a decisive obstacle that prevents the government from legislating its own proposals. On rare occasions, a rebellion within the ranks of the majority party (or coalition) in parliament brings down the cabinet—that is, forces the chief executive to resign. However, one can count such examples on one hand in post–World War II Britain and Germany. The fact that this happens all the time in Italy suggests the value of comparing particular systems, as we do in this book, rather than engaging in generalizations about political systems.

"So what?" you may ask in response to this discussion of political institutions. Good question![5] Ponder what difference the type of system makes as you study parliamentary and presidential systems in this book. And note how rare presidential systems are—a point that may surprise those who think that the U.S. presidential system is typical.

The distinction between presidential and parliamentary systems does not exhaust the range of institutional variation within industrial democracies. You will discover that France's hybrid semipresidential system is quite different from both. France has a dual executive, with both a directly elected president and an appointed prime minister. As you will learn, these differences raise the kinds of questions that are at the heart of comparative politics: How do different political institutions and procedures embody the same democratic values? What consequences do these differences have for the effectiveness of government and the distribution of resources?

Debates about political institutions involve central questions about relations among social groups, for the way that power is organized affects the structure of political conflicts and coalitions and the outcome of governmental decisions and policies. Nor are debates regarding the choice of the appropriate manner of organizing state institutions ever fully settled. Britain, the nation with the longest parliamentary democratic tradition (it is centuries old), has recently modified its basic organizational structure, moving from a unitary state in which all powers were concentrated in the central government to one in which specific authorities were ceded to the constituent units of the United Kingdom (which comprises Scotland, Wales, and Northern Ireland, as well as England). In France, reforms since the 1980s have decentralized political power to regional and local governments, thereby significantly reducing France's centuries-old pattern of state dominance. In East-Central Europe, citizens and political elites evaluate presidential and parliamentary models as they craft new democratic regimes.

What Economic System for Democracy? Capitalism, Socialism, and Democracy

A long-standing political debate involves the question of whether a democratic political system must be associated with a capitalist organization of the economy. To sketch the context broadly, one can identify two ways to organize modern economic life. In a capitalist system, production is organized within the framework of voluntary (market) exchanges between private participants. The bulk of economic decisions—notably, what goods will be produced, by what methods, and by whom—are private, that is, they are made by private individuals (not public officials) who own and control productive assets. Their decisions are based on the goal of reaping the highest possible profits from selling goods in the market. In a socialist system of production, by contrast, key decisions concerning the organization of the economy are considered public, not private. They are made by elected representatives, state planners, and administrators, as well as by workers who produce goods (in the case of the self-managed firm).

Many scholars contend that democratic political institutions cannot flourish unless the economy is organized within a capitalist framework. They believe that democracy requires leaving substantial power in the hands of individual citizens, and citizens cannot have this necessary power if government makes the key decisions involving the organization of production, exchange, and consumption. In this view, public control of the economy is both inefficient and tyrannical. On the other hand, those on the other side of this debate assert that for a system to be democratic, it is not sufficient for democratic procedures to apply in the political sphere; there must also be a significant measure of democratic decision making within the economy. The distinguished democratic theorist Robert Dahl explains why. Private "ownership and control [of business firms] contribute to the creation of great differences among citizens in wealth, income, status, skills, information, control over information and propaganda, [and] access to political leaders. . . . Differences like these help in turn to generate significant inequalities among citizens in their capacities for participating as political equals in *governing the state*."[6] In this view, democracy is crippled when some of the most important decisions affecting the character of the entire society are made by affluent citizens and private business firms that are not democratically chosen or accountable.

The relationship among capitalism, socialism, and democracy is an issue of vital importance.[7] Although the political and scholarly debate on the relationship of capitalism, socialism, and democracy has not been fully settled, all the countries covered in this book, as well as other democracies throughout the world, have capitalist economies. Moreover, you will discover that the countries in this book exhibit a broadly similar relationship between democratic political institutions and capitalist economic institutions. In all stable democracies, there is quite extensive state intervention in the economy alongside extensive market competition by privately owned and controlled firms. The characteristic situation has often been called a mixed economy and was described by political scientist Adam Przeworski as a system "that relies on [state] regulated markets to allocate resources and on the state to assure a minimum of material welfare for everyone."[8]

Within the broadly similar context of a mixed economy, however, we find extensive variation from one democratic country to the next regarding the precise balance between state regulation and free markets. Some of the major political conflicts in democratic regimes—both the longstanding durable regimes in Western Europe and the transitional democracies of East-Central Europe—concern the extent and priorities of state economic intervention, in particular, the optimum trade-offs among a variety of desirable goals: high employment, low inflation, economic growth, provision of welfare, international competitiveness, and so forth. For each country, we discuss the form that these conflicts have taken. Look for the range of policy differences in this arena, consider what difference they make for citizens in these countries, and develop your own position on the most desirable form of political economy.

The Cultural Context

Are there particular historical and cultural conditions that are necessary for democracy? Comparativists have long debated whether democracy requires specific cultural orientations. In an important contribution on this question, *Making Democracy Work*, the political scientist Robert Putnam and his coauthors document the energetic and effective way that Italians in the north used newly created regional governments to improve their situation; by contrast, Italians in the south were less able to exploit the possibilities created by the regional form.[9] What made democracy work better in the north? Putnam suggests there was more abundant *social capital* in the north, that is, a greater capacity by northerners to coordinate their efforts to work for the common good. In the south, in contrast, citizens were less likely to act collectively to make the new regional governments an instrument for economic and social advancement; in other words, social capital was lacking. Putnam claims that a key to why social capital was more prevalent in the north is that northerners were more likely than southerners to trust their fellow citizens in engaging in common public pursuits.

Can we extend Putnam's argument to the global scale? Are some cultures more hospitable to the kind of trust and pragmatic compromises that are essential for democracy to work? Or, as Sidney Tarrow, a sympathetic critic, charged, does Putnam mistake effect for cause? Tarrow suggests that the greater extent of trust and social capital in the north was no accident; it was nurtured by Italian state policies that favored the region.[10] The debate between Putnam and Tarrow in part hinges on the question of which is more important in explaining effective political and economic performance: state policies or political-cultural attitudes. Consider this question as you read about the democratic performance of the countries that are discussed in this book.

A somewhat different question about the cultural base of democracy is whether, for democracy to flourish, there must first be broad agreement or consensus on the democratic rules of the game, notably democratic procedures and the acceptance of the electoral verdict even by those on the losing side. In *The Civic Culture*, a contemporary classic in comparative politics, Gabriel Almond and Sidney Verba claimed, by comparing the distribution of political attitudes in five nations, that citizens in democratic regimes are more likely than citizens in authoritarian regimes to trust government and accept the values of both participating in government and accepting directives from their government.[11] In a rejoinder to this approach, Dankwart Rustow countered, "The basis of democracy is not maximum consensus. It is the tenuous middle ground between imposed uniformity (such as would lead to some sort of tyranny) and implacable hostility (of a kind that would disrupt the community in civil war or secession). There must be a conscious adoption of democratic rules, but they must not be so much believed in as applied, first perhaps from necessity and gradually from habit. The very operation of these rules will enlarge the area of consensus step-by-step as democracy moves down its crowded agenda."[12] Consider the applicability of these two quite distinct claims to each country study and particularly to the case studies of East-Central Europe, where the

development of democratic civic cultures remains an abiding challenge.

The Framework: Four Themes

This book seeks to go beyond "textbook" understandings. However important, politics in the narrow sense of governmental institutions and formal political processes (that is, politics as "how a bill becomes a law") is only part of a far more complex story, which encompasses not only political parties, voting behavior, and the institutions of government, but also the emergence of powerful forces in society, as well as the interaction of international and domestic factors. Within European nations, politics has always involved social movements—from the English Chartists and popular movements on the Continent in the 1830s and 1840s, who demanded rights of political participation and democracy (some of which still have not been achieved), to Green parties in many contemporary Western European nations that struggle for women's rights, nuclear disarmament, and ecological concerns. European politics also involves class conflicts between working people and the financial and business elites, conflicts that force the state to intervene in the economy by regulating market forces, managing industrial disputes through political negotiations, and affecting how the wealth of society is divided among competing social groups. European politics today involves regional, ethnic, racial, and gender divisions, as well as the politics of the EU and the relations between Eastern and Western Europe, within a context of intensified global interdependence, the ever-present influence of the United States, and the ominous threat of transnational terrorist networks.

To make sense of the large volume of information presented in *European Politics in Transition,* we structure our study of European politics around four core themes that we believe are central for understanding the transition that European politics is experiencing now:

1. The interaction of states within the international order
2. The role of states in economic management
3. The particular challenges facing European democracies and the pressures for more democracy
4. The political impact of diverse sources of social identity, including class, gender, ethnicity, and religion

These four themes provide a framework for organizing the extensive information on political institutions, processes, conflicts, policy, and changes that we present in the country chapters. The themes help explain continuities and contrasts among countries. We will also suggest a way that each theme highlights some puzzle in comparative politics that illuminates our understanding of European politics.

Before we introduce the themes, we offer several warnings. First, our four themes cannot possibly capture all of the infinitely varied experience of politics throughout the world. The framework of *European Politics in Transition* provides a guide to understanding many features of contemporary comparative politics. But we urge students (and rely on instructors!), who through study and experience know the politics of the United States and many other countries, to challenge and augment our interpretations. Second, we want to note that a textbook builds from existing theory but does not construct or test new hypotheses, which is the goal of original scholarly studies. The themes are intended to crystallize some of the most significant findings in the scholarly literature on contemporary European politics. Although these themes can usefully be applied to politics anywhere in the world, they serve here as an analytical tool to reveal both the specificity of national experiences and the distinctiveness of a European model of politics.

Theme One: A World of States

The theme that we call *a world of states* highlights the fact that since the beginning of the modern era several centuries ago, states have been the primary actors on the world stage. Although international organizations and private actors like transnational corporations play a crucial role, since the seventeenth century it has been state officials who send armies to conquer other states and territories, states whose legal codes make it possible for business firms to operate within their borders and beyond, and states that regulate, through immigration law and border police, the movement of people across borders. Courses in international relations focus primarily on interaction among states or other cross-border transactions. In *European Politics in Transition*, we emphasize a key feature of the international arena: the impact on a state's domestic political institutions and processes of its relative success or failure in competing economically and politically with other states.

No state, even the most powerful, such as the United States, is unaffected by influences that originate outside its borders. Today a host of processes associated with *globalization* underscore the heightened importance of intensified cross-national influences. The terms *globalization* or *the global era* are frequently applied as general catchphrases to identify the growing depth, extent, and diversity of the cross-border connections that are a key feature of the contemporary world. Discussions of globalization often begin with accounts of economic activities, including the reorganization of production and the global redistribution of the workforce (the "global factory") and the increased extent and intensity of international trade, finance, and foreign direct investment. Globalization involves the movement of peoples due to migration, employment, business, and educational opportunities.

The term *globalization* links a highly diverse set of changes. Consider the attacks in the United States on September 11, 2001. The hijackers were members of Al Qaeda, a thoroughly transnational network that recruits throughout the world and has cells in many continents. The hijackers trained and lived in locations thousands of miles apart. They communicated by cell phone and courier, transferred funds through a sophisticated system linking international banks and traditional moneychangers based in bazaars. Similarly, the network that bombed the Madrid railroads on March 11, 2004, was composed of members from many countries, and the planning and execution of the attack required intricate transnational cooperation.

Globalization includes other profound changes that are less visible but equally significant. For example, applications of information technology (such as the Internet and CNN) blur the traditional distinction between what is around the world and what is around the block, thereby instantly transforming cultures, and eroding the boundaries between the local and global. These technologies make instantaneous communication possible, link producers and contractors, headquarters, branch plants, and suppliers in real time anywhere in the world. Employees may be rooted in time and place, but employers can shop for what will bring them the greatest advantages in a global labor market. Employees who have an apparently secure job today may be unemployed tomorrow as employers downsize or move their operations offshore. But job destruction in one region may be offset by job creation elsewhere.

Globalization forges new forms of international governance, from the European Union to the World Trade Organization. And as described above, international terror networks can strike anywhere—from New York to Bali to Madrid. In an attempt to regulate and stabilize the myriad international flows, an alphabet soup of international organizations—NATO, the UN, IMF, WTO, OECD, NAFTA, to name but a few—has been enlisted. And globalization also involves grassroots movements from around the world that challenge the construction of globalization "from above." The first such challenge occurred when the World Trade Organization sponsored a meeting of government ministers in Seattle in 1999 that was disrupted by 50,000 protesters. Ever since then, conferences called to develop rules for global commerce have been the site of demonstrations by coalitions of environmental, labor-based, and community activists from around the world.[13] To Seattle one can add the names of cities around the world—Washington, D.C., Prague (in the Czech Republic), Nice (France), Davos (Switzerland), Genoa (Italy), Miami (U.S.), Cancún (Mexico), and Potsdam (Germany)—where activists have assembled to protest the activity of international financial and intergovernmental institutions.

The varied elements of globalization erode the ability of even the strongest countries to control their destinies. No state can guarantee economic and life-cycle security for its citizens. None can preserve pristine "national models" of economic governance—or distinctly national cultures, values, understandings of the world, or narratives that define a people and forge their unity. None is safe from violence that target its citizens, public officials, institutions, and territory justified in the name of transcendent religious or political principles.

In the brave new world in which we live, countries face a host of challenges from above and below. The capacities of states to control domestic outcomes and assert sovereignty are compromised by regional and global technological and market forces, as well as by growing security concerns. Countries are simultaneously assaulted by ethnic, nationalist, and religious challenges that often involve both internal and external components. The challenge of democratic self-government is heightened when many of the decisions that fundamentally affect citizens' lives are made by organizations that are located far outside a country's borders.

Today, as they begin to adjust to the changed realities of the twenty-first century, nations are experiencing intense pressures from an expanding and increasingly complex mix of external influences. In every country, politics and policymaking are affected by influences that come from outside its borders. But international political and economic influences do not have the same impact in all countries, and some states help shape the institutional form and policy of international organizations in which they participate.[14] It is likely that the more advantaged a state is—as measured by such factors as level of economic development, military power, and resource base—the more it will shape the global order. By contrast, the policies of less advantaged countries are more extensively shaped by other states, international organizations, and broader international constraints.

When states pool their political and economic resources, they can leverage their influence in the international setting. Perhaps the foremost example in the world today is the EU, to which all the countries analyzed in this book belong. As Part VIII, devoted to the EU, describes, it has been no easy matter for former rivals like France, Britain, and Germany to delegate key decisions to EU institutions. A further daunting challenge that confronts the EU and its member states is to "digest" the ten new countries (eight from East-Central Europe as well as Cyprus and Malta) that joined the EU in 2004 as well as Bulgaria and Romania that joined in 2007. The EU fits uneasily in a world of states, but international organizations like the EU (along with the North American Free Trade Association, the World Trade Organization, and others) are increasingly important actors in world politics.

The theme we identify as *a world of states* includes a second important focus: similarities and contrasts among countries in how they formed as states and how their states are presently organized. We study the ways that states developed historically, diverse patterns in the organization of political institutions, the processes—and limits—of democratization, the ability of the state to control social groups in society and sustain its power, and the state's economic management strategies and capacities. We observe how state formation and the position in the international order of states are linked. For example, compared with other states, the British state had (and continues to have) a less developed capacity to steer British industry. The state was less concerned with the competitiveness of the British domestic manufacturing industry because of the commanding position within international finance enjoyed by the private financial institutions comprising the City of London (London's financial district, equivalent to Wall Street in New York). Moreover, the vast scope of Britain's colonial empire meant that trade with the colonies could sustain the British economy. Consequently, the British state intervened less extensively, and private firms were allowed to develop in a freer fashion than was the case for France and Germany.

A Puzzle: To What Extent Do States Still Remain the Basic Building Blocks of Political Life? Increasingly, the politics and policies of states are shaped by external actors as well as by the more impersonal forces of globalization. At the same time, many states face increasingly restive constituencies that challenge the power and legitimacy of central government. In reading the four country case studies of EU members (Britain, France, Germany and Italy), the analysis of East-Central Europe (Part VII) and that of the EU (Part VIII), try to assess what impact pressures from both above and below have on the role of the state and its capacity to achieve desirable outcomes. Does the EU create a more equal playing field for all the member states, large and small? Or does it enhance the power of the major players at the expense of the weaker members?

Theme Two: Governing the Economy

The success of states in maintaining their authority is greatly affected by their ability to ensure that an adequate volume of goods and services is produced to satisfy the needs of their populations. Certainly the inability of the Soviet economic system to meet this challenge was an important reason for the rejection of communism and the disintegration of the Soviet Union. Conversely, the relatively great political stability

of the wealthy industrialized nations described in this book is closely linked to their superior economic performance. How a country organizes production and exchange—that is, *governs the economy*—is one of the key elements in its overall pattern of development. Countries differ widely in how successful they are in competing with other countries that offer similar products in international markets, and in the relative importance of market forces versus government control of the economy.

An important goal in the contemporary world is to achieve durable economic development. Effective economic performance is near the top of every country's political agenda. The term *political economy* refers to how governments affect economic performance—and how economic performance affects a country's political processes. We accord great importance to political economy in *European Politics in Transition* because we believe that politics in all countries is deeply influenced by the relationship between government and the economy.

Two Puzzles: What Factors Foster Successful Economic Performance? And What Exactly *Is* Successful Economic Performance? These are questions that students of political economy have long pondered—and to which there are no easy answers. Consider the apparently straightforward question of whether states that intervene more vigorously to manage the economy outperform states with less developed capacities for economic management. France developed an extensive array of financial and industrial management tools in the post–World War II period. This directive approach was often praised as a means to promote vigorous economic modernization and growth. British policymakers tried (quite unsuccessfully) to copy French planning institutions. Through unification, Germany's social market economy—a complex interplay of laissez-faire and extremely sophisticated state-centered policies (which formed a very different policy from France's state-centered approach)—created an economy that was the envy of the world. Yet in recent years, Britain's less-is-more approach to governing the economy has been quite successful, while key elements of the French and German models of economic governance have been reformed (with the state yielding more control to markets) in response to the economic and political challenges associated with global economic competition. Indeed, with the disappearance of some of the more distinctive features of French and German economic governance, a frequent topic of discussion among European specialists is whether a convergence is occurring in the economic policies of European countries. There is general agreement both that some of the most important features differentiating economic governance have been dismantled, but that there remain significant contrasts in the varieties of European capitalism (to paraphrase the title of an important study of the question).[15] In reading the country studies as well as the analysis of East-Central Europe and of the EU itself, try to decide what approach to governing the economy is most likely to produce economic success. Has globalization forced a convergence of national models? To the extent that convergence has occurred, is this desirable?

Before resolving the problem of how to achieve maximum economic performance, one must first decide how one knows it when one sees it—and, to further complicate matters, the meaning of economic success is not self-evident. The conventional measure of economic success is the rate at which a country's gross domestic product (GDP) increases from one year to the next, that is, economic growth. Although certainly useful for many purposes, this measure is quite crude and even misleading. For one thing, the GDP growth does not reflect changes in the size of a country's population. A rapidly increasing population may produce a larger GDP at the same time that the average income of each person in the population—that is, per capita income—shrinks (and, thus, people are worse off). Further, measuring economic success by GDP ignores the social value of the products that are produced. GDP lumps together the value of tobacco products along with the value of medical care required to treat the diseases caused by tobacco use. What other measures of economic success are available? One possible yardstick is the United Nations Development Program's Human Development Index (HDI), a composite of qualitative measures like life expectancy along with per capita income and other quantitative measures of equity and well being.

European states have historically prided themselves on giving priority not only to economic growth but also to social equity. The European model of social welfare allocates generous public expenditures to provide adequate income during periods of sickness, unemployment, or old age. But many economists have criticized European governments for devoting too many resources to social purposes and not giving adequate priority to policies that facilitate economic growth and efficiency.

When reading the country sections, ponder the question of how to measure economic performance in alternative ways. Doing so will alert you to the importance of the interaction between politics and economics, for the way that a country organizes the production and distribution of its resources fundamentally affects its economic performance and social equity.

Theme Three: The Democratic Idea

Our comparative studies indicate a surprising level of complexity in the apparently simple theme of the *democratic idea*. We focus first on the near universality of the claim that citizens should exercise substantial control over the decisions that their states and governments make. Especially since the collapse of Soviet communism, democracy has no viable contender as a legitimate basis for organizing political power in the contemporary world. (Perhaps nationalism, especially when fused with religion, might be considered an alternative, but even many forms of religious nationalism claim to be based in democracy.)

In discussing the democratic idea, we focus second on the diverse sources of support for democracy. Democracy has proved appealing for many reasons. In some historical settings, it may represent a standoff or equilibrium among political contenders for power, in which no one group can gain sufficient strength to control outcomes on its own.[16] Democracy may appeal to many people in authoritarian settings because states having democratic regimes often rank among the world's most stable, affluent, and cohesive countries. Another important source of support for democracy is the widespread popular desire for dignity and equality. Even when dictatorial regimes provide some of the benefits often associated with democratic regimes—for example, sponsoring development or using ideological appeals to garner popular support—intense pressures for democracy remain. Although authoritarian governments can suppress demands for democratic participation for a long period, our discussion of East-Central Europe in this book provides abundant evidence that the domestic and, in recent years, international costs of doing so are high.

Third, we emphasize the potential fragility of transitions from authoritarian to democratic rule. Although popular movements and leaders of moderate factions within authoritarian regimes often overthrow undemocratic regimes and force the holding of elections, this does not mean that democratic institutions will endure. As our case studies of Poland, Hungary, and the Czech and Slovak Republics demonstrate, a wide gulf exists between a *transition* to democracy and the *consolidation* of democracy. Historically, powerful groups have often opposed democratic institutions because they fear that democracy will threaten their privileges, whereas disadvantaged groups may oppose the democratic process because they see it as unresponsive to their deeply felt grievances. As a result, reversals of democratic regimes have occurred in the past and will doubtless occur in the future. The country studies in this book do not support a philosophy of history or theory of political development that sees a single (democratic) end point toward which all countries will eventually converge. One important analytical work, published in the early phase of the most recent democratic wave, captured the fragility of the process of democratization in its title: *Transitions from Authoritarian Rule: Tentative Conclusions About Uncertain Democracies.*[17] The difficulty in maintaining democracy once established is captured in the observation that it is easier for a country to hold its first democratic election than its second. The fact that the democratic idea is so powerful does not mean that all countries will adopt or preserve democratic institutions.

Moreover, even when democracy has become relatively secure, we do not believe that it can be achieved in any country once and for all. Indeed, our *democratic idea* theme suggests the incompleteness of democratic agendas even in countries with the longest and most developed experiences of representative democracy (several of which are included in this book). In virtually every democracy in recent years, many citizens have turned against the state when their living standards were threatened by high unemployment and economic stagnation. Social movements have targeted the state's actions or inactions in such varied spheres as environmental regulation, reproductive rights, and race or ethnic relations. Comparative studies confirm that the democratic idea fuels political conflicts even in long-established democracies because there is invariably a gap, even in the most egalitarian and longest-lived democracies, between democratic ideals and the actual functioning of democratic political institutions. Witness, for example, the extensive degree of economic and political inequality in Britain, France, and Germany, countries that are classified as among the most democratic in the world. Nor do challenges to democracy originate only with contentious movements: public officials in even the most stable democracies have violated democratic procedures by engaging in corruption and using illegal force against citizens.

In order to analyze more deeply the underpinnings of democratic stability, *European Politics in Transition* confines its attention to countries with extensive democratic traditions. With the exception of states in East-Central Europe, which adopted democratic institutions after the collapse of communism in 1989, all the countries surveyed in this book have been democratic for longer than a half-century.

A Puzzle: Does Democracy Enhance or Endanger Stability? Comparativists often debate whether democratic institutions contribute to political stability or, on the contrary, to political disorder. On the one hand, democracy by its very nature encourages political opposition. One of its defining characteristics is that competition is legitimate among those who aspire to gain high political office, as well as among groups and parties defending different programs. Political life in democracies is often turbulent and unpredictable. On the other hand, the fact that political opposition and competition are legitimate in democracies paradoxically has the effect of promoting acceptance of the state, even among opponents of a given government. Because opposition movements are free to express their opposition in democratic regimes, the result is greater political stability. Evidence for this claim has been provided by an important study comparing democratic and authoritarian regimes, which finds that economic disruptions are much less destabilizing for democracies.[18] In reading the country studies in this book, look for stabilizing and destabilizing consequences of democratic institutions and the particular challenges that long-standing democracies face.

Theme Four: The Politics of Collective Identity

How do individuals understand who they are in political terms, and on what basis do people form groups to advance common political aims? In other words, what are the sources of group attachments, or *collective political identity?* At one point, social scientists thought they knew. It was generally held that age-old loyalties of ethnicity, religious affiliation, race, gender, and locality were being dissolved by economic, political, and cultural modernization. Comparativists thought that class solidarities based on the shared experience of work, or economic position more broadly, had become the most important source of collective identity. And it was believed that as countries became politically modern or mature, groups would pragmatically pursue their economic interests in ways that were not politically destabilizing. We now know that the formation and interplay of politically relevant collective identities are far more complex and uncertain.

In the industrial democracies, the importance of identities based on class membership has declined, although class and material sources of collective political identity remain significant in political competition and economic organization. In contrast, contrary to earlier predictions in the social sciences, in many countries nonclass identities—affiliations that develop from a sense of belonging to particular groups based on language, religion, ethnicity, race, nationality, or gender—have assumed growing significance.

The politics of collective political identity involves struggles to define which groups will be full participants in the political community and which ones will be marginalized. It also involves a constant tug of war over the relative power and influence—both symbolic and material—among groups. Issues of inclusion and priority remain pivotal in many countries, and are constantly changing as a result of immigration, ideological changes, and changing geopolitics. To cite an example dividing many European countries, recently there have been intense controversies involving the relationship of

Muslim minorities to the wider community. One reason that conflict around the issue of collective identities can be so intense is that political leaders in the state and in opposition movements often seek to mobilize support by sharpening ethnic, religious, racial, or regional rivalries.

A Puzzle: Can You Split the Difference When It Comes to Identity Politics?   Once identity demands are placed on the political agenda, to what extent can governments depolarize them by distributing resources in a way that redresses the grievances of the minority or politically weaker identity groups? Collective identities operate at the level of symbols, attitudes, values, and beliefs as well as at the level of material resources. However, the contrast between material-based identities and demands and nonmaterial-based ones should not be exaggerated. In practice, most groups are animated both by feelings of loyalty and solidarity *and* by the desire to obtain material benefits for their members. But the analytical distinction between material and nonmaterial demands remains useful, and it is worth considering whether the nonmaterial aspects of the politics of collective identities make political disputes over ethnicity, religion, language, or nationality especially divisive and difficult to resolve.

In a situation of extreme scarcity, it may prove well-nigh impossible to find any compromise among groups, even when their conflicts revolve only around clashing material interests. But if at least a moderate level of resources is available, such conflicts may be easier to resolve because groups can "split the difference" and get a share of resources that they find at least minimally adequate. This process, which refers to who gets what, or how resources are distributed, is called *distributional politics.* However, the demands of ethnic, religious, and nationalist movements may be difficult to satisfy by a distributional style of politics precisely because the group demands more than merely a larger share of the economic pie. The distributional style may be quite ineffectual when, for example, a religious group demands that its religious values be imposed on the whole society—or, for that matter, that it be allowed to engage in practices either prohibited by law or widely regarded as illegitimate. A good example is provided by the controversy in French politics over whether to prohibit Muslim girls from wearing headscarves in school. Similarly, can the difference be split when a dominant linguistic group insists that a single language be used in education and government throughout the country? In such cases, political conflict tends to assume an all-or-nothing quality. The country studies in this book examine a wide range of conflicts involving collective identities. It will be interesting (and possibly troubling) to ponder whether and under what conditions such conflicts are subject to the normal give-and-take of political bargaining.

These four themes provide our analytic framework. With the four themes in mind, we can now discuss some of the common features and issues explored in the country studies that comprise *European Transitions in Politics,* as well as how the text is organized.

European Politics in Transition: Critical Junctures

European political systems are dynamic, not frozen. They respond to complex challenges and are shaped by preexisting institutional and cultural legacies, by battles lost and won, and by the challenges of everyday life as it is experienced—and understood—by ordinary citizens, who make a host of messy demands on their governments. In this section we look at some of the major stages and turning points in European political development.

Industrialization, State Formation, and the Great Divide

For several decades following World War II, it was common for students, scholars, and policymakers to think of two Europes: East and West. The meanings we attach to the political arrangements for any part of the globe emerge historically. The words we use are not neutral, and they have important political and ideological implications. For example, expressions like *First World*, which refers to Western Europe, Japan, and the United States, and *Third World*, which refers to the less economically developed states of Latin America, Africa, and Asia, may intentionally or unintentionally reflect a Eurocentrism in which the economically and politically dominant West is given pride of place. And terms like *Western Europe* and *Eastern Europe* are as much political and ideological as they are geographical. In this case, the terms were linked to the cold war divide that pitted the United States against the Soviet Union, each allied with European states.

When we look at the evolution of modern European societies, we see two fundamentally transformative processes at work: the emergence of the modern state and the advent of developed capitalism linked to the Industrial Revolution. Absolutist states emerged in Europe during the sixteenth century. Monarchies with firm, centralized authority replaced the more localized and personal administration of power that characterized the large number of small principalities, city-states, leagues, and so on scattered throughout medieval Europe. The introduction of permanent bureaucracies, codified laws, national taxes, and standing armies heralded the arrival of the first modern European states. In the competition between the widely varied political units of the time, victory went to monarchs who devised more efficient methods of governing—bureaucracies—and more productive economies.[19]

By the eighteenth century, new economic developments associated with capitalist industrialization began to clash with the increasingly archaic monarchical forms of various states. Although bitter feuds between landowners and monarchs were not uncommon, absolutist regimes were generally linked by economic, military, and political ties to the traditional landholding aristocracy. With the Industrial Revolution, the owners of manufacturing enterprises, the bourgeoisie, increasingly gained economic prominence and political influence. A growing incompatibility between old state forms and new economic demands fostered revolutionary upheavals—often violent, as in the French Revolution of 1789; sometimes less violent, as occurred in eighteenth-century Britain (although Barrington Moore's classic study emphasized how Britain's peaceful incrementalism in later periods was facilitated by the violence that occurred at an earlier period—in the Glorious Revolution of 1688).[20] The outcome of eighteenth-century struggles was often the development of more modern constitutional forms of the state. Industrialization and state formation were closely linked historical phenomena, and they developed in tandem.

Another point is crucial to an understanding of both the history of European societies and the organization of this book. Until the Russian Revolution in

1917 and the subsequent post–World War II division of Europe, Europe was not divided into East and West. In earlier centuries, absolutist states in Central or Eastern Europe—Austria, Prussia, and Russia—existed alongside similarly centralized bureaucracies in France, Spain, and England. (The situation in Eastern Europe was complicated by the breakup of the great multinational empires, notably the Ottoman and Austro-Hungarian empires, and the creation of a host of small new nation-states after World War I.)

With the Russian Revolution and the emergence of socialist states in Eastern and Central Europe in the aftermath of World War II, a great divide split Europe into East and West. The iron curtain that divided the continent, in the words of British prime minister Winston Churchill, was linked to the global campaign waged by the United States and the Soviet Union against one another to win allies and secure geopolitical and ideological dominance. For over half a century, profound differences in political and economic processes separated the capitalist democracies of Western Europe from the socialist regimes of Eastern Europe.

The passing of communism in East-Central Europe in the 1990s has created new geopolitical territories—or rather, it has restored the situation that prevailed until the Russian Revolution of 1917. Yet the risk of new and bitter divisions within Europe also exists because the same process of widening the EU means that although some states will be admitted, others will be excluded. The most notable example is Turkey's perpetually stalled application for EU membership. But other countries that have been left standing, hat in hand, at the entrance to the EU include the former Yugoslav republic of Macedonia and Croatia (which gained official candidate status in 2005), and Albania, Bosnia, Kosovo, Montenegro, and Serbia.

To understand the current transition in Europe, a useful historical baseline is the period following World War II. This was when the framework was established that at first regulated political conflict for a generation and then itself proved the source of new challenges beginning in the late 1960s. The result was to press forward the agenda of European integration.

Our account centers on Western Europe, the major focus of *European Politics in Transition*. We also consider briefly the evolution of East-Central Europe. In the West, the key domestic political tension involved the balance between private market forces as opposed to state control over the economy. Linked to the question of states versus markets was the issue of expanding democratic rights, political participation, and social equity.

The solution fashioned after World War II, which set the stage for an unprecedented period of prosperity and political stability, involved the extension of the welfare state and the widespread application of a newly formulated theory of economic management (known as Keynesianism, which we discuss below). The new political formula involved cooperation among the state, organized labor, and organized capital around the quest for economic growth as a way to resolve the problem of class conflict. This pattern of cooperation has been dubbed the postwar settlement. Born from the destruction and the weariness following World War II, the postwar settlement ushered in an era of unprecedented economic growth and prosperity. During a moment that some thought would last forever, it appeared that economic growth organized within a capitalist framework was not only compatible with steadily expanding democratic participation and state-mandated social benefits but actually depended on them.

Postwar stability declined when the social and economic bases of the postwar settlement crumbled. Gradually cooperation among classes gave way to conflict, new non-class-based social actors grew more assertive, and the possibility and desirability of linking economic growth, welfare state expansion, and democratic participation were challenged. This is the story that we now recount in fuller detail.

World War II and the Emergence of the European Model

The years following World War II represented a period of rapid economic growth in Western Europe, sustained by secure and widely popular regimes. In Germany and Italy, the Christian Democrats ruled throughout the period, and in Britain, Labour and Conservative governments shared a mainstream consensus. In contrast to the economic depression and social instability of the interwar period, the years following World War II reflected an unusual degree of social harmony. (These observations must be qualified in the case of southern Europe, as we discuss later in this section.)

During the period of the postwar settlement, many scholars and political elites believed that intense social, economic, and political conflicts were a thing of the past. Sociologist Daniel Bell described "the end of ideology" and the waning of ideological passions; political sociologist Seymour Martin Lipset proclaimed that the fundamental problems of industrial society had been solved. In brief, economic growth seemed to provide the solvent for reducing class antagonisms. Rather than the major economic classes struggling to enlarge their share of a static economic pie, or to gain complete control of the pie, the new approach (which we dub the postwar settlement) postulated that all groups should cooperate to increase the size of the pie—and thereby achieve the gains deriving from economic expansion. To change metaphors, another common observation during this period was that a rising (economic) tide lifted all boats. Given rapidly rising standards of living, the more radical social movements seeking fundamental change in the organization of society and control of economic resources appeared outmoded. "The performance of capitalism since the end of the Second World War has been so unexpectedly dazzling," wrote an observer in 1965, that "it is hard for us to believe that the bleak and squalid system which we knew could, in so short a time, have adapted itself without some covert process of total destruction and regeneration to achieve so many desired objectives."[21]

Although class conflicts persisted in Europe, especially in southern Europe (Italy and France among our studies), the general trend was toward a consensus on the value of state regulation of market forces. The most common approach, often described as *neocorporatism,* involved direct negotiations over prices or incomes between representatives of labor unions and organizations composed of business firms, with the coordination and guidance of the state. A key shift was that the state persuaded organized labor to moderate its demands for substantial wage gains, autonomy, and control of the workplace in exchange for attractive benefits, including full employment, stable prices, welfare programs, and steady wage increases. And the state also persuaded employers to recognize the legitimacy of labor unions, both in representing workers at the workplace and in participating in decisions about the entire economy. The understandings and arrangements of the

postwar settlement helped to end the era of strife associated with the transition to an industrial capitalist order.

The postwar settlement was linked to changes within technology and the organization of production and consumption—what some scholars have termed a shift to a *Fordist system* of mass production and consumption. The American industrialist Henry Ford lent his name to the two key elements of Fordism because he was among the first to introduce the new techniques. In the realm of production, Ford pioneered in reducing the cost of producing that quintessential consumer durable—the automobile. The secret was to simplify production by introducing fewer parts (often interchangeable from one model to another) that were brought together to produce the finished automobile through assembly-line methods that divided the work into repetitive, simple operations. By standardizing the production process and the skills that workers needed, Ford was able to lower the cost of automobiles dramatically.

Fordist production techniques not only affected the way that goods were produced—that is, by mass production—but also facilitated the growth of mass consumption. This occurred because Fordist techniques in industrial production brought the cost of goods within reach of large numbers of consumers. Further, because assembly-line work was so repellent, Ford was forced to pay workers more than the prevailing wage. The indirect result was that, thanks to the greater purchasing power enjoyed by workers at Ford and other large firms, the potential market for goods—automobiles and other mass-produced consumer durables—dramatically expanded. The social consequence of Fordism was to swell the ranks of semiskilled manual-industry workers, a group that came to rank as one of the largest sectors in the societies of Western Europe. The fact that these workers and their families enjoyed some of the material benefits of industrial production cemented their loyalty to the established regime, especially when the postwar settlement integrated them into political arrangements.

With the benefit of hindsight, particularly in light of renewed political conflict since the late 1960s, it becomes evident that the harmony of the postwar settlement derived from an unusual set of circumstances.

Wartime destruction exhausted political passions and placed a premium on cooperation within and among the states of Europe to rebuild their shattered economies and achieve a takeoff into the era of mass production. At the same time, the division of global influence between the United States and the Soviet Union reduced the possibility of pan-European unity and placed the states of Western Europe in a situation of economic and military dependence on the United States. *Pax Americana* meant that Western European nations lacked the material means to challenge the United States's leadership, at the same time that the perceived threat of a Soviet military invasion quelled potential political conflicts.

U.S. military, political, and economic intervention promoted European recovery and was also directed toward preventing the emergence of radical regimes in Western Europe. Nevertheless, despite the aims of some policymakers in the United States, convergence between U.S. and European political systems was limited because historical differences between the two regions were too strong to be overridden. Two factors were particularly important: the difference in the configuration of class forces in Western Europe and the role of the state. European workers were more conscious of their class affiliations and often defined their lives in terms of their participation in political parties and in party- and class-linked subcultures that provided strong bonds of friendship and community. European workers were likely to organize along class lines in the political sphere and support a range of parties—labor, social democratic, socialist, communist—that sought to extend state control over the private market system as well as to expand social provision. Although most such parties were not radical, they did energetically seek to extend state-provided social services in ways that widened the gap separating Europe and the United States.

Moreover, not all workers and worker-supported parties were enthusiastic participants in the postwar settlement. Notably, Communist parties in France and Italy (among the largest parties in the country) were fundamentally, and quite openly, opposed to the entire capitalist system. Thus, contrary to the U.S. experience, political party cleavages within European politics reflected to a considerable extent class divisions dating from the emergence of industrial capitalism in the nineteenth century. In contrast to the United States, a fundamental axiom of European political life involved the continued conflict between working people (organized through trade unions and socialist parties of one variety or another) and the propertied classes (manufacturing elites and those linked to the world of finance, organized through business associations and bourgeois parties). Even when the gulf between classes diminished, it remained a central source of partisan conflict.

The role of the state—the bureaucracy, parliament, and the entire range of national governmental institutions—was far greater in Western Europe than in the United States. In Europe, the state provided substantial welfare benefits, directed fiscal and monetary policy, regulated industrial relations, and engaged in extensive efforts to sponsor industrial growth and restructure failing industries. In the postwar period, states throughout Western Europe extended their activities in the economic and social welfare spheres. For example, in many countries, a wave of nationalization of industry after the war resulted in state-owned enterprises that controlled basic industries like steel, energy, and air and rail transport.

For these reasons, the social harmony of the 1950s and 1960s did not lead to an Americanization of Western European politics. Rather, the two factors that most clearly distinguished Europe from the United States—party mobilization along class lines and activist state institutions—produced a special (Western) European model of politics that was more statist than what occurred in the United States, albeit unmistakably capitalist.

The process of constructing political harmony involved negotiating a set of nationally specific arrangements in each of the Western European countries, in which a wide array of state, business, trade union, and political party elites participated.[22] It was at this time that the welfare state was consolidated, high levels of employment were achieved, anticapitalist forces were marginalized, and an unusual degree of social, industrial, and political consent for mainstream and reformist policies was secured.

Both the nature of political participation and the character of the economic system underwent significant changes as the European model emerged after World War II and developed in the intervening half-century or more. Although contemporary European politics involves fundamental changes in the agreements that were negotiated in the 1940s and 1950s, the postwar settlement remains a critical juncture of great importance. Indeed, the agenda for European integration partially transferred the logic of the postwar settlement from the national to the EU level—since both levels of politics involved negotiations over distributive politics that were sustained by a normative appeal to common fates. Two major challenges involve whether the growth of EU institutions and policies throughout Western Europe can achieve the same result that occurred in the postwar settlement and (perhaps even more daunting) whether the same process can be extended by the eastward expansion of the EU.

The Transformation of Political Parties. Political parties played a key role in organizing political participation and consent within the emergent European model. However, as parties were transformed in the process of organizing and sustaining the postwar consensus, they eventually destabilized its social basis and weakened its underlying foundations.

The structure and behavior of political parties were transformed as parties with explicit organizational and ideological links to the working classes, on the one hand, and parties linked historically to the interests of economic elites, on the other, competed by appealing to broader constituencies. As an alternative to more adversarial ideological appeals, parties of both the left and the right often sought to generate broad-based electoral support. They did so by representing themselves to the electorate not as the party of the working class or the economic elite, but as the best modernizing party—the one that could master technological change and guide the national economy within a complex system of international interdependence. (One scholar termed this a shift from class-based, ideological, mass parties to "catch-all" parties that sought to "catch" support from voters of diverse social classes.)[23]

As parties in the 1960s began seeking interclass support on election day and became less concerned with mobilizing stable subcultures around class-based issues, class identities began to erode relative to non-class forms of self-identification, such as region, age, and religion. Social movements based on these and other non-class-based factors also erupted on the scene beginning in the 1960s to further supplant citizens' class identities.

A New Political Framework. The new political framework that developed in Western European nations after World War II involved a tacit alliance between the organized working class and large-scale business, an arrangement that had not existed in the past and would crumble by the 1970s. Under the guidance of the state, the two groups cooperated in a manner that stimulated economic growth, political moderation, and social harmony. Although states intervened extensively to regulate the economies and ensure nearly full employment, higher wages, and expanded social welfare provision, the working class was asked to accept as its part of the bargain severe limits on both its industrial and political demands.

The political scientist Adam Przeworski has elaborated a theoretical model that illuminates the conditions for the emergence and functioning of the postwar settlement. The political arrangements organizing this model are known as social democracy, in which a center-left party closely allied with the labor movement controls the government to orient state policy along the lines described here. According to the social democratic model that Przeworski elaborates (and which is a formalized model of what existed in considerable measure in the postwar period), the working class must be sufficiently organized, cohesive, and centralized to act in a unified, disciplined manner, and workers must gain a reasonable assurance from business and the state that they will receive a steady stream of benefits, including high employment levels, regular wage increases, and generous welfare state benefits. In return, the organized working class, through its leaders within the trade union and socialist party spheres, finds it worthwhile to moderate demands in ways that enable business to carry on profitable activities.[24]

Working-class moderation had several elements. In contrast to a past marked by intense class conflict, workers came to accept the prerogatives of capitalist control in the overall organization of the economy and within the production process. In effect, demands for annual wage increases and welfare state programs became substitutes for the satisfaction of demands that were more threatening to capitalist production (for example, workers' control over the pace, content, and conditions of work or over investment decisions, industrial policy, and technological innovations).

The model specifies that business must also accept constraints for the new agreement to work. Business firms must renounce the arbitrary exercise of their power in the workplace and political sphere, accept the legitimacy of unions, and provide workers with high levels of wages and employment. Finally, for the agreement to succeed, the state must do its part—for example, by vigorously pursuing policies that aim to maximize employment levels, price stability, social equity, and economic growth. More generally, the state must appear to be a neutral arbiter serving the general interest, rather than siding unduly with either employers or workers. If the state were seen as favoring business interests, workers would protest rather than cooperate; if the state were seen as favoring workers' interests, capitalists would refuse to invest (what has been dubbed a capital strike), and economic stagnation would result.

In Przeworski's model, the postwar settlement pattern of class relations appears to represent a situation of positive-sum cooperation, in which citizens from both major classes, as well as other groups, gain from mutual cooperation and restraint. In fact, however, the appearance of universal benefit was misleading. Not all classes and social forces gained from participating in the new, rationalized capitalist order. Although industrial workers (whether in blue-collar or office positions) began to enjoy the benefits of the consumer society, they continued to be subjected to the harsh conditions of industrial labor. Given a shortage of labor, owing to rapid economic expansion, millions of immigrant workers were recruited to northern Europe from southern Europe (Portugal, Spain, Italy, Greece, and Turkey) and Eastern Europe (especially Poland and Yugoslavia), as well as from Africa and Asia. Immigrant workers were assigned the most menial positions and received low wages and meager welfare benefits. They were denied citizenship rights and were subjected to discrimination in housing and educational opportunities. Women also received fewer benefits from the new order as a result of their unequal position in employment, in the domestic sphere, and in welfare state provisions.

Labor Movements, Social Democracy, and Western European Politics. The reforms, which resulted from the cross-class and cross-party political settlements that ushered in the postwar order of European politics, were first set in place in the 1950s. However, important political and economic differences generally divided the capitalist democracies in Western Europe by a north-south dimension: the nations of northern Europe (represented in this book by Britain and Germany) and those of southern Europe (represented by France, a mixed case, and Italy).

Workers in northern Europe were more likely to gain citizenship rights early and to be included within the dominant system. In West Germany (but not in Britain), labor unions were more unified, and workers gained greater benefits from the system. As a result, they were more likely to be moderate in their political stance. In contrast to southern Europe, working-class elements were not excluded from the decision-making process, nor did they remain hostile to the existing economic and political order in significant numbers. Indeed, social democratic governments in northern Europe were in the vanguard and sponsored most of the major policy innovations that composed the postwar settlement. Then, moderate conservative governments elsewhere emulated these reforms.

Labor movements in southern Europe were divided internally by ideological and religious differences that found expression in rival national confederations engaging in bidding wars for members at the workplace, firm, and industry levels. National union leaders had neither the authority nor the mandate to negotiate with business representatives and the state, and rank-and-file workers often refused to abide by whatever agreements were struck. Business was likely to be opposed to unions on ideological grounds, and, in any event, unions could not, and were not inclined to, offer management the kinds of benefits that unions routinely provided in northern Europe. Thus, the working class was relatively excluded from the ongoing economic order, which strengthened its tendency toward oppositional values and protest activity.

This comparison of labor movement dynamics in northern and southern Europe finds an important parallel in workers' political activity. For example, in the two northern European nations covered in this book, Britain and Germany, two-thirds or more of all workers were unified in a single socialist party, and these parties were either the first or second most powerful in their respective party system. The British Labour Party and the West German Social Democratic Party alternated as the governing party with center-right parties and played crucial roles in promoting progressive reforms. These social democratic parties made a vital contribution to forging the class compromise that prevailed in northern Europe. Within social democracy, the state provided more expansive welfare benefits, tax laws were more progressive so that income inequalities were somewhat narrowed, and state policies placed a higher priority on full employment.

In southern Europe, workers divided their support about equally among communist, socialist, and more conservative Christian democratic parties. As a result, the right governed in these countries, although sometimes in complex and unstable coalitions. This circumstance reinforced workers' exclusion from the political community and also fostered more conservative state policies.

France is a mixed case in our analysis of the north-south split during the postwar settlement. Although it industrialized rapidly after World War II, and thus in this respect converged with northern Europe, its political and cultural patterns—notably a high degree of ideological conflict, labor militancy, and political fragmentation—were reminiscent of southern Europe.

Despite important differences in the way that political conflict was structured in the various Western European nations and the north-south split that we have identified, there was a broad convergence in the policies sponsored by the major Western European governments. The rapid industrialization associated with the postwar settlement fueled the expansion of housing, education, old-age pensions, and unemployment insurance. Far more than in the United States, Western European governments shared major responsibility for providing all citizens with basic services, including housing, medical care, and old-age pensions. The means varied through time and from country to country. By the late 1950s, the European Economic Community (EEC), forerunner of the EU, which provided for lower tariffs and a harmonization of economic policies among member states, provided additional impetus toward convergence.

Nonetheless, national differences persisted as a result of variations in historical evolution, political culture and institutions, and the specific balance among social forces and political parties. In the country sections of this book, we review the particular policy orientation adopted by each state. Nevertheless, there were some common elements on the postwar policy agenda of all the Western European states covered in the book.

Economic Regulation and the Keynesian Welfare State.　Within the economic realm, the state engaged in ambitious efforts to achieve the goals of full employment, growth, economic modernization, and assistance to export-based industries. The European model of economic regulation, as it informally came to be known, involved vigorous state intervention with the twin aims of maximizing economic growth *and* ensuring that the fruits of economic growth would be diffused throughout the population. Two key terms summarize the policy mix: *Keynesian economics* and *the welfare state.* Taken together, the policy package is sometimes referred to as the *Keynesian welfare state.*

The distinguished English economist John Maynard Keynes inspired Keynesian economics. His work centered around understanding the causes of the Great Depression of the 1930s, when the industrialized economies of Europe and North America stagnated, living standards plummeted, and unemployment soared to unprecedented levels, reaching as high as 20 percent. Keynes sought to devise policies to end the depression and prevent the recurrence of future depressions. Rather than accepting fiscal orthodoxy, which stipulated that governments should cut spending when times were hard, Keynes advocated precisely opposite policies. According to Keynes, when governments cut spending, which orthodox economics claimed was necessary for governments to live within their reduced means, this *further* reduced demand, thereby contributing to the downward spiral of dwindling demand and investment. On the contrary, Keynes claimed, governments should boost spending during hard times—thereby countering the "natural" movement of the business cycle—in order to bolster demand and stimulate new investment. (This is why Keynes's economic recommendation is often called *countercyclical* demand management.) In brief, he posited that a more vigorous, activist government stance would reverse the trend toward stagnation and provoke upward growth.

Keynes's name is also associated with the welfare state, the second leg of the new policy orientation that developed during the Great Depression and following World War II. He argued that the provision of welfare service, that is, an expanded welfare state, provided an ideal outlet for the additional government spending. Before the 1930s, government spending for the most part was devoted to defense, the maintenance of internal order (police), and education. Keynes argued that a desirable way to increase government spending during economic downturns was to redistribute resources to those most in need—the unemployed, sick, and economically dependent members of society. The term *welfare state* refers to the series of programs that transfer funds to citizens to meet social needs (transfer payments, such as unemployment insurance, pensions, and family allowances) or involve direct government provision of goods or social services (housing, medical care, job training, and the like). Although the origins of such programs lie earlier than the Great Depression, it was during the 1930s, and especially after World War II, that the welfare state expanded to alter the political economies of European countries fundamentally.

Modernization of Political Institutions.   After World War II, power shifted from parliamentary to executive institutions within the state. This shift involved two elements. First, the balance of power within the state shifted from parliament to the bureaucracy. The decline of legislative bodies was justified by the presumed need for speed and cohesion in policymaking. Parliamentary institutions are designed to represent diverse interests and to promote debate among options, but they move quite slowly and are fragmented. The executive, on the other hand, is organized to act decisively in order to implement decisions effectively. Second, there was a shift of decision-making power within the executive. On the one hand, with the state involved in more far-flung activities, power gravitated upward, with prime ministers and their staffs exercising greater power of oversight and control over their cabinet associates and line agencies. On the other hand, because of the state's increased involvement in

macroeconomic and policy activities, economic ministries gained greatly increased influence in the day-to-day administration of governmental policy.

The European Model: Crises, Variations, and Challenges

Through the late 1960s, the European model we have described prevailed (with variations from nation to nation) throughout Western Europe as governments successfully managed economic and welfare policies and the major social classes maintained their modernizing alliance with the state. For the most part, the central trade-off of the national postwar settlements held: governmental steering mechanisms promoted full employment and economic growth, while increased social and welfare expenditures helped purchase relative social harmony and labor peace. The tension between democracy (now meaning participation through interest associations and cross-class political parties) and capitalism (now meaning politically regulated "modern capitalism" with extensive public holdings) was reduced—some thought forever.

Suddenly, and virtually without warning, this social harmony shattered, and a new era of political uncertainties began. The critical juncture unfolded in two stages. It was succeeded in the 1990s by a whole new era in European politics.

Stage One—From the Late 1960s Through the Mid-1970s: The Price of Success.   In a way, the renewal of political conflict was rooted in the process of economic growth itself, which generated a host of political tensions that had been obscured by the strong grip of organized labor, capital, and the state. Since state regulation was aimed at forcing the pace of economic growth rather than reducing its damaging social consequences, the balance of costs and benefits shifted. Urban sprawl, traffic jams, and congestion became common. Forests were destroyed and rivers poisoned by industrial pollution. Migrants from rural areas and "guest workers," the euphemism for immigrant workers, jammed into hastily constructed blocks of high-rise flats that began to ring older central cities.

Women were drawn into the paid labor force in high numbers as a result of a tight labor market and an increase in clerical and governmental service positions, but they were recruited to poorly paid, subordinate positions. Economic growth was achieved in part through the introduction of new technology, which displaced skilled workers and posed threats to workers' health and safety.

The rapid expansion of the educated, urban middle class helped spark the early phase of militant protest. Many university students were radicalized by opposition to the U.S. military action in Vietnam as well as to the rigid authority patterns they encountered closer to home in their universities, political parties, and families. Many sought nontraditional goals: they wanted production to be democratically organized, resisted the traditional demands of marriage and career paths, and were the first to warn of environmental dangers from corporate abuses.

The political scientist Ronald Inglehart has coined the term *postmaterialism* to describe the values espoused by many educated youths in the postwar generation.[25] He discerns an intense generational cleavage created by the very different conditions under which prewar and postwar generations reached political maturity. Those born before World War II craved material and physical security because this was what they most lacked as a result of the Great Depression and military cataclysm. In contrast, Europeans born after the war were raised in a period of relative material security that was linked to the postwar settlement. They were more likely to be highly educated and to have the confidence born of expecting to gain stable and well-paid jobs.

Rather than expressing satisfaction and political quiescence, the postwar generations took their material advantages for granted and developed higher expectations. They resented, more than their parents did, being forced to submit to hierarchy, whether, for working-class youth, the tedium and mindlessness that characterized assembly-line production jobs, or, for middle-class youth, the tedium of the rigid hierarchies they encountered in corporations, universities, and government. Postwar youth were more likely than their elders to reject the human and physical costs of military confrontation and economic growth. They sought to pursue nonmaterial goals, including self-expression, a sense of community, and autonomy. Because they were less integrated within established

institutions, they were inclined to express their frustration through unruly protest.

We should beware of assuming that the rebellion of the late 1960s was confined to the new middle class. A key element contributing to the outbreak of protest in the late 1960s, which scholars often overlook in their fascination with new sources of opposition, was the rebellion of the industrial core of the working class. As the pace of economic change increased, workers were forced to endure intensified work tempos, increased occupational hazards, and tedious work.

In order to understand the 1960s rebellion, we need to appreciate how it represented a confluence of diverse sources, somewhat in the manner of "the perfect storm" described in Sebastian Junger's book (and later film) of that name. That is, although there were some common grievances linking the diverse groups that protested in the 1960s, the sources were also quite diverse. "The movement" was a sprawling coalition of industrial workers; newly militant white-collar working classes; urban, educated middle-class youth; and women and nonwhites who had been neglected by traditional unions and leftist parties.

In the late 1960s and 1970s, there was a massive and unexpected eruption of what one study termed the "resurgence of class conflict in Western Europe." The most dramatic instance occurred in France in May 1968, when nearly half of all French workers, students, professionals, and civil servants staged the largest general strike in history. In Italy, during the "hot autumn" of 1969, workers and allied groups waged widespread grassroots struggles, outside established political party or legislative channels, for workplace control, political influence, and provision of social necessities like health care and housing. In Sweden, industrial relations became far more conflictual in the 1970s than previously and culminated in a general strike/lockout in May 1980.

A "crisis of governability" accompanied increasing electoral volatility. At the same time, increasingly influential political ideas and campaigns emerged outside and against conventional parties from the New Left and New Right: the women's movement; both neofascist and antiracist responses to immigration; nuclear disarmament agitation; environmental protest; and taxpayers' revolt.

If economic growth had continued unabated in the 1970s, social harmony might have been restored. However, the slowdown of Western Europe's economies reinforced the crisis of the postwar settlement. Many causes contributed to the continued erosion and replacement of the postwar settlement, and each made it more difficult for governments to maintain popular support.

Changes in the organization of production further eroded the postwar settlement. Fordism became an inefficient way to produce in the new era of the microelectronic revolution. As production shifted from mass-produced goods to diverse and often smaller-scale production strategies and to service-based industries, the semiskilled (often male) industrial working class began to shrink as a proportion of the employed population. On the one hand, this fragmented the working population and complicated neocorporatist bargaining that had been based on unified social actors. On the other hand, technological change brought about new collective identities that were based on new skills and social groups newly involved in production; for example, the number of female workers expanded rapidly. These changes were difficult to accommodate within the framework of privileged institutionalized bargaining with the state by the representatives of labor and business (neocorporatism) associated with the European model.

Western Europe was affected by the wider recession that began with the sharp increase in oil prices in 1973–1974. The cost of petroleum exports by the oil-producing developing countries grew at the expense of the industrialized nations of the West. The extremely high levels of popular support for the welfare state in Western Europe meant that most governments were unable to reduce welfare state benefits significantly. Meanwhile, trade union power limited labor market adjustments, and the increasingly global scale of production encouraged an outflow of investment from flagging Western European economies.

More generally, increasing economic integration meant that national governments were less able to regulate their domestic economies. In general, though with notable exceptions (among the larger European nations, West Germany was especially dynamic), Western Europe suffered a decline in international competitiveness. The result was higher rates of unemployment and inflation, slower productivity growth, and meager increases in living standards. The golden years of the postwar settlement were over.

Stage Two—From the Mid-1970s to the Mid-1980s: Experimentation and a Rightward Turn. Provoked by the political protest and poor economic performance that began in the late 1960s, a relatively brief phase of political experimentation occurred from the 1970s to the mid-1980s, when governments of the left and right promising new departures were elected in many Western European nations. Initially, political momentum took a leftward turn. For example, northern European regimes devised mechanisms that enabled workers to participate in decisions regarding technology change and occupational health and safety. In France, the Socialist government of François Mitterrand, elected in 1981, substantially expanded the nationalized industrial and financial sectors.

Political momentum soon shifted toward the right as constraints deriving from the international economy and the opposition of conservative domestic forces brought a halt to radical reforms. Although no Western European government was highly successful in either mobilizing political support or promoting successful economic performance, the left failed utterly to develop a new beginning—especially when measured against the high expectations that had been created by the election of radical reformist socialist regimes in France, Spain, and Greece.

If the postwar settlement was intimately associated with social democracy, the 1980s were an opportunity for a conservative counterattack. For example, in Britain the Conservative government of Margaret Thatcher mounted a massive and quite successful assault on the power of labor unions and privatized both public housing facilities and nationalized industrial firms. Equally significant, it fostered important changes in British political culture, increasing support for initiative and entrepreneurship at the expense of collectivity. Rightist coalitions promising tax reductions were elected in Denmark, Norway, and elsewhere, often replacing social democratic incumbents.

The uncertainty, loss of confidence, instability, and general decline that prevailed in Western Europe in the early 1980s was captured by the pungent term *Eurosclerosis*, which began to be heard at the time. Europe had lost its bearings following the long period of postwar reconstruction and growth, and where the drifting was destined to stop, nobody knew. Yet ever since the late 1980s and 1990s, there has been a revitalization of Europe, amid new issues, problems, and challenges.

From the 1990s to the Twenty-First Century: A New European Model?

Sometime in the 1980s, the vitality disappeared from the European model that was inspired by the postwar settlement of social democratic mixed economies and national policy models. Although significant elements of the European model remain—Europe's welfare state sector remains far more extensive than its counterpart in the United States—a new model of politics has emerged since the 1990s, the product of both a renewal of the process of European integration and a distinctive new domestic policy mix, which is pursued by governments that reject Keynesian economic policies. The present period is also marked by the reinvigoration and expansion of the EU, an intensification of economic globalization, the ever-present menace of terrorism, and the unrivaled power of the United States that often creates friction with European allies—as in the run-up to the war in Iraq or in perpetual trade disputes at the WTO or over the Kyoto protocols and efforts to reduce climate change. We are now living through a critical juncture in European political development of historic proportions.

From State to Market to the Third Way. Across the political spectrum, there has been a significant shift in expectations about the role of the state in economic management. Unions have lost power, and middle-class politics is ascendant. The state continues to play an important role in the new political economy, but the role consists of activity to bolster rather than curtail the operation of markets. The dominant tendency in Western European politics currently seems to be a powerful backlash against the principles of compromise and the balance of public and private power that were presupposed by the postwar settlement and the welfare state. There is general agreement on lowering taxes, reducing state economic intervention, and relying more on market forces to shape socioeconomic outcomes (an orientation widely referred to as

neoliberalism). Although many of the state steering mechanisms and welfare programs that were put in place during the postwar settlement have survived, the momentum for expanding political regulation of the marketplace is gone; instead, the dominant tendency is for the welfare state to cut back (roll-back of provisions and tightened eligibility) and the reinvigoration of private market forces wherever politically feasible.

This shift toward neoliberalism does not sweep other political concerns off the board. Many of the concerns that began to undermine the postwar settlement in the late 1960s, including environmental and other quality-of-life matters, the demand for autonomy and community, and opposition to intrusive public and private bureaucracies, continue to fuel social and political movements. And conservative parties are often less suited than left-of-center ones to respond effectively to these new issues on the policy agenda. In fact, it has become increasingly difficult to define left and right in traditional pro-market or pro-state terms.

Into the breach, a new policy orientation emerged in Europe as center-left politicians and parties, led by Britain's Tony Blair, with Germany's Gerhard Schröder a powerful ally, tried to go "beyond left and right." This *third way* attempts to transcend distributional politics, which it considers unsuited to an era of intensified global competition, and to combine the best of traditional appeals of left and right: the social justice concerns of classic social democracy with reliance on the economic dynamism of the right.[26] Ralf Dahrendorf, a distinguished observer of European affairs, has commented, "In fact, the Third Way debate has become the only game in town—the only hint at new directions for Europe's politics in a confused multitude of trends and ideas."[27] Thus far, the changing of the guard in Europe—with Angela Merkel replacing Schröder in Germany, Nicolas Sarkozy replacing Jacques Chirac in France, Gordon Brown taking over from Blair in Britain, and Romano Prodi replacing Silvio Berlusconi in Italy—has largely reinforced this third way orientation.

To be sure, the arrival of a new political orientation that challenges and significantly recasts the European model does not mean the eradication of the old model. Class and occupational boundaries remain politically important, although sometimes in unusual ways. For example, as jobs become scarce, an important cleavage pits those occupying stable jobs against those with precarious employment or none at all. As private sector jobs become unstable, an important cleavage pits private sector workers against public sector workers, who usually enjoy the security of lifetime employment. At the same time, the waning of long-standing debates between socialists and conservatives means neither the end of political ideologies nor the consecration of a centrist consensus. Witness the rise of new forces, groups, and parties that challenge the established order. Without wishing to equate them, we observe other orientations that have gained increased importance: the environmental movements and their political expression (the Greens are now solidly represented in the European Parliament), plus anti-immigrant xenophobic forces in virtually every country. Thus, although the third way may not be the only game in town, it casts a long shadow over Europe.

September 11, Iraq, the Old and New Europe, March 11, and Beyond.   In the unfinished story of European politics in transition, the most recent chapter began on the fateful morning of September 11, 2001, when four planes hijacked by Al Qaeda militants were transformed into bombs and used to attack strategic targets in the United States. Initially, most Europeans shared Americans' sense of shock, grief, and outrage. Numerous European states provided military assistance, including troops or supplies, during the United Nations–authorized attack led by the United States on the Taliban regime in Afghanistan, the base of Al Qaeda operations. However, international support turned to opposition the following fall as the United States began preparations to invade Iraq. The overwhelming majority of Europeans opposed the U.S. invasion, and the three Western European governments that supported the action—Britain, Italy, and Spain—paid dearly. The pro-U.S. Spanish government of José Aznar was turned out of office in the 2004 parliamentary elections. Italian prime minister Silvio Berlusconi also suffered a steep loss of support and lost his premiership in April 2006. Tony Blair's passionate support for the Iraq invasion severely damaged his credibility at home. He never recovered his former popularity and was ultimately forced to resign in June 2007.

The situation was very different in East-Central Europe, where most governments supported the U.S. military action in Iraq. One reason advanced was that the postcommunist regimes in the region were repaying the United States for its contributions in the 1980s to the demise of communist dictatorships. Unlike most countries in Western Europe, Poland and other countries in East-Central Europe contributed military assistance and political support to the U.S.-led war in Iraq.

So sharp was this cleavage that, in the diplomatic campaign by the United States to win support for the war in Iraq that was to be launched in March 2003, U.S. Secretary of Defense Donald Rumsfeld distinguished between what he called the "new Europe" and the "old Europe." Rumsfeld suggested that the center of gravity in Europe had shifted east, toward the states preparing to join the EU and NATO, who he implied represented the wave of the future. The old Europe—notably France and Germany, whose leaders and populations firmly opposed an invasion of Iraq—were, in Rumsfeld's view, out of step with a new emerging European sensibility that embraced American values and global leadership. As you read the country-by-country analyses, think about Rumsfeld's observation—and consider how 9/11 and the war in Iraq have shaped each country's foreign policy and relationship to the United States.

The European Union, the Failed Constitution, and the Prospects Ahead[28]

When the Treaty of Rome created the European Economic Community in 1957, many scholars confidently predicted the steady growth of European economic and political integration. Despite steps in this direction, the path was far more tortuous than many expected. Indeed, the economic turbulence beginning in the mid-1970s brought the process to a crashing halt as European states became more concerned with protecting their domestic economies than with cooperating on a European-wide level. By the early 1980s, this had produced the Eurosclerosis noted earlier.

The same forces that drove domestic political change in the 1980s also impelled political leaders and prominent business executives to cast their lot with a strengthened EU. When French president François Mitterrand reluctantly concluded in 1983 that France could not revive its sluggish economy by itself, he decided to join forces with German chancellor Helmut Kohl in a joint effort to revive France and Germany's ailing economies through increased European economic cooperation. In so doing, the leaders of Western Europe's two major states, along with prominent business leaders and officials in the EU, rescued the EU from stagnation.

When the Maastricht Treaty on European Union was ratified in 1993, a new era began in Western European politics. Maastricht deepened economic integration; incorporated some aspects of foreign relations, defense policy, and policing; and addressed the persistent demands for greater internal democracy. Since the early 1990s the regulatory and institutional changes in the framework of the EU have ranged from specific provisions expanding the organization's scope—which mandate the free movement of commodities, capital, technology, and labor—to infrastructural concerns of standardizing technical production norms and redrafting labor and other codes, as well as unresolved issues, such as the Social Charter to enhance workplace and social rights. These changes include the creation of the European Central Bank; the launching of the euro in 1999; the Stability and Growth Pact (which specifies limits on the debt and deficit of member states) negotiated in 1997 and revised in 2005 to provide more flexibility; and the enlargement of the EU in 2004 and again in 2007. All these developments signal new life and great hopes for the EU, but they also introduce significant political and institutional challenges. And nothing captures this yeasty brew of challenges and opportunities better than the story of the May–June 2005 rejection of the EU Constitution, in quick succession, by France and then the Netherlands.

The EU Constitution: "Non" for Now—or Forever?

In the early years of the new century, the EU seemed poised to take another leap forward as the result of a new initiative to promote closer economic integration, streamlined decision making, and a common security and foreign policy. The new reforms were proposed in the first draft of what was entitled the "Treaty Establishing a Constitution for Europe." The proposal was developed by the Convention on the Future of Europe, a body convened by the EU Commission and composed of distinguished European political figures. The Member States then convened an Intergovernmental Conference (IGC) in October 2003, taking the draft prepared by the Convention as their starting point. In June 2004, facing the prospect of a rancorous defeat, agreement was reached, and in October 2004, the document was signed in Rome by all the member states.

In order to go into force, the treaty establishing the constitution had to be approved by all member states, at the time 25. By May 2005, ten countries had ratified the treaty: Austria, Germany, Greece, Hungary, Italy, Latvia, Lithuania, Slovakia, and Slovenia approved it by parliamentary vote; Spain approved it by referendum. And then . . . the unthinkable happened. France, one of the founding members of the EU—and, along with Germany, the most influential country advocating closer European integration—rejected the draft treaty. In a nationwide referendum sponsored by President Chirac, an ardent supporter of the treaty, 55 percent of French voters opposed ratifying the treaty. (The reasons are analyzed in Chapter 30.)

Three days after the French "non," 62 percent of Dutch voters also rejected the treaty—a significantly larger majority than the French outcome. Many in the Netherlands feared that the new Constitution would reinforce the power of larger member states in the EU at the expense of the smaller ones. There was also some Dutch anxiety that Europe might "harmonize" out of existence some of Dutch society's social liberalism (tolerance for soft drugs and euthanasia, for example). The Dutch were in the midst of a major crisis of conscience about immigration. The discovery that immigrants were not learning Dutch and were resisting assimilation plus the assassinations of public figures who had taken strong positions on immigration had stimulated deep debate about past and future policies. It was a bad moment to ask the Dutch about Europe.

A devastating one-two blow, the resounding French and Dutch no votes provoked a huge European crisis. With resentments over the war in Iraq spilling over into EU politics, Tony Blair and Jacques Chirac engaged in bitter mutual recriminations. These two rivals were the lightening rod, but the bitterness of the defeat was far more widespread. Acrimony between national leaders around major disagreements about the EU's future foretold difficult years to come. Clearly, the French "non" helped precipitate a new, uncertain, and possibly ominous moment of transition in European politics. What are the roots of that crisis, its character, and possible outcome?

The Constitution: Sowing the Seeds of Failure

The European Convention was intended to bring the European Union closer to European peoples. It was designed, above all, to resolve the serious problems of popular lack of interest and disenchantment. What a bitter irony that the "Treaty Establishing a Constitution for Europe" would become a lightning rod for every perceived slight and every discontent about Europe and about national politics, political elites, and economic problems as well.

The idea was to gather a broadly representative group of leaders and organizations, who were mandated to consult as widely as they could, to propose solutions to EU institutional problems tied to the Union's Central and Eastern European enlargement, to work on important unresolved policy matters (such as defense and foreign policy and key "justice and home affairs" issues such as immigration), and to recodify the EU's existing legal and institutional foundations in ways that ordinary citizens could understand.

Valéry Giscard d'Estaing, the Convention president and former president of France, was a distinguished and intelligent politician, but he was too haughty, aristocratic, and elderly to communicate with Europe's newer generations. His assistants, Giuliano Amato and Jean-Luc de Haene, the former prime ministers of Italy and Belgium, respectively, were seasoned wheeler-dealers. The consultation was trapped in a world of insiders: EU officials, intellectuals, and political elites and those interest and pressure groups who functioned at European levels. The Convention did not solve the EU's broader problem of communicating beyond such insiders—in fact it deepened the problem.

Nor could the Convention satisfy the reservations and confusions many European citizens harbored about EU institutions and decision-making processes. At the EU level, there are three key institutions:

- The European Commission that serves as the executive, proposes legislation, and advances the broad agenda for the EU
- The Council of the European Union, the main decision-making body, which represents the member states through the direct participation of one minister from each member country
- The European Parliament, directly elected by EU citizens every five years, which passes laws in many policy areas with the Council, and provides democratic oversight and legitimacy for other institutions and for the EU as a whole—but does not autonomously legislate in the manner of national parliaments

The Constitution proposed a number of institutional changes to cope with enlargement—in particular, changes in the composition of the European Commission. It also proposed new powers for the European Parliament and a new approach to weighting national votes in the European Council (the so-called dual majority procedure—of states and of populations—that better reflected the relative sizes of member states). These changes were really matters of institutional tinkering and did not create a great deal of elite conflict, even though they caused apprehension among smaller member states, who were afraid of domination by larger ones.

There were also a few broader proposals. For example, one called for the creation of a Council president and a foreign minister, offices intended to enhance the capacity of the EU to represent its interests externally and to speak more or less authoritatively with national counterparts. In addition, the Constitution included some slippery wording on moving from unanimity to qualified majority decision making in certain areas. In general, however, the proposed Constitution was remarkable for its lack of bold new initiatives.

In its first two parts, the Constitution presented the European Union in simple and persuasive ways. Part One, which was a readable fifteen pages, set out the core values and objectives of the European Union in terms that had broad appeal. Among other things, Europe was for peace and freedom, against poverty, social exclusion, and discrimination of all kinds. It was in favor of equality between men and women, solidarity between generations, and the protection of children. Europe stood for cohesion between its different regions, enhanced social protection and justice, and a competitive "social market economy." Part Two was a five-page Charter of Fundamental Rights, guaranteeing wide-ranging human, social, economic, and political rights. All well and good.

Had the Constitution ended after Part Two it might have been spared the indignities that the French and Dutch inflicted upon it. Alas, there was also Part Three, a long, detailed, and dense recapitulation of what the EU could do, and how it should do it institutionally. This made the Constitutional document into 200 pages, 448 articles, 36 protocols, and 50 declarations. Part Three was necessary to integrate the EU's many previous treaties, but it added nothing useful and was full of references to liberalization and market building. It was read and denounced endlessly in France, the Netherlands, and elsewhere, even though it did little more than recapitulate the arcane details of fifty years of integration.

The prospects for the success of the Constitution were not helped when European citizens were asked to ratify the Constitution at the worst possible time. Economies were in the dumps. Unemployment was painfully high. The European social and economic models—which promised extensive social protections—were under assault from all sides. A proposed directive from the Commission for liberating the market for services was portrayed as a threat to health care and to national controls over professional certification for private services. The directive fed intense fears that immigrants from the new Eastern and Central European member states would swamp the EU-15. The prospect of Turkish accession to the EU, which was widely opposed, provided another red flag, provoking fears and mobilizing opposition to the Constitution.

In retrospect, the politics of the EU Constitution seem to confirm the famous maxim of Tip O'Neill, the former Speaker of the U.S. House of Representatives that "all politics is local." As we turn to our country-by-country analysis of key EU members it becomes clear that the broad themes identified above are in play in every national context but—no surprise!—each case reveals a unique relationship between national and EU factors.

Where Will the EU Go from Here?

EU cynics are having a field day. It's the economy, stupid. It's the lack of democracy and transparency. It's global competitive pressures and neoliberalism chipping away at the European social and economic model. It's the distant, arrogant, and aloof European bureaucrats—or the national politicians, who are no better!

National leaders have played a deceptive two-level game—and have finally been caught! They have been using Europe as a lever to create EU-level programs that oblige their constituencies to undergo reforms—mainly cuts in social protections—which they would never have permitted at the national level. In the end, the no votes delivered a simple message to the political elites: You can try to fool the people all the time, but it won't work, especially if you call referendums to ask them how they feel about being fooled!

There is an old maxim in sports, "Your team is never as good as it looks when you are winning—or as bad as it looks when you are losing." For now, the EU looks pretty bad, but it is worth remembering its extraordinary record of achievements.

Against the horrifying backdrop of World War II, the founders of the European Coal and Steel Community (1950) and then the European Economic Community (1958) calculated that promoting economic cooperation would enable member countries to bury past differences and become political allies. For half a century—despite some important bumps in the road—the plan has worked brilliantly, contributing significantly to stability, peace, and prosperity for the member states.

The French and Dutch veto in 2005 was a significant setback for the EU, signaling that the Union was likely to remain stuck in place for a number of years. Without a reform treaty, it would be difficult to achieve intergovernmental consent to move forward in foreign policy and defense, on the budget, on enlargement, or on streamlining decision making. After two years of stalemate, EU officials and diplomats negotiated a slimmed-down version of the draft constitution in 2007. If ratified by all 27 EU member states, the compromise document will help promote a more unified and energetic EU.

The EU's future will be significantly affected by what key member states do about their domestic problems. And on this, the effect of the Constitution should not be exaggerated. Even had France provided a reverberating "oui," it would not have been easy to reform the European "social model" to spur more growth and greater competitiveness without destroying all that is unique and good about Europe, starting with the economic security and social solidarities that Europeans demand.

The defeat of the Constitution makes solving these problems more difficult. But it should not—and must not—justify inertia or extreme pessimism. After all, it is just possible that the period of turmoil and reflection that the no votes inspired will provoke some hard thinking and productive political mobilizations to revitalize the Union, narrow the gap between citizens and elites, and resolve the institutional and programmatic challenges of enlargement and competitiveness. With new leadership in several of the most influential EU countries comes hope that the constitutional deadlock will be broken, but the consolidation of a new political and institutional settlement for Europe will require exceptional resolve and diplomacy, and more than a little luck.

Conclusion

The EU is not only a source of economic progress and political optimism. It has also become a target for popular discontent by reshaping European economies, involving the standardizing of production norms, ending state subsidies for domestic producers, and promoting austerity policies. The new European model that has developed since the deepening of European integration in the 1990s—in tandem with the dramatic enlargement of members—is very much a mixed blessing: on the one hand, a revival of Europe's economic fortunes and geopolitical influence; on the other hand, widening divisions between European citizens who are winners and those who are losers—depending on education, training, and occupation. The shift in power toward the EU has also limited the capacity of the member states to regulate their own economies and societies, increased tensions over the definition of citizenship and national identity, and produced a "democratic deficit"—concerns over citizen control and institutional transparency and accountability—at the level of EU institutions.

Europe faces a host of stresses and unanswered questions, including how to reconcile regional and ethnic diversity with national unity, national cultural differences with the evolving EU, persistent (and often disappointed) demands for economic growth with concerns about inequality and unemployment as well as environmental and social costs. How can European countries and the EU participate in the U.S.-sponsored war on terrorism—and other American foreign policy initiatives with far-reaching consequences for Europe—without becoming hostage to decisions made in Washington? How can the EU and member countries muster the necessary unity and muscle to help reduce renewed conflicts between the United States and Russia, for example over the U.S. plan to build an antimissile shield in Eastern Europe?

European politics is in transition from a stable postwar past to an uncertain future; from a set of conflicts dominated by class-based politics to a more complex political dynamic defined by both centrist and more radical versions of a politics beyond left and right: a transition from a situation of national autonomy to a web of European integration. Can EU Europe emerge from its constitutional crisis and the challenges posed by rapid enlargement with the necessary institutional reforms and a renewed sense of purpose? The answer to this daunting question is not yet clear.

As the failed ratification of the Constitution demonstrated, whatever occurs at the level of the domestic politics of EU member countries will heavily affect the future of the EU and the challenges European countries may face. Although the current transition in European politics signals the emergence of the EU as a transnational polity, understanding European politics in transition requires close attention to the political systems, institutions, and processes of national states in Europe.

This is the task that we seek to accomplish in *European Politics in Transition*. Directly following the Introduction, we describe the political economy, institutions, participants, and processes of major Western European nations: Britain, France, Germany, and Italy. We then analyze developments in Russia, in many ways the most powerful European country, whose fate has enormous repercussions for the EU and the entire region. We then analyze developments in East-Central Europe, where we focus on Poland, Hungary, and the

Czech and Slovak Republics (and consider Yugoslavia), the most important nations in East-Central Europe. Finally, we provide a comprehensive analysis of developments in the EU and their consequences for the understanding of national politics.

In each country study, we begin with a description of the historical legacy of state formation, which continues to have a significant impact on political forces and policies, and a broad overview of contemporary political institutions and challenges. The second chapter in each part analyzes the historically specific features of both the postwar settlement and the shift since the 1970s toward the more market-oriented political economy. The third chapter in each part analyzes institutions of policy formation and implementation: the government and executive generally, public and semi-public agencies, local government, and the judiciary. The fourth chapter in each part analyzes institutions of political representation, notably legislatures, political parties and elections, modes of organizing interests, and contentious movements. The last chapter in each country part focuses on the current transition: new political forces, cleavages, and policies; the impact of the EU; and likely directions of change. The interplay of the EU and domestic politics and policy is highlighted in each country study.

It is quite a challenge to understand the political systems and changing dynamics of contemporary Europe. We hope that the timely information and thematic focus of *European Politics in Transition* will both prepare and inspire you to explore further the endlessly fascinating terrain of European politics.

Notes

[1] Ralph Atkins, "Eurozone Trumpets Its Perfect Economic Recovery," *Financial Times*, March 31–April 1, 2007, p. 2.

[2] Samuel Brittan, "Almost a New Economic Miracle," *Financial Times*, April 13, 2007, p. 13.

[3] "Europe's Mid-Life Crisis," *The Economist*, March 17, 2007, p. 13.

[4] For a superb study of this issue, see David Stark and Laszlo Bruszt, *Postsocialist Pathways: Transforming Politics and Property in East Central Europe* (Cambridge: Cambridge University Press, 1998).

[5] For attempts to answer this question, see Alfred Stepan and Cindy Skach, "Constitutional Frameworks and Democratic Consolidation: Parliamentarism Versus Presidentialism," *World Politics* 46, no.1 (October 1993): 1–22, and Juan J. Linz and Arturo Valenzuela, eds., *The Failure of Presidential Democracy* (Baltimore: Johns Hopkins University Press, 1994).

[6] Robert A. Dahl, *A Preface to Economic Democracy* (Berkeley and Los Angeles: University of California Press, 1985), pp. 54–55 (emphasis in the original).

[7] For a classic discussion of this issue, see Charles Lindblom, *Politics and Markets: The World's Political Economic Systems* (New York: Basic Books, 1977).

[8] Adam Przeworski, *Democracy and the Market: Political and Economic Reforms in Eastern Europe and Latin America* (Cambridge: Cambridge University Press, 1991), p. xi.

[9] Robert Putnam, with Robert Leonardi and Raffaella Y. Nanetti, *Making Democracy Work: Civic Traditions in Modern Italy* (Princeton, N.J.: Princeton University Press, 1992).

[10] Sidney Tarrow, "Making Social Science Work Across Space and Time: A Critical Reflection on Robert Putnam's *Making Democracy Work*," *American Political Science Review* 90, no. 2 (1996): 389–399.

[11] Gabriel Almond and Sidney Verba, *The Civic Culture: Political Attitudes and Democracy in Five Nations* (Boston: Little, Brown, 1963). See also Gabriel Almond and Sidney Verba, eds., *The Civic Culture Revisited* (Boston: Little, Brown, 1980).

[12] Dankwart Rustow, "Transitions to Democracy: Toward a Dynamic Model," *Comparative Politics* 2, no. 3 (April 1970): 363.

[13] For recent descriptions by sympathetic participant-observers, see John Cavanagh and Jerry Mander, eds., *Alternatives to Economic Globalization: A Better World Is Possible* (San Francisco: Berrett-Koehler, 2004), and Robin Broad, ed., *Global Backlash: Citizen Initiatives for a Just World Economy* (Lanham, Md.: Rowman & Littlefield, 2002). For a spirited defense of globalization, see Jagdish Bhagwati, *In Defense of Globalization* (New York: Oxford University Press, 2004).

[14] For a superb analysis, see Saskia Sassen, "The State and Globalization," in Rodney Bruce Hall and Thomas J. Biersteker, eds., *The Emergence of Private Authority in Global Governance* (Cambridge: Cambridge University Press, 2002), chap. 5.

[15] Peter A. Hall and David Soskice, eds., *Varieties of Capitalism: The Institutional Foundations of Comparative Advantage* (New York: Oxford University Press, 2001). Also see Herbert Kitschelt, Peter Lange, Gary Marks, and John D. Stephens, eds., *Continuity and Change in Contemporary Capitalism* (Cambridge: Cambridge University Press, 1999).

[16] This view was first put forward in Dankwart Rustow's classic article, "Transitions to Democracy . . . ," reprinted in Lisa Anderson, ed., *Transitions to Democracy* (New York: Columbia University Press, 1999). More recently, it has been developed by Dietrich Rueschemeyer, Evelyne Huber Stephens, and John D. Stephens, *Capitalist Development and Democracy* (Chicago: University of Chicago Press, 1992), and Adam Przeworski, *Democracy and the Market*.

[17] Guillermo O'Donnell and Philippe C. Schmitter, *Transitions from Authoritarian Rule: Tentative Conclusions About Uncertain Democracies* (Baltimore: Johns Hopkins University Press, 1986).

[18]Adam Przeworski et al., *Democracy and Development: Political Institutions and Well-Being in the World, 1950–1990* (Cambridge: Cambridge University Press, 2000), chap. 4. For a classic statement of the opposing view, see Samuel Huntington, *Political Order in Changing Societies* (New Haven, Conn.: Yale University Press, 1968).

[19]Perry Anderson, *Lineages of the Absolutist State* (London: New Left Books, 1974); Douglass North, *Structure and Change in Economic History* (New York: Norton, 1981); Hendrick Spruyt, *The Sovereign State and Its Competitors: An Analysis of Systems Change* (Princeton, N.J.: Princeton University Press, 1994); and Charles Tilly, *Coercion, Capital and European States, A.D. 990–1992* (Cambridge, Mass.: Blackwell, 1993).

[20]Barrington Moore, Jr., *The Social Origins of Dictatorship and Democracy* (Boston: Beacon Press, 1966).

[21]Andrew Shonfield, *Modern Capitalism: The Changing Balance of Public and Private Power* (Oxford: Oxford University Press, 1980), p. 3.

[22]The general process has been exquisitely described by Claus Offe, *Contradictions of the Welfare State* (Cambridge, Mass.: MIT Press, 1984), chap. 8 and *passim.*

[23]Otto Kirchheimer, "The Transformation of the Western European Party Systems," in Joseph La-Palombara and Myron Weiner, eds., *Political Parties and Political Development* (Princeton, N.J.: Princeton University Press, 1966), chap. 6.

[24]Adam Przeworski, *Capitalism and Social Democracy* (New York: Cambridge University Press, 1985).

[25]See Ronald Inglehart, *The Silent Revolution: Changing Values and Political Styles Among Western Publics* (Princeton, N.J.: Princeton University Press, 1977), *Culture Shift in Advanced Industrial Society* (Princeton, N.J.: Princeton University Press, 1990), and *Modernization and Postmodernization: Cultural, Economic, and Political Change in 43 Societies* (Princeton, N.J.: Princeton University Press, 1997).

[26]For the classic statement of this approach, see Anthony Giddens, *The Third Way: The Renewal of Social Democracy* (Cambridge: Polity Press, 1998).

[27]Ralf Dahrendorf, "The Third Way and Liberty: An Authoritarian Streak in Europe's New Center," *Foreign Affairs* 78, no. 5 (September–October 1999): 13.

[28]This discussion of the European Constitution is drawn from Mark Kesselman and Joel Krieger, eds., *The European Union Constitution: "Non" for Now—or Forever?* (Boston: Houghton Mifflin, 2006). The analysis and commentary included here is drawn from the contribution of George Ross to this pamphlet.

Part 1 Bibliography

Anderson, Perry. *Lineages of the Absolutist State.* London: New Left Books, 1974.

Berger, Suzanne, ed. *Organizing Interests in Western Europe: Pluralism, Corporatism, and the Transformation of Politics.* Cambridge: Cambridge University Press, 1981.

Coates, David, ed. *Varieties of Capitalism, Varieties of Approaches.* London: Palgrave, 2005.

Dalton, Russell J., and Manfred Kuechler, eds. *Challenging the Political Order: New Social and Political Movements in Western Democracies.* New York: Oxford University Press, 1990.

Eichengreen, Barry. *The European Economy since 1945: Coordinated Capitalism and Beyond.* Princeton, N.J.: Princeton University Press, 2007.

Esping-Andersen, Gøsta. *Social Foundations of Post-Industrial Economies.* New York: Oxford University Press, 1999.

Hall, Peter A., ed. *The Political Power of Economic Ideas.* Princeton, N.J.: Princeton University Press, 1989.

Hall, Peter A., and David Soskice, eds. *Varieties of Capitalism: The Institutional Foundations of Comparative Advantage.* New York: Oxford University Press, 2001.

Hobsbawm, Eric. *The Age of Extremes: The Short Twentieth Century, 1914–1991.* New York: Vintage Books, 1994.

Hollingsworth, J. Rogers, and Robert Boyer, eds. *Contemporary Capitalism: The Embeddedness of Institutions.* New York: Cambridge University Press, 1997.

Hollingsworth, J. R., Philippe C. Schmitter, and Wolfgang Streeck, eds. *Governing Capitalist Economies: Performance and Control of Economic Sectors.* New York: Oxford University Press, 1994.

Huber, Evelyne, and John D. Stephens, *Development and Crisis of the Welfare State: Parties and Policies in Global Markets.* Chicago: University of Chicago Press, 2001.

Inglehart, Ronald. *Culture Shift in Advanced Industrial Society.* Princeton, N.J.: Princeton University Press, 1990.

Iversen, Torben. *Capitalism, Democracy, and Welfare.* Cambridge: Cambridge University Press, 2005.

Judt, Tony, *Postwar: A History of Europe since 1945.* New York: Penguin, 2005.

Marglin, Stephen A., and Juliet R. Schor. *The Golden Age of Capitalism: Reinterpreting the Postwar Experience.* New York: Oxford University Press, 1990.

Martin, Andrew, et al. *The Brave New World of European Unions: European Trade Unions at the Millennium.* New York: Berghahn, 1999.

Moore, Barrington, Jr. *The Social Origins of Dictatorship and Democracy.* Boston: Beacon Press, 1966.

Offe, Claus. *Contradictions of the Welfare State.* Cambridge, Mass.: MIT Press, 1984.

Portusson, Jonas. *Inequality and Prosperity: Social Europe versus Liberal America.* Ithaca: Cornell University Press, 2005.

Putnam, Robert D., with Robert Leonardi and Raffaella Y. Nanetti. *Making Democracy Work: Civic Traditions in Modern Italy.* Princeton, N.J.: Princeton University Press, 1992.

Rueschemeyer, Dietrich, Evelyne Huber Stephens, and John D. Stephens. *Capitalist Development and Democracy.* Chicago: University of Chicago Press, 1992.

Schmidt, Vivien A. *The Futures of European Capitalism.* New York: Oxford University Press, 2002.

Schofield, Norman. *Multiparty Government: The Politics of Coalition in Europe.* Oxford: Oxford University Press, 1990.

Shonfield, Andrew. *Modern Capitalism: The Changing Balance of Private and Public Power.* Oxford: Oxford University Press, 1980.

Stark, David, and Laszlo Bruszt. *Postsocialist Pathways: Transforming Politics and Property in East Central Europe.* Cambridge: Cambridge University Press, 1998.

Swank, Duane. *Global Capital, Political Institutions, and Policy Change in Developed Welfare States.* Cambridge: Cambridge University Press, 2002.

Tarrow, Sidney. *Power in Movement: Social Movements and Contentious Politics.* New York: Cambridge University Press, 1998.

Tilly, Charles. *Coercion, Capital and European States, A.D. 990–1992.* Cambridge, Mass.: Blackwell, 1993.

Tilly, Charles. *Contention and Democracy in Europe, 1650–2000.* Cambridge: Cambridge University Press, 2003.

PART 2

Britain

Joel Krieger

CHAPTER 1

The Making of the Modern British State

Politics in Action

They met innocently enough, Tony Blair and Gordon Brown, but their tempestuous political relationship at the helm of Britain's New Labour government from 1997 to 2007, while Blair was prime minister and Brown was chancellor of the exchequer (an exceedingly powerful finance minister or treasury secretary), preoccupied the country almost as much as that of Charles and Diana in their heyday—and with far greater political consequences. Born in 1953 to a mother from Donegal, Ireland (who moved to Glasgow after her father's death), and a father from the Clydeside shipyards, Tony Blair moved to Durham in the north of England when he was five but spent much of his youth in boarding schools. Then, when he was old enough to set out on his own, Blair moved south to study law at Oxford; specialized in employment and industrial law in London; and then returned to the north only to enter the House of Commons from Sedgefield in 1983. Born in 1951, Gordon Brown, on the other hand, is the son of a Church of Scotland preacher. By all accounts an imposing and rigorous

intellectual figure, he attended Edinburgh University at the age of sixteen where he achieved first-class honors. He earned a doctorate (he wrote on the Labour Party in Scotland in the early part of the twentieth century) and served as a lecturer at Edinburgh and at Caledonian University. He then worked for Scottish television before moving on, full-time, to the world of Scottish and British Labour party politics.

Blair and Brown first met when they were newly elected members of parliament (MPs) after the 1983 election. They formed a friendship and shared an office: Blair was charming, intuitive, telegenic; while Brown was more bookish, intense, cautious, and dour. Both were rising stars in the party, Blair pushing the party to modernize and expand its political base well beyond its heritage as a labor party and Brown taking on the role of shadow chancellor (the opposition party's spokesman on the economy and potential chancellor should Labour return to office).

After the death in 1994 of John Smith, the leader of the Labour party, their ambitions inevitably clashed as both sought to replace Smith as leader—the person who would become prime minister upon a Labour Party

Blair's 2005 victory was both historic and humbling. In an image that promised to be replayed endlessly on television whenever the 2005 election was discussed, Blair visibly blanched as a defeated independent candidate, whose son died in Iraq, asked Blair to make amends to the families of those who lost loved ones in the war.
Source: © Jeff J. Mitchell/ Reuters/Corbis

victory in a national election. With the Conservatives in power since 1979, Labour had been in the political wilderness for a lengthy period, and both men were eager to take on the Tories (as the Conservatives are commonly called) and lead a new version of the Labour Party (what has been dubbed "New Labour") into office.

The next step in this relationship, which was to shape British politics for a generation or more, has been endlessly discussed, filled endless newspaper columns, and been the subject of TV docudramas. Although never confirmed by Blair or Brown (if true, it was doubtless the worst-kept secret in Britain), within weeks of Smith's death, as the process of selecting his successor as Labour leader was unfolding, the two met at a restaurant in London (the exact day and restaurant are widely known). It is said that Brown agreed to withdraw from the leadership contest in favor of Blair. In return (although Blair supporters have routinely denied it), Blair promised one day to resign as prime minister in favor of the chancellor.

In the intervening years the two have achieved considerable success, with Blair as prime minister

inaugurating a "third way" alternative to traditional left and right politics and Brown as chancellor overseeing the longest continuous period of growth in Britain since the industrial revolution. In the early years after New Labour came to government in 1997 and was riding a wave of popularity, the rivalry was muted and seldom spilled beyond the inner sanctums of government. But Brown chafed at how long it was taking for Blair to make good on his promise, and policy splits—first and foremost over British participation in the euro zone—spilled out into the open. (Although Blair, who was initially more optimistic on the European common currency, conceded that Brown would decide when a number of economic benchmarks were met, they never have been.) Increasingly, the British government began to look and feel like a dual executive, with Blair responsible for foreign affairs and Brown for domestic policies.

Blair's decision to support the U.S.-led war in Iraq was very unpopular in Britain, increasingly so when weapons of mass destruction—the key justification for war—never were found. Recurring questions about

After what must have felt like an interminable wait, on June 24, 2007, Gordon Brown succeeded Tony Blair as Labour party leader—and a few days later became prime minister. How much change would the new prime minister bring to British politics—and to the special relationship with the United States? *Source:* Paul Ellis/AFP/Getty Images

the war in Iraq hounded Blair right through the campaign leading to his third electoral victory in May 2005—a feat never before achieved by the leader of Britain's 105-year-old Labour Party.

Blair's victory, however, was bittersweet, and the slashing of his parliamentary majority by nearly 100 seats was not even the worst of it. British election night tradition has each candidate in a constituency standing side by side as the results are announced. Thus, television cameras captured a stony-faced prime minister standing just behind Reg Keys, an independent antiwar candidate whose son had been killed in Iraq, as Keys solemnly intoned: "I hope in my heart that one day the prime minister will be able to say sorry . . . to the families of the bereaved."

By then, Blair and Brown were barely on speaking terms, and Brown loyalists in government were growing increasingly impatient with Blair's unwillingness to set a date for his departure. Before the final results were tabulated, the guessing game that would engulf Blair's third term began, as pundits and Labour Party critics of the prime minister openly speculated about when Blair should resign in favor of Gordon Brown. By late summer 2006, a full-scale succession crisis was underway. Blair first insisted as he returned from a Caribbean vacation that he would not set a date for leaving but then, by early September, announced that he would depart within a year. Under relentless pressure, in June 2007 Blair tendered his resignation to the Queen who immediately summoned Gordon Brown (who had run unopposed in a leadership election in the Labour party) to become prime minister.

Geographic Setting

Britain is the largest of the British Isles, a group of islands off the northwest coast of Europe, and encompasses England, Scotland, and Wales. The second-largest island includes Northern Ireland and the independent Republic of Ireland. The term *Great Britain* encompasses England, Wales, and Scotland, but not Northern Ireland. We use the term *Britain* as shorthand for the United Kingdom of Great Britain and Northern Ireland.

Covering an area of approximately 94,000 square miles, Britain is roughly two-thirds the size of Japan, or approximately half the size of France. In July 2007,

the population of the United Kingdom was estimated to be 60.8 million people. To put the size of this once immensely powerful country in perspective, it is slightly smaller than Oregon.

Although forever altered by the Channel Tunnel, Britain's location as an offshore island adjacent to Europe is significant. Historically, Britain's island destiny made it less subject to invasion and conquest than its continental counterparts, which afford the country a sense of security. The geographic separation from mainland Europe has also created for many Britons a feeling that they are both apart from and a part of Europe, a factor that has complicated relations with Britain's EU partners to this day.

Critical Junctures

This study begins with a look at the historical development of the modern British state. History shapes contemporary politics in very important ways. Once in place, institutions leave powerful legacies, and issues that were left unresolved in one period may present challenges for the future.

In many ways, Britain is the model of a united and stable country with an enviable record of continuity and resiliency. Even so, the history of state formation reveals how complex and open-ended the process can be. Some issues that plague other countries, such as religious divisions, were settled long ago in Great Britain proper (although a similar settlement is only now taking shape in Northern Ireland). But others, such as multiple national identities, remain on the agenda.

British state formation involved the unification of kingdoms or crowns (hence the term United *Kingdom*). After Duke William of Normandy defeated the English in the Battle of Hastings in 1066, the Norman monarchy extended its authority throughout the British Isles. With the Acts of Union of 1536 and 1542, England and Wales were legally, politically, and administratively united. The unification of the Scottish and English crowns began in 1603, when James VI of Scotland ascended to the English throne as James I. After that, England, Scotland, and Wales were known as Great Britain. Scotland and England remained divided politically, however, until the Act of Union of 1707. Henceforth, a common Parliament of Great

Britain replaced the two separate parliaments of Scotland and of England and Wales.

At the same time, the making of the British state included a historic expression of constraints on monarchical rule. At first, the period of Norman rule after 1066 strengthened royal control, but the conduct of King John (1199–1216) fueled opposition from feudal barons. In 1215, they forced the king to consent to a series of concessions that protected feudal landowners from abuses of royal power. These restrictions on royal prerogatives were embodied in the Magna Carta, a historic statement of the rights of a political community against the monarchical state. Soon after, in 1236, the term *Parliament* was first used officially to

Critical Junctures in Britain's Political Development	
1688	Glorious Revolution establishes power of Parliament
ca. 1750	Industrial Revolution begins in Britain
1832	Reform Act expands voting rights
1837–1901	Reign of Queen Victoria; height of British Empire
1914–1918	World War I
1929–1939	Great Depression
1939–1945	World War II
1945–1979	Establishment of British welfare state; dismantling of British Empire
1973	Britain joins the European Community
1979–1990	Prime Minister Margaret Thatcher promotes "enterprise culture"
1997–2007	Prime Minister Tony Blair and Chancellor Gordon Brown lead New Labour in government
2001	Under Blair's leadership, Britain "stands shoulder to shoulder" with America in war against terror
2007	Gordon Brown becomes prime minister and promises to renew the party and the nation

refer to the gathering of feudal barons summoned by the king whenever he required their consent for special taxes. By the fifteenth century, Parliament had gained the right to make laws.

The Seventeenth-Century Settlement

The making of the British state in the sixteenth and seventeenth centuries involved a complex interplay of religious conflicts, national rivalries, and struggles between rulers and Parliament. These conflicts erupted in the civil wars of the 1640s and the forced abdication of James II in 1688. The nearly bloodless political revolution of 1688, subsequently known as the Glorious Revolution, marked the "last successful political coup d'état or revolution in British history."[1]

By the end of the seventeenth century, the framework of constitutional (or limited) monarchy, which

would still exercise flashes of power into the nineteenth century, was established. For more than three hundred years, Britain's monarchs have answered to Parliament, which has held the sole authority for taxation and the maintenance of a standing army.

The Glorious Revolution also resolved long-standing religious conflict. The replacement of the Roman Catholic James II by the Protestant William and Mary ensured the dominance of the Church of England (or Anglican Church). To this day, the Church of England remains the established (official) religion, and approximately two dozen of its bishops and archbishops sit as members of the House of Lords, the upper house of Parliament.

Thus, by the end of the seventeenth century, a basic form of parliamentary democracy had emerged. Except in Northern Ireland, the problem of religious divisions, which continue to plague many countries throughout the world, was largely settled (although Catholics and Jews could not vote until the 1820s). As a result of settling most of its religious differences early, Britain has taken a more secular turn than most other countries in Western Europe. The majority of Britons do not consider religion a significant source of identity, and active church membership in Britain, at 15 percent, is very low in comparison with other Western European countries. These seventeenth-century developments became a defining moment for how the British perceive their history to this day. However divisive and disruptive the process of state building may have been originally, its telling and retelling have contributed significantly to a British political culture that celebrates democracy's continuity, gradualism, and tolerance.

In Britain, religious identification has less political significance in voting behavior or party loyalty than in many other countries. By contrast to France, where devout Catholics tend to vote right of center, there is relatively little association between religion and voting behavior in Britain (although Anglicans are a little more likely to vote Conservative). Unlike Germany or Italy, for example, politics in Britain is secular. No parties have religious affiliation, a factor that contributed to the success of the Conservative Party, one of the most successful right-of-center parties in Europe in the twentieth century.

As a consequence, except in Northern Ireland, where religious divisions continue, the party system in the United Kingdom has traditionally reflected class distinctions and remains free of the pattern of multiple parties (particularly right-of-center parties) that occurs in countries where party loyalties are divided by both class and religion.

The Industrial Revolution and the British Empire

Although the British state was consolidated by the seventeenth century, the timing of its industrial development and the way that process transformed Britain's role in the world radically shaped its form. From the mid-eighteenth century onward, the Industrial Revolution involved rapid expansion of manufacturing production and technological innovation. It also led to monumental social and economic transformations and created pressures for democratization. Externally, Britain used its competitive edge to transform and dominate the international order. Internally, the Industrial Revolution helped shape the development of the British state and changed forever the British people's way of life.

The Industrial Revolution. The consequences of the Industrial Revolution for the generations who experienced its upheavals can scarcely be exaggerated. The typical worker was turned "by degrees . . . from small peasant or craftsman into wage-labourer," as historian Eric Hobsbawm observes. Cash and market-based transactions replaced older traditions of barter and production for local need.[2]

Despite a gradual improvement in the standard of living in the English population at large, the effects of industrialization were often profound for agricultural laborers and certain types of artisans. With the commercialization of agriculture, many field laborers lost their security of employment, and cottagers (small landholders) were squeezed off the land in large numbers. The mechanization of manufacturing, which spread furthest in the cotton industry, upset the traditional status of the preindustrial skilled craft workers and permanently marginalized them.

The British Empire. Britain had assumed a significant role as a world power by the end of the seventeenth century, building an overseas empire and engaging actively in international commerce. But it

was the Industrial Revolution of the eighteenth century that established global production and exchange on a new and expanded scale, with special consequences for the making of the British state. Cotton manufacture, the driving force behind Britain's growing industrial dominance, not only pioneered the new techniques and changed labor organization during the Industrial Revolution but also represented the perfect imperial industry. It relied on imported raw materials, and, by the turn of the nineteenth century, the industry already depended on overseas markets for the vast majority of its sales of finished goods. Growth depended on foreign markets rather than on domestic consumption. This export orientation fueled an expansion far more rapid than an exclusively domestic orientation would have allowed.

With its leading industrial sector dependent on overseas trade, Britain's leaders worked aggressively to secure markets and expand the empire. Toward these ends, Britain defeated European rivals in a series of military engagements, culminating in the Napoleonic Wars (1803–1815), which confirmed Britain's commercial, military, and geopolitical preeminence. The Napoleonic Wars also secured a balance of power on the European continent, which was favorable for largely unrestricted international commerce (free trade). Propelled by the formidable and active presence of the Royal Navy, international trade helped England to take full advantage of its position as the first industrial power. Many scholars suggest that in the middle of the nineteenth century, Britain had the highest per capita income in the world (certainly among the two or three highest), and in 1870, at the height of its glory, its trade represented nearly one-quarter of the world total, and its industrial mastery ensured highly competitive productivity in comparison with trading partners (see Table 1.1).

During the reign of Queen Victoria (1837–1901), the British Empire was immensely powerful and encompassed fully 25 percent of the world's population. Britain presided over a vast formal and informal empire, with extensive direct colonial rule over some four dozen countries, including India and Nigeria. In addition, Britain enjoyed the advantages of an extensive informal empire—a worldwide network of independent states, including China, Iran, and Brazil—whose economic fates were linked to it. Britain ruled as a hegemonic power, the state that could control the pattern of

Table 1.1

World Trade and Relative Labor Productivity

	Proportion of World Trade (%)	Relative Labor Productivity[a] (%)
1870	24.0	1.63
1890	18.5	1.45
1913	14.1	1.15
1938	14.0	0.92

[a]As compared with the average rate of productivity in other members of the world economy.

Source: Robert O. Keohane, *After Hegemony: Cooperation and Discord in the World Economy*, p. 36. Copyright © 1984 by Princeton University Press. Reprinted by permission of Princeton University Press.

alliances and terms of the international economic order, and that often could shape domestic political developments in countries throughout the world. Overall, the making of the British state observed a neat symmetry. Its global power underwrote industrial growth at home. At the same time, the reliance of domestic industry on world markets, beginning with cotton manufacture in the eighteenth century, prompted the government to project British interests overseas as forcefully as possible.

Industrial Change and the Struggle for Voting Rights.   The Industrial Revolution shifted economic power from landowners to men of commerce and industry. As a result, the first critical juncture in the long process of democratization began in the late 1820s, when the "respectable opinion" of the propertied classes and increasing popular agitation pressed Parliament to expand the right to vote (franchise) beyond a thin band of men, mainly landowners, with substantial property. With Parliament under considerable pressure, the Reform Act of 1832 extended the franchise to a section of the (male) middle class.

In a very limited way, the Reform Act confirmed the social and political transformations of the Industrial Revolution by granting new urban manufacturing centers, such as Manchester and Birmingham, more substantial representation. However, the massive urban working class created by the Industrial Revolution and populating the cities in the England of Charles Dickens remained on the outside looking in. In fact, the reform was very narrow and defensive. Before 1832, less than 5 percent of the adult population was entitled to vote—and afterward, only about 7 percent. In extending the franchise so narrowly, the reform underscored the strict property basis for political participation and inflamed class-based tensions in Britain. Following the Reform Act, a massive popular movement erupted in the late 1830s to secure the program of the People's Charter, which included demands for universal male suffrage and other radical reforms intended to make Britain a much more participatory democracy. The Chartist movement, as it was called, held huge, often tumultuous rallies, and organized a vast campaign to petition Parliament, but it failed to achieve any of its aims.

Expansion of the franchise proceeded slowly. The Representation of the People Act of 1867 increased the electorate to just over 16 percent but left cities significantly underrepresented. The Franchise Act of 1884 nearly doubled the size of the electorate, but it was not until the Representation of the People Act of 1918 that suffrage included nearly all adult men and women over age thirty. How slow a process was it? The franchise for men with substantial incomes dated from the fifteenth century, but women between the ages of twenty-one and thirty were not enfranchised until 1928. The voting age for both women and men was lowered to eighteen in 1969. Except for some episodes during the days of the Chartist movement, the struggle for extension of the franchise took place without violence, but its time horizon must be measured in centuries. This is British gradualism—at its best and its worst (see Figure 1.1).

World Wars, Industrial Strife, and the Depression (1914–1945)

With the issue of the franchise finally resolved, in one sense the making of the British state as a democracy was settled. In another important sense, however, the development of the state was just beginning in the twentieth century with the expansion of the state's direct responsibility for management of the economy and the provision of social welfare for citizens. The

Figure 1.1

Expansion of Voting Rights

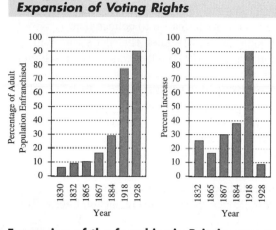

Expansion of the franchise in Britain was a gradual process. Despite reforms dating from the early nineteenth century, nearly universal adult suffrage was not achieved until 1928.

Source: From Jorgen S. Rasmussen, *The British Political Process,* First Edition, p. 151. Copyright © 1993. Reprinted with permission of Wadsworth, an imprint of the Wadsworth Group, a division of Thomson Learning.

making of what is sometimes called the *interventionist state* was spurred by two world wars.

The state's involvement in the economy increased significantly during World War I (1914–1918). It took control of a number of industries, including railways, mining, and shipping. It set prices and restricted the flow of capital abroad and channeled the country's resources into production geared to the war effort. After World War I, it remained active in the management of industry in a rather different way. Amid tremendous industrial disputes, the state wielded its power to fragment the trade union movement and resist demands for workers' control over production and to promote more extensive state ownership of industries. This considerable government manipulation of the economy obviously contradicted the policy of laissez-faire (minimal government interference in the operation of economic markets). The tensions between free-market principles and interventionist practices deepened with the Great Depression (which began in 1929 and continued through much of the 1930s) and the experiences of World War II (1939–1945). The fear of depression and

the burst of pent-up yearnings for a better life after the war helped transform the role of the state and ushered in a period of unusual political harmony.

Collectivist Consensus (1945–1979)

In the postwar context of shared victory and common misery (almost everyone suffered hardships immediately after the war), reconstruction and dreams of new prosperity and security became more important than ideological conflict. In Britain today, a debate rages among political scientists over whether there was a postwar consensus. Critics of the concept contend that disagreements over specific policies concerning the economy, education, employment, and health, along with an electorate divided on partisan lines largely according to social class, indicated politics as usual.[3] Nevertheless, a broad culture of reconciliation and a determination to rebuild and improve the conditions of life for all Britons helped forge a postwar settlement based broadly on a collectivist consensus that endured until the mid-1970s.

The term *collectivism* was coined to describe the consensus that drove politics in the harmonious postwar period when a significant majority of Britons and all major political parties agreed that the state should take expanded responsibility for economic governance and provide for the social welfare in the broadest terms. They accepted as a matter of faith that governments should work to narrow the gap between rich and poor through public education, national health care, and other policies of the welfare state, and they accepted state responsibility for economic growth and full employment. Collectivism brought class-based actors (representatives of labor and management) inside politics and forged a broad consensus about the expanded role of government.

Throughout this period, there was a remarkable unity among electoral combatants. Both the Labour and Conservative mainstream endorsed the principle of state responsibility for the collective good in both economic and social terms. Although modest compared to policies in Europe, the commitment to state management of the economy and provision of social services marked a new era in British politics. In time, however, economic downturn and political stagnation caused the consensus to unravel.

Margaret Thatcher and the Enterprise Culture (1979–1990)

In the 1970s, economic stagnation and the declining competitiveness of key British industries in international markets fueled industrial strife and brought class-based tensions near the surface of politics. No government appeared equal to the tasks of economic management. Each party failed in turn. The Conservative government of Edward Heath (1970–1974) could not resolve the economic problems or the political tensions that resulted from the previously unheard-of combination of increased inflation and reduced growth (stagflation). The Labour government of Harold Wilson and James Callaghan (1974–1979) fared no better. As unions became increasingly disgruntled, the country was beset by a rash of strikes throughout the winter of 1978–1979, the "winter of discontent." Labour's inability to discipline its trade union allies hurt the party in the election, a few months later, in May 1979. The traditional centrist Conservative and Labour alternatives within the collectivist mold seemed exhausted. Many Britons were ready for a new policy agenda.

Margaret Thatcher more than met the challenge. Winning the leadership of the Conservative Party in 1975, she wasted little time in launching a set of bold policy initiatives, which, with characteristic forthrightness, she began to implement after the Conservatives were returned to power in 1979. Reelected in 1983 and 1987, Thatcher served longer without interruption than any other British prime minister in the twentieth century and never lost a general election.

Thatcher transformed British political life by advancing an alternative vision of politics. She was convinced that collectivism had led to Britain's decline by sapping British industry and permitting powerful and self-serving unions to hold the country for ransom. To reverse Britain's relative economic slide, Thatcher sought to jump-start the economy by cutting taxes, reducing social services where possible, and using government policy to stimulate competitiveness and efficiency in the private sector.

The term *Thatcherism* embraces her distinctive leadership style, her economic and political strategies, as well as her traditional cultural values: individual responsibility, commitment to family, frugality, and an affirmation of the entrepreneurial spirit. These values combined nostalgia for the past and rejection of permissiveness and disorder. Taken together, they were referred to as the *enterprise culture.* They stood as a reproach and an alternative to collectivism.

In many ways, Margaret Thatcher's leadership as prime minister (1979–1990) marks a critical dividing line in postwar British politics. She set the tone and redefined the goals of British politics like few others before her. In November 1990, a leadership challenge within Thatcher's own Conservative Party, largely over her anti-EU stance and high-handed leadership style, caused her sudden resignation and replacement by John Major. Major served as prime minister from 1990 to 1997, leading the Conservative Party to a victory in the 1992 general election before succumbing to Tony Blair's New Labour in 1997.

New Labour's Third Way. Some twenty electoral records were toppled as New Labour under the leadership of Tony Blair (see the box on facing page) won 419 of the 659 seats in Parliament, the largest majority it has ever held. Blair was propelled into office as prime minister with a 10 percent swing from Conservative to Labour, a postwar record. The Conservative Party, which had been in power since Margaret Thatcher's 1979 victory and was one of Europe's most successful parties in the twentieth century, was decimated.

New Labour aspired to recast British politics, offering what it referred to as a "third-way" alternative to Thatcherism and the collectivism of traditional Labour. Everything was at issue, from the way politics was organized to the country's underlying values, institutions, and policies. In electoral terms, New Labour rejected the notion of interest-based politics, in which unions and working people naturally look to Labour and businesspeople and the more prosperous look to the Conservatives. Labour won in 1997 by drawing support from across the socioeconomic spectrum. It rejected the historic ties between Labour governments and the trade union movement and chose instead to emphasize partnership with business.

In institutional and policy terms, New Labour's innovations were intended to reverse the tendency of previous Labour governments in Britain to provide centralized statist solutions to all economic and social problems. Blair promised new approaches to economic, welfare, and social policy; British leadership in Europe;

TONY BLAIR

orn in 1953 to a mother from Donegal, Ireland (who moved to Glasgow after her father's death), and a father from the Clydeside shipyards, Tony Blair lacks the typical pedigree of Labour Party leaders. It is very common in the highest ranks of the Labour Party to find someone whose father or grandfather was a union official or a Labour MP. The politics in the Blair family, by contrast, were closely linked to Conservatism (as chairman of his local Conservative Party club, his father Leo had a good chance to become a Conservative MP). Often, like Tony Blair's two predecessors—Neil Kinnock from Wales and John Smith from the West of Scotland—leaders of the Labour Party also have strong regional ties. In contrast, Blair moved to Durham in the north of England when he was five but spent much of his youth in boarding schools, moved south when he was old enough to set out on his own, studied law at Oxford, specialized in employment and industrial law in London—and returned to the north only to enter the House of Commons from Sedgefield in 1983. Thus, Blair has neither the traditional political or regional ties of a Labour Party leader.*

Coming of political age in opposition, Blair joined the shadow cabinet in 1988, as shadow minister of energy, then of employment, and finally as shadow home secretary. An MP with no government experience, he easily won the contest for party leadership after his close friend and fellow modernizer John Smith died of a sudden heart attack in the summer of 1994. From the start, Blair boosted Labour Party morale and raised expectations that the party would soon regain power. As one commentator observed, "The new Leader rapidly made a favorable

impression on the electorate: his looks and affability of manner appealed to voters whilst his self-confidence, lucidity and clarity of mind rendered him a highly effective communicator and lent him an air of authority."[†] As prime minister, Blair combined firm leadership, eclectic beliefs, and bold political initiatives as he transformed the Labour Party to "New Labour."

Even before the war in Iraq, his lack of familiar roots and ideological convictions made Blair an enigmatic figure. His very personal decision to support the U.S.-led invasion of Iraq deepened the impression that Blair would follow his own inner voice above the preferences of party. After the 2005 election, many both within and outside the party hoped that the prime minister would live up to his end of a deal with Gordon Brown, which had been long rumored: that in exchange for Brown backing Blair for party leadership in 1994, Blair would at some point in the future resign and hand the leadership of party and country to Brown. Now that he is retired as prime minister, Blair will doubtless be remembered as a towering figure in British politics. But two questions remained. In light of the war in Iraq, what would be Blair's legacy? And would he leave the scene gracefully, handing power to his rival, while the economy was still robust and Brown would still have the opportunity to make his mark as prime minister for a couple of years before having to face the electorate?

---

*See Andy McSmith, *Faces of Labour: The Inside Story* (London: Verso, 1997), pp. 7–96.

†Eric Shaw, *The Labour Party Since 1945* (Oxford: Blackwell, 1996), p. 195.

---

and far-reaching constitutional changes to revitalize democratic participation and devolve (transfer) certain powers from the central government to Scotland, Wales, and Northern Ireland.

In his early months in office, Blair displayed effective leadership in his stewardship of the nation during the period after Lady Diana's death and in his aggressive

efforts to achieve a potentially historic peace agreement for Northern Ireland, with far-reaching constitutional implications. By the summer of 2000, however, many began to say that New Labor was better at sounding innovative than at delivering the goods (better at spin than substance). In addition, a series of crises—from a set of fatal train crashes since 1997 to protests over the cost of gasoline in September 2000 to an outbreak of mad cow disease in spring 2001—made Blair seem a little shopworn. Nevertheless, until the war in Iraq, Blair remained a formidable leader, and a few months before the cataclysmic events of September 11, 2001, New Labour won what it most sought: an electoral mandate in June 2001 for a second successive term.

Britain in the Euro Era

In May 1998, eleven EU countries, led by Germany, France, Italy, and Spain—but not Britain—signed on to the single EU currency, the euro. One month later, the European Central Bank was established, operating with considerable institutional and political independence, and charged primarily with maintaining price stability and advancing the economic policies of the EU. Britain's decision not to join the euro zone remains a significant nondecision in both economic and broader political terms, for it reflects the United Kingdom's ambivalent posture toward Europe.

Blair came to office determined to rescue Europe for Britain by redressing the problems caused by Thatcher's anti-Europe stance. He was an enthusiast for the Common Foreign and Security Policy (CFSP), has helped galvanize the European role in Kosovo, and has worked with France and Germany to develop a more robust European military capability. But Britain remains stuck on the outside when it comes to the euro and has made little or no progress in changing the mindset of Britons. With Brown's extreme caution about the euro while he was chancellor there is little reason to anticipant a sudden change of course.

Britain after September 11

In the aftermath of the September 11, 2001, attacks on the World Trade Center and the Pentagon, Blair showed decisive leadership in assuming the role of a key ally to the United States in the war on terrorism. Since Britain was willing and able to lend moral, diplomatic, and military support, September 11 lent new credence to the special relationship—a bond of language, culture, and national interests, which creates an unusually close alliance—that has governed U.S.-UK relations for fifty years and catapulted Blair to high visibility in world affairs. Before long, however, especially when

the central focus of the war on terrorism moved from Afghanistan to Iraq, many Britons became disenchanted. Blair's willingness to run interference with allies and add intellectual ballast to President George W. Bush's post-9/11 plans was a big help to the United States. But it locked Britain into a set of policies over which it had little or no control, it vastly complicated relationships with France and Germany (which opposed the war), and it generated hostility toward the United Kingdom in much of the Arab and Muslim world.

The devastating London bombings on July 7, 2005, were perpetrated by UK citizens who were Muslim and were timed to correspond with the G-8 summit in Gleneagle, Scotland. They appeared to confirm that Britain faced heightened security risks because of its participation in the war. Attempted terror attacks in London and Glasgow in July 2007 increased the sense of insecurity. Finally, the war in Iraq, which had grown even more unpopular in the UK, eroded Blair's popularity beyond redemption. In addition, the conviction

A PLACE IN THE HISTORY BOOKS

In the early years of his premiership it seemed likely that Blair would leave a glittering legacy behind as modernizer and architect of the Third Way. But Blair's commitment to the "special relationship" led Britain into the war in Iraq, and when no weapons of mass destruction were found he seemed trapped, his legacy falling down around him.

Source: © Ingram Pinn, Cartoonists and Writers Syndicate, from *The Financial Times*, May 12, 2007.

among many Britons that Blair led them into war under false premises permanently weakened his credibility and tarnished the legacy of New Labour while Blair was at the helm.

As Brown became prime minister, many on both sides of the Atlantic wondered how Brown—who has kept a low profile on the war in Iraq—would reshape the special relationship between the United States and the United Kingdom. What steps will he take to limit the casualties to British forces in Iraq and Afghanistan and to separate his policy in Iraq from that of his predecessor?

Britain after the French and Dutch Veto of the European Constitution

The issue of a European constitution has taken a back seat in Britain. In the May 2005 general election Europe was barely an issue. With Blair's political capital depleted by the war in Iraq, he suddenly announced in April 2004 that Britain would hold a referendum on the Constitution. It was one thing, apparently, to ram an unpopular war through parliament, quite another to risk pushing through the EU Constitution!

As the French and Dutch votes approached, everyone assumed that Blair was hoping for a "no" vote before the UK went to the polls, so the UK could not be blamed. And defeat in the UK was almost a forgone conclusion. Ladbrokes, the famous British bookmakers who take bets on almost anything, placed the odds for passage of the EU Constitution in Britain at 8:1 against!

In the end, even the French and Dutch defeats didn't save Britain in general—and Blair in particular—from the wrath of Schröder and Chirac, if not directly for the Constitution, then for defiantly demanding that agricultural subsidies and Britain's rebate be joined at the hip in budget negotiations.

Until the end of his time as prime minister, Blair remained Europe's favorite scapegoat—for advancing an economic and social model that challenges European social protection traditions, demanding budgetary reforms, and supporting the war in Iraq. Since Brown has a lower-key style and pays more attention to detail, perhaps he will develop better relationships with key European allies and mend the rift. But even Ladbrokes may not want to cover that bet.

Themes and Implications

The processes that came together in these historical junctures continue to influence developments today in powerful and complex ways. The four core themes in this book, introduced in Part I, highlight some of the most important features of British politics.

Historical Junctures and Political Themes

The first theme suggests that a country's relative position in the world of states influences its ability to manage domestic and international challenges. Weaker international standing makes it difficult for a country to control international events or insulate itself from external pressures. Britain's ability to control the terms of trade and master political alliances during the height of its imperial power in the nineteenth century confirms this maxim. In a quite different way, Blair's temptation to cling to the special relationship with the United States and Britain's reduced standing and influence today also confirm the theme of the world of states.

As the gradual process of decolonization defined Britain's changing relationship to the world of states, Britain fell to second-tier status during the twentieth century. Its formal empire began to shrink in the interwar period (1919–1939) as the "white dominions" of Canada, Australia, and New Zealand gained independence. In Britain's Asian, Middle Eastern, and African colonies, the pressure for political reforms that would lead to independence deepened during World War II and in the immediate postwar period. Beginning with the formal independence of India and Pakistan in 1947, an enormous empire of dependent colonies more or less dissolved in less than twenty years. Finally, in 1997, Britain returned the commercially vibrant crown colony of Hong Kong to China. The process of decolonization ended any realistic claim that Britain was still a dominant player in world politics.

Is Britain a world power or just a middle-of-the-pack country in Western Europe? It appears to be both. On the one hand, as a legacy of its role in World War II, Britain sits as a permanent member of the United Nations Security Council. On the other hand, Britain invariably plays second fiddle in its special relationship to the United States, a show of relative weakness that has exposed British foreign policy to extraordinary pressures since September 11.

In addition, British governments face persistent challenges in their dealings with the EU. As Margaret Thatcher learned too late, Europe is a highly divisive issue. Can Britain afford to remain aloof from the fast-paced changes of economic integration—symbolized by the headlong rush toward a common currency, the euro, which has already been embraced by every other leading member state—as well as several of the newer members from East-Central Europe? It is clear that Britain cannot control EU policy outcomes, and the schism over the war in Iraq, for a time at least, weakened the United Kingdom's influence as an honest broker between the United States and Europe. Under Brown's leadership, will Britain find the right formula for limiting the political fallout of EU politics, using the special relationship with the United States to extend British influence, and, at the same time, find the best approach to economic competitiveness?

A second theme examines the strategies employed in governing the economy. Since the dawn of Britain's Industrial Revolution, prosperity at home has relied on superior competitiveness abroad. This is even truer in today's environment of intensified international competition and global production. When Tony Blair took office in 1997, he inherited a streak of prosperity in Britain that dated from 1992—an enviable legacy. The Blair government could thus work to modernize the economy and determine its budgetary priorities from economic strength. Will Britain's "less-is-more" laissez-faire approach to economic governance, invigorated by New Labour's business partnerships, continue to compete effectively in a global context? Can Britain achieve a durable economic model with—or without—fuller integration into Europe? How can we assess the spending priorities and distributive implications of the third-way politics of Blair and Brown? Britain will never again assume the privileged position of hegemonic power, so a great deal depends on how well it plays the cards it does have.

A third theme is the potent political influence of the democratic idea, the universal appeal of core values associated with parliamentary democracy as practiced first in the United Kingdom. Even in Britain, issues about democratic governance, citizen participation, and

constitutional reform have been renewed with considerable force.

As the royal family has been shaken by scandal and improprieties, questions about the undemocratic underpinning of the British state have taken on greater urgency. Few reject the monarchy outright, but questions about the role of the monarchy helped place on the agenda broader issues about citizen control over government and constitutional reform. As a result, in November 1999, a bill was enacted to remove hereditary peers from Britain's upper unelected chamber of Parliament, the House of Lords. Although the final form of a reformed second chamber is not settled, the traditional House of Lords has been abolished.

Long-settled issues about the constitutional form and unity of the state have also reemerged with unexpected force. How can the interests of England, Wales, Scotland, and Northern Ireland be balanced within a single nation-state? Tony Blair placed squarely on the agenda a set of policies designed to reshape the institutions of government and reconfigure the fundamental constitutional principles. Key policy initiatives have included the formation of a Scottish Parliament and a Welsh Senedd (the Welsh Assembly). Has the perpetual crisis in Northern Ireland finally been resolved? It seems that it has (we will discuss developments in Northern Ireland further in Chapter 5). Clearly, even in the United Kingdom, democracy can be a highly politicized and potentially disruptive process, as constitutional reform has assumed an important role in New Labour's governing agenda and an historic settlement in Northern Ireland may well be remembered as Tony Blair's greatest achievement.

Finally, we come to the fourth theme, collective identity, which considers how individuals define who they are politically in terms of group attachments, come together to pursue political goals, and face their status as political insiders or outsiders. In Britain, an important aspect of collective identity is connected to Britain's legacy of empire and its aftermath. Through the immigration of its former colonial subjects to the United Kingdom, decolonization helped create a multiracial society, to which Britain has adjusted poorly. Issues of race, ethnicity, and cultural identity have challenged the long-standing British values of tolerance and consensus, and they now present important challenges for policy and the prospects of cohesion in Britain today.

Especially after the London bombings in July 2005 (referred to in Britain as 7/7), with the possible exception of Iraq, there has been no more hot-button issue than nationality and immigration. Indeed, the concept of "Britishness"—what the country stands for and who comprises the political community—has come under intense scrutiny. At the same time, gender politics remains significant, from voting patterns to questions of equality in the workplace and positions of political leadership. Moreover, the specific needs of women for equal employment opportunities and to balance the demands of work and family have assumed an important place in debates about social and employment policies.

Implications for Comparative Politics

Britain's privileged position in comparative politics textbooks (it almost always comes first among country studies) seems to follow naturally from the important historical firsts it has enjoyed. Britain was the first nation to industrialize, and for much of the nineteenth century, the British Empire was the world's dominant economic, political, and military power, with a vast network of colonies throughout the world. Britain was also the first nation to develop an effective parliamentary democracy (a form of representative government in which the executive is drawn from and answers to an elected national legislature). As a result of its vast empire, Britain had tremendous influence on the forms of government that were introduced in countries around the globe. For these reasons, British politics is often studied as a model of representative government. Named after the section of London that is home to the British legislature, the Westminster model emphasizes that democracy rests on the supreme authority of a legislature—in Britain's case, the parliament. Finally,

Britain stands out as a model of gradual and peaceful evolution of democratic government in a world where transitions to democracy are often turbulent, interrupted, and uncertain.

Today, more than a century after the height of its international power, Britain's significance in comparative terms must be measured in somewhat different ways. Even in tough times, as today, the advantages bestowed on prime ministers by the formidable levers of power they control and the relative strength of the British economy provide a platform for success. Especially in the aftermath of September 11, with signs of intolerance rampant, all economies facing new challenges, and European center-left politics in disarray, the stakes are high. Britain's ability to succeed (or not) in sustaining economic competitiveness, resolving the euro dilemma, and revitalizing the center-left will send important signals to governments throughout the world. Is significant innovation possible in established democracies? Can a politics beyond left and right develop coherent policies and sustain public support? Can constitutional reforms bind together a multiethnic, multinational state? What geopolitical sphere of maneuver does any state have in a global order dominated by the United States (where it is not easy to tell whether the "special relationship" is a blessing, a curse, or a one-way street with little benefit for the United Kingdom)? In fact, contemporary Britain may help define what the prospects are for middle-rank established democracies in a global age.

Notes

[1] Jeremy Black, *The Politics of Britain, 1688–1800* (Manchester: Manchester University Press, 1993), p. 6.

[2] E. J. Hobsbawm, *Industry and Empire* (Harmondsworth, UK: Penguin/Pelican, 1983), pp. 29–31.

[3] See Duncan Fraser, "The Postwar Consensus: A Debate Not Long Enough?" *Parliamentary Affairs* 53, no. 2 (April 2000): 347–362.

CHAPTER 2

Political Economy and Development

The timing of industrialization and of a country's insertion into the world economy are important variables in explaining both how and how successfully the state intervenes in economic governance. Both the specific policies chosen and the relative success of the economic strategy have significant political repercussions. Economic developments often determine political winners and losers. They also influence broad changes in the distribution of resources and opportunities among groups in society and affect a country's international standing.

To take up our "governing the economy" theme, some scholars have suggested that states that have institutionalized effective relationships with organized economic interests (such as France and Germany in Europe) have enjoyed more consistent growth and stronger economic competitiveness. It is true that Britain's annual growth rates were lower than those of Germany and France from the end of World War II through the 1970s. Rather than institutionalizing a dense network of relationships among government agencies, business, and labor, Britain has preserved arm's-length state relationships with key economic actors. Since British political culture has trumpeted the benefits of free-market individualism and New Labour has reinforced Thatcherism's appeal to entrepreneurship, competition, and industriousness in the private sector, the British experience becomes a critical test case for analyzing the relative merits of alternative strategies for governing the economy.

In the first decade of the new century, it appears that the trend in Europe regarding the management of the economy is moving in the UK's direction, breathing new life into the old economic doctrine of laissez-faire. The pressures of global competitiveness and the perceived advantages of a "one size fits all" style of minimalist government have encouraged a movement toward neoliberalism (free markets, free trade, welfare retrenchment, and an attractive investment climate as the end game of every state's politics). Despite the traditions of extensive state regulation of the economy and the political interests, led by trade unions, to maintain tradition social protections, even Germany and France are working hard to implement promarket reforms. So too is the European Union more generally. In part this trend is due to the demonstration effects that have resulted from the relative success of the British and U.S. economies. Neoliberalism is a touchstone axiom of New Labour. Government policies aim to promote free competition among firms, to interfere with the prerogatives of entrepreneurs and managers as little as possible, and to create a business-friendly environment to help attract foreign investment and spur innovation.

This chapter begins with a historical overview of Britain's economic development and its experience of the postwar settlement. It then considers, in turn, the principles of British economic management, the social consequences of economic developments, and the political repercussions of Britain's position in the international economic order.

The Postwar Settlement and Beyond

To understand the postwar settlement in Britain and come to terms with the contemporary debate about economic management, we must first step backward to analyze the historical trajectory of British economic performance. In addition to its claim as the first industrial nation, Britain is also the country with the longest experience of economic decline. It has been a victim of its own success and approach to economic development. From the eighteenth century onward, Britain combined its naval mastery and the dominant position created by the Industrial Revolution to fuel expansion based on the foreign supply of raw materials and foreign markets. With plenty of profits available from this traditional overseas orientation, British entrepreneurs became complacent about keeping up with the newest industrial techniques and investing in machinery at home. Secure in the advantages of empire and the priority of international trade over domestic demand, the government stuck to its belief in free trade (low tariffs and removal of other barriers to open markets) in the international realm and a hands-off approach at home. With low investment in the modernization of industrial plants and little effort to boost efficiency by grouping small-scale firms into cartels and trusts as the United States and Germany were doing, eventually Britain slipped behind its competitors in crucial areas: technological innovation, investment in domestic manufacturing, and scale of production facilities.

By the 1890s, Britain's key export, textiles, was slipping, and the international position of the machine-tool industry, which Britain also had dominated, was collapsing even more rapidly. Both Germany and the United States had overtaken Britain in steel production, the key indicator of competitiveness at the time, and the gap was widening. In 1901, the largest U.S. steel company alone was producing more steel than all of England![1] Thus, Britain has been concerned about relative economic decline for more than a century.

Forty years ago, there was not much to admire in the British economy. Growth and domestic investment were low and unemployment high. In 1976 the government even received a Third World–style bailout from the International Monetary Fund to help stabilize the economy. Britain was routinely called the "sick man of Europe." However, throughout the 1980s and 1990s, Britain's growth rate was right in the middle of the pack of the seven richest countries, or G7 (see Figure 2.1). During the same period, which spans the Conservative governments of Margaret Thatcher and John Major, as well as that of Labour's Tony Blair, living standards (whether measured by gross domestic product per capita or purchasing power parity) also placed Britain in the middle of the G7 and the group of twenty-nine Organisation for Economic Co-operation and Development (OECD) industrialized countries. Although living standards were significantly below those of the United States and Japan, they roughly corresponded to others in Western Europe. As the *Economist* observed in 2000, "Britain is neither an economic paradise nor a wasteland."[2]

The economy New Labour inherited after eighteen years of Conservative stewardship was both prosperous and troubled. It was still in decline relative to the performance of key competitors, but it exhibited a long and significant growth performance relative to British performance. But despite New Labour's best efforts to claim full credit for the longest run of uninterrupted growth since 1701 (trumpeted by Brown in his March 2005 budget), in fact more than a third of that run came under the Conservatives.[3]

Despite this success, the British economy had been going through—and was continuing to experience—a set of radical shifts that created great political challenges—and headaches. In a few unsettling decades, it had shifted from semiautomated standardized heavy industry to a predominantly service economy. It was rapidly shedding labor and, from 1983, for the first time since the industrial revolution it became (as it remains today) a net importer of manufactured goods. So New Labour inherited growth, but economic troubles, as well: relatively weak competitiveness and key industrial sectors that were losing ground to rivals. In short, when Gordon Brown took ultimate responsibility for the economy in 1997, he found a platform for economic stability in the making but, at the same time, not just an economy, but also a society in need of reform—one that was not so easy to govern.[4]

It was an aging society, one with gender gaps in voting (in which women favored the Conservatives) and in experiences of work (with women very significantly overrepresented in part-time and nonstandard work). It was, in many ways, a troubled society in which social and political life was still powerfully shaped by social class. Historically, the Labour party in Britain relied on a core working-class base of support who tended to view the world in an "us" (workers, pensioners) versus "them" (the wealthy, entrepreneurs, and managers) framework. But the meaning and political implications of class had changed. New Labour "faced a working class whose members largely shared the concerns of middle England."[5]

In addition, New Labour found a society in which class was increasingly understood and experienced in consumption terms (defined by whether the big-ticket consumption items such as housing, education, health care, and pensions were provided by the state or the market).[6] David Coates aptly describes this troubled economic, social, and political context marked by tensions and frustrations, a "patchwork Britain," of vastly disparate experiences of life—with some, especially in London, enjoying a style of life and living standards as elevated as any in the world, while others lived in Second World (the term used for the Soviet Bloc during the cold war) conditions of grim run-down housing estates and the near-certainty of long-term unemployment.

Figure 2.1

Britain's Relative Economic Performance: Annual Percentage Growth of Gross Domestic Product

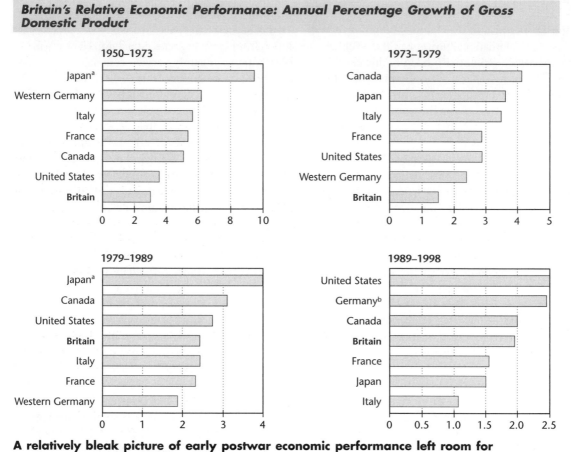

A relatively bleak picture of early postwar economic performance left room for improvement in the 1980s and the 1990s as Britain began to catch up with and then overtake its European competitors.

[a]1952–1973.

[b]Western Germany before 1991.

Source: Economist, March 25, 2000. Copyright © 2000 The Economist Newspaper Group, Ltd. Reprinted with permission. Further reproduction prohibited. www.economist.com.

State and Economy

Neoliberalism has driven the economic policy orientation of New Labour during the premierships of both Blair and Brown and the economic performance of the UK economy today, in its sustained growth as well as its high inequality (discussed below in "Society and Economy"), reflects both the strengths and the weaknesses of that model. Government policies aim to promote free competition among firms, to interfere with the prerogatives of entrepreneurs and managers as little as possible, and to create a business-friendly environment to attract foreign investment and spur innovation. At the same time, Britain's Labour government insists that its third way—as distinct from Conservative or conventional center-left projects—can blend the dynamism of market forces with the traditional center-left concern for social justice and commitment to the reduction of inequalities. How "new" is New Labour's approach to economic management? Are Britons across the spectrum enjoying the fruits of relative prosperity? How have the growing importance of the EU and the economic processes of globalization changed the political equation? The next section analyzes the politics of economic management in Britain and considers the implications of Britain's less-is-more, laissez-faire approach.

Since the mid-1990s, Britain has avoided the high unemployment and recession that haunt many of the member nations of the European Union (EU). The pattern of growth reveals the two-track character of the UK economy, with growth in the service sector—the UK is especially competitive in financial services—offsetting a much weaker industrial sector performance. But in general the British economy exhibits overall strength, and stands up well in knowledge-intensive high-technology industrial sectors, which account for one-quarter of the country's total exports. The British economy is a strong performer, with an enviable record of growth, low inflation, low unemployment, and strong international competitiveness, especially in the service sector. Both supporters and fair-minded critics would agree that New Labour has been successful in governing the economy.

Although many now wonder how much longer the good times will continue to roll, with low unemployment, low interest rates, low inflation, and sustained growth, the UK performance profile through the century's first decade was one of the best in the OECD. (In spring 2007, for the first time since New Labour came to power, inflation topped 3 percent).

There is cause for concern about a productivity gap between the United Kingdom and key competitors, the persistent deficit in the UK balance of trade, as well as endemic concerns about low rates of domestic investment and spending on research and development. Also, the British model encompasses far greater inequality than its west European counterparts, and it relies on a system of production that produces non-standard and insecure jobs without the traditional social protections associated with the European social and economic model. Women and ethnic minorities are significantly overrepresented in this sector. As a result, within EU Europe (at least before the May 2004 enlargement eastward), Britain assumed a specialized profile as a producer of relatively low-technology, low-value-added products made by a comparatively low-paid, segmented, weakly organized, and easily dismissed labor force.[7]

In addition, housing prices have escalated rapidly beyond the reach of many middle-class Britons as home mortgage refinancing has fueled a huge boom in consumer spending for the "haves" and—augmented by a frenzy of credit card borrowing—pushed record numbers onto the edge of personal bankruptcy. Working-class families were largely excluded from this new affluence, which was spurred by a rapid rise in the equity generated by home ownership.[8]

Two central dimensions, economic management and social policy, capture the new role of the state. Analysis of these policy areas also reveals how limited this new state role was in comparative terms.

Economic Management

Like all other states, whatever their commitment to free markets, the British state intervenes in economic life, sometimes with considerable force. However, the British have not developed institutions for state-sponsored economic planning or industrial policy. Instead, the British state has generally limited its role to broad policy instruments designed to influence the economy generally (macroeconomic policy) by adjusting state revenues and expenditures to achieve short-term goals. The Treasury and the Bank of England dominate economic policy, which has often seemed reactive and relatively ineffectual. Despite other differences, this generally reactive and minimalist orientation of economic management strategies bridges the first two eras of postwar politics in Britain: the consensus era (1945–1979) and the period of Thatcherite policy orientation (1979–1997). How has the orientation of economic policy developed and changed during the postwar period?

The Consensus Era. When it took control of crucial industries during World War I and assumed active management of industry in the interwar years, the state assumed a more interventionist role that belied its laissez-faire traditions. After World War II, the sense of unity inspired by the shared suffering of war and the need to rebuild a war-ravaged country crystallized the collectivist consensus as the British state broadened and deepened its responsibilities for the overall performance of the economy.

The state nationalized some key industries, assuming direct ownership of them. It also accepted the responsibility to secure low levels of unemployment (a policy of full employment), expand social services, maintain a steady rate of growth (increase the output or GDP), keep prices stable, and achieve desirable balance-of-payments and exchange rates. The approach is called Keynesian demand management, or Keynesianism (after the British economist John Maynard Keynes, 1883–1946). State budget deficits were used to expand demand in an effort to boost both consumption and investment when the economy was slowing. Cuts in government spending and a tightening of credit and finance, by contrast, were used to cool demand when high rates of growth brought fears of inflation or a deficit in balance of payments. Taken together, this new agenda of expanded economic management and welfare provision, sometimes referred to as the Keynesian welfare state, directed government policy throughout the era of the collectivist consensus.

Before Thatcher became leader of the Conservative Party in 1975, Conservative leaders in Britain generally accepted the terms of the collectivist consensus. By the 1970s, however, public officials no longer saw the world they understood and could master; it had become a world without economic growth and with growing political discontent. Edward Heath, the Conservative centrist who governed from 1970 to 1974, was the first prime minister to suffer the full burden of recession and the force of political opposition from both traditional business allies and resurgent trade union adversaries. In an era marked by increased inflation and reduced growth (stagflation), Heath could never break out of the political constraints imposed on him by economic decline.

From 1974 to 1979, the Labour government of Harold Wilson and James Callaghan reinforced the impression that governments could no longer control the swirl of events. The beginning of the end came when trade unions became increasingly restive under the pinch of voluntary wage restraints that had been pressed on them by the Labour government. Frustrated by wage increases that were well below inflation rates, the unions broke with the government in 1978. The number of unofficial work stoppages increased, and official strikes followed—all fueled by a seemingly endless series of leapfrogging pay demands that erupted throughout the winter of 1978–1979 (the "winter of discontent"). There is little doubt that the industrial unrest that dramatized Labour's inability to manage its allies, the trade unions, contributed a great deal to Thatcher's electoral victory a few months later in May 1979. The winter of discontent helped write the conclusion to Britain's collectivist consensus and discredit the Keynesian welfare state.

Thatcherite Policy Orientation. In policy terms, the economic orientations that Thatcher pioneered and that Major substantially maintained reflected a growing disillusionment with Keynesianism. Monetarism emerged as the new economic doctrine. Keynesian demand management assumed that the level of unemployment could be set and the economy stabilized through decisions of government (monetary and fiscal or budgetary policy). By contrast, monetarism assumed that there is a "natural rate of unemployment" determined by the labor market itself. Monetary and fiscal policy should be passive and intervention should be limited (so far as this was possible) to a few steps that would foster appropriate rates of growth in the money supply and keep inflation low.

By implication, the government ruled out spending to run up budgetary deficits as a useful instrument for stimulating the economy. On the contrary, governments could contribute to overall economic efficiency and growth by reducing social expenditure and downsizing the public sector, by reducing its work force or privatizing nationalized industries. Monetarism reflected a radical change from the postwar consensus on economic management. Not only was active government intervention considered unnecessary; it was seen as undesirable and destabilizing.

New Labour's Economic Policy Approach. Can New Labour thinking on macroeconomic policy end the short-term thinking of economic policy and provide the cohesion previously lacking? British commentaries on

New Labour make much of the influence of revitalized Keynesian ideas and reform proposals.[9] In some ways, government policy seems to pursue conventional market-reinforcing and probusiness policies (neoliberalism). In other ways, the New Labour program stands as an alternative to both Thatcherite monetarism and traditional Keynesianism. Whether New Labour's approach to economic management constitutes a distinctive third way or a less coherent blend of disparate elements is the subject of endless political debate.

The first shot in the Blair revolution was the announcement within a week of the 1997 election by Gordon Brown, who was then the chancellor of the exchequer (equivalent to the minister for finance or secretary of the treasury in other countries), that the Bank of England would now have "operational independence" in the setting of monetary policy, and charged with maintaining low inflation (which has been achieved). The decision transferred from the cabinet a critical, and highly political, prerogative of government. Since Brown was attuned to the pressures of international financial markets, and the control of inflation and stability the key goals of macroeconomic policy, the transfer of authority over monetary policy confirmed the neoliberal market orientation of economic policy.

Central to the concerns of Brown and his Treasury team from 1997 were issues of macroeconomic stability. Brown (the "iron chancellor") insisted on establishing a "platform of stability" through explicit acceptance of the preexisting (and Conservative-specified) limits on public spending, and he gave a very high priority to policies that were designed to reduce the public debt. Only as he turned that debt into a surplus did the iron chancellor reinvent himself as a more conventionally Labour and social democratic chancellor. Deciding to use economic growth to increase spending on key social policies (rather than cut taxes), spending on the National Health Service (NHS), which was 6 percent of GDP, jumped to 8 percent of GDP in 2005. Similarly, annual expenditure on education is scheduled to nearly double between 2002 and 2008.[10] Both Brown's success in achieving growth and economic stability and the credit he is given for a commitment to fund social policy positioned the chancellor well to succeed Blair as leader of the Labour Party and prime minister.

Does the third way represent a genuine departure in economic policy? Although there is no ready agreement on how best to answer this question, the claim of a distinctive policy design is quite clear in the way Blair and Brown have articulated their priorities. Just as Keynesianism inspired Old Labour, new growth theory allowed New Labour to embrace globalization as something positive, to be welcomed, as a rising historical tide—one that the center-left was uniquely well placed to understand and exploit. According to this theory, which Gordon Brown embraced and vigorously applied, a high-skill labor force tilted toward high-tech applications spurs growth and competitiveness.

Armed and emboldened by new growth theory, New Labour insisted that they could sustain and enhance the growth inherited from the Conservatives—and at the same time marry efficiency to a more equal distribution of wealth—and gain by promoting growth in knowledge-driven sectors and by increasing the education, training, and skill of the workforce from top to bottom. If anything did, new growth theory contributed the "new" to New Labour.

Since capital is international, mobile, and not subject to control, industrial policy and planning that focus on the domestic economy alone are futile. Rather, government should improve the quality of labor through education and training, maintain the labor market flexibility inherited from the Thatcher regime, and attract investment to Britain. Strict controls of inflation and tough limits on public expenditure help promote both employment and investment opportunities. New Labour is very focused on designing and implementing policies that will create new jobs and get people, particularly young people, into the work force in increasingly high-skill and high-tech jobs.

Political Implications of Economic Policy. Differences in economic doctrine are not what matter most in policy terms. In fact, British governments in the past have never consistently followed any economic theory, whether Keynesianism or monetarism. Today, the economic policy of New Labour is pragmatic and eclectic. The political consequences of economic orientations are more significant: each economic doctrine helps to justify a broad moral and cultural vision of society, provide motives for state policy, and advance alternative sets of values. Should the government intervene, work to reduce inequalities through the mildly redistributive provisions of the welfare state, and sustain the ethos of a caring society (collectivism/"Old Labour")? Should it back off and allow the market to function competitively and in that way promote entrepreneurship, competitiveness, and individual autonomy (Thatcherism)? Or should it help secure an inclusive "stakeholder" economy in which business has the flexibility, security, and mobility to compete and workers have the skills and training to participate effectively in the global labor market (New Labour)? As these questions make clear, economic management strategies are closely linked to social or welfare policy.

Social Policy

The social and political role of the welfare state depends as much on policy goals and instruments as on spending levels. Does the state provide services itself or offer cash benefits that can be used to purchase services from private providers? Are benefits universal, or are they limited to those who fall below an income threshold (means-tested)? Are they designed to meet the temporary needs of individuals or to help reduce the gap between rich and poor?

The expanded role of government during World War II and the increased role of the Labour Party during the wartime coalition government led by Winston Churchill prepared the way for the development of the welfare state in Britain. The 1943 Beveridge Report provided a blueprint for an extensive but, in comparative European terms, fairly moderate set of provisions. The principal means-tested program is social security, a system of contributory and noncontributory benefits to provide financial assistance (not services directly) for the elderly, sick, disabled, unemployed, and others similarly in need of assistance.

In general, welfare state provisions interfere relatively little in the workings of the market, and policymakers do not see the reduction of group inequalities as the proper goal of the welfare state. The NHS provides comprehensive universal medical care and has long been championed as the jewel in the crown of the welfare state in Britain, but it remains an exception to the rule. Compared with other Western European countries, the welfare state in Britain offers relatively

few comprehensive services, and its policies are not very generous. For the most part, Britons must rely on means-tested safety net programs that leave few of the recipients satisfied.

The Welfare State Under Thatcher and Major. The record on social expenditure by Conservative governments from 1979 to 1997 was mixed. Given Britons' strong support for public education, pensions, and health care, Conservative governments attempted less reform than many at first anticipated. The Thatcher and Major governments encouraged private, alongside public, provision in education, health care (insurance), and pensions. They worked to increase efficiency in social services, reduced the value of some benefits by changing the formulas or reducing cost-of-living adjustments, and contracted out some services (purchasing them from private contractors rather than providing them directly). In addition, in policy reforms reminiscent of U.S. "workfare" requirements, they tried to reduce dependency by denying benefits to youths who refused to participate in training programs. Despite these efforts, the commitment to reduced spending could not be sustained, partly because a recession required increases in income support and unemployment benefits.

To some degree, however, this general pattern masks specific and, in some cases, highly charged policy changes in both expenditures and the institutionalized pattern of provision. In housing, the changes in state policy and provision were the most extensive, with repercussions in electoral terms and in changing the way Britons think about the welfare state. By 1990, more than 1.25 million council houses (public housing maintained by local government) were sold, particularly the attractive single-family homes with gardens (quite unlike public housing in the United States). Two-thirds of the sales went to rental tenants. Thatcher's housing policy was extremely popular. By one calculation, between 1979 and 1983 there was a swing (change in the percentage of vote received by the two major parties) to the Conservative Party of 17 percent among those who had bought their council houses.[11]

Despite great Conservative success in the campaign to privatize housing, a strong majority of Britons remain stalwart supporters of the principle of collective provision for their basic needs. And so there were limits on the government's ability to reduce social spending or change institutional behavior. For example, in 1989, the Conservative government tried to introduce market practices into the NHS, with general practitioners managing funds and purchasing hospital care for their patients. Many voiced fears that the reforms would create a two-tier system of medical care with one system for the rich and one for the poor.

More generally, a lack of confidence in the Conservatives on social protection hurt Major substantially in 1992, and it has continued to plague the party. Nothing propelled the Labour landslide in 1997 more than the concern for the "caring" issues. The traditional advantage Labour enjoys on these issues also helped secure victory for Blair in June 2001 and again, in 2005, when he needed a boost from traditional Labour supporters to offset their opposition to the prime minister on the war in Iraq.

New Labour Social Policy.   As with economic policy, New Labour sees social policy as an opportunity for government to balance pragmatism and innovation, while borrowing from traditional Labour as well as from Thatcherite options. Thus, the Blair government rejected both the attempted retrenchment of Conservative governments that seemed mean-spirited as well as the egalitarian traditions of Britain's collectivist era that emphasized entitlements. Instead, New Labour focuses its policy on training and broader social investment as a more positive third-way alternative. At the same time, New Labour draws political strength from the "Old Labour" legacy of commitment on the "caring" social policy issues.

For example, following Bill Clinton, Blair's New Democratic counterpart in the United States, prime minister Blair promised a modernized, leaner welfare state, in which people are actively encouraged to seek work. The reform of the welfare state emphasizes efficiencies and tries to break welfare dependency. Efforts to spur entry into the labor market combine carrots and sticks. A signature policy initiative of chancellor Brown, the government offered positive inducements to include training programs, especially targeted at youth, combined with incentives to private industry to hire new entrants to the labor market. The threats include eligibility restrictions and reductions in coverage. Referred to as the "New Deal" for the young unemployed, welfare reform

in the United Kingdom has emphasized concerted efforts to create pathways out of dependence. Although beginning with a focus on moving youth from welfare to work, New Deal reform efforts expanded in several directions.

The New Deal quickly extended to single parents and the long-term unemployed. In 1999, the government launched a "Bridging the Gap" initiative to provide a more comprehensive approach for assisting sixteen- to eighteen-year-olds not in education, employment, or training to achieve clear goals by age nineteen through a variety of "pathways" (academic, vocational, or occupational). "Better Government for Older People" was launched in 1998, which was followed quickly by "All Our Futures," a government report issued in the summer of 2000 with twenty-eight recommendations to improve the quality of life and the delivery of public services for senior citizens. A new initiative, The IT New Deal, was launched in 2001 as a government-business partnership to address skill shortages in information technologies.

Although doubts remain about the follow-through and effectiveness of New Labour social and welfare policy initiatives, the intent to create innovative policies and approach social policy in new and more comprehensive ways is clearly there. Late in 1997, the government inaugurated the Social Exclusion Unit, staffed by civil servants and external policy specialists. Initially located in the Cabinet Office and reporting directly to the prime minister, the Social Exclusion Unit moved to the Office of the Deputy Prime Minister in May 2002. It was charged broadly with addressing "what can happen when people or areas suffer from such problems as unemployment, poor skills, low incomes, poor housing, high crime environments, bad health, and family breakdown." The Social Exclusion Unit has been actively involved in developing the New Deal initiative as well as in writing reports and recommending policies to address problems such as truancy and social exclusion, homelessness, neighborhood renewal, and teenage pregnancy. This effort to identify comprehensive solutions to society's ills and reduce the tendency for government to let marginalized individuals fall by the wayside captures the third-way orientation of the New Labour project.

Nevertheless, New Labour, like all governments in Britain and in many other countries, will be accountable above all for the failure or success of more traditional social policies, especially health care and education. By 2004, there was mounting evidence that record growth in the NHS budget had netted results. Despite the report of a House of Commons select committee on the health dangers of obesity (particularly for children), there was widespread confidence that NHS quality and performance were improving, with shorter waiting lists and significant advances in the treatment of life-threatening diseases. After years of skepticism about New Labour's ability to deliver on promised improvements in providing key public services, by 2005 the tides of opinion—and massive budgetary increases—were beginning to have the desired effect. New Labour had gained considerable credibility on health care as well as education, and increasing success on core policies gave Labour a huge boost heading into the 2005 election. Nevertheless, Gordon Brown has also inherited some significant problems with the delivery of key public services, such as health care. Despite the unprecedented increase in resources, health care remains a huge headache for New Labour and Gordon Brown. New Labour's internal market health care reforms have left the system with increasingly untenable deficits. Some hospital trusts are ominously near collapse. Brown needs to find the recipe to provide health care—and other public services such as education—on a sound financial footing and to reassure a restive electorate that the quality of services is high and access equitable. His success or failure in these areas will say a lot about the overall success of his premiership—and whether he will rival Blair's longevity as prime minister.

Society and Economy

What were the *distributional effects* of the economic and social policies of Thatcher and Major—the consequences for group patterns of wealth and poverty? To what extent have the policies of the Labour governments headed by Blair and Brown continued—or reversed—these trends? How has government policy influenced the condition of minorities and women? It is impossible to be sure when government policy creates a given distribution of resources and when poverty increases or decreases because of a general downturn or upswing in the economy. The evidence is clear, however, that eco-

nomic inequality grew in Britain during the 1980s before it stabilized or narrowed slightly in the mid-1990s, and that ethnic minorities and women continue to experience significant disadvantages.

In general, policies initiated by the Conservative Party, particularly during the Thatcher years, deepened inequalities. The economic upturn that began in 1992, combined with Major's moderating effects on the Thatcherite social policy agenda, served to narrow inequality by the mid-1990s. Since 1997, as one observer noted, Labour has "pursued redistribution by stealth, raising various indirect levies on the better-off to finance tax breaks for poorer workers."[12] As a result, Britain has witnessed a modest downward redistribution of income since 1997. Attention to social exclusion in its many forms, a 1999 pledge by the prime minister to eradicate child poverty (even though Britain at the time had one of the highest rates of child poverty in EU Europe), and strong rates of growth seemed to bode well for a further narrowing of the gap between rich and poor in Britain, especially among children.

Especially in Blair's third term, there were clear indications that the government was committed to an ambitious agenda to reduce childhood poverty through a new set of inclusive tax credits for children and other measures to transfer resources to poor families. In addition, since January 2005, the payment of vouchers to the parents of all British children born since 2002, with a promise to top up the funds periodically, represented an innovative effort to provide a sizeable nest egg of savings available for eighteen-year-olds. This "asset-based" welfare held the promise of reducing poverty and providing a new generation with new economic opportunities.

Finally, the *Innocenti Report Card* (2007), recently published by UNICEF, puts a very sobering spotlight on New Labour's high-profile commitment to end childhood poverty in the UK. In addition, it indirectly raises questions about the broader efficacy of its economic and social model.[13] In this careful assessment of the comparative performance of twenty-one OECD countries in securing the well-being of children, European countries generally score very well. In fact, in the rankings based on an index that includes measures of relative income poverty, households without jobs, and reported deprivation, to assess the material well-being of children, four European countries— Netherlands, Sweden, Denmark, and Finland, are at the top of the league tables comparing the twenty-one countries analyzed. However, both the United States and the United Kingdom are in the bottom third for five of the six dimensions under review. Worse still, in the summary table that presents the overall rankings, the UK comes in dead last, just behind the United States (see Figure 2.2).

Inequality and Ethnic Minorities

Poverty and diminished opportunity disproportionately affect ethnic minorities (a term applied to peoples of non-European origin from the former British colonies in the Indian subcontinent, the Caribbean, and Africa). Official estimates place the ethnic minority population in Britain at 4.7 million or 7.9 percent of the total population of the United Kingdom. Indians comprise the largest ethnic minority, at 21.7 percent; Pakistanis represent 16.7 percent, Bangladeshis, 6.1 percent, and Afro-Caribbeans and other blacks, 27.1 percent.[14] Because of past immigration and fertility patterns, the ethnic minority population in the United Kingdom is considerably younger than the white population. More than one-third of the ethnic minority population is younger than sixteen, nearly half is under twenty-five, and more than four-fifths is age forty-five. Despite the common and often disparaging reference to ethnic minority individuals as "immigrants," the experience of members of ethnic minority groups is increasingly that of a native born population.[15]

Britain has adjusted slowly to the realities of a multicultural society. The postwar period has witnessed the gradual erosion of racial, religious, and ethnic tolerance and a chipping away at the right of settlement of postcolonial subjects in the United Kingdom. During the Thatcher era, discussion of immigration and citizenship rights was used for partisan political purposes and assumed a distinctly racial tone. Ethnic minority individuals, particularly young men, are subject to unequal treatment by the police and suffer considerable physical harassment by citizens. They have experienced cultural isolation as well as marginalization in the educational system, job training, housing, and labor markets. There is considerable concern about the seeming rise in racially motivated crime in major metropolitan areas with significant ethnic diversity. Recognizing these problems, in 2000 the government introduced a bill to amend the Race Relations Act 1976 by outlawing direct and indirect discrimination in all public bodies and placing a "positive duty" on all public officials and authorities to promote racial equality. The Race Relations (Amendment) Act 2000 received final parliamentary approval in November 2000.

In general, poor rates of economic success reinforce isolation and distinct collective identities. Variations among ethnic minority communities are quite considerable, however, and there are some noteworthy success stories. For example, among men of African, Asian, Chinese, and Indian descent, the proportional representation in the managerial and professional ranks is actually higher than that for white men (although they are much less likely to be senior managers in large firms). Also, Britons of South Asian and, especially, Indian descent enjoy a high rate of entrepreneurship. Despite some variations, however, employment opportunities for women from all minority ethnic groups are limited.[16] In addition, a distinct gap remains between the job opportunities available to whites and those open to ethnic minorities. It is clear that people from ethnic minority communities are overrepresented among low-income households in the United Kingdom (see Figure 2.3). Almost 60 percent of Pakistani or Bangladeshi households are in low-income households (defined by income below 60 percent of the median). Just under half of black non-Caribbean households also live on low incomes after housing costs are deducted, as do nearly one third of black Caribbeans. In contrast, only 16 percent of white people live in such low-income households before housing costs are deducted, and 21 percent after housing costs are deducted.[17]

The human side behind the statistics reveals how difficult it remains in Britain for ethnic minorities to achieve top posts and how uneven the prospects of success are, despite some pockets of modest success. It seems that the police have been more effective in recent years in recruiting and retaining ethnic minority police officers, and moving them up through the ranks, but the further-education colleges (non-degree-giving institutions providing mainly vocational training for sixteen- to eighteen-year-olds not headed to university) have not done so well. "We don't have one black

Figure 2.2

Child Well-being in Rich Countries: A Summary Table

Countries are listed here in order of their average rank for the six dimensions of child well-being that have been assessed.*
A light gray background indicates a place in the top third of the table; mid-gray denotes the middle third; and dark gray the bottom third.

Dimensions of Child Well-being	Average Ranking Position (for all 6 dimensions)	Dimension 1 Material Well-being	Dimension 2 Health and Safety	Dimension 3 Educational Well-being	Dimension 4 Family and Peer Relationships	Dimension 5 Behaviors and Risks	Dimension 6 Subjective Well-being
Netherlands	4.2	10	2	6	3	3	1
Sweden	5.0	1	1	5	15	1	7
Denmark	7.2	4	4	8	9	6	12
Finland	7.5	3	3	4	17	7	11
Spain	8.0	12	6	15	8	5	2
Switzerland	8.3	5	9	14	4	12	6
Norway	8.7	2	8	11	10	13	8
Italy	10.0	14	5	20	1	10	10
Ireland	10.2	19	19	7	7	4	5
Belgium	10.7	7	16	1	5	19	16
Germany	11.2	13	11	10	13	11	9
Canada	11.8	6	13	2	18	17	15
Greece	11.8	15	18	16	11	8	3
Poland	12.3	21	15	3	14	2	19
Czech Republic	12.5	11	10	9	19	9	17
France	13.0	9	7	18	12	14	18
Portugal	13.7	16	14	21	2	15	14
Austria	13.8	8	20	19	16	16	4
Hungary	14.5	20	17	13	6	18	13
United States	18.0	17	21	12	20	20	–
United Kingdom	18.2	18	12	17	21	21	20

*OECD countries with insufficient data to be included in the overview: Australia, Iceland, Japan, Luxembourg, Mexico, New Zealand, the Slovak Republic, South Korea, Turkey.

Despite a strong commitment by New Labour to end child poverty, Britain comes in last in a comparison of child well-being among twenty-one wealthy countries.

Source: UNICEF, Child poverty in perspective. An overview of child well-being in rich countries. *Innocenti Report Card 7,* 2007. UNICEF Innocenti Research Centre, Florence. © The United Nations Children's Fund, 2007.

Figure 2.3

Distribution of Low-Income Households by Ethnicity

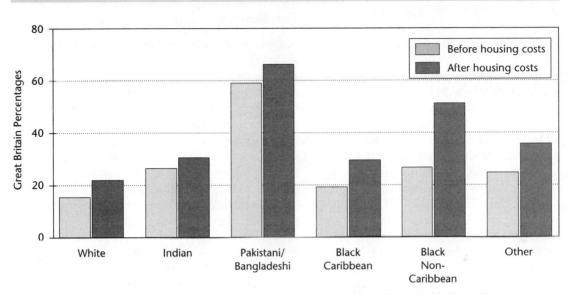

Households on low income: by ethnic group of head of household, 2001–02

People from Britain's ethnic minority communities are far more likely than white Britons to be in lower-income households, although there are important differences among ethnic minority groups. Nearly 60 percent of Pakistani or Bangladeshi households are low-income households, while about one-third of black Caribbean households live on low incomes.

Source: National Statistics Online: www.statistics.gov.uk/CCI/nugget.asp?ID=269&Pos=1&ColRank=2&Rank=384

college principal in London in spite of having one of the most ethnically diverse student populations in the country," observed the mayor of London's senior policy director in 2004. "There are many more young Afro-Caribbean men in prison than there are in university, and more black Met [London police] officers than there are teachers."[18] Ethnic minority police officers now make up 3 percent of the United Kingdom's 122,000-member police force, but only 2 percent of junior and middle managers in the more than four hundred colleges in Britain, only five of which have ethnic minority principals. It speaks volumes about the level of ethnic minority inequality that a 3 percent representation of ethnic minority police officers is considered evidence that "the police have in recent years been undertaking a much-needed overhaul of equal opportunities."[19]

Inequality and Women

Women's participation in the labor market when compared to that of men also indicates marked patterns of inequality. In fact, most women in Britain work part-time, often in jobs with fewer than sixteen hours of work per week and often with fewer than eight hours (in contrast, fewer than one in every fifteen men is employed part-time). More than three-quarters of women working part-time report that they did not want a full-time job, yet more women than men (in raw numbers, not simply as a percentage) take on second jobs. Although employment conditions for women in Britain trail those of many of their EU counterparts, the gap in the differential between weekly earnings of men and women in the United Kingdom has narrowed. In fact, the gender gap in pay based on median hourly earnings has narrowed from 17.4 percent in 1997 to 12.6 percent in 2006, the lowest value since records have been kept. That's the good news. The bad news is that the part-time gender pay gap (based on a comparison of the hourly wage of men working full-time and women working part-time) for 2006 was 40.2 percent.[20]

New Labour remains committed to gender equality in the workplace and has affirmed its resolve to address women's concerns to balance work and family responsibilities. The government has implemented a set of family-friendly work-related policies, including parental leave and flexible working arrangements and working times. Most of these initiatives only reached the minimum EU standard as required by treaty commitments (once the UK under Blair signed on to part of the Social Chapter of the 1991 Maastricht Treaty to which previous UK governments had opted out, and further took on the obligations under the 1997 Amsterdam Treaty). Other measures include a commitment in principle to filling half of all public appointments with women, a review of the pension system to ensure better coverage for women, draft legislation to provide for the sharing of pensions after divorce, tax credits for working families as well as for child care, and a National Childcare Strategy, to which the Blair government committed extensive financial support and gave high visibility. Nevertheless, the gap between childcare supply and demand is considerable, and the cost for many families remains prohibitive. Moreover, despite its efforts to make it easier for women to balance work and family obligations, "Labour has focused its efforts on persuading employers as to the 'business case' for 'family friendly' working conditions."[21]

This approach limits New Labour's agenda, as witnessed by the government's willingness to let employers opt out of a forty-eight-hour ceiling on the work week (a serious impediment to a healthy family-work balance, especially since UK fathers work the longest hours in Europe).[22] Thus, New Labour's core commitment to management flexibility makes it likely that the general pattern of female labor market participation will change relatively little in the years ahead. A report commissioned by the Cabinet Office's Women's Unit confirms that there is a significant pattern of inequality in lifetime earnings of men and women with an equal complement of skills, defined by both a gender gap and a "mother gap."

The Generation Gap

Another widely discussed and equally significant gap shapes British politics: the generation gap. In fact, its dimensions are most clear at the point where gender and generational differences come together, and they have done so acutely in elections. The issue of a gender gap in voting behavior has long been a mainstay of British electoral studies. From 1945 to 1992, women were more likely than men to vote Conservative. In addition, since 1964 a gender-generation gap has become well established and was very clear in the 1992 election. Among younger voters (under thirty years old), women preferred Labour, while men voted strongly for the Conservatives, producing a fourteen-point gender gap favoring Labour; among voters over sixty-five years old, women were far more inclined to vote Conservative than were their male counterparts, creating a gender gap of eighteen points favoring the Conservatives.

The modest all-generation gender gap that favored the Tories in 1992 (6 percent) was closed in 1997 as a greater percentage of women shifted away from the Conservatives (11 percent) than did men (8 percent). As a result, women and men recorded an identical 44 percent tally for Labour. The gender-generation gap continued, however, with younger women more pro-Labour than younger men and the pattern reversing in the older generation. Furthermore, one of the most striking features of the 1997 election was the generational dimension: the largest swing to Labour was among those in the age group eighteen to twenty-nine years (more than 18 percent), and among first-time voters; there was no swing to Labour among those over age sixty-five.[23]

What are the implications of this overlay of gender and generational voting patterns? For one thing, it seems that a party's ability to recognize and satisfy the political agendas of women in Britain may offer big political dividends. Studies suggest, first, that issues at the top of the list of women's concerns (such as child care, the rights and pay of part-time workers, equal pay, support for family caregivers, domestic

violence) do not feature strongly in the existing policy agendas of the political parties. Second, to the
extent that women and men care about the same
broadly defined issues, women often understand the
issues differently from the way men do and express
different priorities. For example, while men (and the
three major parties) consider unemployment the central employment issue, women emphasize equal pay
and pensions, access to child care, and the rights of
part-time workers. Third, research indicates that distinct sets of issues concern different groups of women.
For example, older women are most concerned about
pensions and transportation. Because of the overrep-
resentation of women in lower-paid part-time jobs,
working women express particular concern about the
minimum wage and the treatment of part-time workers. Mothers find the level of child benefits more
important than tax cuts. Finally, younger women
strongly support policies that would help them balance
the responsibilities of work, family, and child care.
This last point may be the most critical. Like the
perennial focus on "working families" in U.S. presidential campaigns, political parties in Britain recognize that the successful political management of the
gender-generation gap is becoming a critical electoral
battleground. Winning the support of working mothers or younger women who plan to become working
mothers could pay huge political dividends.

Other aspects of the generation gap are far less
clear. The political apathy and self-interested materialism of the "youth of today" receive wide comment, but there is little evidence that can disentangle
the attitudes of the millennium generation from the
different stages and accompanying social and political attitudes each generation acquires during its life
cycle.

After the 2001 election, analysts pointed to a generation gap in turnout. BBC exit polls revealed that
young voters had the lowest turnout, most often saying the election "didn't matter." The new home secretary, David Blunkett, worried aloud that youth had
"switched off politics." Polling data generally confirm
that there is a generation gap in the connection
between citizens and mainstream politics and that
younger Britons are more divorced from politics.
Three-quarters of young people aged fifteen to twenty-

four have never met their local councillor, compared
with just over half of those aged fifty-five or older.
Also, older citizens are more than twice as likely to
say that they know the name of their local councillor
(46 percent compared with 20 percent of fifteen- to
twenty-four-year-olds).[24] That said, the unprecedented
participation of British youth in the massive antiwar
protests in February and March 2003 tells a different
story, one of young people with strong political views
and an unexpected taste for political engagement. A
BBC poll of schoolchildren in February 2003 reported
80 percent opposed to war, while Britain as a whole
was more evenly divided. On March 5, thousands of
teenagers across the country walked out of school and
congregated in city centers, while some five hundred
protested at the Houses of Parliament. "What's shocking isn't their opposition but the fact they're doing
something about it," noted one electronic journalist on
a youth-oriented website. "Considering that most
18–25 year olds couldn't even be bothered to put a
cross in a box at the last general election this is a pretty
big thing."[25] It was a big enough thing that New
Labour strategists were left to ponder the consequences, knowing that the mobilization of support
among young people, which was already a cause for
concern, could become more difficult in the aftermath
of the war in Iraq.

What are the gender and generational storylines in
Blair's historic third electoral victory in May 2005? The
most talked about theme regarding youth was their continued disaffection from electoral politics. According
to MORI, Britain's highly regarded political polling
organization, only 37 percent of the possible voters
between eighteen and twenty-four turned out to vote in
2005 (down from 39 percent in 2001). But this is only
one side of the generational story. The other side is that
the "grey vote" rose. Voters fifty-five and older made
up 35 percent of the electorate in 2005 (up 2 percent
from 2001) and since 75 percent voted, they represented
42 percent of those casting ballots. As for women—
they delivered a very big chunk of Blair's majority.
While men split evenly between Conservatives and
Labour an identical 34 percent (and 23 percent for the
Lib Dems), women swung decisively to Labour, giving
them a 10 percent advantage over the Conservatives (32
percent to 22 percent).[26]

The Dilemmas of European Integration

Since the beginning of the Industrial Revolution in the eighteenth century, Britain has been more dependent than most other countries on international commerce. Because Britain's economy is more interdependent with the global economy than most other leading industrial powers, it faces considerable external pressures on its economic policy. The dilemmas of European integration vividly illustrate the interplay between economics and politics in an era of global interdependence.

In 1963, and again in 1967, Britain was humbled when France blocked its applications for membership in the European Community (EC). Worse, since its admission in 1973, Britain's participation in the EC (in November 1993, it became the EU) has tended to underscore its reduced international power and ability to control regional and global developments. Many Britons remain skeptical about Britain's political and economic integration with Europe and are uneasy about the loss of sovereignty that resulted from EU membership.

Economic Integration and Political Disintegration

During the Thatcher and Major years, the issue of economic integration bedeviled the prime minister's office and divided the Conservative Party. The introduction of the European Monetary System (EMS) in 1979 set the stage for the political dramas that followed. The EMS fixed the exchange rates among member currencies (referred to as the Exchange Rate Mechanism, or ERM), and permitted only limited fluctuation above or below. Intended to stabilize European economies and promote trade among members, its success depended on the willingness of member states to pursue compatible economic strategies—and on their ability to maintain similar growth rates and levels of inflation. In retrospect, this plan seems highly unrealistic. How likely were Spain, Portugal, and Greece—or even Britain—to keep pace with Germany in the period of heady economic competitiveness before unification? But there was tremendous pressure to set up the ERM before political disagreements or recession could close the window of opportunity.

Thatcher opposed British participation in the ERM throughout the 1980s and insisted on British control of its economic policy. However, when her domestic economic policy failed to stem Britain's rampant inflation, Thatcher's anti-EC stance pitted her against senior ministers and leaders of Britain's EC partners, as well as against the bulk of the British business community. It seemed that everyone but Thatcher thought participation in European integration would ease inflation in Britain and enhance its competitiveness. In the end, Thatcher succumbed to the pressure to give up a measure of economic sovereignty, in effect, to Germany and its central bank (the Bundesbank), whose decisions would force Britain to follow in lockstep. She permitted Britain to join the ERM in October 1990. Ironically, just one month later, Thatcher was toppled from office in a coup led by those in her own party who most deeply resented her grudging attitude toward integration.

For the new government of Prime Minister John Major, participation in the ERM held enormous symbolic and political significance. As chancellor of the exchequer, he had quietly pressed Thatcher to join, and as prime minister, he staked his reputation on its success. He hoped that participation would stabilize European trade, reduce inflation, and pull Britain out of a stubborn recession.

Implications of Maastricht and the Common Currency

The Treaty on European Union (usually called the Maastricht Treaty for the small Dutch town where it was negotiated in 1991) represented a bold agenda for economic and monetary union and for deeper cooperation on foreign policy and security matters. Maastricht also established a plan to phase in a single EC currency and to give control of national monetary policy to a European central bank. In addition, Maastricht gave treaty status to the Community Charter of the Fundamental Social Rights of Workers, more commonly known as the Social Charter.

Unlike Thatcher, Major positioned himself as pro-Europe and was solicitous of his allies. But he stood his ground at Maastricht. Negotiating well, Major secured a crucial opt-out clause for Britain. The United

Kingdom would not be bound by the Social Charter or by any single-currency plans. Unfortunately for Major and the Conservatives, almost before he could enjoy his Maastricht victories, Major's integration strategy faced a nearly fatal setback.

In September 1992, the EMS collapsed under the downward pressures in the British economy and the strains of German unification. The prime minister's reputation was badly damaged, and the momentum for economic unity among EC countries abruptly stalled. The Thatcherite anti-Maastricht hard core in the Conservative Party dug in against Major on the key issues of economic and monetary union, thereby undermining his leadership and forcing him to squander political capital on the lost cause of party unity on Europe. Major never recovered, and it took several years before plans for economic integration in the EU came on track. Remarkably, a single European policy (the ERM) led to Thatcher's downfall and politically haunted John Major throughout his premiership.

Developments in European integration presented a formidable hurdle for Tony Blair and seem certain to present complications for Gordon Brown. On the one hand, few in Britain find it easy to countenance a common currency in place of the pound sterling (the British currency), a symbol of empire and national autonomy. Britons are also extremely reluctant to lose direct control over monetary policy to the European Central Bank (ECB). While he was chancellor in Blair's government, Gordon Brown insisted on a cautious approach to British participation in the euro zone and has controlled the political terrain of the Labour Party position on participation. On the other hand, Britain under Blair wanted to assume leadership in Europe and expand the foreign policy and military capabilities of the Union. Brown, like Blair before him, supports a strong EU role in meeting the challenge of climate change, narrowing the development gap, and taking on the challenge of AIDS in Africa. And, of course, Brown wants to position Britain on the cutting edge of globalization, with the EU an important player in this process.

Britain faces a significant dilemma over European integration. Although the defeat of the 2005 EU Constitution took the pressure off Britain, the EU reform treaty in October 2007 put Brown on the hot seat. Should he try to get it through Parliament, claim it was a treaty and not a constitution, and be accused of reneging on a promise to put an EU Constitution to a referendum? Or have a referendum and risk an almost certain defeat?

Britain in the Global Economy

Is Britain making the most of globalization? The answer begins with the understanding that Britain plays a special role within the European and international economy, one that has been reinforced by international competitive pressures in this global age. For a start, foreign direct investment (FDI) favors national systems, like those of Britain (and the United States), that rely more on private contractual and market-driven arrangements and less on state capacity and political or institutional arrangements. Because of such factors as low costs, political climate, government-sponsored financial incentives, reduced trade union power, and a large pool of potential non-unionized recruits, the United Kingdom is a highly regarded location in Europe for FDI.

From the mid-1980s onward, the single-market initiative of the EU has attracted foreign investment by according insider status to non-EU-based companies, so long as minimum local content requirements are met. Throughout this period, all British governments have, for both pragmatic and ideological reasons, promoted the United Kingdom as a magnet for foreign investment. For the Thatcher and Major governments, FDI was a congenial market-driven alternative to state intervention as a way to improve sectoral competitiveness. It had the added benefit of exposing UK producers to lean production techniques and to management cultures and strategies that reinforced government designs to weaken unions and enforce flexibility. New Labour has continued this approach, which advances its key third-way strategy orientation to accept globalization and to seek ways to improve competitiveness through business-friendly partnerships.

The FDI is only one part of a bigger picture. In important ways, New Labour accepted the legacy of eighteen years of Conservative assaults on trade union powers and privileges. It has chosen to modernize, but not reshape, the system of production in which non-standard and insecure jobs without traditional social protections proliferate—a growing sector in which women and ethnic minorities are significantly over-represented. As a result, within EU Europe Britain has assumed a specialized profile as a producer of medium-technology, relatively low-value-added mass-market products through the use of a comparatively low-paid, segmented, weakly organized work force that can be easily dismissed.

The competitive strengths of the UK economy are confirmed in some key benchmarks used in *The Global Competitiveness Report, 2005–2006*, published by the World Economic Forum.[27] The UK ranked thirteenth in Growth Competitiveness and sixth in Business Competitiveness, with very high rankings for the quality of the national business environment (6), financial market sophistication (1), and, perhaps a mixed blessing, the extent of incentive compensation (1). Britain displays areas of competitive excellence, but also of competitive disadvantage: national savings rate (98), real effective exchange rate (87), and government success in ICT promotion and quality of math and science education (47). This last point was both generalized and reinforced by the results of an executive opinion survey in which respondents rated an inadequately educated work force as the most troubling factor for doing business in the UK.[28]

On balance, the Report indicates success in economic competitiveness, but does not provide heartening news on the new growth theory, since competitive disadvantages are clustered in the key areas of education and technology acquisition and diffusion, not to mention the availability of scientists and engineers, where the UK ranks 41, below Vietnam and Romania and just above Turkey and Ghana.

Nor does the OECD improve the assessment. The most recent OECD UK survey (2005) states categorically, "A wide range of indicators suggests that UK innovation performance has been mediocre in international comparisons," (it ranks sixth among the G7, down from second, behind Germany, in the early 1980s). The OECD survey also emphasizes the UK's considerable strength in knowledge-intensive services, and points to success in an area that Blair and Brown hold dear. The UK achieves a double first—among the G7 and among the 30 OECD countries—in liberal product market regulation. But it achieves only a fifth among the G7 and

a seventeenth among the OECD countries for the percentage of adults having more than low skills.[29]

Britain preaches a globalization-friendly model of flexible labor markets throughout EU Europe, and its success in boosting Britain's economic performance in comparison with the rest of Europe has won some reluctant admirers, even converts. For example, Chancellor Gerhard Schröder's economic reform package, Project 2010, had much in common with Blair's neoliberal approach to economic governance, and the new French President, Nicolas Sarkhozy, seems determined to introduce neoliberal economic reforms. Thus, Britain has been shaped by the international political economy in important ways and hopes to take full advantage of the economic prospects of globalization, even as it tries to reshape other European national models in its own image.

As the world-of-states theme suggests, a country's participation in today's global economic order diminishes autonomous national control, raising unsettling questions in even the most established democracies. Amid complicated pressures, both internal and external, can state institutions retain the capacity to administer policy effectively within distinctive national models? How much do the growth of powerful bureaucracies at home and complex dependencies on international organizations such as the EU limit the ability of citizens to control policy ends? We turn to these questions in Section 3.

Notes

[1]See Paul M. Kennedy, *The Rise and Fall of British Naval Mastery* (Atlantic Highlands, N.J.: Ashfield Press, 1992), pp. 186–189.

[2]"A British Miracle?" *Economist,* September 16–22, 2000, pp. 57–58.

[3]See David Smith, "The Treasury and Economic Policy," in Seldon and Kavanagh (eds), *The Blair Effect 2001–5* (New York: Cambridge University Press, 2005), p. 177.

[4]See David Coates, *Prolonged Labour* (London: Palgrave, 2005), chap. 1.

[5]Ibid, p. 13.

[6]See Joel Krieger, "Class, Consumption, and Collectivism: Perspectives on the Labour Party and Electoral Competition in Britain," in Frances Fox Piven (ed), *Labor Parties in Postindustrial Societies* (New York: Oxford University Press, 1992), pp. 47–70.

[7]The discussion of the UK economy is drawn largely from previous work. See Joel Krieger, *British Politics in the Global*

Age: Can Social Democracy Survive? (New York: Oxford University Press, 1999); Joel Krieger and David Coates, "New Labour's Model for UK Competitiveness: Adrift in the Global Economy?" paper presented to the Wake Forest Conference on the Convergence of Capitalist Economies, September 27–29, 2003 (unpublished, available from the authors); and Joel Krieger, *Globalization and State Power: Who Wins When America Rules?* (New York: Longman, 2005), chap. 3.

[8]Coates, *Prolonged Labour*, p. 172.

[9]Will Hutton, *The State We're In* (London: Jonathan Cape, 1995).

[10]Andrew Gamble, "The British Economic Miracle: New Labour and the Economy," paper presented at the Conference on *Cool Britannia: Britain After Eight Years of Labour Government*, Montreal, Cerium, May 4–6, 2005.

[11]Ivor Crewe, "Labor Force Changes, Working Class Decline, and the Labour Vote: Social and Electoral Trends in Postwar Britain," in Frances Fox Piven, ed., *Labor Parties in Postindustrial Societies* (New York: Oxford University Press, 1992), p. 34. See also David Marsh and R. A. W. Rhodes, "Implementing Thatcherism: Policy Change in the 1980s," *Parliamentary Affairs* 45, no. 1 (January 1992): 34–37.

[12]Steven Fielding, "A New Politics?" in Patrick Dunleavy et al., eds., *Developments in British Politics* 6 (New York: St. Martin's Press, 2000), p. 2.

[13]UNICEF, *Child Poverty in Perspective: An Overview of Child Well Being in Rich Countries* (UNICEF Innocenti Research Centre, 2007); www.unicef.org/media/files/ChildPovertyReport. pdf.

[14]National Statistics Online, "Population Size: 7.9% from a Minority Ethnic Group," February 13, 2003; www.statistics. gov.uk/cci/nugget.asp?id=273.

[15]Office of National Statistics Social Survey, *Living in Britain: Results from the 1995 General Household Survey* (London: The Stationery Office, 1997).

[16]Gail Lewis, "Black Women's Employment and the British Economy," in Winston James and Clive Harris, eds., *Inside Babylon: The Caribbean Diaspora In Britain* (London: Verso, 1993), pp. 73–96.

[17]National Statistics Online, "Low Income for 60% of Pakistanis/ Bangladeshis," December 12, 2002; www.statistics.gov.uk/CCI/ nugget.asp?ID=269&Pos=1&ColRank=2&Rank=384.

[18]"All White at the Top," *Guardian,* May 25, 2004; education.guardian.co.uk/egweekly/story/0,5500,1223478,00. html.

[19]Ibid.

[20]Women & Equality Unit, "What is the Pay Gap and Why Does It Exist?"; www.womenandequalityunit.gov.uk/pay/pay_ facts.htm.

[21]Jane Lewis, "The Pursuit of Welfare Ends and Market Means and the Case of Work/Family Reconciliation Policies," p. 10, paper presented at the Conference on *Cool Britannia: Britain After Eight Years of Labour Government*, Montreal, Cerium, May 4–6, 2005.

[22]Ibid.

[23]Pippa Norris, *Electoral Change in Britain Since 1945* (Oxford: Blackwell, 1997), pp. 133–135; ibid., "A Gender-Generation Gap?" in Pippa Norris and Geoffrey Norris, eds., *Critical Elections: British Parties and Voters in Long-Term Perspective* (London: Sage, 1999).

[24]MORI, "Many Councillors 'Divorced' from the Electorate," April 30, 2002; www.mori.com/polls/2002/greenissues.shtml.

[25]David Floyd, "British Youth Oppose 'Bomber Blair,'" *WireTap,* March 28, 2003; www.wiretapmag.org/stories/15505.

[26]Robert Worcester, "Women's Support Give Blair the Edge," *Guardian Unlimited,* May 8, 2005; politics.guardian.co.uk/ election/story/0,15803,1479238,00.html#article_continue.

[27]Klaus Schwab and Michael Porter (eds), *The Global Competitiveness Report 2004–2005* (World Economic Forum/ Palgrave Macmillan, 2005).

[28]Ibid., pp. 454–455.

[29]OECD Economic Surveys (United Kingdom, 2005), chap. 7.

CHAPTER 3

Governance and Policymaking

Understanding of British governance begins with consideration of Britain's constitution, which is notable for two significant features: its form and its antiquity. Britain lacks a formal written constitution in the usual sense; that is, no single unified and authoritative text has special status above ordinary law and can be amended only by special procedures. Rather, the British constitution is a combination of statutory law (mainly acts of Parliament), common law, convention, and authoritative interpretations. Although it is often said that Britain has an unwritten constitution, this is not accurate. Authoritative legal treatises are written, of course, as are the much more significant acts of Parliament that define crucial elements of the British political system. These acts define the powers of Parliament and its relationship with the Crown, the rights governing the relationship between state and citizen, the relationship of constituent nations to the United Kingdom, the relationship of the United Kingdom to the EU, and many other rights and legal arrangements. It is probably best to say, "What distinguishes the British constitution from others is not that it is unwritten, but rather that it is part written and uncodified."[1]

More than its form, however, the British constitution's antiquity raises questions. It is sometimes hard to know where conventions and acts of Parliament with constitutional implications began, but they can certainly be found as far back as the seventeenth century, notably with the Bill of Rights of 1689, which helped define the relationship between the monarchy and Parliament. "Britain's constitution presents a paradox," a British scholar of constitutional history has observed. "We live in a modern world but inhabit a pre-modern, indeed, ancient, constitution."[2] For example, several European democratic countries, including Spain, Belgium, and the Netherlands, are constitutional monarchies, in which policymaking is left to the elected government and the monarch fulfills largely ceremonial duties. In fact, Europe contains the largest concentration of constitutional monarchies in the world. However, Britain alone among western democracies has permitted two unelected hereditary institutions, the Crown and the House of Lords, to participate in governing the country (in the case of the Lords, a process of reform began in 1999, but where the reforms will lead remains unclear).

More generally, constitutional authorities have accepted the structure and principles of many areas of government for so long that appeal to convention has enormous cultural force. Thus, widely agreed-on rules of conduct, rather than law or U.S.-style checks and balances, set the limits of governmental power. This reality underscores an important aspect of British government: absolute principles of government are few. At the same time, those that exist are fundamental to the organization of the state and central to governance, policymaking, and patterns of representation. Yet, the government is permitted considerable latitude.

Organization of the State

The core constitutional principle of the British political system and cornerstone of the Westminster model is parliamentary sovereignty: Parliament can make or overturn any law; the executive, the judiciary, and the throne do not have any authority to restrict or rescind parliamentary action. In a classic parliamentary democracy, the prime minister answers to the House of Commons (the elected element of Parliament) and may be dismissed by it. That said, by passing the European Communities Act in 1972 (Britain joined the European Economic Community in 1973), Parliament accepted significant limitations on its power. It acknowledged that European law has force in the United Kingdom without requiring parliamentary assent and acquiesced to the authority of the European Court of Justice (ECJ) to resolve jurisdictional disputes. To complete the circle, the ECJ has confirmed its prerogative to suspend acts of Parliament.[3]

Second, Britain has long been a unitary state. By contrast to the United States, where powers not delegated to the national government are reserved for the states, no powers are reserved constitutionally for subcentral units of government in the United Kingdom. However, the Labour government of Tony Blair introduced a far-reaching program of constitutional reform that created, for the first time, a quasi-federal system in Britain. Specified powers have been devolved (delegated) to legislative bodies in Scotland and Wales and, with the end to decades of conflict, to Northern Ireland as well. (The historic developments in Northern Ireland will be discussed in Chapter 5). In addition, some powers have been redistributed from the Westminster Parliament to an authority governing London with a directly elected mayor, and additional powers may be devolved to regional assemblies as well.

Third, British government operates within a system of fusion of powers at the UK level: Parliament is the supreme legislative, executive, and judicial authority and includes the monarch as well as the House of Commons and the House of Lords. The fusion of legislature and executive is also expressed in the function and personnel of the cabinet. Whereas U.S. presidents can direct or ignore their cabinets, which have no constitutionally mandated function, the British cabinet bears enormous constitutional responsibility. Through its collective decision making, the cabinet, and not an independent prime minister, shapes, directs, and takes responsibility for government. This core principle, cabinet government, however, may at critical junctures be observed more in principle than in practice.

Finally, sovereignty rests with the Queen-in-Parliament (the formal term for Parliament). Britain is a constitutional monarchy. The position of head of state passes by hereditary succession, but the government or state officials must exercise nearly all powers of the Crown. Taken together, parliamentary sovereignty, parliamentary democracy, and cabinet government form the core elements of the British or Westminster model of government, which many consider a model democracy and the first effective parliamentary democracy.

Even so, such a venerable constitutional framework is also vulnerable to uncertainty and criticism. Can a willful prime minister overstep the generally agreed-upon limits of the collective responsibility of the cabinet and achieve an undue concentration of power? How well has the British model of government stood the tests of time and radically changed circumstances? These questions underscore the problems that even the most stable democracies face. They also identify important comparative themes, because parliamentary (rather than presidential) systems have been adopted widely by the former Communist states of East-Central Europe, for example, in Hungary, the Czech Republic, and Slovakia.

The Executive

The term *cabinet government* emphasizes the key functions that the cabinet exercises: responsibility for policymaking, supreme control of government, and coordination of all government departments. However, the term does not capture the full range of executive institutions or the scale and complexity of operations. The executive reaches well beyond the cabinet. It extends from ministries (departments) and ministers to the civil service in one direction, and to Parliament (as we shall see in Chapter 4) in the other direction.

Cabinet Government

After a general election, the queen (or king) invites the leader of the party that emerges from the election with control of a majority of seats in the House of Commons to form a government and serve as prime minister. The prime minister usually selects approximately two-dozen ministers to constitute the cabinet. Among the most significant assignments are the Foreign Office (equivalent to the U.S. Department of State), the Home Office (ministry of justice or attorney general), and the chancellor of the exchequer (a finance minister or a more powerful version of the U.S. treasury secretary).

The responsibilities of a cabinet minister are immense. "The Cabinet, as a collective body, is responsible for formulating the policy to be placed before Parliament and is also the supreme controlling and directing body of the entire executive branch," notes S. E. Finer. "Its decisions bind all Ministers and other officers in the conduct of their departmental business."[4] In contrast to the French Constitution, which prohibits a cabinet minister from serving in the legislature, British constitutional tradition *requires* overlapping membership between Parliament and cabinet. (In fact, this point was made in dramatic fashion after Blair's 2005 electoral victory when he appointed a former head of his policy unit to the House of Lords so that he could appoint him as a junior education minister.) Unlike the informal status of the U.S. cabinet, its British counterpart enjoys considerable constitutional privileges and is a powerful institution with enormous responsibility for the political and administrative success of the government.

The cabinet room at 10 Downing Street (the prime minister's official residence) is a place of intrigue as well as deliberation. From the perspective of the prime minister, the cabinet may appear as loyal followers or as ideological combatants, potential challengers for party leadership, and parochial advocates for pet programs that run counter to the overall objectives of the government. Despite this potential for division, the convention of collective responsibility normally ensures the continuity of government by unifying the cabinet. In principle, the prime minister must gain the support of a majority of the cabinet for a range of significant decisions, notably the budget and the legislative program.

The only other constitutionally mandated mechanism for checking the prime minister is a defeat on a vote of no confidence in the House of Commons (discussed in Chapter 4). Since this action is rare and politically dangerous, the cabinet's role in constraining the chief executive remains the only routine check on his or her power. Collective responsibility is therefore a crucial aspect of the Westminster model of democracy. But does collective responsibility effectively constrain the power of prime ministers, or does it enable the prime minister to paint "presidential" decisions with the veneer of collectivity?

As a politician with strong ideological convictions and a leadership style to match, Margaret Thatcher often attempted to galvanize loyalists in the cabinet and either marginalize or expel detractors. In the end, Thatcher's treatment of the cabinet inspired the movement to unseat her as party leader and stretched British constitutional conventions. John Major returned to a more consultative approach, in keeping with the classic model of cabinet government.

Tony Blair, like Thatcher, narrowed the scope of collective responsibility. Cabinet meetings were often dull and perfunctory, and debate was rare. The prime minister, a few key cabinet members, and a handful of advisers made decisions in smaller gatherings. In a striking example of this process early in the Blair premiership, right after the election when the full cabinet had not yet met, the government announced the decision to free the Bank of England to set interest rates. Blair accentuated the tendency for shorter cabinet meetings (they were usually less than an hour) that couldn't seriously consider (much less resolve) policy differences.

In particular, the role of the cabinet in the decision to go to war in Iraq underscores its weakened capacity to exercise constitutional checks and balances. The subject was often discussed in cabinet—and endlessly in bilateral meetings with key ministers and unelected policy advisers—but was never subjected to the full-scale debate and formal cabinet approval that is associated with the model of cabinet government and collective responsibility. "We have not had cabinet government in the textbook sense for a very long time," affirmed Bernard Crick in *The Guardian*. "To gain assent for the Iraq war the prime minister had summoned cabinet ministers individually."[5] In addition, when the cabinet did take up the issue of the war in Iraq, the conversation was more desultory than the strict exercise of cabinet responsibility would imply.

The point is not that Blair lacked a majority in cabinet support of the UK role in the war in Iraq, but that cabinet meetings had become largely beside the point. In addition, with eyes turned toward bruising debates in Parliament, where, as Blair acknowledged, defeat would compel him to resign, the prime minister took no steps to discipline ministers who spoke out against the war plan. In fact, Blair permitted both Robin Cook (former foreign secretary and the leader of the House of Commons) and Clare Short (secretary of state for international development) each to resign in a manner and at a time of their own choosing in protest of the decision to go to war. In March 2003, Blair won the formal support of Parliament he sought. In so doing, he may have set a precedent that the presumed prerogative power of the prime minister or Crown to declare war had been handed over to Parliament.[6] Alternatively, many contend that the real decision to go to war in Iraq had been taken by the prime minister and President Bush long before, probably at President Bush's ranch in April 2002. Either way, the cabinet played a minor, almost incidental role.[7]

As the decision to go to war in Iraq underscores, both Blair and his close aides seemed skeptical about the effectiveness and centrality of the cabinet as well as cabinet committees. As prime minister, Blair preferred to coordinate strategically important policy areas through highly politicized special units in the Cabinet Office such as the Social Exclusion Unit, the Women's Unit, and the UK Anti-Drugs Co-ordination Unit. In June 2001, the Prime Minister's Delivery Unit

Figure 3.1

The Cabinet System

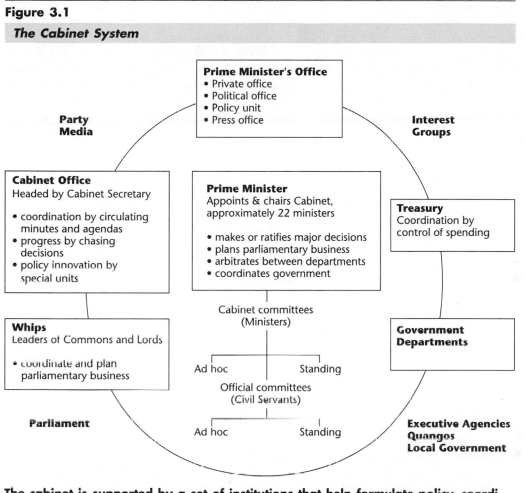

Prime Minister's Office
- Private office
- Political office
- Policy unit
- Press office

Party
Media

Interest
Groups

Cabinet Office
Headed by Cabinet Secretary

- coordination by circulating minutes and agendas
- progress by chasing decisions
- policy innovation by special units

Prime Minister
Appoints & chairs Cabinet, approximately 22 ministers

- makes or ratifies major decisions
- plans parliamentary business
- arbitrates between departments
- coordinates government

Treasury
Coordination by control of spending

Cabinet committees
(Ministers)

Ad hoc   Standing

Official committees
(Civil Servants)

Ad hoc   Standing

Whips
Leaders of Commons and Lords

- coordinate and plan parliamentary business

**Government
Departments**

Parliament

**Executive Agencies
Quangos
Local Government**

The cabinet is supported by a set of institutions that help formulate policy, coordinate operations, and facilitate the support for government policy. Acting within a context set by the fusion of legislature and executive, the prime minister enjoys a great opportunity for decisive leadership that is lacking in a system of checks and balances and separation of powers among the branches of government.

Source: Her Majesty's Budget Bulletin as found in *British Politics: Continuities and Change,* Third Edition, by Dennis Kavanagh, p. 251, Oxford University Press, 1996.

was introduced to take strategic control of the delivery of public services, a central commitment of Blair's second term of office and one with great significance since it further eroded the principles of collective responsibility and the centrality of the cabinet even further.

On balance, cabinet government represents a durable and effective formula for governance, although

the cabinet does not always function in the role of supreme directing and controlling body it occupies in constitutional doctrine. It is important to remember that the cabinet operates within a broader cabinet system or core executive as it is sometimes called (see Figure 3.1) and that the prime minister holds or controls many of the levers of power in the core executive. Because the prime minister is the head of the cabinet, his or her office helps develop policy, coordinates operations, and functions as a liaison with the media, the party, interest groups, and Parliament. As Martin J. Smith puts it, "The culmination of a long-term process of centralization of power in the hands of the Prime Minister is seen in the declining role of the Cabinet and the increased development of resources inside Number 10."[8]

Before taking office as prime minister, Gordon Brown promised, as a priority, to restore trust in government and indicated that he would make government and ministers more responsible to parliament. But this is easier said than done! Brown likes to rely on a small group of trusted advisers, tends to be secretive, and prefers a very strong top-down management style—none of which make it likely that Prime Minister Brown will operate with the kind of transparency that would restore trust in government or breathe new life into the collective responsibility of the cabinet.

Both cabinet committees (comprising ministers) and official committees (made up of civil servants) supplement the work of the cabinet. In addition, the Treasury plays an important coordinating role through its budgetary control, while the Cabinet Office supports day-to-day operations. The *whips,* leaders in both the Commons and the Lords, smooth the passage of legislation sponsored by the government, which is more or less guaranteed by a working majority.

The cabinet system, and the complex interplay of resources, interdependencies, and power within the core executive that tend to concentrate power at the top, ensure that there is no Washington-style gridlock (the inability of legislature and executive to agree on policy) in London. On the contrary, if there is a problem at the pinnacle of power in the United Kingdom, it is the potential for excessive concentration of power by a prime minister who is prepared to manipulate the cabinet and flout the conventions of collective responsibility.

Bureaucracy and Civil Service

Policymaking at 10 Downing Street may appear to be increasingly concentrated in the prime minister's hands. At the same time, when viewed from Whitehall (the road which encompasses parliament Square and many of the government ministries) the executive may seem to be dominated by its vast administrative agencies. The range and complexity of state policymaking mean that in practice, the cabinet's authority must be shared with a vast set of unelected officials.

How is the interaction between the civil service and the cabinet ministers (and their political assistants) coordinated? A very senior career civil servant, called a permanent secretary, has chief administrative responsibility for running a department. Other senior civil servants, including deputy secretaries and undersecretaries, in turn assist the permanent secretaries. In addition, the minister reaches into his or her department to appoint a principal private secretary, an up-and-coming civil servant who assists the minister as gatekeeper and liaison with senior civil servants.

Successful policy must translate policy goals into policy instruments. Since nearly all legislation is introduced on behalf of the government and presented as the policy directive of a ministry, civil servants in Britain do much of the conceptualizing and refining of legislation that is done by committee staffers in the U.S. Congress. Civil servants, more than ministers, assume operational duties, and, despite a certain natural level of mutual mistrust and misunderstanding, the two must work closely together. In the eyes of the impartial, permanent, and anonymous civil servants, ministers are too political, unpredictable, and temporary—*they* are tireless self-promoters who may neglect or misunderstand the needs of the ministry. To a conscientious minister, the permanent secretary may be protecting *his* or *her* department too strenuously from constitutionally proper oversight and direction.

Whatever they may think, however, no sharp line separates the responsibilities of ministers and civil servants, and they have no choice but to execute policy in tandem. Like ministers, civil servants are servants of the Crown, but they are not part of the government (taken in the more political sense, like the term *the administration* in common American usage). The ministers, not the civil servants, have constitutional responsibility for policy and are answerable to Parliament and the electorate for the conduct of their departments.

Since the early 1980s, the pace of change at Whitehall has been very fast, as governments have looked to cut the size of the civil service, streamline its operations, replace permanent with casual (temporary) staff, and enhance its accountability to citizens. As a result of the ongoing modernization of Whitehall (known as new public management, NPM), the civil service inherited by New Labour is very different from the civil service of thirty years ago. It has been downsized and given a new corporate structure (divided into over 120 separate executive agencies). Few at the top of these agencies (agency chief executives) are traditional career civil servants. The old tradition of a career service is fading, a service in which nearly all the most powerful posts were filled by those who entered the bureaucratic ranks in their twenties. Nowadays many top appointments are advertised widely and filled by outsiders. The Blair government has continued the public management reform trends toward accountability, efficiency, and greater transparency in the operations of the executive bureaucracy.

In recent years, many observers have expressed concern, however, that New Labour has done—and will continue to do—whatever it can to subject the Whitehall machine to effective political and ministerial direction and control.[9] A related concern is that the centrality and impartiality of civil servants is being eroded by the growing importance of special advisers (who are both political policy advisers and civil servants). This issue came to a head as Blair made the case for war in Iraq. Key special advisers played critical roles in making the case in the famous "dodgy dossier" of September 2002 that the threat of weapons of mass destruction justified regime change in Iraq. In recent years, many observers have noted that the political neutrality of the civil service is a core element in British governance and policymaking. Some have expressed concern that the boundaries between ministers and civil servants as well as between special advisers and civil servants are not as clearly drawn as they should be.

Public and Semipublic Institutions

Like other countries, Britain has institutionalized a set of administrative functions that expand the role of the state well beyond the traditional core executive functions and agencies. We turn now to a brief discussion of semipublic agencies—entities that are sanctioned by the state but without direct democratic oversight.

Nationalized Industries. The nationalization of basic industries—such as coal, iron and steel, gas and electricity supply—was a central objective of the

Labour government's program during the postwar collectivist era. By the end of the Thatcher era, the idea of public ownership had clearly run out of steam. For New Labour, a return to the program of public ownership of industry is unthinkable. Instead, when thinking of expanding state functions, we can expect a growing set of semipublic administrative organizations and public/private partnerships.

Nondepartmental Public Bodies and Public/Private Partnerships. Since the 1970s, an increasing number of administrative functions have been transferred to bodies that are typically part of the government in terms of funding, function, and appointment of staff, but operate at arm's length from ministers. They are officially called nondepartmental public bodies (NDPBs) but are better known as quasi-nongovernmental organizations or quangos. Quangos have increasing policy influence and enjoy considerable administrative and political advantages. They take responsibility for specific functions and can combine governmental and private-sector expertise. This allows ministers to distance themselves from controversial areas of policy. Key areas of public policy previously under the authority of local governments are now controlled by quangos, which are nonelected bodies. Increasingly, the debate about NDPBs is less about the size of the public, semipublic, or private sector, and more about the effective delivery of services.

Alongside quangos, in recent years the government has looked for ways to expand the investment of the private sector in capital projects such as hospitals and schools that provide public-sector goods. Thus New Labour continued the private finance initiative (PFI) it inherited from the Conservatives as a key part of its signature modernization program and as a means to revitalize public services. The results are controversial: critics and supporters disagree about the quality of services provided and whether taxpayers win or lose by the financial arrangements. In addition, the tendency of PFI initiatives to blur the line between public and private raise important and controversial issues. Do these initiatives, as Labour modernizers insist, bring welcome resources, expertise, and skills to crucial public sector provisions? Or, as critics contend, do they distort priorities in education and health care, erode vital traditions of universal provision of public goods, and chip away at the working conditions for public sector employees?[10]

Other State Institutions

This section examines the military and the police, the judiciary, and subnational government.

The Military and the Police

From the local bobby (a term for a local police officer derived from Sir Robert Peel, who set up London's metropolitan police force in 1829) to the most senior military officer, those involved in security and law enforcement have enjoyed a rare measure of popular support in Britain. Constitutional tradition and professionalism distance the British police and military officers from politics. Nevertheless, both institutions have been placed in more politically controversial and exposed positions in recent decades.

In the case of the military, British policy in the post–cold war period remains focused on a gradually redefined set of North Atlantic Treaty Organization (NATO) commitments. Still ranked among the top five military powers in the world, Britain retains a global presence, and the Thatcher and Major governments deployed forces in ways that strengthened their political positions and maximized Britain's global influence. In 1982, Britain soundly defeated Argentina in a war over the disputed Falkland/Malvinas Islands in the South Atlantic. In the Gulf War of 1991, Britain deployed a full armored division in the UN-sanctioned force arrayed against Iraq. Under Blair's leadership, Britain was the sole participant alongside the United States in the aerial bombardment of Iraq in December 1998. In 1999, the United Kingdom strongly backed NATO's Kosovo campaign and pressed for ground troops. Indeed, the Kosovo campaign and Blair's "doctrine of international community," which the prime minister rolled out in a major speech in Chicago on the eve of NATO's fiftieth anniversary in 1999, assumed an important role in Blair's justification for the war in Iraq.[11] According to Blair, global interdependence made isolationism obsolete and inspired a commitment to a new ethical dimension in foreign policy. Throughout the war in Iraq and its bloody aftermath, Blair has persistently characterized Iraq as an extension of Kosovo, an effort to liberate Muslims from brutal dictatorships, whether Serbia's Milosevic or Iraq's Saddam Hussein.

Until Blair's decision to support the American plan to shift the venue of the war on terror from Afghanistan to Iraq, the use of the military in international conflicts generated little opposition. Indeed, even in the case of the 2003 war in Iraq, the role of the military (as distinct from the decision to go to war) has generated relatively little controversy. Allegations of mistreatment raised far fewer questions than those directed at the United States for its abuse of prisoners at Abu Ghraib. In addition, UK forces are widely credited with operations in and around Basra that have been as culturally sensitive and effective as could be expected under such difficult circumstances. In September 2007, less than three months after Brown became prime minister, and with little fanfare, British troops completed a pull-out from Basra.

As for the police, which traditionally operate as independent local forces throughout the country, government control, centralization, and the level of political use have increased since the 1980s. During the coal miners' strike of 1984–1985, the police operated to an unprecedented, and perhaps unlawful, degree as a national force coordinated through Scotland Yard (London police headquarters). Police menaced strikers and hindered miners from participating in strike support activities. This partisan use of the police in an industrial dispute flew in the face of constitutional traditions and offended some police officers and officials. During the 1990s, concerns about police conduct focused on police-community relations, including race relations, corruption, and the interrogation and treatment of people held in custody. In particular, widespread criticism of the police for mishandling their investigation into the brutal 1993 racist killing of Stephen Lawrence in South London resulted in a scathing report by a commission of inquiry in 1999.

The Judiciary

In Britain, the principle of parliamentary sovereignty limits the role of the judiciary. Courts have no power to judge the constitutionality of legislative acts (judicial review). They can only determine whether policy directives or administrative acts violate common law or an act of Parliament. Hence, the British judiciary is generally less politicized and influential than its U.S. counterpart.

Jurists, however, have participated in the wider political debate outside court, as when they have headed royal commissions on the conduct of industrial relations, the struggle in Northern Ireland, and riots in Britain's inner cities. Some observers of British politics worry that governments have used judges in these ways to secure partisan ends, deflect criticism, and weaken the tradition of parliamentary scrutiny of government policy. Nevertheless, Sir Richard Scott's harsh report on his investigation into Britain's sales of military equipment to Iraq in the 1980s, for example, indicates that inquiries led by judges with a streak of independence can prove highly embarrassing to the government and raise important issues for public debate. The intensely watched inquiry conducted by Lord Hutton, a senior jurist, into the death of David Kelly, a whistle-blower who challenged the government's case for weapons of mass destruction as a justification for going to war in Iraq, confirmed this important public role of judges in the United Kingdom. At the same time, the question of Hutton's independence became very controversial in light of a "verdict" that exonerated the prime minister.

Beyond the politicization of jurists through their role on commissions and public inquiries, potentially dramatic institutional changes in law and the administration of justice are under consideration. In June 2003, Blair announced the government's intention to abolish the office of Lord Chancellor and move the law lords (who hold the ultimate authority of appeal in British law) from the House of Lords to a new "supreme court." The constitutional reform bill, introduced in 2004, faced strong opposition in the Lords and the prospects for ultimate passage remain clouded.

Subnational Government

Since the United Kingdom is a state comprised of distinct nations (England, Scotland, Wales, and Northern Ireland), the distribution of powers involves two levels below the central government: national government and local (municipal) government. Because the British political framework has traditionally been unitary, not federal, no formal powers devolved to either the nation within the United Kingdom or to subnational (really subcentral or sub-UK) units as in the United States or Germany.

Although no powers have been constitutionally reserved to local governments, they have historically had considerable autonomy in financial terms and discretion in implementing a host of social service and related policies. In the context of increased fiscal pressures that followed the 1973 oil crisis, the Labour government introduced the first check on the fiscal autonomy of local councils (elected local authorities). The Thatcher government then tightened the fiscal constraints on local government. Finally, in 1986, the Thatcher government abolished the multicultural-oriented city government (the Greater London Council, GLC) under the leadership of Ken Livingstone, as well as several other metropolitan councils. In 1989, the Thatcher government introduced a poll tax, an equal per capita levy for local finance, to replace the age-old system of local property taxes. This radical break with tradition, which shifted the burden of local taxes from property owners and businesses to individuals, and taxed rich and poor alike, was monumentally unpopular. The poll tax proved a tremendous political liability, made local politics a hot-button national issue, and led to Thatcher's departure.

Although much of New Labour's agenda concerning subcentral government is focused primarily on the political role of nations within Britain, devolution within England is also part of the reform process. Regional Development Agencies (RDAs) were introduced throughout England in April 1999 as part of a decentralizing agenda, but perhaps even more to facilitate economic development at the regional level. Despite the fairly low-key profile of RDAs and their limited scope (they are unelected bodies with no statutory authority), they opened the door to popular mobilization in the long term for elected regional assemblies. Thus far, however, despite opinion polls that indicate some English resentment about devolution in Scotland and Wales, there has been little enthusiasm in England when referenda for regional government in several regions were offered—and a November 2004 referendum in the North-East was soundly defeated.

In addition, the Blair government placed changes in the governance of London on the fast track. The introduction of a directly elected mayor of London in May 2000 proved embarrassing to Blair, since the government's efforts to keep Livingstone out of the contest backfired and he won handily. Livingstone has introduced an expansive agenda to spur long-term sustainable growth and advance a policy agenda that emphasizes ethnic diversity and the enhanced representation and leadership of women in London public life. In addition, London's determined effort to reduce traffic congestion by levying per day per vehicle charges within a central London zone have won widespread admiration for one of England's most controversial political leaders.

The European Dimension

The delegation of more and more authority to the EU has fundamentally restructured British politics. The European dimension has significantly influenced law and the administration of justice. Parliament passed the European Communities Act in 1972 to seal Britain's entry into the European Community (EC), with the provision that existing EC law be binding on the United Kingdom. In any conflict between British law and EC (now EU) law, EU law prevails. The act specifies that British courts must adjudicate any disputes of interpretation that arise from EU law. In addition, the Treaty of Rome (the treaty that formed the EC, to which the United Kingdom is bound by the terms of its membership) specifies that cases that reach the highest domestic appeals court—the House of Lords—be sent to the European Court of Justice (ECJ) in Luxembourg for final ruling.

As a member of the EU, Britain is bound to abide by the European Court of Justice (ECJ), as it applies and develops law as an independent institution within the EU. For example, two decisions by the ECJ led to the enactment of the Sex Discrimination Act of 1986, since previous legislation had not provided the full guarantees of women's rights in employment mandated to all members by the EU's Equal Treatment Directive.

Moreover, with the passage of the Human Rights Act in 1998, Britain must comply with the European Convention on Human Rights (ECHR) as well as with the rulings of the European Court of Justice on Human Rights (ECJHR). This has far-reaching potential for advancing a "pluralistic human rights culture" in Britain

and providing new ground rules in law for protecting privacy, freedom of religion, and a wider respect for human rights.[12] Perhaps an indication of its broad influence to come, the adoption of the ECHR forced Britain to curtail discrimination against gays in the military. (The Ministry of Defense confirmed in 2007 that none of its initial fears about gays in the military have occurred.) The Human Rights Act has also provided the judiciary with a legal framework (which Parliament cannot rescind) for addressing specific concerns such as asylum.[13] In addition, the UK Parliament's Joint Committee on Human Rights now reviews all bills for their compatibility with the Human Rights Act, which imposes an important filter on controversial legislation as well as reporting on positive steps to secure human rights—for example, through a bill prohibiting the physical punishment of children.[14]

The pace of supranational influences on Britain, in legal as in other policy areas, will doubtless increase as EU measures of economic and political integration proceed. Politically, the binding nature of EU laws and regulations has fueled the fear that Britain is losing sovereign control, to jurists in Luxembourg and bureaucrats in Brussels. Moreover, the expanding scope of EU influences is likely to widen the role of the judiciary within British affairs. Since the EU's dispute resolution process relies to a much greater degree on legal instruments than has the domestic UK political system, the growing role of the ECJ as an agent of European integration promises to expand the role of the legal and judicial process in British political disputes.[15]

In administrative and political terms, the consequences of the European dimension are equally profound. Both ministers and senior civil servants now spend a great deal of time in EU policy deliberations and are constrained, directly and indirectly, by the EU agenda and directives. Although still effectively in charge of many areas of domestic policy, more than 80 percent of the rules governing economic life in Britain are determined by the EU. Even when the United Kingdom has opted to remain outside an explicit policy regime, as in the case of the common currency, European influences are significant. Decisions by the Council of Finance Ministers and the European Central Bank shape British macroeconomic, monetary, and fiscal policies in significant ways.

Nor are foreign and security policy, the classic exercises of national sovereignty, immune from EU influences, since multilevel governance has been extended to these spheres by the EU's Common Foreign and Security Policy. Perhaps to offset its euro-outsider status, Britain has been especially active in advancing EU policy agendas such as climate change, where its views are in accord with the EU mainstream. Little is certain about the processes of European integration, except that they will continue to shape and bedevil British politics for many years to come.

The Policymaking Process

Parliamentary sovereignty is the core constitutional principle of the British political system. However, when it comes to policymaking and policy implementation, the focus is not on Westminster (the legislative arena) but rather on Whitehall (the administrative center of UK government). In many countries, such as Japan, India, and Nigeria, personal connections and informal networks play a large role in policymaking and implementation. How different is the British system?

Unlike the U.S. system, in which policymaking is concentrated in congressional committees and subcommittees, Parliament has little direct participation in policymaking. Policymaking emerges primarily from within the executive. There, decision-making is strongly influenced by policy communities—informal networks with extensive knowledge, access, and personal connections to those responsible for policy. In this private hothouse environment, civil servants, ministers, and members of the policy communities work through informal ties. A cooperative style develops as the ministry becomes an advocate for key players in its policy community and as civil servants come perhaps to over-identify the public good with the advancement of policy within their area of responsibility. This cozy insider-only policy process has been challenged by the delegation of more and more authority to the EU.

As we will see in Chapter 4, not only the broad principles and practices of governance, but also the organization of interests and the patterns of representation and political participation have been fundamentally reshaped in recent years.

Notes

[1] See Philip Norton, *The British Polity,* 3rd ed. (New York: Longman, 1994), p. 59, for a useful discussion of the sources of the British constitution.

[2] Stephen Haseler, "Britain's Ancien Régime," *Parliamentary Affairs* 40, no. 4 (October 1990): 415.

[3] See Philip Norton, "Parliament in Transition," in Robert Pyper and Lynton Robins, eds., *United Kingdom Governance* (New York: St. Martin's Press, 2000), pp. 82–106.

[4] S. E. Finer, *Five Constitutions* (Atlantic Highlands, N.J.: Humanities Press, 1979), p. 52.

[5] Bernard Crick, "Blair Should Beware the Boiling Up of Little Irritations," September 29, 2003; www.guardian.co.uk/comment/story/0,3604,1051720,00.html.

[6] Iain Byrne and Stuart Weir, "Democratic Audit: Executive Democracy in War and Peace," *Parliamentary Affairs* 57, no. 2 (April 2004): 455.

[7] John Kampfner, *Blair's Wars* (London: The Free Press, 2005), p. 294.

[8] Martin J. Smith, "The Core Executive and the Modernization of Central Government," in Patrick Dunleavy et al., eds., *Developments in British Politics* 7 (New York: Palgrave/Macmillan, 2003), p. 60.

[9] See Kevin Theakston, "Ministers and Civil Servants," in Pyper and Robins, eds., *United Kingdom Governance,* pp. 39–60.

[10] See Stephen Driver and Luke Martell, *New Labour,* 2nd ed. (Cambridge, England: Polity, 2006), pp. 125–129.

[11] Tony Blair, "Doctrine of the International Community," speech to the Economic Club of Chicago, Hilton Hotel, Chicago, April 22, 1999. For a detailed discussion of the speech and its implications for the war in Iraq, see David Coates and Joel Krieger, *Blair's War* (Malden, Mass.: Polity Press, 2004), chap. 6.

[12] See Bhiku Parekh et al., *The Future of Multi-Ethnic Britain: The Parekh Report* (London: Profile Books, 2000), pp. 90–102.

[13] See Andrew Gamble, "Remaking the Constitution," in Patrick Dunleavy et al., eds., *Developments in British Politics* 7, pp. 34–36.

[14] Sue Prince, "The Law and Politics: Upsetting the Judicial Apple-Cart," *Parliamentary Affairs* 57, no. 2 (2004): 288.

[15] For a useful discussion of the repercussions of the EU on British governance, see Simon Hix, "Britain, the EU and the Euro," in Dunleavy et al., *Developments in British Politics* 6, pp. 47–68.

CHAPTER 4

Representation and Participation

As discussed in Chapter 3, parliamentary sovereignty is the core constitutional principle defining the role of the legislature and, in a sense, the whole system of British government. The executive or judiciary cannot set aside an act of Parliament, nor is any Parliament bound by the actions of any previous Parliament. Nevertheless, in practice, the control exerted by the House of Commons (or the Commons) is not unlimited. This section investigates the powers and role of Parliament, both Commons and Lords, as well as the party system, elections, and contemporary currents in British political culture, citizenship, and identity. The chapter closes with an analysis of surprising new directions in political participation and social protest.

The Legislature

Is Parliament still as sovereign in practice as it remains in constitutional tradition? Clearly, it is not as powerful as it once was. From roughly the 1830s to the 1880s, it collaborated in the formulation of policy, and members amended or rejected legislation on the floor of the House of Commons. Today, the Commons does not so much legislate as assent to government legislation, since (with rare exceptions) the governing party has a majority of the seats and requires no cross-party voting to pass bills. In addition, the balance of effective oversight of policy has shifted from the legislature to executive agencies. This section discusses, in turn, the legislative process, the House of Commons, the House of Lords, and reforms and pressures for change.

The Legislative Process

To become law, bills must be introduced in the House of Commons and the House of Lords, although approval by the latter is not required. The procedure for developing and adopting a public bill is quite complex. The ideas for prospective legislation may come from political parties, pressure groups, think tanks, the prime minister's policy unit, or government departments. Prospective legislation is then normally drafted by civil servants, circulated within Whitehall, approved by the cabinet, and then refined by one of some thirty lawyers in the office of Parliamentary Counsel.[1]

According to tradition, in the House of Commons the bill usually comes to the floor three times (referred to as *readings*). The bill is formally read upon introduction (the *first reading*), printed, distributed, debated in general terms, and after an interval (from a single day to several weeks), given a *second reading*, followed by a vote. Usually the bill then goes for detailed review to a standing committee of between sixteen and fifty members chosen to reflect the overall party balance in the House. It is then subject to a report stage during which new amendments may be introduced. The *third reading* follows; normally, the bill is considered in final form (and voted on) without debate.

After the third reading, a bill that is passed in the House of Commons follows a parallel path in the House of Lords. There the bill is either accepted without change, amended, or rejected. According to custom, the House of Lords passes bills concerning taxation or budgetary matters without alteration, and can add technical and editorial amendments to other bills (which must be approved by the House of Commons) to add clarity in wording and precision in administration. After a bill has passed through all these stages, it goes to the Crown for royal assent (approval by the queen or king, which is only a formality), after which it becomes law and is referred to as an Act of Parliament.

The House of Commons

In constitutional terms, the House of Commons, the lower house of Parliament (with 646 seats at the time of the 2005 election), exercises the main legislative power in Britain. Along with the two unelected elements of Parliament, the Crown and the House of Lords, the Commons has three main functions: (1) to pass laws, (2) to provide finances for the state by authorizing taxation, and (3) to review and scrutinize public administration and government policy.

In practical terms, the Commons has a limited legislative function. Nevertheless, it serves a very important democratic function. It provides a highly visible arena for policy debate and the partisan collision of political worldviews. The high stakes and the flash of rhetorical skills bring drama to the historic chambers, but one crucial element of drama is nearly always missing: the outcome is seldom in doubt. The likelihood that the Commons will invoke its ultimate authority, to defeat a government, is very small. MPs from the governing party who consider rebelling against their leader (the prime minister) are understandably reluctant in a close and critical vote to force a general election, which would place their jobs in jeopardy. Only once since the defeat of Ramsay MacDonald's government in 1924 has a government been brought down by a defeat in the Commons (in 1979). Today, the balance of institutional power has shifted from Parliament to the governing party and the executive.

The House of Lords

The upper chamber of Parliament, the House of Lords (or Lords), is an unelected body that is comprised of hereditary peers (nobility of the rank of duke, marquis, earl, viscount, or baron), life peers (appointed by the Crown on the recommendation of the prime minister), and law lords (life peers appointed to assist the Lords in its judicial duties). The Lords also include the archbishops of Canterbury and York and some two-dozen senior bishops of the Church of England. There are roughly 700 members of the House of Lords, but there is no fixed number, and membership changes with the appointment of peers. At present, there are approximately 200 Labour and 200 Conservative members, and a roughly equivalent number of members (called Crossbenchers) who are not affiliated with any political party. There are approximately 75 Liberal Democrat members. The House of Lords has served as the final court of appeal for civil cases throughout Britain and for criminal cases in England, Wales, and Northern Ireland. This judicial role, which is performed by the law lords, drew international attention in 1998 and 1999 when a Spanish court attempted to extradite General Augusto Pinochet of Chile on charges of genocide, torture, and terrorism. As discussed in Chapter 5, in modern times, however, the House of Lords, which has the power to amend and delay legislation, has served mainly as a chamber of revision, providing expertise in redrafting legislation. Recently, for example, the Lords, which considered the Nationality, Immigration and Asylum Bill too harsh, battled the government for weeks and forced revisions before approving the legislation.

In 1999, the Blair government appointed a Royal Commission on the Reform of the House of Lords (the Wakeham commission) and in the same year introduced legislation to remove the right of hereditary lords to speak and vote. With the passage of House of Lords Act 1999, the number of hereditary peers was reduced to ninety-two. In January 2000, the commission recommended a partly elected second chamber, enumerating alternative models. In February 2003, the Commons rejected seven options, ranging from a fully appointed chamber (Blair's preference) to an entirely elected one. If made into law, the constitutional reform bill, which was introduced in 2004, would transfer that function from the Lords to a new "supreme court." The failure of a joint committee of MPs and peers to achieve consensus has left reform plans in tatters. For now, the future of House of Lords reform has been consigned to the "What is Brown likely to do?" guessing game.

Reforms in Behavior and Structure

How significant are contemporary changes in the House? How far will they go to stem the tide in Parliament's much-heralded decline?

Behavioral Changes: Backbench Dissent. Ever since the 1970s, backbenchers (MPs of the governing party who have no governmental office and rank-and-file opposition members) have been markedly less deferential than in the past. A backbench rebellion against the Major government's EU policy damaged the prestige of the prime minister and weakened him considerably. Until the war in Iraq was on the horizon, Blair seemed less likely to face significant rebellion from Labour MPs, although divisions did occur—relatively early in his premiership, for example, over social welfare policy and the treatment of trade unions. As Blair's political capital was depleted with the war in Iraq, he faced some bruising rebellions. In January 2004, an education bill, which called for increased tuition fees, produced massive opposition from Labour MPs. It scraped through parliament by only 5 votes on the second reading and 28 on the final reading in March—despite a 161 Labour majority in the Commons and prime minister Blair's statement that defeat on the education bill would be treated as a vote of no confidence and likely result in Blair's resignation. One-third of Labour MPs defected on key votes in February and March 2003 authorizing the use of force in Iraq. This represents a far more historic rebellion. Looking ahead, it is likely that any vote to adopt the euro—or on any attempt to introduce a new more limited constitutional treaty for the EU—would inspire significant backbench dissent once more.

Structural Changes: Parliamentary Committees. In addition to the standing committees that routinely review bills during legislative proceedings, in 1979 the Commons revived and extended the number and "remit" (that is, responsibilities) of select committees. Select committees help Parliament exert control over the executive by examining specific policies or aspects of administration.

The most controversial select committees are watchdog committees that monitor the conduct of major departments and ministries. Select committees hold hearings, take written and oral testimony, and question senior civil servants and ministers. They then issue reports that often include strong policy recommendations that may be at odds with government policy. As one side effect of the reform, the role of the civil service has been complicated. For the first time, civil servants have been required to testify in a manner that might damage their ministers, revealing culpability or flawed judgments. As discussed in Chapter 3, the powerful norms of civil service secrecy have been compromised and the relationship with ministers disturbed. On balance, the committees have been extremely energetic, but not very powerful.

Political Parties and the Party System

Like the term *parliamentary sovereignty,* which conceals the reduced role of Parliament in legislation and the unmaking of governments, the term *two-party system,* which is commonly used to describe the British party system, is somewhat deceiving. It is true that since 1945 David Lloyd George, leader of the Liberal party who served as prime minister in a coalition government from 1916–1922, only leaders of the Labour or Conservative parties have served as prime ministers. Focusing on the post-World War II period, from 1945 through 2001, the Conservative and Labour parties each won eight general elections, with

2005 tipping the lead to Labour. It is also true that throughout the postwar period, these two parties have routinely divided at least 85 percent of the seats in the House of Commons. But since the 1980s center parties have assumed a high profile in British electoral politics, with the Liberal Democrats (Lib Dems) sometimes emerging as an important alternative to Conservative and Labour—or perhaps a coalition partner with Labour in the event of a general election which produces no single party with a parliamentary majority (what the British call a "hung parliament"). In addition, Britain has several national parties, such as the Scottish National Party (SNP) in Scotland or the Plaid Cymru in Wales as well as a roster of parties competing in Northern Ireland. (These parties are described below under "Trends in Electoral Behavior.")

The Labour Party

As one of the few European parties with origins outside electoral politics, the Labour Party was launched by trade union representatives and socialist societies in the last decade of the nineteenth century and formally took its name in 1906. But it would be decades before the Labour Party became a contender for government leadership. Its landslide 1945 victory made the party a major player. At the same time, Labour began moderating its ideological appeal and broadening its electoral base by adopting the collectivist consensus described in Chapter 1. In the 1950s and early 1960s, people who were not engaged in manual labor voted Conservative three times more commonly than they did Labour; more than two out of three manual workers, by contrast, voted Labour. During this period, Britain conformed to one classic pattern of a Western European party system: a two-class/two-party system.

The period since the mid-1970s has been marked by significant changes in the party system and a growing disaffection with even the moderate social democracy associated with the Keynesian welfare state and Labourism. The party suffered from divisions between its trade unionist and parliamentary elements, constitutional wrangling over the power of trade unions to determine party policy at annual conferences, and disputes over how the leader would be selected. Divisions also spilled over into foreign policy issues as well. On defense issues, there was a strong pacifist and an even stronger antinuclear sentiment within the party. Support for unilateral nuclear disarmament (the reduction and elimination of nuclear weapons systems with or without comparable developments on the Soviet side) was a decisive break with the national consensus on security policy and contributed to the party's losses in 1983 and 1987. Unilateralism was then scrapped.

The 1980s and 1990s witnessed relative harmony within the party, since moderate trade union and parliamentary leadership agreed on major policy issues. Labour has become a moderate left-of-center party in which ideology takes a backseat to performance and electoral mobilization, although divisions over the war in Iraq have inspired some soul searching about what values the party represents.

The Conservative Party

The pragmatism, flexibility, and organizational capabilities of the Conservative Party, which dates back to the eighteenth century, have made it one of the most successful and, at times, innovative center-right parties in Europe. Although it has fallen on hard times in recent years, it would be unwise to underestimate its potential as both an opposition and a governing party.

The association of the Conservative Party with the economic and social elite is unmistakable, but it was the Conservative government of Prime Minister Benjamin Disraeli (1874–1880) that served as midwife to the birth of the modern welfare state in Britain. The creation of a "long-lasting alliance between an upper-class leadership and a lower-class following" made the Conservative Party a formidable player in British politics.[2] Throughout the postwar period, it has also routinely (with some exceptions) provided the Tories, as Conservatives are colloquially called, with electoral support from about one-third or more of the manual working class.

Contemporary analysis of the Conservative Party must emphasize the cost to the party of its internal divisions over Britain's role in the EU. Wrangling among the Conservatives over Europe led to Thatcher's fall from leadership and weakened Major throughout his years as prime minister. The bitter leadership contest

that followed Major's resignation after the 1997 defeat reinforced the impression of a party in turmoil; subsequent rapid departures of party leaders after electoral defeat in 2001 as well as the forced resignation of the leader in 2003 lent an aura of failure and self-doubt to the Conservatives.

Once the combative, experienced, and highly regarded Michael Howard—who had served in the cabinets of both Margaret Thatcher and John Major—assumed the party leadership in 2003, the Conservatives seemed revitalized. But Howard could not translate his assured performances from the front bench in Parliament into popular support. Although Howard pounded Blair on the failures of intelligence in the run-up to the war in Iraq, Conservatives gave the prime minister far less trouble on Iraq than did members of the Labour Party itself. Nor could Howard make much headway against New Labour on central social and economic policy concerns—and thus despite an energetic campaign, one that will likely be remembered for its xenophobic edge, immediately after the 2005 election Howard succumbed to the same fate as his recent predecessors: electoral defeat followed by a quick resignation as party leader. In December 2005, the Conservatives in a landslide elected David Cameron as party leader.

He wasted little time in reorienting the party, modernizing its appeal, and reaching out beyond its traditional core values. Young (he was born in 1966), smart, and telegenic, Cameron acknowledged that New Labour had been right in understanding the mood of Britain and right, also, to insist on achieving both social justice and economic success. Cameron promised to reduce poverty both in Britain and globally, take on climate change as a priority, and ensure security from terrorism. He looked for ways to retain a special relationship with America, but he also promised to recalibrate British foreign policy by forging comparable special relationships with countries such as India. As a testament to Blair's success, as well as the uncertainty about Gordon Brown, Cameron worked hard to reposition the Conservatives as a reforming, more centrist party that could compete effectively with post-Blair New Labour across the economic and social spectrum. Cameron also encouraged the view that Brown would drift toward the discredited Old Labour left and, quite remarkably, Cameron claimed that he was the true heir to Tony Blair.[3]

Liberal Democrats

Since the 1980s, a changing roster of centrist parties has posed a potentially significant threat to the two-party dominance of Conservative and Labour. Through the 1970s, the Liberal Party, a governing party before World War I and thereafter the traditional centrist third party in Britain, was the only centrist challenger to the Labour and Conservative parties. In 1981, the Social Democratic Party (SDP) formed out of a split within the Labour Party. In the 1983 election, the Alliance (an electoral arrangement of the Liberals and the SDP) gained a quarter of the vote. The strength of centrist parties in the mid-1980s led to expectations of a possible Alliance-led government (which did not occur). After the Conservative victory in 1987, the Liberal Party and most of the SDP merged to form the Social and Liberal Democratic Party (now called the Liberal Democrats or Lib Dems). Especially against the backdrop of an ineffectual Tory opposition to New Labour, the Lib Dems have become a major political player.

Their success in the 2001 general election—the party increased its vote tally by nearly one-fifth and won fifty-two seats, the most seats of a third party since 1929—positioned the party as a potentially powerful center-left critic of New Labour. That said, Labour has not made it easy for them. As the Blair government began to spend massively to improve education and health care, it narrowed the range of policy issues on which the Liberal Democrats could take on New Labour. Although Charles Kennedy, party leader since 1999 and a highly regarded figure in British politics, won the political gamble in spring 2003 by opposing the war in Iraq, challenging the weapons of mass destruction (WMD) claim, and even attending the huge antiwar rally in February, it has not been easy for him—or the party—to take electoral advantage of Blair's political weakness. Thereafter, for a time things went downhill badly, as Kennedy resigned due to problems with alcohol, allegations about sexual conduct plagued potential successors, and the new leader, Menzies (Ming) Campbell, a specialist in foreign affairs, appeared uncomfortable on domestic policy issues and performed poorly in parliamentary exchanges. In spring 2006, the morale of the Liberal Democrats rose as Campbell gained some traction by calling for an early withdrawal of British forces from Basra. For a time supporters

dared hope that after the next election Labour and Conservative might be so evenly matched that the Liberal Democrats might be called on to help form a coalition government. But then things went downhill badly as Campbell suddenly resigned in October 2007, and the party faced yet another leadership context.

Elections

British elections are exclusively for legislative posts. The prime minister is not elected as prime minister but as an MP from a single constituency (electoral district), averaging about 65,000 registered voters. Parliament has a maximum life of five years, with no fixed term. General elections are held after the Crown, at the request of the prime minister, has dissolved Parliament. Although Blair has in effect set a precedent of elections with four-year intervals, the ability to control the timing of elections is a tremendous political asset for the prime minister. This contrasts sharply with a presidential system, which is characteristic of the United States, with direct election of the chief executive and a fixed term of office.

The Electoral System

Election for representatives in the Commons (who are called members of Parliament, or MPs) is by a "first-past-the-post" (or winner-take-all) principle in each constituency. In this single-member plurality system, the candidate who receives the most votes is elected. There is no requirement of a majority and no element of proportional representation (a system in which each party receives a percentage of seats in a representative assembly that is roughly comparable to its percentage of the popular vote). Table 4.1 shows the results of the general elections from 1945 to 2005.

This winner-take-all electoral system exaggerates the size of the victory of the largest party and reduces the influence of regionally dispersed lesser parties. Thus, in 2005, with 35.2 percent of the popular vote, Labour won 355 seats. With 22.1 percent of the vote, the Liberal Democrats won only 62 seats. Thus, the Liberal Democrats achieved a share of the vote that was approximately two-thirds of that achieved by Labour, but won less than one-fifth of the seats won

Table 4.1

British General Elections, 1945–2005

	Percentage of Popular Vote						Seats in House of Commons					
	Turnout	Conservative	Labour	Liberal[a]	National Parties[b]	Other	Swing[c]	Conservative	Labour	Liberal[a]	National Parties[b]	Other	Government Majority
1945	72.7	39.8	48.3	9.1	0.2	2.5	−12.2	213	393	12	0	22	146
1950	84.0	43.5	46.1	9.1	0.1	1.2	+3.0	299	315	9	0	2	0.5
1951	82.5	48.0	48.8	2.5	0.1	0.6	+0.9	321	295	6	0	3	17
1955	76.7	49.7	46.4	2.7	0.2	0.9	+2.1	345	277	6	0	2	60
1959	78.8	49.4	43.8	5.9	0.4	0.6	+1.2	365	258	6	0	1	100
1964	77.1	43.4	44.1	11.2	0.5	0.8	−3.2	304	317	9	0	0	4
1966	75.8	41.9	47.9	8.5	0.7	0.9	−2.7	253	363	12	0	2	95
1970	72.0	46.4	43.0	7.5	1.3	1.8	+4.7	330	288	6	1	5	30
Feb. 1974	78.7	37.8	37.1	19.3	2.6	3.2	−1.4	297	301	14	9	14	−34[d]
Oct. 1974	72.8	35.8	39.2	18.3	3.5	3.2	−2.1	277	319	13	14	12	3
1979	76.0	43.9	37.0	13.8	2.0	3.3	+5.2	339	269	11	4	12	43
1983	72.7	42.4	27.6	25.4	1.5	3.1	+4.0	397	209	23	4	17	144
1987	75.3	42.3	30.8	22.6	1.7	2.6	−1.7	376	229	22	6	17	102
1992	77.7	41.9	34.4	17.8	2.3	3.5	−2.0	336	271	20	7	17	21
1997	71.4	30.7	43.2	16.8	2.6	6.7	−10.0	165	419	46	10	19	179
2001	59.4	31.7	40.7	18.3	2.5	6.8	+1.8	166	413	52	9	19	167
2005	61.5	32.3	35.2	22.1	2.1	8.4	+3.0	197	355	62	9	22	65[e]

[a]Liberal Party, 1945–1979; Liberal/Social Democrat Alliance, 1983–1987; Liberal Democratic Party, 1992–2005.

[b]Combined vote of Scottish National Party (SNP) and Welsh National Party (Plaid Cymru).

[c]"Swing" compares the results of each election with the results of the previous election. It is calculated as the average of the winning major party's percentage point increase in its share of the vote and the losing major party's decrease in its percentage point share of the vote. In the table, a positive sign denotes a swing to the Conservatives, a negative sign a swing to Labour.

[d]Following the February 1974 election, the Labour Party was thirty-four seats short of having an overall majority. It formed a minority government until it obtained a majority in the October 1974 election.

[e]Due to the death of a candidate in one constituency, only 645 parliamentary seats were contested in the May 2005 general election, with one additional seat to be filled through a by-election.

Source: Anthony King, ed., New Labour Triumphs: Britain at the Polls (Chatham, N.J.: Chatham House, 1998), p. 249. Copyright © 1998 by Chatham House. Reprinted by permission. For 2001 results, http://news.bbc.co.uk/hi/english/static/vote2001/results_constituencies/uk_breakdown/uk_full.stm. For 2005 results, http://news.bbc.co.uk/1/hi/uk_politics/vote_2005/constituencies/default.stm.

by Labour. Such are the benefits of the electoral system to the victor (as well as the second major party).

With a fairly stable two-and-a-half party system (Conservative, Labour, and Liberal Democrat), the British electoral system tends toward a stable single-party government. However, the electoral system raises questions about representation and fairness. The system reduces the competitiveness of smaller parties with diffuse pockets of support. In addition, the party and electoral systems have contributed to the creation of a Parliament that has been a bastion of white men. The 1997 election represented a breakthrough for women: the number of women MPs nearly doubled to 120 (18.2 percent). The 2001 election saw the number of women MPs decline to 118 (17.9 percent). But a record 128 women were elected in 2005 (19.8 percent). As a result of using women-only shortlists for the selection of candidates in many winnable seats, Labour sent far more women (94) to Parliament than any other party.

In 1992, 6 ethnic minority candidates were elected, up from 4 in 1987, the first time since before World War II that Parliament included minority members. The number of ethnic minority (black and Asian) MPs rose in 1997 to 9 (1.4 percent), to 12 in 2001 (1.8 percent), and to 15 in 2005 (2.3 percent). Despite the general trend of increased representation of women and minorities, they remain substantially underrepresented in Parliament.

Trends in Electoral Behavior

Recent general elections have deepened geographic and regional fragmentation. The British political scientist Ivor Crewe has referred to the emergence of two two-party systems: (1) competition between the Conservative and Labour parties dominates contests in English urban and northern seats, and (2) Conservative-center party competition dominates England's rural and southern seats.[4] In addition, a third two-party competition has appeared in Scotland, where competition between Labour and the Scottish National Party dominates.

The national parties have challenged two-party dominance since the 1970s. The Scottish National Party (SNP) was founded in 1934 and its Welsh counterpart, the Plaid Cymru, in 1925. Coming in a distant second to Labour in Scotland in 1997, the SNP won

21.6 percent of the vote and six seats. In 2001, support for the SNP declined by 2 percent, and the party lost one of its seats. The 2005 election showed some interesting results in Scotland. Labour lost five seats and the SNP gained two seats (for a total of six). But the Lib Dems overtook the SNP's share of the vote. Both electoral and polling data indicate that Scottish voters are more inclined to support the SNP for elections to the Scottish parliament than to Westminster and that devolution may have stemmed the rising tide of nationalism.[5] In both 1997 and 2001, the Plaid Cymru won four seats where Welsh is still spoken widely. In 2005, after an absence of eight years, three Conservative MPs were elected in Wales, as the Plaid Cymru lost one seat.

The May 2005 election was not easy to sum up. All three major parties could claim some kind of victory, but also had to come to terms with elements of failure. Blair secured an historic third term with a cautious campaign, riding a strong economy and improvements in education and health care to victory—with recurrent images of Gordon Brown by his side. But the election nevertheless left Blair humbled, his majority slashed, his support often grudging. New Labour won by putting off tough decisions—on pension reform, public spending, climate change, Europe, and a timetable for the withdrawal of British troops from Iraq. They won, too, by locking in the middle of the electoral sentiment. They are perfectly positioned: slightly center-right on security and immigration; slightly center-left on the economy and social policy.

Hence, the other parties couldn't lay a glove on Blair on the core issues that drive domestic politics. With little to say about the government's solid economic record or about the war in Iraq (which they supported, whatever criticisms they might muster about Blair's credibility), the Conservatives played the race card. As *The Economist* put it, their campaign was an "unseemly scramble for the anti-immigrant vote." The Tories could take solace in the fact that they had a net gain of thirty-one seats, but Michael Howard's hasty departure made it obvious that the campaign was a failure.

One of the most significant features of the 2005 election, an element of continuity with 2001, was the growing importance of the Liberal Democrats. They enjoyed a net gain of ten seats and, perhaps more importantly, their share of the popular vote rose to an impressive 22 percent. On the down side, like Howard, Kennedy could not chip away at Labour's dominant position on the core economic and social policies. But he benefited from a consistent and articulate opposition to the war in Iraq, which paid dividends especially in constituencies with a strong presence of students or Muslims. As noted above, the hopes of Liberal Democrats to parlay this strong showing into a strong role in opposition and improved electoral prospects in the future soon faded.

Both recent trends in electoral behavior in Scotland and truly historic developments in Northern Ireland will be discussed in Chapter 5.

Political Culture, Citizenship, and Identity

In their classic study of the ideals and values that shape political behavior, political scientists Gabriel Almond and Sidney Verba wrote that the civic (or political) culture in Britain was characterized by trust, deference to authority and competence, pragmatism, and the balance between acceptance of the rules of the game and disagreement over specific issues.[6] Looking back, the 1970s appear as a crucial turning point in British political culture and group identities.

During the 1970s, the long years of economic decline culminated in economic reversals in the standard of living for many Britons. Also for many, the historic bonds of occupational and social class grew weaker. Union membership declined as jobs continued to be transferred away from the traditional manufacturing sectors. More damaging, unions lost popular support as they appeared to bully society, act undemocratically, and neglect the needs of an increasingly female and minority work force. At the same time, a growing number of conservative think tanks and the powerful voice of mass-circulation newspapers, which are overwhelmingly conservative, worked hard to erode the fundamental beliefs of the Keynesian welfare state. New social movements (NSMs), such as feminism, antinuclear activism, and environmentalism, challenged basic tenets of British political culture. Identities based on race and ethnicity, gender, and sexual orientation gained importance. A combination of economic strains, ideological assaults, and social dislocations fostered political fragmentation and, at the same time, inspired a shift to the right in values and policy agendas.

Thatcher's ascent reflected these changes in political culture, identities, and values. It also put the full resources of the state and a bold and determined prime minister behind a sweeping agenda for change. As a leading British scholar put it, "Thatcher's objective was nothing less than a cultural revolution."[7] Although most observers agree that Thatcher fell considerably short of that goal, Thatcherism cut deep. It touched the cultural recesses of British society, recast political values, and redefined national identity.

To the extent that the Thatcherite worldview took hold (the record is mixed), its new language and ethos transformed the common sense of politics and redefined the political community. Monetarism (however modified) and the appeal to an enterprise culture of competitive market logic and entrepreneurial values fostered individualism and competition—winners and losers. This worldview rejected collectivism, the redistribution of resources from rich to poor, and state responsibility for full employment. Thatcherism considered individual property rights to be more important than the social rights claimed by all citizens in the welfare state. And so Thatcherism set the stage in cultural terms for the New Labour consolidation of neoliberalism and the core political-cultural orientation in Britain.

Social Class

One of the key changes in political culture in Britain in the last quarter-century has been the weakening of bonds grounded in the experience of labor or, more broadly, the sense of shared fates among people having common socio-economic status. During the Thatcher era, the traditional values of "an honest day's work for an honest day's pay" and solidarity among coworkers in industrial disputes were characterized as "rigidities" that reduced productivity and competitiveness. New Labour has persisted in this view of social class, as an impediment to competitiveness rather than a collective identity that can provide support and a sense of belonging.

As many have noted, being "tough on the unions" is a core premise of New Labour, and this has contributed to a fundamental erosion of the ability of working people in the United Kingdom to improve their lot through collective bargaining or to exert influence over public policy through the political muscle of the trade union movement. Class still matters in the United Kingdom, but not in the dominating way that it did in the nineteenth century or in the collectivist era. Importantly, as noted in Chapter 2, the political meaning has changed as the values of working-class families have become largely middle-class aspirations and concerns: a nice home to bring up kids, a secure job, good education and heath care—whether public or private. As a result, class says far less than it used to about political party preferences in elections: an individual's social class no longer explains more than about 2 percent of voting behavior.

Class still matters, but fewer workers are in unions (in December 2006 the rate of union membership for all workers in the UK was down to 25.8 percent), and unions are focused narrowly on the enforcement of individual legal rights in the workplace. Collective bargaining has been largely relegated to declining private sector industries and the public sector.[8] Strike rates in the UK have generally been below the average of both the OECD and the EU in the last decade, although there are some notable exceptions. For example, a lengthy dispute between local governments and their employees over pension rights produced a massive one-day strike in March 2006, involving between 400,000 (the estimate by employers) and one million (the estimate by union officials) workers.

In recent decades the sources and relative strength of diverse group attachments have evolved in Britain under the combined pressures of decolonization, which created a multiethnic Britain, and a fragmentation of the experiences of work, which challenges a simple unitary model of class interest. National identity has become especially complicated in the United Kingdom. At the same time, gender politics has emerged as a hot-button issue.

Citizenship and National Identity

Questions about fragmented sovereignty within the context of the EU, the commingled histories of four nations (England, Scotland, Wales, and Ireland/Northern Ireland), and the interplay of race and nationality in postcolonial Britain have created doubts about British identity that run deep. As ethnicity, intra-UK territorial attachments, and the processes of Europeanization and globalization

complicate national identity, it becomes increasingly difficult for UK residents automatically to imagine themselves Britons, constituting a resonant national community.

Thus, the British political community has fragmented into smaller communities of class, nation, region, and ethnicity that exist side by side but not necessarily in amiable proximity. Can New Labour recreate a more cohesive political culture and foster a more inclusive sense of British identity? Unlike Thatcher, Blair worked hard to revitalize a sense of community in Britain and to extend his agenda to the socially excluded. But the results were mixed, with every effort to eradicate an emerging underclass, it seems, offset by the divisive aftereffects of 9/11 and fingers pointed at ethnic minorities, immigrants, and asylum seekers.

Race and Ethnicity

Britain is a country of tremendous ethnic diversity. Beyond the numbers—nearly 8 percent of the people who live in Britain are of African, African-Caribbean, or Asian descent—there is the growing reality of life in a multiethnic society. A recent commission report on multiethnic Britain explained: "Many communities overlap; all affect and are affected by others. More and more people have multiple identities—they are Welsh Europeans, Pakistani Yorkshirewomen, Glaswegian Muslims, English Jews and black British. Many enjoy this complexity but also experience conflicting loyalties."[9]

Although there are many success stories, ethnic minority communities have experienced police insensitivity, problems in access to the best public housing, hate crimes, and accusations that they are not truly British if they do not root for Britain's cricket team against the West Indies team or Pakistan. In addition, harsh criticism directed at immigrants and asylum seekers, in the wake of intense scrutiny of the Muslim community since September 11, contributes to the alienation of the ethnic minority community, particularly sections of the Muslim citizenry. And yet, in the aftermath of the attack on the World Trade Center and the Pentagon, public debate included a range of articulate, young, and confident Muslims from a variety of perspectives. It is true that ordinary law-abiding

Muslims—or people perceived to be Muslims—have experienced intensified mistrust and intimidation since the terror attacks by British Muslims in London in July 2005. But it is equally true that Muslim university graduates are assuming leading roles in the professions, while there are more than 160 Muslim elected city councilors, and British society has become increasingly sensitive to Muslim concerns.[10] The contemporary challenges of multiculturalism and diversity in Britain will be discussed in Chapter 5.

Gender

Historically, the issues women care about most—child care, the treatment of part-time workers, domestic violence, equal pay, and support for family caregivers—have not topped the list of policy agendas of any political party in Britain. Has New Labour significantly changed the equation?

It is fair to say that Labour does well among women voters less because of any specific policies and more because it has made the effort to listen to concerns that women voice. Labour stalwarts insist that they have addressed key concerns that women (and men) share concerning health care, crime, and education. They point with pride to the policy directions spurred by the Social Exclusion and Women's units; to the implementation of a national childcare strategy; to policies intended to help women to balance work and family commitments; and to the creation of women-only shortlists in 2005 for candidates to compete in safe Labour constituencies.

As a result, New Labour has obliterated the old gender gap in which women favored the Conservatives and has begun to establish a new pro-Labour women's vote, which may be particularly significant, for its ability to mobilize young women.

Interests, Social Movements, and Protest

In recent years, partly in response to globalization, political protest has increased in Britain, as protesters demand more accountability and transparency from powerful international trade and development agencies. London became the site of protests timed to correspond with the Seattle meeting of the World Trade Organization (WTO), which generated some 100,000 protesters in November 1999.

In addition, since the mid-1990s, the level and intensity of environmental activism took off with the growing attention to genetically modified (GM) crops in the late 1990s. A newly radicalized movement captured the popular imagination with worries that long-term consumption of GM food might be harmful and that once let loose, GM crops—referred to as "Frankenstein food"—might cross-pollinate with "normal" plants. Opinion polls indicated that nearly 75 percent of the population did not want GM crops in the United Kingdom, and in November 1999, the government announced a ban on commercially grown GM crops in Britain.

In a movement that galvanized the country and raised critical questions about Blair's leadership, massive demonstrations in September 2000 to protest high fuel prices cut across constituencies and enjoyed huge popular support. A very successful and well-coordinated week-long protest stalled fuel delivery throughout the country, forced 90 percent of the petrol stations to run out of unleaded gasoline, and required the Queen, on the advice of the prime minister, to declare a state of emergency. By the time the blockades came down, opinion polls for the first time in eight years showed the Conservatives for the moment surging past Labour. In fact, polling data indicates that Blair's popularity has never recovered from the bump it took over fuel prices.[11]

A quite different kind of activism spread to the countryside among a population not usually known for political protest. Farmers who had been badly hurt by the BSE crisis (bovine spongiform encephalopathy, more popularly known as "mad cow disease") and other rural populations concerned about the perceived urban bias of the Labour government launched massive protests.[12] As the banning and licensing of fox hunting roiled Parliament, the Countryside Alliance, which represents country dwellers who see restrictions on fox hunting as emblematic of domineering urban interests, held mass demonstrations in an effort to block restrictive legislation. Even after a law banning the hunt went into effect in 2005, they kept up the heat with legal challenges.

On the far more significant matter of war in Iraq, a series of antiwar rallies were held in London. In September 2002, a huge protest rally was organized in London, led by the Stop the War Coalition and the Muslim Association of Britain. It was one of Europe's biggest antiwar rallies. Another antiwar rally in mid-February 2003 challenged Blair's stand on Iraq with at least 750,000 demonstrators.

Both within the United Kingdom and among observers of British politics and society, many still endorse the view that British culture is characterized by pragmatism, trust, and deference to authority. This may be true, but the persistence and mobilizing potential of a wide range of social movements suggest that quite powerful political subcurrents persist in Britain, posing significant challenges for British government.

Notes

[1] See Dennis Kavanagh, *British Politics: Continuities and Change, 3rd ed.* (Oxford: Oxford University Press, 1996), pp. 282–288.

[2] Samuel H. Beer, *The British Political System* (New York: Random House, 1973), p. 157.

[3] See Stephen Driver and Luke Martell, *New Labour, 2nd ed.* (Cambridge, England: Polity Press, 2006), pp. 8–9

[4] Ivor Crewe, "Great Britain," in I. Crewe and D. Denver, eds., *Electoral Change in Western Democracies* (London: Croom Helm, 1985), p. 107.

[5] John Bartle, "Why Labour Won—Again," in Anthony King et al., eds., *Britain at the Polls, 2001* (New York: Chatham House, 2002), p. 171.

[6] See Gabriel A. Almond and Sidney Verba, *The Civic Culture: Political Attitudes and Democracy in Five Nations* (Princeton, N.J.: Princeton University Press, 1963); Almond and Verba, eds., *The Civic Culture Revisited* (Boston: Little, Brown, 1980); and Samuel H. Beer, *Britain Against Itself: The Political Contradictions of Collectivism* (New York: Norton, 1982), pp. 110–114.

[7] Ivor Crewe, "The Thatcher Legacy," in King et al., eds., *Britain at the Polls 1992,* p. 18.

[8] See Chris Howell, *Trade Unions and the State* (Princeton, N.J.: Princeton University Press, 2005), chap. 6.

[9] Bhiku Parekh et al., *The Future of Multi-Ethnic Britain: The Parekh Report* (London: Profile Books, 2000), p. 10.

[10] For an excellent treatment of the complex experiences of British Muslims, see Philip Lewis, *Islamic Britain* (London and New York: I. B. Tauris, 2002).

[11] David Sanders, "The New Labour and the Electoral Dynamics," paper presented to the Conference on Cool Britain, Montreal, 4–6 May 2005.

[12] See Helen Margetts, "Political Participation and Protest," in Patrick Dunleavy et al., eds., *Developments in British Politics* 6 (New York: St. Martin's Press, 2000), pp. 185–202.

CHAPTER 5

British Politics in Transition

In the fall of 1994, cease-fire declarations made by the Irish Republican Army (IRA) and the Protestant paramilitary organizations renewed hope for a peace settlement in Northern Ireland. Then, in a dramatic new development in early spring 1995, British prime minister John Major and Irish Prime Minister John Bruton jointly issued a framework agreement, inspiring mounting optimism about a political settlement. Although Major did what he could to secure public and parliamentary support, he lacked the political capital to bring the historic initiative to fruition.

After his 1997 landslide victory, Tony Blair did have political capital to spend, and he chose to invest a chunk of it on peace in Northern Ireland. Blair arranged to meet Gerry Adams, president of Sinn Fein, the party in Northern Ireland with close ties to the IRA—and shook his hand. He was the first prime minister to meet with a head of Sinn Fein since 1921. Blair later spoke of the "hand of history" on his shoulder.

Under deadline pressure imposed by Blair and the new Irish prime minister, Bertie Ahern, and thirty-three hours of around-the-clock talks, an agreement was reached on Good Friday 1998. It specified elections for a Northern Ireland assembly, in which Protestants and Catholics would share power, and the creation of a North-South Council to facilitate all-Ireland cooperation on matters such as economic development, agriculture, transportation, and the environment. Both parts of Ireland voted yes in May 1998 in a referendum to approve the peace agreement. It appeared that a new era was dawning in Northern Ireland.

Handshake or not, devastating bombs have exploded from time to time in Northern Ireland since the agreement, and violent turf battles within and among camps have created fear and repeated crises in the peace process. Insisting that Sinn Fein cabinet ministers be barred from discussion until the IRA disarmed, hardliners in the Protestant camp created a rash of challenges for David Trimble, the Ulster Unionist leader who remained committed to the success of the process. Sinn Fein, in turn, accused Trimble of sabotage and warned that the IRA would not be able to control its own dissidents if the power-sharing arrangements were unilaterally dismantled.

In October 2001, the IRA began disarming under the sponsorship of third-party diplomats, and yet violence rose despite cease-fires by paramilitary groups. In October 2002, home rule government was suspended, and British direct rule was reimposed. Since then, on numerous occasions, Tony Blair and his Irish Republic counterpart, Bertie Ahern, have pledged to redouble efforts to get Northern Ireland's faltering peace process back on track, but progress has not been easy.

In January 2005, hope for a settlement was dashed by the blockbuster announcement that linked the IRA to a $40 million bank robbery. In February, the brutal murder of Robert McCartney, a supporter of the IRA's political wing by IRA members in a Belfast bar—who had accused him of looking inappropriately at one of their female companions—may have permanently shattered support for the IRA. McCartney's murder, the wall of silence the IRA imposed on some 70 witnesses, and the IRA's offer to kill the men responsible, have had significant political repercussions. The May 2005 election ousted Unionist moderate David Trimble and strengthened the hands of the more radical parties (Sinn Fein and Democratic Unionist Party, lead by Ian Paisley). But there were increasingly vocal popular demands for an end to sectarian violence. All in all, it seemed increasingly likely, although perhaps too good to be true, that the deadlock might soon be broken. By mid-2005, the IRA had exhausted its leverage, Gerry Adams seemed ready to press for their dissolution, and—despite denials—insiders spoke of a pending settlement or even a secret deal that is all but agreed upon.

At long last, although as always in Northern Ireland, there would be detours and complications, the optimism was well founded. In March 2007, Gerry Adams and Ian Paisley sat at the same table for the first time, declaring they would work together in a power-sharing government in Northern Ireland. This was a hard-earned crowning achievement for Prime Minister Blair, supported by Chancellor Brown's commitment to a handsome "peace dividend" (a financial package of some $100 billion over ten years to support development and public services, reduce poverty and social exclusion, and spur business initiatives). In May 2007, the unimaginable came to pass. Devolution was restored to Northern Ireland. Ian Paisley became first minister of Northern Ireland and Martin McGuinness the deputy first minister. The Northern Ireland executive, although highly dependent on budgetary transfers from the UK central government, took over responsibility for regional development, health, and education.

As Tony Blair beams, and Irish prime minister Bertic Ahcrn shows the fatigue of a very lengthy set of negotiations, sworn enemies Martin McGuinness and Ian Paisley stand side-by-side, ready to assume responsibilities as first ministers in a historic power-sharing government in Northern Ireland. *Source: AFP/Getty Images*

The decades-long crisis in Northern Ireland confirms the important proposition that unresolved tensions in state formation shape political agendas for generations. As Ian Paisley put it in almost biblical terms on the day the power-sharing arrangement was launched, "Northern Ireland has come to a time of peace, when hate will no longer rule." Let us hope that the decades of sectarian strife ("The Troubles") in Northern Ireland are over. But Northern Ireland was only one of a host of challenges that have faced Britain and New Labour, and the rest are quite enough to leave Gordon Brown's in-box overflowing.

Political Challenges and Changing Agendas

As the democratic idea theme suggests, no democracy, however secure it may be, is a finished project. Even in Britain, with its centuries-old constitutional settlement and secure institutional framework, issues about democratic governance and citizens' participation remain unresolved.

Constitutional Reform

Questions about the role of the monarchy and the House of Lords have long simmered on Britain's political agenda. "Why is the House of Commons not sovereign?" wondered one observer somewhat caustically. "Why does it have to share sovereignty with other, unelected institutions?"[1] In addition, the balance of power among constitutionally critical institutions raises important questions about a democratic deficit at the heart of the Westminster model. Britain's executive, whose strength in relation to that of the legislature may be greater than in any other Western democracy, easily overpowers Parliament. Add to these concerns the tendency of willful prime ministers such as Thatcher and Blair to bypass the cabinet on crucial decisions, a tradition Brown seems likely to continue. Add the bias in the electoral system that privileges the two dominant parties, and it seems appropriate to raise questions about the accountability of the British government to its citizens.

In fact, in the heady days after Blair's 1997 election victory, amidst talk of an expanding array of constitutional reforms, it was commonplace to suggest that constitutional reform might become New Labour's most enduring legacy. But the reform agenda has been sidetracked or subjected to powerful political crosscurrents—or administrative complexities—that have slowed or stalled agreement on key elements. For example, the Freedom of Information Act passed in 2002, but a second stage of implementation began only in January 2005. The act was also weakened by the extensive range of information it permitted ministers to withhold and by its limited provision for independent review of such ministerial decisions.[2] The Blair government has begun to implement far-reaching reforms of Parliament, including the removal of the right of hereditary peers to speak and vote in the House of Lords, and the redesign of the historic upper chamber, but as discussed in Section 4, the form of the new upper chamber has yet to take shape. In addition, the European Convention on Human Rights has been incorporated into UK law, and, more controversially, plans have been announced for the creation of a "supreme court," but strenuous opposition in both chambers has clouded the prospects for passage. New systems of proportional representation have been introduced for Welsh and Scottish elections, as well as for the European Parliament. But the potential use of proportional representation in UK general elections will probably come, if at all, only after a very close election in which no party can constitute a majority in the House of Commons on its own and the Lib Dems are able to wrest a commitment to proportional representation from Labour as a condition for backing Labour or forming a Labour–Lib Dem government. Such is political life in a country without an entrenched constitution!

Finally, the power-sharing initiatives in Northern Ireland and arrangements among Westminster, the Welsh Assembly, and, most importantly, the Scottish Parliament represent basic modifications of UK constitutional principles. Devolution implies both an element of federalism and some compromise in the

historic parliamentary sovereignty at the heart of the Westminster model. Thus far the unsettling consequences feared by some have not come to pass, but 2007 elections in both Wales and Scotland put national parties into power. And with Alex Salmond, leader of the SNP, promising to hold a referendum on Scottish independence by 2010, territorial politics in the UK could become very interesting.

New Labour's constitutional reform agenda represents a breathtaking illustration of a core premise of our democratic idea theme: that even long-standing democracies face pressures to narrow the gap between government and citizens. At the same time, the relatively limited results and slowed pace of reforms are an important reminder that democratic changes are not easy to implement.

Identities in Flux

Although the relatively small scale of the ethnic minority community limits the political impact of the most divisive issues concerning collective identities, it is probably in this area that rigidities in the British political system challenge tenets of democracy and tolerance most severely. With Britain's single-member, simple-plurality electoral system and no proportional representation, minority representation in Parliament is very low, and there are deep-seated social attitudes that no government can easily transform.

The issues of immigration, refugees, and asylum still inspire a fear of multiculturalism among white Britons and conjure up very negative and probably prejudiced reactions. In fall 2000, the report of the Commission on the Future of Multi-Ethnic Britain raised profound questions about tolerance, justice, and inclusion in contemporary UK society. In a powerful and controversial analysis, the report concluded that "the word 'British' will never do on its own . . . Britishness as much as Englishness, has systematic, largely unspoken, racial connotations."[3]

Against the backdrop of intensified finger pointing directed at the Muslim community, the period since September 11 has witnessed a hardening of government policy on asylum, refuge, and immigration. This controversial process culminated in the formal announcement in November 2003 that the Asylum Bill would force a heart-wrenching choice on failed asylum seekers: they must either "voluntarily" accept a paid-for return flight to the country from which they fled or see their children taken into government care.[4] By spring 2004, race, immigration, and asylum issues were even stealing headlines from the war in Iraq. There were charges that there had been widespread fraud in the treatment of East European applications for immigration, as well as efforts by the minister in charge of immigration and asylum, Beverly Hughes, to mislead Parliament. These accusations led to her resignation. Official government data revealed record levels of hate crimes in England and Wales. After an episode in which British-born Muslims set fire to the Union Jack in London, debate raged about the validity of "separateness" among ethnic communities, and the chairman of the Commission for Racial Equality, Trevor Phillips, even called for a return to "core British values" and the abandonment of the government's commitment to building a multicultural society. As Britain experienced increased ethnic tension, polls indicated widespread unease with ethnic diversity. By the start of the election campaign in April 2005, nearly one-quarter (23 percent) of the British people ranked immigration and asylum as the single most important issue facing the nation—nearly double the percentage who thought health care (13 percent) was the biggest issue. A strong majority thought that laws on immigration should be tougher (nine out of ten supporters of the Conservatives, but also six out of ten Labour supporters).[5]

Since the London bombings by British Muslims on 7/7 that killed fifty-six people, intense scrutiny has focused on the Muslim community, which faces endless finger pointing and harassment. According to police, the number of hate crimes primarily affecting Muslims soared 600 percent in the weeks after bombings. There were 269 hate-motivated attacks in the three weeks following the bombings, compared to 40 in the same time period in 2004. In October 2006, Jack Straw, a highly visible MP and former foreign minister, sparked a controversy and angered Muslim groups, when he said that the full facial veil worn by some Muslim women had become a "visible statement of separation and difference"—and urged them to remove the veil when they came to see him in his constituency office in Blackburn. There is increasing concern across the political spectrum that Britain must find a way to deepen the ties of shared political culture and values that hold society together as well as to ensure security.

With other dimensions of collective identity, the situation is fluid. In political terms, the gender gap has tilted quite strongly toward Labour, as it has responded to concerns about women's employment, the disparate impact of social policy, the problems of balancing family and work responsibilities, and parliamentary representation. The electoral force of class identity has declined almost to the vanishing point. By Labour's second term and into the third, however, the country was facing an upsurge in industrial action. Public sector workers such as local government staff and firefighters have led the unrest. A new generation of militant leaders in two railway unions, the postal workers' union, and the government and health workers' union has created new challenges for the government. Any downturn in the economy will likely intensify union militancy and create significant challenges for Gordon Brown.

British Politics, Terrorism, and Britain's Relation to the United States

In the immediate aftermath of the terror attacks on the United States, Blair's decisive support for President Bush struck a resonant cord in both countries and (despite some grumbling) boosted Britain's influence in Europe. But by the spring and summer of 2002, Blair's stalwart alliance with Bush was looking more and more like a liability.

As Britons' instinctive post–September 11 support for America faded, many wondered whether Tony Blair had boxed himself into a corner by aligning himself too closely with George W. Bush—without knowing where the president's foreign policy initiatives might lead in the Middle East and Asia—and in a host of policy areas from trade policy to the conduct of the continuing campaign in Afghanistan, to global warming, to the International Criminal Court. Yet, throughout the diplomatic disputes in the run-up to war in early 2003, Blair persevered in his staunch support for Bush's decision to go to war—even despite Blair's strong preference for explicit Security Council authorization for the use of force and his strong preference that significant progress in resolving the Israeli-Palestinian dispute be made before any military intervention to topple the Saddam Hussein regime.

Nonetheless, even though he could not achieve either of these preferences, Blair refused all advice (including advice from members of his cabinet as well as his chief of defense staff) to make support of the war conditional on achievement of these ends. Blair was convinced that the threats of weapons of mass destruction (WMDs), Al Qaeda terrorism, and rogue states justified the invasion of Iraq and that Britain should and must support the United States in its leadership of a global war against terrorism. Despite initial denials by the prime minister, most Britons instinctively drew a connection between the war in Iraq and the bombs that exploded in London on 7/7. Britons, who displayed enormous resolve in the face of terrorism, were shaken by a set of troubling revelations—first, that the July 7th bombers were all British and, second, after a botched bombing attempt two weeks later, that London police had shot and killed an innocent man on a subway. The repercussions of Iraq continued.

There can be no doubt that when Tony Blair came to office as a modernizer offering a "third way" alternative to the tired Tory and Old Labour recipes for governing the economy, no one anticipated that he would leave office likely to be remembered most (especially in America) for his foreign policy, once the die was cast and the special relationship with the United States became the defining feature of Blair's government after 9/11. It is in Gordon Brown's interest to distinguish his premiership from Blair's in this regard and this would likely involve a constructive reconsideration of the "special relationship" between the United States and the United Kingdom.

The Challenges of European Integration

Tony Blair came to office determined to rescue Europe for Britain—to redress the problems caused by Thatcher's anti-Europe stance and to reposition the United Kingdom both as a major player in Europe and as a powerful interlocutor, respected in both camps, to build bridges between the United States and EU Europe. To advance his agenda, Blair enthusiastically supported initiatives for a common foreign and security policy and helped bring

Europe into the war in Kosovo in accordance with Blair's doctrine of international community, which insisted on military interventions when necessary to prevent or contain humanitarian catastrophes, such as ethnic cleansing. As one lesson of Kosovo, Europe tried to come to terms with its reliance on America's military muscle and unrivaled wartime technological capacities. Hence, Blair worked with France and Germany to develop a more robust European military capability.

But the ambivalence of Britain toward Europe remains very strong. Britain remains on the outside looking in when it comes to the euro (it is one of but three of the fifteen members of the EU before enlargement on May 1, 2004, to remain outside the euro zone). Right from the start in 1997, Blair ceded the decision on the euro to Brown, and Brown, as chancellor, has insisted that the economic tests for participation have never been met. In particular chancellor Brown held firm on the view that Britain's prosperity and economic stability would be undermined by Europe's one-size-fits-all monetary policy. With this history and deeply held set of convictions, it seems unlikely that Prime Minister Brown will bring the UK into the euro zone anytime soon. It is too early to judge how successful Brown will be in shaping any new constitution-like document to Britain's liking, but Britain's stance on any new enabling treaty for the EU will significantly shape UK-EU relations in the years ahead.

British Politics in Comparative Perspective

Until the Asian financial crisis that began in 1997, it was an axiom of comparative politics that economic success required a style of economic governance that Britain lacks. Many argued that innovation and competitiveness in the new global economy required the strategic coordination of the economy by an interventionist state. Interestingly, however, the United Kingdom escaped the recession that plagued the rest of Europe for much of the 1990s and the first decade of the twenty-first century. Although by 2007, the euro zone, led by a resurgent Germany, was picking up economic momentum, Britain is outperforming most major world economies and exhibits good overall performance with low unemployment and inflation (although inflation is rising) and with steady growth. Britain is not an economic paradise, but there is cause for continued optimism, despite persistent poverty, weak investment, problems with productivity, trade imbalances, and the first run on a bank in more than 100 years.

In many countries throughout the world, politicians are looking for an economic model that can sustain economic competitiveness while improving the plight of the socially excluded. New Labour's third way—a political orientation designed to transcend left and right in favor of practical and effective policies—has been carefully watched for more than ten years. Observers have seen in New Labour a historic intellectual and political realignment, not only in Britain, but in Clinton's America, Cardoso's (and later Lula's) Brazil, even as it was refashioning Schroeder's Germany in its own image and, in time, drawing others, such as Nigeria's Obasanjo into its orbit.

At the annual Labour party conference in September 2007, the mood was unusually upbeat. The Blair-Brown feuds seemed a distant memory and Labour supporters felt good about the way the new prime minister had handled a set of crises that tested his early leadership, from attempted terror attacks in London and Glasgow, to horrible flooding that displaced thousands in the north of England, to an outbreak of foot and mouth disease in cattle that created havoc for farmers in the south of England, to the collapse of one of the premier banks that provided mortgages to increasingly worried homeowners. Suddenly, with Gordon Brown at the helm, New Labour was on the upswing and the country was buzzing with talk about an early election to give Brown a proper mandate. Then, even more suddenly, Brown appeared to get cold feet and dropped plans for a snap election (none is required until spring 2010 and none now expected until 2009). The resurgent Tories made much of Brown's retreat, putting the new prime minister on the defensive not only on the timing of an election but on his decision to sign the EU reform treaty in October 2007 without committing the UK to a referendum (a promise made by Blair, before the EU constitutional treaty was rejected by French and Dutch voters in 2005).

If the third way can be sustained, through the transition from Blair to Brown, despite these setbacks, it seems destined to be even more widely emulated and assume considerable historic significance in comparative perspective. If not, for the first time in a long time, real two-party competition seems likely to return to British politics.

Notes

[1] Stephen Haseler, "Britain's Ancien Régime," *Parliamentary Affairs* 40, no. 4 (October 1990): 418.

[2] Iain Byrne and Stuart Weir, "Democratic Audit: Executive Democracy in War and Peace," *Parliamentary Affairs* 57, no. 2 (2004): 453–468.

[3] Bhiku Parekh et al., *The Future of Multi-Ethnic Britain: The Parekh Report* (London: Profile Books, 2000), p. 38.

[4] See Liza Schuster and John Solomos (and respondents), "Debate: Race, Immigration and Asylum," *Ethnicities* 4, no. 2 (June 2004): 267–300.

[5] Ipsos-MORI, "State of the Nation," April 10, 2005; www.ipsos-mori.com/publications//rmw/state-of-the-nation.shtml.

Part 2 Bibliography

Beer, Samuel H. *Britain Against Itself: The Political Contradictions of Collectivism.* New York: Norton, 1982.

Coates, David. *Prolonged Labour.* London: Palgrave/Macmillan, 2005.

Coates, David, and Joel Krieger. *Blair's War.* Cambridge, UK, and Malden Mass.: Polity Press, 2004.

Coates, David, and Peter Lawler, eds. *New Labour in Power.* Manchester: Manchester University Press, 2000.

Cook, Robin. *The Point of Departure.* London: Simon & Schuster, 2003.

Cronin, James E. *New Labour's Pasts.* Harrow, UK: Pearson/Longman, 2004.

Driver, Stephen, and Luke Martell. *New Labour*, 3rd ed. Cambridge: Polity Press, 2006.

Dunleavy, Patrick, et al. *Developments in British Politics* 7. New York: Palgrave/Macmillan, 2003.

Gamble, Andrew. *Between Europe and America: The Future of British Politics.* London: Palgrave/Macmillan, 2003.

George, Bruce. *The British Labour Party and Defense.* New York: Praeger, 1991.

Giddens, Anthony. *The Third Way: The Renewal of Social Democracy.* Cambridge: Polity Press, 1998.

Gilroy, Paul. *"There Ain't No Black in the Union Jack": The Cultural Politics of Race and Nation.* Chicago: University of Chicago Press, 1991.

Hall, Stuart, and Martin Jacques, eds. *The Politics of Thatcherism*. London: Lawrence and Wishart, 1983.

Hobsbawm, E. J. *Industry and Empire*. Harmondsworth, UK: Penguin/Pelican, 1983.

Howell, Chris. *Trade Unions and the State: The Construction of Industrial Relations Institutions in Britain, 1890–2000*. Princeton: Princeton University Press, 2005.

Kampfner, John. *Blair's Wars*. London: Free Press, 2003.

Kavenagh, Dennis, and Anthony Seldon. *The Powers Behind the Prime Minister: The Hidden Influence of Number Ten*. London: Harper-Collins, 1999.

Keegan, William. *The Prudence of Mr. Gordon Brown*. Chichester: John Wiley & Sons, 2004.

King, Anthony, ed. *Britain at the Polls, 2001*. New York and London: Chatham House, 2002.

Krieger, Joel. *British Politics in the Global Age. Can Social Democracy Survive?* New York: Oxford University Press, 1999.

———. *Globalization and State Power*. New York: Pearson Longman, 2005.

Landes, David S. *The Unbound Prometheus: Technological Change and Industrial Development in Western Europe from 1750 to the Present*. Cambridge: Cambridge University Press, 1969.

Lewis, Jane and Rebecca Surrender, eds. *Welfare State Change: Towards a Third Way?* Oxford: Oxford University Press, 2004.

Lewis, Philip. *Islamic Britain: Religion, Politics and Identity Among British Muslims*. London and New York: I. B. Taurus, 2002.

Marsh, David, et al. *Postwar British Politics in Perspective*. Cambridge: Polity Press, 1999.

Marshall, Geoffrey. *Ministerial Responsibility*. Oxford: Oxford University Press, 1989.

Middlemas, Keith. *Politics in Industrial Society: The Experience of the British System Since 1911*. London: André Deutsch, 1979.

Modood, Tariq. *Multicultural Politics: Racism, Ethnicity, and Muslims in Britain*. Minneapolis: University of Minnesota Press, 2005.

Norris, Pippa. *Electoral Change in Britain Since 1945*. Oxford: Blackwell Publishers, 1997.

Parekh, Bhiku, et al. *The Future of Multi-Ethnic Britain: The Parekh Report*. London: Profile Books, 2000.

Riddell, Peter. *The Thatcher Decade*. Oxford: Basil Blackwell, 1989.

Särlvik, Bo, and Ivor Crewe. *Decade of Dealignment: The Conservative Victory of 1979 and Electoral Trends in the 1970s*. Cambridge: Cambridge University Press, 1983.

Seldon, Anthony and Dennis Kavanagh, eds. *The Blair Effect 2001–5*. Cambridge: Cambridge University Press, 2005.

Shaw, Eric. *The Labour Party Since 1945*. Oxford: Blackwell Publishers, 1996.

Thompson, E. P. *The Making of the English Working Class*. New York: Vintage, 1966.

Thompson, Noel. *Political Economy and the Labour Party*, 2nd ed. London and New York: Routledge, 2006.

Websites

Directgov—Portal to public service information from the UK government:
www.direct.gov.uk

National Statistics Online—Home of official UK statistics:
www.statistics.gov.uk

The UK Parliament:
www.parliament.uk

The Cabinet Office:
www.cabinet-office.gov.uk

The Scottish Parliament:
www.scottish.parliament.uk

The British Broadcasting Corporation (BBC):
www.bbc.co.uk

Ipsos MORI (Market & Opinion Research International), Britain's leading political polling organization:
www.ipsos-mori.com

PART 3

France

Mark Kesselman

CHAPTER 6

The Making of the Modern French State

Politics in Action

In most ways, the evening of May 2, 2007, was like any other in France. But it was far from being business as usual. Normally lively cities and towns throughout the country were oddly quiet. Streets were deserted. So too were cafés, movie theaters, and restaurants. Why did France come to a halt? The answer is that a majority of the French were glued to their television sets watching the two candidates in the runoff election for president of France face off in the only televised debate of the campaign.

The stakes in the debate were high. According to polls, only a few percentage points separated conservative frontrunning candidate Nicolas Sarkozy from Socialist Ségolène Royal. If "Ségo" could outperform "Sarko"—or provoke him into losing his proverbially bad temper—the debate could decide the election.

For over two hours, the candidates analyzed the state of France, identified what they regarded as its most pressing problems, presented their reform proposals, and—above all—probed for weaknesses in their opponent. As the underdog and a woman, Royal had the harder job: she needed to demonstrate that she possessed the authority and technical competence to become the first female president of France. But Sarkozy also had challenges to overcome: for a starter, he needed to remain cool under fire. Further, because he was the hard-line candidate of the major conservative party—the one that had controlled government for years—he had to demonstrate solidarity with less-fortunate citizens and at the same time persuade voters that he would break with the past and make a fresh start.

When the debate finally ended—it ran well over the allotted two hours—a majority of French judged that Sarkozy was the winner. And several days later, this opinion translated into a 57 to 43 percent victory for Sarkozy. The intense interest in the debate was evident at the polls as well: 85 percent of registered voters turned out to vote. (Turnout in American presidential elections hovers around 50 percent.)

Three factors probably explain voters' judgment, both about the debate and about who was better qualified to govern France. First, Sarkozy appeared more knowledgeable and authoritative. The debate confirmed the widespread view that Royal often improvised or evaded answers to tough questions, for example, how to finance and implement her reform proposals. Second, Sarkozy was supported by France's best-organized and unified party, the Union for a Popular Majority (UMP). Sarkozy had been president of the UMP since 2004, and the party was solidly behind him. By contrast, Royal won the Socialist Party nomination after a bitter struggle; many party leaders and members gave her candidacy only lukewarm support. Finally, Sarkozy's vision of where he wanted to lead France was apparently more coherent and attractive to voters than Royal's. Sarkozy proclaimed the value of unleashing private market forces and individual initiative, deregulating the economy, slimming down the size of government, and cracking down on crime. Royal spoke of protecting welfare state programs and helping the needy. But she did not provide a convincing answer to how she would revive France's ailing economy in order to finance her proposals.

At the same time, Sarkozy and Royal shared certain characteristics. Both were in their early fifties and represented a new generation of politicians, a striking contrast to most French political leaders, who were well over sixty years old and established fixtures of the political scene. Further, both Sarkozy and Royal were unorthodox representatives of their respective political coalition. Although Sarkozy did not emphasize the proposal in his campaign, he had earlier proposed creating affirmative action programs for ethnic minorities—a world away from the traditional conservative approach. And, to the dismay of those on the left, Royal liberally borrowed campaign themes from the conservative camp. For example, she called for French families to display the flag on July 14, the French equivalent of the Fourth of July in the United States. She proposed that juvenile delinquents be incarcerated in rehabilitation camps run by the military.

Will Sarkozy manage to implement his vision in coming years? When other right-wing politicians proposed cutbacks in social benefits, the result was nationwide protests and stalemate. To understand why, we need to study how the four major themes of *European Politics in Transition* have combined to form the exceptional pattern of French politics.

Geographic Setting

France is among the world's favored countries, thanks to its temperate climate, large and fertile land area, and high standard of living. Its natural beauty and superb architecture, culture, and cuisine make France by far the most popular tourist destination in the world. Paris, the country's capital and one of the world's loveliest cities, is visited by millions of tourists each year. With that said, the site that attracts the most visitors is not Notre Dame Cathedral, the Louvre museum, or the Eiffel Tower—but Disneyland-Paris, which in fact is the most popular tourist site in all Europe.

The French have a reputation for living well (*joie de vivre* is the French term), ranging from a love of art, culture, and romance to an appreciation of fine food and wine. On a more mundane level, however, France has its share of social and economic problems. Indeed, a study ranking the happiest countries in the world, based on a synthesis of many public opinion polls and statistical surveys, reported that France ranks only 64th out of 178 countries, on a par with Indonesia and El Salvador and far behind Britain 41st, Germany—35th, and the United States—23rd. (Denmark and Switzerland top the list.)[1]

With a population of 60 million, France is among the most populous countries in Western Europe, but its large size—211,000 square miles, which makes it the third largest country in Europe—means that population density is low (about half that of Britain, Germany, and Italy). An unusual feature of French national boundaries is that five overseas territories—the Mediterranean island of Corsica, the Caribbean islands of Guadeloupe and Martinique, French Guyana in South America, and the island of Réunion in the Indian Ocean—are considered an integral part of France. Their inhabitants are French citizens. For example, they have full voting rights and elect representatives to the French legislature. (Their situation parallels that of citizens of Alaska and Hawaii in the United States political system.)

The gross domestic product (GDP) of over $2 trillion and per capita income of $29,000 make France among the most affluent countries in the world. Nine families in ten own a color television, 97 percent have a telephone, 74 percent a cell phone, and four-fifths an automobile.[2] Over half of all families own their own home. France ranked 16th among the 177 countries of the world in the 2006 United Nations Development Programme's Human Development Index, a widely respected measure of the overall quality of life.

France occupies a key position in Europe, bordering the Mediterranean Sea in the south and sharing borders with Belgium, Switzerland, and Germany on the north and east, Spain in the southwest, and Italy in the southeast. France is Britain's closest continental neighbor. The two are separated by the English Channel, only twenty-five miles at its most narrow stretch. This distance was further narrowed in 1994 following the opening of the "Chunnel," a railroad tunnel under the English Channel linking the two countries. France has quite secure natural borders of mountains and seas everywhere except on the open plains of the northeast bordering Belgium and Germany. The flat, unprotected terrain enabled German forces to invade France three times in the nineteenth and twentieth centuries.

France has a modern economy, and most people work in the industrial and service sectors. But agriculture continues to occupy a significant place in the economy. France is among the world's most important exporters of agricultural products. Moreover, because so many French families lived in villages and small towns until the mid-twentieth century, the countryside occupies a strong place in the nation's collective memory. (A higher proportion of the French still live in rural areas and small towns than do the British and Germans.) No other French city rivals Paris, the capital, in size and influence; Lille, Lyon, and Marseille are the only other large cities in France.

Critical Junctures

A central feature of French history—from premodern times to present—has been the prominent role played by the state. France was created by monarchs who laboriously united the diverse regions and provinces of what is present-day France—actions that provoked periodic violent resistance. The French have often displayed great respect for the state's achievements—and intense resentment at its highhanded behavior.

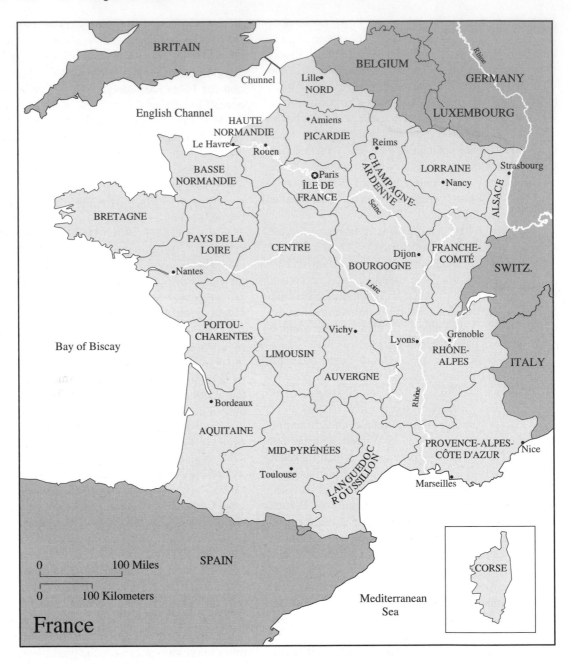

France

However, France's participation in the globalized economy and the EU, along with economic reforms and decentralization measures dating from the 1980s, have jostled the state's preeminence. Nowadays, Paris—the national capital and seat of the ministries that govern French life—must vie with regional and local governments throughout France, as well as with Brussels, headquarters of the EU; Frankfurt, where the European Central Bank is located; and Strasbourg, home of the European Parliament.

Critical Junctures in Modern French Political Development

Until 1789	*Ancien régime* (Bourbon monarchy)
1789–1799	Revolutionary regimes
	Constituent Assembly, 1789–1791
	(Declaration of Rights of Man, Aug. 26, 1789)
	Legislative, 1791
	Convention, 1792–1795: Monarchy abolished and First Republic established, 1792
	Directory, 1795–1799
1799–1814	Consulate and First Empire (Napoleon Bonaparte)
1814–1830	Restoration
1830–1848	July Monarchy
1848–1851	Second Republic
1852–1870	Second Empire (Louis Napoleon)
1871	Paris Commune
1871–1940	Third Republic
1940–1944	Vichy regime
1946–1958	Fourth Republic
1958–Present	Fifth Republic

Creating Modern France

For five centuries at the beginning of the modern era, the area that is now France was part of the Roman Empire. The Romans called the area Gaul (the source of the term *Gallic*, sometimes used to describe the French). France took its current name from the Franks, a Germanic tribe who conquered the area in the fifth century A.D., after the breakup of the Roman Empire. The Frankish Merovingian dynasty ruled France for several centuries, during which time most of the population became Christian. It was succeeded by the Carolingian dynasty, whose most noteworthy ruler, Charlemagne, founded the Holy Roman Empire in the ninth century; it extended throughout Western Europe.

Several decades after Charlemagne's death in 814, his three grandsons divided the empire. Charles the Bald, as he was known, obtained most of the area of present-day France. Hugues Capet was chosen king in 987, by nobles who judged that he would be a more effective ruler than Charlemagne's successors, the Carolingian dynasty. During the next three centuries, Capetian monarchs struggled to subdue powerful provincial rulers in Burgundy, Brittany, and elsewhere. The country was invaded and nearly conquered by the English during the Hundred Years' War (1337–1453). Joan of Arc, a peasant who believed she had a divine mission, led French forces to victory against the English army, although Joan herself was captured and burned at the stake. Her defeat of the English at Orléans has made her a symbol of intense national pride ever since.

France flourished during the next several centuries, especially after Henri IV (who ruled from 1589 to 1610) eased religious conflict between Catholics and Huguenots (Protestants) by issuing the Edict of Nantes in 1598 granting Protestants limited religious toleration. Protestants lost many of these rights when the edict was later revoked in 1685 under Louis XIV. For a century and a half, France and England competed to gain control of North America. The rivalry ended with France's defeat in the French and Indian Wars. The Treaty of Paris in 1763 signified France's acceptance of British domination in North America and India. (At a later period, France engaged in further colonial conquests in Africa, Asia, and the Caribbean.)

The seventeenth and eighteenth centuries were the high point of French economic, military, and cultural influence throughout the world. France was the most affluent and powerful country in continental Europe. It was also the artistic and scientific capital of Europe, home of the Enlightenment in the eighteenth century, the philosophical movement that emphasized the importance of scientific reason rather than religious belief or folk wisdom.

The Ancien Régime

A turning point in the struggle between French monarchs and provincial rulers came when Louis XIV (r. 1643–1715) sponsored the creation of a relatively efficient state bureaucracy, separate from the Crown's personal domain. France began to be administered according to a legal-rational code applied throughout the country.

The absolutist state created by Louis XIV and his successors coexisted with a complex system of taxes and feudal privileges that weighed heavily upon peasants, urban workers, and a rising middle class. Another target of popular discontent was the Catholic Church—a large landowner, tax collector, and ally of the feudal authorities. This complex patchwork of institutions was later described as the *ancien régime*, or old regime.

Pressure on the regime increased as Louis XIV and his successor, Louis XV, engaged in military adventures in Europe and colonial conquests overseas. From the mid-seventeenth to the mid-eighteenth century, France was usually at war with its neighbors. As the historian Simon Schama notes, "No other European power attempted to support both a major continental army and a transcontinental navy at the same time."[3] When Britain began to reap the benefits of the Agricultural and Industrial Revolutions and France's economy remained stagnant, the French monarchy was forced to borrow heavily to compete with Britain. By 1788, interest on past French loans consumed over one-half of current state expenditures.[4] When Louis XVI tried to raise taxes in 1789, he provoked a violent reaction that sealed the fate of the French monarchy.

The Two Faces of the French Revolution, 1789–1815

The angry crowd that burst through the gates of Paris's Bastille prison on July 14, 1789, to free the prisoners helped launch the French Revolution. In short order, the French monarchy and the entire *ancien régime* of nobility and feudal privileges were abolished. A succession of revolutionary regimes quickly followed, including the Constituent Assembly (which in 1789 issued the world-famous Declaration of the Rights of Man and the Citizen), the Legislative Assembly, the Convention, and the Directory.

It is difficult to overestimate the impact of the Revolution on French and world history. Historian Lynn Hunt observes, "The chief accomplishment of the French Revolution was the institution of a dramatically new political culture. . . . The French Revolution may be said to represent the transition to political and social modernity, the first occasion when the people entered upon the historical stage to remake the political community."[5] The First Republic, created in 1792, was the

first modern European regime based on the principle that all citizens, regardless of social background, were equal before the law.

The Revolution of 1789 was at the same time a *national* revolution, which affirmed the people's right to choose their own political regime; an *international* revolution, which inspired national uprisings elsewhere in Europe, often promoted by French armed intervention; a *liberal* revolution, which championed individual liberty in the political and economic spheres, as well as secularism and religious freedom, instead of state-mandated dominance by the Catholic Church in religious affairs; and a *democratic* revolution, which proclaimed that all citizens have the right to participate in making key political decisions. The Revolution's provocative ideas have spread far beyond France's borders and have become part of our universal heritage.

The Revolution exhibited serious flaws. Although the revolutionary regime proclaimed the values of liberty, equality, and fraternity, it treated opponents with brutality. During the Reign of Terror, the Jacobin state—the radical faction that triumphed over moderates within the revolutionary camp—guillotined opponents of the Revolution, along with many revolutionaries from its own and other factions. Despite some reforms that were in women's interests (for example, short-lived divorce legislation), the Revolution was quite hostile to women: "The [First] Republic was constructed against women, not just without them, and nineteenth-century Republicans did not actively counteract this masculinist heritage of republicanism."[6]

In other ways, too, the Revolution left a complex legacy. Alexis de Tocqueville, a brilliant French aristocrat and writer in the nineteenth century, identified two quite opposite faces of the Revolution: it both produced a rupture with the *ancien régime* and powerfully strengthened state institutions, a goal pursued by French monarchs. Many of the centralizing institutions that were created by the revolutionary regime and by Napoleon Bonaparte, the popular general who seized power in 1799 and proclaimed himself emperor in 1802, remain to this day. For example, the Napoleonic Code of Law is a detailed legal framework; its two hundredth anniversary was celebrated with great pomp in 2004. Since Napoleon's defeat in 1815, French politics has often involved the question of how to reconcile state autonomy—the state's independence from pressure coming from groups within society—with democratic participation and decision making.

The Revolution produced enduring scars. First, the Revolution's hostility toward organized religion, in particular the Catholic Church, deeply polarized French society. Further, the Revolution's disdain for pragmatism and compromise has intensified political conflict. Scholars often compare the French style of historical development described here with the British. Although Britain saw its share of instability in an early period (notably, the Revolution of the 1640s and 1650s), since then it has exhibited a pattern of relatively peaceful, incremental change that contrasts dramatically with France's political style.

Many Regimes, Slow Industrialization: 1815–1940

During the nineteenth and twentieth centuries, France confronted the powerful and complex legacy of the Revolution of 1789. Following Napoleon's defeat in 1815, the monarchy was restored (hence the name, the Restoration). It was overthrown in a popular uprising in July 1830, and the king's distant cousin, Louis Philippe, assumed the throne. (This regime is known as the July Monarchy.) In 1848, another revolution produced the short-lived Second Republic. Louis Napoleon, the nephew of Napoleon Bonaparte, overthrew the republic after three years and proclaimed himself emperor. When France lost the Franco-Prussian War of 1870–1871, a revolutionary upheaval produced the Paris Commune, a brief experiment in worker-governed democracy. The Commune was violently crushed after a few months, to be succeeded by the Third Republic, which was created after France's military defeat and civil war in 1871. Thus, in the century following the Revolution of 1789, France oscillated between monarchy and radical democracy. Ever since the creation of the Third Republic, however, France has been ruled by democratic republics, save for a brief period during World War II.

The Third Republic was a parliamentary regime with a feeble executive. Given the legacy of Napoleon's illegal seizure of power and the ideologically fragmented state of French society, the republic was designed to prevent decisive leadership. The Third Republic never commanded much support. (It was described, in a famous phrase by conservative politician Adolphe Thiers, as the regime "that divides us [French] least.") Yet it proved France's most durable modern regime. It survived the terrible ordeal of World War I and held firm against extremist forces on the right during the 1920s and 1930s, when republics were crumbling in Germany, Italy, and Spain. However, the Third Republic collapsed when it failed to check the Nazi invasion of France in 1940.

The regime changes in the nineteenth and twentieth centuries highlight the sharp cleavages and the absence of political institutions capable of regulating conflict. However, in sharp contrast with the dizzying pace at which regimes came and went, the rate of economic change in France during this period was quite gradual. Compared with Germany, its dynamic neighbor to the northeast, France chose economic stability over modernization.

Although France began the nineteenth century as the world's second economic power, close behind Britain, by 1900 it had fallen to fourth, after Britain, the United States, and Germany. A large peasantry acted as a brake on industrialization, as did the fact that France was poorly endowed with coal, iron, and petroleum. Historians have also pointed to the relatively underdeveloped entrepreneurial spirit in France. French manufacturers excelled in producing custom-made luxury goods, such as silk fabrics and porcelain, which did not lend themselves to mechanized production and for which mass markets did not exist.

Another factor inhibiting industrial development was the slow growth of the French population. In the mid-nineteenth century, France was the most populous nation in Europe after Russia. However, although the British population tripled in the nineteenth century and the number of Germans doubled, France's population increased by less than one-half.[7] Slow population growth meant smaller demand, less incentive for businesses to invest, and a relatively weaker state compared to Britain and Germany.

State policies also played a key role in explaining France's lag in economic modernization. In Britain, the government removed restrictions on the free operation of market forces, and in Prussia (later Germany), the powerful chancellor, Otto von Bismarck, imposed industrialization from above. Economic historian Richard Kuisel observes that "rarely, if ever, did [the French state] act to promote economic expansion, plan development, or advance economic democracy." Instead, the state aimed to "maintain an equilibrium among industry, commerce, and agriculture and attempt[ed] to insulate France from the distress and upheaval that had struck other nations bent upon rapid economic advance."[8] In order to shield farmers, manufacturers, and artisans from foreign competition, France retained some of the highest tariff barriers in Western Europe in the nineteenth and early twentieth centuries.

Yet the state did not simply prevent economic modernization. In a tradition dating back to Colbert, the finance minister of Louis XIV who directed the creation of the French merchant marine, the state did sponsor several large-scale economic projects. For example, in the 1860s under Louis Napoleon, the state organized an integrated national rail network; encouraged the formation of the Crédit Mobilier, an investment bank to finance railroad development; and guaranteed interest rates on bonds sold to underwrite railroad construction.

From the seventeenth through the nineteenth centuries, alongside its role in maintaining order within France, the state carved out colonies in North and South America, the Caribbean, North Africa, sub-Saharan Africa, and South and Southeast Asia. By the end of the nineteenth century, France was second only to Britain as a colonial power. Under the pretext of bringing civilization to "backward" areas—the French term was *la mission civilisatrice*"—France extracted resources from its colonies and transformed the colonies into protected markets for French exports. Most colonies eventually gained their independence in the 1960s, in some cases after armed struggle. But the legacy of colonialism occasionally generates controversy. In 2005, over the opposition of the left and of President Chirac, right-wing deputies amended a proposed law requiring public schools to teach about the "positive role of [French] colonization."

To sum up, through much of the nineteenth century and well into the twentieth century, the state sought to preserve political stability rather than promote economic modernization. Slow economic growth did not prevent political conflict. But it did contribute to France's humiliating defeat by Germany in 1940.

Vichy France (1940–1944) and the Fourth Republic (1946–1958)

World War II was one of the bleakest periods in French history. When France was overrun by Germany in 1940, Marshall Henri Philippe Pétain, an aged World War I military hero, destroyed the Third Republic by signing an armistice with Hitler. The agreement divided France in two. The north was under direct German occupation; in the south, Pétain presided over a puppet regime, whose capital was at Vichy. The Vichy regime attacked progressive elements in the Third Republic. It collaborated with the Nazi occupation, for example, sending one million French workers to factories in Germany and shipping enormous quantities of manufactured goods and food to Germany. It was the only political regime in Western Europe not directly under German occupation that actively assisted the Nazi campaign against Jews. It rounded up 76,000 French and foreign Jews, including 12,000 children, and shipped them to German death camps.

Contrary to a myth created after the war that there was widespread opposition to Vichy, the vast majority of French citizens accepted the Vichy government's authority. However, small numbers of Communists, Socialists, and progressive Catholic forces took up arms against the Vichy regime and the German occupation. At immense personal risk, its members provided intelligence to the Allied war effort, blew up bridges, and assassinated Vichy and Nazi officials. Charles de Gaulle, an army general and junior cabinet minister, who had opposed the armistice and escaped to England when it was signed, gained control over the resistance movement. At the war's end, he succeeded in gaining recognition from allied governments as France's legitimate leader.

After World War II, a widely shared view held that the Vichy regime had been isolated and despised. It took fully half a century for a French president to publicly acknowledge French responsibility for the horrors of the Vichy regime. In 1995, President Jacques Chirac declared, "Those dark hours will forever tarnish our history and are a disgrace to our past and to our tradition. We all know that the criminal madness of the [German] occupying forces was assisted by the French, that is, the French state."

In 1945, following the German defeat, de Gaulle, the heroic symbol of French patriotism, proposed a new regime to avoid the errors that he believed had produced France's moral decline and military defeat. In his view, the Third Republic's parliamentary system, with its many parties, shifting alliances, and frequent changes of government, had blurred responsibility for governing and prevented forceful leadership. He proposed a regime with a powerful and independent executive. When French citizens, with the memory of the authoritarian Vichy regime still fresh, rejected de Gaulle's plan, he abruptly retired from politics.

The Fourth Republic, which was created in 1946 and survived for a dozen years, embodied an extreme form of parliamentary rule with a weak executive. The constitution gave parliament a near-monopoly of power, which it exercised in quite destructive fashion: governments were voted out of office about once every six months! An important reason for the absence of stable governing coalitions in the National Assembly, the powerful lower house of parliament, was that elections were held by proportional representation (PR). This is a procedure by which seats in the legislature are distributed in proportion to the number of votes that parties receive. The result is that many parties were represented in parliament. As in the Third Republic, rapid shifts in party alliances meant that governments lacked the cohesion and authority to make tough decisions and develop long range policies. Despite these handicaps, the Fourth Republic can be credited with some important achievements, notably setting France on the road to economic expansion and modernization. Moreover, the Fourth Republic would doubtless have survived had it dealt effectively with a rebellion by forces seeking independence in Algeria, a territory in North Africa that the French considered part of France.

De Gaulle cleverly exploited the military stalemate in Algeria to regain power in 1958. When the French army threatened to topple the republic to protest what it claimed was indecisive leadership, de Gaulle persuaded parliament to name him prime minister and propose a new regime that embodied the strong executive leadership that he considered essential.

The Fifth Republic (1958 to the Present)

The contrast between the Fourth and Fifth republics provides a textbook case of how institutions shape political life. The Fourth Republic could be described as all talk and little action: parliament endlessly debated, and voted to make and unmake governments; political leaders were unable to address the nation's pressing problems. On the other hand, in the Fifth Republic, political leaders are empowered to act decisively, but the regime lacks adequate mechanisms to hold leaders accountable to parliament and public opinion.

Despite the fact that de Gaulle seized power under unsavory circumstances, he commanded wide popular support. Resistance hero and commanding presence, de Gaulle persuaded the French to accept a regime that endowed the executive with extensive power. However, his high-handed governing style as president provoked increasing opposition.

The most dramatic example came in May 1968, when students and workers engaged in the largest general strike in Western European history. For weeks, workers and students occupied factories, offices, and universities, and the regime's survival hung in the balance. Although de Gaulle regained control of the situation, he was discredited and resigned from office the following year.

The Fifth Republic was again severely tested in 1981. For twenty-three years, the same broad political coalition, representing the conservative forces that took power in 1958, had won every single national election. In 1981, economic stagnation and divisions among conservative forces enabled Socialist Party candidate François Mitterrand to be elected president. In the parliamentary elections that followed, Mitterrand's supporters won a decisive victory. The peaceful transition demonstrated that the institutions of the Fifth Republic were sturdy enough to accommodate political alternation.

President Mitterrand's Socialist government sponsored an ambitious reform agenda that included strengthening the autonomy of the judiciary, the media, and local governments. The centerpiece was a substantial increase of industrial firms, banks, and insurance companies in the public sector. However, at the very moment that Mitterrand captured the presidency, conservative leaders Margaret Thatcher in Britain and Ronald Reagan in the

"What!?? The president's a Socialist and the Eiffel Tower is still standing!??" "Incredible!"
Source: Courtesy Plantu, Cartoonists and Writers Syndicate, from *Le Monde,* May 1981.

United States were elected to leadership positions on an opposite platform. After the Socialist experiment began to provoke a crisis in 1983–1984, because of political opposition and the high cost of funding the reforms, Mitterrand reluctantly changed course. Since that time, French governments of left and right alike have pursued market-friendly policies, and the ideological war of left and right in France, which had raged for centuries, has declined.

Does the convergence between center-left and center-right parties mean the end of major political conflict in France? Not at all, as the 2002 presidential elections (and a referendum on the European Union in 2005 described later in this chapter) demonstrate.

The Le Pen Bombshell of 2002

Dramatic evidence of political malaise occurred in the 2002 presidential elections, whose results sent shock waves around the world. Two rounds of elections are usually required to select a French president. If no candidate gains an absolute majority at the first round—the typical case since many candidates compete at this stage—a runoff ballot is held between the two front-runners. When the 2002 election campaign opened, it was universally assumed that the two candidates who would face off in the decisive runoff ballot would be center-left Socialist Prime Minister Lionel Jospin and center-right President Jacques Chirac. They were candidates of the two largest parties, and these parties had alternated in office for decades. It was assumed in 2002 that the first ballot was merely a prelude to the runoff between Chirac and Jospin. On the eve of the election, a *New York Times* reporter explained why the campaign was so lackluster: "Part of the problem, experts say, is that there is little suspense."[9]

However, soon after the polls closed, apathy turned to stupefaction. Although Chirac came in first, according to script, Jospin was nudged out of second place by Jean-Marie Le Pen, the candidate of the Front National (FN), a far-right demagogue whose targets include Muslim immigrants, Jews, gays, and mainstream politicians. Commentators routinely described the first round outcome as a *bombshell* and *earthquake.* *Le Monde,* France's most influential newspaper, spoke for most French when its front-page editorial declared, "France is wounded."[10]

Immediately after the first ballot, virtually everyone who had voted for Jospin and other leftist candidates swallowed their distaste and supported Chirac. At the runoff ballot, Chirac trounced Le Pen 82 to 18 percent, the most lopsided vote in the history of the Fifth Republic. Yet Le Pen's exploit remains a vivid memory, and the FN remains a significant presence in contemporary French politics. Le Pen's exploit highlights a disturbing cleavage in French politics that raises troubling questions about the Fifth Republic's institutions.

Five years later, in 2007, another presidential election occurred. The memory of Le Pen's success in 2002 was still fresh. This time, Le Pen received only 10.5 percent of the first ballot vote and came in fourth. Did he fare less well because voters rejected his ultra-conservative positions? Probably not. The main reason was that Nicolas Sarkozy, the candidate from the major mainstream center-right party, appropriated some of the themes from Le Pen's playbook, including the value of patriotism, the need to safeguard national identity,

***Le Monde's* cartoonist compares Le Pen's attack on Chirac and Jospin to the bombing of the twin towers of the World Trade Center.**
Source: Courtesy Plantu, Cartoonists and Writers Syndicate, from *Le Monde*, April 23, 2002, p. 1.

and tough measures to reduce crime and illegal immigration. Many former Le Pen supporters calculated that voting for Sarkozy would be the most effective way to defend their conservative values.

France after September 11

Following the terrorist attacks on the United States of September 11, 2001, France has been deeply involved in conflicts involving terrorism. France is home to about five million Muslims, the largest Muslim population in West Europe. The vast majority are peaceful. And no deadly attacks have occurred in France in recent years comparable to those that occurred in Madrid in 2005 and London in 2006. However, a few French citizens have been implicated in radical Islamic terrorist activity. (There are also two French separatist movements using violent methods, described in Chapter 10.) In 2001, a plan was foiled to bomb the U.S. Embassy in Paris. In 2003, French antiterrorist police detained eighteen Algerians and Pakistanis in the Paris area on charges that they were linked to Al Qaeda. In 2004, a French suicide bomber attacked U.S. forces in Falluja, Iraq. During this period, seven French citizens were imprisoned at the U.S. detention center in Guantanamo. In 2006, Zacarias Moussaoui, a French citizen, was convicted and sentenced to life imprisonment in the United States on charges that he had helped plan the September 11 attacks. In 2007, French antiterrorism police charged eleven people with participating in an Iraqi insurgency network linked to Al Qaeda.

France has energetically targeted terrorism, and French and U.S. intelligence agencies cooperate closely in antiterrorism activities. President Chirac was the first foreign leader to visit the United States after September 11, 2001. He toured ground zero in New York with President Bush a week after 9/11. France supported the U.S. military action against Al Qaeda and the Taliban regime in Afghanistan in 2001, and French troops served in Afghanistan during and after the initial invasion. However, France intensely opposed the U.S. plan to topple the regime of Saddam Hussein in Iraq in 2003. In a speech at the United Nations shortly before the war, French foreign minister Dominique de Villepin (who later became prime minister) denounced the U.S. plan, and France led an international coalition opposing the war.

The roots of French anti-Americanism predate the Iraq war or George W. Bush's presidency. French distrust of the United States has deep social, cultural, and geopolitical roots. French public opinion surveys report that the French are "apprehensive about the United States acting as world leader, fearful of its hegemony, and mistrustful of its alleged ambitions and its motives. They, moreover, dislike many of America's social policies and are critical of our values."[11]

Yet French and the United States are not simply at loggerheads. American films, television programs, and popular music are enormously popular in France. France and the United States have close economic ties. For example, the United States is the largest foreign investor in France. American companies with operations in France employ 550,000 workers, and French companies with operations in the United States employ 600,000 American workers.

The French "Non"—Now or Forever?

The last critical juncture involves France's relationship to Europe. Throughout the history of the European Union (EU), the organization of twenty-seven European countries that seeks to promote economic and political integration, the French have been a guiding force. From the beginning, France was among the most influential voices within the EU, usually throwing its weight behind closer cooperation among member states. France has taken the lead in setting European agendas and initiating new measures to strengthen European integration. A French citizen, Jean Monnet, was informally known as the Father of Europe: he conceived the European Coal and Steel Community after World War II that replaced a century of French-German hostility with economic cooperation. In the 1980s, another Frenchman, Jacques Delors, as president of the European Commission, provided the energy and vision to breathe new life into the Union.

In 2005, the French again influenced the shape of the EU, but this time in a very different way. After two years of difficult negotiations, an EU commission chaired by former French president Valéry Giscard d'Estaing produced a draft EU constitution. It streamlined decision making, increased the influence of the European parliament, and created the offices of president and foreign minister. It was also an extraordinarily long and complicated document. Few citizens and probably not many political leaders bothered to read its 448 articles. But the symbolic and substantive message delivered by the draft constitution was clear: it was intended to represent another giant step forward in the process of European integration.

EU regulations require that all member states approve changes in its organization and powers. By May 2005, ten member states had approved the draft constitution. No country had rejected it. French president Jacques Chirac could have requested that the French parliament ratify the treaty and approval would

have been a forgone conclusion. Instead, he asked French citizens to ratify the treaty in a nationwide referendum. At the time, polls suggested that it would be approved by a wide margin. However, as months passed, opposition swelled. By early 2005, it was clear that Chirac had blundered. Despite the fact that the major French governing parties—bitter opponents on most issues—campaigned hard for a yes vote, French voters defeated the referendum in May 2005 by the wide margin of 55 to 45 percent. Their action precipitated one of the greatest crises in the EU's fifty-year history. Two factors explain the defeat of the referendum.

The EU's Impact on the Economy. Polls suggested that nearly half of those opposing the draft constitution did so because they feared that it would further increase France's already high unemployment rate. The most economically vulnerable sections of the population, those most in danger of losing their jobs, were most likely to oppose the treaty: an astonishingly high 81 percent of workers and 60 percent of lower-middle-class voters opposed the treaty. Thus, the EU referendum pitted a more prosperous, economically secure France against a France more fearful of the increased insecurity that a stronger EU would produce.

The Partisan Factor. A second factor explaining the defeat of the referendum was a split in the Socialist Party (PS), one of France's major governing parties and a traditional supporter of the EU. Although the PS bitterly opposed conservative President Chirac, most party leaders reluctantly lobbied for approval of the draft constitution. However, many Socialist voters rejected their leaders' advice. Exit polls revealed that 59 percent of the PS electorate voted "no" in the referendum—enough to tip the balance toward rejection.[12]

The outcome of the referendum sent shock waves through France second only to the 2002 presidential election. It suggested that many French citizens feared participation in the EU and perhaps in the wider global arena as well. The vote also highlighted a gulf between mainstream political leaders—most of whom campaigned for a yes vote—and the majority of French voters. The controversy invites us to analyze the character of French political culture and its relation to political institutions, policies, and economy.

The Sarkozy Presidency: Same Old, Same Old—Or a New Beginning?

Did a new era begin in 2007 with the election of Nicolas Sarkozy and a pro-Sarkozy majority in parliament? Will the Sarkozy presidency constitute a critical juncture or the "same old, same old"? By "same old" is meant a continuation of an enduring pattern in French politics, the gulf between the state and civil society. As we have seen, the state has played a central role in French historical development—at the same time that citizens often resist state directives. In extreme cases, opposition has taken a revolutionary form. Nowadays, citizens more commonly mount strikes and demonstrations to block state action. The result is often stalemate.

President Sarkozy was elected in large part because he promised a fresh start. He advocated bold new approaches to deal with an ailing economy, high unemployment, undocumented immigration, crime, and threats to social cohesion and national identity. The French agree that much needs to be done—but they intensely disagree about what precisely *should* be done! Given his reputation for being boundlessly ambitious, short-tempered, and impetuous, Sarkozy seemed ill-equipped to engage in the kind of broad consultation necessary to nurture cooperative solutions to these problems. The bold new approaches that he promised could quickly provoke crisis. At the same time, President Sarkozy's first initiatives after his election suggested that he might break the logjam that has characterized French politics for decades. For example, he appointed several prominent Socialist politicians to positions in his administration, including Bernard Kouchner to the key cabinet position of foreign minister. Kouchner is co-founder of Médecins Sans Frontières—Doctors Without Borders—the humanitarian organization that was awarded the Nobel Peace Prize. He was a leading member of the Socialist party and had campaigned for Ségolène Royal during the presidential election. President Sarkozy also met with France's labor unions right after his election in an attempt to jump-start social policy initiatives. If he

acts as a conciliator and not as a gladiator, the result may indeed be a fresh start, rather than "same old, same old."

Themes and Implications

Our analysis of the evolution of French development has identified some key turning points in French history. It is useful to highlight the distinctive ways that France has addressed the four key themes that provide our framework for analyzing comparative politics.

Historical Junctures and Political Themes

Analyzing the four themes that frame *European Politics in Transition* reveals dramatic changes in French politics in the past few decades.

France in a World of States. For over a century following Napoleon's defeat in 1815, the country displayed an inward-looking, isolationist orientation by maintaining high tariff barriers to minimize international trade. At the same time, France aggressively increased its colonial possessions beyond North Africa to Southeast Asia, sub-Saharan Africa, and the Pacific. Until the 1950s, France had access to the mineral resources of its colonies while the colonies served as a protected market for French manufactured exports. But in the long run this exploitative relationship was harmful not only to the colonies but to the French economy as well because it sheltered France from international competition and stifled technological and industrial development. France's integration in the EU and participation in the global economy have enabled the French economy to become more modern and efficient and helped France compete in the international economy. Yet, as will be described in Chapter 7, the French economy has developed significant weaknesses.

France's tortured relationship with Germany—the two countries fought three devastating wars in less than a century—has weighed heavily on state development. The fact that France and Germany have had cordial relations since the end of World War II, thanks to the EU and the expansion of the European and world economies, has provided France with vastly increased

The world's longest and tallest multispan bridge, Millau, France.   *Source:* © Chris Hellier/Corbis

security. The alliance between the two countries has been vital in promoting European economic and political integration. The countries also sponsored a joint military force that served in Afghanistan—a project that would have been unthinkable during the century of mutual hostility. They also jointly opposed the U.S. and British military intervention in Iraq in 2003.

Although a middle-rank power, France remains an important player on the world stage. For example, it has developed nuclear weapons and sophisticated military technology. France is among the world's leading arms exporters. It is a major participant in the Western alliance led by the United States. But, in contrast to Britain and Germany, it has often been a gadfly to the United States.

The French state has been a powerful, capable instrument, helping the country adapt to the challenges posed by global economic competition. In recent decades, the state has promoted internationally acclaimed high-tech industrial projects, including rapid rail travel (the TGV, that is, *train à grande vitesse*); leadership in the European consortium that

developed the Airbus wide-bodied airplane; and relatively safe and cheap nuclear-powered electricity.

France's high-tech achievements rank among the world's best. For example, TGVs carry passengers from one end of France to the other at average speeds of nearly 200 miles an hour! In a test run of the latest version of the TGV in 2007, the train set a world speed record of 261 miles an hour on a newly constructed line between Paris and Strasbourg, in eastern France. In 2004, the tallest and longest multispan bridge in the world was built in central France. These projects were made possible by France's powerful and well-financed state. But they may also represent the end of a wave of state-sponsored innovation. International economic competition, EU and other treaty commitments, ideological shifts, and citizens' demands for more autonomy have challenged France's statist tradition.

Governing the Economy.   The heyday of statism followed World War II. Thanks to state planning, loans and subsidies to private business, and crash programs to develop key industries, the French economy soared. However, the postwar style of state direction, useful in an era when France was relatively underdeveloped, is problematic in the current period, when rapidly changing technology and economic globalization put a premium on flexibility. Chapter 7 describes the state's more modest role.

At the same time, citizens fiercely resist the state's attempt to retrench when they judge that the result lowers living standards. In particular, government initiatives to reduce state spending on social programs, such as medical care, pensions, and unemployment insurance, have provoked popular explosions that, although often successful in preventing change in the short run, only postpone dealing with the very real problem of how to pay for costly social programs.

The Democratic Idea.   France has a complex relationship to the democratic idea. On the one hand, an antidemocratic orientation linked to France's strong statist tradition tends to assume that popular participation and decision making hamper rational direction by qualified, objective leaders. On the other hand, France has passionately promoted two quite different democratic currents. The first, inspired by philosopher Jean-Jacques Rousseau in the eighteenth century, stipulates that citizens should participate directly in political decisions rather than merely choose leaders. This idea nourishes the protests, like those of May 1968, that periodically challenge established institutions. A second democratic current, identified with republican values, rejects direct democracy in favor of representative or parliamentary government. Opponents of de Gaulle regarded him as trampling on representative democracy and exercising *le pouvoir personnel* (personal power).

France's democratic theory and institutions face important challenges. The no vote in the referendum of 2005 on the EU constitution highlights that French citizens fear entrusting their fate to distant and, in their view, undemocratic institutions. Another problem involves the chronic difficulty of reconciling state autonomy and democratic participation within France. The concrete form of this problem, as we will describe in Chapter 8, is defining the appropriate powers and relationship of the executive and legislature within the French political system.

Politics of Collective Identity.   French national identity has always been closely linked to state formation. The Revolution championed an inclusive assimilationist orientation that welcomed newcomers into the political system—as long as they accepted dominant republican values. The French approach stresses the importance of shared political values rather than inherited racial or ethnic characteristics. At the same time, it is generally believed that ethnic, racial, religious, or gender identities should remain confined to the private sphere and play no role in the public arena. The French typically regard multiculturalism as a destructive approach that fragments the body politic.

Nevertheless, France can hardly be considered a unified society. Indeed, it has typically been deeply divided by social, economic, and cultural cleavages. In the period after World War II, there was sharp opposition between a working-class subculture, closely linked to the powerful French Communist Party (Parti communiste français—PCF), and a Catholic subculture, in which the Church played a key role. In recent decades, these subcultures have declined in importance. The PCF has become a small and insignificant splinter party, and nowadays only 12 percent of French Catholics attend mass weekly.[13]

As old cleavages declined, however, new ones have developed. French national identity has been destabilized recently by ethnic conflict and globalization. Jean-Marie Le Pen and the FN gained widespread support by charging that unemployment, crime, and urban decay are caused by Muslim immigrants and their children. At the same time, many second-generation immigrants (native-born French citizens whose parents are immigrants) consider themselves fully French, but are often treated as second-class citizens. A particularly disturbing development has been a wave of violence against French Jews by neo-Nazis and Muslim youth. French national identity has also been jostled by French participation in the EU and globalization.

Implications for Comparative Politics

The study of French politics offers rich lessons for the study of comparative politics. Scholars have coined the term *French exceptionalism* to highlight that French politics is distinctive. A central feature is intense ideological conflict, which in turn has fueled political instability reflected in frequent regime change. Does the exceptional character of French politics rule out comparison? Quite the contrary! For without comparison, we cannot identify and explain what is exceptional about France.

Because France has continually tried to reshape its destiny by conscious political direction, it provides a natural laboratory to test the importance of variations in institutional design. To illustrate, because France's political institutions have often changed within a brief period, comparativists can measure the impact of institutions on political outcomes. One fascinating example was a 1999 constitutional amendment that mandated gender parity in political recruitment. From one election to the next, the proportion of women on municipal and regional councils ballooned. These councils now have virtually equal numbers of men and women.

At a more general level, the French have often expected the state to pursue important economic and political goals. In countries without a strong statist tradition (for example, the United States and Britain), private groups must rely on their own efforts. What can we learn from comparing the two approaches? What are the strengths and weaknesses of statism?

A place to begin our analysis of current French politics is with France's political economy, for the way that a country organizes economic governance deeply influences the functioning of its political system.

Notes

[1] *Le Monde*, March 20, 2007.

[2] INSEE, *Tableaux de l'Économie Française, 2003–2004* (Paris: INSEE, 2003), pp. 45–47. GDP, per capita income, and cell phone statistics from the UNDP, *Human Development Report 2006*.

[3] Simon Schama, *Citizens: A Chronicle of the French Revolution* (New York: Knopf, 1989), p. 62.

[4] Perry Anderson, *Lineages of the Absolutist State* (London: New Left Books, 1974), p. 111. See also Theda Skocpol, *States and Social Revolutions: A Comparative Analysis of France, Russia, and China* (New York: Cambridge University Press, 1979).

[5] Lynn Hunt, *Politics, Culture, and Class in the French Revolution* (Berkeley and Los Angeles: University of California Press, 1984), pp. 15, 56.

[6] Joan B. Landes, *Women and the Public Sphere in the Age of the French Revolution* (Ithaca, N.Y.: Cornell University Press, 1988), pp. 171–172.

[7] William H. Sewell Jr., *Work and Revolution in France: The Language of Labor from the Old Regime to 1848* (Cambridge: Cambridge University Press, 1980), p. 199.

[8] Richard F. Kuisel, *Capitalism and the State in Modern France* (Cambridge: Cambridge University Press, 1981), pp. 15–16.

[9] Suzanne Daley, "As French Campaign Ends, Many Focus on Next Round," *New York Times*, April 20, 2002.

[10] *Le Monde*, April 23, 2002.

[11] Richard Kuisel, "What Do the French Think of Us? The Deteriorating Image of the United States, 2000–2004," *French Politics, Culture, and Society* 22, no. 3 (Fall 2004): 107.

[12] *Le Monde*, May 30, 2005.

[13] *New York Times*, April 19, 2005.

CHAPTER 7

Political Economy and Development

France's gross national product (GNP) makes it the world's sixth-largest economy. It has accomplished this feat by a combination of skill, state management, and favorable historical and geographic circumstances. (France is in the center of one of the world's most economically developed regions.) Prior to the 1980s, the state played a key role in shaping and steering the economy. Since then, there has been a sharp increase in the importance of markets and a corresponding decline in the state's role because of an ideological shift, EU commitments, and globalization. Accompanying these changes has been a shift from an inward-looking economic posture to an export orientation that has transformed France into a major participant in the global economy. France now ranks among the top few countries in the world in the amount of capital invested abroad and as a location for foreign investment.

Yet the French economic record is not simply one of success. Unemployment has hovered around 10 percent for decades, although it has declined in the past several years. In the 1990s, France was the fourth-largest economy in the world and ranked seventh in per capita income. Today it has slipped to sixth-largest and seventeenth in per capita income of its citizens. The purchasing power of French citizens has recently fallen below the median for the EU. France is now outranked by, among other countries, Britain, Belgium, Norway, Finland, and Ireland.[1] To account for both the successes and failures of the French economy, a good place to start is the period following World War II, when the French economy began a rapid ascent.

The New French Revolution

During the nineteenth century, when Britain and Germany were becoming the leading industrial powers in Western Europe, the French state sought to preserve traditional groups and contain political conflict. The Third Republic's humiliating failure to meet the Nazi threat in 1940 proved a turning point.

When France was liberated and the Fourth Republic was created in 1946, influential groups active in the Resistance concluded that economic and social modernization was essential, both to rebuild after the ravages of war and to ensure that the country would remain on the path of progress. They judged that the

project required a fundamental transformation in the state's relationship to the economy. "After the war," Richard Kuisel observes, "what was distinctive about France was the compelling sense of relative economic backwardness. This impulse was the principal stimulus for economic renovation and set France apart from other countries."[2] The modernizers were enormously successful. One study described the postwar shift as "a new French Revolution. Although peaceful, this has been just as profound as that of 1789 because it has totally overhauled the moral foundations and social equilibrium of French society."[3]

State and Economy

The new French Revolution involved sweeping changes in the economy, society, and values. As a result of its statist tradition of economic management, France was potentially able to develop the institutional capacity to steer the economy—once the goal shifted from economic protection to economic expansion. From guardian of the established order, the state became the sponsor of social and economic progress, an approach often described as *dirigisme*. The project was brilliantly successful. In a few decades, France was transformed into a dynamic industrialized economy.

French-Style Economic Management

The French developed a variety of techniques to foster economic modernization. In the French model of economic management, the state was a (indeed, *the*) chief player.

Planning. After World War II, the French developed techniques of state economic management. A key element was indicative planning, in which a national Planning Commission of civil servants appointed by the government established broad national economic and social priorities for the next four or five years. The Planning Commission was assisted by modernization commissions, whose members were public and private officials. Unlike the coercive style of Soviet planning, indicative planning was developed and implemented by democratic procedures. Successive plans established maximum feasible rates of economic growth, proposed crash programs for the development of specific industries and regions, and identified social priorities such as educational targets.

De Gaulle's Leadership.   Planning began in the Fourth Republic, but the process was given a shot in the arm in 1958 when Charles de Gaulle, the most influential politician in twentieth-century French history, returned to power. A complex, controversial, and contradictory figure, de Gaulle was a faithful representative of traditional France, deeply attached to the values of order and hierarchy, which earned him the enmity of the left. Yet he was also a rebel: he believed that if France was to play a leading role on the world stage, shock therapy was needed to strengthen the French economy.

Dirigisme.   General de Gaulle extended the style of state-led industrialization and growth originating in the Fourth Republic. The state financed favored industrial sectors and firms, and it encouraged the creation of large firms, which were dubbed "national champions." Key economic decisions were made in governmental ministries and the planning agency. State leadership compensated for the relatively weak role played by private entrepreneurs. Among the tools that the state deployed were subsidies, loans, and tax write-offs. The state also restructured key sectors, including steel, machine tools, and paper products, by steering credit and pressuring medium-sized industrial firms to merge to create "national champions" able to compete in world markets. And it created and managed entire industries. Some state-created and state-managed firms were in the vanguard of technological progress throughout the world. A prime example was nuclear power. The state reduced its dependence on imported petroleum by developing safe and reliable nuclear energy. Most of France's electricity is produced by nuclear reactors, and France is a world leader in designing, building, operating, and exporting nuclear power installations.

France's Economic Miracle

During the period that a French economist called "the thirty glorious years" (1945–1975), the planners and their allies were remarkably successful. French economic growth was among the world's highest during

Table 7.1

Average Growth Rates in Gross National Product, 1958–1973

Average Growth Rates in Gross National Product, 1958–1973

Japan	10.4%
France	5.5
Italy	5.3
West Germany	5.0
Belgium	4.9
Netherlands	4.2
Norway	4.2
Sweden	4.1
United States	4.1
United Kingdom	3.2

Source: Reprinted by permission of the State University of New York Press, from *The Fifth Republic at Twenty* by William G. Andrews and Stanley Hoffmann (eds). © 1981 State University of New York. All rights reserved.

this period—a striking contrast to the 1930s, when the French economy declined at the rate of over 1 percent annually (see Table 7.1). Economic growth produced higher living standards and the birth of a consumer society. Average yearly income nearly tripled between 1946 and 1962. After a century of economic stagnation, France leapfrogged into the twentieth century.

May 1968 and Beyond: Economic Crisis and Political Conflict

And yet, despite the dramatic economic growth of the 1950s and 1960s—or because of the way that economic restructuring was carried out—economic change generated political conflict. The Gaullist regime was superbly equipped to direct change. But by its arbitrary style and refusal to consult widely, it eventually provoked an explosive reaction.

The most dramatic challenge was a massive wave of strikes and demonstrations in May 1968, which immobilized the entire country for weeks. What united diverse groups—students, workers, artists, and professionals—was anger at the high-handed style of authority in universities, political institutions, and workplaces. Other European countries were also modernizing during this

Students and workers unite in a mass demonstration on the Left Bank of Paris, May 27, 1968.
Source: AP Images.

period. But, with the exception of Italy, no other country experienced such intense opposition movements.

The May movement was followed by years of intense labor mobilization. Strikes in the early 1970s were frequent and militant. A rapid increase in female employment, beginning in the early 1970s (see Figure 7.1), also provoked some important strikes by women protesting unequal treatment.

Economic Instability

Discontent increased when economic growth slowed in the mid-1970s. First, the shift of workers out of agriculture and from rural to urban areas began to reach its limit. Second, France was affected by steep increases in petroleum prices. The restructuring of international

capitalism in the 1970s further challenged French industry. When developing nations, including Taiwan, South Korea, and Brazil, developed basic industries, such as textiles, steel, and shipbuilding, the result was to eliminate hundreds of thousands of French jobs in these three industries alone. Entire regions were devastated. At the same time, advanced industrialized nations outstripped France in high-tech sectors like microelectronics, bioengineering, and robotics.

These trends provoked a crisis in the French model of development. The postwar state-centered approach helped promote crash programs for industrial reconstruction and modernization. But it was poorly suited to helping the French economy to decentralize decision making and compete effectively in the global economy.

Figure 7.1

Women in the Labor Force

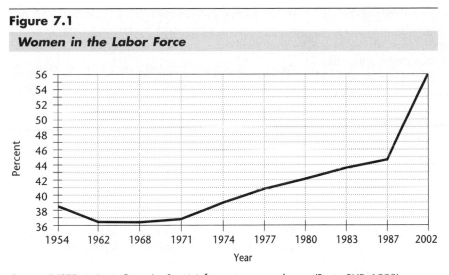

Source: INSEE, in Louis Dirn, *La Société française en tendances* (Paris: PUF, 1990), p. 108; 2002 data from INSEE, *Tableaux de l'Économie Française, 2003–2004* (Paris: INSEE, 2003), p. 77.

French Socialism in Practice— and Conservative Aftermath

After right-wing governments failed to meet the economic challenges of the 1970s, the left finally got the chance to try. A new era began when, after twenty-three years of conservative governments, Socialist candidate François Mitterrand defeated incumbent president Valéry Giscard d'Estaing in the 1981 presidential election, and elections to the National Assembly (the more powerful legislative chamber) weeks later resulted in a Socialist Party victory. The government quickly sponsored an array of radical reformist measures to revive the ailing economy, create jobs, and recapture domestic markets. They included the following:

- Sharp increases in social benefits, including hikes in the minimum wage, family allowances, old-age pensions, rent subsidies, and state-mandated paid vacations.
- The creation of public sector employment.
- State assistance to develop cutting-edge technologies (including biotech, telecommunications, and aerospace).
- The nationalization of many firms in the industrial and financial sectors. Following the nationalization measures, public sector firms accounted for 28 percent of

France's gross domestic production, 23 percent of French exports, and 36 percent of investments.[4] Thirteen of France's twenty largest industrial firms and most banks were integrated into the public sector.

The Socialist program extended the postwar *dirigiste* approach to economic governance, expanded social benefits, and created mechanisms for participation by rank-and-file workers and labor unions in economic decision making. Many citizens achieved significant gains from the Socialist program, and many of the newly nationalized firms were strengthened by the infusion of government subsidies.

The Socialist reform agenda helped modernize the French economy, society, and state in the long run. However, in the short run, it drove France to the brink of bankruptcy. Business interests in France bitterly opposed the government's Socialist policy orientation, and international investors avoided France like the plague. Private investment by French and foreign firms declined sharply in the early 1980s. Further, an international economic recession in the early 1980s reduced the demand for French exports, just when increased social spending enabled French consumers to buy foreign imports. The result was a severe trade imbalance. France's international currency reserves were rapidly exhausted. Something had to give—and fast.

The crisis cruelly demonstrated how limited was the margin of maneuver for a medium-rank power like France. Mitterrand reluctantly ordered an about-face in economic policy in 1983 and set France on a conservative course from which it has not departed since.

France's failure to achieve autonomous state-sponsored development in the early 1980s has often been cited as demonstrating the futility of nationally based radical or democratic socialist reforms. Within France, it helped discredit the traditional *dirigiste* pattern.

An indirect effect of the 1983 "right turn" was to propel European integration forward. Concluding that France could not exercise global power on its own, Mitterrand turned to the EU as the next-best alternative. Abandoning his initially lukewarm attitude toward European integration, Mitterrand energetically began to promote European economic, monetary, and political integration in the mid-1980s.

France's Neoliberal Modernization Strategy

Although the state has continued to play an important role in economic governance since 1983, it has scaled back its commanding role and often defers to private decision makers. The major elements in this market-friendly "neoliberal modernization strategy" are privatization, deregulation, and liberalization.[5]

Privatization.   Since 1983, governments of left and right alike have sponsored a sweeping privatization program. The decision to support privatization was especially wrenching for the Socialists, who had long championed nationalization and, as we have seen, had sponsored an extensive increase in public sector firms when elected in 1981.

Although privatization involves a drastic shift from public to private control, the change is less substantial than meets the eye. For example, there is considerable continuity in managerial ranks when firms are privatized. Many of France's largest private firms are directed by executives trained in state-run elite schools and belong to cohesive elite networks, described in Chapter 8, that span the public-private divide.

Employees of firms slated for privatization often mount strikes in key sectors like transportation and power supply. Employees fear cutbacks in wages and fringe benefits, job security, and rights to representation within the firm. These fears have often been justified.

Deregulation and Liberalization.   Until the right turn in 1983, state administrators were often responsible for defining technical standards for manufactured products; allocating market shares among firms; setting prices, interest rates, and terms of credit; and determining the type and location of investment. The state regulated labor markets by restricting employers' freedom to schedule work time and lay off workers.

State management could be highly effective. For example, the public railway network has a superb record for safety and performance. State labor inspectors limited arbitrary employer actions. However, critics claimed that the French economy was being strangled by kilometers of red tape.

A key element in the Socialists' right turn, extended by governments of left and right since then, was the deregulation of commodity, financial, and labor markets. Price controls have been largely eliminated. Government controls have been dismantled in the financial sector, where market forces, not ministry of finance officials, now determine how loans and investments will be made. Labor markets have become much more flexible, in that employers have greater freedom to hire, promote, deploy, and fire workers. Yet critics charge that deregulation has not gone far enough and that French labor markets remain overly rigid. Some claim that this contributes to France's high unemployment rate because employers are reluctant to hire new workers. President Sarkozy promises to revive economic growth and boost employment by loosening restrictions on employers' right to hire, supervise, and dismiss workers.

Impact of the European Union.   France's participation in the EU has further reduced the state's role in economic management. The Single European Act in 1987, the Maastricht Treaty in 1991, and the Growth and Stability Pact in 1997 have tied France more tightly to its European neighbors and limited state discretion.

EU directives encountered stiff popular resistance in France beginning in the 1990s. In 1995, when Prime Minister Alain Juppé proposed austerity measures to trim the budget deficit, the initiative provoked massive strikes by public sector workers that threatened the Juppé government's very existence. In 2003, Prime

GLOBAL CONNECTION: France and the European Union

France has been a charter member and one of the most powerful states in the European Union since it was founded in 1958. (The EU was originally known as the European Economic Community.) Before World War II, France had preferred isolation to international cooperation. But three devastating wars in less than a century between France and Germany taught both countries that there was no alternative but to cooperate. The EU was a resounding success in fostering closer ties between the two countries and the other member states of the organization. (The number of members has steadily increased to twenty-seven by 2007.)

The EU enjoyed widespread support in France during the first decades of its existence because it was credited with contributing to economic prosperity and political stability. French farmers received the largest share of the EU's lavish program of agricultural subsidies. As a result of the EU's adoption of a common currency, the euro, its sponsorship of lower tariffs among member states, as well as other measures to liberalize trade and investment, France developed extremely close economic relations with other countries in West Europe.

Yet French participation in the EU became increasingly controversial. Many French citizens fear that France's distinctive culture and identity,

as well as extensive welfare state programs, are threatened by membership in the EU. Citizens railed against what they regarded as unreasonable directives by faceless and arbitrary eurocrats in Brussels. Moreover, some of the EU decisions (agreed upon, it should be emphasized, by the French government) involve the need for sacrifice, notably, a requirement to limit government deficits.

When economic prosperity turned to stagnation in the 1980s, the EU began to be seen less as a blessing and more as a liability. A referendum sponsored by President Mitterrand in 1991 to ratify the Maastricht Treaty, which involved closer economic integration, barely passed.

As was described above, President Chirac's decision to hold a referendum to ratify the draft European constitution backfired.

The French veto did not mean the end of the EU: the many thousands of pages of EU treaty regulations and directives remain in force. But the French vote halted forward momentum for closer European integration and revealed a wide chasm between rank-and-file French voters and the governing parties.

President Sarkozy tried to end the stalemate produced by the French veto by proposing a scaled-back version of the draft constitution. However, conflict among EU members persists and the fate of the proposal hangs in the balance.

Minister Jean-Pierre Raffarin pushed through a pension reform despite massive strikes and demonstrations. In the 2005 referendum, popular opposition to what was regarded as the heavy hand of the EU helped tip the balance toward a no vote. (See "Global Connection: France and the European Union.")

The End of *Dirigisme*?   Although since the middle 1980s French governments have sponsored reforms to free market forces, they have done so in a distinctively French manner. For better or worse, statism is alive and well in France. Political scientist Vivien Schmidt observes that France has not "abandoned its statist model. . . . Governments have not stopped seeking to

guide business . . . even as they engineer the retreat of the state.[6]

Assessing French Economic Performance

The French economy faces daunting problems. For a starter, the French economy has stalled: during President Chirac's second term, economic growth was less than 2 percent annually, second only to Portugal within the EU. France has not been adept in shifting from an industrial society based on manufacturing to a postindustrial economy geared to the production of services. France's declining ability to remain at the top of world-class economies is reflected in a decline in competitiveness, as measured by France's export performance. One cause is that France has been devoting fewer resources than other leading countries to technological innovation. Other problems include persistent budget deficits, rising public debt, high taxes, and rigidities in a variety of economic sectors.

Underemployment also contributes to France's lagging economic performance. The average workweek for French workers employed full time is 39.1 hours, compared to 42.4 hours for British workers, and 40.3 hours for German workers. Moreover, this is only part of the problem of underemployment. We have stressed the importance of France's persistently high unemployment rate—second highest in the EU in 2007.

Underemployment is especially high among older and younger age groups. Whereas 49 percent of Germans and 58 percent of British between 55–64 years old are employed, the comparable figure for French workers is 38 percent. Whereas 15 percent of Germans and 14 percent of British under age 25 are unemployed, the comparable figure for young French is 21 percent.[7]

In order to reverse economic decline, drastic reforms are needed. However, disagreement rages over precisely which reforms are needed. For example, the two leading candidates in the 2007 presidential election held sharply opposing views. Socialist Ségolène Royal called for wage increases for the lowest paid workers and measures to promote cooperation among business groups and labor unions. Nicolas Sarkozy advocated unleashing free market forces, shrinking the size of the state, increasing the workweek, and postponing the retirement age. Sarkozy's election, along with that of a solid parliamentary majority, enabled him to implement his approach. Whether the result will be an improvement in economic performance—and/or intense opposition and stalemate—remains an open question.

Social Policy

The French have enacted some of the most extensive welfare state programs in the world. Cradle-to-grave social services begin before birth, with pregnant women entitled to free prenatal care. Preschool facilities, supported by public subsidies, are excellent. So too are public schools, and all students passing the baccalauréat, a stiff high school graduation exam, are entitled to attend a public university, with tuition costing $300

a year. Extensive public housing and rent subsidies make housing affordable for most citizens. The minimum wage is far higher than the level prevailing in the United States, and employers are legally required to provide their employees with six weeks of paid vacation annually. The unemployed receive substantial unemployment insurance benefits and job retraining. The long-term unemployed are eligible to participate in a minimum income program for two years. Many citizens are eligible to retire at age 60, and pensions come close to matching the wage or salary levels of employed workers. A key element of the social security system, as the welfare state sector is known in France, is health insurance, financed mostly by payroll taxes on employers and employees. In return for modest co-payments, most French have coverage for prescription drugs as well as outpatient, specialized, and hospital care. In 2000, the World Health Organization ranked the French health care system first in the world. And the results speak for themselves. Infant mortality rates are about half those in the United States. Life expectancy is 81 years. No wonder Michael Moore's documentary film *Sicko*, released in 2007, praised the French public health care system so lavishly!

A journalist described the French system "as a global ideological rival" to the American model of social provision.[8] Many of the social benefits described here—guaranteed as a right either to all citizens or (depending on the particular program) to full-time workers—would be the envy of most people in the world.

However, although the French model is highly popular, it has been under great stress recently. First, it is terribly expensive: social expenditures account for nearly one-third of France's gross domestic product (GDP), second only to Sweden among EU countries.[9] Moreover, tax revenues to finance social programs are perennially outstripped by soaring medical costs, high levels of unemployment, and a demographic imbalance between retired workers and actively employed workers. The result is that the public debt in France has soared, because the state must borrow to close the gap between tax revenue and expenditures. (Not all the debt, it should be noted, is the result of social spending.) Within the past thirty years, the public debt has increased from about one-fifth to two-thirds of the GDP.[10] (This level violates France's EU treaty obligation and is comparable to the debt level of the United States, a country often criticized for tolerating an excessive amount of public debt.)

These structural problems are predicted to worsen because of demographic factors. For every retired worker at present, there are three adults with jobs; by 2050, the ratio will drop to 1.5 employed workers for every retired worker. Under France's pay-as-you-go system, currently employed workers mostly pay taxes to finance pensions for the elderly—that is, citizens do not save for retirement—so strains on social programs are bound to increase.

Second, hefty social spending may deter economic growth and inhibit job creation. For decades, French growth rates have been anemic. The result is a low rate of social mobility and increased economic inequalities. In 1975, the wealthiest 10 percent of French households owned 40 percent of all assets; thirty years later, the wealthiest tenth owned 54 percent. Economic stagnation also explains why, for thirty years, France has had some of the highest levels of unemployment among industrialized countries. For years, joblessness hovered around 10 percent. (It has recently declined to about 8 percent.) Because the social security system is mostly financed by payroll taxes, which adds to wage costs, employers are deterred from hiring new workers. For years, voters have consistently ranked unemployment among the most pressing problems in France. The failure of successive governments to bring down unemployment has contributed to frequent electoral gyrations.

The Socialist government of Lionel Jospin (1995–2002) sought to encourage employers to create jobs by reducing the standard workweek from thirty-nine to thirty-five hours. Since the reform also contained a provision enabling employers to schedule work more flexibly, it provided benefits to both business firms and workers. And later reforms relaxed restrictions on overtime work, such that by 2007 the average workweek for full-time workers was 39 hours. The reform continues to be blamed for damaging the French economy. President Sarkozy promised to sponsor an increase in the legal definition of the workweek.

Third, there are important inequalities and inequities involving access to social benefits. Two groups of unusually well-organized French citizens have obtained the lion's share of social benefits: full-time, stably employed workers (especially civil servants) and older citizens. Retirees receive relatively generous pensions; they represent the most costly category of social spending. Yet large numbers of deserving citizens are shortchanged by the system of social provision. The French have coined the term *the social fracture* to describe the opposition between more secure, protected groups and more vulnerable citizens, roughly one-third of the population, who are likely to be young, poor, less-educated, and from immigrant backgrounds. Historian Timothy B. Smith, a strong critic of the French welfare state, claims that "French public policy, despite its rhetoric of solidarity, creates or aggravates as many inequalities as it corrects."[11]

Environmental Policy

France has a mixed record on ecology. The state has traditionally given higher priority to industrial development and economic growth than to environmental concerns. The environment movement has scored some notable successes, but these victories were the exception that proved the rule. For example, activists forced the French military to evacuate a base at the Larzac plateau in central France which it had used as a weapons test site. But a powerful state was quite indifferent to environmental concerns, as was the general public: ecology ranked low on the list of issues that captured public attention. To illustrate: although France has more nuclear power plants than any other country in the world, the French antinuclear movement is far weaker than its German counterpart. The French Green party (or, rather, parties, since there are several) is far weaker than the German Greens. Although the government created a ministry of the environment several decades ago, until it was upgraded in 2007 it ranked among the weakest cabinet departments.

In recent years, the issue of environmental protection has gained increased importance. Among the reasons are the growing evidence of climate change, the high price of petroleum, and fears concerning the safety of the food supply, in part linked to concerns about genetically modified organisms (GMOs). President Chirac sponsored a constitutional amendment in 2005 that integrated in the constitution a Charter of Environmental Protection. A key provision is the "precautionary principle." It stipulates that genetically modified changes should be authorized only if there is convincing evidence that they will not be harmful.

President Sarkozy passionately championed ecological concerns. He created a superministry of ecology and sustainable development, and he requested that officials from public agencies, farm and business groups, labor unions, and environmental protection advocates develop "green" proposals. They recommended halving the use of agricultural pesticides, banning incandescent lightbulbs by 2010, subsidizing "green" construction, and reducing use of nuclear power. Implementing these measures would make France a world leader in confronting global warming and environmental degradation.

Society and Economy

French economic performance has traditionally been hindered by stormy relations between management and labor. Economists claim that this situation helps explain France's economic difficulties. Typically, employers refused to bargain collectively with unions, and workers resorted to strikes and pressured the state to mandate gains. French labor unions have long had a beleaguered existence. For example, they obtained the legal right to organize plant-level locals only as a result of the May 1968 uprising. Employers were not legally required to bargain collectively with unions over wages and hours until the Socialist government passed reform legislation in 1982. The labor movement has historically been quite weak. It was further weakened when economic growth slowed and industrial restructuring destroyed labor's traditional bastions of organized labor. Currently, less than 10 percent of the wage-earning population belongs to a labor union.

Inequality and Ethnic Minorities

In the postwar period through the 1970s, when labor was scarce and low-skilled jobs were plentiful in manufacturing, textiles, and construction, France actively sought to recruit immigrants from North Africa to do the heavy lifting needed for economic growth. Since the 1980s, however, the situation has become very different. Suddenly, the issue of integrating Muslims into French society became prominent.

Two specialists observe that the roots of the difficulty may not be religious as much as economic. "Many of the challenges of integration—perhaps most of them—have

nothing to do with Islam. . . . And everything to do with the poor social conditions and lack of educational capital of recent immigrants and their children and grandchildren."[12] A government study in 2002 reported the existence of widespread job discrimination toward immigrants and second-generation French citizens.[13] A dramatic illustration was provided in a recent research project. Researchers mailed 2,000 applications for job openings using fictitious names and identical CVs. When "Thomas Lecomte" and "Guillaume Dupont" (the names of "traditional" Frenchmen) applied for jobs, they received one invitation to a job interview for every nineteen applications that were sent. When "Youssuf Belkacem" and "Karim Brahimi" (obviously, Muslim names) applied for the same jobs, they received one invitation to a job interview for every fifty-four applications.[14]

Inequality and Women

Women's economic position is double-edged. On the one hand, France has adopted a number of family-friendly social policies. Mothers are entitled to four to six months of paid maternity leave; fathers to two weeks of paid paternity leave. A sliding scale of family allowances eases the financial cost of parenting. France has been at the forefront of enabling women to work outside the home by the provision of excellent day care facilities staffed by highly qualified teachers. These measures have had a significant impact. The proportion of women aged twenty-five to forty-nine in the paid labor force has soared—from 49 percent in 1970 to 82 percent in 2003.[15]

On the other hand, French women are far from achieving economic and social equality. France ranks fourteenth among countries in the world on a Gender-related Development Index compiled by the United Nations Development Programme. The proportion of female managers and administrators in France is among the lowest of industrialized countries. More broadly, the gender wage gap—that is, the disparity between what men and women are paid for comparable work—is a hefty 20 percent. Although laws mandate gender equality in the workplace, the absence of adequate enforcement mechanisms explains why France falls so far short of achieving this goal. As will be described in Chapter 9, when legislation was passed in 2000 providing for gender equality in some elected offices, stiff penalties were imposed for political parties that did not comply with the law. As a result, female representation soared. However, the law applies only to elected positions, not jobs in the civil service or private sector.

The Generation Gap

France's extensive welfare state arrangements, coupled with France's low growth rate, have created a sharp generation gap. The protections enjoyed by older, stably employed workers limit job creation and fall especially hard on first-time job seekers. Over one-fifth of young adults—more than twice the national average—are unemployed. This situation is relatively recent. Whereas in 1982, only one-tenth of young French failed to land a stable job within three years of leaving school, nowadays the proportion is about one-quarter.

One reason for this situation is that large numbers of youth, especially those from immigrant and modest backgrounds, lack needed skills. Many young people leave high school before obtaining a diploma. Many high school graduates who enroll in universities either fail to obtain a degree or specialize in fields for which there is little demand. French universities have been widely criticized for their outdated curriculum and teaching methods. (Of course, not all young French have difficulty finding a good job. Young French from more affluent backgrounds, especially those who graduate from elite universities, are in great demand.)

Recent government measures to deregulate labor markets have proved a mixed blessing for the young. Although the greater flexibility that managers possess to schedule work encourages new hiring, two-thirds of new hires are offered temporary or part-time jobs, which provide low wages and few fringe benefits. Whereas in the past twenty years the number of stable full-time jobs has increased by 12 percent, the number of part-time jobs has increased by 400 percent and the number of fixed-term jobs has increased by 600 percent.[16] In brief, it does not pay to be young in France: one-fifth of all households headed by those under twenty-five years old have incomes below the poverty line—double the proportion in 1979.[17]

One response by young people to this disturbing situation is to emigrate in search of jobs. The most popular destination is London, home to 86,000 French expatriates.[18]

The Dilemmas of European Integration

A government-commissioned study observes, "[EU] legislation has assumed an increasingly important place in French economic and social life."[19] In such varied domains as the organization and governance of business firms, labor relations, food and medicines, and even cultural life, the EU provides a regulatory framework. EU membership has fundamentally altered France's trade orientation. Whereas the bulk of France's international trade and investment in the postwar period were with its former colonies in Asia and Africa, over 60 percent of its imports and exports are currently with other member states of the EU. Membership in the EU has contributed to French economic growth and assisted particular sectors of the French economy. For example, French farmers receive the largest subsidies of any single group in the EU. (However, reforms of the subsidy program will severely cut these benefits in the future.)

Yet the EU provides challenges as well as opportunities. The EU's emphasis on deregulation has harmed vulnerable economic groups and challenged the state-led pattern by which France achieved economic success and cultural distinctiveness. The style of economic governance in the EU is closer to that in Britain or Germany than to the French model. EU regulations prohibit states from engaging in the kind of *dirigisme* that was the hallmark of the French state in the postwar period. For example, in 2002 Jacques Chirac proposed reducing French income taxes by 5 percent. The EU Commission promptly warned that doing so might violate the government's agreement to reduce budget deficits and balance the budget by 2004. After first blustering at the EU's warning, the government fell into line. Another example: when France passed a law limiting the possibility for foreign companies to engage in hostile takeovers of firms in industrial sectors that the government deemed of strategic importance, the Commission ordered the law overturned, on the grounds that it violated EU regulations ensuring free economic competition.

These examples demonstrate how EU membership has forced France to modify its style of economic management. Along with Paris, Brussels—the seat of the EU—can now be considered a site of decision making for French politics; the weight of the EU is evident in virtually every policy area imaginable.

France in the Global Economy

France is highly integrated in the global economy, and has benefited enormously from globalization. Imports and exports of capital and goods account for fully half of French GDP, among the highest proportion of any country in the world. Foreign investors, especially American pension funds, own nearly half of all shares traded on the French stock exchange. About one-third of all French workers are employed in firms that are at least partly foreign-owned. Contrary to the stereotype of France as a bucolic, rural economy, only about 3 percent of the population is employed in agriculture. At the same time, the agricultural sector is highly productive; France is the world's third-largest agricultural exporter. France can boast a large number of world-class industrial, banking, and high-tech firms. In 2003, the business magazine *Forbes* compiled a list of the world's four hundred best-performing companies. France was second only to the United States in the number of companies on the list.[20]

Yet French participation in the global economy, as well as the performance of the French economy more generally, has caused intense political strains. The impact of economic factors on domestic politics depends heavily on the shape of political institutions and partisan coalitions. We analyze these issues in the next two chapters.

Notes

[1] Michel Dollé, "Niveau de vie, 'La France perd des points,' " *Le Monde 2*, April 7, 2007, p. 46.

[2] Richard F. Kuisel, *Capitalism and the State in Modern France* (Cambridge: Cambridge University Press, 1981), p. 277.

[3] Henri Mendras with Alistair Cole, *Social Change in Modern France: Towards a Cultural Anthropology of the Fifth Republic* (Cambridge: Cambridge University Press, 1991), p. 1.

[4] Laurent Ménière, *Bilan de la France, 1981–1993* (Paris: Hachette, 1993), p. 18.

[5] Peter A. Hall described the new economic orientation since the mid-1980s as a "neo-liberal modernization strategy." Hall, "From One Modernization Strategy to Another: The Character and Consequences of Recent Economic Policy in France" (paper presented to the Tenth International Conference of Europeanists, Chicago, March 15, 1996).

[6] Vivien A. Schmidt, *From State to Market? The Transformation of French Business and Government* (Cambridge: Cambridge University Press, 1996), p. 442.

[7] Eurostats, *Le Monde*, March 13, 2007.

[8] Roger Cohen, "Paris and Washington Speak Softly," *International Herald Tribune*, October 20, 1997.

[9] INSEE, *Tableaux de l'Économie Française, 2003–2004* (Paris: INSEE, 2003), p. 103.

[10] Académie des Sciences Morales et Politiques, *La France prépare mal l'avenir de sa jeunesse* (Paris: Editions du Seuil, 2007), p. 103.

[11] Timothy B. Smith, *France in Crisis: Welfare, Inequality and Globalization since 1980* (Cambridge: Cambridge University Press, 2004), p. 6.

[12] Jonathan Laurence and Justin Vaisse, *Integrating Islam: Political and Religious Challenges in Contemporary France* (Washington, D.C.: Brookings Institution Press, 2006), p. 10.

[13] *Le Monde*, June 4, 2002.

[14] *Metro*, March 15, 2007.

[15] Commissariat général du plan, *Rapport sur les perspectives de la France* (Paris: La Documentation Française, 2000), p. 54.

[16] Jacques Rigaudiat, "A propos d'un fait social majeur: la montée des précarités et des insécurités sociales et économiques," *Droit Social*, no. 3 (March 2005).

[17] Fondation Abbé Pierre pour le logement des Défavorisés, "L'Etat du mal logement en France," rapport annuel 2006.

[18] *New York Times*, June 2, 2006.

[19] *Rapport sur les perspectives de la France*, p. 45.

[20] Sophie Meunier, "Free-Falling France or Free-Trading France?" *French Politics, Culture and Society* 22, no. 1 (Spring 2004): 98–107.

CHAPTER 8

Governance
and Policymaking

Charles de Gaulle, founding father of the Fifth Republic, did his work well—too well, many now believe. He was completely successful in designing the Fifth Republic to enable a strong executive to govern relatively free of parliamentary and other restraints. He may have succeeded too well in that the imbalance in power between the executive and parliament may have created a design flaw in the institutional architecture of the Fifth Republic. Ever since the creation of the republic in 1958, there has been criticism of unchecked executive power.

At the same time, fundamental changes in the character of the French state are occurring in three key respects. The first change involves the centralized state. Article 2 of the French constitution specifies, "France is a Republic, *indivisible,* secular, democratic and social." For many years it was generally assumed that an indivisible state meant a centralized state. However, in the 1980s, the Socialist government transferred substantial governmental powers to local, departmental, and regional authorities. In 2003, a conservative government transferred additional powers to subnational governments and sponsored a constitutional amendment affirming the principle of decentralization. These changes involved an important reinterpretation of "indivisible." There is now a broad consensus on the value of decentralization. It is widely agreed that the French state can become stronger and more effective when subnational governments share governmental responsibilities.

Second, as described in Chapter 7, the state's relation to the economy has shifted. Although the state continues to have an exceptionally important role, it now consults and persuades more—and commands less.

The third change involves constitutional mechanisms that limit state action. Until recently, the French accorded little importance to the principle of constitutional supremacy. A nation that emphasizes the importance of formalized legal codes and that boasts the modern world's second-oldest written constitution (after the United States) did not consider that the constitution should be scrupulously respected. French democratic theory held that the government, chosen by democratic elections, should have a free hand to govern and should not be hindered by constitutional texts. Similarly, the executive and legislature considered that, as the elected branches, they could safely ignore the judiciary, since that branch lacked democratic legitimacy. This too has changed. The constitution of the Fifth Republic has come to be regarded as the authoritative source for allocating power among political institutions, and the Constitutional Council has gained the vital power of judicial review: that is, the power to nullify legislation and sanction executive actions that it judges to violate the constitution.

These recent changes require analyzing French political institutions with a fresh eye.

Organization of the State

The Fifth Republic is usually described as a semi-presidential system that combines elements of presidential and parliamentary systems. In a presidential system, such as in the United States, the executive and the legislature are elected separately, and the two branches have independent powers, although they also share responsibility in important areas, for example, regarding the passage of legislation. Neither branch selects the other, is directly accountable to the other, or controls the other's agenda. Moreover, both institutions have fixed terms in office, and neither one can force the other to resign and face new elections. The one exception in a presidential system is that the legislature can impeach and force the president to resign when it deems that he or she has committed treason or other grave misdeeds. There is a similar impeachment procedure in the French Fifth Republic, although it has never been used: an absolute majority of both houses of parliament must vote articles of impeachment. The president's case is then judged by a High Court of Justice made up of twelve members apiece from the two legislative chambers.

In a parliamentary system, the executive and legislature are linked organically. The government is accountable to parliament and must resign if parliament passes a motion of no confidence. At the same time, the government has substantial control over the parliamentary agenda and can dissolve parliament, thereby necessitating new elections.

In the Fifth Republic, both the president and parliament are popularly elected. In contrast to both presidential and parliamentary systems the French system provides for a dual executive: the president appoints a prime minister and government. As in parliamentary systems, the parliament can force the government to resign (but, recall, not the president) by voting a motion of no confidence—what the French call a *motion of censure.*

Why is the Fifth Republic considered a semi-presidential (and not a semiparliamentary) system? Because whenever the Fifth Republic deviates from a purely parliamentary or presidential model, the result is to strengthen the executive. The fusion of executive and legislative powers characteristic of parliamentary regimes enables the executive to control the parliamentary agenda and dissolve parliament. The executive is further strengthened because the French parliament cannot vote censure of the president, in contrast to parliamentary regimes. (As described below, however, the National Assembly, the more powerful house of parliament, can vote a motion censuring the government, thus forcing it to resign.) Thus, the president—the key office within the dual executive—is not answerable to parliament. This feature reflects the separation of powers found in presidential systems, and it provides the executive with exceptional power in the Fifth Republic.

Ever since the creation of the Fifth Republic, there has been controversy about the imbalance between the executive and parliament. Although several reforms have partially redressed the balance, controversy continues to this day. Despite the lopsided relationship, however, the Fifth Republic has proved among the most stable regimes in modern French history. Support for the regime has been bolstered by France's economic prosperity and a peaceful international context.

Since the early 1980s, the Fifth Republic has overcome two daunting political challenges. The first was a shift in political control (alternation) between opposing partisan coalitions in 1981, when François Mitterrand defeated incumbent president Valéry Giscard d'Estaing. Contrary to widespread fears, the institutions of the Fifth Republic proved quite adequate to the challenge. Since then, alternation has occurred several times.

The second challenge arose when the president led one political coalition and a rival political coalition elected a majority in parliament. The French call this situation *cohabitation,* or power sharing. In the early years of the Fifth Republic, many predicted that, if it were to happen, it would produce stalemate or even a crisis of the regime. The Gaullist party's dominance of both the presidency and parliament prevented a test from occurring. However, the unthinkable finally came to pass in 1986, during the presidency of François Mitterrand, when parliamentary elections produced a right-wing majority in the National Assembly. President Mitterrand immediately bowed to political realities by appointing Jacques Chirac, leader of the conservative coalition, to be prime minister. The event proved to be the mouse that roared. The two seasoned politicians quickly devised workable solutions to governing, and despite a few tremors the regime held firm. As with alternation, cohabitation has occurred several times since then.

However, the most recent experience of cohabitation, in 1997–2002, provoked an important institutional reform designed to minimize the chances of it occurring again. When the Socialists and their allies won the 1997 parliamentary elections, Jacques Chirac, who had been elected president only two years earlier, was forced to name Socialist leader Lionel Jospin as prime minister. The long cohabitation—five full years—proved highly unpopular. In an attempt to prevent a repeat performance, major parties agreed to reduce the president's term from seven to five years, the same length as that of the National Assembly, and to hold elections for the two branches at about the same time. Doing so would greatly increase the chance that the same political coalition would win both elections. The 2007 presidential and parliamentary elections completely fulfilled these expectations.

The Executive

France was the first major country to adopt a semi-presidential system. After the Soviet Union crumbled and communism was abandoned, Russia was inspired by France's semipresidential model when creating a new political system. Other countries that have adopted the semipresidential system include Austria, Finland, Portugal, Sri Lanka, Iceland, and (most recently) Iraq.

In parliamentary regimes, the head of state—either a president or a monarch—is mostly a figurehead who symbolizes the unity of the nation and exercises purely ceremonial duties. The bulk of executive power, involving the making and implementation of policy, is wielded by the prime minister and cabinet (collectively known as the government). In France, the president combines the two roles. He (there has never been a female president) is head of state. But unlike the head of state in a parliamentary regime, he also has important formal and informal power to direct the executive and shape policy. At the same time, he shares executive power with the prime minister and cabinet—who are appointed by the president but are responsible to parliament. The complex relationship between the president and prime minister will be analyzed below.

The President

When both the executive and the legislature are controlled by the same party coalition—what we will term *united control*—the president combines the powers of the U.S. president—notably, command of the executive branch and independence from the legislature—with the powers that the government possesses in a parliamentary regime—namely, control of parliament's agenda and the ability to dissolve parliament. During periods of united control—the situation since 2002 and one that will probably persist for many years—the president's power exceeds that of the chief executive in virtually any other democratic nation.

The presidency is such a powerful position because of (1) the ample powers that the constitution has conferred on the office; (2) the towering personalities of Charles de Gaulle, the founder and first president of the Fifth Republic, and François Mitterrand, the Socialist president from 1981 to 1995; and (3) political practices of the Fifth Republic.

The Constitutional Presidency. The president is the only political leader directly elected by the entire French electorate. This provides an enormously important source of personal support. In order to be eligible to run, a candidate must be a French citizen and at least twenty-three years old. Presidents are eligible for re-election without limit. The office of vice president does not exist in France; if a president dies in office, the president of the Senate (the upper house of parliament) acts as interim president, and a new election is held within a short time.

In order to run for president, a candidate must be nominated by five hundred mayors or regional legislators. Because there are about 40,000 such officials, it is not too difficult to qualify; thus, many candidates typically compete in presidential elections. The record was 2002, when the field contained sixteen candidates! In 2007, there were twelve.

A two-ballot system of election is used for presidential elections. To win on the first ballot, a candidate must obtain an absolute majority: that is, over 50 percent of those voting. If no candidate receives a first-ballot majority, the case in every presidential election to date, a runoff election is held two weeks later between the two front-runners.

Although only candidates nominated by major political parties stand a realistic chance of winning, minor-party candidates can affect which candidates make it to the runoff ballot. The most dramatic example occurred in 2002, when Lionel Jospin, the major center-left candidate, came in third, behind Chirac and far-right candidate Jean-Marie Le Pen. A large number of other leftist candidates that year had gained enough votes to prevent Jospin from making the runoff.

The constitution of the Fifth Republic endows the president with the ceremonial powers of head of state. He resides in the resplendent Élysée Palace, in a fashionable section of Paris, and represents France at international diplomatic gatherings. The constitution also grants the president important political powers. The president:

- names the prime minister, chooses or approves the prime minister's choice of cabinet officials, and names high-ranking civil, military, and judicial officials.
- presides over meetings of the Council of Ministers (the government). Note that the constitution charges the president, not the prime minister, with this responsibility.
- conducts foreign affairs, through the power to negotiate and ratify treaties, as well as to name French ambassadors and accredit foreign ambassadors to France.
- directs the armed forces, bolstered by a 1964 decree that grants the president exclusive control over France's nuclear forces.

- is empowered to dissolve the National Assembly and call for new elections.
- appoints three of the nine members of the Constitutional Council, including its president, and can refer bills passed by parliament to the council to determine if they conform to the constitution.

Four other constitutional grants of power strengthen the president's position. Article 16 authorizes the president to assume emergency governing powers when, in his or her judgment, France's independence is threatened. It is unthinkable that a president would invoke Article 16 except in a very grave crisis. (The one time that this occurred was when President de Gaulle assumed emergency powers in 1962 following a threat of a military coup linked to the war in Algeria.)

Article 89 authorizes the president, with the approval of the prime minister, to propose constitutional amendments. Each chamber of parliament must approve the amendment. It must then be ratified either by a national referendum or by a three-fifths vote of both houses of parliament meeting together as a congress. The amendment procedure has been used with increasing frequency in recent years. President Chirac sponsored fourteen amendments in the twelve years of his presidency, more than any other president.

Article 11, which was amended in 1995, authorizes the president to organize a referendum to approve important policy initiatives or reorganize political institutions, provided that the proposed change is first approved by the government. (This procedure is distinct from the use of the referendum to amend the constitution.)

President de Gaulle successfully sponsored several referenda in the early years of the Fifth Republic, all of which were approved by voters. However, a referendum he called in 1969 to restructure the Senate was rejected by voters—in large part because of citizens' growing discontent with de Gaulle's high-handed style of governing. (The referendum came a year after the May 1968 uprising described in Chapter 6.) Immediately after the referendum was defeated, de Gaulle resigned from office. He judged that voters' rejection of the referendum signified a vote of no confidence in his leadership. Following the defeat of the 1969 referendum up until 2005, all referenda called by de Gaulle's successors had been approved, several by narrow margins.

When the referendum on the EU in 2005 was rejected, President Chirac's decision not to resign was in stark contrast with de Gaulle's departure in 1969—and further diminished Chirac's standing. President Sarkozy has announced that he has no plans to sponsor a referendum, probably wishing to avoid risking the kind of damage suffered by President Chirac.

Article 5 directs the president "to ensure, by his arbitration, the regular functioning of the governmental authorities, as well as the continuance of the State." This clause bolsters the president's authority by making him or her the sole official responsible for arbitrating among state institutions and guaranteeing national independence.

Presidential Personalities.   The constitution grants the president extensive powers—on paper. But the use that presidents make of these powers depends in large part on leadership skills. Charles de Gaulle, the first president in the Fifth Republic, made full use of his constitutional power and set the standard for his successors. (Table 8.1 lists the Fifth Republic's presidents and their terms of office.)

De Gaulle was the most influential politician in modern French history. After leading the Resistance forces in France during World War II and helping to topple the Fourth Republic in 1958, he designed the Fifth Republic to ensure strong leadership. He established the precedent that presidents could define goals for the state to pursue, dominate the policymaking process, represent France in foreign relations, and supervise the government and bureaucracy.

The two presidents following de Gaulle—Georges Pompidou and Valéry Giscard d'Estaing—were not

Table 8.1

Presidents of the Fifth Republic

President	Term
Charles de Gaulle	1958–1969
Georges Pompidou	1969–1974
Valéry Giscard d'Estaing	1974–1981
François Mitterrand	1981–1995
Jacques Chirac	1995–2007
Nicolas Sarkozy	2007–present

highly influential, in part because they did not have a clear vision of what they hoped to accomplish. The next president to make full use of presidential powers was President Giscard's successor, François Mitterrand. Mitterrand was a youthful leader in the Resistance during World War II and an ally of de Gaulle. But when de Gaulle returned to power in 1958, Mitterrand joined many on the left in opposing de Gaulle as undemocratic. Mitterrand ran for president against de Gaulle in 1965 and against Giscard in 1974, losing both times. He did, however, fashion a coalition led by the Socialist Party into a major alternative to the Gaullist coalition, and defeated incumbent President Giscard in 1981. Mitterrand was re-elected in 1988 and remained in office until 1995, the longest presidential term in the history of the Fifth Republic.

On becoming president, Mitterrand ruled in an autocratic manner strikingly similar to that of his archrival, de Gaulle. However, he was also the first president to have to swallow the bitter pill of cohabitation. When conservative forces won the 1986 parliamentary elections, he appointed Jacques Chirac, who was leader of the winning party, to be prime minister.

Mitterrand was succeeded as president by Jacques Chirac, who had been a fixture on the French political scene for decades. By the time he was elected president in 1995, Chirac had served as prime minister twice and mayor of Paris for eighteen years. Chirac served two terms as president, retiring in 2007. He proved more adept at gaining power than in using it once in office to pursue bold goals. He was notorious for changing positions, for example, shifting from opposing European

POLITICAL LEADERS: Nicolas Sarkozy

Nicolas Sarkozy is an audacious, tireless, and controversial figure. He is the first French president from an immigrant background. Although he was born in Paris, his father was Hungarian, his mother of Greek Jewish background. His parents settled in France following Hungary's communist takeover after World War II. Nicolas Sarkozy was not a child of privilege. He attended the University of Paris, along with hundreds of thousands of other students, not one of the selective elite schools with small enrollments (described in this chapter) that have produced many of the leading members of France's political establishment.

Sarkozy decided at an early age to pursue a political career. In his youth, he reportedly boasted that one day he would be elected president. He has few interests other than politics—and living well. (On election night, he celebrated his victory by dining at one of France's most famous—and expensive—restaurants. He then left for a holiday on a luxurious yacht, hosted by a billionaire friend.)

As a young man, Sarkozy joined the party that later became the UMP. He quickly rose to

Source: © Horacio Villalobos/epa/Corbis.

become leader of the party's youth organization. At a UMP meeting in 1975, young Sarkozy was allotted two minutes to make a speech. Instead, he spoke for ten minutes. The speech so impressed Jacques Chirac, prime minister at the time, that

(continued)

POLITICAL LEADERS: Nicolas Sarkozy (cont.)

Chirac invited Sarkozy to lunch the next day and took him under his wing.

Sarkozy was elected to parliament in 1988 (at the ripe age of 33) and was appointed a cabinet minister while still in his thirties. Throughout his career, he reveled in breaking taboos and making headlines. As minister of the interior, responsible for law and order within France, he ordered a crackdown on crime that, according to critics, encouraged the police to harass youth, especially those from immigrant backgrounds. In 2005, he famously remarked, when visiting the site of a violent crime in a shabby suburban neighborhood near Paris, that local criminal elements—mostly from immigrant backgrounds— were "scum." He later proclaimed that such neighborhoods should be "disinfected." The harsh language did more than make headlines. When youths from slum neighborhoods in Paris and other cities went on a rampage several weeks later, burning cars and damaging public buildings, they hurled his insults back at him.

Sarkozy has long stressed the importance of being tough on crime. As minister of the interior, he sponsored a drive to deport undocumented immigrants. Soon after being elected president, he made it possible for juvenile delinquents between sixteen and eighteen years old to be tried as adult offenders. At the same time, President Sarkozy has been among the few mainstream politicians to support affirmative action programs that aim to assist immigrants to achieve social and economic mobility. And he was the first French president to appoint men and women of color to cabinet positions.

Sarkozy rose through the political ranks by gaining the support of more senior politicians,

and then betraying his patrons when he judged that the time was ripe. The first example was when, at age twenty-eight, he outmaneuvered his mentor, the mayor of a posh Paris suburb where he lived, to capture the mayor's office. A more famous example was in 1995, when he supported Edouard Balladur, a rival of Jacques Chirac, in the presidential election that year. Chirac won the election, and he never forgave Sarkozy's infidelity. For the next dozen years, Chirac did all he could to check Sarkozy's rise. For example, when Sarkozy gained control of the UMP in 2004, Chirac ordered him to choose between retaining his cabinet position and leading the UMP. However, in the long-running dispute, Sarkozy proved more politically astute than both Chirac and the three successive prime ministers whom Chirac tried to groom as his successor. Sarkozy's prospects became brighter as their prospects faded. One (Alain Juppé) was convicted of corruption, a second (Jean-Pierre Raffarin) was lackluster, and a third (Dominique de Villepin) displayed monumental political misjudgment by proposing a youth employment program that provoked massive opposition. (The controversy is described in Chapter 10.)

By 2007, at the young age (for French politicians) of fifty-two, Sarkozy had the conservative field to himself. Assisted by his leadership of the UMP, France's most powerful political party, he ran a brilliant presidential campaign, won the all-important televised debate with Ségolène Royal which opened this section, and . . . the rest was history. Or rather, these events were the prehistory that enabled the history of Sarkozy's presidency to begin. Stay tuned to observe how it will fare.

---

integration to supporting closer integration, and from defending Gaullist-style state economic intervention to defense of free markets and a smaller role for the state. Rather than noteworthy achievements, Chirac's presidency will be remembered for some major political blunders that he committed. (Several are described in Chapter 10.) When he retired in 2007, *Le Monde* editorially

commented, "the French have the impression that the country was immobilized for the twelve years of the Chirac presidency."[1]

Time will tell if Nicolas Sarkozy, Chirac's successor, will leave a distinctive stamp on the presidency. He has made no secret of his desire to do so. Upon his election in 2007, he ensured that the conservative government and cabinet ministers would be directly answerable to him. He ordered cabinet ministers to provide him with an annual report evaluating how effectively their departments had accomplished their mission. He announced that he planned to deliver an annual speech to parliament, modeled after the U.S. president's State of the Union Address. (Until this point, French presidents have not been authorized to address parliament directly.) He sponsored a flurry of policy initiatives, intervened in the everyday business of government, and dominated media coverage to an extent never seen before. (Analysts suggested that François Fillon, whom Sarkozy appointed as prime minister, functioned more as Sarkozy's chief of staff than as prime minister.) In brief, Nicolas Sarkozy clearly aimed to be a highly activist president, eager to wade into the thick of the fray rather than remaining on the sidelines as a distant and majestic figure. If he succeeds, he will compile an impressive legacy of accomplishments and enhance the president's power. But at least in the short run, his whirlwind of activity at the start of his presidency has further imbalanced political institutions.

The Political President. The constitution creates a powerful office whose exercise depends on the personality of the president. In addition, political factors affect the extent of presidential power. By far the most important is whether presidents command a parliamentary majority. When they do, their actual power is far greater than the formal powers specified by the constitution.

When the president enjoys a parliamentary majority, he has a commanding position with respect to the prime minister, government, and legislature. For example, in addition to the constitutional power to designate prime ministers, presidents have successfully claimed the ability to dismiss them. The effect is to make the government responsible not only to the National Assembly, as specified in the constitution, but also to the president. During periods of unified control, presidents have successfully assumed the power, which is assigned to the government by the constitution, to shape policy in virtually any domain they choose. The prime minister and government exercise important functions by translating political priorities in concrete policy proposals and by directing the day-to-day operation of the far-flung executive. But although these tasks are vitally

important, presidents usually chart the overall political course and arbitrate the most important political conflicts within the government.

The Prime Minister and Government

Although the constitution provides the president with ample powers, it authorizes the prime minister and government to make many key policy decisions. The constitution designates the government, not the president, to be the preeminent policymaking institution. Article 20 states that the government "shall determine and direct the policy of the nation. It shall have at its disposal the administration and the armed forces." And Article 21 authorizes the prime minister to "direct the action of the government. He [the prime minister] is responsible for national defense. He assures the execution of the laws." Thus, prime ministers accept presidential leadership, as they invariably do during periods of unified control, because of *political dynamics* rather than *constitutional directive.*

The constitution authorizes the president to appoint the prime minister, who is usually the leader of the major party in the dominant coalition in the National Assembly, in order to ensure parliamentary support for the prime minister and government. (The boxed feature on institutional intricacies further explores the complex relationship of presidents and prime ministers.)

Although the respective responsibilities of presidents and prime ministers vary according to political and personality factors, an informal division of labor exists. During periods of unified control, the president formulates the state's overall policy direction, while the prime minister is responsible for translating these general policies into specific programs and supervising the implementation of policy. Presidents retain predominant responsibility for overall defense and foreign policy, but the prime minister determines the government's specific policy orientation and legislative timetable. The prime minister is also responsible for coordinating and supervising the work of the cabinet, as well as arbitrating conflicts among cabinet ministers over policy and budget priorities.

The prime minister nominates, and the president appoints, members of the cabinet or government, a collective body under the prime minister's direction. The constitution specifies that members of the National

INSTITUTIONAL INTRICACIES: Of Presidents and Prime Ministers

The relationship between the president and prime minister is a key element in the Fifth Republic. There are two possible situations: (1) the periods of unified control, when the president and prime minister are political allies and (2) the periods of cohabitation, when the two are political opponents. The first situation is characterized by undisputed presidential supremacy. Presidents select the prime minister from the ranks of leaders of the majority party coalition. Most prime ministers during periods of unified control have been prominent politicians and close associates of the president. For example, in 2007 newly elected President Sarkozy appointed as prime minister François Fillon, a former cabinet minister. More important, Fillon was a close friend (and jogging partner) of Sarkozy and he served as Sarkozy's presidential campaign director. Loyal and effective prime ministers provide the president with important political assets: parliamentary support for the government's policies, skill in gaining sympathetic media treatment, and experience in directing the government and the state bureaucracy. A competent prime minister frees the president to conduct international affairs and focus on the most important policy questions.

Prime ministers also serve as lightning rods to protect the president. By taking the heat for controversial decisions, they partially shield the president from criticism. Political scientist Robert Elgie describes the prime minister's thankless position: "When things go well, the President often receives the credit. When things go badly, the Prime Minister usually takes the blame. If things go very badly and the President starts to be criticized, then the Prime Minister is replaced. If things go very well and the Prime Minister starts to be praised, then the Prime Minister is also replaced."[2] Serving as prime minister is regarded as a stepping stone to the presidency. This dynamic explains why presidents generally dismiss prime ministers after several years and name a fresh replacement. Indeed, when a prime minister loses popularity and is not replaced, the president's standing suffers. For example, Prime Minister Dominique de Villepin provoked enormous opposition in 2006 by sponsoring an unpopular youth employment reform. (The incident is described in Chapter 10.) When President Chirac decided not to replace de Villepin, Chirac himself was greatly weakened.

During cohabitation, when the president and prime minister are political rivals, the balance shifts from cooperation to competition. At such times, the prime minister has some powerful resources: he or she controls the government, the parliament, and the bureaucracy, and is not inclined to defer to the president. At these times, the president is forced to beat a dignified retreat although he retains major responsibility for foreign and defense policy. But the prime minister now assumes the responsibility—and risks—for leadership in other policy areas.

The constant jockeying for power between the president and prime minister that occurred during the seemingly endless period of cohabitation between 1997 and 2002 proved highly unpopular. It provoked a constitutional reform in 2000 designed in part to minimize the chance that cohabitation would recur. The reform reduced the president's term to five years, the same length as the term of deputies in the National Assembly. Holding presidential and parliamentary elections within a month of each other, and making the terms of the president and members of parliament identical, made it highly likely that the same political coalition would win both elections. It worked. In 2002 and 2007, conservatives swept the presidential and parliamentary elections. Unified control will doubtless endure until at least 2012, when the next presidential and parliamentary elections are scheduled. Thus, cohabitation has become a distant memory. Few lament its passing.

Assembly who are named to the cabinet must resign their parliamentary seat. Most cabinet members, also known as ministers, are senior politicians from the parties forming the dominant parliamentary coalition. Positions in the cabinet are allotted to political parties in rough proportion to their strength in the majority parliamentary coalition. An attempt is also made to ensure regional balance.

Until President Sarkozy's election in 2007, nearly all cabinet ministers were white men. Sarkozy broke with this long-standing tradition by appointing women to fully half the senior cabinet positions in Prime Minister François Fillon's government. The most noteworthy choice was Minister of Justice Rachida Dati, a Muslim woman whose parents were North African immigrants of humble circumstances.

Presidents and prime ministers shape the cabinet to convey political messages. For example, President Sarkozy symbolized his intention to broaden his conservative political coalition when he appointed several Socialist politicians to Prime Minister Fillon's government. The most prominent was Bernard Kouchner, co-founder of Doctors Without Borders, who was named Foreign Minister.

Cabinet ministers direct government departments and propose policy initiatives in their domain. If the government and president support these proposals, the proposals are included on the legislative and administrative agenda. One way for ambitious politicians to rise is by dynamic performance as ministers. Cabinet positions differ widely in power. Key ministries include Finance, Defense, Foreign Affairs, and Interior.

The prime minister and other government ministers have extensive staff assistance to help them supervise the immense and far-flung bureaucracy. For example, the prime minister's office includes, in addition to his personal staff, the General Secretariat of the Government, the General Directorate for Administrative and Financial Services, and the General Secretariat for National Defense. These powerful agencies are charged with coordinating and supervising policy implementation by government ministries.

The prime minister and other cabinet ministers are assisted by a personal staff, known as a *cabinet*, to help them supervise departments and provide policy assistance. (Note that the *cabinet*, italicized here, is a wholly different body from the cabinet, composed of government ministers.) Members of the *cabinet* are usually drawn from the ranks of the most talented civil servants—graduates of elite schools described below. Their mission is to serve as the minister's eyes and ears: while serving in the *cabinet*, they are not part of the line bureaucracy (although they often return to bureaucratic positions after leaving the *cabinet*). *Cabinets* are an invaluable resource enabling French cabinet ministers to wield considerable power.

Even more than is the case for cabinets in other political regimes, the French cabinet is not a forum for searching policy debate or collective decision making. Cabinet meetings are occasions where constitutional requirements are met—for example, authorizing appointment of key administrative officials—and where the president and prime minister announce decisions. Important policies are shaped at a higher level—at the Élysée or Matignon (the official residence of the prime minister)—or by interministerial committees, that is, informal working groups of ministers and high administrators that are directed by the president, prime minister, or their staff.

Bureaucracy and Civil Service

Although France is often described as having a dual executive, the bureaucracy in fact constitutes a third important element of the executive. The bureaucracy is a large and sprawling organization that reaches far and wide to regulate French society. These three elements of the executive provide the motor force of the French state.

The most prominent administrators in the French state are found in the Élysée, the Matignon, and the ornate government ministries scattered throughout Paris. The day-to-day work of the state, however, is performed by an army of civil servants, including 2.3 million in the state administration and another 2.7 million who staff public hospitals, semipublic agencies, and subnational governmental bureaucracies. In brief, about one in five French wage earners works in the public sector.

The bureaucracy plays a key role in shaping the country's social and economic life. The Fifth Republic bolstered its influence by limiting parliament's legislative power and extending the government's authority to issue binding administrative regulations that had the force of law. Securing a position in the bureaucracy has traditionally provided lifetime employment and considerable prestige, along with good pay and fringe benefits.

The top administrative positions, on which we focus here, offer among the most prestigious and powerful careers in France. Recruitment to these posts is limited to graduates of elite educational institutions known as a *grande école.* While over 1 million students are enrolled in higher education at any given time (mostly at public universities), only 40,000 students attend a *grande école,* and an even smaller number— about 3,000—study at the few most selective *grandes écoles.*[3] Among the most prestigious are the École Polytechnique (popularly known as X), which trains engineers and scientists; the École Nationale d'Administration (ENA), which trains top civil servants and executives (graduates of the ENA are popularly known as *énarques*); and the École des Mines, which trains engineers and other technical specialists. Mention should also be made of the Institut d'Études Politiques (popularly known as Sciences Po), which prepares students for admission to the *grandes écoles.*

Despite the small size of the elite schools, they receive nearly one third of all public expenditures on higher education. It is not surprising that the nonelite track—that is, the universities, in which most students are enrolled—are starved for funds, bursting at the seams, and often ill-equipped to provide adequate guidance or training. Further, although French political discourse emphasizes the importance of meritocracy, children from culturally and economically favored milieux have an immense advantage in the fierce competition for admission to the *grandes écoles.* Only a handful of students from modest backgrounds, even fewer if they are second- or third-generation immigrants, pass the demanding entrance exams.

Students who graduate in the top tier of their class at a *grande école* are admitted into an even more select fraternity: a *grand corps.* These are small, cohesive networks with particular administrative specialties, such as the financial inspectorate or diplomatic service. Membership in a *grand corps* is for life and guarantees a relatively ample salary, high status, and considerable power. Recently, members of the *grands corps* have also filled top executive positions in public and private corporations and banks. Many members enter politics, serving in parliament or the cabinet. Cabinet ministers often appoint members of the *grands corps*

to their *cabinets* (the personal staff described above). Over half of all prime ministers in the Fifth Republic were members of *grands corps,* as were presidents Giscard d'Estaing and Chirac.

The state and the bureaucracy, which is the primary organizational instrument for implementing state policies, remain a formidable presence in French society. However, in recent years they have experienced a decline in prestige, power, and morale because of the diminished scope of state activity, the increased power of the private sector, ideological changes, and the growing importance of the EU. One of President Sarkozy's initiatives was to reduce the size of the bureaucracy by decreeing that not all those retiring in certain sectors, for example, the military and education, would be replaced by new recruits.

Public and Semipublic Institutions

The past two decades have sharply reduced the size of the public sector, following the privatization of state-owned industrial enterprises like automobiles (the Renault auto company), banking, transportation (for example, Air France), energy, and telecommunications. Large and powerful semipublic agencies remain—for example, Electricity of France, the agency that monopolizes the distribution of electricity throughout France, which has been described as a state within the state. But like the civil service, semipublic agencies no longer enjoy the prestige and power of yesteryear.

Other State Institutions

Given the far-flung reach of the French state, many state institutions warrant close attention. We focus here on those with great power or that are described in the constitution.

The Military and the Police

In all countries, the military and police are the executive agencies that employ coercive force to enforce law and order. Unlike some countries, where the armed forces play an important role in shaping policy and directing the state, the French army has traditionally played only a minor role in politics. However, the army has occasionally intervened to influence civilian authorities, most recently in 1958 when it helped de Gaulle return to power by threatening to topple the Fourth Republic because of the government's failure to quell the Algerian uprising.

France is a middling-rank power nowadays, with nowhere near the resources to rival the United States. But de Gaulle and later presidents have tried to pursue an independent foreign policy. Unlike Britain and Germany, for example, who have generally been loyal members of the military alliance led by the United States, France has maintained a studied distance. For example, following World War II, the United States had several military bases in France. De Gaulle ordered the United States to close them and evacuate its troops from France. He also announced that France was withdrawing from the integrated command structure of the North Atlantic Treaty Organization (NATO). De Gaulle and his successors have sponsored an independent French nuclear striking force, with sophisticated delivery systems that include missiles, aircraft, and nuclear submarines. France is among the world's major arms exporters.

Africa has been the one region of the world where France retains major influence. French troops were dispatched on numerous occasions in recent decades to prop up friendly dictators in former French colonies that became nominally independent in the 1960s. France has sponsored extensive assistance programs in these countries—what is called francophone Africa. French teachers, engineers, and business firms are dispatched both to promote development and encourage these countries to remain allies. France's influence in the region has been waning recently, however.

In recent years, France has sought to enhance its international standing by playing a major role in United Nations–sponsored peacekeeping operations in post-conflict situations, such as in Bosnia, Afghanistan, and Lebanon. France has committed more troops to peacekeeping forces than any other country in the world.

Within France, the police have great power and operate with considerable freedom—too much, according to critics. Alongside the police forces that are under the control of local governments, a national police force is located in the ministry of defense. It is garrisoned throughout France and has a reputation for tough tactics. Judges and executive officials have rarely reined

in the police. The "forces of order," as they are called in France, have a reputation for engaging in illegal surveillance, arbitrary actions, racism, and torture. Young men of immigrant backgrounds from North Africa, black Africa, and the Caribbean are especially likely to be subject to identity checks and strip searches. This constant tension occasionally erupts in ugly confrontations. In 2007, for example, when security agents at a Paris railroad station arrested an African immigrant who was traveling without a ticket, a pitched battle occurred between the police and bystanders. Before the tear gas settled and the battle ended, scores of police and demonstrators had been injured. For several nights following Nicolas Sarkozy's election as president in 2007, there were demonstrations, car burnings, and clashes with police in Paris, Marseille, Lyon, Nantes, Bordeaux, and Toulouse. The most dramatic example of an urban uprising, involving thousands of car burnings in 2005, will be described in Chapter 10. Although clashes between demonstrators and the police are often violent and result in injuries on both sides, France's tough gun control legislation limits the use of guns, and deaths are extremely rare.

The Judiciary

Traditionally the French judiciary possessed little autonomy and was considered an arm of the executive. In the past two decades, however, this condition has changed dramatically. The Constitutional Council has assumed central importance and independent administrative regulatory authorities have been created in such varied sectors as broadcasting, stock market transactions, and commercial competition.

The Constitutional Council. The Constitutional Council might be considered the Cinderella of the Fifth Republic, a Cinderella who has now come into her own. Two scholars observe, "Originally an obscure institution conceived to play a marginal role in the Fifth Republic, the Constitutional Council has gradually moved toward the center stage of French politics and acquired the status of a major actor in the policymaking system."[4]

The nine members of the council are named for staggered nine-year nonrenewable terms. The president of the republic and the presidents of the National Assembly and Senate each appoint three members. The president of the republic names the council's president. Those named to the Constitutional Council are generally distinguished jurists or elder statesmen. Ex-presidents are entitled to sit on the council. The first woman ever named to the council was appointed in 1992.

Three factors contributed to the substantial increase in the power of the Constitutional Council and of the judiciary more generally:

- Broadening access to the Constitutional Council. At first, only the president of the republic and the presidents of the two houses of the legislature could bring cases to the council. A constitutional amendment passed in 1974 authorized sixty deputies or sixty senators to bring suit. As a result, the council now rules on most important new legislation.
- Broadening the council's jurisdiction to include the power of judicial review—that is, the power to invalidate legislation that a majority of the council judges to be in violation of the constitution. The council exercises judicial review in a more limited way than does the U.S Supreme Court. It can only strike down recently enacted legislation before the law is officially implemented. If it fails to do so, the legislation can never be reviewed. But it is unprecedented in France that a judicial body should be able to overrule the legislature, and the council now exercises this sweeping power in a bold and continuous fashion. If a major innovation of the Fifth Republic in the first years of the republic was to establish the dominance of the executive over the legislature, a major development since then has been to establish the primacy of the constitution, as interpreted by the Constitutional Council, over both the legislature and executive. The change has substantially expanded the powers of the council and has provided greater balance among political institutions. However, after the Council issued a ruling that the government disliked, it sponsored a constitutional amendment in 1995 that prevents the council from reviewing (and overturning) legislation passed by a referendum.
- Transferring the power to appoint judges from the executive to magistrates elected from among the rank of judges. This change required a constitutional amendment in 1993. The same amendment created

a new Court of Justice of the Republic to try cases against government ministers who are accused of criminal acts committed while in office. The court comprises six deputies and six senators, elected by the two chambers of the legislature, and three senior judges.

Critics charge that the judiciary continues to be unduly subject to political influence. Two institutional factors are that the minister of justice, a cabinet minister, exercises important power over judges, and the president (not an independent judge) presides over the *Conseil supérieur de la magistrature*, the highest judicial governing body.

The French judicial system of Roman law, codified in the Napoleonic Code and similar codes governing industrial relations and local government, differs substantially from the pattern prevailing in Britain, the United States, and other nations that are inspired by the common law system. French courts accord little importance to judicial precedent; what counts is legislative texts and the codification of legislation in specific subfields. The trial system also differs from that in the United States. French judges play an active role in questioning witnesses and recommending verdicts to juries. A judicial authority, the *juge d'instruction*, is delegated responsibility for preparing the prosecution's case. Criminal defendants enjoy fewer rights than in the U.S. or British system of criminal justice.

State Council.   France has a system of administrative courts whose importance is linked to the great power of the bureaucracy and the wide scope of administrative regulations. (Keep in mind that many areas regulated by laws in other democratic systems are the subject of administrative regulation in France.) There are about thirty administrative courts. The most important is the *Conseil d'État* (State Council), whose role as a watchdog on the executive is especially important in the French political system, where the executive has such great power. Members of the State Council belong to one of the most powerful and prestigious *grand corps*. The council hears cases brought by individuals alleging that their rights have been violated by administrative regulations and actions, and it can order appropriate remedies. The State Council also provides advice to the government about the constitutionality, legality, and coherence of proposed laws. Although the government can overrule the State Council, it rarely does so because the council's opinions command enormous respect.

The Economic and Social Council

The constitution designates the Economic and Social Council as a consultative body composed of representatives from business, agriculture, labor unions, social welfare organizations, and consumer groups, as well as distinguished citizens from cultural and scientific fields. The council has issued influential reports on important public issues, including job discrimination toward immigrants and reorganization of the minimum wage system. However, it has no legislative power and occupies a modest role within the regime.

Subnational Government

There are three layers of subnational elected governments in France: municipal, departmental, and regional. With 36,000 municipalities, France has more local governments than all other Western European countries combined! Although the system seems unusually cumbersome, citizens are deeply attached to local government. Public opinion polls consistently demonstrate that local politicians command far greater respect than do national officeholders. Until the 1980s, local governments were quite weak. Responsibility for regulating local affairs lay in the hands of nationally appointed field officers of government ministries, such as prefects, supervisors of civil engineering, and financial officers.

The Socialist government sponsored a fundamental overhaul of local government in the 1980s. The national government's supervision of local governments was reduced, regional governments were created, and localities were authorized to levy taxes and sponsor economic, social, and cultural activities. A constitutional amendment in 2003 further extended the scope of decentralization, enshrines the principle of decentralization in the constitution, and requires the national government to provide local governments with adequate revenues when local governments are delegated responsibilities.

The decentralization reforms have enabled regional, departmental, and city governments to gain significant responsibility for education, transportation, social welfare, and cultural activity. Subnational governments have sponsored public transportation facilities that link cities in the provinces, thereby modifying the characteristic wheel-and-spokes pattern by which all French roads and railroads formerly led to Paris! The reforms have brought government closer to citizens. They have enabled local governments to sponsor joint public-private economic development projects.

Yet decentralization has created new problems. The greater autonomy and authority of local officials has provided tempting opportunities for corruption. Many local officials have been convicted of taking kickbacks in return for authorizing questionable land development schemes and for granting contracts for public works projects. The reforms have also increased economic inequalities among localities and regions.

The European Dimension

Political institutions in France, like those in other member states of the EU, are closely integrated with the corresponding EU institutions. French public officials spend considerable time participating in and implementing EU decisions. The process begins at the top: the president, prime minister, and cabinet constantly participate in shaping EU decisions. The cabinet includes a minister responsible for European affairs. An agency within the prime minister's office is charged with coordinating French governmental policies, legislation, and regulations that relate to EU affairs. Most government ministries have a bureau specializing in EU regulation. Whether the topic is the quantity of fish that French commercial trawlers are permitted to haul or standards for French pharmaceuticals, French legal and administrative regulations must conform to EU treaties and directives. (With that said, France has been among the countries that have been slowest to transpose EU directives into national regulations and legislation.)

The French judiciary has played an important role in promoting the Europeanization of France's political institutions. French courts give EU directives and rulings by the European Court of Justice and the European Court of Justice on Human Rights precedence over French regulations and legislation. In 2004 the French Constitutional Council went one step further; the State

Council concurred in a ruling in 2007. They declared that EU directives trump the French constitution (although the Council hinted that some fundamental features of the constitution, for example, those involving human rights, remain supreme). As a result of the close integration of France in the EU, it is difficult to unravel where the "EU" begins and "France" leaves off.

The Policymaking Process

The policymaking process differs substantially between periods of unified control and cohabitation. We describe the pattern in which control is united, the current situation. At these times, the president formulates most major policy initiatives, usually after consulting with the prime minister and powerful cabinet ministers. Government ministers, assisted by top civil servants, develop legislative proposals and administrative regulations that translate broad policy into concrete action. The parliament nearly always approves the government's initiatives, with few changes.

There are fewer opportunities in France, compared with most other democratic regimes, for public and private actors outside government to influence policymaking. The constitution enshrines executive dominance at the expense of the legislature and popular participation. The bureaucracy is large, expert, and often domineering. Points of access for private interests are fewer than in most democratic regimes.

Yet the fact that a particular policy is adopted does not mean that it will be fully and smoothly implemented. The details of policy *outcomes* cannot be predicted merely by knowing the content of policy *decisions*. The bureaucracy may be divided by competition among different ministries, and bureaucrats may use their expertise and power to protect their own and their agency's interests. Moreover, private interests have resources to resist legislative and bureaucratic directives, as evidenced by strikes and popular protests described in Chapter 9. And the Constitutional Council may intervene to require the modification or even abandonment of policy initiatives.

The position of the executive and the French state more generally have been deeply affected by France's participation in the global economy. EU commitments have limited France's freedom of action, although EU membership has also enabled France to leverage its power by gaining a leading voice in this influential multilateral organization. EU membership has also redistributed power among the political institutions of the French state. For example, judicial authorities, notably the Constitutional Council and State Council, have gained an authoritative role in interpreting and applying EU treaty commitments and directives. Executive agencies have gained power relative to the French parliament, since the executive represents France in EU decision making and parliament has little choice but to accept the results.

As France has become more integrated within the EU and the wider global arena, the gulf has widened between political decision makers and ordinary citizens. This has created additional stress on the system of political representation. Despite reforms described above, including limiting the president's term to five years and strengthening the autonomy of the judiciary, France's institutional structure remains the target of widespread criticism. Chapter 10 describes several proposals for institutional reform.

Notes

[1]Editorial, "Chirac, sans Regret," *Le Monde*, May 16, 2007.

[2]Robert Elgie, *The Role of the Prime Minister in France, 1981–91* (New York: St. Martin's Press, 1993), p. 1.

[3]Ezra Suleiman, "Les élites de l'administration et de la politique dans la France de la Ve République: Homogénéité, puissance, permanence," in Ezra Suleiman and Henri Mendras, eds., *Le recrutement des élites en Europe* (Paris: La Découverte, 1995), p. 33.

[4]John T. S. Keeler and Alec Stone, "Judicial-Political Confrontation in Mitterrand's France: The Emergence of the Constitutional Council as a Major Actor in the Policy-making Process," in Stanley Hoffmann, George Ross, and Sylvia Malzacher, eds., *The Mitterrand Experiment: Continuity and Change in Mitterrand's France* (New York: Oxford University Press, 1987), p. 176.

CHAPTER 9

Representation and Participation

The construction of the Fifth Republic was inspired by Charles de Gaulle's belief that political parties and parliament had overstepped their proper role in the Third and Fourth Republics and had thereby prevented vigorous executive leadership. To correct what he regarded as this dangerous imbalance, the Constitution of the Fifth Republic grants the executive an astonishing array of powers and severely limits popular participation, representation, and legislative autonomy.

Although de Gaulle did succeed in limiting parliament's role, he completely failed to curb political parties. Ironically, however, the development of strong, well-organized, centralized parties early in the Fifth Republic—squarely contrary to de Gaulle's intentions—has helped provide decisive leadership and political stability, which were de Gaulle's highest priorities.

What explains this curious turn of events? De Gaulle's decision to provide for popular election of the presidency powerfully contributed to the development of strong parties. What he did not anticipate was that, in order to win the all-important presidential contest, the formerly decentralized parties of the Fourth Republic were forced to become centralized, unified organizations. The result facilitated strong executive leadership, although parties have not been especially useful in fostering popular participation and representation. As a result, France's centuries-old tradition of popular protest against state authority persists.

The Legislature

Parliaments everywhere have been described as ceding power to the executive. But the French parliament began (in the Third and Fourth Republics) with a higher degree of power than other legislative bodies have generally enjoyed and has sunk lower (in the Fifth). The operative assumption in the Fifth Republic has apparently been that parliament should be neither seen nor heard.

The French parliament is bicameral and consists of the National Assembly and the Senate. The National Assembly is the more powerful of the two houses since it alone can censure the government, and it has the decisive role in passing legislation. Since the Senate's approval is required for constitutional amendments to pass, it is coequal in this important domain with the National Assembly.

In France's semipresidential system, parliament lacks the independence that legislatures enjoy in presidential systems. Moreover, since the president is not responsible to parliament, it cannot hold the executive fully accountable. Parliament in the Fifth Republic has lost power to the president, government, bureaucracy, judiciary, television, subnational governments, and the EU!

Article 34 of the constitution, which defines the scope of parliament's legislative jurisdiction, represented a revolution in French constitutional law. Rather than authorizing parliament to legislate in all areas except those explicitly designated as off-limits—true to the tradition of parliamentary sovereignty prevailing most of the time since the French Revolution—the constitution enumerates those areas in which parliament *is* authorized to legislate; it prohibits legislation on other matters. Furthermore, outside constitutionally specified areas, the executive can issue legally binding regulations and decrees without need for parliamentary approval. Even within the domain of parliamentary competence, the government can request parliament to authorize it to issue ordinances with the force of law. Governments requesting this have been delegated authority when they wish to save time, avoid extensive parliamentary debate, or limit unwelcome amendments. Yet another procedure by which the executive can bypass parliament is by calling a referendum.

Within the limited area of lawmaking, the constitution grants the government extensive powers to control legislative activity. The government is mostly responsible for establishing the parliamentary agenda. As in other parliamentary regimes, the government, not backbenchers or the opposition, initiates most bills that eventually become law—about 90 percent in a typical legislative session.

Parliament has especially limited control over the budgetary process. Members of parliament are prohibited from introducing budget amendments that will raise expenditures or lower revenues. Furthermore, parliament must approve the budget within seventy days after it has been submitted by the government or the government can enact it by decree (although this has never occurred in the Fifth Republic).

The executive can dissolve the National Assembly before its normal five-year term ends, which necessitates new elections. (The executive cannot dissolve the

Senate, but this matters little since, as stated above, the Senate lacks two vital powers enjoyed by the National Assembly: the right to pass legislation and the ability to force the government to resign by voting censure.) If the executive dissolves the National Assembly, it cannot do so again for a year.

The government's control over parliament's legislative and other activity is bolstered by additional measures. Under Article 44, the government can call for a single vote—known as the *vote bloquée* ("blocked vote," or package vote)—on all or a portion of a bill. The government can select which amendments to include with the text. Governments have used—or, according to the opposition, abused—the package vote procedure to restrict debate on many key legislative texts.

The government can further curb parliament by calling for a confidence vote on either its overall policies or a specific piece of legislation (Article 49, clause 3). This provision applies only to the National Assembly since the Senate is not authorized by the constitution to pass a motion of no-confidence (that is, censure). When the government calls for a confidence vote on a text, the measure is considered approved unless the National Assembly passes a censure motion by an absolute majority of all deputies within twenty-four hours. (Members of the National Assembly are known as deputies; members of the Senate are known as senators.) In effect, deputies who abstain are counted as voting with the government. If an absolute majority of deputies do vote against the measure, it is defeated and—more significant—the government is required to resign.

Deputies can also submit motions to censure the government (and thereby force it to resign) on their own initiative. A motion must be signed by one-tenth of all deputies in the National Assembly. The procedure for passing this kind of censure motion is the same as the one called by the government. However, deputies who sign a censure motion of this kind cannot do so again during the life of the legislature. This limits the number of parliament-initiated censure motions.

Given that the government normally commands majority support in the National Assembly, it need not worry about being forced to resign by a vote of censure. In fact, only one censure motion has ever passed in the fifty-year history of the Fifth Republic.

Because of the severe restrictions under which parliament functions, it is widely perceived as a rubber stamp. The result is to limit the opportunity for useful national debate. Because opposition parties cannot air grievances effectively, discontented groups often calculate that they must take to the streets rather than channel demands through parliament.

Voting in the National Assembly is generally along party lines, and there is strong party discipline: that is, deputies from each party vote as a bloc. This means that the government can generally count on obtaining majority support for proposed legislation.

In some parliamentary systems, parliamentary committees—the French term them commissions—play a vital role. But not in the Fifth Republic. There are six permanent commissions: Foreign Policy; Finances and Economy; Defense; Constitutional Changes, Legislation, and General Administration; Cultural, Family, and Social Affairs; and Production and Exchange. Commissions are responsible for reviewing proposed legislation. Although they may propose amendments, the government can reject those it dislikes. The constitution also authorizes parliament to create commissions of inquiry to investigate the executive, but the few that have been created were ineffective.

In recent years, parliament has modestly increased its role. For example, in the early years of the Fifth Republic, only one session a week was reserved for members of parliament to pose oral questions to the government; a constitutional amendment in 1995, however, added two more periods a week. A 1990 reform increased the possibility for members of parliament to initiate legislation.

The imbalance between executive and legislature remains a fundamental flaw in the constitutional architecture of the Fifth Republic. Although there is wide agreement on this point, it is difficult to correct. When political parties are in the opposition, they usually lead the charge for change. However, when they win presidential and parliamentary elections, and are therefore in a position to rectify the imbalance, they develop a sudden appreciation of the virtues of the status quo!

How a Bill Becomes a Law

We provide here a simplified version of how legislation is enacted. Following a bill's introduction in one of the two houses of parliament (usually the National Assembly), the bill is reviewed by a parliamentary commission in that chamber and is then submitted to the full chamber for debate, possible amendment, and vote. If the text is approved, it goes to the second chamber, where the same procedure is followed.

If a bill is passed in identical form by the two houses, it becomes law (unless subsequently struck down by the Constitutional Council). If the two houses vote different versions of a bill, the process begins again in which bills are introduced into both chambers. If the two houses pass a different version of a text twice—or after one reading, if the government declares the bill a priority matter—a joint commission composed of members from the two houses seeks to negotiate a compromise text. If the commission reaches agreement on such a text, it is again considered by both houses. If the two chambers do not pass an identical text at this reading, the government can request the National Assembly to have the last word. If the National Assembly approves its version of the bill, the measure is considered to have passed despite having failed to gain approval by the Senate.

Once a bill passes, the constitution authorizes the president of the republic, the president of either chamber of the legislature, or sixty deputies or senators to request the Constitutional Council to review the text. The council can strike down the entire text or approve some portions and strike down those that it judges to violate the constitution. The council must be asked to rule within one month after a bill is passed. After this period, the bill becomes law and can never be reviewed by the council. (This is an important difference from the procedure followed by the American Supreme Court; it can review legislation no matter how long ago it was passed.)

Why would the National Assembly and Senate hold different positions on a policy issue? One reason is that the two houses are elected by different procedures and represent different interests.

Electing the Legislature

Elections in the 577 single-member districts of the National Assembly are held according to a two-ballot plurality election procedure, similar in most respects to the one for presidential elections. District boundaries are drawn by nonpartisan procedures that quite accurately reflect the distribution of the population throughout France. To be elected at the first ballot, a candidate

must receive over 50 percent of the votes cast in the district. In most districts, no candidate obtains a majority at the first ballot because France's multiparty system means that there are many candidates running. However, some popular candidates—usually incumbent deputies—are elected at the first ballot. If no candidate receives a majority at the first ballot, a runoff election is held the following week. Unlike presidential elections, in which only the two front-runners may compete at the runoff, all candidates receiving at least 12.5 percent of the votes can compete at the second ballot. Although some "triangular" runoffs occur, in which three candidates compete, most runoff elections pit one candidate on the left against one on the right.

Since party alliances typically reflect the left-right divide, the system used to elect the National Assembly contributes to polarization within French politics. The system also maximizes the chances that a cohesive coalition will gain a majority in parliament, and it bolsters political stability in the entire political system. Political scientist Jean Charlot claims that the two-ballot single-member district system "has proved . . . one of the most solid underpinnings of the Fifth Republic."[1]

There are 343 members of the Senate. Most are elected for six-year terms by mayors and town councilors from France's 100 *départements* (the administrative districts into which mainland and overseas France is divided) as well as from several overseas territories. Since there are many small towns and villages in France, this procedure ensures that the Senate will be particularly conservative and zealous in defending rural interests. (This situation has produced frequent demands to reform the composition of the Senate.) When the National Assembly is controlled by center-right parties, the Senate and National Assembly usually agree on proposed legislation. When the National Assembly has been controlled by the Socialist party, the two chambers often clashed and the National Assembly was more likely to pass legislation over senatorial opposition.

Political Parties and the Party System

France has a multiparty system: that is, one in which more than two parties capture a significant share of the popular vote. We have described how powerful political parties have promoted political stability in the Fifth Republic. Parties have facilitated stable leadership and political alternation in office. In recent years, there has been a decline in the ideological distance between the major parties on the center-left and center-right. Although this has reduced tensions between center-left and center-right parties, many French citizens do not consider that these governing parties represent their interests. As a result, they have gravitated to fringe parties at the ideological margins.

The result of this development is that one can identify two different axes of competition in the sphere of electoral politics in contemporary France. The first axis involves competition in presidential and parliamentary elections between two major governmental parties, one on the center-left, the other on the center-right. Smaller parties present candidates in presidential and parliamentary elections in the Fifth Republic, but most of the time candidates from the two major parties have won the presidency and the lion's share of seats in parliament.

The second axis pits the two major governing parties against a large number of small, fringe parties, often located at the extremes of the political spectrum. This logic was evident in the 2005 referendum on the EU draft constitution, when the center-left and center-right parties joined forces to advocate approval of the referendum, while fringe parties throughout the spectrum recommended a no vote. This axis pits the prosystem parties against the parties calling for radical change of one kind or another.

Nicolas Sarkozy won the 2007 presidential election because he performed effectively on both dimensions. On the one hand, he was the candidate of one of France's major political parties, the center-right Union pour un mouvement populaire (UMP), and he represented order, stability, and continuity. Having served as an influential cabinet minister for years, he was clearly an insider. At the same, he reflected the second logic by presenting himself as an outsider and appealing to voters sympathetic to the National Front. He did so by calling for a "rupture" (his term) with the established system, advocating extensive change, and highlighting themes traditionally championed by Le Pen: the value of work, patriotism, and law and order.

The 2007 election did not exclusively involve competition between the center-left and the center-right.

The main surprise of the first round of the election was the strong showing of centrist candidate François Bayrou. Although he was a seasoned cabinet minister in center-right governments, Bayrou broke ranks and advocated rejecting both center-left and center-right. Unlike other fringe candidates, who were located on the extremes of left and right, he led a centrist party. However, as he proclaimed during the 2007 campaign, he was a *radical* centrist! What he meant was that he squarely opposed the left-right logic that has shaped the Fifth Republic, but he was not an ideological extremist of left or right. Instead, he advocated transcending left-right cleavages in favor of a centrist coalition that would unite moderates on both sides. The fact that he gained nearly 20 percent of the vote and came in third was further confirmation that the French are tired of business as usual and are looking for a new approach.

The Major Parties

Two major parties—the Union pour un mouvement populaire (UMP) and the Parti socialiste (PS)—currently vie for national dominance. For the past several decades, each one has been the largest party within a coalition that includes smaller, separate, but allied parties. The UMP has led a center-right coalition, the PS a center-left coalition. The two coalitions have alternated control of key political institutions in the Fifth Republic. The two parties are continually challenged by a host of smaller parties. Many of the smaller parties ally with one or the other major party, others, at the ideological flanks, oppose both parties. We review here the UMP and PS and, more briefly, two of the most important small parties.

Union pour un Mouvement Populaire (UMP). Until General de Gaulle reached power in 1958, there were a large number of parties on the center-right of the French political spectrum. Under de Gaulle's leadership, a new party was created. Largely thanks to his popularity, it was the keystone of the Fifth Republic in the early years. Although the party lost its commanding position in the mid-1970s, it has re-established its dominance in the current period.

The Union for a Popular Majority, or UMP, is the current name of the party. (Its name and political orientation have gone through many changes since the party was first created.) It was originally created to support de Gaulle's personal leadership and his goals of championing France's national independence, while providing strong political leadership for modernizing French society and economy, while preserving the country's distinctive cultural heritage. The party has never had a precise program, and its positions have frequently changed.

Beginning in the mid-1970s, the UMP slipped from first place. Jacques Chirac, who became leader in 1974, lost presidential bids in 1981 and 1988. With Chirac still in control, the UMP regained its premier role in the 1990s. Chirac was elected president in 1995 and re-elected president in 2002, while Nicolas Sarkozy, who became leader of the party in 2002, was elected president in 2007. Sarkozy's popularity contributed to the party's victory in elections to the National Assembly held a month after the presidential elections. However, the UMP's majority was smaller than in the previous legislature and less than polls had predicted. The party's support slumped shortly before the election when news leaked out that the government was considering raising taxes to finance social programs.

President Sarkozy promised bold leadership and a fresh start, following President Chirac's lackluster presidency. Given Sarkozy's dynamic personality, the UMP's control of the government and National Assembly—along with the disarray of the Socialist Party, as will be described in a moment—the UMP will likely retain political dominance until at least the next presidential elections in 2112.

Demographic changes further contribute to improving the UMP's future prospects. The party's social base generally reflects its conservative orientation. It enjoys strong support from business executives, shopkeepers, professionals, farmers, the elderly, the wealthy, and the highly educated. The UMP's popularity with elderly voters provides the party with a strong advantage, as the population is becoming increasingly composed of older people.

Parti Socialiste (PS). The PS has a long history, stretching back a century. In the early years of the Fifth Republic, it was a perpetual and ineffective opposition party. However, under the leadership of François Mitterrand, it achieved a stunning reversal. When Mitterrand was elected president in 1981, and the PS swept parliamentary elections, it played a key role in shaping present-day France by embracing the institutions of the Fifth Republic (many on the left opposed the legitimacy of the Fifth Republic in the early years) and sponsoring sweeping reforms in the 1980s and 1990s that helped modernize the French economy and society.

However, as described in Chapter 7, the party lost its ideological bearings after the right turn of 1983 and has yet to define a coherent new identity. It lost the last two legislative elections, in 2002 and 2007, and the last three presidential elections, in 1995, 2002, and 2007. A major reason is that the PS is deeply divided by ideological and personal conflicts. When Ségolène Royal ran for president in 2007, she tried to synthesize the party's warring factions, but she succeeded only in antagonizing all camps and giving the impression of incoherence. The party was further battered following the 2007 elections when President Sarkozy persuaded several leading PS politicians to accept cabinet positions in Prime Minister Fillon's government and membership on blue-ribbon government commissions.

The PS remains a powerful force in French politics. Although it lost the last several presidential and parliamentary elections, it remains the largest opposition party in the National Assembly (and the number of PS deputies elected to the legislature in 2007 increased by fifty-five). The PS controls twenty of France's twenty-two regional governments, the Paris city hall, and many other subnational governments. But if the party is to regain dominance, it will need to unify around a new and attractive program, mount a credible opposition to the Sarkozy administration, and renew its leadership.

The PS draws support from public sector workers, notably teachers and civil servants, and members of the liberal professions. Despite the differences between the electorates of the PS and UMP, both parties tend to represent the more secure strata of French society. The most vulnerable and excluded groups, including unskilled workers, the unemployed, and school dropouts, have been especially likely either to support fringe parties or to remain on the political sidelines.

Small Parties

At the same time that the UMP and PS have consolidated the center-right and center-left of the spectrum, a backlash has occurred among voters who believe that neither party is responsive to their concerns. An array of small parties (sometimes known as splinter parties) appeal for support from this large group. The extreme case was the 2002 presidential election, when Jospin and Chirac, the PS and UMP candidates, received only 36 percent of the first ballot vote. In 2007, the PS and UMP candidates received over half the first ballot votes—but candidates from smaller parties received a hefty 43 percent of the vote. The strength of splinter or fringe parties means that the current French party system exhibits strongly conflicting tendencies between consolidation and fragmentation.

Splinter parties contribute to the diversity, vitality and confusion—of French political life. Among the most significant are les Verts (Greens), several ultraleft Trotskyist parties, and the Parti communiste français (PCF). Special mention should be made of the PCF, which was the largest party in France in the first years after World War II. It steadily declined and is now a shadow of its former self. (Its presidential candidate in 2007 received less than 2 percent of the vote.) Given space limitations, we limit our analysis to the two largest splinter parties.

Front national (FN).   The FN was among the first political parties in Western Europe since World War II to promote racist themes. The party's fortunes have been tied to the popularity of its founder, Jean-Marie Le Pen, a flamboyant orator whose speeches blend folksy humor and crude attacks. Le Pen's first success in the 1980s came from targeting immigrants, primarily Arabs from Algeria, as the cause of France's problems. His answer was to deport them or, at the least, deprive them of social benefits.

In recent years, Le Pen and the FN broadened their focus to make political hay from an increase in France's crime rate, the corruption of mainstream politicians, economic insecurity, and the problems caused by European integration. Le Pen has proposed protectionism, pulling France out of the EU, eliminating the income tax, and outlawing abortion. In the 1990s, he added Jews to his list of scapegoats, characterizing the Holocaust as a "historical detail" and making crude anti-Semitic jokes. Le Pen has been convicted several times of violating laws that make it a crime to incite racial and religious discrimination as well as defend war crimes.

Le Pen's biggest breakthrough occurred in 2002, when he skillfully capitalized on citizens' apathy, disgust with the status quo, and lurid media coverage of some violent crimes during the election campaign. He nosed out Socialist candidate Lionel Jospin to come in second at the first round, and thus qualified to compete in the runoff ballot against frontrunner Jacques Chirac.

Le Pen could not repeat his 2002 exploit in the 2007 elections. By gaining 14 percent of the vote, he came in fourth. One reason for his fairly poor showing, as already described, is that Nicolas Sarkozy stole Le Pen's thunder by appropriating some of his principal campaign themes. Another reason was Le Pen's advanced age (he was seventy-nine during the 2007 election).

Although the FN has apparently passed its peak, it remains an important political force. Moreover, Le Pen's greatest achievement was not winning elections but reshaping France's political agenda by highlighting issues like immigration and crime. For this reason, the editor of an influential newsweekly described Le Pen's movement as "the most important political phenomenon of the last 25 years . . . ."[2]

Nouveau Centre (NC).   The Nouveau Centre (NC)—New Center—is the modest remnant of major centrist and Christian Democratic political parties in the Fourth and Fifth Republics. In the first years of the Fifth Republic, these parties maintained a separate existence from the Gaullist party because they opposed de Gaulle's strong opposition to European integration. For many years, the major centrist party was called the Union des démocrates pour la France—UDF. The high point of the UDF's influence came when its leader, Valéry Giscard d'Estaing, was elected president in 1974. However, after Giscard was defeated by François Mitterrand in 1981,

Both Ségolène Royal and Nicolas Sarkozy seek François Bayrou's endorsement. *Source:* Plantu, *Le Monde*, April 24, 2007.

and the UMP became more pro-European in the 1980s and 1990s, the UDF seemed headed for extinction.

In 2002, the UMP attempted to persuade the UDF to merge, but UDF leader François Bayrou refused. At the same time, the UDF served as a junior partner of the UMP. For example, UDF deputies elected in 2002 owed their victory to an alliance with the UMP; in turn, they supported UMP governments. And to cement UDF support, UMP prime ministers usually appointed several UDF politicians to their government.

In 2005, Bayrou became increasingly critical of the UMP and by 2006 ended his support for UMP Prime Minister Dominique de Villepin's government. When Bayrou came in third in the 2007 presidential election, with a very respectable 18.6 percent of the vote, he produced the greatest surprise of the election.

In the 2007 parliamentary elections that followed the presidential elections, most UDF deputies running for re-election threw in their lot with the UMP in order to gain the UMP's support. (Without UMP support, it was certain they would not be re-elected.) The UDF renamed itself the Nouveau Centre and succeeded in electing twenty-two deputies to the National Assembly. However, Bayrou opposed an alliance with the UMP

and formed a new party, the Mouvement Démocratique (popularly known as MoDem). He announced his aim of remaining independent and positioning the MoDem as an alternative to both major political camps. In the short run, the strategy failed: the MoDem elected only four deputies in 2007. However, commentators have noted that Bayrou has his sights fixed on the 2012 presidential elections. His strategy is to be available in the event that Sarkozy proves unpopular.

Elections

French voters go to the polls nearly every year to vote in a referendum or in elections for municipal, departmental, or regional councilor, deputy to the European Parliament or National Assembly, and president. The most important elections are the legislative and presidential elections (see Tables 9.1 and 9.2).

After the Socialist Party's right turn and the PCF's decline in the 1980s, scholars identified a trend toward the "normalization" and "Americanization" of French politics. This involves a trend toward a two-party system, with both parties converging toward the political

Table 9.1

Electoral Results, Elections to National Assembly, 1958–2007 (percentage of those voting)

	1958	1962	1967	1968	1973	1978	1981	1986	1988	1993	1997	2002	2007
Far Left	2%	2%	2%	4%	3%	3%	1%	2%	0%	2%	2%	3%	2%
PCF	19	22	23	20	21	21	16	10	11	9	10	5	4
Socialist Party/ Left Radicals	23	21	19	17	22	25	38	32	38	21	26	25	26
Ecology	—	—	—	—	—	2	1	1	1	12	8	4	3
Center	15	15	18	10	16	21*	19*		19*	19*	15*		8
Center-Right	14	14	0	4	7			42*				5*	4
UNR-RPR-UMP	18	32	38	44	24	23	21	—	19	20	17	34	40
Far Right	3	1	1	0	3	0	3	10	10	13	15	12	7
Abstentions	23	31	19	20	19	17	30	22	34	31	32	36	40

*Number represents the percentage of combined votes for Center and Center-Right parties.

UNR = Union pour la nouvelle République; RPR = Rassemblement pour la République.

Percentages of parties do not add to 100 because of minor-party candidates and rounding errors.

Sources: Françoise Dreyfus and François D'Arcy, *Les Institutions politiques et administratives de la France* (Paris: Economica, 1985), p. 54, *Le Monde*, March 18, 1986; *Le Monde, Les élections législatives* (Paris: Le Monde, 1988); Ministry of the Interior, 1993, 1997; *Le Monde*, June 11, 2002; www.electionresources.org/fr/deputies.php?election=2007&region=fr, accessed 6/18/2007.

center. In France's case, this involved the UMP on the center-right; the PS on the center left. Parties that were significant and independent players in the past tended to become junior partners of the two major parties. In most elections, the UMP and PS captured the largest share of the vote at the first ballot. Further, the Americanization of French politics involved a tendency to elevate the personalities of political leaders over ideological issues.

While there is strong evidence for these developments, France is far from having a two-party system and the French political style continues to be quite different from that found in American politics. As for a two-party system, in the 2007 presidential election only 57 percent of those voting chose Sarkozy and Royal at the first ballot. The remaining 43 percent of votes were cast for the other ten candidates. As for whether French politics is now a carbon copy of American politics, recall the presidential debate between Sarkozy and Royal. For well over two hours, the two candidates went head-to-head debating the details of their policy differences—cogent evidence that France has resisted the sound-bite style of American political discourse!

Yet recent developments have caused scholars to speak of a crisis in the French party system. Among the elements:

- The ample support for fringe parties not part of the select "cartel" of governmental parties. Recall that, although the major governing parties vigorously campaigned for a "yes" vote in the 2005 referendum on the European constitution, 55 percent of the electorate opposed their position. A public opinion poll during the 2007 presidential election campaign highlighted the unpopularity of the established parties of center-left and center-right. When voters were asked whether they trusted the left or the right to govern the country, three-fifths of respondents replied that they trusted neither camp.[3] This finding foreshadowed the election returns themselves, where (as we have seen) the two major candidates received only a bare majority of first-ballot votes.

Table 9.2

Presidential Elections in the Fifth Republic (percentage of those voting)							
December 1965		June 1969		May 1974		April–May 1981	
Candidate	Ballot Percentage	Candidate	Ballot Percentage	Candidate	Ballot Percentage	Candidate	Ballot Percentage
Extreme Right							
Center-Right							
de Gaulle (Center-Right)	44 (55)	Pompidou (UNR)	44 (58)			Chirac (RPR)	18
Center							
Lecanuet (Opposition-Center)	16	Poher (Center)	23 (42)??	Giscard	33 (51)	Giscard	29 (49)
Center-Left							
Mitterrand (Socialist-Communist)	32 (46)	Defferre (PS)	5	Mitterrand (PS)	43 (49)	Mitterrand (PS)	26 (52)
Left							
		Duclos (PCF)	22			Marchais (PCF)	15
Abstentions	15 (16)		22 (31)		15 (12)		19 (14)

Note: Numbers in parentheses indicate percentage of vote received in second ballot. Percentages of votes for candidates do not add to 100 because of minor party candidates and rounding errors.

Sources: John R. Frears and Jean-Luc Parodi, *War Will Not Take Place: The French Parliamentary Elections of March 1978* (London: Hurst, 1976), p. 6; *Le Monde, L'Élection présidentielle: 26 avril–10 mai 1981* (Paris: Le Monde, 1981), pp. 98, 138; *Le Monde,* April 28 and May 12, 1998; *Journal officiel,* May 14, 1995; *Le Monde,* May 5–6, 2002; *Le Monde,* April 24 and May 7, 2007.

- Voting patterns have been increasingly unstable. Political scientist Pascal Perrineau notes, "A new type of voter is emerging, less docile to social and territorial allegiances, less faithful to a party or political camp, and less involved in the act of voting. . . . Voters are likely to change their minds from one election to

April–May 1988		April–May 1995		April–May 2002		April–May 2007	
Candidate	Ballot Percentage	Candidate	Ballot Percentage	Candidate	Ballot Percentage	Candidate	Ballot Percentage
Le Pen (FN)	14	Le Pen (FN)	15	Le Pen (FN)	17 (18)	Le Pen (FN)	11
						De Villiers	22
Chirac (RPR)	20 (46)	Chirac (RPR)	21 (53)	Chirac (RPR)	20 (82)	Sarkozy (UMP)	31 (53)
Barre	17	Balladur (UDF)	19	Bayrou (UDF)	7	Bayrou (UDF)	19
				Saint-Josse (CNPT)	4		
				Madelin (PR)	4		
Mitterrand (PS)	34 (54)	Jospin (PS)	23 (47)	Jospin (PS)	16	Royal (PS)	26 (47)
				Mamère (Greens)	5	Voynet (Greens)	2
				Chevèrement	5		
Lajoinie (PCF)	7	Hue (PCF)	9	Hue (PCF)	3	Buffet (PCF)	2
				3 candidates (Extreme Left)	11	3 candidates	7
			21		28 (20)		15 (15)

another, or even from one ballot to another in the same election."[4] In every one of the six legislative elections held between 1981 and 2002, the governing majority swung between the center-left and center-right parties. In the 2007 presidential elections, half the electorate remained undecided about which candidate to support until the closing weeks of the campaign.

At the same time, for the first time in nearly three decades, there was no alternation in 2007 in the majority coalition that controlled the National Assembly. Further, the presidency also remained in the hands of the center-right. This is partly a result of the center-left's divisions, partly a result of the unity of the center-right under Nicolas Sarkozy's leadership. Another factor is demographics: the proportion of older voters, who tend to vote conservative, has been steadily increasing in the French population. Whatever the full explanation, the 2007 election outcome suggests a majority of French these days are more comfortable with center-right governments.

• Senior politicians from across the political spectrum, including former Prime Minister Dominique de Villepin, many cabinet ministers, a president of the Constitutional Council, and prominent mayors, have been accused and in some cases convicted of corruption. Worse yet, President Chirac has been the target of corruption charges. Clear evidence exists that, while mayor of Paris between 1977 and 1994, he received illicit political contributions and kickbacks from companies doing business with the Paris city government. Chirac escaped prosecution

Allegations of corruption by President Chirac.
Source: Photo © Philippe Wojazer/Reuters/Corbis; cover © 2001 The Economist Newspaper Ltd. All rights reserved. Reprinted with permission. Further reproduction prohibited. www.economist.com

only because the Constitutional Court ruled that a sitting president has legal immunity. After leaving the presidency in 2007, Chirac was forced to testify about these cases in closed-door investigations. Further, Alain Juppé, who served as prime minister under Chirac from 1995–1997, was convicted of political corruption in cases in which Chirac was directly involved.

Political Culture, Citizenship, and Identity

For close to a century, French political culture was structured in a quite stable fashion. Since the 1980s, however, two of the major traditional subcultures have disintegrated: a predominantly working-class subculture, structured by the strong grip of the PCF and the PCF's trade union ally, the CGT; and a subculture comprising religiously observant, politically and socially conservative French people linked to the Catholic Church and its affiliated social organizations.

Both subcultures comprised a dense network of organizations in diverse spheres, including sports, culture, mutual aid, and professional activities; they provided their members with distinctive (and opposed) political orientations and social identities. The decline of the communist and Catholic subcultures has produced a vacuum that helps explain the increased volatility in electoral behavior described above. We analyze here changing forms of French political and social identity.

Social Class

For centuries, France was among the countries in which class cleavages periodically fueled intense political conflict. Under the impact of economic change and ideological reorientation, however, there was a rapid decline of class identification in the 1970s, especially among manual workers (see Table 9.3). One reason is the downsizing since the 1970s of basic industries, including steel, shipbuilding, automobiles, and textiles. This has produced a drastic reduction in the size of the industrial work force. Another reason is the decline of the trade union movement, a traditionally important source of working-class identity and activity.

Table 9.3

Proportion of French Citizens Identifying Themselves as Members of a Social Class

	1976	1983	1987
Total	68%	62%	56%
Occupation of respondents			
Higher executives, professionals	68%	67%	60%
Middle executives, school teachers	57%	66%	63%
Office workers	64%	62%	59%
Manual workers	74%	71%	50%

Source: L'Expansion, March 20–April 27, 1987, in Louis Dirn, La Société française en tendances (Paris: PUF, 1990), p. 63.

Citizenship and National Identity

France has a two-sided approach to citizenship and national identity that dates back to the Revolution of 1789. On the one hand, the inclusionary aspect of what has been termed "the republican model" specifies that any immigrant who accepts French political values and culture is entitled to citizenship. Political sociologist Charles Tilly observes that France has "served as Europe's greatest melting pot."[5]

On the other hand, the French republican model is quite restrictive. It dictates that cultural identities should remain private and play no role in the public sphere. France has stiff laws outlawing racial and religious discrimination, hate crimes, and incitement to racist violence, and welfare state programs distribute substantial benefits to individuals who qualify. Yet political scientist Robert Lieberman notes that the French approach to racial and ethnic inequality "has not gone beyond the color-blind frame and the model of individual discrimination to embrace a more collective approach that attempts to compensate for inequalities between groups."[6]

Most French regard the American conception of multiculturalism as dangerous because, in their view, it threatens to fragment the political community and erode common ties of citizenship. Yet France's dominant color-blind and ethnic-blind model functions in a quite exclusionary way in practice. For example, few members of

ethnic minorities hold positions in the Constitutional Council, National Assembly, or upper reaches of the administration. (President Sarkozy's appointment of several members of ethnic minorities to the government in 2007 was a dramatic break with past practice.)

Flaws in the republican model were highlighted by a controversy in 2003–2004 involving the display of religious symbols in public places. In 2003, French president Jacques Chirac delivered a major nationwide television address on educational reform. Did his proposal involve the curriculum, educational standards, or school finance? Guess again. President Chirac proposed banning the display of "conspicuous signs of religious affiliation" in public schools. (The phrase is from the law overwhelmingly passed by parliament in 2004 to implement the proposal.)

The principal target of the reform was the *hidjab* (headscarf) worn by some Muslim girls. The president explained that the reform aimed to preserve religious neutrality in public schools, in accordance with France's secular, republican tradition. Banning headscarves was an attempt to combat Muslim fundamentalism and protect Muslim girls from intimidation, since the headscarf symbolizes their subordinate status.

About 80 percent of the French polled on the question supported the ban. Although only several thousand of nearly one million Muslim schoolgirls wore the headscarf to school, most French citizens considered that they represented a disturbing challenge to France's secular values.

The ban was quite effective. One study found that, since passage of the law, fewer than 300 Muslim girls have been expelled for defying the ban.[7] Teachers and principals report that tensions have been greatly reduced since the ban went into effect, although a study found that many Muslim girls regret having to remove the headscarf.[8]

Conflicts persist about the appropriate boundary between the freedom to practice one's religion and the defense of secular standards in the public sphere. For example, should Muslim girls be required to participate in co-ed gym classes? Can a female patient in a public health clinic refuse treatment from a male doctor? Should female Muslim medical students be prohibited from wearing a headscarf? These are not hypothetical questions: every one has recently provoked public debate and conflict. And a framework has not yet been developed that would handle these issues in a satisfactory way.

Race and Ethnicity

Issues of race and ethnicity in France are intertwined with immigration. France has traditionally attracted large numbers of immigrants. Indeed, in 1930, the proportion of immigrants was higher than in the United States.[9] Today, one French person in four has at least one parent or grandparent who is foreign-born. The most prominent example is President Sarkozy, whose Hungarian parents immigrated to France after World War II. (Sarkozy himself was born in France.)

As discussed above, the republican model proclaims that immigrants are welcome, on condition that they accept dominant French values. Yet anti-immigrant sentiment in contemporary France is widespread. One poll reported that a majority of respondents believe that there are too many immigrants in France. These attitudes have deep historical roots. Historian David Bell observes, "The Belgians and Italians met as much hostility and prejudice in their time as Algerians and black Africans have done in contemporary France, and sometimes more."[10]

Opposition to immigrants is often linked to racism. In one recent poll, over 60 percent of respondents claimed that racist reactions are sometimes justified. Only one-third declared that they would notify the police if they witnessed a racist attack.[11]

Most first- and second-generation immigrants nowadays are from the Maghreb, the term used to describe France's three former North African colonies of Algeria, Morocco, and Tunisia. Other immigrants are from sub-Saharan (black) Africa, Portugal, and Turkey. The majority of recent immigrants are Muslim, and roughly half the Muslims are of Arab background.

There are about five million Muslims in France, about one-third of all Muslims in Western Europe. French Muslims are a diverse group. Although most are from North Africa, others hail from over 100 countries. About half are French citizens. They differ considerably in the extent and character of their religious observance and political beliefs. But what many do share are distressed socioeconomic circumstances. Many immigrant families live in dilapidated public housing projects that are located on the outskirts of Paris, Marseille, and Lyon. For example, about one-quarter of Marseille's residents are Muslim.

These low-income neighborhoods (the French call them *cités*) are desolate places. There are few public services, unemployment is sky-high, and tensions are strong. In late 2005, the accidental death of two adolescents of Algerian background in a *cité* outside Paris sparked a widespread uprising. For weeks, gangs of young men in the low-income neighborhoods of many cities torched cars and public buildings and attacked buses and trains. (The crisis will be described more fully in Chapter 10.)

Recent governments have limited new immigration to France, expelled undocumented immigrants, and tightened requirements for obtaining French citizenship. An immigration reform in 2006 required immigrants to learn French, limited the possibility for family members of immigrants to enter France, and tightened procedures for obtaining residence permits. During the 2007 presidential campaign, Nicholas Sarkozy capitalized on anti-immigrant sentiment by proposing the creation of a ministry of immigration and national identity. Critics charged that linking immigration and national identity implies that immigrants are responsible for France's social unrest.

The government's harsh approach has provoked criticism. When in 2003 the government ratcheted up procedures for those seeking political asylum because of abusive treatment in their home country, Amnesty International charged the French government with violating the human rights of asylum seekers.[12]

To summarize, France has benefited immensely from the presence of immigrants. And it has granted immigrants, or at least their children, the right to citizenship and social benefits, including access to day care facilities and schools, public health programs, and public housing.

However, on an informal level, immigrants have often been regarded as second-class citizens. They are expected to abandon their own cultural practices. They are given the least desirable jobs or not offered jobs at all. The public housing projects and neighborhoods in which they live are often in shabby condition.

The position of immigrants is an extreme case of how public and private institutions can both set a high standard of quality but also inadequately represent the interests of many groups in French society. The result of the design flaws in public institutions and the rigidity of political culture is that what appears as a calm political situation may be the calm before the storm. The pattern of disruptive popular protests described later in this chapter is thus closely linked to the design of French political institutions and cultural attitudes.

Gender

France was the birthplace of modernist feminist thought. Philosopher and novelist Simone de Beauvoir's *The Second Sex*, published after World War II, is a landmark study of women's subordinate position that analyzed how gender differences are socially constructed. In the 1960s and 1970s, French feminist theorists played a major role in reshaping literary studies around the world. However, there is considerable gender inequality in France, and women's movements, like many other French social movements, have been relatively weak.

Women, the largest "minority"—in reality, 53 percent of the population—have traditionally been highly underrepresented in the French political system. Although women are over half the electorate, there has never been a female president of the republic and only one prime minister. Ségolène Royal was the first woman to be a major presidential contender fifty years after the creation of the Fifth Republic. Although she was defeated by Nicolas Sarkozy, her candidacy may alter future political equations. Yet, women remain underrepresented in national political institutions. For example, France has been at the low end of EU countries with respect to women's legislative representation.

France took a giant step toward increasing women's representation by amending the constitution in 1999 and passing legislation in 2000 that mandates gender equality for many elected bodies. The parity law requires political parties to nominate an equal number of male and female candidates in legislative bodies whose members are chosen by elections using a list system. These include municipal councils, regional councils, and the European Parliament. Parties that violate the law may be disqualified. The parity law has been enormously effective in rectifying the traditional gender imbalance in these important institutions.

Roughly equal numbers of men and women now serve on these elected bodies.

Although the glass ceiling in French political institutions has been cracked, it is far from shattered. For one thing, the law is much less demanding when it comes to elections held in single-member districts, that is, institutions that are not filled by the list system of election. In these bodies—above all, the National Assembly—the penalty for parties that fail to nominate an equal number of men and women is mild: they receive smaller public campaign subsidies. Since large parties receive lavish private contributions, it costs them little to violate the law. For example, only 19 percent of deputies elected to the National Assembly in 2007 were women. (At the same time, this represents a significant increase from the 12 percent of female deputies in the previous legislature.)

Further, the parity law does not apply to executive offices—and men continue to monopolize these positions. For example, although female representation on regional councils soared after the 2004 regional elections, only one of mainland France's twenty-two regional councils elected a female president—Ségolène Royal. Moreover, the parity law does not apply to the offices of prime minister, government, or president—the most powerful positions in French politics.

Although the parity law has not produced full political equality, it has put the issue of gender equality front and center. It doubtless helped Ségolène Royal obtain the PS nomination in the 2007 presidential elections. Indeed, four of the twelve candidates running for president in 2007 were women, a record number. And a new era began when newly elected President Nicolas Sarkozy appointed seven women to the fifteen-person government headed by Prime Minister François Fillon, including the dynamic Rachidi Dati as minister of justice and Christine Lagarde as minister of economy, finance, and employment, among the most powerful cabinet posts.

Interests, Social Movements, and Protest

The political party system represents one arena for citizen participation and representation. Other ways that citizens pursue their interests include collective action and protest.

Organized Interests

The overbearing French state has typically tried to restrict interest groups and social movements. Although some interest groups, such as the farm lobby (the FNSEA) and the umbrella business group (Medef), participate in consultative commissions and have easy access to policy makers, many interest groups have little influence. One important example: French labor unions are quite weak. (See boxed feature: "Citizen Action: French Trade Unions.")

CITIZEN ACTION: French Trade Unions

The character of the French trade union movement and its relationship to politics explain much about protest in France. French unions never organized as large a proportion of workers as did unions in other Western European countries, and they have steadily declined in strength from their postwar high: the proportion of the active labor force belonging to a union has plummeted from a high of over 30 percent in the postwar period to under 10 percent nowadays—the lowest figure of any industrialized democracy. The bulk of union members are found among public sector workers.

Moreover, the trade union movement is highly fragmented. There are five umbrella trade unions that group unions based in industries throughout the economy, as well as independent unions in specific sectors (such as teachers). The confederations compete with each other in recruiting members. They also nominate candidates in elections to representative bodies (called works councils) based in shop floors and offices. Traditionally, most confederations were loosely allied with one or another political party. The largest confederation was closely allied with the Communist Party, while other confederations had links to the Socialist and centrist parties. The confederations have ended their ties to political parties, but their rivalry with each other continues. Consequently, save for exceptional moments, such as when the government proposes a cutback in social benefits that all unions oppose, organized labor rarely speaks with one voice.

France's economic difficulties have often been linked to the conflictual state of industrial relations. As opposed to the situation in Germany, for example, French unions and employers do not cooperate to regulate wage levels, working conditions, and retirement arrangements. The result is a contest between the two sides over these issues—mutual animosity and stalemate—often followed by state-imposed solutions.

This description suggests that because of their small numbers, organizational and political divisions, and meager clout, unions are a weak force in French politics and society. And much of the time French unions do indeed play a marginal role. But in some respects, unions are very powerful. First, they play a key role in some public and private institutions. For example, union nominees often dominate the elected works councils of French business firms. Unions have participated in managing the social security, health, pension, and unemployment insurance funds. Second, when unions oppose government proposals, they can mobilize large numbers of members, other workers, and the general citizenry, to demonstrate in support of their position. And strikes and demonstrations have periodically brought France to a halt. At these crisis points, French unions are the only organized actor with which employers and the state can negotiate in order to restore order.

Thus, one needs to distinguish two periods. During normal periods, French employers and the state often ignore unions, calculating that they are not a significant force. But when unions organize strikes and demonstrations that shut down plants, firms, economic sectors, and even large regions or the entire country, employers and the state must court union leaders. At such times, feverish all-night negotiations take place among management, government officials, and union leaders. The outcomes are often settlements that provide wage gains and institutional reforms, after which the cycle of "normalcy" resumes—until the next explosion.

Social Movements and Protest

Although the institutions of the Fifth Republic were designed to discourage citizens from acting autonomously, France's centuries-old tradition of direct protest persists. According to the World Values Survey, France is second only to Italy in the proportion of citizens who have participated in demonstrations. (We review some examples in Chapter 10.) Groups that have engaged in strikes and demonstrations in recent years include farmers, fishing interests, postal workers, teachers and professors, high school and university students, truckers, railway workers, health care workers, the unemployed, those from immigrant backgrounds, research workers, and actors—to provide a partial list! These protests reflect citizens' attempts to press their demands when institutional channels of representation are inadequate. At the same time, France has relatively fewer civic associations than other affluent democracies. The two points are quite consistent: citizens may be more likely to engage in protest precisely because they do not consider that political parties and civic associations are effective in representing their interests.

To sum up the last two chapters, the Fifth Republic has strengthened the state at the expense of citizen participation and representation. This situation raises unsettling questions about the capacity of the political system to address current challenges.

Notes

[1] Jean Charlot, *La Politique en France* (Paris: Livre de Poche, 1994), p. 21.

[2] *L'Express*, September 14, 2006.

[3] *Le Monde*, March 14, 2007.

[4] Pascal Perrineau, "Election Cycles and Changing Patterns of Political Behavior in France," *French Politics and Society* 13, no. 1 (Winter 1995): 53.

[5] Charles Tilly, Foreword to Gérard Noiriel, *The French Melting Pot: Immigration, Citizenship, and National Identity* (Minneapolis: University of Minnesota Press, 1996), p. vii.

[6] Robert C. Lieberman, "Weak State, Strong Policy: Paradoxes of Race Policy in the United States, Great Britain, and France," *Studies in American Political Development* 16 (Fall 2002): 139.

[7] *Le Monde*, April 8–9, 2007.

[8] Ibid.

[9] Patrick Weil, *La France et ses étrangers* (Paris: Gallimard, 1991), p. 28.

[10] David A. Bell, *The Cult of the Nation in France: Inventing Nationalism, 1680–1800* (Cambridge: Harvard University Press, 2001), p. 210.

[11] *Le Monde*, March 22, 2006.

[12] *Le Monde*, May 28, 2004.

CHAPTER 10

French Politics in Transition

Two recent social upheavals demonstrate the troubled state of French politics and society. Both demonstrate widespread distrust of political institutions.

Two Upheavals

In November 2005, France erupted in flames following a tragic incident in a shabby Paris suburb. Two young French citizens of Algerian background, fleeing from the police, were accidentally electrocuted after entering an electrical power substation. Critics charged that the police had chased the young men in order to carry out yet another of the identity checks to which Arab youth are frequently subjected. The police claimed that they had done nothing to provoke the boys' flight.

News of the accident triggered riots in *cités* throughout France. For three weeks, bands of young men roamed nightly to torch cars, schools, and public buildings. (Ten thousand cars were burned.) The cycle of destruction ended when heavy police reinforcements were dispatched to the turbulent neighborhoods.

Why did the deaths of two young men provoke such widespread destruction? An underlying cause is France's persistently high rate of unemployment, described in Chapter 7. Moreover, young Muslim men were especially likely to be unemployed, many had little education, and many were victims of racial discrimination. A contributing factor was that, shortly before the accident, then-minister of the interior Nicolas Sarkozy described criminals as "scum." His remark proved incendiary and for years afterward he could not enter suburban neighborhoods without provoking a violent reaction.

After the riots ended, the government announced (yet another) crash program of assistance for low-income neighborhoods. Yet the underlying problems that caused the crisis persist.

Several months after the suburban riots, a government reform initiative triggered another massive wave of opposition. Although the issues and participants in the two uprisings are very different, the two disturbances share some common features.

In early 2006, Prime Minister Dominique de Villepin sponsored a youth employment scheme that was designed to bring down the high unemployment rate among young people, especially the less educated.

(The plan was called the First Employment Contract; its French initials were CPE.) He pointed to the suburban riots the previous fall as a reason why the CPE was needed. The government hoped to encourage the hiring of young workers by authorizing employers to dismiss new hires without having to show cause. Labor unions and student organizations fiercely opposed the plan. They charged that the reform would give employers a free hand to carry out arbitrary dismissals and would be the first step toward enabling employers to dismiss workers of all ages without adequate cause.

Parliament's passage of the CPE produced an explosion. High school and university students throughout France voted to strike. Before long half of all French universities were shut down. When unions joined the student movement, the conflict spilled over beyond college campuses. Prime Minister de Villepin's refusal to compromise fanned the flames of opposition. Weeks passed, and there was no letup in the opposition movement. At one point, two million citizens in Paris, Lyon, Marseille, and cities throughout the country took part in a massive demonstration. At this point, the government reluctantly admitted defeat and cancelled the CPE. Among the consequences was that Prime Minister de Villepin's hopes to run for president were shattered.

The two crises highlight political challenges in present-day France. Both call attention to the difficulties that young French people face as they navigate the transition from school to work. The problem is most acute for school dropouts, many of whom participated in the wave of car burnings in 2005. But even those with a high school diploma or college degree may be unable to land a job.

Nor is this an exclusively economic problem. Public authorities are often criticized for the inadequate state of France's educational system. For a country that pioneered indicative planning after World War II (see Chapter 7), the failure of schools to provide the skills needed to run a technologically advanced economy is scandalous.

More generally, the two uprisings suggest the gulf between the state and many French citizens. Although successive governments have sponsored endless programs targeting what the French call "troubled neighborhoods"—an antiseptic designation for slums—citizens in these areas consider themselves abandoned by public agencies. And although Prime Minister de Villepin presented the CPE as a response to citizens' social and economic concerns, his government failed to consult student organizations and labor unions when elaborating the program.

The third feature that the uprisings share is the response of citizens to a seemingly distant state. Although the character of the two uprisings, as well as the social characteristics of participants, were very different, in both cases citizens engaged in direct action to oppose an unresponsive state.

Political Challenges and Changing Agendas

The incidents in 2005 and 2006 are extreme cases, but they were not unique events. They belong to a tradition of popular protest in France that originated in the French Revolution of 1789 and has flourished for centuries. The May 1968 protest movement was another important example in recent decades. More recently, when the government tried to ram through cutbacks in social benefits in 1995, strikes shut down railroads, buses, the Paris *metro*, the postal system, and trash collection. After 2 million people throughout France turned out to demonstrate solidarity with the strikers, the government abandoned many of the proposed changes. Other important strikes and demonstrations have occurred in the trucking industry in 2002, the health care sector in 2003 and 2004, the cultural sector in 2003, in opposition to pension reforms in 2003 and 2005, the electrical power industry in 2004, and the two uprisings that opened this chapter. Yet another important strike may be making news while you read this book!

Oui *to Roquefort Cheese,* Non *to Genetically Engineered Products*

The issue of globalization has generated a durable opposition movement among far-leftists, intellectuals, farmers, environmentalists, and ordinary citizens. The movement's best-known leader is José Bové, a sheep farmer sporting a handlebar mustache who comes from southwestern France, where Roquefort cheese is produced from sheeps' milk. Bové helped found a small farmers' movement that opposes standardized methods of farming by agribusiness corporations (including the use of genetically modified seed), as well as farmers'

loss of autonomy when large corporations centralize food processing and distribution. He became a media hero when he ransacked a McDonald's construction site near his home in 1999, for which he was sentenced to a six-week prison term. Bové received wide support from across the political spectrum for his action. He also traveled to Seattle, Washington, in 1999, to join the protests against the World Trade Organization (WTO), an international financial institution that promotes global trade and investment. In the years since then, Bové was sentenced to four additional prison terms (most recently in 2007) for destroying genetically modified crops. However, his popularity as a folk hero has not translated into electoral support: when he ran for president in 2007, he garnered a meager 1.3 percent of the vote.

The French antiglobalization movement, which Bové helps lead, claims that it is not trying to stop globalization. It designates itself as the *mouvement altermondialiste*—that is, a movement seeking another kind of globalization. The movement has wide appeal

Globalization. "And if Roquefort and Microsoft were to merge?" "Let's discuss it with José!" This cartoon appeared when José Bové traveled to the Seattle meeting of the World Trade Organization in 1999. *Source:* Plantu, Cartoonists & Writers Syndicate, from *Cassettes, Mensonges et Vidéo* (Paris: Le Seuil, 2000), p. 36.

in France. Many French fear that globalization, as presently organized, is eroding the benefits associated with the "French social model." They are also concerned that the invasion of American companies, products, and values will decimate France's distinctive culture and cherished way of life. At the same time, France is a major participant in the global economy, and, while many French are disdainful of American culture and public policy, Hollywood movies are box office hits!

One of the major organizations leading opposition to globalization is Attac, which stands for the Association in Support of the Tobin Tax. (Nobel economics prize laureate James Tobin first proposed the idea of a tax on short-term capital movements in order to deter international financial speculation.) Attac has been a sponsor of the World Social Forum, an annual assembly of antiglobalization activists from around the world, who usually meet in Porto Alegre, Brazil.

The Challenge of Le Pen and the FN

The antiglobalization movement is only one response to France's position in a changing world. Another is Le Pen's Front National. The Front National (FN) has reaped a political harvest from the presence of Muslims in French society. Political sociologist Pierre Birnbaum observes, "What the National Front proposes to the French people . . . is a magical solution to their distress, to their loss of confidence in grand political visions of the nation."[1]

The FN's success may be due less to the substance of its ideas than to its position as critic of the established system. Polls suggest that many of the party's supporters do not share its positions but vote for the FN as a way to challenge the established system of parties and politicians. Le Pen enjoyed especially strong support among native-born citizens on the margins of French society. In the 2002 presidential elections, one-third of Le Pen's electorate were unemployed, and more workers voted for Le Pen than for any other candidate.[2] Nicolas Sarkozy adapted to this situation in 2007 by shaping his campaign to stress themes like patriotism, law and order, and conservative social values that are popular among Le Pen supporters.

Muslim-Jewish Tensions

France has the largest number of both Muslims (5 million) and Jews (600,000) of any country in Europe. Although tension between Jews and Muslims has existed for years, the second Palestinian Intifada against Israel and Israel's occupation of the West Bank in 2002 provoked a wave of anti-Semitic violence, including attacks on Jews and synagogues, Jewish cemeteries, schools, kosher restaurants, and sports clubs. Although these attacks peaked in 2004, a particularly horrific anti-Semitic attack occurred in 2006 when a Jewish man was kidnapped, tortured, and set on fire.

Interethnic tension and hostility is especially common in lower-class neighborhoods with significant numbers of Jews and Muslims. Jewish children are often harassed in schools in these neighborhoods. According to one specialist, these "incidents are linked to some very real social problems in France, where many Arabs who are having a hard time or are frustrated with what is going on in Palestine are taking it out on Jews."[3]

Not all anti-Semitic violence is committed by Muslims. In some cases, skinheads and neo-Nazis have been behind the attacks, and they have targeted Muslims as well as Jews. For example, in 2007 skinheads desecrated Jewish and Muslim tombstones in several cemeteries in northern cities. And Muslims, especially from North Africa, are often the target of discrimination by mainstream French society.

France Falling?

The French have not minimized the challenges they face. Indeed, the country has been wracked by self-doubt in recent years, as illustrated by a cottage industry of books with titles like *France Falling* and *France's Disarray*. For example, *France Falling,* a relentless critique of France's political and economic system, which totally ignored anything positive, was on the best-seller list for months.[4] A public opinion poll in 2006 found that three-fourths of the French believe that the next generation will have fewer opportunities than their elders. Another poll reported that 63 percent of the French believe their country is in decline. Indeed, political analyst Sophie Meunier chides the French for being unduly self-critical![5]

A balanced assessment requires taking account of the many aspects of France's situation that are enviable, as well as of successful reforms, such as the parity law and decentralization. France's formerly hierarchical pattern of state-society relations has shifted toward a more pluralist pattern and away from the older pattern in which most decisions originated in Parisian government ministries and were implemented by civil servants. Local governments have greater freedom to experiment. Citizens have greater freedom of choice in areas like television programming and telephone service.

A reform enacted in 1999 further enlarged citizens' freedom of choice. The civil solidarity pact (*pacte civil de solidarité,* or PACs) involves civil union between unmarried couples of the same or opposite sex. The PACs provides many of the legal rights formerly enjoyed only by married couples. These days, about 10 percent of couples choose the PACs over traditional marriage. The innovation reflects a liberalization of French cultural attitudes. It is also a reflection of the weakening of the institution of traditional marriage. For example, the government's official statistical agency reported that 47 percent of all French children in 2004 were born out of wedlock; this compares with 6 percent in 1965.[6]

The French are quite accepting of diverse forms of partnership. Although it was public knowledge that Ségolène Royal and Socialist party leader François Hollande were unmarried partners and parents of four children, this situation provoked little commentary. However, a book about the 2007 election made headlines when it reported that one reason for the intense tension between Royal's campaign team and the Socialist party organization, headed by Hollande, was Royal's outrage when she discovered that her partner had cheated on her. Right after the 2007 elections, the couple announced that they were separating.

The meaning of the developments described here is not self-evident. Have recent economic and social changes produced a welcome pluralism or a disturbing fragmentation of French society? A new spirit of initiative and enterprise or an assault on equality and cherished benefits? Can the positive features of the past be preserved while reforms are introduced to address pressing problems? What must be sacrificed to achieve benefits? What benefits?

Socioeconomic and Institutional Reforms

Given France's high unemployment rate, declining international competitiveness, and daunting deficit in financing social programs, it is widely agreed that sweeping reforms are needed. However, there is intense debate over the causes of these problems and what should be done to resolve them. To what extent are cherished social benefits to blame, such as the thirty-five-hour work week, ample paid vacations, universal health coverage, the relatively young retirement age, generous pensions, and legal protections for stably employed workers? How significant is inadequate public funding of R & D? How important is the government's failure to reshape the educational system to meet the needs of a high-tech postindustrial society? What is the impact of the poor quality of what the French call social dialogue, that is, consultation and negotiation between organized business groups and labor unions?

French politics has been dominated for decades by the issue of how to reverse France's relative economic decline. French voters elected President Sarkozy in 2007 because they judged that he was more likely to possess the energy and vision needed to break the logjam in French politics that has not addressed these problems adequately. At the same time, the election did not signify a desire for a wholesale elimination of the French social model. As Olivier Roy, a French scholar, pointed out to Americans soon after President Sarkozy's election, "Americans misunderstand what a 'conservative' France could be: it does not mean a drastic shift toward a free market . . . but a balance between a welfare (and strong) state and a more flexible labor market."[7] In order to do so, President Sarkozy seeks "to give more flexibility to business, but without dismantling the minimum wage; to give more autonomy to the universities, but without privatizing them; to redefine the welfare state, but without eliminating it; to decrease the power of the unions, but without snubbing them." Among President Sarkozy's first proposals after his election were limiting the right to strike; reducing income, business, and estate taxes; and providing tax incentives to encourage employees to work longer hours. How history evaluates his presidency will in large part hinge on whether these proposed reforms are implemented and whether they promote greater economic growth and competitiveness.

France's political institutional framework is a second arena that urgently requires reform. Here are two indications of why *Le Monde* pointed to "a profound crisis of the French political regime."[8] First, polls reveal that political leaders and institutions are held in pitifully low esteem. Between 1977 and 2006, the proportion of the French who judged that politicians "are very little or not at all concerned" with what ordinary citizens think increased from 42 to 69 percent. Fewer than half of those polled during the 2007 presidential campaign judged that the election results would improve living conditions in France. And 61 percent reported not trusting either major party to govern the country.[9] Also disquieting is the fact that a majority of citizens judge that French democracy is functioning poorly.

A second indication of the crisis of political institutions is the frequency and extent of antigovernment demonstrations protesting the government's reform proposals. On the one hand, as described earlier, the tendency to engage in direct and widespread protest has deep roots in French political culture. However, this tendency has been nourished for the last half century by design flaws in the institutional structure of the Fifth Republic, notably, the imbalanced relations of executive and legislature.

The issue of institutional reform continues to rank high on the political agenda despite recent significant changes, such as the reduction in the president's term to five years and (more modestly) a 2005 constitutional amendment slightly increasing parliament's role in EU affairs.

Scholars generally agree that the major culprit is the Fifth Republic's semipresidential system, which endows the executive with too much power and the legislature with too little. As described in Chapter 8, the president has enormous power as a result of constitutional theory and political practice.

The most drastic reform proposals involve creating a Sixth Republic, either a fully presidential or fully parliamentary system. If a presidential regime were installed, the executive could no longer dissolve parliament, dominate the parliamentary agenda and limit debate (article 44), control parliament's scrutiny of the budget, or call for a confidence vote on legislative texts (Article 49[3]) of the Constitution. The office of prime minister might

be eliminated altogether. In brief, there would be a separation of institutional powers, with parliament becoming a far more powerful branch of government.

If a parliamentary regime were created, similar to Britain's Westminster model, the president might become accountable to parliament; that is, parliament could force the president to resign by passing a censure motion. Alternatively, if the president remained unaccountable, the office might become ceremonial, that is, the president would exercise merely symbolic powers, as is the case for the British monarch or German president. In this case, the prime minister and government would assume the powers that are presently exercised by the president.

President Sarkozy appointed a nonpartisan commission headed by former prime minister Eduard Balladur to recommend constitutional reforms. The commission proposed 77 changes; they would increase the president's already considerable power and strengthen authorities outside the executive. First, the Balladur Commission recommended that the president, rather than, as is presently the case, the prime minister, should be authorized to define the nation's policy orientation. The prime minister's role would be reduced to executing policies elaborated by the president. Second, the commission proposed buttressing the independence of the judiciary, promoting the expression of diverse views in the media, and increasing the role of opposition parties in parliament. It is uncertain which proposals will be enacted and whether the resulting changes will promote greater balance between leadership and representation in the French political system.

French Politics, Terrorism, and France's Relation to the United States

France's relationship to terrorism is quite different from that of the United States. The United States was the site of foreign terrorist attacks in 1993 and 2001. By contrast, France was the target of numerous domestic and international terrorist attacks long before and after 9/11.

Two violent movements having nothing to do with radical Islam have launched attacks in France for decades. One is a separatist movement seeking independence for the Basque region in southwestern France; the other seeks independence for the Mediterranean island of Corsica, which is an integral part of the French state. In 2004, 361 people were incarcerated in French prisons for terrorist activity; two-thirds were members of these separatist movements.[10]

France's troubled relationship to Algeria, the former colony that gained independence in 1964 after a brutal war with France, has been another source of terrorism dating back to the 1950s. France has been targeted by militants seeking Algerian independence (before independence was granted in 1962), by disaffected French military officers and colons (settlers) from Algeria who opposed the French decision to grant Algeria independence, and, in the 1990s, by radical Islamists of Algerian background who oppose the French government's support for the anti-Islamist Algerian government.

Although French intelligence services dismantled all these terrorist networks, the growth of Al Qaeda and other radical Islamic-based organizations in the last several years has posed a new threat to French security. France has reacted vigorously, expelling radical imams (preachers), engaging in extensive surveillance of mosques and the Islamic community more generally, and conducting frequent identity checks and sweeps to dismantle terrorist networks. One such operation in 2004 resulted in the arrest of several young French Arabs who had been recruited to fight American forces in Iraq.

Although counterintelligence agencies, located in the ministries of defense, interior, and justice have been quite effective, they have also caused concern. They operate in secret with little accountability and have been accused of corruption, religious and ethnic discrimination, and abuses of human rights. One study identifies two activities that have attracted particular criticism: "the preventive roundups and the associated indiscriminate detention of suspects; and the broad powers given to the magistrates to conduct the sweeps and detentions with very little oversight."[11] Human rights groups warn that the high-powered search for a few militants can lead to profiling all Muslims, reinforcing religious stereotypes, and fueling religious discrimination.

France has been a close partner with the United States in the international antiterrorist campaign. The two helped form a multilateral antiterrorist apparatus based in Paris. On a more general level, however, the two countries remain troubled allies—to quote the title of a book about their relationship that was published a half century ago![12] A low point in French-American relations came in the months before the United States attack on Iraq in 2003, when President Chirac threatened to veto a U.S.-sponsored resolution that sought UN support for the impending war and Prime Minister Dominique de Villepin blasted the United States in a speech at the UN. France has also criticized the United States for not signing the Kyoto Protocol on global warming and has voiced reservations about the antimissile defense system that President Bush proposed building in Europe.

There has been a partial change in French–U.S. relations following the election of Nicolas Sarkozy. In an election-night speech in 2007, he called for an end to French-American tensions and pointedly alluded to France's "American friends." He declared that "France will always be at [Americans'] side when they need her." President Sarkozy made headlines in both countries when he spent his summer vacation in 2007 at a friend's rented estate in New Hampshire—something quite unthinkable for any previous French president! But, like his predecessors, President Sarkozy continues to express important policy disagreements with the United States, and France continues to chafe at American power. The two countries will doubtless remain "troubled allies" for the foreseeable future.

The Challenges of European Integration

The EU and globalization pose particular challenges for French national identity and political, economic, and cultural autonomy. It is no coincidence that support for fringe parties of the left and right—which are uniformly critical of France's participation in the EU—has increased with the deepening of European integration in the past two decades.

An important reason why voters rejected the European draft constitution in 2005 was because they feared that it would require cuts in French social benefits, as well as because of its democratic deficit and its alleged threat to French independence and identity. The coalition opposing the EU constitution stretched from

Le Pen's FN through the *altermondistes* to far-left parties. Political scientist Pascal Perrineau has pointed out that there are no major political leaders nowadays like former presidents Mitterrand and Giscard d'Estaing who "describe Europe as a project, a dream, a utopia." Instead, Perrineau observes, "Europe is now widely regarded as a constraint."[13] With that said, immediately after his election, President Sarkozy tried to revive the process of European integration that had been stalled by the French veto of the draft EU constitution.

A key question, to which a satisfactory answer has not yet been found, is whether French national identity can be refashioned within the EU just when the French republican values of liberty, equality, and fraternity have become widely shared, and when the dominant model of cultural assimilation has been fiercely challenged in both word and deed.

French Politics in Comparative Perspective

France has long provided a fascinating case for comparative analysis. A few of the many issues involving the study of France that comparativists have analyzed include

- French exceptionalism. What is the character and extent of French exceptionalism? Is French politics becoming less exceptional? In what ways? Why or why not?

    One reason some scholars claim that political patterns in France are becoming less exceptional is that *dirigisme* and ideological conflict, two of the central features of the exceptionalist model, have declined in recent years. On the other hand, we have described how *dirigisme* has been transformed but not abandoned. Further, if "classic" left-right divisions have declined, new cleavages have developed.
- What can we learn from analyzing the tensions between the French social model and economic governance? What are the strengths and weaknesses of the French welfare state? What is the desirable balance for French citizens between time devoted to work and other spheres of social life (family, leisure, and so forth)? Must France curtail relatively extensive social protections in order to remain competitive internationally and to assure equity between

younger and older French? Might economic performance be improved without substantial cutbacks in social programs? How?

- What are the strengths and weaknesses of France's semipresidential system? We have stressed the difficulties caused by an imbalance between executive and legislature. What are the benefits of the configuration of French political institutions? For example, might the dual executive provide a model for other countries? How does the French semipresidential system compare with that of Russia?
- What does the rise of fringe parties tell us about the relationship between political parties, and social and ideological cleavages? Does France's multiparty system provide a model to be emulated—or avoided?
- How significant has been the Le Pen phenomenon? What does it say about the functioning of the French political system?
- How adequately does the French political system reconcile the conflicting values of cohesion and national unity versus toleration, indeed celebration, of diversity? How does the secular, republican model of integration compare with other modes of social integration?
- France provides an exciting opportunity to study the extent to which public policy can reduce gender inequality. What are the pros and cons of the parity law?
- French school children are taught to revere the Declaration of the Rights of Man and the Citizen of 1789 and to take pride in the fact that France has championed the values of liberty, equality, and fraternity. However, the fact that these values are now the heritage of people throughout the world means that they no longer serve as markers to identify what is distinctively French. How well has France managed the dilemma of preserving national identity at the same time that the country has become part of the European Union and a participant in the global economy? How well do French political culture and institutions equip the country to confront these challenges?

These issues will shape the French political agenda in coming years—and provide ample opportunities for comparative analysis! In brief, forty years after youthful French protesters chanted in May 1968, "The struggle continues," the words have lost none of their relevance.

Notes

[1]Pierre Birnbaum, *The Idea of France* (New York: Hill & Wang, 2001), pp. 278–279.

[2]*Le Monde*, April 30, 2002.

[3]*New York Times*, February 26, 2002.

[4]Nicolas Baverez, *La France qui tombe* (Paris: Perrin, 2003); Alain Duhamel, *Le Désarroi français* (Paris: Plon, 2003).

[5]The first poll was reported in Académie des Sciences Morales et Politiques, *La France prépare mal l'avenir de sa jeunesse* (Paris: Editions du Seuil, 2007), p. 9; the second in Sophie Meunier, "Free-Falling France or Free-Trading France?" *French Politics, Culture and Society* 22, no. 1 (Spring 2004): 98–107.

[6]*Le Monde*, February 16, 2005.

[7]Olivier Roy, "Friend or Faux?" *New York Times*, May 15, 2007.

[8]*Le Monde*, March 14, 2007.

[9]*Le Monde*, March 26–27, 2006.

[10]Jonathan Laurence and Justin Vaisse, *Integrating Islam: Political and Religious Challenges in Contemporary France* (Washington, D.C.: Brookings Institution Press, 2006), p. 245.

[11]Ibid., p. 262.

[12]Edgar S. Furniss, *France, Troubled Ally* (New York: Praeger, 1960).

[13]Pascal Perrineau, interview with Agence France Presse, reported at http://abonnes.lemonde.fr/web/dh/0,14-0@2-3224, 39-23054751,0.html; accessed June 7, 2004.

Part 3 Bibliography

Bell, David A. *The Cult of the Nation in France: Inventing Nationalism, 1680–1800.* Cambridge: Harvard University Press, 2001.

Birnbaum, Pierre. *The Idea of France.* New York: Hill & Wang, 2001.

Bleich, Erik. *Race Politics in Britain and France: Ideas and Policymaking since the 1960s.* Cambridge: Cambridge University Press, 2003.

Brubaker, Rogers. *Citizenship and Nationhood in France and Germany.* Cambridge: Harvard University Press, 1992.

Célestin, Eliane DalMolin, and Isabelle de Courtivron, eds. *Beyond French Feminisms: Debates on Women, Politics, and Culture in France, 1981–2001.* New York: Palgrave Macmillan, 2003.

Chapman, Herrick, Mark Kesselman, and Martin A. Schain, eds. *A Century of Organized Labor in France: A Union Movement for the Twenty-First Century?* New York: St. Martin's Press, 1998.

Daley, Anthony. *Steel, State, and Labor: Mobilization and Adjustment in France.* Pittsburgh: University of Pittsburgh Press, 1996.

Duyvendak, Jan Willem. *The Power of Politics: New Social Movements in France.* Boulder, Colo.: Westview, 1995.

Elgie, Robert. *Political Institutions in Contemporary France.* New York: Oxford University Press, 2003.

Gopnik, Adam. *Paris to the Moon.* New York: Random House, 2000.

Gordon, Philip H., and Sophie Meunier. *The French Challenge: Adapting to Globalization.* Washington, D.C.: Brookings Institution Press, 2001.

Hall, Peter A. *Governing the Economy: The Politics of State Intervention in Britain and France.* New York: Oxford University Press, 1986.

Haus, Leah. *Unions, Immigration, and Internationalization: New Challenges and Changing Coalitions in the United States and France.* London: Palgrave, 2002.

Hayward, Jack, and Vincent Wright. *Governing from the Centre: Core Executive Coordination in France.* New York: Oxford University Press, 2002.

Huber, John D. *Rationalizing Parliament: Legislative Institutions and Party Politics in France.* Cambridge: Cambridge University Press, 1996.

Ireland, Patrick. *The Policy Challenge of Ethnic Diversity: Immigrant Politics in France and Switzerland.* Cambridge: Harvard University Press, 1994.

Kastoryano, Riva. *Negotiating Identities: States and Immigrants in France and Germany.* Princeton: Princeton University Press, 2002.

Knapp, Andrew. *Parties and the Party System in France: A Disconnected Democracy?* Hampshire: Palgrave Macmillan, 2004.

Laurence, Jonathan, and Justin Vaisse. *Integrating Islam: Political and Religious Challenges in Contemporary France.* Washington, D.C.: Brookings Institution Press, 2006.

Lebovics, Herman. *Bringing the Empire Back Home: France in the Global Age.* Durham, N.C.: Duke University Press, 2004.

Levy, Jonah. *Tocqueville's Revenge: State, Society, and Economy in Contemporary France.* Cambridge: Harvard University Press, 1999.

Lewis-Beck, Michael S., ed. *The French Voter: Before and After the 2002 Elections.* London: Palgrave Macmillan, 2004.

Noiriel, Gérard. *The French Melting Pot: Immigration, Citizenship, and National Identity.* Minneapolis: University of Minnesota Press, 1996.

Pierce, Roy. *Choosing the Chief: Presidential Elections in France and the United States.* Ann Arbor: University of Michigan Press, 1995.

Robb, Graham. *The Discovery of France: A Historical Geography from the Revolution to the First World War.* New York: W. W. Norton, 2007.

Rosanvallon, Pierre. *The Demands of Liberty: Civil Society in France since the Revolution.* Cambridge: Harvard University Press, 2007.

Sa'adah, Anne. *Contemporary France: A Democratic Education.* Lanham, Md.: Rowman & Littlefield, 2003.

Sarkozy, Nicolas. *Testimony: France, Europe, and the World in the Twenty-First Century.* New York: Harper Perennial, 2007.

Schmidt, Vivien A. *From State to Market? The Transformation of French Business and Government.* Cambridge: Cambridge University Press, 1996.

Shields, James G. *The Extreme Right in France: From Pétain to Le Pen.* London: Routledge, 2007.

Smith, Timothy B. *France in Crisis: Welfare, Inequality and Globalization since 1980.* Cambridge: Cambridge University Press, 2004.

Smith, W. Rand. *The Left's Dirty Job: The Politics of Industrial Restructuring in France and Spain.* Pittsburgh: University of Pittsburgh Press, 1998.

Tiersky, Ronald. *François Mitterrand: The Last French President.* New York: St. Martin's Press, 2000.

Tilly, Charles. *The Contentious French: Four Centuries of Popular Struggle.* Cambridge: Harvard University Press, Belknap Press, 1986.

Treacher, Adrian. *French Interventionism: Europe's Last Global Player?* Brookfield, Vt.: Ashgate, 2003.

Websites

Embassy of France in the United States:
www.ambafrance-us.org.

French Ministry of Foreign and European Affairs:
www.diplomatie.gouv.fr/en/.

French National Assembly:
www.assemblee-nationale.fr/english/index.asp.

French President:
www.elysee.fr/elysee/english/welcome.2.html.

French Prime Minister:
www.premier-ministre.gouv.fr/en.

Le Monde newspaper:
www.lemonde.fr.

Libération, a center-left newspaper:
www.liberation.fr.

Le Figaro, a conservative newspaper:
www.lefigaro.fr.

PART 4

Germany

Christopher S. Allen

CHAPTER 11

The Making of the Modern German State

Politics in Action

In June 2005 Angela Merkel, the Christian Democratic (CDU/CSU) chancellor candidate had a 23 point lead in opinion polls and appeared well on her way to an easy victory in the German election that was less than three months away. Her opponent, Gerhard Schröder, the leader of the Social Democratic Party (SPD) had been chancellor for seven years with the environmentalist Greens party and faced such a growing crisis that he was forced to call elections a year ahead of schedule. His unpopular market-oriented reform proposals had angered the base of his own party, and had even caused some left-wing party members to join with the former eastern German communists to form the new Left Party (Die Linke). While Schröder faced mounting troubles, Merkel was a rising political star. She was the first woman candidate for chancellor in Germany, she was from the economically-depressed east, and she was a new face in a Christian Democratic movement that had been plagued with scandals after their last term in power that ended in 1998.

Yet on election night on September 18, Merkel's star had fallen dramatically. The CDU/CSU vote (35.2 percent) was only 1 percent more than that of Schröder's SPD (34.2 percent) and, more seriously, the CDU/CSU and its preferred coalition partner, the free-market FDP, had together received only 45 percent of the vote, not enough to form a center-right coalition. Rather than conceding defeat, the "loser" Schröder claimed that Merkel and the Christian Democrats had no mandate to govern. In the weeks following the election, Germany did not have the usual predictable outcome with one of the two major parties entering an alliance with its preferred small party partner.[1] Rather, tortuous negotiations ensued between the CDU/CSU and SPD about who would lead the new so-called Grand Coalition. Merkel emerged as Germany's first female chancellor, but her mandate was very uncertain.

In the two years following the surprise election of the CDU/CSU-SPD coalition, Chancellor Merkel has had good news and bad news. The German economy enjoyed a surprising recovery compared to the doldrums it faced during the first half of the decade. Unemployment dropped below 10 percent for the first time in several years, and German economic growth rebounded sharply in the first half of 2007. And for the first time in several years, German trade unions were able to sign wage contracts that produced tangible increases that were tied to increases in productivity. Whether this was due to some of former chancellor Schröder's reforms or to the longstanding adaptive

Chancellor Angela Merkel
Source: © Jens Buettner/epa/Corbis

skills of Germany's brand of organized capitalism was a matter of some debate. The problem for Chancellor Merkel is that she did not seem to receive much credit.

As the leader of a Grand Coalition that comprised the two largest political forces in the country, Merkel faced the same problem as leaders of other governments when divided government is present; namely determining who gets credit when things go well and who gets blamed when things go poorly. To be sure, she was able to use her position as head of government to establish her own political profile in such areas as EU leadership and environmental issues, and in June 2007 she oversaw Germany's hosting of the G8 Summit. Despite this, her party's status in opinion polls remained continuously under 40 percent since her election. Her coalition partner, the SPD, fared even worse, dropping to 30 percent or below for almost the entire period since the last election. Filling in the political gaps were the three, once small, parties of the opposition: Free Democratic Party (FDP), the Greens and the Left Party, each of which was regularly polling over 10 percent in opinion polls. The main problem with Merkel's increasingly not-so-Grand Coalition was that the search for political stability that such an alliance promised created a more diverse multiparty system that was most unusual in post–World War II Germany.

Geographic Setting

Germany is located in Central Europe and has been as much a Western European nation as it has an Eastern European one. The Federal Republic of Germany is divided into sixteen federal states (or *Bundesländer* in German). It has a total area of 137,803 square miles (slightly smaller than the state of Montana) and a population of 82.4 million—the largest population of any wholly European country. (Table 11.1 presents a brief profile of Germany.) About 90 percent of present-day Germans have family roots within the borders of modern Germany; all of this group speak German as their primary language, and they are roughly evenly divided between Catholics and Protestants, approximately one-third each, with the remainder religiously unaffiliated or members of other religions. Until quite recently Germany has been relatively ethnically homogeneous; however, the presence of almost three million Turks in Germany, first drawn to the Federal Republic as "guest workers" (*Gastarbeiter*)—foreign workers who had no citizenship rights—in the 1960s, suggests that ethnic diversity will continue to grow. The early 2000s saw a familiar echo of the importing of foreign workers in the 1960s. A shortage of information-age workers among the German population induced former

Table 11.1

Profile

Land and Population		
Capital		Berlin
Total area (square miles)		137,803 (slightly smaller than Montana)
Population	2005	82.4 million
Economy		
Gross national product (GNP) per capita	2006	$31,400
GDP growth rate	2006	2.2%
Women as percentage of total labor force	2003	46.7%
Income gap: GDP per capita (U.S.$) by percentage of population	2004	
Richest 20 percent		37.1%
Poorest 20 percent		8.2%
Share of trade in GDP	2004	35.6%

Sources: German Information Office; German Statistical Office; OECD; CIA; Human Development Reports.

Germany

chancellor Gerhard Schröder's government to permit the immigration of several thousand Indian information technology professionals. Furthermore, increased migration across borders by EU citizens has also decreased cultural homogeneity, since approximately 10 percent of the country's population traces its origins from outside the Federal Republic.

For a densely populated country, Germany has a surprisingly high proportion, 54 percent, of its land in agricultural production. The country comprises large plains in northern Germany, a series of smaller mountain ranges in the center of the country, and the towering Alps to the south at the Austrian and Swiss borders. It has a temperate climate with considerable cloud cover and precipitation throughout the year. For Germany, the absence of natural borders in the west and east has been an important geographic feature. For example, on the north Germany borders both the North and Baltic Seas and the country of Denmark, but to the west, south, and east, it has many neighbors: the Netherlands, Belgium, Luxembourg, France, Switzerland, Austria, the Czech Republic, and Poland. Conflicts and wars with its neighbors were a constant feature in Germany until the end of World War II.

Germany's lack of resources, aside from iron ore and coal deposits in the Ruhr and the Saarland, has shaped much of the country's history. Since the Industrial Revolution in the nineteenth century, many of Germany's external relationships, both commercial and military, have revolved around gaining access to resources not present within the national borders. The resource scarcity has produced an efficient use of technology since the industrial age, but in the past, the lack of resources also tempted German leaders to launch military aggression against neighboring countries to obtain scarce resources. This era appears to have ended, especially with the arrival of the EU.

Critical Junctures

Examining critical historical junctures from the eighteenth to the twenty-first centuries lets us better understand Germany's dynamic evolution, including the havoc that earlier German regimes caused the country's neighbors and its own citizens. This short review of the key periods that shaped modern Germany extends

Critical Junctures in Germany's Political Development

1806–1871	Nationalism and German unification
1871–1918	Second Reich
1919–1933	Weimar Republic
1933–1945	Third Reich
1945–1990	A divided Germany
1990–1998	The challenge of German unification
1998–2001	Germany in the euro era
2001–2005	Germany after September 11
2005–Present	Germany after the French and Dutch veto of the European Constitution

through the volatile history of the country's nineteenth-century unification, the creation of an empire, a first world war, a short-lived parliamentary democracy, twelve years of Nazi terror and a second world war, military occupation after that war, forty years as a divided nation, and the uncertainties of European integration (see "Critical Junctures" table).

Nationalism and German Unification (1806–1871)

The first German state was the Holy Roman Empire, founded by Charlemagne in A.D. 800 (sometimes referred to as the First Reich). But this loose and fragmented "*Reich*" (empire) bore little resemblance to a modern nation-state. For more than one thousand years, the area now known as Germany was made up of sometimes as many as three hundred sovereign entities. Only in 1871 did the powerful Prussian military leader Otto von Bismarck unite the separate states into a united German nation-state.* Bismarck called it the Second Reich because the name suggested a German state that was both powerful and able to draw on centuries-old traditions.

There are three main points to make about state formation generally and about German state formation in

---

*Prussia no longer exists as a state or province. It was an independent principality for hundreds of years until the end of World War II in what is now northeast and northwest Germany and part of Poland.

particular.[2] First, state building requires an extension of collective identity beyond the family, village, and local region to one encompassing a broader collection of peoples. Clear geographic boundaries may define such an identity. But Germany occupied central European plains with few natural lines of demarcation.

Moreover, religious, linguistic, or ethnic differences can hinder the development of a national identity. The Protestant Reformation, led by the German Martin Luther in 1517, split western Christianity into two competing sects, Catholics and Protestants. Each side viewed the conflict as both a military and a spiritual war that needed forceful leadership. This religious division retarded the development of any liberal or democratic impulses in Germany. In the absence of clear geographic boundaries or shared religious and political experiences, "racial" or ethnic and cultural traits came to define Germans' national identity to a much greater extent than for other European peoples. For many nineteenth-century Germans, the lack of political unity stood in sharp contrast to the strong influence of German culture in such literary and religious figures as Goethe, Schiller, and Luther. For many German-speakers, romanticism thus remained a powerful organic counterpoint to secular French revolutionary values, which exercised a powerful influence on the fragmented German lands after the French Revolution of 1789.

A second point is that nation-states can promote economic growth more easily than fragmented political entities can. By the time Germany joined the global economy, it lagged behind Britain and France in industrializing and securing access to the natural resources of the developing world. Germany was forced to play catch-up with these other developed states.[3] Nineteenth-century leaders felt that Germany needed access to more raw materials than it possessed within its own borders. Combined with the awakened German nationalism of the late nineteenth century, this pursuit of fast economic growth produced an aggressive, acquisitive state in which economic and political needs overlapped. Whereas Britain and France entered the nineteenth century as imperial powers, Germany's late unification and late industrialization prevented it from embarking on this quest for raw materials and empire until the late nineteenth century.

Third, military strength is a fundamental tool that many nation-states use in their formation and consolidation. Yet the rise of militarism and a corresponding authoritarian political culture were tendencies that were exaggerated in Germany for several reasons.[4] The map of Germany shows a country with many neighbors and few natural geographic barriers. This exposed position in the central plains of Europe encouraged an emphasis on military preparedness by nineteenth-century German state builders, since virtually any of Germany's neighbors could mount an attack with few constraints. And the lack of a solid democratic or liberal political culture in the various German-speaking lands before unification in 1871 allowed Prussian militarism an even greater influence over political and civic life.

German nationalism grew stronger in the early nineteenth century following the defeat of Napoleon's empire in 1814 by a British-led coalition. During his reign Napoleon had consolidated many of the smaller German-speaking principalities, particularly those from the northwest to the northeast of what is now Germany. The Prussians, under the leadership of Friedrich Wilhelm III, conducted a "war of liberation" against French forces and further consolidated German-speaking states, but now under Prussian control.

In 1819, authoritarian Prussian leaders confidently expanded trading relationships with neighboring German states that by 1834 had produced a *Zollverein* (customs union) that encompassed almost all of the German Confederation except Austria. This greatly expanded Prussian influence at Austria's expense. Political and economic currents such as free-market capitalism and democracy did not find strong roots in the Prussian-dominated Germanic principalities. Rather, the dominant features of Prussian rule were a strong state deeply involved in economic affairs (an economic policy known as *mercantilism*), a reactionary group of feudal lords called *Junkers*, a patriotic military, and a political culture dominated by virtues such as honor, duty, and service to the state.

In 1848, German democrats and liberals (*liberal* in the original European sense of favoring free markets) challenged Prussian dominance by attempting to emulate the democratic revolutionary movements in France and other European countries. However, German democratic forces were even weaker than in France because the Prussian state and authoritarian political culture were so strong. Thus, free-market and revolutionary democratic movements were violently suppressed. Yet Prussia—and eventually a united Germany—were to experience a different kind of revolution—a "revolution from above," as the political sociologist Barrington Moore has called it.[5]

After the democratic revolution failed in 1848, the most famous of the Prussian leaders, Otto von Bismarck, continued to forge unity among the remaining German-speaking independent principalities. However, after the turmoil of the 1848 revolution, a democratic and free-market approach was not possible. Bismarck then put together an unlikely, and undemocratic, coalition of the feudal, grain-growing *Junkers* in the northeast and the new industrial barons from the growing coal and iron ore industries in the northwestern Ruhr River valley. This alliance relied on an alliance of elites rather than a mobilization of the democratic working-class and peasant/farmers, which had supplied the armies of the French and American revolutions.

Very simply, Bismarck was contemptuous of democracy, preferring "blood and iron" as political tools to accompany his strong diplomatic skills. He was also as good as his word, launching three short wars—against Denmark (1864), Austria (1866), and France (1870)—that culminated in the unification of Germany. The so-called Second Reich, excluding Austria and with the King of Prussia as *Kaiser* (emperor), was proclaimed in 1871.

Second Reich (1871–1918)

The Second Reich (a term not used at the time but only retrospectively in the twentieth century) was an authoritarian regime that had some of the symbols of a democratic regime but very little of the substance. Bismarck's regime was symbolically democratic in that the Iron Chancellor allowed for universal male suffrage for the lower house (*Reichstag*) but real power lay in the hands of the *Landtag* (upper house), which Bismarck controlled.

The Second Reich saw as its primary goal rapid industrialization augmented by state power and a powerful banking system that was geared to foster large-scale industrial investment. Thus, it did not rely on British and American trial-and-error free markets. Germany became a leading industrial power by 1900, following the development of such key industries as coal, steel, railroads, dyes, chemicals, industrial electronics, and machine tools. The production of consumer goods was a lower priority. This pattern created an imbalance in which the industrialists reaped large profits while the majority of Germans did not directly benefit from the economic growth led by heavy industry. The resulting lack of a strong domestic consumer goods economy meant that a substantial portion of what Germany produced was directed toward world markets.

The rapid transformation of a largely feudal society in the 1850s to an industrial one by the turn of the twentieth century created widespread social dislocation and numerous forms of opposition. One was a general pressure to democratize the authoritarian system by providing basic rights for liberal (that is, free-market) and middle-class forces. A second was the growth of the working class and the corresponding rise of the militant Social Democratic Party (*Sozialdemokratische Partei Deutschlands*, SPD). The SPD's primary goals were economic rights in the workplace and democratization of the political system. Socialist philosophy argues that workers, as producers of society's goods and services, should receive a greater share of economic and political power. Greatly influenced by the writings and the active participation of the Germans Karl Marx and Friedrich Engels, the SPD grew as fast as the pace of German industrialization.

As chancellor from 1871 to 1890, Bismarck alternately persecuted and grudgingly tolerated his democratic and socialist opposition. He banned the SPD in 1878, but he also created the world's first modern welfare state in the early 1880s to soften the rough edges of rapid economic growth. Social welfare benefits included health insurance and the first forms of state-sponsored old-age pensions. This combination of welfare and political repression is sometimes referred to as Bismarck's "iron fist in a velvet glove."

Bismarck also powerfully influenced Germany's political culture, with its state-centered emphasis that came to characterize the united Germany. The *Kulturkampf* (cultural struggle) was a prime example of Prussian, and Protestant, dominance. Led by Bismarck,

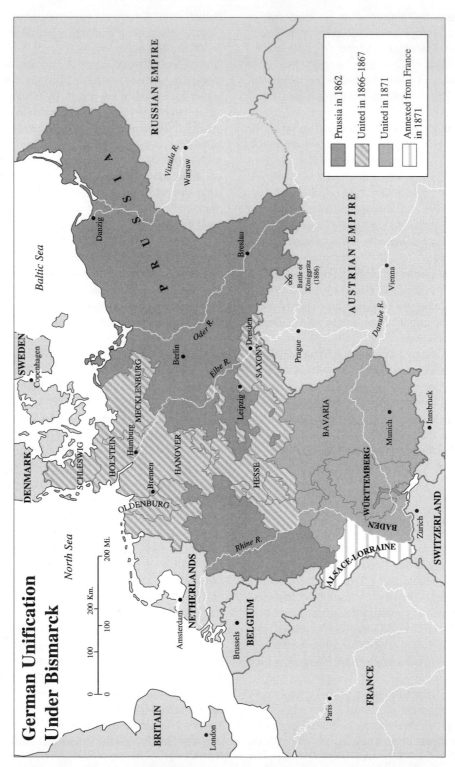

German Unification Under Bismarck

it was essentially a movement against the Catholic Church, aimed at removing educational and cultural institutions from the church and conferring them on the state. This campaign against the church and many Catholic Germans left a significant political legacy.

As the German economy grew during the latter part of the nineteenth century, German business and political leaders faced an immediate problem. How could rapid economic growth continue if they could not be certain of obtaining needed raw materials or having access to world markets to sell their finished goods? Germany participated in what historian Geoffrey Barraclough has called "the scramble for Africa."[6] However, Germany was a latecomer in this region and was able to obtain only four resource-poor colonies in southwestern and eastern Africa. From 1871 until World War I, the foreign policy of the German state was primarily concerned with extending its colonial and economic influence, only to be repeatedly checked by other colonial powers. This situation inflamed German nationalists, causing German leaders to invest in the rapid development of the ship building industry to equip a commercial shipping fleet and a powerful navy that could secure German economic and geopolitical interests.

An undemocratic domestic political system, the lack of profitable colonies, an exposed geopolitical position on the central European plains—all these factors joined with an increasingly aggressive nationalism to heighten Germany's aggression toward other nations. This volatile combination proved to be a blueprint for disaster and caused Germany to declare war in 1914.

World War I cost Germany its colonial possessions, hundreds of thousands of citizens who died in combat, and its imperial social order. The combination of weak leadership (Bismarck's successors were poor imitations of the original), lack of resources, and overconfidence in Germany's military prowess brought the Second Reich to an end at the conclusion of World War I. Germany's defeat and the collapse of the Second Reich in 1918 left very weak foundations for the country's first attempt to establish a parliamentary democracy.

Weimar Republic (1918–1933)

Kaiser Wilhelm II, abdicated the throne at the end of World War I when the army told him that they would no longer obey his orders, and the Second Reich ended. The political vacuum was filled by the large but politically inexperienced SPD, which hastily drafted a new constitution in the provincial city of Weimar. All other leading parties of the Second Reich had been discredited by Germany's defeat, so in 1918, this new leadership proclaimed Germany's first democratic government. Its first, thankless task was to surrender to the Allies.

The Weimar Republic was a procedural democracy in the sense of holding regular elections and contained a broad spectrum of political parties, from the far left to the far right. Yet its eventual fatal weakness was that too many of the rightwing political parties and social forces, as well as the Communists on the left, did not accept the legitimacy of democratic government and actively tried to destabilize and undercut it.

The SPD leadership was weakened from the beginning of the Republic; it asked the undemocratic army to "defend democracy," and it signed the Treaty of Versailles with its huge reparations payments and the demilitarization of the Rhineland. This inauspicious beginning allowed German nationalists to brand the Weimar leaders as "Jews, democrats, and socialists" who had sold out Germany's honor. Further destabilizing the Weimar Republic was a severe economic crisis in 1923, which was exacerbated by the reparations that caused the government to print nearly worthless *Reichmarks* to repay the huge debt.

In the early 1920s, Adolf Hitler, a little-known Austrian-born former corporal in the German army during World War I, joined the nascent Nazi Party. *Nazi* is a German abbreviation derived from *Nationalsozialistische Deutsche Arbeiterpartei*, the National Socialist German Workers Party. Although this sounds like the name of a leftwing party, the word *national* is important here. Taking advantage of a deepening economic crisis and a weakened democratic opposition, the Nazis mobilized large segments of the population by preaching hatred of the left, of "internationalism" (the key philosophical underpinning shared by parties of the left), and of "inferior, non-Aryan" races.

After the Great Depression spread to Europe in 1931, Germany became even more unstable, with none of the major parties of Weimar able to win a majority or even form durable governing coalitions. The last several months of the Weimar Republic (1932–1933) witnessed no fewer than six elections, all resulting in minority governments. At no time did the Nazis receive a majority. Their high point in free and fair elections was 230 seats out of 608 in the vote of July 1932, but the Nazis lost ground between then and the next Reichstag election four months later. They relentlessly pressed for political power, while most Germans continued to underestimate Hitler's real intentions and to view his hate-filled speeches as merely political rhetoric. The Nazis were rewarded in early 1933 when they and their conservative allies induced Weimar's aging president Hindenburg, a former World War I general, to allow the Nazis to obtain cabinet positions in the last Weimar government. Hitler immediately demanded the chancellorship from President Hindenburg, and received it on January 30. Once in power, the Nazis began to ban political parties and took advantage of a fire at the Reichstag that they tried to blame on the Communists. Hitler then demanded that President Hindenburg grant— by "emergency" executive order—broad, sweeping powers to the Nazi-dominated cabinet. This act made the Reichstag irrelevant as a representative political body.

Thus, the parliamentary democracy of the Weimar Republic was short-lived. From its shaky beginnings in 1918, the very stability of the state was mortgaged to forces that wished its destruction. Ironically, the constitutional structure of the Weimar regime was relatively well designed. The two significant exceptions were the "emergency" provisions allowing for greater executive power in crises and the lack of a mechanism to form and maintain stable governing coalitions among the various political parties. The more elementary problem with Weimar, however, was that not enough political parties and social forces were committed to democracy. The Weimar constitution was an elegant document, but without broad-based popular support, the regime itself was continually under attack.

Third Reich (1933–1945)

Once the Nazis controlled the chancellorship, their next priority was establishing total control of the political system and society. The initial step was the systematic banning of political parties and then controlling most civic and religious organizations. Ultimately the Nazis used propaganda, demagoguery, and the absence of a democratic opposition, which had been relentlessly hounded and then banned, to mobilize large segments of the German population. Through mesmerizing

speeches and the relentless propaganda ministry led by his aide Joseph Goebbels, Hitler used his total control of political power and the media to reshape German politics to his party's vision. This vision did not allow opposition, even within the party.

Domestic policy during the first few years of Nazi rule focused on two major areas: consolidating and institutionalizing centralized political power, and rebuilding an economy that had suffered through the monetary chaos of the 1920s and the Great Depression of the early 1930s. The Nazis chose to centralize all political authority in Berlin by making all regional and local authorities subject to tight, autocratic control. The main purpose of this top-down system was to ensure that Nazi policy on the repression of political opposition and of Jews and other racial minorities was carried out to the minutest detail.

The Nazis' economic program was also autocratic in design and execution. Since free trade unions had been banned, both private and state-run industries forced workers—and eventually slave laborers during World War II—to work long hours for little or no pay. The industries chosen for emphasis were primarily heavier industries that required massive investment from the banking system, from the state itself, and from the large cartels that formed in each industry. Some segments of big business initially feared Hitler before he came to power. Yet with free trade unions suppressed, most of German industry endorsed Nazi economic policies. The Nazis also emphasized massive public works projects, most with direct military application, such as creating the *Autobahn* highway system, upgrading the railroad system, and erecting grandiose public buildings to represent Nazi greatness.

During the Third Reich, Hitler fanned the flames of German nationalism by glorifying the warrior tradition in German folklore and exulting in imperial Germany's nineteenth-century victories. Extolling a mythically glorious and racially pure German past, he made scapegoats out of homosexuals, ethnic minorities, and, especially, Jews. Anti-Semitism proved an important political force that let Hitler blame any political problems on this "external" international minority and to target them as enemies who should be relentlessly persecuted and suppressed.

The Nazis refused to abide by the provisions of the Treaty of Versailles, began to produce armaments in

"Enemies of the Third Reich"   *Source:* Courtesy of The Trustees of the Boston Public Library, Rare Books and Manuscripts. Reproduced with the permission of Alexandra Szyk Bracie, daughter of Arthur Szyk, in cooperation with The Arthur Szyk Society; www.szyk.com.

large quantities, and remilitarized the Rhineland. The Nazis also rejected the territorial divisions of World War I, since Hitler claimed that a growing Germany needed increased space to live (*Lebensraum*) in eastern Europe. He engineered a union (*Anschluss*) with Austria in March 1938 and the occupation of the German-speaking Sudetenland section of Czechoslovakia in September 1938. The Third Reich's attack on Poland on September 1, 1939, finally precipitated World War II.

Hitler's grandiose visions of world domination were dramatically heightened by the German conquests of much of Europe during 1939 and 1940. In 1941, Hitler attacked the Soviet Union, assuming that defeating the Soviet Union would be as easy as his other conquests. The attack was not successful in defeating the Soviets and foreshadowed the Third Reich's defeat, a process that would culminate almost four bloody years later.

The most heinous aspect of the Nazi movement was the systematic execution of 6 million Jews and the imprisonment of millions of other civilians in the concentration camps. The Nazis placed most of the extermination camps in occupied countries like Poland; the

most infamous one in Germany was Dachau, just outside Munich. Hitler explicitly stated in his book *Mein Kampf* (*My Struggle*) that the Germans were the "master race" and all other non-Aryan races, especially the Jews, were "inferior." But as with a lot of his other statements during his rise to power, many Germans chose to ignore the implications of this hatred or thought it was mere exaggeration as political scientist Daniel Goldhagen suggested.[7] Critics of this position, however, have argued that Germany was much less single-minded about Jews and that divisions among the left were a significant reason for Hitler's ascension to power.[8] The magnitude of Nazi plans for other races, religions, opposing political views, homosexuals, and Gypsies, among others, became apparent after Hitler came to power, but by then any chance of domestic opposition had passed. Persecution of Jews and other racial and ethnic minorities grew steadily more atrocious until Germany's defeat in 1945.

A Divided Germany (1945–1990)

Germany was occupied by the four Allied powers from 1945 to 1949. But the realities of the cold war soon offered a different and more powerful reason for Germany's division into the Federal Republic of Germany (FRG) in the west and the communist German Democratic Republic (GDR) in the east.

This division was not expected in 1945, but since the Allies (Britain, France, and the United States) had such radically different economic and political systems from the USSR, postwar Germany took on the respective postwar visions of the two victorious sides. The major German cold war focal point was the city of Berlin, like Germany itself, divided between Allied- and Soviet-supported governments.

In the years of the postwar occupation, both German and Allied officials reduced the powers of the central state in domestic politics, replaced in part by strong regional governments. Western German reformers rebuilt the party system, creating parties that were broader and less driven by narrow ideological considerations. The most significant reform was the merger of Catholic and Protestant forces into the Christian Democratic Union (CDU) and the Christian Social Union (CSU), the Bavarian branch of this movement. During Weimar, the Catholics and Protestants had their

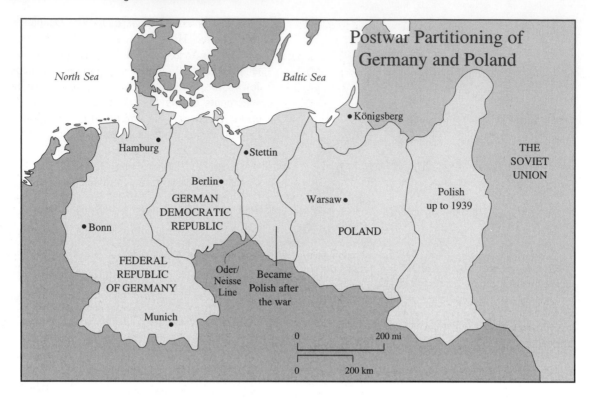

own parties, which were often uncooperative with each other as well as with other parties. However, postwar Christian Democracy radically reshaped German political conservatism by embracing democracy, social welfare, antinationalism, and antimilitarism. The party governed alone, or in coalition, for the first twenty years of the FRG.

While nation-statehood was restored to the two Germanys in 1949, neither of the two parts of divided Germany was fully sovereign. The FRG deferred to the United States in matters of international relations, as did the GDR to the Soviet Union. Neither of the two Germanys joined the cold war's international alliances—NATO (North Atlantic Treaty Organization) and the Warsaw Pact, respectively—until 1955.

The Federal Republic became a parliamentary democracy, characterized by constitutional provisions for free elections, civil liberties and individual rights, and an independent judiciary. The Federal Republic's democratic system produced rapid economic growth and remarkable political stability for its first forty years. Alternation from a moderate center-right government to

a moderate center-left one, and back again, produced high standards of living and a truly democratic regime. The development of this set of institutional and political structures—a mixed economy, democratic corporatism, and a generous welfare state—in Germany, as elsewhere in Western Europe, has been called the *postwar settlement*. The German version differed, however, from its counterparts in other Western European nations. Among the most significant were the highly organized nature of the business community; a weak central state and strong regional governments; an active tradition of worker participation within a strong labor movement (corporatism); influential quasi-public institutions shaping and implementing public policy at all levels of society; and a continued commitment to the welfare state by both major parties. The postwar period saw the development of *Modell Deutschland* (the German model), a term used beginning in the 1970s and 1980s to describe the FRG's distinctive political and socioeconomic features: coordinated banking and industrial relations, export-oriented growth of high-quality manufactured goods, democratic participation by workers on the job, and extensive public sector benefits.[9]

Under Christian Democratic chancellors Konrad Adenauer (1949–1963) and Ludwig Erhard (1963–1966), the FRG saw the establishment of a new parliamentary regime. Under Social Democratic chancellors Willy Brandt (1969–1974) and Helmut Schmidt (1974–1982) the FRG enjoyed robust full employment and saw a large increase in social services since the SPD also advocated a more equal distribution of income. But later in the 1970s, two economic recessions produced increased unemployment and forced Chancellor Schmidt to introduce moderate cutbacks in social services. Unlike many Western capitalist countries in the 1980s, however, West Germany's postwar welfare state retained many of its social services and most of its public support.

The Christian Democrats returned to power in 1982 under the leadership of Chancellor Helmut Kohl, who formed a center-right coalition with the Free Democratic Party (FDP), a moderate centrist party that had allied with both of the two major parties in most governments since 1949. The 1949–1990 period established the viability of constitutional democracy in the Federal Republic, as the country maintained a firm commitment to parliamentary government and political stability.

The German Democratic Republic (a "people's democracy," in communist parlance) was established in Soviet-occupied East Germany in 1949. The GDR was a one-party state under the control of the Communist Party, which was known as the Socialist Unity Party (SED, *Sozialistische Einheits Partei*). Although the state provided full employment, housing, and various social benefits to its citizens, it was a rigid, bureaucratic, Stalinist regime that tightly controlled economic and political life under the leadership of party chairmen Walter Ulbricht, Willi Stoph, and finally Eric Honnecker. East Germany assumed a universal consensus about the correctness of communism and suppressed public dissent as deviationist and undermining the "true path of socialism." East Germans caught trying to escape to the West were subject to execution on the spot. In August 1961, East Germany erected the Berlin Wall to keep its citizens from fleeing to West Germany.

For more than forty years, the international role of the two Germanys was limited. Because of NATO's geopolitical restrictions, West German energies were focused on rebuilding the economy and pursuing European economic integration. East Germany was similarly restricted. Although it became the strongest of the Warsaw Pact's economies, it also loyally toed the Soviet line in international affairs.

Helmut Kohl and the Challenge of German Unification (1990–1998)

Germany's unification in 1990 took place rapidly, surprising West and East Germans alike. When the Berlin Wall was opened in November 1989, the two German states envisioned a slow process of increased contacts and cooperation while maintaining separate sovereign states for the short term. When a currency reform provided East Germans with valuable West German deutsche marks, however, this move fueled the migration westward in the summer of 1990. After a referendum on unification and intense negotiations in the late summer, the former East Germany was incorporated into the FRG as five new West German states (*Länder*). This was clearly not a merger of equals.

Formal unification took place in the fall of 1990 as Chancellor Kohl, the "unification chancellor," won a strong re-election victory for his center-right Christian Democratic–Free Democratic coalition. But unification

"Unification Agreement." West German Chancellor Helmut Kohl and East German Minister President Lothar de Maizière agreeing to unification.
Source: Cartoon by Walter Hanel, courtesy Walter Hanel

euphoria did not last, since its costs placed increased stress on Germany's budget and democratic institutions. Reunification has proved much more difficult than many observers first anticipated. Before unification, East Germany was considered the strongest of the Eastern European Communist economies. But the border opening and eventual unification soon showed that the East German economy was far more backward than most economists had thought. The communist planned economy (sometimes called a *command economy*) was not sensitive to market signals, since production of goods was determined more by rigid government dictates than by consumer needs. The East German level of technology was decades behind, and the current unified German government has spent billions just to rebuild communication networks.

Incorporating the disadvantaged East Germany had an adverse impact on a wide range of public policies, including unemployment expenses, structural rebuilding funds, and the large tax increases necessary to pay for it all. The large number of unemployed in eastern Germany—approximately 20 percent, more than double the figure in the prosperous West—fueled scattered ultra-right-wing political movements. They sought out foreigners (often Turks) as scapegoats, and there were several vicious attacks on minority groups in the 1990s.

The difficulties of unification were complicated by raised expectations by the Kohl governments throughout the 1990s. In order to win the support of eastern Germans, he sugarcoated the enormity of the unification process as well as its duration. In order to win the support of western Germans, he had to convince them that the 7.5 percent "unification tax" imposed on them in the early 1990s would be money well spent. Unfortunately for Kohl, the longer the unification process remained incomplete, the less willing the German electorate was to give him continued support.

By the 1998 election, Kohl's center-right government had exhausted its mandate. Successfully convincing Germans that a change was necessary, newly elected SPD chancellor Gerhard Schröder, a generation younger than Kohl, entered into a coalition government with the Greens for the first time in the nation's history. Significant too was the continued high support for the former Communist Party in eastern Germany, renamed the Party of Democratic Socialism (PDS)

(over 20 percent), which enabled it to gain more than 5 percent of the total German vote. With almost 54 percent of the electorate voting for parties of the left, clearly a new era had arrived in Germany.

Germany in the Euro Era (1998–2001)

Germany's leaders from Konrad Adenauer, the first postwar chancellor, through Schröder have all been strongly enthusiastic toward European integration. In its relations with other states after World War II, however, Germany has faced two different kinds of criticism. First was the fear of a too-powerful Germany, a country that had dominated its European neighbors for most of the first half of the twentieth century. Second is the opposite problem, the so-called economic giant–political dwarf syndrome in which Germany was accused of benefiting from a strong world economy for much of the past fifty years while taking on none of the political responsibility. The fact that these are mutually contradictory points of view did not spare Germany from criticism.

Yet an integrated Europe promised the possibility of solving both problems simultaneously. Germany remains the economic anchor of the EU, and its membership in the EU enables it to do things and take on needed political responsibilities that it would be unable to do on its own. Former chancellor Kohl (1982–1998) realized this and was a firm advocate of all measures that would assist in a smooth, stable, and comprehensive EU.

The accelerating pace of European integration, however, with its movement toward a common monetary policy, a European Central Bank, and a single (virtual) currency in 1999, was followed by the physical elimination of eleven European currencies in favor of the euro in 2002. These changes placed additional pressures on the Federal Republic. Many Germans wondered whether the anchor of stability represented by the redoubtable deutsche mark (DM) and the inflation-fighting Deutsche Bundesbank would begin to drift in the uncertain sea of the EU. In the early years of the twenty-first century, many Germans began to realize the costs associated with European integration that might threaten the economic and political stability they had so long prized during the first fifty years of the Federal Republic. The fall in value of the euro by some

25 percent in relation to the dollar in 1999 and 2000—and its subsequent rise to more than 40 percent greater than the dollar seven years later—was worrisome to Germans long accustomed to a stable and predictable DM. More structurally, the lack of complete domestic control of Germany's monetary and fiscal policies (the latter due to the EU requirement that member states not run deficits greater than 3 percent of GDP) placed significant constraints—particularly with respect to social spending—on Chancellor Schröder.

With respect to open borders and seemingly free-flowing immigration, Germans also wondered whether Europeanization threatened to erode what it meant to be German. At the same time that immigration and political asylum increased in Germany during the 1990s, the birthrate, particularly in the former GDR, dropped precipitously. Far-right and even some moderate rightwing politicians used these demographic changes to whip up nationalist support for decreasing the flow of migrants to the FRG. Ironically, these demographic changes also coincided with the inability of the highly regarded secondary educational system to produce enough skilled workers for the information age. Germany's vocational educational system and integrated apprenticeship system have worked exceptionally well for traditionally strong German industries, but they have been less effective in producing highly qualified workers for the information sector.

Finally, the issue of democratic governance was an additional European challenge. With fiscal and monetary policy essentially determined by either Brussels or the European Central Bank, where does democratic governance really lie?

Germany after September 11

The terrorist attacks in the United States had several significant effects on German domestic and international politics. Among the most significant were immigration/globalization, antiterrorist measures, and the German relationship with the United States.

The enlargement of the EU with the addition of twelve central and eastern European countries since 2004 highlighted the challenge that immigration poses for Germany. During the *Gastarbeiter* period after World War II, immigration to Germany was comparatively straightforward. Workers came from southern Europe and Turkey, supposedly for limited periods and returned home when economic conditions no longer required their services. Of course, several generations of Turkish Germans remain in the Federal Republic, illustrating the principle of unintended consequences. But in the first decade of the twenty-first century, migrants to a much more open Germany were coming not only for economic opportunities in a globalizing world but also for political asylum.

The discovery that some of the 9/11 terrorists had lived in Germany prior to the attacks only added to the tension. Germany's sensitivity to the excesses of the Nazi regime was responsible for the liberal asylum laws because postwar German governments viewed with pride the country's openness to people facing repression. Yet the discovery of an Al Qaeda cell in Hamburg, where several of the terrorists lived before going to the United States, and the thwarting of a terrorist plot in September 2007, have created uneasy discussion in Germany on the issue of freedom versus security. Clearly the Schröder and Merkel governments in the wake of 9/11 increased domestic surveillance to locate additional terrorist cells, and made a series of arrests and detentions. But such aggressive actions by police and security forces—while essential to identify potential threats to domestic and international security—rest uneasy with considerable segments of the German population.

Germany's lack of support for the Iraq war drove a large wedge between the United States and the Federal Republic. The tension was exacerbated by the conduct of Gerhard Schröder during his 2002 re-election campaign. His leading issue in the final weeks of the campaign—largely reflecting the preferences of the German public in avoiding an attack on Iraq—was direct opposition to the Bush administration's Iraq policy in the run-up to the war in early 2003. While never reaching the depths of American-French bitterness, the long-standing strong relationship between Germany and the United States took a significant hit because of this dispute. Further exacerbating these tensions were the acquittals of two Moroccan alleged terrorists in Germany in February 2004. Because the United States refused to release witnesses—who were being held in detention in the United States—who could potentially exonerate the two Moroccan suspects in Germany, the judges in the two German courts were forced to release the two defendants because they could not present a proper defense. As the American position in Iraq deteriorated in 2004, Germany and its continental European allies did not rush to embrace the idea of either EU or NATO action in an increasingly volatile and unstable Iraq.

Germany after the French and Dutch Veto of the European Constitution

In May 2005, with 569 yes votes, 23 no votes and 2 abstentions, the German Bundestag approved the new European Union Constitution, but the situation is more complicated than this vote might suggest.

Germans want the EU, but not this EU. Most Germans would like to try to find a way to resuscitate the social market economy. This was made all the more difficult by a Social Democratic Party that marched resolutely to the right, for instance, in the Agenda 2010 and the Hartz IV reforms that many SPD members believed had gutted the heart of what the social market economy was. The fact that this departure was led by Social Democratic Chancellor Schröder is even more bizarre, since he has a constituency that actually likes and wants the kind of social protection that they used to have. The problem is that nobody has any idea how to get it, Schröder least of all, who lost his gamble with this policy in the September 2005 election.

There are three big exogenous problems and one big endogenous one.

First, a high-everything model of ever-higher skills producing ever higher-quality products may be finally meeting its match because the newly industrializing countries, particularly India and China, can catch up too fast. German firms do not have a very good answer for this, other than going offshore to places that pay lower wages and may or may not have the quality of labor that they need. Despite this challenge there is still a tremendous amount of human capital that remains in Germany, but is not being effectively tapped.

Second, the costs of German unification have been a huge drag on the capacity of the organized capitalist model to regain competitiveness. Economic stagnation will likely continue for the better part of the next decade. This has produced in its wake the Left Party (*die Linke Partei*) a merger of the PDS, the successor to the former eastern German Communist Party, and a group of left-wing western German Social Democrats

and the beginnings of right-wing movements that are for the moment still considerably smaller than similar right-wing movements in other European countries.

Third, the institutional architecture of the EU is the antithesis of the old social market economy model, which involved a coordinated set of institutions working with actors from the private sector in ways that fostered relationships, not deals, and produced high economic growth, high living standards, and considerable labor market and political peace. However, the policy of economic liberalism has been embraced heartily by both the Schröder and Merkel governments. When combined with restrictive monetary policy and a 3 percent fiscal straitjacket (that only now is beginning to be ignored), they represent the antithesis of what the German model used to be about. The larger point is that markets move much faster than institutions, and it takes time to establish institutions when a new market reality develops. The question of the day is whether Germans can resuscitate a revised set of institutions to deal with the new reality because Germans are very ineffective at economic liberalization and free market policies.

The large endogenous problem is that Germans have lost their institutional memory. In the past decade and a half the ability to develop innovative ideas to adapt their organized capitalist social market economy to economic challenges has atrophied. Most policymakers have reflexively based their responses to these challenges on old prevailing practices and not on a purposeful response to specific contemporary challenges. It is quite unclear whether Germany can find a twenty-first-century version of its once redoubtable institutional model. Much about the fate of Germany and the future of the EU hangs in the balance.

Themes and Implications

We now step back and reexamine the historical junctures in light of the four political themes that constitute our analytical framework.

Historical Junctures and Political Themes

Germany's role in the world of states, the first theme, is contentious. For all states, military strength is a basic tool used to shape and consolidate. But in Germany, the rise of militarism and a corresponding authoritarian political culture were exaggerated. In short, late unification accompanied by war created a state that caused tremendous fear among Germany's neighbors. The conduct of World War I and the crimes of the Third Reich during World War II intensified this fear. Although more than fifty years have passed since the end of World War II and although Germany's independent political actions are constrained by the EU, many Europeans remain wary of Germany's international role.

The second theme, *governing the economy,* has been colored profoundly by Germany's late-nineteenth-century state building. Clearly, nation-states can promote economic growth more easily than can politically fragmented entities. Delayed unification and industrialization prevented Germany from embarking on the race for empire and raw materials until the late nineteenth century. Thus, pursuit of fast economic growth combined with the awakened sense of German nationalism in the late nineteenth century produced an aggressive, acquisitive state in which economic and political needs overlapped. This fusion of state and economic power enabled Hitler to build the Third Reich. Consequently, after World War II policymakers and political leaders sought to remove the state from actively governing the economy. In this way, the postwar period saw the development of *Modell Deutschland* (the German Model), a term often used to describe the Federal Republic of Germany's distinctive political and socioeconomic features. It remains an open question whether previously successful German economic institutions will continue to function well in a unified Europe.[10]

The *democratic idea,* our third theme, developed much later in Germany than in most other advanced industrialized countries. It was not until 1918 and the shaky Weimar Republic that Germany first attained democracy at all. And Germany's fragile democratic institutions were crushed by the Nazi takeover less than two decades later. Despite a formal democratic constitution, Weimar was a prisoner of forces bent on its destabilization. Unlike stable multiparty political systems in other countries, the Weimar Republic was plagued by a sharp and increasing polarization of political parties. The constitution of the Federal Republic in 1949 was designed to overcome Weimar's shortcomings. A system of federalism, constitutional provisions to encourage the formation and maintenance of

coalitions, and a streamlined political party system proved solid foundations for the new democracy. Electoral turnout of between 80 and 90 percent for almost all elections since 1949 suggests that Germans have embraced democracy, although skeptics argue that Germans were voting more out of duty than anything else.[11] However, five peaceful electoral alterations in the past fifty-five years in which both government and opposition functioned more smoothly than most other democratic regimes may finally put to rest doubts about German democracy. The remaining uncertainty is how well and how quickly the democratic culture will penetrate formerly Communist East Germany.

The fourth theme, the *politics of collective identities,* offers a unique look at the intersection of democracy and collectivity. More than in other democratic countries, German political institutions, social forces, and patterns of life emphasize collective action rather than the individualism characteristic of the United States. This does not imply that German citizens have less personal freedom compared with those in other developed democracies or that there is no conflict in Germany. It means that political expression, in both the state and civil society, revolves around group representation and cooperative spirit in public action. Certainly Germany's history from Prussian militarism through Nazism has led many observers to believe that collectivist impulses should be eradicated. However, to expect Germany to embrace a liberal, individualistic democracy as in the United States with no deep history of this is misguided. Germany's development of a collective identity since 1945 has relied on a redefinition of Germany in a European context. For example, one of the first provisions of the Social Democratic–Green coalition agreement was to alter Germany's restrictive immigration policies. The new law finally enabled long-established immigrants to gain German citizenship. Thus, German collective identity is changing.

Implications for Comparative Politics

Germany differs from other developed countries in substantial ways. Germany—like Japan—was late to industrialize and late to democratize. But the most significant difference between Germany and other Western European states is, of course, the Nazi period and the destruction that the Third Reich wrought.

Concerns about this period, however, have been somewhat allayed by the passage of time, Germany's stable democratic experience since 1949, and Europe's postwar development.

Germany's significance for the study of comparative politics lies in several areas: the contrast between its nationalistic history and democratization in an integrating Europe; its unique form of organized capitalism that is neither state-led nor laissez-faire; its successful form of representative democracy that combines widespread participation and representation of the entire electorate in a stable parliamentary regime; and a politics of identity that builds on existing collectivities in an increasingly multifaceted political culture.

Some suggest that to enjoy sustained economic growth, a state should have a balanced relationship among its various social and economic interests and between the means of production and exchange. The state should promote an independent economic strategy but work closely with influential economic sectors within society, including financial institutions, trade unions, and business elites, in order to make better-informed decisions. According to this theory, neither state nor market interests should overpower the other. The Federal Republic of Germany comes close to approximating this model. Germany has taken a development path that emphasizes cooperative interaction between the state and a dense interest group network made up of key social and economic participants.

Notes

[1] Wolfgang Streeck, "A State of Exhaustion: A Comment on the German Election of 18 September," *The Political Quarterly* 77 (2006): 79–88.

[2] Charles Tilly, ed., *The Formation of National States in Western Europe* (Princeton, N.J.: Princeton University Press, 1975).

[3] David Blackbourn, *The Conquest of Nature: Water, Landscape, and the Making of Modern Germany* (New York: Norton, 2006).

[4] Gordon Craig, *The Politics of the Prussian Army* (Oxford: Oxford University Press, 1955).

[5] Barrington Moore, *Social Origins of Dictatorship and Democracy* (Boston: Beacon Press, 1965).

[6] Geoffrey Barraclough, *An Introduction to Contemporary History* (Baltimore: Penguin, 1967).

[7] Daniel Goldhagen, *Hitler's Willing Executioners: Ordinary Germans and the Holocaust* (New York: Knopf, 1996).

[8] Robert R. Shandley, ed., *Unwilling Germans? The Goldhagen Debate* (Minneapolis: University of Minnesota Press, 1998).

[9] William E. Paterson and Gordon Smith, *The West German Model: Perspectives on a Stable State* (London: Cass, 1981).

[10] Richard Deeg, "The Comeback of Modell Deutschland? The New German Political Economy in the EU," *German Politics* 14 (2005): 332–353.

[11] Ralf Dahrendorf, *Society and Democracy in Germany* (Garden City, N.Y.: Anchor, 1969).

CHAPTER 12

Political Economy and Development

The Federal Republic of Germany (FRG) has taken a distinctive development path that emphasizes cooperative interaction with key social and economic actors. Ever since the end of World War II, Germany has largely avoided the imbalances that sometimes plague other countries: for example, the American pattern in which powerful private interests "capture," or dominate, state policy; and the French pattern in which the state plays this role. Germany's organized capitalism, combined with the social market economy, has generally avoided the imbalance of state economic strategies that are subject to unpredictable changes and boom-and-bust cycles. This relative stability has been all the more remarkable in the face of the triple challenges beginning in the 1990s: German unification, European integration, and globalization.

The Postwar Settlement and Beyond

The postwar settlement in Germany long seemed to be almost an immutable fact of nature. After emerging from its horrendous history during the first half of the twentieth century, the new FRG produced something quite different: a set of structures and institutions consisting of an organized-capitalist, mixed-economy welfare state with a high degree of labor union involvement; and a stable multiparty democracy. Yet like all other institutional arrangements, those in the FRG were neither immutable nor without tensions. A number of challenges to the postwar settlement arose in the 1970s, at the end of the economic boom years, and have continued through unification and the era of European integration. This chapter characterizes the consolidation and maturing of the postwar settlement and contrasts it with the new political economy from the mid-1980s to the present. The new patterns are not simply a rejection of the old, for there are important continuities between the two.

The revitalization of the postwar settlement took place throughout the 1980s as the political economy of the Federal Republic emerged from a period of economic uncertainty—what some called Eurosclerosis.[1] By the end of the decade, however, Germany had become the leading nation in the process of European integration and accomplished its unification with the former German Democratic Republic (GDR). Yet

Helmut Kohl, the CDU chancellor for most of the decade, was consistently underestimated by his critics as he led his center-right coalition to enthusiastically embrace the concept of the single European market and pragmatically moved to consolidate the former GDR into the Federal Republic. The opposition (SPD, Greens, and the former eastern German communist party—then called the PDS) was much slower to embrace either of these two momentous developments, to their political detriment.

How did the Germans adapt their supposedly "sclerotic" system? One formidable challenge lay in labor market policy, an area that embodied the core of the long-standing institutional relationships of the postwar settlement. This issue has also suggested that the institutional capacity to address such problems, although sharply challenged, has not fundamentally eroded.

The most serious problem that Kohl faced upon becoming chancellor was increased unemployment, which was largely driven by the residue of the twin oil shocks of the 1970s. One immediate task required the government to shoulder the cost of sustaining the long-term unemployed through general welfare funds. But cost was not the only problem; there were larger structural concerns. How could the Federal Republic's elaborate vocational education and apprenticeship system absorb all of the new entrants into the labor market? In a country that prides itself on its skilled and highly paid workforce, one of the linchpins of the German model, this issue could have undermined the core of the economy, the continued supply of skilled workers.

Despite these threats in the early and mid-1980s, the unemployment compensation system and the vocational education and apprenticeship system both weathered this period during the first years of the Kohl government. In a concentrated effort, the national and state (*Länder*) governments, employer associations, trade unions, and works councils, using a variety of formal and informal institutional mechanisms, found ways to reinvigorate one of the core foundations of the Federal Republic's labor market. They did so by a series of regionally specific industrial policies. They targeted such industrial needs as automobiles and machine tools in the Stuttgart area, industrial electronics in Munich, and the declining steel industry in the Ruhr Valley. They used such existing institutions

as codetermination (*Mitbestimmung*), the works councils (*Betriebsräte*), which are present in almost all
German firms, and the country's elaborate vocational
education system. In total, 40 percent of all Germans
between fourteen and twenty-one attend vocational
school. This system allows employers, unions, and
governments to participate in shaping the curriculum
to meet the needs of particular regions. Although some
regions lagged, principally northern German regions
such as the heavy-industry Ruhr Valley and the shipbuilding cities of Bremen and Bremerhaven, other
regions prospered. Among the more successful regions
was the southwestern state of Baden-Württemberg,
where firms such as Daimler-Benz and Bosch have
their headquarters outside the region's largest city,
Stuttgart. The city of Munich and the *Land* of Bavaria
(where the giant electronics firm Siemens is located)
also prospered during the latter part of the 1980s to
the mid-1990s.

The FRG has relied heavily on its skilled blue-
collar workers throughout the postwar period. There has
been less erosion of this segment of the working class
because it plays a crucial role in the flexible-system
production processes of such industries as machine
tools, automobiles, chemicals, and industrial electronics. Sometimes called "flex-spec," this process relies
on a manufacturing workforce that is continually
requiring new skills, and the system is greatly aided
by such democratic corporatist institutions as the
works councils. Although some semi-skilled workers
have suffered job erosion in weaker industries such as
steel and shipbuilding, where there have been major
job losses, blue-collar workers in Germany have not
seen losses comparable to those in either Britain or
the United States.

Because of this reliance on high-skill and high-
wage manufacturing, the FRG has seen only a small
growth of jobs in the service sector. Unlike the United
States, where a large proportion of the new jobs since
the 1980s has been created in the service sector,
Germany has resisted this option, largely owing to the
belief that low wages would result. The plan for high-
productivity, high-wage unionized employment had
sustained the economy for many years, and most labor
market actors preferred to retain their dependence on
that policy path. The U.S. "solution," they believed,
was the wrong choice. From the mid-1980s until the

first years of unification, German industry had not listened to the siren song of service sector jobs to replace
manufacturing ones and had slowly reduced unemployment by relying on a traditional postwar pattern:
manufacturing jobs in export-earning sectors helping
to fuel economic growth and prosperity.[2] An additional
institutional factor that prevented the erosion of the
working class was the residual strength of organized
labor.[3] (The role of unions is treated at greater length
in subsequent chapters.) Their well-thought-out response to the economic downturn of the late 1970s and
early 1980s, by fortifying the institutions of worker participation (codetermination and the works councils)
prevented the erosion of union strength that took place
in other industrialized countries.

More serious strains on the social market economy
began in the early 1990s, in the wake of a false boom
immediately after unification, which was fueled by a
currency exchange that gave eastern Germans instant
hard currency to spend. These policies exacerbated the
huge costs of unification, especially the costs of
rebuilding the eastern German infrastructure. The postwar settlement was under enormous strain as Germany
reached the upper limits of its capacity to pay for such
expenses. Larger budget cuts than ever previously proposed in the FRG became imperative by the early
1990s. The completion of the European Union's (EU)
single market, supposedly the grand culmination of a
post–cold war spirit of German and European unity,
proved more difficult to realize than its planners first
thought. The immediate impact in the early 1990s
seemed only likely to strengthen the trends toward
decentralization and deregulation already under way in
Western Europe. Expanding markets is easier than
building stable and durable political institutions, as the
rapid expansion of the EU to twenty-seven countries
in 2006 has demonstrated.

More significant for Germany, the market-based EU
expansion threatened to disturb the organized capitalism
of Germany's small and large businesses. Organized
capitalism in Germany consists of an intricate, mutually
reinforcing pattern of government and business self-
regulation. Clearly, an Anglo-American push for deregulation would undermine these patterns because such a
push relies more on fast-moving transactions, not the
carefully constructed longstanding institutions characteristic of the German model. Further, the rapid

Germany has long been an organized-capitalist country in which two sets of business groups, representing industry generally and employers specifically, are powerful and coordinated.[7] Rather than emphasizing the importance of either individual entrepreneurship and small business or large corporate firms as the defining characteristic of its economy, Germany has relied on an organized network of small and large businesses working together.[8] In addition, the banking system and financial community have played a direct role in private investment. Until recently they have engaged in little of the financial speculation characteristic of Wall Street. Traditionally, they have seen their primary role as providing long-term investments for the health of the internationally competitive manufacturing industries, which are the foundation of the economy. This model generally holds for the regional and savings banks. However, a bifurcation has developed in the industry as the largest and best known of the German banks (Deutsche, Dresdner, and Commerzbank) have begun to move away from their traditional role and to behave like large banks in New York, London, and Tokyo, unfettered by long-term relationships to domestic manufacturing firms.[9]

Government economic policy is indirect and supportive rather than heavy-handed and overly regulatory. It sets broad guidelines but often leaves the implementation of policies to coordinated negotiations among organized interests such as employers, banks, trade unions, and regional governments. This does not mean the government avoids becoming involved in economic policymaking; it just does so more flexibly. The flexibility is produced in two ways. First, the German pattern of regulation addresses the general framework of competitiveness rather than the minute details more commonly addressed in other countries. In many cases, if the framework patterns are effectively drawn, microregulation is much less necessary. Second, among the major European economies such as Britain, France, and Italy, Germany has the smallest share of industry in government hands. This condition is accomplished by a cooperative federalism that delegates to the states the administrative powers of laws and regulations passed at the federal level. Both are integral parts of Germany's social market economy (*Soziale Marktwirtschaft*), discussed more fully later in this chapter.

Such policies are based on the German system of framework regulation and can best be explained in the words of one of the shapers of post–World War II economic policy, economist Wilhelm Röpke:

> [Our program] consists of measures and institutions which impart to competition the framework, rules, and machinery of impartial supervision which a competitive system needs as much as any game or match if it is not to degenerate into a vulgar brawl. A genuine, equitable, and smoothly functioning competitive system can not in fact survive without a judicious moral and legal framework and without regular supervision of the conditions under which competition can take place pursuant to real efficiency principles. This presupposes mature economic discernment on the part of all responsible bodies and individuals and a strong impartial state.[10]

By this method, German economic policy after World War II has avoided the sharp lurches between laissez-faire-led and state-led economic policy that have characterized Britain.

Germany is a prime case of a high-wage, high-welfare country that, despite slower growth since the turn of the century, has maintained its competitive world position far better than other advanced industrialized states for more than three decades since the oil crisis of 1973. In its success in combining strong competitiveness with high wages and social spending, Germany has surpassed even Japan. A high-skill emphasis in key export-oriented manufacturing industries has been the specific path that German economic policy has taken to maintain its competitive position. The foundation stones of this system are the elaborate system of vocational education combined with apprenticeship training. This education is implemented through the works councils, which are elected by all employees in all German firms with five or more employees. This system of advanced skill training enabled Germany to resist the full-scale postindustrial, service sector orientation that countries such as the United States and Britain have tried. Relying extensively on this elaborate apprenticeship training program, Germany has maintained competitive positions in such "old" manufacturing industries as automobiles, chemicals, machine tools, and industrial electronics.

The Federal Republic's strategy for international competitiveness was not to develop new high-tech industries, thereby deemphasizing the fulcrum sectors, but to employ high-technology *processes* in these comparatively old-fashioned industries. Economist Michael Piore and political sociologist Charles Sabel have called such process innovation "flexible-system manufacturing" because it emphasizes the high skill levels and flexibility of the German work force, thereby enabling these industries to find crucial niches in world markets.[11] To Americans, Mercedes-Benz, Audi, and BMW automobiles have been the most visible examples of the success of this strategy. By stressing the value that its highly skilled work force adds to raw materials, Germany has defied predictions for more than thirty years that its industrial economy would erode, as have many other formerly manufacturing-oriented developed economies. Despite being poor in natural resources (like most of the rest of Europe), Germany maintains a surplus balance of trade and still has a large working-class population, which historically has *not* favored protectionism. With one in every three jobs devoted to exports (one in two in the sectors of automobiles, chemicals, machine tools, and industrial electronics), protectionism for German unions would be self-defeating. The skills of its workers allow German industry to overcome the costs of acquiring resources and paying high wages because German industry has emphasized high quality and high productivity as offsetting factors.

Enhancing this set of policies has been Germany's research and development strategy. It preferred not to push for specific new breakthroughs in exotic technologies or for inventing new products that might be years from market. Instead it chose to adapt existing technologies to its traditional, already competitive sectors. This has been the exact opposite of U.S. research and development strategy. During the postwar years, this policy has enabled Germany to maintain a favorable balance of trade and a high degree of competitiveness. But can this model continue?

Early in the twenty-first century, however, the German political economy was much less rosy than in previous decades. European integration, German unification, and globalization have forced German industry and policymakers to examine whether their model remains appropriate or needs fundamental reexamination.

Depending on others to make core discoveries and then quickly applying the technology to production is a delicate task that requires coordinated policies among all producer groups. Trying to institute the western German policy among former GDR workers who come from a different industrial culture has proven difficult. In fact, the speed with which the information technology has penetrated into all facets of economic and public life has caught the German model somewhat unprepared. Are Germany's prevailing economic practices and policy styles still relevant for the new information industries, and for existing industries that are being transformed by the process? Can the vocational and apprenticeship system produce the kind of workers needed in the new century? The answer is uncertain, because despite unemployment at 9 percent in early 2007, German industry had to recruit programmers, web designers, and network specialists from India to meet gaping shortages in these fields. However, the deregulation of Deutsche Telekom, the formerly state-run telephone service, has begun to spur a belated development in Internet and information infrastructure technology. The question for observers of the German political economy is whether the traditional German industrial pattern of integrating and applying innovations first developed elsewhere will work well in the information age economy. In general, however, Germany still seems well positioned among those developed countries to which the term *postwar settlement* applies in the sense of the embedding of a capitalist economic system within a parliamentary democratic polity. An economic upturn in early 2007 gave the Merkel government hope.

In response to Germany's volatile history, these political and institutional arrangements were first imposed by the Allied powers to prevent extreme economic and political outcomes. Once instituted, they were soon adapted and embraced by most of the major West German interest groups and political parties. The German state has played a guiding, though not imposing, role in developing and supporting the postwar settlement. Fearful of the excesses of centralized state control, manifested in extreme form by the Nazis of the Third Reich and the Communists of the GDR, German state policy has preferred to shape and frame outcomes rather than to control them directly. In general, social identities—the guest workers excepted—and political regulation remained relatively consistent from the founding of the Federal Republic until the 1990s. Here, too, though, the post-unification turmoil has created a much greater strain on the democratic political institutions of the Federal Republic.

Social Policy

The German social market economy and its related concept of framework regulation are at the core of state-society relations and are unique contributions to democratic practice. These institutional arrangements characterize the relationship between private and public sectors and among major interest groups in German society. Rather than the state-centered polity of France and Japan or the market-centered polity of Britain and the United States, Germany has adopted a fluid, interpenetrated set of policies that govern state and market relationships. Democratic corporatism and the role of interest groups in shaping public policies (not just through state policies) are two examples. In effect, these processes of "negotiated adjustment" allow the state to delegate certain public functions to private actors in return for these private actors' taking responsibility for implementing public policy.[12] Also, Germany enjoys a kind of overlapping federalism—in the sense of national and regional governments explicitly coordinating policies with many federal laws actually implemented by regional and local governments. This produces strong institutional continuity and avoids some of the duplication that plagues relations among different levels of government in the United States. This German framework of regulation has been maintained for much of the postwar period, though the tensions produced by unification have clearly strained this system.

Such strains are particularly evident in the newer Länder that composed the former GDR. The complex network of institutions that evolved in western Germany for over forty years had to be created from scratch in the former GDR. Western German policymakers attempted to transplant successful FRG models in such policy areas as labor market, educational, welfare, housing, and regulatory institutions. Virtually all of them were less successful in the five new Länder than in the western Länder. To scholars of institutional analysis, this lack

of fit was no surprise. Wade Jacoby has written eloquently about just such "transplantation difficulty."[13] It is very difficult to impose institutional structures from outside. As Jacoby argues, successful adaptation of institutional change must be "pulled in" by indigenous actors in eastern Germany. That takes time. Furthermore, one usually organized segment of German society, business, also suffered from organizational fragmentation. Competitive pressures, principally in the east but also in the west, weakened the solidarity that had long characterized organized capitalism and began to complicate the usually smooth-running industrial relations system.[14]

Clearly the organized-capitalist model is not an unadulterated success in the minds of all Germans. Both the Greens and the small free-market-oriented sector feel that the organized, and perhaps closed, nature of producer groups gives advantages to those who are inside the loop (such as industry organizations, employer groups, and the banking community) and excludes those outside. Moreover, the Greens are also critical of many business policies that they feel do not sufficiently guard against environmental consequences. The primary critique from the small-business sector is that the organized nature of large-firm dominance is not flexible enough in the creation of new products and industries. However, neither the Greens nor advocates of a more laissez-faire approach to economic policies have dislodged the dominant position of German organized capitalism in the shaping of economic policy. And the apparent limitations of the German model for eastern Germany have been largely responsible for the continued presence of the former Communist Party, called the Party of Democratic Socialism (PDS) until 2005, and now part of the new Left Party (Die Linke). This party serves as an important tribune for Germans who would like greater resources from the federal government to offset economic dislocation.

Beginning in the early 1990s, a sharp three-pronged challenge began to undermine the idea of a smoothly functioning German socioeconomic model.

First, the Kohl government badly misjudged the costs of unification and the institutional resources that would be needed to integrate the five new Länder. Second, the structural challenges that the German political economy faced in the mid-1990s were far more extensive than any the Federal Republic had experienced since the 1950s. The amount budgeted in the early 1990s for reconstruction in Germany was approximately 20 percent of the entire FRG budget. There remains today a large gap in productivity levels between the two regions. Third, the West German integrated institutions (even when working well) became difficult to transfer as a model to eastern Germany.[15] Some 1.2 million persons were officially unemployed, and another 2 million were enrolled in a government-subsidized short-time program (part-time work with full-time pay) combined with job training. Yet the latter program had its funds cut as part of an austerity budget. In short, the problems in eastern Germany have threatened to overwhelm the FRG's institutional capacity to handle them.

The German political economy seemed in a precarious position by the turn of the century since its prowess resided in certain export-oriented manufacturing industries that faced sharper competition. In these industries, many technologies had to be constantly upgraded, and the cost of wages continued to rise. Depending on other countries to make core discoveries and then quickly applying the technology to production is a delicate task that requires coordinated

policies among all producer groups. Great problems arose. This poor economic performance created the *Wirtschaftsstandort* debate (literally, location for economic growth), which argued that the combination of domestic and international factors had made Germany a much less attractive place for investment by either international or German capital. In direct response to this challenge, the Schröder government passed a tax reform package in July 2000, followed in 2003 by Schröder's Agenda 2010—a further reform package that challenged many traditional labor market institutions to become more "flexible" along Anglo-American lines, a challenge that seemed to address directly the major criticism of the *Wirtschaftsstandort* criticism by offering both personal and corporate tax cuts. These contentious issues were significant turning points for German social democracy and the social market economy, and helped precipitate the early election (one year ahead of schedule) in September 2005. Although the reforms seemed to mollify the equities markets, they were bitterly opposed by the left-leaning rank and file of the Red-Green coalition and were a major cause of the SPD's defeat in the election. For

High Point of the Summer Concert Season. "Egon, when is the coal miners' choir finally coming out?" The sign on the tree says, "Bono, Geldof, Groenemeyer proudly present SPD-AID: Your Voice Against Low Poll Numbers." (Groenemeyer is a German rock musician.) *Source:* Cartoon by Herbert Lenz, courtesy Greser and Lenz

many, Schröder's programs represented an abandonment of fundamental principles and directly led to some SPD members, most notably former SPD Finance Minister Oskar Lafontaine to join with the former communist Party of Democratic Socialism (PDS) from eastern Germany to form the new Left Party (*die Linke Partei*) just before the 2005 election.

Thus, although the German model of economic growth has proved remarkably durable through almost all of the postwar period, the specific and demanding requirements of unification, European integration, and globalization have put new pressures on this model. The huge demands of unification are daunting enough. Complicating them is the need to align Germany's economic policies with those of its European neighbors and to respond to a competitive global economy.

Society and Economy

The social component of the social market economy also differs from those of other countries. Although the Federal Republic has always been generous with welfare benefits, they serve more than just distributive income-transfer purposes. For example, two of the most important provisions, government savings subsidies to individuals and a comprehensive vocational education system, have direct and positive benefits for the competitiveness of the German economy. They create a stable pool of investment capital and a deep pool of human capital that enables Germany to produce high-quality goods.

During the boom years of the mid-twentieth century, German economic growth provided a sound foundation for social development. The social market economy of the Christian Democrats was augmented by the SPD-led governments from 1969 to 1982, which extended and elaborated the supportive social programs of the 1950s and 1960s. Such growth and corresponding social policies helped avoid much the occupational and regional conflict common to many other countries. However, the strong role of trade unions and the unwillingness of employers to attack their workers on wage and workplace issues (perhaps owing to trade union strength) minimized stratification of society and the workplace until the 1990s. Nevertheless, German unification, European integration, and new global competitive pressures on the German economy placed increasing strains on the social market economy by slightly increasing inequalities compared with the long pre-unification period of postwar prosperity. Such change increased German *Angst* about whether their social state could support citizens at levels they had come to expect.

Inequality and Ethnic Minorities

One indelible image of Germany in the post-unification years is that of neo-Nazi skinheads setting fire to a hostel containing newly arrived immigrants in the early 1990s while chanting *"Ausländer raus"* (foreigners out) as local German residents looked on without intervening. Although such heinous acts have been relatively rare in Germany—and have also occurred in other European countries—Germany's history during the Third Reich causes alarm bells to ring at the slightest hint of racial intolerance. Thus, the issue of the role of ethnic minorities in Germany grew in prominence throughout the 1990s and has continued into this decade as unification and European integration intensify and as immigration to Germany continues. The most contentious concepts are those of nationalism and ethnicity. Exacerbating the problem is the fact that the inhabitants of the former GDR were raised in a society that did not value toleration or dissent. They were also part of a society in which official unemployment did not exist. The average GDR citizen rarely encountered, not to mention worked with, foreign nationals. West Germany, in contrast, had encouraged the migration of millions of guest workers from throughout southern Europe since the 1960s. At the same time, the FRG has provided generous provisions for those seeking political asylum, in large part to try to overcome the legacy of Nazi persecution of non-Germans from 1933 to 1945. East Germany, on the other hand, was a much more closed society, as were most other Communist regimes. Thus, when unification arrived—and was complicated by the migration of different ethnic minorities into both the east and west—few former GDR citizens responded positively to the contact with foreign nationals.

Former GDR citizens were expected, first, to adopt completely Western democratic habits of debate and toleration of diversity without missing a beat. Second, they were expected to deal with a labor *market,* which sometimes did not supply an adequate number of jobs. In other words, gone was a world of lifetime employment, and in its place was one where structural unemployment claimed as much as 25 percent of the work force in the five new *Länder*. Third, they were faced with a much more open and ethnically diverse society than they had ever known, and they often blamed the lack of employment on immigrants and asylum seekers. Consequently, many of those German citizens who were beginning to fall through the cracks of the German welfare state were also susceptible to racist pronouncements from demagogues who wished to blame ethnic minorities for all the major changes that had taken place in such a short time. The immigration of IT workers from India in 2000 only added to the tensions.

Ethnic minorities—even long-term legal residents and new citizens of Germany—often face on-the-job discrimination, particularly in occupations unprotected by a trade union or a works council. Not surprisingly, ethnic minorities—in Germany as in most other developed countries—have found themselves often employed in workplaces where they are required to perform menial and often thankless work.

Inequality and Women

Women's role in the German workplace is a growing issue. First, the increase in female participation in the labor force (see Table 12.1) has created a departure from traditional German experience. Although still at lower rates than in the United States, the participation of increasing numbers of female employees has created new tensions in an area where men had dominated virtually all positions of authority in both management and unions. The unions, however, have

made far greater strides than management in providing women with expanded opportunities with responsibility and authority. Further adding to this tension in eastern Germany has been an increase in migration by young women in much larger numbers than young men. The women are often better educated than their male counterparts and have better job opportunities in the west, leaving some of the young men susceptible to far-right political movements.[16]

Perhaps the most significant obstacle that German women have to overcome is not so much the substance of the benefits that they receive but the premise on which women's role in German society is defined.[17] By any measure, Germany's universal welfare state benefits are generous to all citizens, including women, but it is helpful to understand the context within which rights are granted. Benefits are generally cash-based rather than service-based (such as public day care), which means they are less women-friendly and do not encourage women to enter the paid labor force. This is in sharp contrast to a country like Sweden, which has publicly provided day care and a larger number of women in the workforce.

German welfare was created by conservatives and Christian Democrats, not by the left. It was Bismarck who created the foundations of the first modern welfare state in the late nineteenth century—not out of the goodness of his heart but to stave off socialist revolution and preserve traditional German cultural values. Similarly, the postwar Christian Democratic creation of the social part of the social market economy was based on Christian values and envisioned a world of male breadwinners and women at home caring for— and having more—children. To be sure, the years of Social Democratic governance (1969–1982 and 1998– 2005) have expanded benefits for women, but at their foundation women's benefits in German society have been tied more to their roles within the family than as individuals. This means that within the context of the labor market, individual German women face discriminatory aspects and assumptions about their career patterns that some American women have overcome. In comparison, Sweden's experience suggests that there can be a third option that provides positive, collective women-friendly measures.[18] As increasing numbers of women enter the German work force, it is harder for them to achieve positions of power and responsibility

Table 12.1

Labor Force Participation Rates, Ages Fifteen to Sixty-Five, 1993–2005 (in percentages)

	1993	1995	1997	1999	2001	2003	2005
Male	81.3	81.0	80.3	80.2	80.1	79.2	80.4
Female	62.3	62.6	62.8	63.5	64.9	65.1	66.8

Source: Federal Statistical Office, Germany, 2007.

than it is for some of their American counterparts. Perhaps this is owing to the difference between a welfare state with paternalistic origins and a society that allows some women to achieve positions of authority. Even though Angela Merkel is the first female German chancellor, she had a surprising weakness among women voters, especially in the east where she lives. This was due to her changing positions on the abortion issue; once favoring the liberal eastern policy, she changed her position to a more restrictive one as she rose within the CDU.

The Generation Gap

Modern generational issues first achieved political significance in the FRG with the emergence of the new social movements in the late 1960s. Several issues drove these movements, culminating in a wave of protests throughout West Germany in 1968, but here we concentrate on those that have affected the economy.

These social movements grew increasingly influential in the early 1980s when elements of diverse citizen action groups became core supporters of the Green Party, formed in the late 1970s. In 1982, these groups—both the Greens and the young social movements outside the SPD—contributed to the exhaustion of the SPD as a party of government for sixteen years. Willy Brandt, the first SPD chancellor, reflecting during the early 1980s on these developments, termed these movements "the SPD's lost children," meaning, in retrospect, that the SPD ought to have listened to and incorporated their concerns into party policy.

Although increasingly important in the Federal Republic, these youth-led social movements were seen as "post-materialist," in the sense that their concerns were not those of traditional Marxist materialism.[19] In fact, in Germany youth have not relied on class as a primary category to define themselves, since many tend to be university-educated children of the middle class. They have thus not been able to create an identity strong enough to challenge the highly skilled working-class's dominance in the structure of the Federal Republic. If there is a new working class, it has arisen within the trade unions as members have increased their skills to engage in the flexible system of manufacturing. The still-dominant working-class

culture of the Federal Republic has, to some extent, prevented the post-materialist social movement from attaining further influence. However, the movement has attained an important vehicle for systematic political representation in the Green Party.

The second aspect of the generation gap comprises pensioners and older workers. The German birthrate fell markedly in the last decade of the twentieth century, particularly in the former GDR. This placed great demographic pressure on the German welfare state because the low birthrate and the increasing age of the baby boom generation meant that fewer younger workers now contribute to the welfare and retirement benefits of an increasing elderly population. This time bomb is just hitting German politics in the early twenty-first century, largely because the Kohl government during the 1980s and 1990s essentially ignored it. In 2000 the Schröder government began to address it in the context of the tax reform package. But pensions continue to be one of many unresolved issues with which the new CDU/CSU-SPD Grand Coalition struggles. It is unclear how far the new government will augment the beleaguered public pension system with additional tax funds that will help Germans diversify their retirement options by developing tax-supported private pensions to accompany the public ones.

The Dilemmas of European Integration

The EU was embraced by most Germans and by the political and industrial establishment, especially in the first few years after unification. As Europe's leading power, Germany stands to benefit greatly from successful European integration, since its position of strength will likely expand through wider market opportunities. Germany realizes that actions taken as a member of a twenty-seven-nation European Union will be much more palatable to its neighbors than if Germany were using its size and economic power to dominate Europe.

From its international position in the early twenty-first century, Germany has confronted a number of difficult issues. One open question regarding the EU for Germany has been whether successful German-specific institutional arrangements will prove adaptable or durable in a wider European context. Its institutionalized system of worker (and union) participation in management, its tightly organized capitalism, and its elaborate apprenticeship training will all be challenged. What may work well inside Germany may be dependent on German-specific institutional, political, or cultural patterns that will not travel well outside the Federal Republic.

The challenge for Germany in the EU is difficult. EU economic policy seems modeled more on the British free-market policies reminiscent of Conservative 1980s prime minister Margaret Thatcher than on successful postwar German patterns. What explains this anomaly? The short answer is that institutions take longer to build and establish than do laissez-faire markets. Moreover, German-style organized capitalism developed in a context specific to Germany and has been reinforced by thousands of overlapping and mutually reinforcing relationships built since the end of World War II. In short, German institutional practice is unlikely to extend beyond the borders of the FRG. The dilemma for the Germans is that success in the EU economy will mean adopting the more free-market practices of the Anglo-U.S. model. The question for Germany is whether it will continue to flourish in Europe using the "German model," at a time when most economies are being pressed by more deregulatory patterns.

As for the question of the speed of European integration, countries that might see the value of emulating German institutions require not just strategies but also the means of implementing them. The lack of a cohesive European-wide institutional framework would severely hinder efforts to develop strategies appropriate to meeting the domestic and international challenges of European unification. Most other European nations know the goals to which they must aspire. They need a highly skilled workforce that can compete in international markets on some basis other than a combination of low labor costs and high-tech production strategies. But whether they can or want to emulate Germany's example remains to be seen, especially in the face of recent German uncertainty about which economic model to pursue. The preoccupation of Germans with their immediate domestic issues, plus the German-specific nature of the institutions of their political economy, has partially diminished the luster of German-style policies for the new Europe.

Germany in the Global Economy

The post-unification years have altered Germany's political role on the world stage. As a mature democracy and the leading European power, more is now expected from it. Germany's economic and political power continued through the postwar period and reached its high point between 1960 and 1990. Yet after the momentous events of German unification and European integration, many observers in Europe, Japan, and North America assumed that Germany would take on greater political responsibility based on its position of economic strength and newfound political unity. However, the international indecision and inaction of recent governments suggested that Germany was not yet willing or able to do so. Examples of this inaction can be seen—in the eyes of the G. W. Bush administration—its failure to support the 2003 Iraq war. Thus, some still believed that Germany would remain a "political dwarf," at least in a geopolitical sense.

Clearly Germany is being pressed to take greater political responsibility, both within the EU and as a sovereign nation-state, based on its economic resources and its political power as the leading European nation. Yet its first steps in the post–cold war arena of Eastern Europe demonstrated its lack of diplomatic skill, when in the 1990s the former Yugoslavia came apart in waves of ethnic killing. As a united entity, Europe might find it easier to develop a region-wide geopolitical policy if more skillful leadership came from Germany. But leadership requires working with one's allies and not simply taking an independent position diametrically opposed to their interests. Obviously future military issues are very much bound up with this question of leadership in the EU. Whether the United Nations, the North Atlantic Treaty Organization (NATO), or the EU itself are to take military responsibility for Europe remains uncertain, even more so in the wake of Iraq and the fissures it produced between the United States and the United Kingdom on the one hand and France and Germany on the other. This uncertainty has been prolonged by Germany's own ambivalence about its international political role. In their defense, the Germans have stressed the strains and huge costs of unification, as well as the difficulty of dealing with the issue of political asylum. But Germany is experiencing nothing more than the obligations of political responsibility. Great nations have to find a way to do extremely difficult things at inconvenient times, but Germany is only beginning to develop these skills.

However, the arrival of both Gerhard Schröder and Angela Merkel as chancellors seems to have moved Germany's foreign policy in a more decisive direction, much to the chagrin of the Bush administration. As the first chancellor with no direct memory of World War II (he was born in 1944), Schröder was less willing to defer to the United States and NATO on all international issues, and his more independent foreign policy expanded Germany's international political role. Germany participated in the United Nations peacekeeping mission in Bosnia and Kosovo in the late 1990s and sent forces to Afghanistan to attack Al Qaeda sites after the 9/11 attacks against the United States among other examples. While the Merkel government is less openly antagonistic toward the United States, she was harshly critical of the Bush Administration's position on global warming prior to the G8 meetings held in Germany in June 2007. While some European neighbors might express anxiety about increased German political power in Europe, the alternative is a political vacuum caused by an indecisive EU, hardly a better option. All of these extra-German involvements are part of a larger vision of Germany and the EU expanding their world economic responsibilities.

Other issues, such as global trade, the type of monetary policy to be favored by the EU, and the general pace of economic integration, remain areas of major concern. Serious U.S.-EU trade differences exist in such areas as genetically modified organisms (GMOs), agricultural subsidies, and steel tariffs, among many others. To its benefit, Germany, as a goods-exporting nation, has always favored an open trading system and has retained its role as the world's leading exporter in 2006. Both its management and its unions have realized that exports represent both profits and jobs, and that to seek refuge in protectionism would be self-defeating. Germany had developed a different strategy to deal with

the Japanese economic challenge from those of other Western nations. Instead of believing, as Britain and the United States did, that older manufacturing industries should be given up in the face of the Japanese competitive onslaught, the Germans felt that these industries could remain competitive with a high-skill, high-value-added approach. This approach has generally succeeded, but slow growth and lingering stagnation in some regions and industries may raise questions about how thoroughly the German economy can bounce back.

As seen above, global warming has become one of Germany's primary concerns. Recent reports emphasizing the acceleration of man-made contributions to climate change have galvanized German policymakers, even among the center-right Merkel government. Obviously the presence of the Greens in parliament for twenty-five years has been important, but even more important is Germany's understanding that it is a densely-populated nation and must use its natural resources as efficiently as possible if it is to maintain its generous living standards.

Germany has enjoyed a higher degree of economic performance and institutional political stability since World War II than at any other time in its history, despite the large amount of *Angst* that permeates the political culture. Even the momentous European and German changes, beginning in the late 1980s and continuing to the present, do not seem to have fundamentally undermined the political structure, although new parties have emerged. Part of the reason for this stability has been the ability of dominant economic and political leaders to retain a balance between the private and public sectors. Nineteenth-century history showed Germans the important role that the state played in the unification of the country and the development of an industrial economy. By contrast, twentieth-century German history—both the Nazi years and the GDR experience—have shown Germans the dangers in placing too heavy a reliance on centralized state authority. Even the left now realizes that it must maintain a strong presence in both public and private sectors. The social welfare measures are important for the left's constituents, but so too are the institutions that workers have obtained within the workplace, and these institutions will be strongly tested as the five eastern *Länder* struggle to attain the material benefits that the rest of Germany enjoys. The combination of Germany's pre–World War II undemocratic legacy, the GDR experience, and the FRG's post–World War II parliamentary practices have taught the major actors in the Federal Republic's political economy an important lesson. A balance must be struck between the public and private sectors if the country is to deal with the challenges of globalization. As this chapter suggests, Germany's response to economic challenges takes place as the public and private sectors work together. It is not likely that this pattern will substantially change.

Notes

[1]Mancur Olson, *The Rise and Decline of Nations: Economic Growth, Stagflation, and Social Rigidities* (New Haven, Conn.: Yale University Press, 1982).

[2]Steven Cohen and John Zysman, *Manufacturing Matters* (New York: Basic Books, 1987).

[3]Andrei S. Markovits, *The Politics of the West German Trade Unions* (Cambridge: Cambridge University Press, 1986).

[4]Peter J. Katzenstein, ed., *The Politics of Industry in West Germany: Toward the Third Republic* (Ithaca, N.Y.: Cornell University Press, 1989).

[5]Alexander Gerschenkron, *Bread and Democracy in Germany*, 2nd ed. (Ithaca, N.Y.: Cornell University Press, 1989).

[6]Colleen A. Dunlavy, *Politics and Industrialization: Early Railroads in the United States and Prussia* (Princeton, N.J.: Princeton University Press, 1994).

[7]Rudolf Hilferding, *Finance Capital: A Study of the Latest Phase of Capitalist Development* (London: Routledge and Kegan Paul, 1981).

[8]Gary Herrigel, *Industrial Constructions* (Cambridge: Cambridge University Press, 2000).

[9]Richard Deeg, *Finance Capitalism Unveiled* (Ann Arbor: University of Michigan Press, 1999).

[10]Wilhelm Röpke, "The Guiding Principles of the Liberal Programme," in Horst Friedrich Wünche, ed., *Standard Texts on the Social Market Economy* (Stuttgart: Gustav Fischer Verlag, 1982), p. 188.

[11]Michael Piore and Charles Sabel, *The Second Industrial Divide* (New York: Basic Books, 1984).

[12]Kathleen Thelen, *A Union of Parts* (Ithaca, N.Y.: Cornell University Press, 1992).

[13]Wade Jacoby, *Imitation and Politics: Redesigning Germany* (Ithaca, N.Y.: Cornell University Press, 2000).

[14]Steven J. Silvia, "German Unification and Emerging Divisions Within German Employers' Associations," *Comparative Politics* 29, no. 2 (January 1997): 194–199.

[15]Jacoby, *Imitation and Politics.*

[16]"Lack of Women in Eastern Germany Feeds Neo-Nazis," *Der Spiegel*, May 31, 2007, http://www.spiegel.de/international/germany/0,1518,485942,00.html.

[17]Joyce Mushaben, "Challenging the Maternalist Presumption: Gender and Welfare Reform in Germany and the United States," in Ulrike Liebert and Nancy Hirschman, eds., *Women and Welfare: Theory and Practice in the U.S. and Europe* (Rutgers, N.J.: Rutgers University Press, 2001).

[18]Christina Bergqvist, "Gender (In)equality, European Integration and the Transition of Swedish Corporatism," *Economic and Industrial Democracy* 25 (2004): 125–146.

[19]See Ronald Inglehart, *The Silent Revolution: Changing Values and Political Styles Among Western Publics* (Princeton, N.J.: Princeton University Press, 1977); Serge Mallet, *The New Working Class* (New York: Monthly Review Press, 1968).

CHAPTER 13

Governance and Policymaking

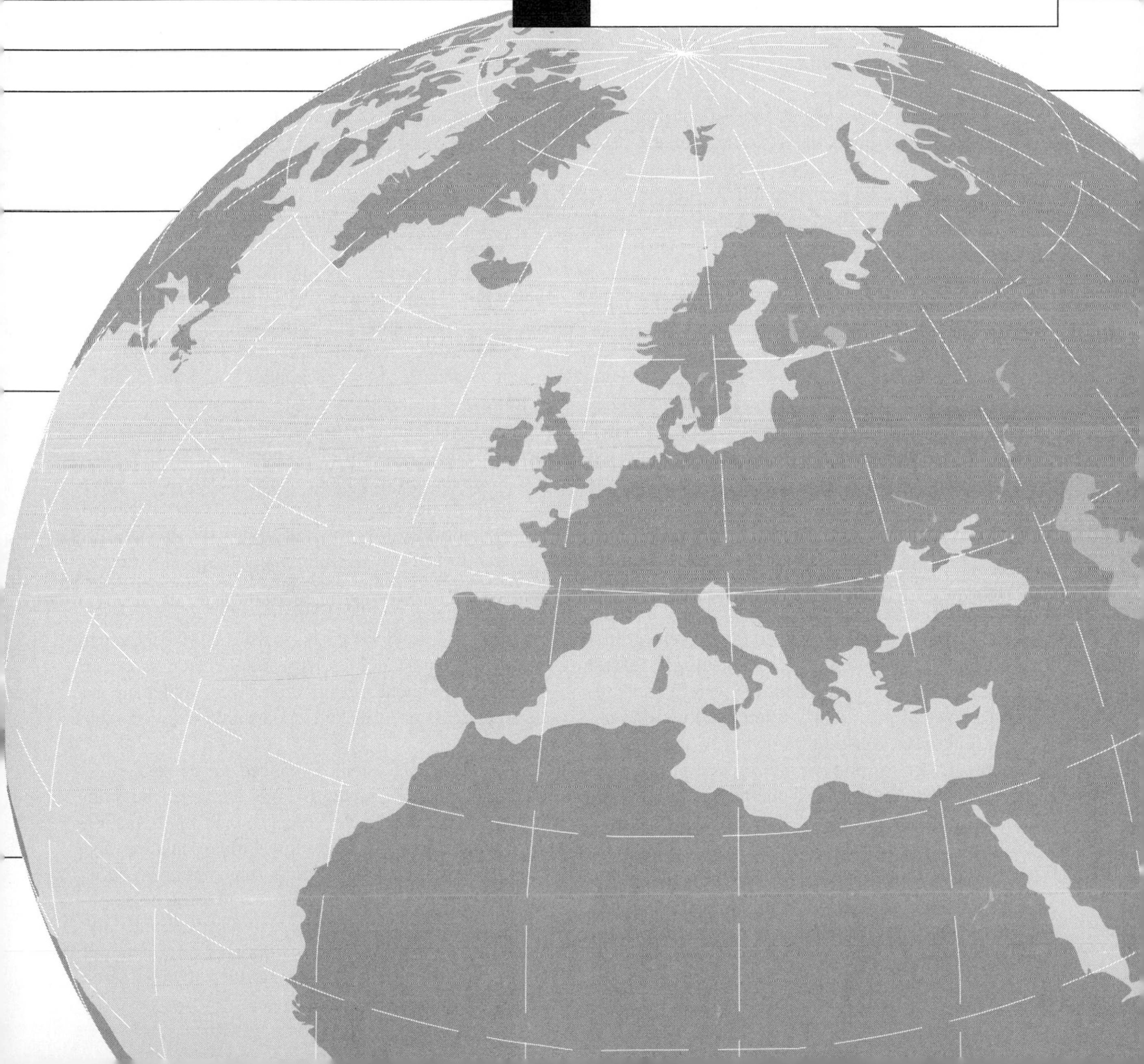

The political scientist Ralf Dahrendorf once stated that until the arrival of the Federal Republic, Germany had been a premodern country, having never developed a liberal democracy.[1] Between 1949 and unification in 1990, Germany had become much more like other Western industrialized countries, developing a stable parliamentary democracy. With the difficulty in integrating the two regimes after unification in 1990 and with the increasing uncertainty regarding the pace and scope of European integration, some of the more optimistic assumptions that Germany had purged its politics of antidemocratic elements came under greater scrutiny.

The governing principles of the Federal Republic of Germany (FRG) are a clear reaction to the catastrophic experiences that beset previous regimes in Germany. When the Federal Republic was established in 1949, the primary goals of the founders were to work toward eventual unification of the two Germanys and, more important, to avoid repeating the failure of Germany's only other experiment with democracy, the Weimar Republic.[2] Unable to accomplish immediate unification, the founders formulated the *Grundgesetz* (Basic Law) as their compromise. It symbolized the temporary nature of disunited Germany, since the founders preferred to wait until Germany could be reunited before using the term *constitution* (*Verfassung*).* However, their goal of ensuring a lasting democratic order was more complicated. Two fundamental institutional weaknesses had undermined the Weimar government.

One principal weakness was that provisions for emergency powers enabled leaders to centralize authority and arbitrarily suspend democratic rights. The founders of the postwar system sought to remedy the abuse of centralized power by establishing a federal system in which the states (*Länder*) were given considerable powers, particularly administrative powers. It is unusual that a constitution owing so much to the influence of foreign powers has proved so durable. Under the Basic Law of the Federal Republic, many functions that had formerly been centralized during the imperial, Weimar, and Nazi periods—the educational system, the police, and the radio and television

networks—now became the responsibility of the states. Although the federal Bundestag (the lower house) became the chief lawmaking body, the implementation of many of these laws fell to the *Länder* governments. Moreover, the *Länder* governments sent representatives to the Bundesrat (the upper house), which was required to approve bills passed in the Bundestag.

There was little opposition from major actors within the Federal Republic to this shift from a centralized to a federal system. The Third Reich's catastrophic abuse of power was the primary reason. Furthermore, the development of a federal system was not a departure but a return to form. Before the unification of Germany in 1871, the various regions of Germany had formed a decentralized political system that had developed such autonomous institutions as banks, universities, vocational schools, and state administrative systems.

The second weakness of the Weimar government was the fragmentation of the political party system, which prevented stable majorities from forming in the Reichstag. This instability encouraged the use of emergency powers to break legislative deadlocks. The new system overcame party fragmentation and the inability to form working majorities in several ways. The multiplicity of parties was partially overcome by changes in electoral laws that reduced the number of small parties and have resulted in a more manageable system. Only two large parties and four small ones have ever gained representation. In this way, the Bundestag has always managed to achieve working majorities, a situation in striking contrast to the chronic government instability in the Weimar Republic. Election laws require that the interval between elections be four years (except under unusual circumstances). This requirement gives an elected government the opportunity to implement its electoral goals and to take responsibility for success or failure.

The electoral system, explained in the section on the Bundestag in Chapter 14, was also changed from Weimar's unstable "pure" proportional representation to a combination of proportional representation and single-member electoral districts, which is now one of the most emulated models in the world for democratizing countries. New constitutional provisions limited the possibility for the Bundestag to vote a government out of office; in Weimar negative majorities often garnered

---

*Since unification in 1990, the term *Basic Law* has been retained because most Germans rightly associate the "temporary" term with the country's longest and most successful experience of democracy.

enough votes to unseat the chancellor but could not provide a mandate to install a replacement. The FRG's Basic Law requires that a chancellor cannot be voted out of office unless there is majority support for a successor; furthermore as the leader of the dominant party or coalition of parties, the chancellor now has control over the composition of the cabinet. The federal president is merely the ceremonial head of state and has limited powers. Under the Weimar constitution, the president could wield emergency powers such as those Hitler used to manipulate the system under aging president Paul Hindenburg in 1932–1933.

The principles of the Federal Republic's government contained in the Basic Law give the regime a solid foundation that has helped the FRG assimilate the five former GDR *Länder* after 1990 and fulfill the FRG founders' original unification goals. Nevertheless, the increase in far-right movements and racist violence, mostly in the east since unification, surprised many observers who thought these sentiments had long since been purged from German politics.

Organization of the State

Germany is a parliamentary democracy with a chancellor as head of government and a ceremonial president as head of state (see Figure 13.1). Bonn was the capital beginning in 1949, but following unification, the capital was eventually fully transferred to Berlin, in 1999.

The German state is organized as a federal system, with the sixteen *Länder* having considerable authority independent of the federal government. Most important are the powers that authorize *Länder* governments to raise revenue independently through the ability to own and operate firms, usually in partnership with private industry. Regional and local governments in Britain, Italy, and France have far fewer such powers. The functioning of the German federal government, however, is more like the parliamentary systems of its European neighbors. There is a fusion of powers in that the chancellor (the executive) is also the leader of the leading party (or coalition) in the Bundestag. This contrasts with the U.S. separation of powers, in which neither the

Figure 13.1

Constitutional Structure of Germany's Federal Government

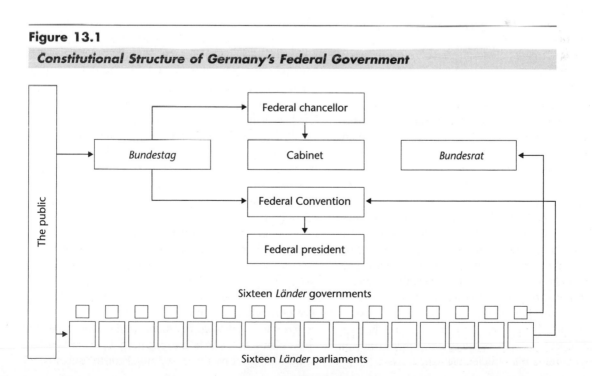

president nor his cabinet officials can simultaneously serve in the Congress. Generally in the Federal Republic, the executive dominates the legislature, but this authority comes from the chancellor's role as party leader, coupled with a high level of party discipline. Most members of the governing parties support the chancellor at all times, since their own positions depend on a successful government. This circumstance has the significant result of avoiding the "lone ranger" syndrome, so common in the U.S. House of Representatives and Senate, where individual members of the House or the Senate act as independent political entrepreneurs.

The Executive

The division between the head of government (the chancellor) and the head of state (the president) was firmly established in the Federal Republic, with major political powers delegated to the chancellor. Responsibilities and obligations were clearly distinguished. For example, the chancellor could be criticized for the government's policies without the attack being perceived as a frontal assault against the state itself. In this sense, the division of the executive branch was crucial in gaining respect for the new West German state at a time when most of its neighbors remained suspicious of Germany's Nazi past.

The President

As head of state, the German president holds a much weaker position than that of the chancellor. Like constitutional monarchs in Britain, for example, German presidents stand above the political fray, which means that they take more of a ceremonial role than an active political one. Federal presidential powers are not autonomous but are constrained by the formal provisions of the Basic Law. The distinction between executive functions in the Federal Republic can be contrasted with the confluence of the roles of head of state and head of government in the United States. The president of the United States fills both of these roles, the implications of which have not always been positive for the country. Lyndon Johnson, Richard Nixon, and, some say, George W. Bush have hidden behind the head-of-state mantle by suggesting that criticism of their government's policies was unpatriotic.

The German president has the following duties. As head of state, the president represents Germany in international affairs, concluding treaties with other countries and receiving the credentials of foreign ambassadors and envoys. He or she formally appoints and dismisses federal civil servants, federal judges, and officers of the Federal Armed Forces and may exercise the right of presidential clemency. He or she participates in the legislative process through the promulgation of laws, the dissolution of the Bundestag, and the formal proposal, appointment, and dismissal of the federal chancellor and the ministers. The political system of Germany assigns the president a nonpartisan, largely ceremonial role, with powers that rest largely on the moral authority of the office rather than on political power. One exception, however, occurs during a parliamentary crisis when no candidate can command the support of an absolute majority of Bundestag members. In this case, the president can decide whether the country is to be governed by a minority government under a chancellor elected by a plurality of deputies or whether new elections are to be called (although the German president has never had to use the last provision in FRG history).[3] The presidential term is five years, and a president may serve only two terms.

On July 1, 2004, Horst Köhler, an economist and former head of the International Monetary Fund (IMF), assumed the presidency after having been elected in May by a procedure specified in the Basic Law—that is, by the Federal Convention (*Bundesversammlung*), an assembly of all Bundestag members and an equal number of delegates elected by the state legislatures (much like an electoral college) according to the principle of proportional representation. Köhler, sponsored by the opposition Christian Democratic Union (CDU)–Christian Social Union (CSU), and Free Democratic Party (FDP), defeated Gesine Schwann, sponsored by the then-governing Social Democratic Party (SPD)–Green coalition in a narrow vote of 604 to 598. Schwann would have been the first female federal president.

The Chancellor

The chancellor is elected by a majority of the members of the Bundestag. In practice, this means that the chancellor's ability to be a strong party leader (or leader of a coalition of parties) is essential for the success of the government. A government is formed after a national election or, if the chancellor leaves office between elections, after a majority of the Bundestag has nominated a new chancellor, such as in the transition from Helmut Schmidt to Helmut Kohl in 1982. The new leader consults with other party and coalition officials to make up the cabinet. These party leaders have considerable influence in determining which individuals receive ministries. In the event of a coalition government—there has been only one noncoalition majority government, the CDU-CSU from 1957 to 1961—party leaders often earmark, even before the chancellor's election, members of their party who will receive certain ministries.[4] Negotiations on which policies a coalition will pursue often become heated, so the choice of ministers is made on policy as well as personal grounds.

Once the cabinet is formed, however, the chancellor has considerable authority to govern, owing to the power of the Federal Chancellery (*Bundeskanzleramt*). This office is, the first among equals of all of the cabinet ministries, enabling the chancellor to oversee his or her entire government efficiently, as well as to mediate conflicts among the other ministries. It is a kind of superministry with wide-ranging powers in many areas. The chancellor uses this office and its professional staff to supervise and coordinate policy among the other cabinet departments, such as the Ministries of Economics, Finance, Interior, and Labor, and the Foreign Office, as well as less influential departments. The chancellor draws the cabinet officials largely from the high ranks of the majority party or coalition partner. Germany's party system and its parliamentary legislative body place a premium on long service, which is expected before advancement is possible. Consequently, party officials often develop specific areas of expertise, which the majority party or the chancellor's office can draw upon when positions need to be filled. Rather than relying on outsiders from other professions for cabinet positions (as the U.S. executive often does), the chancellors draw their cabinet officials from a pool of individuals with long experience in both government and the party in power.

The Federal Republic has had a history of strong chancellors, although this has not always been the case. The first was Konrad Adenauer, who, as the leader of the CDU, served as the head of government from 1949

to 1963 and established the social market economy. A former mayor of Cologne in the Weimar years, he was known as *Der Alte* (the old man) and played a reassuring role at a critical time. His successor, Ludwig Erhard (CDU), had been economics minister under Adenauer and was widely credited with formulating the social market economy policies that produced the economic miracle during the 1950s and early 1960s. As chancellor from 1963 to 1966, Erhard was much less effective, however. Still weaker was Kurt Kiesinger (CDU), the chancellor of the 1966–1969 Grand Coalition of the CDU and CSU with the Social Democratic Party (SPD). He was not a resolute leader, and his task was hindered by the increasing conflicts between the CDU-CSU and the SPD, and the strong foreign policy posture of Vice Chancellor Willy Brandt (SPD). His leadership was also hindered by the growth of the Extraparliamentary Opposition (Ausserparliamentarische Opposition—APO) on the left and by the National Democratic Party of Germany (NPD), a reconstituted neo-Nazi party, on the right. Although the Grand Coalition had fused the two major parties in government, it also meant that there was no authentic opposition party. This "consensus" government proved short-lived.

Following the 1969 election, the SPD became the dominant coalition partner until 1982. Its thirteen-year tenure was largely due to the strong leadership of chancellors Willy Brandt (1969–1974) and Helmut Schmidt (1974–1982). Brandt was mayor of West Berlin during the 1960s, and during his years as chancellor, he emphasized *Ostpolitik* (encouraging relations with East Germany and the Soviet bloc countries). Brandt, however, was forced to resign in 1974 when one of his personal assistants was discovered to be a spy for East Germany; yet he remained party chairman through the mid-1980s and was a unifying figure for the party after the Christian Democrats came to power in 1982. Helmut Schmidt replaced Brandt in 1974 and during his term was highly regarded for his skill in managing the economy. Schmidt steered the West German economy through the first oil crisis and through troubled economic straits during the late 1970s and early 1980s. Under his chancellorship, the German economy performed better than those of other European countries. As leaders of the SPD, both Brandt and Schmidt were adept at brokering difficult conflicts between the left wing of the party and the centrist FDP coalition partner;

both also expanded and consolidated the welfare state. Schmidt's primary weakness was his inability to retain a close relationship with the rank and file of the Social Democrats.

Helmut Kohl took office in 1982. He expertly used the power of the chancellor's office to hold the CDU/CSU-FDP coalition together; to fend off an attack from the right by the Republikaner (the Republican Party); and to keep the opposition SPD and Greens from making effective challenges to him in the elections of 1987, 1990, and 1994. By the time Kohl left office in 1998, he was the longest-serving and among the most influential chancellors in the history of the FRG.

Gerhard Schröder, elected chancellor in 1998, was the first German political leader truly of the postwar generation, having been born at the end of the war in 1944. During the 1998 election campaign, he was compared with British prime minister Tony Blair and U.S. president Bill Clinton. Observers stressed one apparent thread that tied the three young (all were in their forties or fifties) political leaders together. As heads of "left" parties on their countries' respective political spectrums, they seemed to share an affinity for moving their parties toward more centrist positions. In fact, the SPD slogan for the 1998 campaign was "*die neue Mitte*" (the new middle), which suggested just such a moderate tendency on Schröder's and the SPD's part. Schröder had a generally successful first term, but the second was more problematic, forcing him to call for new elections in 2005 a year ahead of schedule. The major reason for the early election was the unpopularity among his party and his constituents concerning portions of his conservative economic reforms in 2003 and 2004.

The current chancellor Angela Merkel, fifty-one years old when she became the first female chancellor in 2005, has had a remarkable road to the pinnacle of German politics. A clergyman's daughter, a physicist by profession, a latecomer to political life, an eastern German, a Protestant in a party dominated by Catholics, and a woman who has eschewed feminist positions, Merkel surprised many Germans when she finally became Germany's head of government after the most inconclusive election in the fifty-six-year history of the Federal Republic of Germany.

A quick political learner, Merkel rose through the ranks of the Christian Democrats. Western German parties that wanted to establish a presence in eastern Germany desired skilled and astute easterners who would help these parties establish a political foundation there. She held several regional Christian Democratic Party positions and soon caught the political eye of four-time CDU chancellor Helmut Kohl. She won a seat in the Bundestag and was named the Environment minister in 1994. After the Christian Democrats were defeated in the 1998 election, Merkel rapidly moved into the political vacuum in the wake of Helmut Kohl's departure from the Christian Democratic leadership.

Despite her considerable accomplishments, Merkel is not a natural political leader. She seems awkward and stiff on the political stump, which many analysts have suggested almost cost her the 2005 election. She also failed to develop two potential advantages, namely her gender and her background in eastern Germany. She pointedly avoided feminist positions, perhaps necessary in the male-dominated CDU/CSU. However, she lost considerable political support from women when she chose to support the much more restrictive West German abortion law instead of the more liberal law that had prevailed in East Germany. She also has not been effective in recruiting large numbers of women from her party to run for seats in the Bundestag. In fact, the three parties of the left (SPD, Greens, and Left) have 41.2 percent women among their deputies while the parties of the right (Christian Democrats and FDP) have only 20.9 percent women in the Bundestag. She also failed to use her background to alleviate the fears of eastern Germans, who suffer from much higher unemployment (15–20 percent) than do the states of the former West Germany (7 percent). In numerous campaign appearances in eastern Germany, she would address the crowds using the pronoun "you" instead of "we." In the 2005, the CDU finished third in the five eastern German states behind the SPD and the Left parties. Merkel's achievement in becoming the first female chancellor was most impressive, but she faced formidable obstacles in the first years of her government.

The office of chancellor has played a pivotal role in the Federal Republic. The clearly defined role of the chancellor within the federal framework has resulted in a far more effective office than was the case in the Weimar period. One feature of this change, however, is that the chancellor's more limited role within the context of a federal system has constrained the ability of the central government to take sweeping action. Many Germans have seen this limitation of centralized executive power as a welcome improvement.

As in all other parliamentary systems, in Germany the head of government is the dominant member of a governing team. Chancellors select a cabinet of ministers who can best support and strengthen the executive branch. The most significant cabinet ministries are those of finance, economics, justice, interior, and foreign policy (the Foreign Ministry). Chancellors generally select cabinet members from leaders of their own party or of coalition partners. In many cases, chancellors rely on strong ministers in key posts, but some chancellors have often taken ministerial responsibility themselves in areas such as economics and foreign policy. Helmut Schmidt and Willy Brandt, respectively, fit this pattern. The Economics and Finance Ministries always work closely with the Bundesbank, Germany's central bank.

Perhaps the most significant source of the chancellor's powers is the constitutional *constructive vote of no confidence*. To overcome the weakness of the cabinet governments of Weimar, the Federal Republic's founders added a twist to the practice, which is familiar in most other parliamentary systems, in which a prime minister is brought down on a vote of no confidence. In most systems, if prime ministers lose such a vote they are obliged to step down or to call for new elections. In the Federal Republic, however, such a vote must be "constructive" in the sense that a chancellor cannot be removed unless the Bundestag *simultaneously* elects a new chancellor (usually from an opposition party). This constitutional provision strengthens the chancellor's power in at least two ways. First, it means that chancellors can more easily reconcile disputes among cabinet officials without threatening the chancellor's position. Second, it forces the opposition to come up with concrete and specific alternatives to the existing government and prevents them from being oppositional just for the sake of opposition. The there have been only two such occurrences: the first was in 1982, with the transition from Helmut Schmidt to Helmut Kohl; the second was in 2005 when Gerhard Schröder called for a new election a year ahead of schedule when his SPD party lost a major *Land* election that spring. In a maneuver subsequently

ruled legal by the Federal President and the Constitutional Court, Schröder intentionally lost a vote of confidence in order to hold an early election. He argued that the loss in the *Land* election, thereby changing the balance of power in the Bundesrat, or upper house (see below for details), required a new election to clarify his coalition's mandate.

Nonetheless, chancellors face significant limits on their power, one of which involves the passage of legislation. As discussed in Chapter 14, the Bundesrat must ratify all legislation passed in the Bundestag, unless overridden by a two-thirds vote in the lower house. In addition, the Bundesrat generally implements most legislation passed in the Bundestag, so it is important for chancellors to consider the position of the upper house on most issues, as Schröder was forced to do in 2005.

Bureaucracy and Civil Service

The tradition of a strong civil service has deep roots that long predate the introduction of democracy. Particularly in a country like Germany, where the state stubbornly resisted democratic politics, the civil service was regarded as serving the state and not necessarily all citizens. Even in the democratic parliamentary Federal Republic, the perception remains strong among civil servants that their responsibility is first to the state and only secondly to the citizens. In Germany, positions in the bureaucracy are very powerful and are protected by long-standing civil service provisions. Moreover, German civil servants (*Beamten*) have long had an historical reputation for being inflexible and rigid in the performance of their duties. During the Federal Republic, when the bureaucracy has been under democratic supervision, there remain certainly inefficiencies in the Federal Republic's public sector, as in all other public and private bureaucracies. Yet civil servants view the work that they perform as a profession—that is, more than just a job.

Only about 10 percent of civil servants are employed by the federal government. The vast majority are employed by the various state and local governments. Before the founding of the Federal Republic, most of the civil servants were recruited from the families of the reactionary nobility, but selection of bureaucrats in the Federal Republic takes a more modern form. Most are either graduates of major German universities or from positions within the political parties. The federal bureaucrats are primarily policymakers and work closely with their ministries and the legislature. The bureaucrats at the state and local levels are the main agents for implementing policy, because the states bear most of the responsibility for carrying out policies determined at the national level. This overlapping of national, regional, and local bureaucracies is enhanced by the belief that certain crucial functions can be performed only by the public sector and that the civil servants' mandate is to perform these duties as well as possible. The continuing institutionalized relationship among the various levels of the bureaucracy has produced more consistent and effective public policy than in some countries where federal and state governments are often at odds with one another. Social policy, particularly health care and education, is a good example. Policy is designed at the federal level but implemented at the *Land* level; however, it occurs as part of an institutionalized process of formal and informal discussion.

The German bureaucracy has high—albeit grudging—political respect from the population. It is generally seen as efficient, although sometimes arcane. Selection of some bureaucrats is based on party affiliation. This derives from the traditional German pattern of *Proporz* (proportionality), in which all major political groups are represented in the bureaucracy. In the 1970s however, attempts were made to purge the bureaucracy of suspected radicals. The results—notably requiring civil servants to take loyalty oaths, arbitrarily dismissing many bureaucrats—tarnished the reputation of the bureaucracy for impartiality and fairness. Those who are chosen based on party politics—largely top federal officials—are in the minority. Selection to the status of civil servant is generally based on merit, with elaborate licensing and testing for those who advance to the highest professions. German bureaucrats are well known for a high degree of competence.

Public and Semipublic Institutions

Public and semipublic institutions in Germany are powerful and efficient, and are responsible for much national policymaking. In countries that had a feudal guild system of representation, such as Germany, an inclusionary, often corporatist form of representation is common. Semipublic institutions combine aspects of both representation and implementation.[5] The corporatist interest groups are also closely intertwined with the Federal Republic's parapublic agencies, which we argue are institutions crucial for the functioning of the German political economy. Occupying a gray area that encompasses both public and private responsibilities, these semipublic (or parastatal) institutions are an apparently seamless web that shapes, directs, implements, and diffuses German public policy.

In the late 1940s, the idea of a strong central state in Germany was discredited for two reasons: the excesses of Nazism and the American occupation authorities' strong affinity for the private sector. West German authorities faced a dilemma. How would they rebuild society if a strong public sector role had been ruled out? The answer was to create modern, democratic versions of those nineteenth-century institutions that blurred the differences between the public and private sectors. These institutions have played a crucial, and long unrecognized, role in the German political economy.

Political scientist Peter Katzenstein has described these parapublic agencies as "detached institutions." He argues that they reduce the influence of the central state by acting as primary mediating entities that operate from a principle of engaging all relevant actors in the policy community in continuous dialogue until appropriate policies are found.[6] Katzenstein finds that they have tended to work best in areas of social and economic policy, but less well in their interaction with the university system. Among the most important parapublic agencies are the Chambers of Industry; the Council of Economic Advisers (known colloquially as the Five Wise Men); the vocational education system, which encompasses the apprenticeship training system; and the institutions of worker participation (codetermination and the works councils). Even parts of the welfare system are parapublic, since the system for distributing welfare benefits is often administered by organizations that are not officially part of the state bureaucracy. The most significant example is the *Krankenkassen* (sickness funds), which bring all major health interests together to allocate costs and benefits through an elaborate system of consultation and group participation.

Historically, the most important semipublic German institution for shaping economic policy, the politically independent Bundesbank, is not formally part of the government. Prior to the arrival of the euro in 1999, this institution was both the bankers' bank (in that it set interest rates) and the agency that determined the amount of money in circulation. This last point proved contentious during the 1980s and 1990s. The Bundesbank's preference was for low inflation, both because this is a traditional demand of all central bankers and because of Germany's history of ruinous inflation during the Weimar Republic. The relevance for economic policy is that when the government wishes to expand the economy through increased spending or reduced taxes, the Bundesbank has always preferred policies that favor monetary restrictions ahead of fast economic growth. In other words, the government and the Bundesbank can be of opposite minds on economic policy, which has happened in the years since unification.

However, the introduction of the euro has also been accompanied by the creation of the European Central Bank (ECB). Modeled after the Bundesbank, the ECB would seem to be poised to favor Germany. But because it serves all of Europe, the ECB has caused the Bundesbank to lose some of its former power and luster as a result of the new European-wide monetary regime. The ECB now sets exchange and interest rates. Some Germans worry not only about future monetary stability but also about whether European and German monetary interests will continue to be harmonious.

One of the policy areas already mentioned merits more extensive discussion: the parastatal (or parapublic) institutions involved in the implementation of policy that is concerned with industrial relations. This system of codetermination (*Mitbestimmung*) contrasts sharply with Anglo-American patterns. We cover this set of institutions here because the area of industrial relations in Germany is more than just a system of interest representation. It also shapes public policy.

Providing for the institutionalized representation of workers—including, but not restricted to, union members—on the supervisory boards of directors of all medium-sized and large firms, codetermination gives unions an inside look at the workings of the most powerful firms in the Federal Republic. Codetermination gives workers and unions up to one-half of the members of these company boards. Labor representatives are chosen by democratic election among the workers of the companies where they work. Unions can thus learn, if not control, how and why major corporate decisions are made on such issues as investment and application of technology. What difference does codetermination make? A major benefit of representation is that it provides information about the operation of the company and forces management to defend its decisions. Even though the unions can challenge management positions on contentious issues, however, the laws always provide management with one more seat than workers have.

An additional institutional structure represents German workers and gives them access to the policy implementation process. In notable contrast to the trade unions' industrywide role of representation, all shop-floor and plant-level affairs such as social and personnel matters—but not collective bargaining, which is a union function—are the exclusive domain of the works councils (*Betriebsräte*). These are internal bodies of worker representation that exist in most German firms. Such lines of demarcation were much clearer before the late 1980s and early 1990s, when more flexible workplaces developed, in the sense of team work groups and multiple tasks within specific job categories. In fact, some of the structural economic reforms implemented by Schröder's 2004 economic reforms eroded some of the powers of these unique labor market institutions under the goal of increased flexibility to deal with globalization.

The unions' legitimacy derives from a countrywide, multi-industry representation of a large number of diversified workers. The works councils, on the other hand, owe their primary allegiance to their local plants and firms. The two distinct and separate bodies definitely cause rivalries, periodic rifts, and different representations of interest. Despite the 85 percent overlap in personnel between unions and works councils and despite a structural entanglement between these two major pillars of labor representation, these divisions produce tensions among organized labor. A period of general flux and plant-related, management-imposed flexibility exacerbated these tensions, particularly in the east. Specifically, micro (plant-level) concerns sometimes clashed with macro (industrywide) ones, which partially threatened the broad labor solidarity that the unions desired.

Other State Institutions

The chancellor, the president, the bureaucracy, and semipublic institutions are not Germany's only important state agencies for governance and policymaking. Among other state institutions that deserve attention are the military and police, the judiciary, and subnational governments.

The Military and the Police

From the eighteenth century through World War II, the German military was powerful and aggressive. After World War II, the military was placed completely under civilian control and tightly circumscribed by law and treaty. The end of the cold war produced two other important changes that have affected German military policy: the reduction in U.S. armed forces stationed in Germany and the payments made to Russia for removal of soldiers and materiel from the former East Germany.

Germany has a universal service arrangement requiring all citizens over the age of eighteen to perform nine months of military or civilian service. In 1990, Germany had about 600,000 men and women in the military, but in 1994 the Federal Government fixed the figure at approximately 340,000. Germany now spends approximately 1.5 percent of its GDP on the military. Its armed forces have been legally proscribed from extranational activity, first by the Allied occupation and later by the German Basic Law. Under the provisions of the Basic Law, the German military can be used only for defensive purposes within Europe, and then in coordination with NATO authorities. Only very limited military activity under tightly circumscribed approval (via NATO) has altered the general prohibition. German participation in the UN peacekeeping mission in Bosnia was one example. Agreeing to participate in opposition to Serbian aggression in Kosovo in 1999, a decision made by the Red-Green government, was another, and sending troops to Afghanistan—even forming a joint Franco-German brigade—was a third.

Discussion of the German police should focus on three areas. The first is that of the postwar experience in the FRG, where police powers have been organized on a *Land* basis and, after the excesses of the Third Reich, have been constitutionally restricted to ensure that human and civil rights remain inviolate. To be sure, there have been exceptions. For example, during the dragnets for the Red Army *Faktion* terrorists in the late 1970s, many critics argued that German police forces were compromising civil liberties in their desire to capture the terrorists.

The second area is that of the GDR's notorious secret police, the *Stasi*. The Ministry for State Security (the *Stasi*'s formal name) included some 91,000 official employees; in addition, by 1989 more than 180,000 East Germans and perhaps 4,000 West Germans worked as informants for the *Stasi*.[7] In proportion to the 16 million GDR citizens, the *Stasi* was more encompassing in the GDR than the Gestapo had been during Nazi rule. The *Stasi* spied on virtually the entire society and arbitrarily arrested and persecuted thousands of citizens. Since unification, *Stasi* archives have been opened to all, because the East Germans and later the FRG believed that full and open disclosure of *Stasi* excesses was essential in a democratic state. In the process, however, names of informants were made public, which created bitter confrontations among former friends and neighbors.

The third area is the heightened concern for security in Germany in the wake of 9/11. Germany is particularly concerned about terrorism, since numerous members of al Qaeda, including several of the 9/11 bombers, lived for years in Hamburg and other German cities, where they lived clandestine lives. Germany will need to balance the pressing demand for terrorist surveillance with the preservation of civil liberties.

The Judiciary

The judiciary has always played a major role in German government because of the state's deep involvement in political and economic matters. But the worst abuses of the judiciary for political purposes came during the Nazi regime, when it carried out a wide range of antidemocratic, repressive, and even criminal decisions. Among these were banning non-Nazi parties, allowing the seizure of Jewish property, and sanctioning the deaths of millions.

The Federal Republic's founders were determined that the new judicial system would avoid these abuses.

One of the first requirements was that the judiciary explicitly safeguard the democratic rights of individuals, groups, and political parties, with emphasis on some of the individual freedoms that had long been associated with the American and British legal systems. In fact, the Basic Law contains a more elaborate and explicit statement of individual rights than exists in either the U.S. Constitution or in British common law.

However, the Federal Republic's legal system differs from the common law tradition of Britain, its former colonies, and the United States. The common law precedent-based system is characterized by adversarial relationships between contending parties, in which the judge (or the court itself) merely provides the arena for the struggle. In continental Europe, including France and Germany, the legal system is based on a codified legal system with roots in Roman law and the Napoleonic code.

In the Federal Republic, the judiciary is an active administrator of the law rather than solely an arbiter. Specifically, judges have a different relationship with the state and with the adjudication of cases. This judicial system relies on the concept of the responsibility of the state to identify and implement certain important societal goals. And if the task of the state is to create the laws to attain these goals, then the judiciary should safeguard their implementation. In both defining the meaning of very complex laws and in implementing their administration, German courts go considerably beyond those in the United States and Britain, which supposedly have avoided political decisions. The German courts' role in shaping policy has been most evident in the ruling on whether to allow the unions to obtain increased codetermination rights in 1976. The court allowed the unions to obtain near parity on the boards of directors but stated that full union parity with employers would compromise the right of private property.

The German judiciary is an independent institution, since judges are appointed by federal or state governments (depending on the court) and are drawn from practitioners of the law, similar to the pattern in other countries. In 2004, there were over 20,000 judges in Germany, almost one-third of them female. The German judiciary remains outside the political fray on most issues, although a ruling in 1993 limiting access to abortion for many women, in direct opposition to a more liberal law in East Germany, was a clear exception to the general pattern. The judiciary was also criticized in the 1990s for showing too much leniency toward perpetrators of racist violence.

The court system in the Federal Republic is three-pronged. One branch consists of the criminal-civil system, which has the Federal High Court at its apex. It is a unified rather than a federal system and tries to apply a consistent set of criteria to cases in the sixteen states. The Federal High Court reviews cases that have been appealed from the lower courts, including criminal and civil cases, disputes among the states, and matters that would be viewed in some countries as political, such as the abortion ruling.

The Special Constitutional Court deals with matters directly affecting the Basic Law. It was founded after World War II to safeguard the new democratic order. Precisely because of the Nazis' abuses of the judiciary, the founders of West Germany added a layer to the judiciary, basically a judicial review, to ensure that the democratic order was maintained. However, several subsequent rulings have caused concern about the judiciary's commitment to protecting civil liberties from arbitrary executive actions.

The Administrative Court system is the third branch of the judiciary. Consisting of the Labor Court, the Social Security Court, and the Finance Court, the Administrative Court system has a much narrower jurisdiction than the other two branches. Because the state and its bureaucracy have such a prominent place in the lives of German citizens, this level of the court system acts as a check on the arbitrary power of the bureaucracy. Compared to Britain, where much public policy is determined by legislation, German public policy is more often determined by the administrative actions of the bureaucracy. Citizens can use these three courts to challenge bureaucratic decisions—for example, if authorities improperly take action with respect to labor, welfare, or tax policies.

In the 1990s, the courts came under great pressure to resolve the intractable policy issues that arose from unification and European integration. As they were drawn deeper into the political thicket, their decisions came under increased scrutiny. Clandestine searches for terrorists in the late 1970s left many observers believing that the rights of citizens who were unaffiliated with any terrorist organizations had been compromised. Many critics wish that today's courts would show the same diligence and zeal in addressing the crimes of neo-Nazism, not to mention potential al Qaeda terrorists, as the courts did in the 1970s, when Germany was confronted with violence from small ultraleftist groups. The judicial system as a whole must now walk a very fine line between maintaining civil rights in a democratic society and providing security from various sources of extremist violence. The antiterrorist measures in the wake of 9/11 have placed additional pressures on the courts. For example, alleged Moroccan terrorists on trial in Germany for 9/11-related acts were released by the German court because the U.S. government would not allow the Moroccans to call witnesses on their behalf. These witnesses were being detained by the U.S. government as enemy combatants.

Subnational Governments

There are sixteen states in the Federal Republic; eleven from the old West Germany and five from the former East Germany. Unlike the weakly developed regional governments of Britain and France, German state governments enjoy considerable autonomy and independent powers. Each state has a regional assembly (*Landtag*), which functions much as the Bundestag does at the federal level. The governor (*Minister-Präsident*) of each *Land* is the leader of the largest party (or coalition of parties) in the *Landtag* and forms a government in the *Landtag* in much the same way as does the chancellor in the Bundestag. Elections for each of the sixteen states are held on independent, staggered four-year cycles, which generally do not coincide with federal elections and only occasionally coincide with elections in other *Länder*. Like the semipublic institutions, subnational governments in Germany are powerful and are responsible for much national policy implementation.

Particularly significant is Germany's "marble-cake" federalism—the interaction among state and federal government that sees the former implement many of the laws passed by the latter.[8] In fact, from its hybrid beginnings, German federalism has become one of the most imitated systems in the world among newly democratized countries. A good way to show how German federalism works in a specific policy arena is to cite the example of industrial policy (*Ordnungspolitik*). Regional governments are much more active than the national government in planning and targeting economic policy. For this reason, they have greater autonomy in administering industrial policy. Since the *Länder* are constituent states, they are able to develop their own regional versions of industrial policy. Because the different regions have different economic needs and industrial foundations, most voters see these powers as legitimate and appropriate.

The state governments encourage banks to make direct investment and loans to stimulate industrial development. They also encourage cooperation among regional firms, many in the same industry, to spur competition with other countries. State governments also invest heavily in vocational education to provide the skills needed for manufacturing high-quality goods, the core of the German economy. Organized business and organized labor have a direct role in shaping curricula to improve worker skills through the vocational education system. These *Land* governments have improved industrial adaptation by shaping the state's competitive framework rather than by adopting a heavy-handed regulatory posture. The states do not pursue identical economic policies, and there are various models of government involvement in economic policy.

In the Federal Republic, state politics is organized on the same political party basis as the national parties. This does not mean that national politics dominates local politics. However, the common party names and platforms at all levels let voters see the connection among local, regional, and national issues. Because parties adopt platforms for state and city elections, voters can see the ideological differences among parties and not be swayed solely by personalities. This does not mean that personalities do not play a role in German regional politics. Instead, the German party system encourages national political figures to begin their careers at the local and state levels. Regional and local party members' careers are tied closely to the national, regional, and local levels of the party. The system rewards ideological and policy continuity across levels of government. Some observers suggest that this connection in the Federal Republic among national, regional, and local politics may be one reason that voter turnout in German state elections far exceeds that of equivalent U.S. elections.

Local governments in the Federal Republic can raise revenues by owning enterprises, and many do. This has partly resulted from the historical patterns of public sector involvement in the economy but also from the assumption that these levels of government are the stewards of a collective public good. For instance, by operating art museums, theater companies, television and radio networks, recreational facilities, and housing complexes, and by providing various direct and indirect subsidies to citizens, local governments attempt to maintain the quality of life in modern society. The post-unification period has placed strains on these governments, particularly in the east, but Germans still look to regional governments for basic public infrastructure needs.

The European Dimension

The increased prominence of the EU offers both challenges and opportunities for FRG governance issues.[9] German policy formation at the European level is constrained because a much larger number of actors are involved in policies directly affecting the FRG. More significant, however, these actors generally operate in an environment that is quite different from the institutional continuity of German-style organized capitalism and democratic corporatism. Because pragmatic pluralist relationships are much easier to establish at the EU level than the deeply entrenched institutional continuities of the FRG, the shared understanding among German actors who have long years of interpenetrated relationships is much harder to establish at the EU level. For instance, both the role of the Bundesbank and the cozy bank-firm relationships so long characteristic of the German model become less and less significant as the ECB usurps the role of the Bundesbank. In addition, the organized capitalist German mode—at least among the largest firms and banks—is also giving way to a more Anglo-American deregulatory model. In that sense, what was unique about the German political economy in the postwar period is becoming much less so the further European integration proceeds.

On the other hand, Germany possesses a significant institutional advantage over other European states as European integration continues. According to the political scientist Vivien Schmidt, "To the extent that German institutional actors are now part of the larger, quasi-federal decision-making system that is the EU, this additional level of decision-making basically complements traditional German notions of democratic representation."[10] Unlike unitary states such as Britain, France, and Italy, Germany has experienced fifty years of modern federalism. To the extent that the institutional structure of the EU is based on federalism, the organizational landscape for both German federal and regional actors is most definitely known territory. One exceptionally important area within the EU is the complex of regional policies that sometimes enables Brussels to bypass national governments and implement directives within the regions of sovereign nation-states. While Britain and France have belatedly developed degrees of regional autonomy, the FRG has experienced regional political actors who can integrate themselves much more easily into the multilevel governance structures of the EU.

The Policymaking Process

The chancellor and the cabinet have the principal responsibility for policymaking, but their power cannot be wielded arbitrarily. Policymaking in Germany is largely consensus-based, with contentious issues usually extensively debated within various public, semipublic, and private institutions. Although the legislature has a general role in policymaking, the primary driving forces are the respective cabinet departments and the experts on whom they call.

Policy implementation is similarly diffuse. Along with corporatist interest groups and various semipublic organizations, the Bundesrat (upper house) also plays a significant role. Among the areas of policy most likely to be shaped by multiple actors are vocational education, welfare, health care, and worker participation. Germany is a federal state that is populated by a broad range of democratic corporatist groups and parapublic institutions. This means that policy implementation has many participants. Even in such areas as foreign and security policy, the federal cabinet departments sometimes rely on business interests in policy implementation. EU policy is shaped by both national and regional governments, as well as by private sector interests that use corporatist institutions to participate in the process.

The extraordinary nature of unification and the increasing significance of the EU in policymaking have greatly challenged this consensual system. Both changes have put this informal style of policymaking under tremendous pressure. Among the issues that proved most intractable at the domestic level are those of political asylum, racist violence, and scandals that have tarnished the reputations of major public figures in the political system and in major interest groups. At the European level, issues such as the euro and counterterrorism remain difficult. Moreover, for all of its system-maintaining advantages, the German consensual system contains a certain intolerance of dissent. The structure of the party system forces politicians to work slowly through the organization, there is a 5 percent threshold for party representation, and some political parties have been judicially banned. This intolerance helps to explain the protest from outside the parties that started in the 1960s and has continued on and off ever since.

Notes

[1] Ralf Dahrendorf, *Society and Democracy in Germany* (Garden City, N.Y.: Anchor, 1969).

[2] Gerhard Ritter, *The German Problem* (Columbus: Ohio State University Press, 1965).

[3] German President, official site, http://eng.bundespraesident.de.

[4] Michaela Richter, "Continuity or *Politikwechsel*? The First Federal Red-Green Coalition," *German Politics and Society* 20, no. 1 (Spring 2002): 1–48.

[5] Parastatal institutions differ greatly from pluralist representation in countries such as the United States, where interest groups petition public authority for redress of grievances but themselves often stay at arm's length from the implementation process. See Robert Dahl, *Dilemmas of Pluralist Democracy: Autonomy vs. Control* (New Haven, Conn.: Yale University Press, 1982).

[6] Peter Katzenstein, *Policy and Politics in West Germany: The Growth of a Semi-Sovereign State* (Philadelphia: Temple University Press, 1987).

[7] John O. Koehler, *Stasi: The Untold Story of the East German Secret Police* (Boulder, Colo.: Westview Press, 1999).

[8] Daniel Ziblatt, *Structuring the State: The Formation of Germany and Italy and the Puzzle of Federalism* (Princeton: Princeton University Press, 2005).

[9] Vivien A. Schmidt, *Democracy in Europe: The EU and National Polities* (Oxford: Oxford University Press, 2006).

[10] Vivien A. Schmidt, "European 'Federalism' and its Encroachments on National Institutions," *Publius* 29, no. 1 (Winter 1999): 36.

CHAPTER 14

Representation and Participation

In the new century of an expanded European Union, Germany still struggles with issues surrounding collective identities and representation. Its history with its European neighbors combined with recent immigration has brought these concerns to the surface once again. Socializing disparate political cultures, especially when respect for dissent and dialogue is not deeply ingrained, is problematic for any society. In the wake of unification and European integration, the key issue for Germany is how to develop a system of democratic participation among newly arrived groups to Germany that encompasses both extrainstitutional protest and flexible and responsive democratic political institutions.

The Legislature

The legislature occupies a prominent place in the political system in Germany, with both the lower house (Bundestag) and the upper house (Bundesrat) having significant and wide-ranging powers. The Federal Republic's legislature is bicameral; the lower house—the Bundestag—has 614 members, and the upper house—the Bundesrat—has 69 members. Unlike the U.S. Senate and the British House of Lords, the Bundesrat is made up of elected and appointed officials from the sixteen *Länder*. In this sense, Germany's constitutional system allows more governmental institutional overlap than in many other countries that are either unitary (France, Italy, and Britain) or that believe in sharp separation of powers within the federal government and a separation of powers between federal and state governments (the United States). The Bundestag members are elected in a basically proportional representation system (explained below), in which the leader of the major party, usually the leader of the largest party in a two- or three-party coalition, is the chancellor. As in most parliamentary systems, the chancellor must maintain a majority for his or her government to survive.

The electoral procedures for choosing members of the two houses differ substantially. German citizens elect members of the Bundestag both by choosing individual district representatives and selecting the political parties that represent their interests. The Bundesrat's members, on the other hand, are officials who are elected or appointed to the governments of the states (*Länder*). Both branches of the legislature are broadly representative of major interests in society, although some interests in the Bundestag, such as business and labor, are somewhat overrepresented and ecological and noneconomic interests are somewhat underrepresented. By design, the Bundesrat tends to represent principally regional interests.

The executive initiates important specific legislative proposals, since such issues as the federal budget and taxation are required by the Basic Law to come from the executive. That most bills are initiated in the cabinet does not diminish the influence of Bundestag or Bundesrat members, however, since party and coalition unity is important to ensure support for legislation. Also, many different groups, both inside and outside the legislature, can propose different policies. However, the chancellor and the cabinet are prominent. Since parties are generally ideologically coherent, there is usually strong consensus within parties and within coalitions about both the input and output of the legislative process. Parties and coalitions depend on party discipline to sustain majorities, which places high priority on agreement about major legislation.

When the chancellor and his or her cabinet propose a bill, it goes to a relevant Bundestag committee. Most of the committee deliberations are held behind closed doors, so the individual committee members have significant latitude to shape the details of legislation. The committees call on their own considerable expertise, but also solicit the expertise of relevant government ministries as well as testimony from affected interest groups. This system appears to be a kind of insiders' club, and to some degree it is. However, the committees generally call on a wide range of groups, both pro and con, that are affected by the proposed legislation. By consulting the corporatist interest groups, a more consensus-oriented outcome emerges. In contrast, legislative sessions in countries with a more pluralist (less inclusive) form of lobbying, such as Britain and the United States, tend to be contentious and less likely to produce agreement. Under pluralism, it is relatively easy for groups to articulate issues, but without a coordinated institutional structure policymaking is more haphazard.

After emerging from committee, the bill has three readings in the Bundestag. The debate in the Bundestag often produces considerable criticism from the opposition and sharp defense by the governing parties. The primary purpose of the debate is to educate the public about the major issues of the bill. Following passage in the Bundestag, the Bundesrat, must approve the bill.

A majority of the national legislature is composed of male, middle-class professionals, even in the supposedly working-class Social Democratic Party, which had a much greater proportion of blue-collar deputies in the 1950s. There were few women lawmakers until the 1980s and 1990s, when the Greens elected an increasing number of female Bundestag members, and women began to gain slots on the Social Democrats' electoral lists.[1] Fewer than 10 percent of Bundestag members were women through the 1983 election, but since 1987, the number of women has increased substantially, reaching 31.8 percent with the 2005 election (see Table 14.1). The addition of newer parties such as the worker-oriented Left Party (die Linke Partei, a fusion of the former eastern German ex-communist party and dissident leftwing social democrats) and the continued presence of the Greens with their counterculture lifestyles have increased the variety of backgrounds among Bundestag members. In fact, the proportional representation system increases the number of women and minorities elected to the Bundestag. Many parties, particularly the Social Democrats, the Greens, and the Left Party, select candidates for their electoral lists based on gender and diversity.

The Bundestag

The lower house of the legislature consists of 614 seats (see Figure 14.1), approximately half elected in single-member districts and half elected by proportional representation from lists compiled by the political parties. Citizens have two votes, one for an individual candidate in a local district, and one for their preferred political party.

The German parliamentary system represents a synthesis of the British and U.S. tradition of a single legislator representing one district and the proportional representation (PR) method that is more common in continental Europe, in which a group of party members represent a given region depending on the percentage of the party's vote there. The German hybrid system, which is known as mixed-member (or personalized) proportional representation, requires citizens to cast two votes on each ballot: the first one for an individual member of a political party, almost always from the district, and the second for a list of national and regional candidates grouped by party affiliation (see Figure 14.2).This system has the effect of personalizing list voting because voters have their "own" representative but also can choose among several parties. To ensure that only parties with significant support are represented, only those winning 5 percent of the vote or having three candidates who win individual seats directly gain representation in the Bundestag (or in any Land or municipal government). This provision exists because in the late Weimar period, sharp conflict among parties opened the door for the Nazi rise to power. Under the 5 percent rule, from the founding of the FRG until 1983, smaller parties tended to disappear as most of their adherents gravitated toward the three major parties. But then the Green Party broke the 5 percent barrier and attained twenty-seven seats in the Bundestag in 1983. In the 1990 federal election, the former East German communists (then called the PDS) won seats to become the fifth party in the Bundestag. With the 2005 election, the five-party system seems well-established.

Allocation of seats by party in the Bundestag, however, functions more like proportional representation.

Table 14.1

Percentage of Women Members of the Bundestag, 1949–2005

Year	Percentage	Year	Percentage
1949	6.8	1980	8.5
1953	8.8	1983	9.8
1957	9.2	1987	15.4
1961	8.3	1990	20.5
1965	6.9	1994	26.3
1969	6.6	1998	30.2
1972	5.8	2002	32.2
1976	7.3	2005	31.6

Source: Bundeszentrale für Politische Bildung, 2004 (http://www.bpb.de/suche/?all_search_action=search&all_search_text=%22Frauen%22+und+%22Bundestag%22); Women in National Parliaments, 2007 (http://www.ipu.org/wmn-e/classif.htm).

Figure 14.1

Distribution of Seats in the Sixteenth Bundestag (2005)

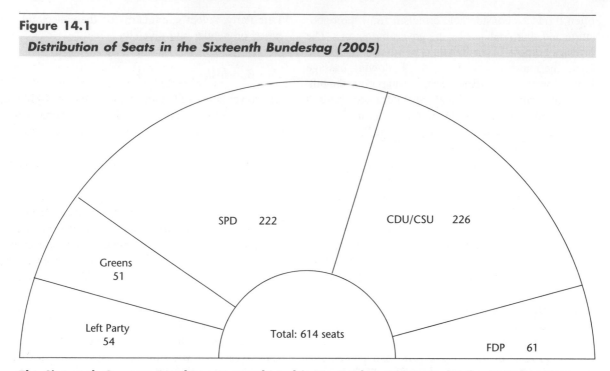

The Sixteenth German Bundestag was elected in September 2005. Currently, 614 deputies represent the Federal Republic of Germany's 61 million voters.

Specifically, the percentage of total seats won by each party corresponds to the party's percentage of the popular vote (providing the party receives the 5 percent minimum percentage to attain seats). For example, if a party's candidate wins a seat as an individual member, the candidate's party gains one fewer candidate from the list. In practice, most of the district seats are won by the two large parties, the Social Democrats and Christian Democrats (CDU), since the district vote is winner-take-all. The smaller parties' representatives, on the other hand, are almost always elected from the party lists. The list system creates stronger, more coherent parties. In countries with fragmented, individualistic parties, it is often harder to gain and hold effective majorities.

This combination of two systems was unique when it was first devised, but its results have proven so successful in achieving a variety of views and producing a stable majority, that it has been widely imitated, particularly in democratizing countries, because it combines local (geographical) representation with representation by ideology, class, gender, and/or religion. The list system enables party leaders to provide representation to diverse groups by placing individuals with different characteristics and attributes on the list, something harder to do when there are single-member districts. Single-member-district voting systems tend to produce a two-party system, and the PR system was melded with the single-member district of plurality voting because Germany wanted to ensure that all major parties, not just two, were represented.

Bundestag members belonging to the same parliamentary party almost always vote alike because general ideological coherence is essential. Party unity contributes to consistency in the parties' positions over the course of a four-year legislative period, and this enables voters to identify each party's stance on a range of issues. Consequently, all parties and their representatives in the Bundestag can be held accountable by voters based on their support for their party's positions

Figure 14.2

1990 Bundestag Election Ballot

Stimmzettel

für die Wahl zum Deutschen Bundestag im Wahlkreis 136 Kreisfreie Stadt Wiesbaden am 2. Dezember 1990

Sie haben 2 Stimmen

hier 1 Stimme
für die Wahl
eines/einer Wahlkreis-
abgeordneten

Erststimme

hier 1 Stimme
für die Wahl
einer Landesliste (Partei)
- maßgebende Stimme für die Verteilung der
Sitze insgesamt auf die einzelnen Parteien -

Zweitstimme

	Erststimme				Zweitstimme	
1	**Rönsch,** Hannelore Angestellte 6200 Wiesbaden **CDU** Carl-von-Ossietzky-Str. 38	Christlich Demokratische Union Deutschlands	○	○	CDU	Christlich Demokratische Union Deutschlands Dr. Alfred Dregger, Hannelore Rönsch, Dr. Christian Schwarz-Schilling, Dr. Heinz Riesenhuber, Bernhard Jagoda	1
2	**Wieczorek-Zeul,** Heidemarie Lehrerin 6200 Wiesbaden **SPD** Walkmühlstraße 39	Sozialdemokratische Partei Deutschlands	○	○	SPD	Sozialdemokratische Partei Deutschlands Heidemarie Wieczorek-Zeul, Rudi Walther, Dr. Dietrich Sperling, Ute Zapf, Karsten Voigt	2
3	**Koch,** Ulrich Friedrich Sozialarbeiter 6200 Wiesbaden **GRÜNE** DIE GRÜNEN Feldstraße 27		○	○	GRÜNE	DIE GRÜNEN Ulrike Riedel, Hubert Kleinert, Marina Steindor, Dietrich Wetzel, Freya Klier	3
4	**Dr. Funke-Schmitt-Rink,** Margret Studienrätin 6200 Wiesbaden **F.D.P.** Sonnenberger Straße 3	Freie Demokratische Partei	○	○	F.D.P.	Freie Demokratische Partei Dr. Hermann Otto Prinz zu Solms-Hohensolms-Lich Hans-Joachim Otto, Dr. Gisela Babel, Ekkehard Gries, Dr. Heinrich Kolb	4
				○	DIE GRAUEN	DIE GRAUEN Initiiert vom Senioren-Schutz-Bund "Graue Panther" e.V. ("SSB-GP") Ludwig Neise, Sibylle Schöning, Karl Röth, Dr. Hildegard Malecki-Anna Hildebrand	5
6	**Langer,** Herbert Prokurist 6200 Wiesbaden **REP** DIE REPUBLIKANER Sonnenberger Str. 27		○	○	REP	DIE REPUBLIKANER Gert Feldmeier, Herbert Langer, Brigitte Wurnert, Peter Münch, Günter Hämer	6
7	**Deubert,** Ernst Wilhelm Rentner 6000 Frankfurt/Main 60 **NPD** Bergerstraße 234	National- demokratische Partei Deutschlands	○	○	NPD	Nationaldemokratische Partei Deutschlands Winfried Krauß, Dora Zull, Hans Schmidt, Dieter Fuhrmann, Volker Sachs	7
				○	ÖDP	Ökologisch-Demokratische Partei Gerhard Mahnke, Waltraud Schunck, Monika Zickwolff, Dr. Wolfgang Günther, Rolf-Dewel Klar	8
				○	PDS/ Linke Liste	Partei des Demokratischen Sozialismus/Linke Liste Manfred Coppik, Angela Kraft, Heike Schmuser, Manfred Alter, Reinhold Rückert	9

on the issues. This party discipline, in turn, helps produce more stable governments.

One direct result of party discipline is that the Federal Republic has high electoral participation (80 percent at the federal level). Some observers once argued that German citizens voted in such high numbers out of habit or duty.[2] Given the remarkable stability in the voting patterns of the three main postwar parties—and now the Greens and the Left parties—with little deviation in each party's electoral outcome from election to election, it is more likely that high electoral participation is due to clear party ideology. For the FRG's fifty years, voting participation rates have matched or exceeded those of all other Western European countries.

The tradition of strong, unified parties in the Bundestag has had some drawbacks, however. The hierarchy within parties relegates newer members to a comparatively long period of apprenticeship as backbenchers (the rear seats are for newly elected members). In fact, some of the Federal Republic's most prominent postwar politicians at the national level built up their visibility and political skill through long service in *Land* or local government service before using their experience as a springboard for national political power.

Although this system does educate younger members in party ideology, it also frustrates ambitious young legislators. They can become even more frustrated when their party is in power, because the dominance of the party elders increases at that time. The chancellor and the party leadership need to understand the dynamics of the organization, or they can lose touch with the backbench members of their party.

The Bundesrat

The Bundesrat occupies a position quite different from those of the U.S. Senate and the British House of Lords. The Bundesrat is the mechanism by which the federal system of the country actually works. It is responsible for the distribution of powers between national and state levels, and grants to the states the right to implement federal laws. It is the institutional intersection of the national and state governments, for it consists of members of the sixteen *Länder* governments. The total number of seats is sixty-nine, with each *Land* sending at least three representatives, depending on its population. States with more than 2 million residents have four votes, and states with more than 6 million have five. This system gives disproportionate representation to small *Länder* although nothing close to the disproportionate representation the U.S. Senate gives to small American states. One might think that smaller states would be more conservative, but three of the small states are city-states (Berlin, Hamburg, Bremen) and usually vote for the left, so the political composition of the German *Länder* does not vary appreciably by size.

The political composition of the Bundesrat at any given time depends on which parties are in power in the states. Each state delegation casts its votes in a bloc in the Bundesrat, reflecting the views of the party or coalition in control of the state government. Consequently, the party controlling the majority of *Länder* governments can have a significant effect on legislation passed in the Bundestag. And because *Länder* elections usually take place between Bundestag electoral periods, the Bundesrat majority can shift during the course of a Bundestag legislative period.

The Bundesrat must approve all amendments to the constitution, as well as all laws passed in the Bundestag that address the fundamental interests of the *Länder*, such as taxes, territorial integrity, and basic administrative functions. It also can exercise a *suspensive veto;* that is, if the Bundesrat votes against a particular bill, the Bundestag can pass the measure again by a simple majority to override the Bundesrat's veto. If a two-thirds majority of the Bundesrat votes against a bill, the Bundestag must pass it again by a two-thirds margin. In usual practice, however, the Bundesrat has not acted as a force of obstruction or gridlock. When the legislation is concurrent—that is, when the state and national governments jointly share administrative responsibilities for implementing the particular policy—there is almost always easy agreement between the two houses. Furthermore, if a party or coalition has a stable majority in the Bundestag, then any possible obstruction by the Bundesrat can be overcome.

The Bundesrat introduces comparatively little legislation, but its administrative responsibilities are considerable. Most members of the Bundesrat are also *Land* government officials and are well experienced in the implementation of particular laws. Their expertise is frequently called on in the committee hearings of the Bundestag, which are open to all Bundesrat members. This overlapping policy process (*Politikverflechtung*) is a unique feature of the Federal Republic. Many Americans make the mistake of equating German and U.S. federalism. Yet because of *Politikverflechtung*, the relationship between national and *Länder* governments differs qualitatively from the relationship between the federal and state governments in the United States.

The Bundesrat's strong administrative role is a crucial component of the government. For example, the Bundesrat coordinates the regional and national links between economic policies, vocational education systems, and the components of a major television network (ARD). The Bundesrat's structure positions it closer to the concerns and needs of the entire country and provides a forum for understanding how national legislation will affect each *Land*.

Although the Bundesrat was originally envisioned to be more technocratic and less politically contentious than the popularly elected Bundestag, in the 1970s debates in the Bundesrat became strongly politicized. The most common conflicts occurred when regional elections caused a change in control of the Bundesrat, especially when this change gave more influence to the party, or group of parties, that was in opposition to the Bundestag. For example, part of Helmut Kohl's difficulty in his last term (1994–1998) resulted from the Social Democrats' controlling a majority of state governments, where they occasionally blocked national legislation. After Schröder's narrow victory in the 2002 Federal elections and the CDU victory in several *Land* elections since then, similar conflicts occurred in the remainder of the SPD-Green second term and caused the election in 2005, a year ahead of schedule.

The Bundesrat has a role to play as the European Union (EU) becomes increasingly significant. It promotes representation for the *Länder* in EU institutions, most notably in the Council of Regions. It also successfully insisted on the German federal government's accepting that it could have a veto power over certain German positions on EU decisions.

Political Parties and the Party System

Germany has often been called a party democracy because its parties are so important in shaping state policy. Its multiparty system has proved quite stable for most of the period since World War II. Until the early 1980s, Germany had a "two-and-a-half" party system, composed of a moderate-left Social Democratic Party (SPD), a moderate-right Christian Democratic grouping (CDU in all of West Germany except Bavaria, where it is called the CSU), and a small centrist Free Democratic Party (FDP). During their time as the main parties in politics (1949–1983), these groups presided over a stable, growing economy and a broad public consensus on economic and social policies.

During the 1980s and 1990s, two new parties emerged to challenge the "two-and-a-half" major parties and to complicate Germany's comparatively tidy political landscape.[3] These were the Bündnis '90/The Greens, generally of the left and promoting ecological, environmental, and peace issues; and the

Table 14.2

German Political Parties

Christian Democratic Union (CDU)/Christian Social Union (CSU) (moderate-right)

Social Democratic Party (SPD) (moderate-left)

Bündnis '90/Greens (left-environment)

Free Democratic Party (FDP) (center)

The Left Party (LinksPartei) (left)

Deutsche Volks Union (DVU) (far right)*

National Democratic Party (NPD) (far right)*

---

*The latter two parties (DVU & NPD) have not attained the 5 percent of the vote necessary for representation in the Bundestag.

Left Party (*die Linkepartei*). This was formerly the Party of Democratic Socialism (PDS), and previously the former Communist Party of East Germany. In 2005, the latter merged with a group of former left-wing Social Democrats who believed that Schröder's reforms were undermining social democracy and formed the Left Party. Two other small right-wing parties, the German Peoples Union (*Deutsche Volksunion*, DVU) and the National Democratic Party (*Nationaldemokratische Partei Deutschlands*, NPD), also have emerged. (See Table 14.2.) Much more conservative than the CDU/CSU, they emphasized nationalism, aggression, intolerance and sometimes violence toward immigrants and ethnic minorities. Neither of these two right-wing parties has yet won seats in the Bundestag because of the 5 percent rule. In 2006, however, both exceeded the 5 percent threshold in two separate eastern German regional elections and have won seats in those bodies.

Christian Democrats

The Christian Democrats combine the Christian Democratic Union (CDU, in all *Länder* except Bavaria) and the Christian Social Union (CSU, the affiliated Bavarian grouping). Unlike the older parties (SPD and FDP) of the Federal Republic, the CDU/CSU was founded immediately after World War II and united Catholics and Protestants in one confessional (Christian) party and served as a catchall party of the center-right. During Weimar, the two Christian denominations had been divided politically, with the Catholics in the Catholic Center Party and the Protestants in several other parties.

Programmatically, the CDU/CSU stressed the social market economy, involving pro-capitalist elements as well as a paternalistic sense of social responsibility.[4] Under chancellors Adenauer and Erhard, the Christian Democrats held political power for almost twenty years. Its social policies during this period were paternalistic and moderately conservative. The CDU/CSU even explicitly codified this approach with the phrase *Kinder, Kirche, Kuche* (children, church, and kitchen), which defined the Christian Democrats' view of women's primary roles and had originally been a motto of the last Kaiser's wife.

After the SPD and FDP established their center-left coalition in 1969, the CDU/CSU spent thirteen years as the opposition party. Returning to power in 1983 under Helmut Kohl, the CDU/CSU with their FDP coalition partners retained power through four elections until 1998.[5] The most significant and historic accomplishments—truly twin legacies—of the long Kohl regime are German unification and Germany's integration into the EU.

Although Angela Merkel became Germany's first female chancellor after the 2005 election, her victory was much less glorious than either she or her Christian Democratic colleagues originally expected. Instead of the preferred coalition with the FDP, their traditional coalition partner, the CDU/CSU was forced into a "Grand Coalition" with the SPD for only the second time in the Federal Republic's history. Merkel only emerged as chancellor three weeks after the election, after the CDU/CSU and SPD had contentiously negotiated their agreement. It came at a heavy price for the Christian Democrats; in return for Gerhard Schröder stepping aside as the SPD's chancellor candidate, the Christian Democrats agreed to take only six of the fourteen cabinet seats, leaving the remaining eight to the SPD.

Social Democratic Party

As the leading party of the left in Germany, the *Sozialdemokratische Partei Deutschlands* (SPD) has had a long and durable history. The SPD was founded in 1875 in response to rapid industrialization. After surviving Bismarck's attempts in the 1880s to outlaw it, the SPD grew to be the largest party in the *Reichstag* by 1912.[6] Following World War I, it became the leading party—but without a majority—of the Weimar Republic during its early years.

Despite strong influence in postwar Germany from 1945 to 1948, the SPD was able to obtain only about 30 percent of the popular vote from 1949 until the early 1960s. In an attempt to broaden its constituency, the party altered its party at a 1959 conference in Bad Godesberg. Deemphasizing its primary reliance on Marxism, its new goal was to broaden its base and become what the political scientist Otto Kirchheimer has called a "catchall party."[7] The SPD did not relinquish Marxism completely and continued to represent the working class, but it also began to seek and attract support from groups outside the traditional blue-collar working class. The Bad Godesberg conference transformed the SPD into a party similar to other western European social democratic parties.

The SPD finally took office as the leading member of a majority coalition, with the FDP, in 1969 and remained in power for thirteen years under chancellors Willy Brandt and Helmut Schmidt. The SPD brought to the coalition a concern for increased welfare and social spending.[8] This was due partly to pressure by left-wing extraparliamentary opposition groups and student demonstrations in 1968. The FDP brought its support for increased individual freedom of expression at a time when youth in all industrialized societies were seeking a greater voice. The principal factor cementing these two dissimilar parties for such a long time was the strong performance of the economy. The coalition finally broke up in the early 1980s, when an economic recession prevented the increased social spending the SPD left wing demanded.

During the 1980s and 1990s when it was out of power, the SPD failed to formulate clear alternative policies to remain attractive to its members, supporters, and voters. In 1998 Gerhard Schröder enabled the SPD to win the 1998 elections in coalition with the Greens, a government that lasted until 2005.

Bündnis '90/The Greens

The Greens (the party's common name) entered the political scene in 1979 and have won seats at national and regional levels ever since. It is a heterogeneous party that first drew support from several different constituencies in the early 1980s: urban-based Citizens Action Groups, environmental activists, farmers, activists against nuclear power, the remnants of the peace movement, and small bands of Marxist-Leninists. After overcoming the 5 percent hurdle in the 1983 Bundestag elections, the Green Party went on to win seats in most subsequent state elections by stressing noneconomic quality-of-life issues. The electoral successes of this "antiparty party" generated a serious division within the organization between the *realos* (realists) and the *fundis* (fundamentalists). The *realos* believed it was important to enter political institutions to gain access to power; the *fundis* opposed any collaboration with existing parties, even if this meant sacrificing some of their goals.

The realists gained the upper hand, but there was no guarantee of long-term success for the Greens because all the other parties began to include environmental and qualitative issues in their party programs. Until the merger with the eastern German Bündnis '90 in 1993, the Greens' position looked bleak. The squabbling between *fundis* and *realos* undercut the party's credibility. Unable to develop positions to address the problems of unification, the party appeared unwilling to deal with reality. The Greens' failure to motivate its own core constituency during the early 1990s greatly hampered the party. The unexpected suicide of a former party leader—the American-born Petra Kelly, a *fundi*—and the moderation of a former party leader (and foreign minister), Joschka Fischer, signaled the transformation of the Greens into a dependable, innovative coalition partner.[9]

The persistent ecological problems of the former East German states have presented the Greens with a tremendous opportunity. After gaining over 6 percent of the vote in the 1994 and 1998 elections and becoming the junior coalition partner in the SPD-Green coalition, the party's firm base seemed to waver. This was caused by its defending coalition policy on which its own members did not always agree. However, the Greens rebounded and increased their share of the vote to 8.6 percent in 2002 and won 8.1 percent in 2005. They now appear to be a permanent fixture in the German Bundestag.

One of the first ecological changes that the Greens won in coalition with the SPD was the commitment to phase out nuclear power in Germany, although the completion date is at least two decades in the future. In addition, the Greens were able to push for an increase in the gasoline tax. The party also used its position in the cabinet to force the German government to challenge the United States on such policies as genetically modified foods, the American failure to maintain its commitment to the Kyoto protocols, which committed world governments to reduce greenhouse gas emissions on a strict schedule, and military action against Iraq.

After the 2005 election, the Greens returned to the opposition benches in the Bundestag after briefly flirting with the idea of entering a coalition with the Christian Democrats and FDP. However, Green party members rebelled against the idea of a coalition with probusiness parties.

Free Democratic Party

The FDP's major influence for many years was its role as a swing party. It has allied with each of the two major parties (SPD and CDU/CSU) at different periods from 1949 to 1998. Regularly holding the foreign and economics ministries in coalition with the Christian Democrats, the FDP's most notable leaders were Walter Scheel, Count Otto Lambsdorff, and Hans-Dietrich Genscher.[10]

The FDP's perspective encompasses two ideologies, broadly characterized here as economic liberalism (*liberal* in the European sense of laissez-faire individualism) and social liberalism. During the postwar period, the FDP relied on two philosophies to align itself with the two major political groupings, the CDU/CSU and the SPD. The FDP was a member of almost all governing coalitions from 1949 to 1998; but because of its strategy of co-governing with first one major party and then the other, the FDP has occasionally been accused of lacking strong political convictions.

During the years of the SPD-Green governments (1998–2005), the FDP became much more explicitly a free-market party, emphasizing deregulation and privatization. With its 9.8 percent of the vote in 2005, it had hoped to join the Christian Democrats in a right-wing coalition but the CDU's showing was poorer than expected and did not give the CDU/CSU and FDP enough seats to form a majority.

The Left Party (Die Linke)

In June 2005 the former eastern German communist party (Party of Democratic Socialism) merged with a breakaway faction of the SPD that called itself the Wahlalternative Arbeit und Soziale Gerechtigkeit (WASG, or "electoral alternative for labor and social justice") to form the Left Party. The PDS was concentrated in the five states of the former East Germany, and although it received as much as 25 percent of the vote in some regional and local elections, it always drew well under the 5 percent mark in elections in the *Länder* of the former West Germany.[11] Although it was officially a new party concentrated in the former East Germany, it has had a long and volatile history. It was formed from the Communist Party of Germany (Komministische Partei Deutschlands, KPD), which was founded after World War I. In the late 1940s, the Communist Party flourished in the Soviet zone and under USSR acquiescence forced a merger with the Social Democrats in the east. The merged Communist/Socialist party was renamed the Socialist Unity Party (Sozialistische Einheits Partei, SED). It dominated all aspects of life in East Germany and was considered the most Stalinist and repressive regime in Eastern Europe.

With unification in 1990, reality confronted the SED, but it demonstrated considerable tactical agility by changing its name and program. Throughout the 1990s, however, the difficulties of unification strengthened the PDS. It gained over 20 percent of the vote in the five new German states in the Bundestag elections of 1994, 1998, and 2002 and won seats in the Bundestag in four consecutive elections. In the mid-1990s, it formed regional coalitions with the SPD in eastern Germany and even was a junior member of the Berlin city and state governments in 2001.

The WASG, comprised of left-wing dissident former SPD members, led by former finance minister Oskar Lafontaine, offered an attractive option for the PDS. Based primarily in western Germany, the WASG provided electoral support for the PDS precisely where the latter was weakest. Polling as high as 12 percent nationwide prior to the election, the new Left Party obtained 8.7 percent of the vote in September 2005 and represented an intriguing complication for the other parties.

In fact the Left Party's strong showing, largely due to its opposition to budget cuts, is the main reason why neither the SPD and Greens, nor the CDU/CSU and FDP were able to form either a left-wing or right-wing coalition. With a growing base in the west (4.9 percent) combined with its traditional eastern support (nearly 25 percent) it seems solidly entrenched as the fifth party. However, all other parties have ruled out dealing with the Left—including the SPD and Greens—even though the three left of center parties won 51.1 percent of the votes and had a potential 21 seat majority. Schröder resisted because one of the Left's leaders is Oskar Lafontaine, who was purged as his first finance minister in early 1999, and the two have not spoken since. In addition, the Left party is a merger between two different "lefts" (east and west); they are not yet philosophically or organizationally coherent enough to be the key member in an all-left government.[12] Their other leader, the East Berliner Gregor Gysi is much more focused on acting as principled opposition in the Bundestag and actually making the merged entity into a real party with the long-term goal of reaching a united left government with the SPD and Greens.

While the Left Party is still finding its way as a parliamentary party on the opposition benches, it is also performing an important task in eastern Germany. The FRG is one of the few countries in Western Europe that has not had a far right and/or neo-fascist party gain seats in its national legislature. Because the primary support for the Left Party in the east comes from marginalized and/or unemployed people in Germany society, it has provided a left-wing alternative to those whom, under other circumstances, might turn to the far right.

The Far Right

There have been various splinter-group right-wing parties throughout the Federal Republic's history, but with the exception of the National Democratic Party of Germany (NPD), which received 4.3 percent of the vote in 1969, they had never seriously threatened to win seats in the Bundestag. There are two far-right political parties[13] that have won seats in regional parliaments since 2000: the Deutsche Volksunion (DVU), and the neo-Nazi Nationaldemokratische Partei Deutschland (NPD). None, however, have come close to winning seats in the Bundestag. The latter two parties have won *Land* government seats in 2006. They will be discussed more fully in Chapter 15.

Elections

The German electoral system has produced two significant outcomes. The first is coherence among the parties, since the system—and the constitution itself, for that matter—specifically supports the parties as essential organizations for political democracy. Second, the 5 percent hurdle ensures that only parties that command significant support attain seats in the Bundestag. This rule has helped Germany avoid the wild proliferation of parties in such democracies as Italy and Israel, which has made forming coalitions difficult in those countries.

As Table 14.3 suggests, Germany has been a country without volatile electoral swings. There have been five major periods of party dominance (plus two Grand Coalitions) between 1949 and the present:

1. CDU/CSU-FDP coalition (1949–1966) [CDU/CSU majority 1957–1961]
2. Grand Coalition (CDU/CSU-SPD) (1966–1969)
3. SPD-FDP coalition (1969–1982)
4. CDU/CSU-FDP coalition (1982–1998)
5. SPD-Green coalition (1998–2005)
6. Grand Coalition (CDU/CSU-SPD) (2005–)

Political Culture, Citizenship, and Identity

Germany has never had a strong individualistic ethos; rather it is a country dominated by organized collectivities, as shown by the organization of interests and social movements. This characteristic appears not only among major economic producer groups but also among political parties (in which participatory membership is high) and a wide range of social groups. However, the FRG's strong collective identities have enhanced rather than diminished the country's relationship to democracy. Germany's political culture thus offers a strong contrast to the individualism characteristic of Anglo-American countries. German citizenship historically has been based primarily on the ethnicity of one's parents, making the granting of citizenship to those of non-German ethnicity problematic until relatively recently. For much of its history, including much of the period after World War II, Germany has taken a comparatively restrictive—some even say racist—position. The opening of the EU could potentially change this landscape significantly.

Table 14.3

FRG Election Results, 1949–2005

Year	Party	Percentage of Vote	Government	Year	Party	Percentage of Vote	Government
1949	Voter turnout	78.5	CDU/CSU-FDP	1983	Voter Turnout	89.1	CDU/CSU
	CDU/CSU	31.0			CDU/CSU	48.8	
	SPD	29.2			SPD	38.2	
	FDP	11.9			FDP	7.0	
	Others	27.8			Greens	5.6	
1953	Voter turnout	86.0	CDU/CSU-FDP		Others	0.5	
	CDU/CSU	45.2		1987	Voter turnout	84.3	CDU/CSU
	SPD	28.8			CDU/CSU	44.3	
	FDP	9.5			SPD	37.0	
	Others	16.7			FDP	9.1	
1957	Voter turnout	87.8	CDU/CSU		Greens	8.3	
	CDU/CSU	50.2			Others	1.3	
	SPD	31.8		1990	Voter turnout	78.0	CDU/CSU
	FDP	7.7			CDU/CSU	43.8	
	Others	10.3			SPD	33.5	
1961	Voter turnout	87.8	CDU/CSU-FDP		FDP	11.0	
	CDU/CSU	45.3			Greens	3.8	
	SPD	36.2			PDS	2.4	
	FDP	12.8			Bündnis '90	1.2	
	Others	5.7			Others	3.5	
1965	Voter turnout	86.8	CDU/CSU-SPD	1994	Voter turnout	79.0	CDU/CSU
	CDU/CSU	47.6	Grand		CDU/CSU	41.5	
	SPD	39.3	Coalition		SPD	36.4	
	FDP	9.5			FDP	6.9	
	Others	3.6			Greens	7.3	
1969	Voter turnout	86.7	SPD-FDP		PDS	4.4	
	CDU/CSU	46.1			Others	3.5	
	SPD	42.7		1998	Voter turnout	82.3	SPD-Greens
	FDP	5.8			CDU/CSU	35.1	
	Others	5.4			SPD	40.9	
1972	Voter turnout	86.0	SPD-FDP		FDP	6.2	
	CDU/CSU	44.9			Greens	6.7	
	SPD	45.8			PDS	5.1	
	FDP	9.5			Others	6.0	
	Others	16.7		2002	Voter turnout	79.1	SPD-Greens
1976	Voter turnout	90.7	SDP-FDP		SPD	38.5	
	CDU/CSU	48.2			CDU/CSU	38.5	
	SPD	42.6			Greens	8.6	
	FDP	7.9			FDP	7.4	
	Others	0.9			PDS	4.0	
1980	Voter Turnout	88.6	SPD-FDP		Others	3.0	
	CDU/CSU	44.5		2005	Voter turnout	77.7	
	SPD	42.9			CDU/CSU	35.2	
	FDP	10.6			SPD	34.2	
	Others	0.5			FDP	9.8	
					Left Party	8.7	
					Greens	8.1	

Source: German Information Center, 2005.

Social Class

In the analysis of Germany's social forces ever since industrialization in the late nineteenth century, class has been a primary category. Germany's working class remains larger and more prosperous than those of Britain, France, or Italy, and it has thrived as postwar Germany's high-wage, high-skill, export-oriented industries have provided substantial material benefits to its mostly unionized work force. While class remains a salient cleavage, other significant social divisions have been based on religion and region, with the former less significant than the latter. Although the population in the southeast, portions of the southwest, and along the Rhine as far north as Düsseldorf is predominantly Catholic, and although in the northwest, northeast, and portions of the southwest, one finds predominantly Lutheran Protestants, this cleavage is not particularly significant. Collective identities are also determined on regional divisions, which only rarely are based on religious cleavages. Many of the pre-1871 German states have retained considerable autonomy, which is often manifested in different traditions and customs. The creation of a *Federal* (rather than unitary) Republic of Germany was due to these regional divisions. Of course, during the late nineteenth century, and particularly during the first half of the twentieth, ethnicity and race were major lines of social demarcation, with monstrous consequences.

Interest groups behave differently in the Federal Republic than they do in the Anglo-Saxon countries. In the Federal Republic, they have a societal role and responsibility that transcends the immediate interests of their members. Germany's public law traditions, deriving from Roman and Napoleonic legal foundations, specifically allow private interests to perform public functions, albeit within a clear and specific general framework. The *Krankenkassen* (sickness funds), which provide national health insurance, are the best example. Such interest groups are part of the fabric of society and are virtually permanent institutions, and a social premium is placed on their adaptation and ability to respond to new issues. To speak of winners and losers in such an arrangement is to misunderstand the ability of existing interest groups to make incremental changes over time.

Because they are structurally integrated into the fabric of society, German interest groups have an insti-

tutional longevity that surpasses those of interest groups in most other industrialized countries. But how does the German state mediate the relationship among interest groups? Peter Katzenstein observes that in the Federal Republic, "the state is not an actor but a series of relationships," and these relationships are solidified in what he has called "parapublic institutions."[14] As noted in Chapter 13, the parapublics encompass a wide variety of organizations. Under prevailing German public law, rooted in feudal traditions from before 1871, Katzenstein states they have been assigned the role of "independent governance by the representatives of social sectors at the behest of or under the general supervision of the state." In other words, organizations that would be seen as mere interest groups in other countries are combined in Germany with certain quasi-governmental agencies so that together they have a much more parapublic role in the Federal Republic.

Employer associations and trade unions are the key interest groups within German society, but they are not alone.* Other, less influential groups include the Protestant and Catholic churches, the Farmers Association (Deutscher Bauernverband), the Association of Artisans (Handwerk Verein), the Federal Chamber of Physicians (Bundesaerztekammer), and the now nearly defunct League of Expelled Germans (Bund der Vertriebenen Deutschen, BVD), which has represented the interests of emigrants from the GDR and Eastern Europe. Each of these groups has been tightly integrated into various parapublic institutions in order to perform a range of important social functions that in other countries might be performed by state agencies. These organizations are forced to assume a degree of social responsibility as they implement policy that goes beyond what political scientist Arnold Heidenheimer has called the "freewheeling competition of 'selfish' interest groups."[15]

The churches, through the state, assess a church tax on all citizens who have been born into the Protestant or Catholic Church. This tax provides the churches with a

---

*German industry is represented by the BDI (Federal Association of German Industry), and employers are represented by the BDA (Federal Association of German Employers).The former addresses issues pertaining to industry as a whole; the latter focuses specifically on issues of concern to employers. German workers are represented by eight different unions, organized by industry, which belong to the DGB (German Trade Union Confederation).

steady stream of income and ensures institutional permanence, but it also compels the churches to play a major role in the provision of social welfare and in aiding the families of *Gastarbeiter* (guest workers). The Farmers Association has been a pillar of support for both the FDP and the CDU-CSU, and for decades has strongly influenced the agricultural ministry. It has also resisted attempts by the EU to enforce the common agricultural policy and lower the agricultural support provided to European farmers in the form of direct subsidies. The Association of Artisans is a major component of the German chamber of commerce (Der Deutsche Industrieund Handelskammer—DIHK), to which all firms in Germany *must* belong, and the Chamber of Physicians has been intimately involved with both the legislation and implementation of social and medical insurance (social security and general welfare).

These interest groups, and the parapublic agencies within which they function, attempt to contain social conflict through multiple, small-scale corporatist institutions. The Federal Republic's corporatist variant in the 1980s was much more regionalized and industry-specific, and much less centralized, than earlier national-level conceptions of corporatism. Even so, this system of interest groups and parapublics still must express the concerns of member organizations, channel conflict, and recommend (and sometimes implement) public policy.

Citizenship and National Identity

The most contentious issue of citizenship and identity has surrounded the political asylum question. Following World War II, Germany passed one of the world's most liberal political asylum laws, in part to help atone for the Nazis' political repression of millions. The German government granted immediate asylum status to all those who claimed persecution or fear of persecution based on violated political freedoms, and it allowed those asylum seekers to remain in Germany, with considerable monetary support, until each individual's case was heard. Often this process took years. With the end of the cold war and the opening of East European borders, the trickle of asylum seekers turned into a flood in the minds of some Germans. This sentiment caused the Kohl government to curtail drastically the right of political asylum, a step that called into question whether

Germany's democracy was as mature and well developed as it had claimed during the stable postwar period. Germany's commitment to democratic rights appeared to contain some new conditions, and many of them involved a definition of identity that looked remarkably insular in a Europe that was otherwise becoming more international.[16]

Examples of this restrictive aspect of naturalization are evident in the wake of the breakdown of the Eastern bloc. The immigration of ethnic Germans, the presence of *Gastarbeiter* who have been in Germany for two generations and are only now slowly obtaining citizenship, and the volatile political asylum question have all placed strains on the concept of citizenship in the post-unification years. Further, the expansion of the EU to twenty-seven countries threatens to exacerbate questions of both citizenship and national identity. For many poor citizens in those ten new EU countries that are in Eastern Europe, Berlin is a very powerful magnet drawing these individuals in search for a better life. Until now, German history since World War II has acted as a powerful brake on anti-ethnic, nativist sentiment. The FRG's generous asylum laws are a prime example of this commitment. However, the much more fluid world of the EU, in both citizenship and national identity terms, will likely prove a significant challenge for Germany.

Race and Ethnicity

In the late 1980s and the 1990s, some of the optimistic views that Germany had become a "normal" parliamentary democracy were challenged by the nature of anti-ethnic and anti-immigrant violence. The attacks on foreign immigrants and even on *Gastarbeiter* families who had lived in Germany for more than thirty years raised questions among some observers as to how tolerant the Germans really are. Owing to Germany's history of repression toward Jews and most non-Germans during the first half of the twentieth century, such concerns must be taken extremely seriously. More disturbing to many was the lack of leadership coming from the Kohl government at the time and the apathy—and, in some cases, enthusiasm—of some Germans toward the intolerant violence. To be sure, Germany was not alone among industrialized nations in racist violence, but Germany's history imposes a special burden. The Schröder government between

1998 and 2005 was more aggressive in using the bully pulpit of the chancellor's office as well as the German legal system to pursue racist attacks aggressively. On the tenth anniversary of German unification, a group of neo-Nazis attacked a synagogue in Düsseldorf, and the Schröder government issued a statement calling on German citizens to rise up against the "brown scum" in a "revolt of the righteous."

The full development of citizenship, democracy, and participation in Germany is not blemish-free, however. Only in 1999 did Germany alter an extremely restrictive position on immigration, in one of the first acts taken by the Schröder SPD-Greens government. Immigrant workers have generally fared better in German society than those immigrants who are not members of trade unions or works councils and/or the democratic left political parties. Without the granting of German citizenship, such workers remain marginalized residents of the FRG. Unlike many other European nations, Germany had made it difficult for immigrants to be naturalized, no matter how long they had been in the country, and generally denied citizenship to offspring of noncitizens born on German soil. This prejudice was exacerbated by the end of the cold war and the demise of the Soviet Union. For example, "ethnic" Germans whose ancestors had not been in Germany for centuries were allowed to enter Germany legally and assume citizenship rights immediately. Yet the *Gastarbeiter* who had lived in Germany for decades—and at the express invitation of the German governments of the 1960s—were not given the same opportunities for instant citizenship.* The new law, which took effect on January 1, 2000, provided for German citizenship for all children born in Germany, provided their parents had resided lawfully in Germany for eight years or had an unlimited residence permit for three years. Naturalization now is possible after eight years of residence instead of the previous fifteen.

Gender

Gender did not appear to be a politically significant cleavage in Germany until the 1960s, since women had remained politically marginalized for most of the first half of the Federal Republic's history. Gender did not produce political divisions because many women appeared to accept their unequal position in postwar West German society. Taking to heart the Christian admonition of *Kinder, Kirche, Küche* (children, church, and kitchen), many German women were socialized into believing that their status as second-class citizens was appropriate. To be sure, there were pre-FRG exceptions to this pattern—such as the socialist activist and theorist Rosa Luxemburg and the artist Käthe Kollwitz from the 1910s—but until the social explosions of the 1960s, very few women held positions in society outside the home.

Even with the spread of feminism since the 1970s, German women have generally lagged behind their American counterparts by some five to ten years in terms of advancement in business and politics, at least on an individual level. However, as the data in Chapter 13 show, German women have nearly quadrupled their representation in the Bundestag from approximately 8 percent in 1980, to over 31 percent in 2005. The differences between East and West Germany on social policy affecting women provoked great controversy after unification. Women in the former East Germany had far more presence and influence in public life and in the workplace than did their counterparts in West Germany.

In areas outside the formal workplace, the differences between the laws in the GDR and the pre-unification FRG created a huge controversy. In the former East Germany, women had made far greater social and economic progress (relatively speaking) and enjoyed greater government provision for such services as child care and family leave. In fact, one of the hottest items of contention in Germany during the early 1990s was whether to reduce East German–style benefits to women (including abortion) in favor of the more conservative and restrictive ones of the Federal Republic. The more restrictive West German law prevailed after unification, to the consternation of many women, and many men.

Interests, Social Movements, and Protest

Germans engage in significant strikes and demonstrations on a wide range of economic and noneconomic issues. But rather than signs of instability or a failure

---

*Turkish *Gastarbeiter* are disadvantaged because if they accept German citizenship, they generally surrender property rights in Turkey.

of public institutions, these struggles are indicators of success. Political institutions are more than fixed structures that prevent or repress dissent or controversy. A "new institutionalist" approach argues that political organizations shape and adapt to social and political protest and channel such action in ways that are not detrimental to democratic participation but in fact represent its essence.[17]

This distinction has important implications for interest groups and social movements in the Federal Republic. Instead of fractious competition, this system creates a bounded framework within which such groups struggle tenaciously but usually come to an agreement on policy. Moreover, because they are encouraged to aggregate the interests of all members of their association, their policy total—the general interest of the group as a whole—will be greater than the sum of its parts—the aggregated concerns of individual members. These institutions are not omnipotent, however. If they fail and allow conflict to go unresolved, the failure challenges the effectiveness of the institutions and may allow elements of society to go unrepresented. A partial failure of certain interest groups and institutions led to the rise of a series of social movements during the 1960s and 1970s, particularly concerning university reform, wage negotiations, and foreign policy. The very existence of the Green Party is a prime example of a movement that arose out of the earlier inability of existing institutions to address, mediate, and solve contentious issues.

With respect to extrainstitutional participation and protest, a general system of inclusionary proportional representation has left few outside the political arena until recently. Those who are outside belong to political groups that fail to meet the 5 percent electoral threshold. Right-wing groups seem to fit into this category. Similarly, the substantial Turkish population, which accounts for over 5 percent of Germany's inhabitants, might also be included here. Finally, the once-active leftist community of revolutionary Marxists still retains a small presence, mostly in large cities and university towns. Some of these left-wing parties contest elections but never get more than 1 percent of the vote.

Nevertheless, during the years since the student mobilizations of the late 1960s, Germany has witnessed considerable protest and mobilization of social forces outside the established channels of political and social representation. Among the most significant forces in the postwar FRG have been the feminist, peace, environmental, and antinuclear movements. All four, in different ways, have challenged fundamental assumptions about German politics and have pointed to the inability of the institutional structure to respond to the needs and issues that these groups raised. From challenges to a restrictive abortion law in the 1970s, to demonstrations against stationing nuclear missiles on German soil in the 1980s, to climate change in the 1990s, to regular protests against nuclear power plants since the 1970s, the spirit of direct action has animated German politics in ways that were not possible before the late 1960s.

The 1990s, however, witnessed protest less from the left than from the right. Although the DVU and NPD are legitimate parties, illegal neo-Nazi groups have been responsible for numerous racist attacks, increasing since the summer of 2000, the most reprehensible one taking place at a Jewish synagogue on the tenth anniversary of German unification. Significantly, many of these attacks by the right-wing fringe have been met with spontaneous, peaceful marches, sometimes producing demonstrations of from 200,000 to 500,000 people in various cities. This reaction suggests that social protest, now a part of active democratic political discourse, has matured in the face of this new threat from the right. The early twenty-first century has produced an increase in social protest, largely among forces on the left of the governing SPD-Green coalition. Opposition to the Iraq war has been a great focus of protest. Prior to the 2002 election, Schröder used this often vocal opposition to compensate for poor economic performance and secure reelection. The challenge for German politics is to maintain a system of democratic participation that encompasses both extrainstitutional groups and specific organized political institutions in a way that enhances democracy rather than destroying it. Germans would suggest that effective consensus is not something that is imposed from the top; it requires the engagement of contentious issues and the institutional capacity to successfully resolve them.

Notes

[1]Frank Louis Rusciano, "Rethinking the Gender Gap: The Case of West German Elections," *Comparative Politics* 24, no. 3 (April 1992): 335–358.

[2]Ralf Dahrendorf, *Society and Democracy in Germany* (Garden City, N.Y.: Anchor, 1969).

[3]Christopher S. Allen, *Transformation of the German Political Party System: Institutional Crisis or Democratic Renewal?* (New York: Berghahn Books, 1999).

[4]Aline Kuntz, "The Bavarian CSU: A Case Study in Conservative Modernization" (Ph.D. diss., Cornell University, 1987).

[5]Reimut Zohlnhöfer, "Institutions, the CDU and Policy Change: Explaining German Economic Policy in the 1980s," *German Politics* 8 (1999): 141–160.

[6]Carl E. Schorske, *German Social Democracy, 1905–1917: The Development of the Great Schism* (Cambridge: Harvard University Press, 1983).

[7]Otto Kirchheimer, "The Transformation of the Western European Party System," in Roy C. Macridis, ed., *Comparative Politics: Notes and Readings*, 6th ed. (Chicago: Dorsey Press, 1986).

[8]Gerard Braunthal, *The German Social Democrats Since 1969: A Party in Power and Opposition*, 2nd ed. (Boulder, Colo.: Westview Press, 1994).

[9]Thomas Poguntke, "Green Parties in National Governments: From Protest to Acquiescence?" *Environmental Politics* 11 (2002): 133–145.

[10]Thomas Saalfeld, "Coalition Politics and Management in the Kohl Era, 1982–98," *German Politics* 8 (1999): 141–173.

[11]Hans-Georg Betz and Helga Welsh, "The PDS in the New German Party System," *German Politics* 4 (1995): 92–111.

[12]David F. Patton, "Germany's Left Party. PDS and the 'Vacuum Thesis': From Regional Milieu Party to Left Alternative?" *Journal of Communist Studies & Transition Politics* 22 (2006): 206–227.

[13]Hans-Georg Betz, *Radical Right-Wing Populism in Western Europe* (New York: St. Martin's Press, 1994).

[14]Peter Katzenstein, *Policy and Politics in West Germany: The Growth of a Semi-Sovereign State* (Philadelphia: Temple University Press, 1987).

[15]Arnold J. Heidenheimer, *Comparative Public Policy: The Politics of Social Choice in America, Europe, and Japan*, 3rd ed. (New York: St. Martin's Press, 1990).

[16]Joyce Marie Mushaben, "A Search for Identity: The 'German Question' in Atlantic Alliance Relations," *World Politics* 40, no. 3 (April 1988): 395–418.

[17]Sven Steinmo, Kathleen Thelen, and Frank Longstreth, eds., *Structuring Politics: Historical Institutionalism in Historical Perspective* (New York: Cambridge University Press, 1992).

CHAPTER 15

German Politics in Transition

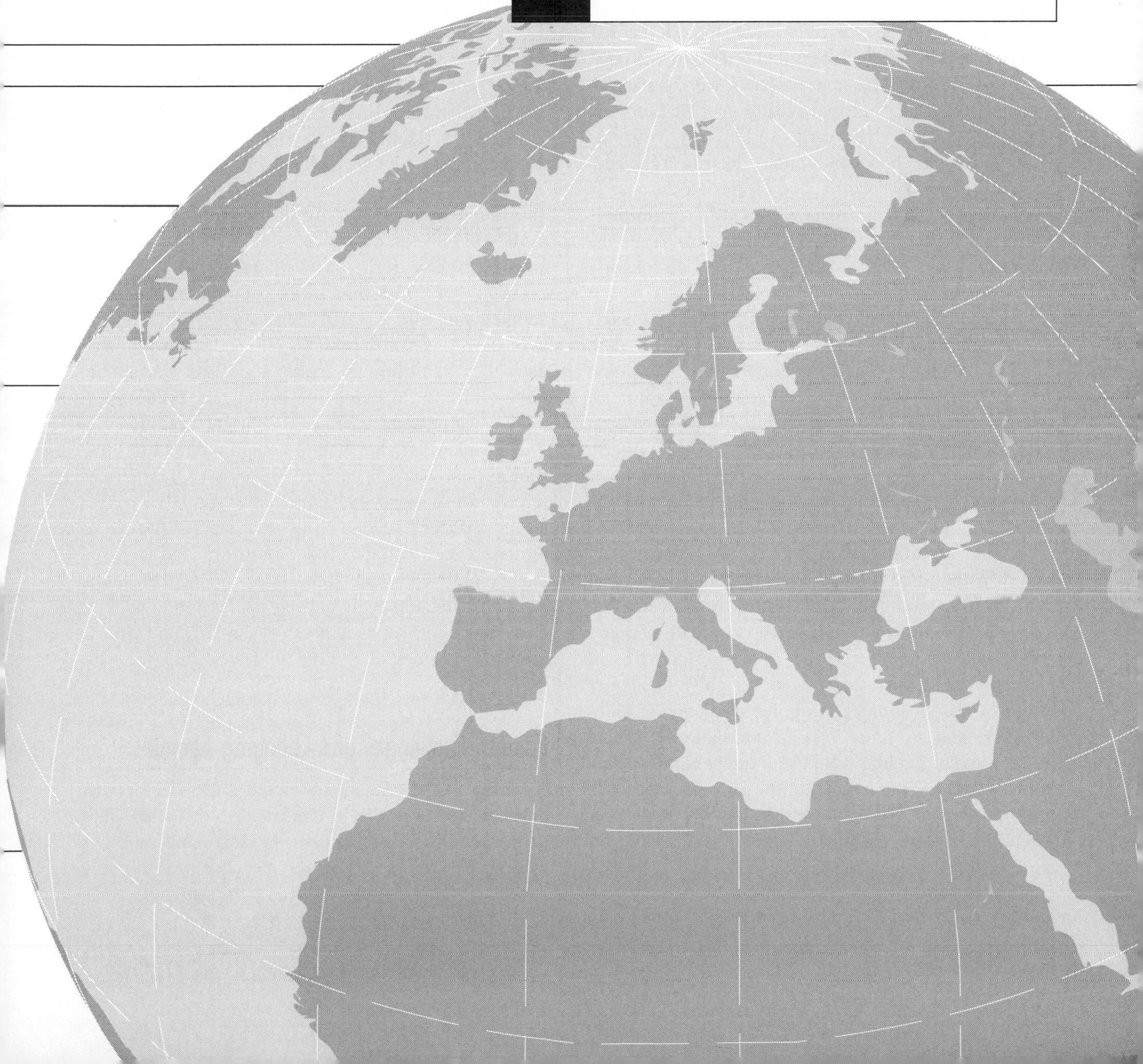

At first glance, the arrival of Angela Merkel as chancellor might signify a refreshing policy change toward a more dynamic economy. The reality of contemporary German politics paints a more complicated picture. The narrow plurality of Merkel's Christian Democrats forced the new chancellor to drastically rein in the party's ambitious plans to reform the labor market. Moreover, in order to become chancellor, Merkel's CDU/CSU had to allow the SPD to have eight of the fourteen cabinet posts, including Labor, Finance, Justice, and the Foreign Ministry. Despite the change in leadership, Merkel still faces the same triple challenges that bedeviled Schröder: (1) the still-formidable uncompleted tasks associated with unification; (2) the rapid expansion of the European Union (EU) and its free-market-style policy focus that is at odds with the institutionally based, organized-capitalist German economy; and (3) the intense pace of globalization that threatens Germany's competitive edge. The question is whether Germany can retain the institutional and political skills to recover its formerly strong position.

The path taken by German politics will be determined by the resolution of the four core themes identified in Chapter 11. The more hopeful outcome would be for Merkel to strike a spirit of genuine compromise with the SPD and bridge the formidable gaps between these two large parties in such a difficult coalition. By finding common ground to address such problems as economic competitiveness, unemployment, and the still gaping East-West divide—among many others—the Grand Coalition could develop the patience and sound institutional foundation to accomplish a great deal. In fact, economic performance through the first half of 2007 augured well, since only with a sound and effective foundation of domestic policy will Germany be able to address successfully the larger issues of European integration, the challenge of globalization, and the more volatile international climate in the wake of the Iraq war. The more pessimistic outcome would see the two coalition partners digging in their heels and failing to move beyond their pre-election campaign platforms—which could only produce continued stalemate. This would further deepen German pessimism, and increase the share of the vote going to the three opposition parties. Despite the improved economy, Merkel has yet to reap much political credit for it.

There are now five significant political parties in Germany's political landscape rather than the three during the 1949–1983 period. Can Germany's organized society and institutional political structure sustain the increased cooperation necessary to maintain a vibrant democracy? What about Germany's "economic giant–political dwarf" syndrome (a phrase once used to describe Germany's failure to assume the political responsibility commensurate with its economic stature)? Do its European neighbors really want it to do so? And what of Germany's high-wage economy and welfare structure in the face of increased economic competition from lower-wage countries in East Asia and elsewhere? Will using the now stronger euro (in terms of its value against the dollar) instead of the deutsche mark enable Germany to thrive, or will it undermine the previous strengths of the German economy? And what is the state of the German economy in the face of domestic structural challenges, as well as globalization of the international economy and the evolution of "Euroland" (the countries that have adopted the euro as their currency)? Following the 2005 elections, the CDU/CSU-SPD government faced daunting pressures to make significant economic policy reforms to overcome a sluggish economy. It remains to be seen whether the Grand Coalition can implement significant economic and political reforms such as Schröder's Agenda 2010 program—sometimes referred to as Hartz IV, named after the labor minister in Schröder's second term—that merged the unemployment and welfare systems reforms and required the unemployed to take jobs either outside their home region or outside their chosen profession. The Left Party and significant segments of the SPD and Greens are likely to block all but the mildest of such reforms.

Political Challenges and Changing Agendas

For many years Germany was touted as a model for other industrialized societies to emulate. Yet the years since unification have seen increases in racial intolerance, as well as the partial erosion of the country's formerly vaunted economic strength. What is the state of German democracy in the face of racist attacks and rising intolerance, and what is the state of the German economy in the face of contemporary structural challenges?

The continuity of democratic institutions has clearly balanced participation and dissent effectively, for the country's turbulent and often racist past has been offset by more than a half-century of well-established multiparty democracy. Despite the challenges of deregulation and the new information economy, Germany has maintained its unique and successful industrialized democracy. The country is a bastion of advanced capitalism, yet it also possesses an extensive welfare state and government-mandated programs of worker, trade union, and works council participation in managerial decision making. Moreover, these economic and political successes have helped Germany participate more effectively in the wider world of other nation-states. Based on the post–World War II idea that neither a laissez-faire nor a state-centered economy was appropriate, the FRG developed its own social market economy. And based on the idea that an organized and integrated labor movement could produce not only worker safeguards but also a high-productivity economy, Germany found a way to produce for over fifty years a "high-everything" (wages, skills, quality goods, competitiveness) political economy.

Let us briefly review the three major contemporary transitional challenges that the Federal Republic faces: unification; Germany's production profile and the welfare state; and immigration and the far right.

First, German unification has been both a tremendous accomplishment and a daunting challenge for all Germans. Few other countries could so quickly add 20 percent to their own population from an adjoining country with a completely different economic and social system. In most other countries, such a challenge would likely have produced either a much less successful unification or far greater social chaos, or both. The fact that official political unification took place within a year of the breaching of the Berlin Wall is an accomplishment of significant proportion. And the formal integration of the former German Democratic Republic (GDR) into the FRG as five new *Länder* is a tribute to organizational and political skills that combined both vision and pragmatism.

United Germany's democracy seems well established after almost sixty years of the Federal Republic and almost two decades of unification. It boasts high voter turnout, a stable and responsible multiparty political system, and a healthy civic culture.[1] Despite the inconclusive 2005 election resulting in an awkward "Grand Coalition," German politicians have negotiated an interim solution that could begin to solve Germany's difficult challenges, and they have done so through constitutional principles common to all multiparty parliamentary systems.

Many observers believe that broad-based participation is part of the fabric of German political life. The overriding challenge for Germany's political institutions is the assimilation of the five eastern states. Can eastern Germans who have lost jobs and benefits in the transition to capitalism understand that ethnic minorities are not the cause of their plight? Can tolerance and understanding develop while a right-wing fringe is preaching hatred and searching for scapegoats to blame for the costs of unification? Also, what is the legacy of a bureaucratic state, which as recently as the 1970s, under a Social Democratic–led government, purged individuals who appeared to have radical tendencies? In other words, if social tensions continue to grow, how will the German state respond?

Beyond the immediate institutional features of unification lie the more difficult issues of integration of economic and social systems and of the quite different political cultures of eastern and western Germany, which will take years to blend together. Furthermore, after the initial wave of construction and the economic mini-boom in the first year after unification, a more sobering mood set in. As unemployment has remained much higher in the five new states than in the others by mid-decade, Germans have realized that unification was far from a quick fix. The process of fully unifying the disparate parts of Germany will continue well into this century.

Second, Germany's famed social market economy, with its characteristic organized-capitalist features and strong emphasis on manufacturing over services, its privileged position for trade unions, and its generous social welfare provisions, has faced renewed pressures in the post-unification years. Some fissures have arisen within business associations and labor unions that may threaten the traditionally solid institutions of organized capitalism. For many years, the German economy was characterized as "high everything" in that it combined high-quality manufacturing with high wages, high fringe benefits, high worker participation, and high levels of vacation time (six weeks per year).[2]

A cynical western German view of money spent to rebuild eastern German.
Source: Janusz Majewski, Cartoonists and Writers Syndicate, from *Frankfurter Allgeneine Zeitung.*

Since the first oil crisis in 1973, however, critics have insisted that such a system could not last in a competitive world economy. Nevertheless, the German economy has remained among the world's leaders and still is the world's leading exporter. But the huge costs of unification, the globalization of the world economy, and the exaggerated emphasis on laissez-faire principles in many of its neighboring countries challenge the German model anew. Together, these problems have caused many of the old criticisms about an extended, inflexible, and overburdened economy to surface again.

Pessimists began to suggest that the stresses of the late 1990s and early 2000s placed the German political economy in a precarious position.[3] The primary economic task of the Merkel government is to address the competitiveness issue and manage the transition to an economy that can confront the technological and globalizing pressures that German firms continue to face. The trend toward Europeanization may be incompatible with the consensus-oriented and coordinated nature of Germany's adjustment patterns. The completion of the single market of the EU has also complicated Germany's relationship with other states. Although the EU was supposedly the grand culmination of a post–cold war spirit of European unity, it has proved more difficult to establish than first anticipated. Rather than enhancing integration, its principal actions in the early twenty-first century have only strengthened the trends toward decentralization and deregulation already under way in Western Europe. More significant for the German economy, such deregulatory tendencies, if spread throughout Europe, could potentially disturb the organized capitalism of Germany's small and large businesses. In addition, the apparent deregulation in European finance threatens Germany's distinctive finance-manufacturing links.

The effects of introducing the euro have also caused uncertainty. Administration of the currency has required a European central bank, a common monetary policy of all twelve "Euroland" nations, and a common set of fiscal policies. In short, fundamental tools, which in the past had defined sovereignty for nation-states, are now subject to European, not national, control. Germany has tried to model the European Central Bank after the *Bundesbank* (it is located in Frankfurt, not Paris or London). However, the coordination of monetary and fiscal policies by the European Central Bank since the introduction of the euro has not always been what German governments and German firms have come to expect.

Third, racist movements and far-right parties, however marginal they may have been in the 1990s, still retain a presence in modern unified Germany in the 2000s. In 2004 eastern German regional elections in Brandenburg, the extreme right-wing party, Deutsche Volksunion (DVU), received 6.1 percent of the vote and gained representation for the second consecutive Land election. Further to the right is the National-demokratische Partei Deutschlands (NPD), which came close to gaining Bundestag representation in 1966 with 4.3 percent of the vote. But after years of relative dormancy, the NPD resurfaced in the 2004 regional election in Saxony, and obtained 9.2 percent of the vote and won seats in the regional parliament. It also won 7.3 percent of the vote in Mecklenburg-Lower Pomerania in 2006. The attacks on foreigners, thought to have peaked in the early 1990s, have returned since the 1990s when a hostel for foreign refugees was firebombed and Jewish synagogues were attacked. While representing a tiny minority of the population, far-right racist movements nonetheless represent a significant concern for a democratic country with its catastrophic past. Whether these far-right regional electoral victories are just protest votes or harbingers of something more ominous bears watching.

In other words, in the area of collective identities, Germany faces numerous unresolved challenges. Germany's guest workers (mostly Turkish) remain essential to Germany's economy, but will the citizenship reforms of the 2000s prove sufficient to integrate them into the fabric of German political and social life? The opening of East Germany produced an influx of refugees and asylum seekers, beginning in the late 1980s, which placed great strains on a country that paradoxically has had generous political asylum laws but significant restrictions on non-Germans' attaining citizenship. Increased ethnic tensions, which had understandably been suppressed since the end of World War II, have produced increased German nationalism and reawakened primal identity issues. The dark side of such a development is manifested by the various extremist groups, which though still small in numbers, preach exaggerated nationalism and hatred of foreigners and minorities. Contributing to this climate is the reluctance of some German firms to settle reparation payments to aging workers who were slave laborers in World War II. Such tendencies are incompatible with a Germany that wishes to play a leading role in European integration.

The future of German politics depends on how the country addresses these challenges, which overlap the four primary themes in this book: a world of states, governing the economy, the democratic idea, and the politics of collective identities. For much of the post–World War II period, Germany enjoyed a spiral of success, in that dealing well with one of these thematic issues enabled the country to confront others successfully. For example, problems of collective identities were handled in a much less exclusionary way as women, ethnic groups, and newer political parties and movements all began to contribute to a stable and healthy diversity in German politics, which had been missing for most of the country's history.

However, in closely examining all four of these major themes, we find Germany at a crossroads. Can the country continue its successes in all four areas, or will tensions and difficulties undermine these successful patterns to produce a period of economic, political, and social instability?

There has been a significant change in the nature of German politics in the twenty-first century. In the four preceding chapters, we reexamined the theme of democratic tolerance and respect for the positions and opinions of other individuals and groups. The question remains. Can Germany evolve peacefully and democratically in a region where increased integration will become more likely? The expansion of the European Union in the 1990s—and once again with twelve more countries in 2007—enabled more European citizens to live and work outside their home countries. What happens to German collective identity? Can the elaborate and, for almost sixty years, effective institutional structure that balances private and public interests be maintained and supported? Will the EU augment or challenge Germany's position in Europe? Will these challenges threaten Germany's enviable economic position in the face of increased competition from newly industrializing countries?

German Politics, Terrorism, and Germany's Relation to the United States

The good news for the Germans with respect to their relationship with the United States is that the Germans are not the French. The bad news is that the Bush administration considers Germany an unreliable ally, almost as "disloyal" as its neighbor to the west. Before the Iraq war, Germany strongly preferred to rely on the United Nations, to take a multilateral approach, and to keep nonmilitary options open as long as possible in dealing with Saddam Hussein. The Schröder government was unconvinced that unilaterally attacking Iraq would have any positive effect in challenging Al Qaeda. Thus the French and Germans prevented the United States from building a broad-based coalition to initiate the war. Britain was the only major country that supported the United States.

For anyone who understands German politics in the past fifty years, however, the German ambivalence about rushing pell-mell into Iraq alongside the United States and a relatively small contingent of British soldiers is completely understandable. Germany was explicitly discouraged by the United States from projecting a strong international political posture after World War II, and was heavily constrained by the structure of the North Atlantic Treaty Organization (NATO), not to mention by the thousands of American troops stationed in Germany for decades after the end of World War II—and even after the end of the cold war. For fifty years Germany was explicitly encouraged to concentrate on economic affairs and to leave geopolitics to the United States. After educating two generations of German citizens about the folly of military adventure, to expect the Federal Republic to sign on to the Iraq invasion on a series of extremely dubious premises about "weapons of mass destruction," and against the wishes of the UN, represents a fundamental misunderstanding of German postwar politics.

For the Germans, the UN and NATO remain the primary international political vehicles for Germany to engage in international relations. It's not that Germany is unwilling to undertake responsibility in the fight against terrorism, as the deployment of forces in Afghanistan under a UN mandate has shown.

As for German domestic politics and terrorism, Germans are embarrassed that several of the 9/11 hijackers lived in Hamburg before moving to the United States. But Germany believes that the fight against terrorism can be better waged via domestic intelligence rather than by the approach that the Bush administration took in Iraq. The discovery in September 2007 of an active terrorist organization within Germany that threatened to target American interests in Germany caused a heightened sense of anxiety. In general, however, Germany believed that the fight against terrorism should not take place at the expense of democratic rights and freedoms. Germans found it ironic that these were rights that the United States encouraged Germany to develop in the wake of the Third Reich.

Finally, it is not as if Germany has not had experience in dealing with its own domestic terrorists of both the left and right. Clearly, some dubious measures were taken against the left-wing Red Army Faktion (RAF) terrorists and other political dissidents in the late 1970s, but successive German governments have engaged in less onerous forms of surveillance and counterterrorist measures. Many Germans would say that most of the provisions of the USA PATRIOT

Act—such as holding suspects, both citizens and noncitizens alike, indefinitely, without formal charges, and without allowing them to consult a lawyer—would never have come close to passing in the Bundestag had a similar 9/11 event taken place in Germany.

The Challenges of European Integration

The challenge that the EU presents offers both opportunities and dangers to the Federal Republic. Although the creation of a single market can clearly benefit the strongest European economy, Germany faces unique problems as it attempts to integrate its economy with that of other economies on the Continent. Clearly the weaker countries, such as Portugal and Greece, will look to strong countries such as Germany for assistance. Moreover, Germany's brand of organized capitalism is clearly out of step with the more free-market sentiments of other European countries. Defenders of the German model might rightfully ask why the economy of all of Europe shouldn't be modeled on Germany rather than on the free-market-oriented United Kingdom? However, transferring the deeply embedded structures of German capitalism to countries that do not understand how they work is much easier said than done, even assuming these countries would want to import the German model. Furthermore, the transition from the redoubtable deutsche mark to the stronger euro has added further worries about export performance to the minds of German citizens.

The completion of the single market of the EU—now along with the enlargement of the EU in 2007 to twenty-seven nations—has also complicated Germany's relationship with other states. The EU was supposedly the grand culmination of a post–cold war spirit of German and European unity. But unity has proved more difficult to establish than first anticipated. The outcome of recent reforms—the single market, the euro, an incomplete EU constitution—has only strengthened the trends toward decentralization and deregulation already under way in Western Europe, rather than initiating EU political institution building. In short, the specific direction that Europeanization is taking may be incompatible with the highly consensus-oriented and coordinated nature of Germany's adjustment patterns.

For much of the period after World War II, Germany's growing international economic prowess was not complemented by a similar level of international political responsibility. Yet since unification in 1990, Germany has confidently, and with the support of its neighbors and allies, taken a leading role in European integration. It is firmly anchored in Western Europe but uniquely positioned to assist in the transition of the formerly Communist East-Central European states toward economic and political modernization. Initial doubts concerning the capacity of Germany's commitment to a deeper and wider EU have been resolved, as Merkel seems to be speaking with an even greater sense of the projection of German responsibility in the EU than did her predecessors.

German Politics in Comparative Perspective

Germany offers important insights for comparative politics. First, how successfully has Germany remade its political culture and institutions in the wake of a fascist past? Countries such as Japan, Italy, and Spain among developed states also bear watching on this point. Many have hoped that Germany's impressive democratic record during the first fifty five years of the Federal Republic has completely exorcised the ghosts of the Third Reich. But not all observers are certain. To what extent have the educational system, civil service, and the media addressed the Nazi past? To what extent do they bear some responsibility for the recent rise of right-wing violence? Have the reforms in the educational system since the 1960s provided a spirit of critical discourse in the broad mainstream of society that can withstand right-wing rhetoric? Can judges effectively sentence those who abuse the civil rights of ethnic minorities? Will the news media continue to express a wide range of opinion and contribute to a healthy civic discourse? Or will strident, tabloid-style journalism stifle the more reasoned debate that any democracy must have to survive and flourish?

Second, Germany's historical importance on the world political stage during the past 150 years means that understanding its transition is essential for comparative purposes. Germany was late to achieve political unity and late to industrialize. These two factors eventually helped produce a catastrophic first half of the twentieth century for Germany and the whole

world. Yet the country's transition to a successful developed economy with an apparently solid democratic political system seems to suggest lessons for other countries. Those that might derive the most benefit may be industrializing nations as they too attempt to achieve economic growth and develop stable democracies.

Third is the role of organized capitalism. Germany offers a model for combining state and market in a way that is unique among advanced industrialized nations. Many models of political analysis choose to emphasize the distinctions between state and market. Debates about whether nationalized industries should be privatized and whether welfare should be reduced in favor of private charity, for example, are symptomatic of the conflict between state and market that informs the politics of most developed countries. Germany's organized capitalism, together with its social market economy, has blurred the distinction between the public and private sectors. It has refused to see public policy as a stark choice between these two alternatives, preferring to emphasize policies in which the state and market work together. The German state pursues development plans that benefit from its cooperative interaction with a dense network of key social and economic participants. Despite Germany's prominence as a powerful, advanced, industrialized economy, this model remains surprisingly understudied. Regardless of Germany's current economic challenges, which have been brought about by unification and the uncertain terrain of Europeanization, it remains a model worthy of comparative analysis.

The fourth insight concerns Germany's development as a collectivist democracy. In other words, it has stressed the role of the individual not as a sole actor in isolation from the rest of society, but as a citizen in a wider set of communities, organizations, and parties that must find ways of cooperating if the nation-state is to maintain its democracy. It is clearly within this complex of policies that Germany is wrestling with its treatment of different groups within the Federal Republic.

Germany offers a fifth insight on the issues of tolerance and respect for the civil rights of ethnic minorities. The Schröder government modified Germany's immigration policies to provide a path for long-time foreign workers to gain citizenship and make a meaningful contribution to German democracy. Can residual ethnic tensions be resolved in a way that enhances democracy rather than undermines it? Clearly, the issue of collective identities offers both powerful obstacles and rich opportunities to address one of the most crucial issues that Germany faces in the new century.

Finally, what is the role of a middle-rank power as the potential leader of a regional bloc of some 450 million people? Germany is facing intense pressures from within its borders, such as conflict among ethnic groups, and from a complex mix of external influences. Its role as both a western and an eastern European power pulls at it in different ways.[4]

Should the country emphasize the western-oriented EU and build a solid foundation with its NATO allies? Or should it turn eastward to step into the vacuum created by the demise and fragmentation of the former USSR? Can Germany's twentieth-century history allow either its western or eastern neighbors to let it play the geopolitical role that its low-profile postwar political status has only postponed? It would be an ironic twist if Germany, the country whose virulent nationalism caused the most widespread destruction and destabilization in the twentieth century, took the lead at the head of the supranational EU in promoting creativity and stability in the twenty-first century.

Notes

[1]Gabriel A. Almond and Sidney Verba, eds., *The Civic Culture Revisited* (Newbury Park, Calif.: Sage, 1989).

[2]Lowell Turner, ed., *Negotiating the New Germany: Can Social Partnership Survive?* (Ithaca, N.Y.: Cornell University Press, 1997).

[3]Wolfgang Streeck and Christine Trampusch, "Economic Reform and the Political Economy of the German Welfare State," *German Politics* 14 (2005): 174–195.

[4]Peter J. Katzenstein, ed., *Tamed Power: Germany in Europe* (Ithaca, N.Y.: Cornell University Press, 1997).

Part 4 Bibliography

Allen, Christopher S., ed. *Transformation of the German Political Party System: Institutional Crisis or Democratic Renewal?* New York: Berghahn, 1999.

Berger, Stefan. *The British Labour Party and the German Social Democrats: 1900–1931.* Oxford: Oxford University Press, 1994.

Braunthal, Gerard. *The Federation of German Industry in Politics.* Ithaca, N.Y.: Cornell University Press, 1965.

————. *The German Social Democrats Since 1969: A Party in Power and Opposition.* 2nd ed. Boulder, Colo.: Westview Press, 1994.

————. *Parties and Politics in Modern Germany.* Boulder, Colo.: Westview Press, 1996.

Craig, Gordon. *The Politics of the Prussian Army.* Oxford: Oxford University Press, 1955.

Dahrendorf, Ralf. *Society and Democracy in Germany.* Garden City, N.Y.: Anchor, 1969.

Deeg, Richard. *Finance Capitalism Unveiled.* Ann Arbor: University of Michigan Press, 1999.

Eley, Geoff. *Reshaping the German Right: Radical Nationalism and Political Change After Bismarck.* New Haven, Conn.: Yale University Press, 1980.

Evans, Peter B., Dietrich Rueschemeyer, and Theda Skocpol. *Bringing the State Back In.* Cambridge: Cambridge University Press, 1985.

Gerschenkron, Alexander. *Bread and Democracy in Germany.* 2nd ed. Ithaca, N.Y.: Cornell University Press, 1989.

Hager, Carol. "Environmentalism and Democracy in the Two Germanies." *German Politics* 1, no. 1 (April 1992): 95–118.

Hesse, Joachim Jens. "The Federal Republic of Germany: From Cooperative Federalism to Joint Policy-Making." *West European Politics* 10, no. 4 (October 1987): 70–87.

Hirschman, Albert O. *Exit, Voice, and Loyalty.* New Haven, Conn.: Yale University Press, 1970.

Inglehart, Ronald. *Culture Shift in Advanced Industrial Society.* Princeton, N.J.: Princeton University Press, 1990.

Jacoby, Wade. *Imitation and Politics: Redesigning Modern Germany.* Ithaca, N.Y.: Cornell University Press, 2000.

Katzenstein, Peter J. *Policy and Politics in West Germany: The Growth of a Semi-Sovereign State.* Philadelphia: Temple University Press, 1987.

————. *Tamed Power: Germany in Europe.* Ithaca, N.Y.: Cornell University Press, 1997.

Kemp, Tom. *Industrialization in Nineteenth Century Europe.* 2nd ed. London: Longman, 1985.

Markovits, Andrei S. "Political Parties in Germany: Agents of Stability in a Sea of Change." *Social Education* 57, no. 5 (September 1993): 239–243.

Moore, Barrington. *Social Origins of Dictatorship and Democracy.* Boston: Beacon Press, 1965.

Piore, Michael, and Charles Sabel. *The Second Industrial Divide.* New York: Basic Books, 1984.

Rein, Taagepera, and Matthew Soberg Shugart. *Seats and Votes: The Effects and Determinants of Electoral Systems.* New Haven, Conn.: Yale University Press, 1989.

Rueschemeyer, Dietrich, Evelyn Huber Stephens, and John D. Stephens. *Capitalist Development and Democracy.* Chicago: University of Chicago Press, 1992.

Rusciano, Frank Louis. "Rethinking the Gender Gap: The Case of West German Elections." *Comparative Politics* 243 (April 1992): 335–358.

Schmidt, Manfred G. "West Germany: The Politics of the Middle Way." *Journal of Public Policy* 7, no. 2 (1987): 135–177.

Schmitter, Philippe C., and Gerhard Lembruch, eds. *Trends Toward Corporatist Intermediation.* Beverly Hills, Calif.: Sage, 1979.

Shirer, William. *The Rise and Fall of the Third Reich.* New York: Simon & Schuster, 1960.

Thelen, Kathleen. *A Union of Parts.* Ithaca, N.Y.: Cornell University Press, 1992.

Tilly, Charles, ed. *The Formation of National States in Western Europe.* Princeton, N.J.: Princeton University Press, 1975.

Wever, Kirsten S. *Negotiating Competitiveness: Employment Relations and Industrial Adjustment in Germany and the United States.* Boston: Harvard Business School Press, 1995.

Websites

American Institute for Contemporary German Studies, The Johns Hopkins University:
www.aicgs.org

German Embassy, German Information Center:
www.germany.info

German News (in English), 1995–present:
www.germnews.de/dn/

German President, official site:
www.bundespraesident.de/en

German Studies Web, Western European Studies Section:
www.dartmouth.edu/~wess

Max-Planck Institute for the Study of Societies, Cologne:
www.mpi-fg-koeln.mpg.de/index_en.asp

WZB, Social Science Research Center, Berlin:
www.wz-berlin.de/default.en.asp

PART 5

Italy

Stephen Hellman

CHAPTER 16

Making the Modern Italian State

Politics in Action

For nearly fifty years, the Italian political system was considered "blocked" or "frozen." One party, Christian Democracy (Democrazia Cristiana, DC), dominated every governing coalition between 1948 and 1992. Others were permanently relegated to the opposition: the largest Communist Party in the West dominated the left, while neofascists occupied the far right of the spectrum.

Then, quite suddenly, the most immobile party system in the West imploded. By the elections of 1994, the governing parties had simply dissolved, and the largest party in the country was one that had not even existed five months earlier. Its creator, Silvio Berlusconi, the richest man in Italy, became prime minister. His partners in a totally new center-right government included former neofascists on the one hand, and another new party that had recently been preaching separatism on the other.

A year after this political earthquake, the leader of the opposition, Massimo D'Alema, published a book in which he hoped Italy could complete its transformation into "a normal country." He looked forward to the day that his own party—created when the Communist Party (Partito Comunista Italiano, PCI) dissolved—would finally be able to govern the country. But he was also expressing the hope that Italy would finally witness the apparently simple act of one government being voted out of office by another.[1]

In the next decade, there were *three* alternations in office, and in 2001 and 2006, two consecutive elections took place in which government and opposition switched places—something that had never before occurred in Italy.

Yet few people today would call Italy's political system "normal." As we will see, many problems have indeed been left behind, but some stubbornly persist. Moreover, an entirely new set of problems has arisen. A number of these revolve around the personal affairs of one individual: Silvio Berlusconi. If the old system was notable for a mass of gray politicos shuffling between positions of power, as though they were in a high-stakes game of musical chairs, the new system has a lightning rod who is anything but gray and anonymous.

Berlusconi is not only immensely rich; even more important is the *nature* of his wealth. In addition to extensive construction and financial interests, he owns three of Italy's four private television networks and its largest advertising agency, along with a newspaper, an Internet company, and the country's largest publishing house. With politics increasingly conditioned (or dominated) by the mass media, this degree of control over a country's commercial means of communications is alarming. But when the person who dominates the private communications sector takes over the government and thus gains control over the public broadcasting sector as well, any normal understanding of fair competition goes by the boards.[2]

His first government collapsed after only seven months. But Berlusconi's second government, elected in 2001, set a record as the longest-lived cabinet in postwar Italy. He showed considerable skill in keeping his often-fractious coalition together. To no one's surprise, much of the legislative agenda of his second government was devoted to writing laws that were nakedly self-serving.[3] The falsification of corporate budgets and the illegal export of capital were effectively decriminalized; a toothless conflict of interest law was passed; an effort to guarantee immunity from prosecution passed, but was declared unconstitutional; and the list could continue. Berlusconi's seeming indifference to the rules of the democratic game was underscored in the 2006 elections. A last-minute change in the electoral law failed to keep him in office: the center-right lost by the narrowest of margins. Instead of conceding defeat, Berlusconi suggested that the vote had been manipulated (even though he held power at the time of the election). And even after finally vacating the prime minister's residence, he contacted various heads of government to assure them he would soon be back in power.

But Italy's problematic transition goes well beyond one problematic personality. The collapse of the old party system has made possible the alternation in power between center-right and center-left blocs. Yet despite the achievement of bipolarity, the party system remains extraordinarily fragmented. The center-left coalition that barely won in 2006 is made up of nine distinct political groupings—ranging from Communists and Greens on the left to rather moderate Catholics on the right-center.

Such fragmentation provides many opportunities for minor partners to jeopardize the entire coalition, and both sides have seen governments fall when a small party abruptly withdraws its support. Berlusconi had to wait six years to return to power after the often-unpredictable Northern League abandoned him seven months into his first term. Prime Minister Romano Prodi lost his job when the Refounded Communist Party (Partito della Rifondazione Comunista, PRC) withdrew its support in 1998. Most recently, Prodi's second term in office almost came to an end early in 2007 when a pair of pacifist left-wing senators voted against Italy's commitment of troops to Afghanistan.

With the country so evenly divided between two major political blocs, ignoring even a seemingly minor player may have major consequences. Like all advanced capitalist democracies, Italy faces problems that would challenge even solid and coherent majorities. Having to do so under these circumstances complicates matters immensely. Normalcy is indeed a long way off.

Geographic Setting

Italy's boot may be the most immediately recognizable outline of any country in the world. Jutting into the Mediterranean, with 4,750 miles (7,600 kilometers) of coastline, it has been a strategic crossroads almost since humans began traveling, and conquering each other, for it dominates the central Mediterranean as well as the southern approaches into western and south-central Europe.[4] Phoenicians, Greeks, Normans, North Africans, Spaniards, and, more recently, Austrians, French, and Germans have all conquered or occupied parts of what became Italy.

Except for the flat, fertile Po Valley, Italy is mountainous. Half of all the Alps, Europe's largest range, are found in Italy. The rugged Apennines run down the rest of the boot, and smaller ranges cover most of the rest of the land. The Po is the only navigable river of any significance. Italy was poorly endowed with the natural resources most central to the age of heavy industry, such as coal, iron, oil, and natural gas, which further delayed its industrialization.

Italy was both a late industrializer and, in West European terms, a latecomer to the family of nation-states. Until unification was finally achieved in 1870,

its weakness and strategic location made it easy prey for more powerful neighbors. The new state was marked by extreme regional differences, reflecting centuries of different political, social, and cultural legacies. Italy's rugged terrain also reinforced regional and local differences until well into the twentieth century, when modern transportation and communications systems finally unified the country culturally and linguistically.

With almost 59 million inhabitants, Italy has roughly the same population as the United Kingdom and France; its territory is somewhat larger than the United Kingdom and a bit smaller than Germany (France is nearly twice the size of Italy). All these countries have rapidly aging populations. Italy has recently been neck and neck with Spain for the lowest birthrate in the world. These trends lend a sense of urgency to the need to confront questions of pensions and welfare state restructuring, as well as immigration.

Italy's location gives it continuing strategic importance. Major U.S. Air Force bases are located in the northeast, and the U.S. Sixth Fleet has its home in Naples. Even in a post–cold war era, Italy remains a vital staging area for the North Atlantic Treaty Organization (NATO).

Critical Junctures

Its strategic location gave Italy a central role in the history of the West. The Romans established an advanced urban society and conquered most of the world (at least as the Romans knew it) two millennia ago. Their impact on the rest of Europe is evident in the Latin-based

Critical Junctures in Italy's Political Development	
1848–1870	The Risorgimento and Unification
1870–1922	The Liberal Regime (Constitutional Monarchy)
1922–1945	Fascism
1945–1948	The Emergence of the Republic
1948–1994	Christian Democratic Dominance ("First Republic")
1994–Present	Transition to the "Second Republic"?

Romance languages, and also in the codified legal system, which they developed. After becoming the religion of the emperor, Christianity spread rapidly and became the most powerful force shaping medieval Europe.

But the rise of the nation-state found Italy lagging behind most of its neighbors. For centuries, the country was carved up by successive waves of emerging powers. By the nationalist era of the mid-nineteenth century, the glorious past served mainly as a unifying myth to patriots chafing under rulers who were either foreign or, as in the Papal States, considered backward and illegitimate by educated opinion. It is significant that Italian nationalists called their movement the Risorgimento (resurgence).

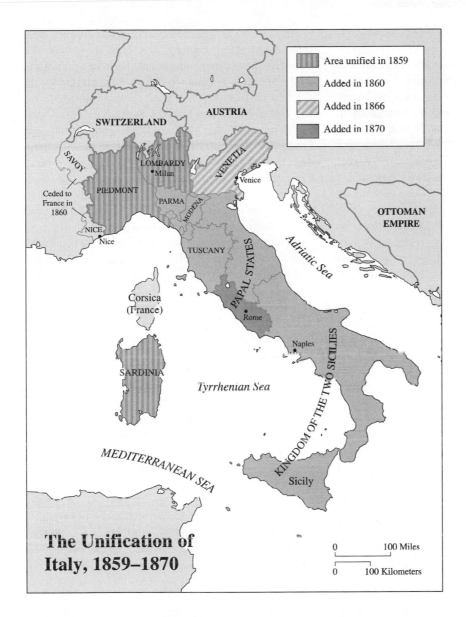

Area unified in 1859
Added in 1860
Added in 1866
Added in 1870

SWITZERLAND

AUSTRIA

SAVOY

LOMBARDY
•Milan

VENETIA

Venice

Ceded to
France in
1860

PIEDMONT

PARMA

MODENA

OTTOMAN
EMPIRE

NICE
•Nice

TUSCANY

PAPAL STATES

Adriatic Sea

Corsica
(France)

•Rome

SARDINIA

Naples

KINGDOM OF THE TWO SICILIES

Tyrrhenian Sea

MEDITERRANEAN SEA

Sicily

**The Unification of
Italy, 1859–1870**

0   100 Miles

0   100 Kilometers

The Risorgimento and Liberal Italy (1848–1922)

In the mid-1800s, northern Italy was divided between the Kingdom of Sardinia under the Savoy monarchy (Piedmont and Liguria) and the Austrian-controlled northeast (Lombardy and Venetia). In the north-center, numerous small duchies and principalities led an uneasy existence. The Papal States dominated most of central Italy. South of Rome down to Sicily was the Kingdom of the Two Sicilies, ruled by descendants of the Spanish Bourbons. This archconservative realm remained secure, in one ruler's words, since it was surrounded "by salt water on three sides and holy water on the fourth."[5]

The Risorgimento triumphed in the second half of the 1800s. Victor Emmanuel II of Savoy and his skilled prime minister, Camillo Cavour, attracted middle- and upper-class moderates with their enlightened liberalism.

Italy was thus created by extending Piedmontese hegemony over the entire boot.

Outside intervention determined the unification of the peninsula. Austria's defeat by France in 1859 forced the Habsburgs to cede part of the north to Victor Emmanuel II, who, in turn, gave Nice and Savoy to France. Eager to strike a deal, the French accepted Piedmont's annexation of some of the Papal States, and limited French presence to a garrison in Rome. A parliament, elected by very limited suffrage, proclaimed the Kingdom of Italy in March 1861. Victor Emmanuel II of Savoy was its first monarch. No new constitution was drawn up: Piedmont's 1848 *Statuto albertino* (named for King Charles Albert of Piedmont, Victor Emmanuel II's father) was extended over the whole country. The *Statuto* gave the crown far more powers than did the more democratic constitutions of 1848.

The remainder of modern Italy's territory was acquired thanks to Prussian military victories over Austria (1866) and France (1870), as the map of the unification of Italy shows. After the French withdrew from Rome, Italian troops seized the historic capital. Difficult church-state relations followed for the next half-century, as the pope refused to recognize the new state.

Because of its narrow bases of support, the Risorgimento left basic social and political problems untouched. Italy's largest social group, the peasantry, was excluded from the independence movement and was then ignored by the new state. The new country's leaders were in no hurry to extend democratic participation in a society with 60 to 80 percent illiteracy rates. Northern elites guaranteed the loyalty of southern landlords by repressing restive peasants and introducing tariffs to protect inefficiently grown southern crops. But these northern leaders otherwise pursued laissez-faire industrial policies, serving their own interests while devastating struggling new firms in the less developed parts of the country.

By the mid-1870s, free-market policies were proving inadequate for a country with so much ground to make up. The government noticed the impressive advances of another new state—Germany—and changed its policies accordingly. In the 1880s, a new economic policy evolved: taxes were lightened, tariff barriers were erected, and the state became more active in the economy.

Italy remained overwhelmingly agricultural well into the twentieth century. Not until the 1950s did industrial employees outnumber those in agriculture. This slow growth produced staggering emigration in the first half-century following unification, mostly to the United States and South America.

Emigration affected the entire country, but was hardest on the south. The outflow of so many young, able-bodied people distorted the population profile. Emigration did serve as a social safety valve, however, and was therefore welcomed by ruling elites, who had good reason to fear the often-brutal class warfare that periodically erupted in the countryside.

Trying to overcome their country's marginal role, Italy's leaders brought the country into World War I following secret negotiations with the Allies. Although secondary by the standards of 1914–1918, the Italian front brought the horrors of trench warfare to millions of (mostly peasant) conscripts: approximately 600,000 died. The war extended Italy's border to the Brenner Pass in the north and to Trieste and Istria on the Adriatic. When more ambitious demands were not met, Italy abandoned the Versailles peace talks, legitimizing rising extreme-right nationalism. Although Liberal Italy emerged from the slaughter of World War I on the winning side, its days were numbered. It lacked the culture, the institutions, and the leadership that could attract mass support or regulate modern class conflict.

Liberal Italy's Political Contradictions and Collapse. The ruling Liberal Party (Partito Liberale Italiano, PLI) relied on local power brokers instead of building modern political organizations or strengthening civil society. It tolerated corruption in the south and practiced repression everywhere, to keep workers and peasants in their place. And the party also practiced *trasformismo* in Parliament—that is, constructing a majority by winning over enough deputies, irrespective of political affiliation, by whatever means proved most effective. What were ultimately "transformed" were differences between parties, groups, and ideologies. If the opposition was absorbed into the government itself, so much the better. *"Trasformismo"* is still used to refer to unprincipled maneuvering by party leaders.

The Roman Catholic Church, deprived of its land and hostile to liberalism, was implacably opposed to the Liberal regime. Pope Pius IX forbade Catholics from participating in Italian politics in 1874, but by the turn of the twentieth century political realism, and a less intransigent pope, led to the creation of an openly Catholic Popular Party (Partito Popolare Italiano, PPI).

The polarized mass politics that followed World War I put the finishing touches on the Liberals' system of power as the Socialists (Partito Socialista Italiano, PSI) and the PPI won more than half the votes in the 1919 elections. When the Socialists then swept local elections in industrial areas, the old parties' bases of support were drastically reduced.[6]

As workers and peasants grew increasingly militant in demanding their rights, frightened bourgeois looked to the extreme right since they felt the state could no longer defend their privileges. Nor did overheated Socialist rhetoric, about a revolution they had no intention of carrying out, help matters. Armed Fascist squads were soon sowing terror in the countryside of Italy's central regions and openly attacked the unions and the PSI in the cities of the north, as the regime stood by and watched.

Fascism (1922–1945)

Benito Mussolini, a charismatic ex-Socialist, built a quasi-military party organization that preached and practiced violence. Within a few years, his denunciations of Italy's "betrayal" after World War I, his open contempt for democracy, and his willingness to attack the left won him support on the right and, more important, among masses of urban and rural property holders who were impatient with what they considered the regime's vacillation.

The Liberal system's fate was sealed following Mussolini's March on Rome in October 1922. This march was a successful act of intimidation. Tens of thousands of armed Fascist Blackshirts (the militia's uniform) paraded through the capital, and King Victor Emmanuel III asked Mussolini to form the next government. With

Italian Fascist dictator Benito Mussolini drew Italy into a very close alliance with Hitler. This photo shows them reviewing SS troops in Germany in 1937.
Source: © Allman Archives/The Image Works.

only 32 of 530 seats in Parliament, the Fascist Party (Partito Nazionale Fascista, PNF) received support from the entire political spectrum (including the PPI), except the left.[7] When Mussolini showed a willingness to compromise with the church and extend it financial aid, Pope Pius XI quickly abandoned the PPI, allowing pro-Fascist Catholics to secede and form their own party.[8]

Democratic freedoms were curtailed; by 1926, following the murder of Socialist leader Giacomo Matteotti by Fascist thugs, a dictatorship was in place. Opposition parties were banned, the independent press was closed or brought to heel, and political opponents—mainly Socialists and Communists—were jailed or forced into exile.

Italian fascism's complexity and inconsistency help explain its broad appeal. Mussolini convinced people he would act decisively to make sure that the left and the trade unions would be crushed. Denouncing the "decadence" of democracy, fascism promised to reclaim Italy's rightful place in the world as a great power, as it invoked the glory of the Romans. (Fasces, a Roman symbol of power and authority, are a bound bundle of rods symbolizing strength in unity.)

Mussolini pursued an aggressive foreign policy. Italy's 1936 conquest of Ethiopia led to condemnation and sanctions by the League of Nations. When the Spanish military rose against the elected Spanish Republican government in 1936, Mussolini and Hitler joined the rebels in the Spanish Civil War. As Italy and Germany drew closer together, anti-Semitic racial laws stripped Jews of rights and property in 1938. Most catastrophic of all was Mussolini's entry into World War II on the side of Nazi Germany and Imperial Japan.

Political Trade-Offs. We must distinguish between the regime's claims and its accomplishments. Fascism's ambitions were openly totalitarian. Citizens were to be made over in a new image, tough and uncorrupted by the materialistic softness represented by liberal democracy (or capitalism, for the really radical Fascists). At the pinnacle of a totally regimented society was il Duce (the Leader), the living embodiment of all Fascist virtues.

Some Fascist reforms did have totalitarian ambitions, but Mussolini was really more of a pragmatic maneuverer than a dedicated ideologue. For instance, he inherited a top-heavy state structure and centralized

it even further. At the same time, local party officials often ran personal fiefs, which il Duce tolerated so long as his popularity was not threatened.

Another trade-off was the Lateran Pacts, a series of agreements in 1929 between church and state, formalizing the Catholic Church's privileged position. The most important pact was the Concordat, naming Roman Catholicism the official state religion, thus entitling the church to special privileges—above all, control over the compulsory weekly hour of religious teaching in Italy's public schools.* In return, the regime was granted the Vatican's full recognition, and frequently its enthusiastic support—even when Mussolini undertook aggressive military action in Ethiopia and Spain. Nor did the Vatican condemn the 1938 anti-Semitic laws.

In the economic sphere, the Great Depression and League of Nations sanctions drove Mussolini to take protectionism to its logical conclusion: autarky, or economic self-sufficiency. His militaristic foreign policy required a heavy industrial sector, and he was committed to this goal even if it meant isolation. These decisions forced more state involvement in economic affairs, especially as the Depression took hold. The Institute for Industrial Reconstruction (Istituto per la Ricostruzione Industriale, IRI) was created in 1933 as a holding company for stocks from distressed firms, which the state bought up as companies slid toward bankruptcy. In 1937, IRI became a permanent holding company geared to furthering rearmament and autarky. By 1940, about a fifth of all capital assets in all joint stock corporations in Italy were in IRI's hands, and the state effectively monopolized vital sectors of the economy (iron, steel, shipbuilding, and banking).

Fascism's End and the Republic's Birth (1945–1948)

With Victor Emmanuel III's support, a military coup deposed Mussolini in 1943. The new regime broke with Germany six weeks later. But by then the Nazis had poured into Italy, set Mussolini up in a puppet regime in the north, and dug in, guaranteeing a drawn-out war

---

*Other parts of the Pacts recognized the Vatican as a sovereign city-state headed by the pope, and paid a large indemnity to the Vatican for property seized during the Risorgimento.

that only ended two weeks before Germany's final surrender. The 1943 declaration of war did legitimize the Resistance against the Nazis and their Fascist allies in areas under German control, where a brutal civil war ensued. The Resistance is of immense symbolic importance: it helped salvage national pride, and it legitimized the left, including Communists, as democratic and patriotic.

The war reinforced historic north-south divisions. The south was spared the worst of the conflict, as well as the brutal German occupation and the unifying liberation struggle. But it was, as a result, cut off from any direct role in yet another critical juncture. This estrangement was apparent in the 1946 referendum to abolish the monarchy. The rest of the country could not forgive the king's early support of fascism and voted solidly for a republic, while a majority in the south opted for the monarchy, making the vote fairly close (53 percent to 47 percent).

At war's end, the Communists and Socialists were close allies. Combined, they accounted for 40 percent of the vote in the 1946 elections. Christian Democracy was the largest party but garnered only 35 percent. Its favored status in the eyes of both the Catholic Church and the United States, and its social base in the smallholding peasantry and urban middle classes, ensured that the DC would not cooperate with the Communists and Socialists for long. In 1946–1947, with the cold war brewing, a tense unity among these parties produced a constitution that reflected the few points of agreement and the many divisions of its writers (Chapter 18).

The 1946 vote, Italy's first exercise in truly universal suffrage, abolished the monarchy and elected a Constituent Assembly to serve as a temporary parliament and write a republican constitution within eighteen months. In 1947, as the constitutional exercise drew to a close, Christian Democrat prime minister Alcide De Gasperi ejected the Communists and the pro-PCI Socialists from the government. With cold war tensions at their peak, the DC won a crushing victory in 1948. This election saw lavish spending, and blatant intervention, by the United States on behalf of the DC. The Catholic Church also intervened heavily. In a totally polarized climate, Italians flocked to the DC as the surest defense against communism. For the only time in the history of the republic, a single party won an absolute majority of parliamentary seats (and over 48 percent of the popular vote).

DC Domination, 1948–1994 (The "First Republic")

Most Western European democracies saw postwar settlements between capital and labor, but in Italy and France, Communist leadership of the workers' movement produced a policy of *labor exclusion*. The left enjoyed political freedom and limited influence in labor relations, but it was condemned to the role of permanent political opposition. The country would develop within the Western sphere of influence, with a more or less liberal-democratic institutional framework, but with little concern for the workers' principal representatives. Even when the Communists rose to over a third of the vote in the mid-1970s and their support was needed in Parliament, they were denied a full share of political power. By the 1980s, union and PCI influence was again reduced, as the tide turned in favor of business interests and the center of the political spectrum. Only the end of the cold war, out-of-control government spending, massive scandals, and the collapse of the party system finally ended the DC-centered system of power in Italy and once more put the question of full governmental participation by the left on the agenda.

Christian Democratic Dominance. The DC's crushing victory of 1948 proved to be exceptional. The DC would dominate every government until 1994, but it always needed allies. From the beginning, De Gasperi resisted intense pressure from the Vatican and his own right wing and looked to the center, not the extreme right, for partners. As it continued to dominate every government, the DC found that it could use Italy's many public resources, inherited from fascism, to build a patronage structure that made the party less dependent on the Vatican, the United States, southern notables, and big industry. Public resources increasingly became part of a spoils system that helped build the party organization, while rewarding the party faithful—beginning with members of one's own faction. These resources helped the DC hold its heterogeneous constituencies together.

The groundwork was laid for what one writer aptly called the DC's "occupation of power."[9] This process accelerated throughout the 1960s and 1970s, contributing to Italy's huge deficits, while setting the stage for truly prodigious amounts of corruption.

By the 1960s, after the PSI had moved away from close collaboration with the PCI, the Socialists had also become part of the government. But the Socialists were too weak to force the passage of serious reforms, while their collaboration with the DC cost them votes and credibility on the left. When the PCI reached its historic high of 34.4 percent in 1976, the DC was forced to make numerous concessions, but the unacceptability of formal Communist participation in a Western government thwarted PCI secretary Enrico Berlinguer's ambitions to construct a "historic compromise" between the PCI and DC. By the end of the 1970s, the PCI was languishing in the opposition, where it steadily lost votes.

Socialist leader Bettino Craxi brought his party back into the government at the end of the 1970s demanding greater influence and a larger share of the spoils. Under Craxi's leadership, the PSI's influence did grow, but it also became mired in a corrupt system of power. In the course of the 1980s, the DC–PSI partnership degenerated into a shameless, increasingly corrupt struggle over political spoils.

Governing the Postwar Economy Through the 1970s. Under *labor exclusion*, the unions were weak and politically divided. At the end of the war, the General Confederation of Italian Labor (Confederazione Generale Italiana del Lavoro, CGIL) was dominated by the PCI and PSI; once the left was expelled from the government, its unity was doomed. Catholics left to found the Italian Confederation of Workers' Trade Unions (Confederazione Italiana Sindacati Lavoratori, CISL), which remained close to the DC. A year later, Social Democrats and Republicans exited the CGIL to form the Union of Italian Labor (UIL), the smallest of the major confederations. These partisan divisions reinforced labor's weakness.

Only the boom of the 1960s finally created conditions of near-full employment, giving unions increased leverage in contract negotiations. Political divisions finally mattered less than enjoying more benefits produced by the so-called Economic Miracle. The result of the unions' new strength and unity was the extremely militant period known as the Hot Autumn

of 1969, which carried over into the 1970s. Divided and demoralized employers made concessions that drove up production costs. Weak governments granted many union demands and then had to make costly commitments to the self-employed and other middle-class categories to guarantee their continuing support. Social spending mushroomed, aggravated by the governing parties' unrestrained use of public resources for partisan purposes. Italy's increasingly distressed public finances are a legacy that the country has still not overcome.

The Politics of Collective Identity. As social mobilization continued, democracy itself appeared threatened. Terrorists of both the extreme right and left tried to destabilize the political system and to provoke a coup (right) or a revolution (left). Although they failed miserably in their broader goals, these groups shook the country to its foundations throughout the 1970s and into the 1980s.

Terrorism was an extreme symptom of the profound changes that Italy's deadlocked political system was unable to resolve. Terrorism was also a distorted reaction by marginal groups to the widespread mass mobilizations that involved millions of Italians in the course of the 1960s and 1970s. Workers, students, and women burst onto the political stage, sweeping aside entrenched values and practices. Nowhere is this more evident than in the 1974 referendum to repeal Italy's 1970 divorce law, which failed by a 40-to-60 margin, shocking everyone. (A 1981 referendum on abortion produced an even worse defeat for the church and DC.)

1992 to the Present: Toward a Second Republic?

Despite their squabbling, the DC and the PSI appeared secure through the 1980s. Yet within a few years, they were fighting for their survival—and losing. The DC, which had averaged almost 40 percent of the vote since World War II, suddenly dropped under 30 percent in 1992; by 1994 it had renamed itself in a last-ditch effort to salvage some credibility, but it barely obtained one vote in ten. The Socialists suffered an even greater collapse: from a more modest starting point, they had risen to almost 15 percent of the vote by 1992, and seemed to be on the verge of replacing the Communists as Italy's second-largest party. Within two years, the PSI had effectively ceased to exist.

What accounts for this turnaround? The answer can be found in the four themes that inform the organization of this book. *The world of states* impinged directly on Italy at the end of the 1980s. Within days of the fall of the Berlin Wall, the largest Communist party in the Western world announced that it would dissolve itself to become a new left-wing actor. This removed the DC's main rationale to be Italy's perennial governing party. And it also encouraged prosecutors to pursue corruption in governing circles with far more purpose, and courage, than they had in the past.

Italy's international placement also had a direct impact on events involved with *governing the economy*. As the DC and PSI were busy squandering public funds to boost their own power, the tide shifted decisively in the opposite direction. As the move toward European integration gained momentum, Italy simply could not continue business as usual. Changes in the *democratic idea* were most evident in the increasingly rapid erosion of support for the ruling parties, whose credibility plummeted, since they appeared oblivious to the changes taking place around them.

Old *collective identities* and ideologies eroded, including the loyalties that had shaped postwar politics. Entirely new identities arose, most notably the various leagues of northern Italy, whose antiparty and anti-Rome rhetoric exerted a strong appeal in areas where the DC had done very well historically. By 1992 the Northern League (Lega Nord) united all these groups, and became the largest party in Lombardy and the Veneto, two of Italy's most dynamic regions.

By the early 1990s, reformers rode a tide of rising public disgust with the ruling parties. In 1991, and again in 1993, referenda (Chapter 18) effectively forced Parliament to rewrite the electoral laws. On both occasions, the public voted overwhelmingly to change the existing laws.[10] A French-style electoral law was instituted in municipal elections. This guarantees a clear personal mandate for mayoral candidates, undercutting the leverage of the parties. Elections held under this system in 1993 and 1994 devastated the DC.

In 1992, so much corruption was exposed that even hardened observers were shocked. As scores of politicians were arrested, the prestige of the ruling parties was obliterated, while investigators and prosecutors became folk heroes. The scandal was dubbed *Tangentopoli* ("Bribesville"). Barely six months after the 1992 elections, five ministers had been forced to resign. Within two years, roughly a fifth of the members of Parliament were in some form of legal trouble; the old style of politics was in terminal crisis. "Operation Clean Hands," as the anticorruption campaign was called, did not cause the ruling parties' downfall, but it certainly delivered the coup de grâce.

Economic problems compounded the political crisis. By 1992, it appeared doubtful that Italy could meet the restrictive Maastricht convergence criteria for membership in the Economic and Monetary Union (EMU). With the party system in a terminal crisis, governments finally began to impose more rigorous budgets. It says everything about how seriously Italy took its economic plight to note that in 1993, Carlo Azeglio Ciampi was named prime minister. A former governor of the Bank of Italy, Ciampi's appointment sent a clear signal to foreign markets that the economy remained in capable hands.

The Emergence of a New Party System.   The new system of electing mayors helped put the finishing touches on the governing parties, producing some surprises in the process. The Northern League continued to grow in the north. The ex-Communist left showed signs of rejuvenation. The true pariah of the First Republic, the neofascist Italian Social Movement (Movimento Sociale Italiano, MSI), appeared to be the only party able to fill the vacuum left by the DC outside the north. The MSI shattered its outcast status by making it into the mayoral runoffs in Rome and Naples. It received over 40 percent of the vote, but the left won handily.

At this point, Berlusconi stepped into the fray. Frightened by the left's successes, he created his own party, called Forza Italia (FI), "Let's Go Italy," the cheer for the national soccer team. Despite his ties to Craxi and the old system, Berlusconi represented something new on the political scene. Far more than a media phenomenon, he was the center-right's political lifeboat. He was a respectable alternative to the Northern League and MSI, and veterans from the discredited parties flocked to FI, ready to trade their much-needed experience for a chance to remain in power.

Berlusconi and his staff understood the logic of the new national electoral system, which assigned 75 percent of parliamentary seats to single-member districts, leaving only a quarter to be chosen by the old proportional list method. He quickly set about finding attractive candidates to stand in the new single-member districts drawn up for the 1994 general election. Because his major coalition partners could not stand each other, he engineered different alliances in the south and north: with the National Alliance (AN), as the MSI was rebaptized, and with the Northern League. Running a slick media campaign, the center-right won an absolute majority in the Chamber of Deputies, and a near majority in the Senate as the ex-DC was relegated to little more than a footnote. The 1994 elections really did seem to signal the end of the First Republic.

Continuity and Change in the Political Sphere. The last fifteen years would seem to leave no room for the term *continuity* when describing the Italian party system. The old parties have been swept away, replaced in the main by forces that either did not exist at all in the 1980s or have undergone radical changes since then. Governments may routinely be defeated by the opposition in most democracies, but in 2001, when the center-left lost to the center-right, there had not been a single occasion in the entire twentieth century when such a transfer had occurred.* That this occurred again in 2006 suggests that Italian politics has indeed changed dramatically.

There were other novelties as well. Although yet another electoral system was introduced in 2006, Italian politics has been personalized as never before. Nowhere is this more apparent than in the case of Silvio Berlusconi.

Where, then, are signs of continuity? Above all they operate in the dynamics of the party system, which remains fragmented and polarized, albeit with many new actors. There may now be two large political blocs, but both are internally divided along several dimensions. Berlusconi's first government lasted

all of seven months before the Northern League pulled out of the coalition. The center-left coalition that won the 1996 elections was led by three different prime ministers in five years. All this maneuvering, sabotaging of one's own side, and alliance switching recalled the First Republic, suggesting that Parliament remained at the mercy of the parties, however new or recycled they might be.

Continuity and Change in the Policy Arena. Reformers hoped that a bipolar system would finally enable real alternatives to be proposed, and acted upon. Yet no coalition elected since 1994 has been internally coherent, and much legislation passed since then reflects the sorts of compromises typical of heterogeneous governments. Some laws have passed only with help from the opposition.

Yet in some ways, the desired result has been achieved. The center-left government of 1996–2001 imposed budgetary discipline that enabled Italy to qualify for membership in the euro zone. The health system was restructured. Administrative reforms began to streamline and simplify one of the West's most inefficient and unresponsive bureaucracies. Italy's entrenched (and, to many, tyrannical) criminal justice procedures were changed through amendments to the constitution guaranteeing that the accused and the prosecution have equal status. Important educational reforms were enacted, and a constitutional amendment changed the way the governments of the regions are elected, which introduced a variant of federalism into the constitution. Berlusconi's second term began inauspiciously, seemingly more concerned with the prime minister's conflicts of interest and legal problems than with enacting important legislation. But his government did eventually pass extensive educational, health care, pension, and labor market reforms, while it also passed more punitive immigration legislation, and took measures that severely restricted medically assisted procreation.

As this quick summary shows, alternation in power by different majorities has indeed produced alternatives, but in doing so alternation has also produced dramatic swings in policy, so that a new set of rules is hardly in place before it is abruptly replaced by another. This dynamic came into play once again immediately after the fall of the second Berlusconi government, when a popular referendum in 2006 overturned constitutional

---

*The previous occasion was 1876. When the center-left won in 1996, it did not replace the center-right, which resigned in 1995 and was replaced by a coalition of "technicians."

changes in the role of the prime minister and the regions, which had been introduced only recently.

Italy in the Euro Era

Confounding many European leaders' rather smug expectations, Italy met the Maastricht convergence criteria in mid-1998 and was thus among the eleven founders when the euro was officially adopted in 1999. When the center-left Olive Tree (Ulivo) coalition won the elections in 1996, Italy was still a long way from meeting the criteria for inclusion in the establishment of the EMU. But the goal was achieved during Prodi's first term in office.

Prodi managed this feat thanks to considerable belt tightening, tax increases, and much cooperation from the unions.[11] His coalition depended on the external support of the far-left Communist Refoundation Party (Partito della Rifondazione Comunista, PRC), which made his tightrope-walking act even more precarious, for the PRC had threatened to bring down the government if it cut social programs. When Prodi's "EU Budget" was presented, Rifondazione voted for it, and even Forza Italia and the Northern League abstained.

This outcome makes sense only in light of Italy's obsession with being included in the monetary union and, more broadly, with being taken seriously on the international stage. After reaching this milestone, Prodi and his successors imposed far more restrictive budgets—in the name of maintaining Italy's commitments—than would have been imaginable a few years earlier. There is no doubt that Prodi's impressive achievements as prime minister paved the way for his selection by the governments of the EU as president of the European Commission once the PRC had pushed him out of the prime minister's office in 1998.

As the domestic problems of Prodi, and his successor, D'Alema, show, Italian parliamentary bickering and maneuvering can still paralyze legislative initiatives and bring down governments, suggesting disturbing continuities with the so-called First Republic. Yet the "European imperative" had obviously introduced a series of constraints on almost the entire political class inside Parliament, as well as on significant actors outside the legislature, like the unions. Some of the most acute observers of Italian policy could, without irony, publish a book called *Rescued by Europe?* in 2004.[12]

But even though Italians number among the most enthusiastic pro-EU publics in Western Europe, we find many of the same skeptical, and even hostile, opinions as elsewhere, above all among workers and small businesspeople. Some of the most militant elements on the left and in the unions have consistently denounced what they call the imposition of a neoliberal project aimed primarily at rolling back the gains of the workers' movement. As the Northern League has grown increasingly xenophobic, its anti-EU rhetoric has escalated. And several groups within Berlusconi's own party—not surprisingly, those most threatened by international competition—have always been critical of the EU.

These attitudes reflect ideological as well as economic interests. Although the goal of gaining entry to the euro zone has been achieved, the center-left's policies inflicted real pain along the way. As a result, Berlusconi had to do some tightrope walking himself. In the first six months of his government, there were so many discordant voices on the EU, and a distinct lack of firmness in bringing the critics to heel on Berlusconi's part, that his foreign minister was effectively forced to resign. Berlusconi's distancing of Italian foreign policy from that of traditional allies France and Germany, including foreign policy initiatives toward Iraq and Russia, fueled further speculation that a real sea change was underway in Italy's European posture. By the end of his second term in office, the consensus was that he had perhaps tilted Italy a bit more toward the United States than toward Europe, but this was a constant tension in Italian foreign policy, dating all the way back to the cold war.[13] With Prodi's return to office, not surprisingly, the tilt can be expected to go in the other direction, most notably with regard to the Middle East.

Italy After the French and Dutch Veto of the European Constitution. Italy has been among the most strongly pro-European countries since the birth of the European Economic Community. The European Constitution rejected in France and the Netherlands in 2005 was passed overwhelmingly several months earlier by the Italian Parliament. The vote was 436–28 in the Chamber, and 217–16 in the Senate. The main open opposition came from the Northern League on the right and Rifondazione Comunista on the left.

There were also some dissenters from the left wing of the DS (Left Democrats, the main opposition party) and from within Berlusconi's own Forza Italia. Yet the strength of Italy's pro-European consensus is evident from the fact that most of these dissenters chose not to show up in Parliament for the vote on the constitution rather than make a public show of their disagreement.

As we have seen, Italy does not lack for Euroskeptics. But it is striking how much lip service continues to be paid to the idea of "Europe" across the board. Thus, following the 2005 referenda, almost everyone (except the Northern League) was at pains to insist that "Europe" had not been defeated, but only a particular version of Europe—the product of far-off, insensitive bureaucrats or those who listened too closely to the banks rather than the people. Because the center-right had just suffered devastating losses in regional elections, the Euroskeptics within Berlusconi's coalition tried to blame their own defeat on the EU. And, with the European Constitution apparently a dead letter, there was very little to be lost politically by sounding a more militant anti-EU position.

When Romano Prodi returned to the prime minister's office in 2006, his last public position had been president of the European Commission. Hence, even if Prodi were a demagogue, which he is not, he could not credibly flirt with the Euroskeptics among his own supporters (and there are quite a few, above all on the left). His government will certainly chafe under EU constraints but because of both his temperament and his convictions we can expect far less open conflict between Rome and Brussels than was the case when Berlusconi was in office.

After September 11

Italy has been no stranger to terrorism. Domestically, the Red Brigades and similar groups killed over four hundred individuals, including five-time prime minister Aldo Moro, because they were considered "class enemies." These attacks peaked in the 1970s, but sporadic murders still take place. Between the Hot Autumn of 1969 and the 1980s, fascist bombs struck more indiscriminately in train stations, banks, and other public places, killing several hundred Italians. International terrorism has also brought the Middle East uncomfortably close to home.

Separate massacres in 1973 and 1985 in Rome's airport killed over thirty people, while the hijacking of the Italian cruise ship *Achille Lauro* made headlines in 1985 when hijackers murdered a disabled Jewish passenger.

Among West European countries, it would be hard to find an ally more loyal to the United States than Italy in the postwar period, due to Italy's historical weaknesses and to the obvious benefits, ideological as well as material, it gained during the cold war. This loyalty—some call it subservience—continued even when the center-left was in power and a former Communist was prime minister. Massimo D'Alema's government approved U.S.-imposed NATO air strikes directed at Serbia during the 1999 Yugoslav-Kosovo conflict, to the consternation of some on the left. But D'Alema was able to argue that the intervention was multilateral, thus keeping Italy within its traditional foreign policy framework. Italy's participation in the overthrow of the Taliban in Afghanistan following September 11, involving the commitment of nearly 3,000 troops, also fit this mold although Afghanistan has had domestic repercussions serious enough to divide the center-left as to how long Italy's commitment can last.

Berlusconi's enthusiastic support for the much less multilateral invasion and occupation of Iraq, and his friendliness toward George W. Bush, put him at odds with his neighbors. And Italy's commitment to Iraq was more than verbal: at its peak, over 3,000 soldiers were sent there (and more than two dozen were killed in action). Berlusconi was eventually forced to begin withdrawing troops from Iraq, as Italian public opinion on that conflict has consistently been among the most hostile in the entire EU. The last contingents were sent home late in 2006, after Prodi's government took office, but the center-left simply completed what had already begun.

Prodi's relatively muted and moderate criticism of U.S. policy in Iraq is notable only for its contrast with Berlusconi's previous support. The most troubling development in terms of both U.S.–Italian relations and domestic Italian politics has concerned the abduction of an Egyptian cleric from Milan, where, under the U.S. policy of "extraordinary rendition," he was sent to Egypt where he claims to have been tortured. (He was eventually released from custody.) The international fallout from this episode resulted in Italian judges issuing arrest warrants for the CIA agents who carried out the abduction. On the domestic front, it emerged that Italy's secret services not only knew about the operation, but resorted to various dirty tricks to mislead investigators as well as the press. Rogue operations by secret services would be cause for concern in any democracy, and this issue is especially sensitive in Italy. In the past, military or civilian agencies had colluded with antidemocratic (or terrorist) elements, with the apparent aim of destabilizing the country and, on at least one occasion, planning a coup d'état.

Themes and Implications

Several of the key themes of this text are discussed more fully in subsequent chapters, but we can quickly review all four here.

Historical Junctures and Political Themes

The democratic idea has been no abstraction in Italian history. Each critical juncture has been marked by deep differences over the very meaning of democracy and how much democracy is desirable. The Risorgimento saw the victory of those with an extremely limited definition of democracy, along with the overt hostility of the Roman Catholic Church. The church's opposition to democracy continued throughout the Liberal regime, which tolerated blatant corruption and backroom deals (*trasformismo*) to keep the masses on the margins of politics. Fascism crushed the workers' movement, which attempted to broaden the meaning of democracy to include social issues, but it also crushed conservative democrats. Because of the painful past, the mass parties that built the postwar republic defined democracy as, above all, a proportional principle of representation with limited executive powers. Cumbersome and prone to paralysis, this system revolved around the DC's ability to pose itself as democracy's most reliable defender against communism.

The "Second Republic" was supposed to enable Italy to become a mature democracy in which government and opposition could alternate in power and in which voters could translate their choices into effective political action. But conflicting visions of democracy continue to dominate Italian political debate as the transition drags on.

The world of states shaped Italy from unification onward. Powerful neighbors dictated the timing of unification and the country's eventual borders. Prussian interventionism provided the economic model, while the colonial successes of others drew Italy into ill-fated adventures in Africa. Exaggerated international ambitions are most apparent in fascist aggression, isolation, and the eventual catastrophe of World War II. After the war, Italy played a modest international role, often abjectly subservient to the United States. But by placing itself squarely in the Western camp, the country's political leadership ensured that the largest opposition party, the PCI—identified with the Soviet camp—would remain excluded from a governing role. Because its party system revolved around this division, the collapse of Soviet-style socialism had profound domestic effects in Italy.

Governing the economy meant, from the 1870s until the re-emergence of free-market ideology in the 1980s and 1990s, extensive state involvement in economic affairs. Italy came out of World War II with the West's largest public sector. The "occupation" of this state by the DC (and its allies) profoundly shaped the postwar political economy. The system that evolved eventually produced budget deficits and accumulated debt unmatched among the major western economic powers. Italy's profligacy made the country vulnerable in the changed international economic situation of the 1980s and contributed significantly to the political crisis of the 1990s.

The politics of collective identity has been an elusive, problematic concept for Italy. At the time of the Risorgimento, Italy was considered more a geographical expression than a true nation-state, and this generalization seemed valid well into the late twentieth century. In a pioneering study of political culture by political scientists Gabriel Almond and Sidney Verba, Italians stood out for their lack of pride in the state or its institutions and instead identified with Italy's artistic heritage and natural beauty.[14] The term for localism—*campanilismo*—expresses the sense that the world that matters is within sound of the town bell tower (*campanile*).

Stereotypes may reflect a partial reality, but they also glide over uncomfortable facts. Mussolini's excesses were enthusiastically supported by most Italians until Allied bombings and invasions brought the war's brutal costs home. Healthy second thoughts and outright embarrassment may account for the lack of nationalistic pride in the postwar period.

Explicitly *political* identities reinforced cold war polarization for nearly two generations following the war. These identities centered around mutually antagonistic subcultures, "white" (Catholic) versus "red" (Socialist and Communist). Deep class divisions fed these subcultures, but neither had a very pure class base. The DC, and even the PCI to a striking degree, were able to win support across social groups on the basis of political allegiance. This explains the longevity of their appeal: each was rooted in and dominated specific areas of the country, guaranteeing a powerful political base. Only the dissolution of cold war polarization, compounded by a rapidly modernizing society that weakened established traditions, finally undermined these subcultures, though it has not eliminated them altogether.

What has replaced the old identities? At times nothing, or, more exactly, a politics based on identifying not with tradition or ideological commitment, but with platforms and concrete policies. In other cases, as the success of the Northern League indicates, new identities based on regionalism have filled the vacuum left by the DC's collapse. The League initially targeted southern Italians, reproducing one of Italy's oldest cleavages. But as the movement unified and tried to expand, it increasingly focused on a new "other": dark-skinned immigrants.

Implications for Comparative Politics

To study Italy is to take a continuing course in comparative politics. For many of its earlier historic junctures, interesting and fruitful comparisons could be drawn with Germany. Unified at about the same time, Italians consciously copied Prussia's interventionist model of development after laissez-faire policies (copied from Britain) failed to move the economy ahead at a satisfactory pace. Italy then was itself the pioneer; it invented fascism. Both countries had this grim legacy to overcome in their postwar democratic experiments, and both were dominated, though in different degrees, by Christian Democracy.

But despite these provocative parallels, comparisons with France in the postwar period are even more telling. Catholic-Socialist-Communist collaboration, followed by the isolation of the Communists, characterized both countries at war's end. But whereas new rules of the game under France's Fifth Republic laid the groundwork for reshaping the party system by the early 1960s, Italy kept the same rules, and Italian politics resembled the Fourth Republic's assembly-style democracy through the 1990s. In France, the Socialists became the dominant party on the left by joining the Communists, as the two-ballot electoral system required. In Italy, the Socialists tried to imitate Mitterrand's success by keeping the PCI at arm's length, but they moved to the center and were crushed when the old system collapsed.

Italy, like other advanced capitalist democracies, faces daunting policy challenges in adjusting to the new international economy, but with distinct handicaps. The first is that in addition to considerable economic difficulties, Italy's political sphere remains in transition. The old party system has disintegrated, and a new one is struggling to be born. The process is fascinating, but it remains uncertain; operating with unsettled and frequently changing rules of the game means one more obstacle on a very difficult course.

The second handicap aggravates the first. Italy's economic challenges are greater than those of other European countries. Its accumulated debt is enormous. And although it has moved, under unrelenting pressure from EU watchdogs, to divest the state of its considerable ownership of the economy, the process has been haphazard. Other members of the EU 15 face similar problems, but none is in worse shape along either of these dimensions.

Finally, Italy used to have an advantage that grew, ironically, out of its historic shortcomings. Because the state was always weak, and coherent direction of the economy so problematic, vast sectors of the economy— above all those characterized by small, flexible firms— flourished by their ability to react quickly to changing market conditions. But as we will see in the next chapter, what worked as recently as fifteen years ago is no longer a guarantee of success, or even of survival.[15]

Notes

[1]Massimo D'Alema, with Claudio Velardi and Gianni Cuperlo, *Un Paese normale: La sinistra e il futuro dell'Italia* (Milan: Mondadori, 1995).

[2]David Hine, "Silvio Berlusconi, i media, e il conflitto d'interesse," in Paolo Bellucci and Martin Bull, eds., *Politica in Italia: Edizione 2002* (Bologna: Il Mulino, 2002), esp. pp. 293–294.

[3]Stefano Fella, "Introduction: One Step Forward or Two Steps Back?—Assessing the Italian Transition," *Journal of Southern Europe and the Balkans* 8 (August 2006): 136–137.

[4]Details obtained from http://www.cia.gov/cia/publications/factbook/geos/it.html#Geo.

[5]Luigi Barzini, *The Italians* (New York: Atheneum, 1964), p. 241, quoted in Sidney G. Tarrow, *Peasant Communism in Southern Italy* (New Haven, Conn.: Yale University Press, 1967), p. 21.

[6]Frank M. Snowden, "From Sharecropper to Proletarian: The Background to Fascism in Rural Tuscany, 1880–1920," in John A. Davis, ed., *Gramsci and Italy's Passive Revolution* (New York: Barnes and Noble, 1979), p. 165.

[7]Paolo Farneti, "Social Conflict, Parliamentary Fragmentation, Institutional Shift, and the Rise of Fascism: Italy," in Juan J. Linz and Alfred Stepan, eds., *The Breakdown of Democratic Regimes: Europe* (Baltimore: Johns Hopkins University Press, 1978), pp. 23–26.

[8]Charles S. Maier, *Recasting Bourgeois Europe* (Princeton, N.J.: Princeton University Press, 1975), p. 548.

[9]Ruggero Orfei, *L'Occupazione del potere: I democristiani '45–'75* (Milan: Longanesi, 1976).

[10]Piergiorgio Corbetta and Arturo M. L. Parisi, "The Referendum on the Electoral Law for the Senate: Another Momentous April," in Carol Mershon and Gianfranco Pasquino, eds., *Italian Politics: Ending the First Republic* (Boulder, Colo.: Westview Press, 1995), pp. 75–92.

[11]James I. Walsh, "L'incerto cammino verso l'Unione monetaria," in Luciano Bardi and Martin Rhodes, eds., *Politica in Italia: Edizione 98* (Bologna: Il Mulino, 1998), pp. 117ff.

[12]Maurizio Ferrera and Elisabetta Gualmini, *Rescued by Europe? Social and Labour Market Reforms in Italy from Maastricht to Berlusconi* (Amsterdam: Amsterdam University Press, 2004).

[13]James Walston, "Italian Foreign Policy in the 'Second Republic.' Changes of Form and Substance," *Modern Italy* 12 (February 2007): 102.

[14]Gabriel Almond and Sidney Verba, *The Civic Culture* (Boston: Little, Brown, 1959).

[15]*The Economist*, April 8, 2006, p. 28.

CHAPTER 17

Political Economy and Development

Italy's late development saw considerable state intervention in the economy by the 1870s. Fascism then reinforced and expanded heavy industry's cozy relationship with the state, leaving huge portions of the economy in public hands by the end of World War II. The Christian Democrats (DC), who dominated politics for forty-five years, had few qualms about the large public sector they inherited. By the 1980s, problems common to all advanced societies were aggravated by the colonization of great chunks of the state-owned parts of the economy by the DC and its Socialist allies. Until events finally caught up with them, they increasingly used public enterprises to award contracts to their cronies, and to siphon off funds or collect kickbacks for the purpose of lining their parties' treasuries (and at times their own pockets). Italy's development was also notable for an unusually large number of small enterprises. Left largely to their own devices, they often proved to be the most dynamic elements in the economy. But as the global economy has evolved, some of their virtues have proven to be liabilities in a world marked by ever more competitive markets.

The Postwar Settlement and Beyond

The republic inherited weak internal markets and a lopsided industrial structure that favored heavy industry. It also had the largest public sector among the Western economies. In some ways, this was an advantage: the challenge of postwar reconstruction could never have been met by reliance on free-market forces alone.

State and Economy from Reconstruction to Crisis

At the end of World War II, laissez-faire ideas were in a distinct minority in Italy. Yet for all its interventionism and high degree of public ownership of the economy, Italy never elaborated policies comparable to France's concerted *dirigisme*, or state-directed economic leadership. Italy's economic policies were fragmented and uncoordinated, although they soon produced impressive results.

Wartime devastation, the Resistance, and Italian capitalism's compromised position under fascism initially favored the workers' movement. But following the expulsion of Communists and Socialists from the government in 1947, Italy's recovery was built on low wages, a large surplus labor pool, and limited social spending. In the late 1940s, the United States launched the European Recovery Plan (ERP, but more commonly known as the Marshall Plan, after Secretary of State George C. Marshall) to set Western European capitalism back on its feet. Italy would eventually receive $1.3 billion.[1]

The State and Private Sectors. Italy's huge state holdings, as well as considerable banking and financial powers that were also inherited from fascism, were initially used in farsighted fashion. Over the protests of both protected oligopolies and free marketers, huge sums were invested in key industries such as steel and chemicals. Managers were allowed to reinvest dividends from state-held stocks, with the result that Italy's industrial infrastructure was greatly strengthened. These policies paid handsome dividends. As Andrew Shonfield, author of an important study of postwar European economies, put it:

> It was another one of the characteristic Latin conspiracies in the public interest, of which France, in particular, has provided some outstanding examples. In Italy such things have to be done with greater stealth, because there is neither the instinctive French respect of the high public official, nor any of the confidence in his moral purpose.[2]

Public sector initiatives meshed well with the most dynamic parts of the private sector. By the 1960s, led by Fiat, aggressive export-oriented firms were churning out low-priced goods for increasingly affluent Europeans. Earlier public sector intervention paid off now, as abundant steel, fuel, and chemicals enabled rapid expansion without the bottlenecks that would have occurred had free marketers won earlier debates about dismantling publicly owned firms. The groundwork for Italy's "Economic Miracle" was complete.

The Economic Miracle. In the early 1950s, a parliamentary investigation described terrible living conditions. One family in eight lived in "utter destitution"; one house in ten had a bath; fewer than half of all Italians had an indoor toilet; and even fewer (38 percent) could

Table 17.1

Occupation in Italy, by Sector of the Economy, 1951–2001

Economic Sector	1951 Employees	1961 Employees	1971 Employees	1981 Employees	1991 Employees	2001 Employees
Agriculture	43.9%	30.7%	20.1%	13.3%	8.4%	5.2%
All industries	29.5	34.9	39.5	37.2	32.0	31.8
All services, including government	26.6	34.4	40.4	49.5	59.6	63.0
Total	100.0	100.0	100.0	100.0	100.0	100.0
Number (000s)	(19,693)	(20,427)	(19,295)	(20,751)	(22,623)	(23,781)

Sources: For 1951, Kevin Allen and Andrew Stevenson, *An Introduction to the Italian Economy* (New York: Harper & Row, 1975), p. 104. For 1961, CISL, *CISL 1984* (Rome: Edizioni Lavoro, 1984), p. 56. For 1971–1991, ISTAT (Italian Statistical Institute), *Italia in cifre, 2000:* "Lavoro," at www.istat.it, p. 2. For 2001, ISTAT, *Approfondimenti:* 12_lavoro.pdf, at ibid., pp. 1, 2.

drink water from their own taps.[3] Yet by the 1960s, Italy's economic growth ranked at the top of all Western European countries. Gross national product doubled between 1950 and 1962, finally reducing chronically high unemployment rates. By the 1970s, illiteracy had been halved. Industrial workers surpassed the entire agricultural population in the 1960s; by 1971, agriculture accounted for barely one-fifth of the work force (see Table 17.1). New car registrations more than quadrupled in the 1960s. By other measures as well, such as televisions and telephones per capita, Italy was finally on a par with other large Western European countries by 1971.[4]

But important problems persisted. Only the steady emigration of (mainly southern) workers had avoided depression-era levels of unemployment in the decade following the war, when net emigration totaled 1.6 million.[5]

Much of the miracle was built on labor's weakness, which was only partially due to high unemployment. When the left was expelled from government, the union movement split along partisan political lines. The General Confederation of Italian Labor (CGIL), which was identified with the Communists and Socialists, was strongest among industrial workers. But its political affiliation hurt the CGIL, and favored the CISL, the predominantly Catholic Confederation of Italian Workers' Unions.[6] The smaller UIL (Union of Italian Labor) consisted of more moderate non-Catholic unions, which tended to ally with the CISL.

The 1960s: The Tide Turns.   By the 1960s, the unions, increasingly united, began to make up for their previous division, isolation, and weakness. Management, used to running roughshod over labor, was demoralized and badly divided. During the Hot Autumn of 1969 through 1970, the unions made impressive gains, and throughout the 1970s, Italy led the industrialized world in both the number and the intensity of strikes and labor disruptions.

The results were dramatic. The Workers' Charter of 1970 guaranteed civil rights on the shop floor and entrenched the major confederations as bargaining agents. General strikes forced passage of a generous pension scheme and massive government commitments to public housing. Contracts saw wages outstrip productivity (and inflation), while overtime, layoffs, and even plant modernization became nearly impossible without union cooperation. A 1975 cost-of-living escalator (*scala mobile*) guaranteed a 100 percent adjustment for inflation every three months. Given the high inflation of the late 1970s and early 1980s, the impact of the *scala mobile* was greatly magnified.

Crisis: The Late 1970s and Afterward

Italy's reliance on imported oil made the shocks of 1973 and 1979 especially severe (see the inflation figures in Table 17.2). But by the mid-1970s, all capitalist economies had to face additional challenges.

Table 17.2

Italian Economic Performance, 1971–2005 (odd-numbered years)

Year	Percentage Change of Real GDP over Previous Year	Percentage Rise in Consumer Prices over Previous Year	Percentage of Total Labor Force Unemployed
1971	1.6	4.8	5.4
1973	7.0	10.8	6.4
1975	3.6	17.0	5.9
1977	1.9	17.0	7.2
1979	4.9	14.8	7.7
1981	0.1	17.8	8.4
1983	1.2	15.0	9.8
1985	2.3	9.2	10.3
1987	3.0	4.7	12.0
1989	3.2	6.3	12.0
1991	1.2	6.2	10.9
1993	0.7	4.5	10.4
1995	3.0	5.2	11.6
1997	1.5	2.0	11.7
1999	2.1	1.7	11.4
2001	1.8	2.8	9.4
2003	0	2.3	8.0
2005	0.3	2.2	7.7

Sources: Real GDP and consumer prices through 1983: OECD and ISTAT figures cited in CISL, *CISL 1984* (Rome: Edizioni Lavoro, 1984), pp. 28, 32. Unemployment figures: ISTAT, *Annuario Statistico, 1983* (Rome: ISTAT, 1984), Table 292 for 1970–1982. For 1985, Ferruccio Marzano, "General Report on the Economic Situation of the Country in 1989," *Journal of Regional Policy* 10 (April–June 1990): 267–268. For 1985–1993: OECD Economic Surveys "Italy" (Paris: OECD, 1995), pp. 144, 150. For 1995–2001, the 1999 ISTAT Yearbook: www.istat.it/Anumital/cifre.pdf, pp. 10, 20; and the 2002 *Rapporto Annuale*, Istat-2002.pdf. For 2003 and 2005, ISTAT, *Rapporto annuale. La situazione del paese nel 2005*, Table 1.2, downloaded from www.istat.it.

Growth slowed, unemployment rose, and labor militancy declined. For Italy, the worst aspect of the crisis was—and remains—the state's fiscal problems. As Italy began to approximate a modern welfare state, costly benefits won by workers were quickly granted by the DC and PSI to their own constituencies.

Meanwhile, an inefficient and irrational bureaucratic and fiscal structure could neither deliver services effectively nor pay its own way.

Successive governments avoided alienating their supporters by running up immense annual deficits, and hence the overall debt. By the end of the 1980s, the national debt had risen above 100 percent of gross domestic product (GDP). Efforts to impose a modicum of austerity alarmed the ruling parties' supporters, further undermining the parties' legitimacy on the very eve of the *Tangentopoli* ("Bribesville") scandals.

The 1980s: The Tide Turns Again. Labor's leverage weakened as hundreds of thousands of jobs disappeared. Socialist leader Bettino Craxi led his party back into government, eroding union unity—and pitting Communists against Socialists in the CGIL. A head-on confrontation in the form of a referendum over limits imposed on the *scala mobile* led to a decisive political defeat in 1985, underscoring the PCI's isolation as well as the severity of the unions' crisis.

The CGIL, strongest among industrial workers, suffered the greatest losses as factory jobs disappeared. By 1983, pensioners replaced industrial workers as the largest group in the CGIL: over half of all CGIL members are retired; the same is true for the CISL. Table 17.1 shows how employees in services now outnumber those in industry by a ratio of roughly two to one. Not surprisingly, white-collar and service-sector workers have become the most militant part of the labor force since the 1980s, with the emergence of so-called autonomous unions that are not affiliated with any of the major confederations. The most militant of these are the Committees of the Base (Comitati di Base, COBAS), found above all in key state sectors such as railroads, air transportation, medicine, and education.[7]

Organized labor thus became increasingly fragmented as its real weight in society shrank. Disruptive tactics fed rising public resentment of unions. These trends help explain why, in the early 1990s, the major confederations agreed to a reform of labor relations that institutionalized tripartite negotiations with management and the state. Also known as corporatism or concertation, this arrangement guaranteed that the unions would be consulted and would be able to defend their interests in hard bargaining. We should note that, while weakened, Italian unions remain relatively strong by international standards, and organize a larger proportion of the labor force (35 percent) than the other countries in this text.

State and Economy

The very large state sector of the economy ensured that Italy's embrace of deregulation and privatization would begin later (often against considerable resistance from within the ruling coalition) and be more limited than that of many other Western democracies.

Economic Management Since the 1980s

As with the unions, meaningful departures from earlier policies only began in the 1980s. Truly dramatic developments took place in the 1990s, when economic and political reality could no longer be ignored.

Privatization, Italian Style.   There was no rush to sell off Italy's immense public holdings in the 1980s because the stakes were enormous. State-owned enterprises employed 38 percent of the entire workforce in industry and services, and accounted for 45 percent of sales in those sectors.[8] But if privatization at first proceeded at a fraction of the British or French rates, it nevertheless did begin in the 1980s.[9] It was then that changes in European Community (EC) rules explicitly excluded the sort of bailout operations Italian governments had routinely practiced. Governments were now required to ensure that troubled companies were restructured—and "restructuring" increasingly meant the privatization of state-owned firms.

Italian privatization has nonetheless had a distinctive character, due to the huge state sector, the weakness of Italian capital markets, and the domination of the private sector by a handful of large firms. These big companies have regularly colluded with Italy's largest private investment bank to dominate the stock market, making it very hard for small investors—as well as outside investors—to exert much influence.

These practices, and other forms of foot dragging, have angered watchdogs in Brussels. But the trend is clear and irreversible. The die was cast when the Ministry of State Holdings was eliminated in 1993. The most extensive sales took place under the center-left government of Romano Prodi between 1996 and 1998 in the aftermath of the Maastricht Treaty. By the end of the 1990s, once-sacrosanct areas of state intervention such as electric energy, steel, petroleum and natural gas, telecommunications, rail transport, autostradas, and innumerable industrial enterprises were sold off or were well on their way to being transferred out of state hands. When Italian Telecom was sold in 1997, it brought 26 trillion lire, or over $15 billion, into the Treasury. The largest such sale in West European history, it was dubbed "the mother of all privatizations."[10] By 2000, IRI, the very symbol of Italian public enterprise, and among the top thirty-five corporations in the world just three years earlier, had been totally liquidated.

Banking was progressively deregulated and privatized starting in the 1980s. The Bank of Italy obtained its independence from the Treasury early in the decade. In the mid-1980s, rules governing investment and borrowing abroad were liberalized. Toward the end of the decade, exchange regulations were loosened, and banks were deregulated, greatly easing the flow of capital into and out of the country. By the end of the decade, experts called the financial sector "Anglo-Saxonized."[11] By the end of the 1990s, all financial markets had been privatized, and the taxation of investments was greatly simplified.

Financial reform has encountered intense resistance all along the way. Collusion between the Bank of Italy and domestic banks has bent and broken the rules in order to keep the financial sector in Italian hands. Such collusion has generated scandals that have seriously damaged Italy's credibility: at the end of 2005, the governor of the Bank of Italy had to resign after two particularly outrageous schemes came to light.[12]

Changing Industrial Relations.   In the course of the 1980s, even as the tide turned against labor, management faced serious problems of its own. By the 1990s, difficulties for both sides were magnified by the growing political crisis and the need to meet the Maastricht convergence criteria. Improved industrial and labor relations were essential to meet these challenges.

The defeat of the PCI and CGIL in the 1985 referendum on the *scala mobile* was clearly a turning point, demonstrating that labor could no longer shape the agenda. As Figure 17.1 shows, the decline in union

Figure 17.1

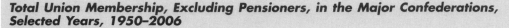

Total Union Membership, Excluding Pensioners, in the Major Confederations, Selected Years, 1950–2006

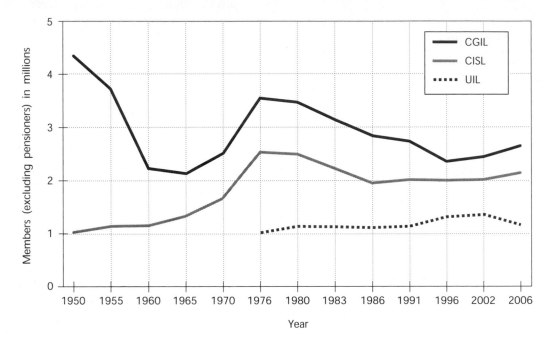

Note: Reliable figures for the UIL are not available for 1950 through 1970.

Sources: For 1950–1970: Guido Romagnoli, ed., *La sindacalizzazione tra ideologia e pratica: Il caso italiano, 1950–1977*, vol. 2 (Rome: Edizioni Lavoro, 1978), Table 1.2. For 1976: Guido Romagnoli, "Sindacalizzazione e rappresentanza," in *Le Relazioni sindacali in Italia: Rapporto 1981*, ed. Guido Baglioni et al. (Rome: Edizioni Lavoro, 1982), Table 2. For 1980–1991: CESOS, *Le relazioni sindacali in Italia: Rapporto 1992–93* (Rome: Edizioni Lavoro, 1994), Table 3, p. 76. For the CISL from 1985–2005: http://www.cisl.it, and then follow the *Gli iscritti e le risorse* link. For the UIL from 2002–06: http://www.uil.vr.it/2007/070126_iscritti.pdf. For the CGIL, go to the home page at http://www.cgil.it/, and then follow the *Tesseramento-dati* link, which provides membership figures between 1997 and 2006.

membership, already notable by 1985, became even more pronounced. By the mid-1980s, industrial jobs were disappearing in such large numbers that not even the vigorous small firms of the north, or the huge submerged economy, could absorb displaced workers. In the first four years of the 1990s, half a million manufacturing jobs disappeared.[13]

Yet management could hardly run roughshod over the unions. For one thing, the DC had always been an ally of convenience, juggling many interests in society; it was never going to implement a nakedly probusiness

agenda. Indeed, Confindustria (the Confederation of Italian Industries, private capital's leading peak organization), had declared its effective political independence from the DC even before the final debacle of *Tangentopoli*.[14] Moreover, this organization had grown much more diverse over the years. Once dominated by large export-oriented firms, by the 1980s it was increasingly giving voice to the small, dynamic industries that had led Italy's recent industrial growth.

At the same time, galloping privatization eliminated a division in employers' ranks. Many of Italy's largest (and most unionized) companies had been in public hands: management in these firms had cooperative relations with the unions and had even organized a separate association. With Italy following EU mandates to eliminate state-owned industry by the 1990s, the logic of separate management associations disappeared, and Confindustria absorbed the others.[15] Concern to keep its heterogeneous base united thus made Confindustria far more circumspect in its relations with the unions. Meanwhile, the pressures of increased global competition persuaded some manufacturers that they needed to worry about the quality of their products (and not just prices) and skilled workers' job satisfaction, which are, of course, related. These employers concluded that having a stable, predictable framework for negotiating with workers was preferable to confrontation—at least for the time being.

Labor Relations Reforms of the 1990s.   The most important reforms were passed in 1993 when concertation was established.[16] The old *scala mobile* was abolished; wage increases now had to be negotiated within projected inflation guidelines and be tied to rises in productivity rather than the cost of living. The new agreement satisfied many of management's long-standing complaints, and gave it more flexibility in hiring and layoffs—something the unions had always fiercely resisted. Furthermore, a larger share of benefit contributions now come from workers' paychecks rather than management's pockets, bringing Italian practices in line with the rest of Europe.

The 1993 reforms also reshaped workers' workplace representation. More inclusive shop floor institutions have been constructed. Two-thirds of the members of the new bodies are elected (by all workers), and the remaining third are appointed by any union taking part in contract negotiations. These changes are intended to increase the representativeness of shop floor organizations (ensuring a place for autonomous unions and COBAS, for instance), in the hope of revitalizing and relegitimizing the unions.

The new framework served the unions well in negotiations over pensions, starting with Lamberto Dini's government in 1995. The unions made concessions, but—particularly when negotiating with center-left governments that needed their support—they were able to dilute many changes and draw out their implementation.

These may seem like minor victories, but they helped the unions regain a measure of legitimacy and support in the shop floor elections of the mid-1990s.

As a final illustration of a changed climate of labor relations, legislation in the spring of 2000 put more teeth into a 1990 law regulating strikes in "essential" public services. These services are primarily in transportation, where the autonomous unions' wildcat strikes have long bedeviled Italians and tourists alike, since trains, ferries, and airports during peak travel periods are preferred targets. Several things stand out about the new rules. One is that public services are broadly defined—for instance, they include the self-employed in certain circumstances (truck drivers, for example). Another is that the major confederations agreed to these changes at the end of 1998, after Massimo D'Alema, the former Communist, replaced Prodi as prime minister. The legislation is a compromise, but it represents a breakthrough for Italy. Strikes are not forbidden, but they are restricted, including the introduction of mandatory cooling-off periods. If a strike does occur in an essential service, 50 percent of services normally delivered must be guaranteed, as must the presence of 30 percent of regular personnel.[17]

These regulations were fiercely opposed by the most left-wing unionists. But the major confederations welcomed the changes. The largest unions have always been sensitive to public opinion and try to avoid strikes that disrupt the lives of citizens and, especially, fellow workers. Those most affected by the new rules are the autonomous unions and COBAS, whose militancy wins them support within the workplace but antipathy among the public.

The center-right has less need of organized labor's support, and, as a result, labor relations during Berlusconi's second term in office were often tense. Backed by Confindustria, the government tightened the rules governing pensions (see below). It also pushed through measures making the labor market more "flexible": it is now much easier to hire people on limited-term or part-time contracts, and layoffs have also been made less cumbersome. The most militant unions tried to use a referendum to reverse, or at least limit, what they saw as an assault on workers' rights in 2003, but this produced the lowest turnout in history, producing another stinging defeat for the workers' movement.[18]

Social Policy

Italy's social policies have distinctive features, but most are typical of other countries as well.

Welfare all'Italiana. Maurizio Ferrera, perhaps the leading authority on the Italian welfare state, has shown that it conforms to a pattern found along the Mediterranean rim of Europe.[19] These welfare regimes have fragmented social services and favor cash transfers over services in kind. Cash payments render such systems especially susceptible to clientelistic abuses and corruption. Most important, following the distinctions introduced by Richard Titmuss,[20] the underlying logic of these systems is particularistic; that is, benefits go to people as members of specific, privileged categories, in contrast to institutional welfare states, which provide (universal) benefits as a condition of citizenship. An example of a universal benefit would be a national health system or guaranteed free public education. Italy has tended to be highly particularistic as well as highly inefficient.

Historically, the Italian state provided limited benefits, leaving most services in the hands of the workers' movement and, especially, the Catholic Church. Under fascism, benefits tended to be granted on an industry-wide basis, with the result that some clerks and workers enjoyed reasonable treatment, while others lacked coverage. When fascism fell, there was no national system of benefits; those who lived off the land (most Italians in 1945) had no entitlements at all.

As the DC sought to build bases of support, it gradually added farmers, businesspeople, and professionals to the rolls. Their benefits were increased in the 1970s and 1980s. In contrast to, say, Scandinavia, the Italian workers' movement did not press for universalistic benefits. Reflecting the Marxist orthodoxy of the period, they demanded that benefits be distributed to people as members of the working class, not as citizens. For this reason, for a long time the unions ignored the claims of many people without benefits—for instance, housewives or part-time employees. Furthermore, as the DC "occupied the state," many services were tied to partisan politics. For example, disability pensions would be awarded not because a person qualified, but because the local pension office was in the hands of a politician willing to trade benefits for votes.

The perpetuation of a fragmented system had long-lasting implications. First, because groups were included for partisan reasons, in piecemeal fashion, there was no sense of urgency that the system as a whole pay its own way. Second, the emphasis on privileged groups and cash transfer payments meant that historically underdeveloped areas remained perpetually underserved. To cite one telling example, Italy traditionally provided a tiny "subsistence" check for the chronically unemployed, paid out of public assistance funds, compared with a guaranteed 80 to 90 percent of the preceding wage, paid out of the main pension fund, for unemployed workers. Southerners, people with large families, and young people (especially women) have been least well served by the system's built-in biases.

The Italian welfare state expanded from the 1970s onward, pushed by the first center-left governments and even more by the militancy of the Hot Autumn. Whenever workers won concessions, the DC lavished similar benefits on its most important constituencies—with no concern as to how they would be funded. By the 1980s, Italy resembled other Western countries in the proportion of gross GDP spent on social programs. But Italy spends far more on pensions, and far less on all other benefits; Italy's nonpension welfare expenditures are less than half that of other highly developed EU members.[21]

Deficit Reduction and Welfare State Reform. The inflation and ballooning deficits of the 1980s only slowed the DC and PSI's intense battle over the spoils of office. The dimensions of the phenomenon are quickly captured with a few figures: in the late 1980s, one in ten Italians—as many as one in three adults in some parts of the south—was receiving a disability pension; 180,000 new ones were being awarded every year.[22] Over 19 million pensions are distributed in Italy,[23] at a cost that amounts to 16 percent of GDP.

Retirement benefits, which can in some cases be very generous, were historically funded out of general revenues, not contribution-based funds. Payments were of the defined-benefit type and were protected by cost-of-living escalators.[24] The budgetary consequences of these arrangements did not take long to make themselves felt. It took the collapse of the ruling parties, however, as well as the exchange rate crisis of 1992, for decisive action to be taken. Between 1992 and 1995, successive governments pushed through extensive budgetary reforms, imposing cuts and slowdowns in the growth of welfare programs.

The key pension reform came in 1995 after lengthy negotiations with the unions, leading many critics to complain that the reforms did not go far enough. The critics have a point. To keep the unions on-side, changes will be brought in very slowly. The new contribution-based system will not apply to everyone collecting a pension until 2036.[25] The minimum age at which someone can retire has increased at a glacial pace, as has the minimum number of years required to qualify for a full pension. Both center-left and center-right governments have nudged these limits upward. Fraudulent pension and other benefit claims have also been sharply reduced.

Prodi had campaigned with the left's (and unions') support, but he was utterly committed to meeting the Maastricht convergence criteria. After winning the 1996 election, he created an economic "superministry," subsuming the budget portfolio under the Treasury and entrusting it to Carlo Ciampi. There can be no doubt that the rigor of successive governments played an important part in these achievements. By the start of the twenty-first century, the accumulated national debt had been steadily reduced, although it remained above 100 percent of GDP, giving Italy the third-highest relative debt in the world.

Tax Evasion.   The *Economist*, no enemy of private enterprise, noted over twenty years ago that Italy is "a country where cheating on taxes by the self-employed is regarded as their entrepreneurial privilege," and it regularly repeats the charge.[26] The problem would be amusing were it not so serious. The total amount of income tax that goes unpaid each year has recently been estimated at a whopping 130 billion euros.[27] The inequities produced by rampant evasion are staggering; roughly half of national income is earned by dependent workers, and the other half goes to the self-employed—above all, shopkeepers and small businesspeople, professionals, and the like. But workers whose taxes are withheld at the source pay 80 percent of all personal income tax.[28]

Evasion was tolerated in the past, and even since the so-called First Republic ended, it has been dealt with erratically. It did not help matters when

Berlusconi announced, while prime minister, that he "understood" why people would try to avoid paying the tax man. Periodic amnesties are routinely employed to recover at least some unpaid taxes without interminable administrative and legal battles. Individuals—and corporations—receive "discounts" on taxes owing if they pay up promptly. Many billions of euros are recovered every year in this fashion, but evasion remains an intractable problem.

Society and Economy

Modern Italy has been marked by profound regional differences, none more serious than those between north and south, which were exacerbated from the Risorgimento onward. Late industrialization and the powerful presence of the Roman Catholic Church meant that Italy encountered modernity later and in different ways from other advanced countries. Italy also suffered from seriously polarized class relations—fascism arose as a response to militancy in the factories and fields—which were then perpetuated and entrenched by cold war divisions.

A Legacy of Polarized Class and Political Relations

For much of the postwar period, Italy was among the world's leaders in strikes. From the left's expulsion from government in 1947 through the 1980s, Italian labor relations mainly revealed whether labor or capital had market conditions in its favor. When labor was weak, it was all but ignored; when it was strong, it played catch-up with a vengeance. When labor's fortunes flagged, capital tried to recoup its losses.

Successive governments, lacking strong ties to the labor movement and themselves internally divided, could not produce a more institutionalized, less contentious framework of labor relations. The welfare state, already fragmented and very uneven in the way it distributed resources, became even more so and was increasingly awash in a sea of red ink. Employed and organized workers, in both the public and private sectors, did relatively well but they carried a crushing tax burden. The self-employed did even better, particularly when authorities looked the other way at tax time. But unprotected groups remained unprotected and often achieved benefits only thanks to willful distortions of the system (such as disability pensions).

It took the end of the cold war, the collapse of the postwar party system, and a disastrous economic inheritance further constrained by external (EU) guidelines before a sustained attack on this legacy could be mounted.

A Legacy of Gender, Generational, and Regional Differences

Italy's social problems have deep and complex roots; this legacy has had a clear impact in the three areas of gender, generational, and regional inequities.

Gender Inequities. Legally sanctioned discrimination against women lasted well into the postwar period. Adultery was a crime that only a woman could commit, women could not apply for passports without their husband's or father's permission, and rape was defined as a crime against public morality. That such a society would ignore women's educational or employment opportunities is hardly surprising, nor would one expect much concern about providing day care or other facilities for working parents. In societies of this type—and they are especially common in southern Europe—women are often actively dissuaded from working at all. Traditionally, the state expected them to produce children, not goods or services.

The assumption was that the family should provide services. And, in this context, "family" is really a euphemism for "women." These attitudes were reinforced by the Catholic Church's "family values," but they were also prevalent for many years in the union movement as well. It took years of struggle by the women's movement, including powerful pressure by feminists within unions, before the major confederations embraced gender-neutral unemployment lists, or demands for day care centers in the workplace.

Here again we see a welfare state skimpy in its provision of services in kind, and hence in its modern infrastructure. Even with some improvement over the past decade, the distortions of Italy's political economy are apparent in low female participation rates—45 percent (the proportion employed in the fifteen–sixty-four age

group). This contrasts with a rate of 70 percent for men, which is also low. At just over 10 percent, women's unemployment rates are nearly double the rate for men (6 percent).[29] And this despite the fact that women outnumber men in university attendance and the completion of degrees.

The low participation rate means that Italy has one of the weakest tax bases of all advanced capitalist nations. The entrenchment of gender-biased practices obviously aggravates the challenges of persistently high unemployment, as in the south.

Generational Inequities. Italian women are disadvantaged compared with men, but this is hardly the only inequity built into the Italian labor market and welfare state. Young people as a whole—men and women—do much worse than their elders, though women always suffer relatively more deprivation. The unemployment rate for youth, officially 24 percent, was at the top of the major EU member states in 2005.

This does not mean that a quarter of all young people find no work at all, for many obtain part-time jobs or limited-term contracts, which recent legislation has facilitated. But they are much less well paid and have few, if any, of the guarantees that those with steady full-time employment enjoy. Since the 1990s, successive governments have encouraged employers to hire young people for traineeships or at least part-time jobs, by paying a portion of their wages. All too often, however, employers fail to extend the contract once government subsidies expire.

Regional Inequities. A north-south gap existed when Italy was unified, and persisted through the postwar period despite massive infusions of funds. Every social and economic indicator shows the south lagging behind. Sidney Tarrow argued forty years ago that the south was not so much "backward" as systematically distorted by the way the DC had created a clientelistic network using the levers of a modern capitalist economy to perpetuate a structurally underdeveloped south.[30] This distortion still exists.

Simply put, ever since the Economic Miracle the north has enjoyed an unemployment rate roughly half that of the nation as a whole, while the rate in the Mezzogiorno (the south) has been about one and a half times the national average.[31] And this regional difference compounds the gender and generational differences, so that young southerners, and especially young female southerners, are the worst off of all.

The south stands out from the rest of the country in many other ways, ranging from birthrates and family size to migratory flows. In the south, births exceed deaths, and the population would in fact grow were it not for a net exodus of inhabitants. In the north, the dynamic is precisely the opposite: deaths exceed births, yet the population continues to increase, mainly because of immigration from outside Italy.[32] As with the employment data, the north and south are at the extremes, while the center tends to resemble the north more than the south.

The Politicization of Regional Identity. Regional differences have been central to many aspects of postwar politics; the red zones of the north-center and the Catholic white zones of the northeast served, respectively, as the PCI's and DC's subcultural anchors (see Chapter 19). But except for a short-lived separatist movement in Sicily at the end of World War II,* local identities never served as the foundation of political movements or parties—that is, until the rise of the leagues. Chapter 18 discusses the phenomenon in more detail, but it is necessary to mention it here, particularly since we address immigration immediately below.

As the DC lost political and moral credibility, the fortunes of the various leagues rose. Some earlier leagues made an unabashed ethnic appeal, first against southerners and then against foreigners. Others expressed more of the middle-class, populist tax revolt mentality that has recently appeared in many advanced capitalist nations. Many northerners felt that the country's prosperity was based on their hard work, while they blamed its problems on spendthrift and corrupt governments that poured funds into an insatiable—and lazy—south. The northeast, where the Northern League is strongest, hosts the most polarized attitudes concerning demands for greater local autonomy and the most negative views toward the welfare state and aid to the poorest regions of the country.[33]

Umberto Bossi created the Northern League (Lega Nord, LN) out of several regional leagues. For a time this was the largest party in the northeast, and occasionally in the north as a whole, before Berlusconi's own party, Forza Italia, displaced it at the turn of the century. Bossi may be mercurial and demagogic, but he has given expression to a political cleavage that waxes and wanes yet shows no signs of fading away.

From a Country of Emigrants to One of Immigrants: Ethnic Tensions

Italians used to think of themselves as a country of emigrants and as therefore highly sensitive to the plight of strangers in a new land. But a rising tide of immigration, beginning in the 1970s and accelerating since the end of the 1980s, has forced them to confront their own intolerance and lack of preparedness.

Immigration is a rapidly growing phenomenon. By the end of 2005, legal residents were just over 3 million, or 5.2 percent of the population.[34] Somewhat less than a million others are estimated to be undocumented. Immigrants follow jobs, so they tend to cluster in the north and center of Italy. The Northern League has played heavily on the idea that a flood of foreigners was invading the country, taking Italian jobs, and boosting crime rates. At the same time, there have been undeniable connections between some immigrants and drug trafficking, forms of petty crime, and prostitution, and public opinion has shown growing sensitivity to immigration-related issues. Violent racist episodes have increased, and anti-Islamic sentiment was increasing even before September 11, 2001. Four separate immigration laws were passed between 1986 and 2002, tightening rules and increasing penalties on each occasion.

Italy at any rate would have had to address this issue because of its desire to be part of the EU's agreements on borders, which require standardized laws, controls, and restrictions on immigration among all participants. The 2002 law, enacted by Berlusconi's second government, tried to soften its most repressive aspects by promising an amnesty for undocumented workers who were already established in Italy. Over half a million people took advantage of the offer.[35] Like

*There was also a separatist movement in the German-speaking Alto Adige in the 1960s, but this took the form of terrorist incidents rather than a mass movement.

all such laws, many aspects of the current legislation are quite unrealistic, establishing arbitrary annual quotas and pretending that immigration can be made to conform neatly to the needs of the labor market. In recent years, the demand for labor in the north has been so great that the annual quotas are routinely exceeded barely halfway through the year.

Public tolerance and bureaucratic incompetence will probably keep Italy from turning into a country that systematically tracks down and expels dark-skinned foreigners, although the willingness of politicians to exploit popular fears is not encouraging. Recent developments show that decision makers are only beginning to grasp the implications of economic trends and migration patterns that have become integral parts of a radically transformed, increasingly interdependent global economy.

The Dilemmas of European Integration

Italy has always occupied a peculiar place in what was originally the European Economic Community (EEC) and then became, in stages, the European Union (EU). Italian governments were among the most enthusiastic supporters of the project of European integration, and the 1957 treaty that established the EEC was, after all, the Treaty of Rome. Italians consistently ranked at the very top of public opinion polls in their enthusiasm for all things European, from positive general attitudes to their desire to see the EU expand more rapidly. Yet in spite of this general and official enthusiasm, Italy's reputation in the Community has always been rather spotty. Time and again, France and Germany simply overshadowed the Italians, who, even as their economic weight increased, left the impression of being political and diplomatic lightweights. Nor was Italy's reputation helped by an erratic and indifferent application of European norms or, for that matter, its inability to collect and spend funds to which it was entitled.[36] As if it were needed, here was yet another illustration of the degree to which the pathologies of the Italian state—in this case the notoriously inefficient bureaucracy—interfered with everything Italians tried to do.

As we have seen, however, by the 1980s Italy could no longer ignore international or European realities. By the early 1990s, the same forces undermining the politics of the First Republic were also pushing economic policy in new directions. As the status quo collapsed, so too did the attitude that had prevented numerous domestic reforms from being realized. The weight of international considerations in Italian economic policymaking is underscored by recalling that two of Italy's recent prime ministers (Lamberto Dini and Carlo Ciampi) were previously top officials of the Bank of Italy. A third (Romano Prodi) is an economist who built his reputation reforming IRI in the 1980s. Ciampi went on to be elected president of the republic, while Prodi became president of the European Commission. By the end of the decade, having made conformity to the Maastricht convergence parameters a top priority, successive center-left governments had enacted far-reaching changes, and Italy appeared to be taking its European obligations much more seriously.

When Berlusconi returned to power in 2001, a more ambivalent attitude toward the EU came to the fore, reflecting the fierce Euroskepticism of some allies (most notably the LN). In fact, Berlusconi had to assume the role of foreign minister himself for nearly a year after his first appointee felt compelled to resign over the constant anti-EU sniping from within his cabinet. But even the return of Romano Prodi, whose European credentials are above suspicion, is no guarantee against critical attitudes being expressed on the left: as is the case throughout the euro zone, pro- and anti-EU sentiment cut across the political spectrum.

Since the mid-1990s, Italy's economic growth has not kept up with even the EU's modest rates, and the Brussels bureaucracy makes a convenient target in uncertain times, as the French and Dutch votes on the EU constitution made clear in 2005. In that same year, Italy's growing deficit pushed the accumulated national debt up after eleven consecutive years of reductions.[37]

Although it is undeniably the case that the coming of the EU and the pressure of conforming to the Maastricht convergence criteria have powerfully conditioned Italian policymakers, it would be a gross oversimplification to attribute all changes in Italy's political economy over the past two decades to the *vincolo esterno* (severe external constraint) imposed by membership in the EU.[38] The European imperative, it is clear, has been powerful, but it has served to reinforce trends that were already underway both domestically and internationally.

Italy in the Global Economy

Italy's postwar economy, like that of its neighbors, was built on an aggressive policy of exporting manufactured goods. Unlike its neighbors, however, Italy's investment in research and development was always relatively scanty; its comparative advantage was largely a reflection of lower labor costs in the mass production of durable consumer items. With the growth of international competition, particularly from Asia, and the opening up of once-protected economies to increasing foreign penetration, many of these advantages started to slip away, as can be seen in a dramatic loss of markets for Italian household appliances, office machines, and, especially, automobiles.[39] Some large corporations adapted to new conditions, and many smaller firms also responded very well to a more competitive international climate—for a time. Italian industrial and agricultural machinery, textiles and clothing, and specialized metallurgy helped the country maintain a generally favorable balance of trade, but over the past decade Italy has seen a notable shrinkage of its share of the global export market.

Reversing these trends in the face of growing Chinese encroachment into many areas where Italy has done quite well would be a daunting challenge in any event. By general consensus, the Italian economy's chronic weaknesses happen to be in areas that are central to the new international economic order. One such area is research and development. Another is that Italian corporations remain, on the whole, family-run firms of rather limited dimensions. This perpetuates an undercapitalized stock market, and the fragmentation of the sector makes sustained research and development extremely difficult. It also limits the country's attractiveness to foreign investment—as do corporate scandals that draw attention to practices that were once hidden from general view, including extremely lax rules regarding corporate audits and the monitoring of market operations. As noted earlier, collusion among the country's largest corporations and key segments of financial institutions (including, recently, the Bank of Italy) further tarnished a reputation that was not very strong in the first place.

In sum, domestic and international pressures combined to set Italy's economic governance on a new path in the 1990s, but recent challenges raise many questions as to whether long-established practices, and shortcomings, may prove to be serious impediments to future progress.

Notes

[1] Kevin Allen and Andrew Stevenson, *An Introduction to the Italian Economy* (New York: Harper & Row, 1975), p. 10.

[2] Andrew Shonfield, *Modern Capitalism* (Oxford: Oxford University Press, 1969), pp. 186–187.

[3] Allen and Stevenson, *Introduction to the Italian Economy*, pp. 11–12.

[4] Ibid., p. 28.

[5] George H. Hildebrand, *Growth and Structure in the Economy of Modern Italy* (Cambridge, Mass.: Harvard University Press, 1965), p. 117.

[6] Guido Romagnoli, ed., *La sindacalizzazione tra ideologia e pratica: Il caso italiano, 1950–1977*, vol. 2 (Rome: Edizioni Lavoro, 1978), Table 2.2.

[7] Lorenzo Bordogna, "'Arcipelago COBAS': Frammentazione della rappresentanza e conflitti di lavoro," in Piergiorgio Corbetta and Robert Leonardi, eds., *Politica in Italia: Edizione 88* (Bologna: Il Mulino, 1988), pp. 260–262.

[8] Anthony C. Masi, "Il complesso siderurgico di Bagnoli: La ristrutturazione e le relazioni industriali," in Raimondo Catanzaro and Raffaella Y. Nanetti, eds., *Politica in Italia: Edizione 89* (Bologna: Il Mulino, 1989), p. 213.

[9] Patrizio Bianchi, Sabino Cassese, and Vincent Della Sala, "Privatisation in Italy: Aims and Constraints," *West European Politics* 11 (October 1988): 88.

[10] Guglielmo Raggozino, "Italia i miliardi delle privatizzazioni," *Il manifesto*, July 21, 1998.

[11] Gerald Epstein and Juliet Schor, "The Divorce of the Banca d'Italia and the Italian Treasury: A Case Study of Central Bank Independence," in Peter Lange and Marino Regini, eds., *Stato, Market and Social Regulation: New Perspectives on Italy* (New York: Cambridge University Press, 1989), p. 147.

[12] Marcello Messori, "Le aggregazioni bancarie e il ruolo della Banca d'Italia," in Grant Amyot and Luca Verzichelli, eds., *Politica in Italia: Edizione 2006* (Bologna: Il Mulino, 2006), pp. 178–179.

[13] OECD Economic Surveys, "Italy" (Paris: OECD, 1995), Table H, p. 151.

[14] Liborio Mattina, "Abete's Confindustria: From Alliance with the DC to Multiparty Appeal," in Stephen Hellman and Gianfranco Pasquino, eds., *Italian Politics: A Review*, vol. 8, pp. 151–164.

[15] Marino Regini and Ida Regalia, "Employers, Unions and the State: The Resurgence of Concertation in Italy?" in Martin Bull and Martin Rhodes, eds., *Crisis and Transition in Italian Politics* (London: Frank Cass, 1997), pp. 221–222.

[16]Richard M. Locke, "The Abolition of the Scala Mobile," in Carol Mershon and Gianfranco Pasquino, eds., *Italian Politics: Ending the First Republic* (Boulder, Colo.: Westview Press, 1994), pp. 185–196.

[17]Riccardo De Gennaro, "Scioperi, da oggi si cambia," *La Repubblica*, April 19, 2000, p. 28.

[18]Ferruccio Sansa, "Referendum senza quorum il centrodestra canta vittoria," *La Repubblica*, June 17, 2003, p. 2. A turnout of 50 percent + 1 of the electorate is required for an abrogative referendum to be valid: see Chapter 19.

[19]Maurizio Ferrera, "The Uncertain Future of the Italian Welfare State," in Bull and Rhodes, *Crisis and Transition in Italian Politics*, pp. 231–249.

[20]Richard Titmuss, *Social Policy: An Introduction* (London: Allen and Unwin, 1974).

[21]Ferrera, "The Uncertain Future of the Italian Welfare State," pp. 232–233.

[22]*L'Unità*, December 3, 1994, p. 9.

[23]The data are from 2004. Another 3.7 million pensions are classified as social assistance. ISTAT, *Annuario statistico italiano 2006: Cap. 4, Assistenza e previdenza sociale*, p. 126. Downloaded from www.istat.it.

[24]Giuliano Cazzola, *Lo stato sociale tra crisi e riforme: Il caso Italia* (Bologna: Il Mulino, 1994), p. 66.

[25]Marco Mira D'Ercole and Flavia Terribile, "Spese pensionistiche: Sviluppi nel 1996 e 1997," in Luciano Bardi and Martin Rhodes, eds., *Politica in Italia: Edizione 98* (Bologna: Il Mulino, 1998), p. 226.

[26]"Will *la dolce vita* Turn Sour?" *Economist*, January 5, 1985, p. 58, for the quote. For a recent restatement, see the issue of July 8, 2006, p. 67.

[27]Maria Stella Conte, "Un paese con sempre più poveri," *La Repubblica*, February 1, 2003, p. 12.

[28]Enzo Forcella, "Un paese senza ricchi," *La Repubblica*, January 4, 1990, p. 8.

[29]All figures are for 2005. ISTAT, *Annuario statistico italiano 2006: Capitolo 9, Lavoro*, p. 238. Downloaded from www.istat.it.

[30]Sidney G. Tarrow, *Peasant Communism in Southern Italy* (New Haven, Conn.: Yale University Press, 1967).

[31]ISTAT, *L'Italia in cifre, 2005*, p. 24.

[32]ISTAT, *L'Italia in cifre, 2005*, p. 2.

[33]Ferrera, "The Uncertain Future of the Italian Welfare State," pp. 245–247.

[34]Figures cited in *Il manifesto*, October 26, 2006, p. 6.

[35]For a good discussion of regularization efforts over the years, see Ferruccio Pastore, "A Community Out of Balance: Nationality Law and Migration Politics in the History of Post-Unification Italy," *Journal of Modern Italian Studies* 9 (Spring 2004): 44, n. 31.

[36]A good synthetic treatment of Italy's involvement in the EEC-EU can be found in Paul Ginsborg, *Italy and Its Discontents* (London: Penguin, 2001), pp. 232–242.

[37]"Romano Prodi's Government Faces Up to the Need for Fiscal Austerity," *The Economist,* June 10, 2006, p. 41.

[38]Vincent Della Sala, "The Italian Model of Capitalism: On the Road between Globalization and Europeanization?" *Journal of European Public Policy* 11 (December 2004): 1055.

[39]Paolo Guerrieri, "La collocazione internazionale dell'economia italiana," in Paul Ginsborg, ed., *Stato dell'Italia* (Milan: Il Saggiatore, 1994), pp. 379–387.

CHAPTER 18

Governance
and Policymaking

The *Statuto albertino* mandated a highly centralized state structure with extensive executive powers. It allowed the king to appoint Mussolini as prime minister, and it allowed Mussolini to use emergency decrees to install a dictatorship. Therefore the authors of the 1948 republican constitution tried to ensure that such abuses could never happen again. As time passed, the framers appeared to have succeeded all too well: they gave so much power to the legislature that it hampered the executive's ability to act effectively.

But it would be a serious error to blame all of Italy's governing problems on faulty constitutional design. Italian prime ministers do have less formal power than their counterparts in other parliamentary systems (such as Britain or Germany), although those powers have been strengthened over the years. But if fragmented and incoherent policy has been the hallmark of Italian governments for half a century, this reflects the fragmented and often fractious nature of Italian cabinets. Governing majorities have often been internally divided, and it is hard to produce coherent policies when different parties—or factions of the same party—are trying to outmaneuver each other.

Another chronic obstacle to coherent governance has been Italy's notoriously inefficient bureaucracy, which was then rendered even more inefficient by the way the ruling parties (again, above all the DC) occupied the state machinery for partisan ends. Here, too, institutional design certainly contributed to the problem, for instance, in concentrating so much power in the hands of a central administration. But most serious pathologies are less the product of formal arrangements than the result of the way these arrangements were used, and abused, by political elites.

When the old party system began to crumble in the 1990s, serious reform finally appeared to be on the political agenda. But although changes have been implemented in the past fifteen years, some chronic problems persist, starting with a party system that is more fragmented than ever (Chapter 19). The reform process has also taken on a see-saw character as successive majorities have displaced one another. In the old days, majorities never changed, and dramatic new laws never appeared. Now, one majority can pass new laws, and even amend the constitution, only to have its successor immediately undo its handiwork while introducing entirely new legislation. So we can add unpredictability to an already problematic situation.

Organization of the State

Although people refer to the First Republic of 1946–1993, and a Second Republic since 1994, this is political shorthand. Formally, there has only been one Italian Republic—a parliamentary republic with a bicameral legislature. Both chambers of Parliament are elected at the same time and have identical powers; the Chamber of Deputies has 630 members, while the Senate has 315. It has a dual executive, with an indirectly elected head of state, the president of the republic. The presidency is largely ceremonial, although its incumbents exerted considerable influence in the tumultuous 1990s. The far more important executive office is the head of government, whose formal title is President of the Council of Ministers (as the cabinet is called), but who is generally referred to as the prime minister.

The republic inherited a unitary, centralized administrative structure, based on the French model, including prefects in its 106 provinces who are agents of the Ministry of the Interior in Rome. The constitution of 1948 decentralized some powers to the twenty regions of the country, which have become the most important subnational level of government. But it took the rise of the Northern League to put serious decentralization, and federalism, on the political agenda. In 2000, a rather weak form of federalism was instituted by the center-left; in 2004, a more ambitious form of federalism was passed by the center-right, but was then rejected in a referendum in 2006.

The judicial system has evolved dramatically, reflecting the interplay of conscious design and politics. Judicial review was not part of the continental legal tradition, based in Roman law, but it was inserted into the postwar constitution because of past Fascist abuses and U.S. influence. In another reaction against the past, the Italian judiciary was granted far more autonomy than its counterparts in France or Germany, but it acquired that autonomy very slowly. Eventually, however, the judiciary helped bring down the old party system thanks to its relentless—for some, reckless—prosecution of corruption during *Tangentopoli*.

As this summary suggests, Italy's institutional framework has been in flux, and the rate of change has accelerated greatly since the 1990s.

The Executive

Throughout the First Republic, the executive was at the mercy of the parties—including the prime minister's own party. When the old party system collapsed, many hoped to leave old problems behind. While changes have occurred, many old patterns persist.

Chronic Problems of Cabinet Government

Italian governments are formed according to the rules of most parliamentary democracies. Following an election, the president of the republic designates the prime minister. The designee constructs a cabinet by consulting the leaders of the various parties that support the proposed government. In an effort to guarantee the collective responsibility of the government, the framers stipulated that the entire cabinet, and not just the prime minister, must then win the confidence of both the Chamber of Deputies and the Senate.

Governments are sworn in and remain in office until they no longer command Parliament's confidence or, much more common, the support of the governing coalition. In fact, only once since 1946 (Romano Prodi in 1998) has a government resigned after a no-confidence vote. All other cabinet crises have resulted from internal divisions within the majority. When the prime minister no longer commands a majority, he (so far, there has never been a female prime minister) notifies the president, who can choose the incumbent or someone else to form a new government. If no coalition then obtains a majority or if Parliament's five-year term is near its end, the president dissolves the legislature and calls general elections, which must be held within ten weeks of dissolution (Article 61).

During the First Republic, the outcome of elections was rarely in doubt because of a nearly "pure" proportional representation electoral system. Nevertheless, it often took months to choose a prime minister and distribute ministerial portfolios because of postelectoral bargaining within the winning coalition.

Since 1994, this situation has changed. Electoral reforms have forced the parties to construct their alliances before the general elections (see Chapter 19). These alliances, to be effective, must also preselect the prime ministerial candidate around whom they will rally. Although doling out ministerial posts to all members of the winning coalition may still take a long time, there is no longer any mystery about the prime minister's identity once an election is decided.

Since World War II, Italy has had over sixty governments and twenty-six different prime ministers; the average cabinet of the First Republic lasted nine months. Until the early 1990s, this very high cabinet turnover actually masked the remarkable underlying stability of the party system. The same parties, and indeed many of the same people, occupied the key ministries of every government for over forty years. This situation reflected postwar Italy's political arithmetic: in a fragmented Parliament, 35 to 40 percent of the seats regularly went to parties (Communists and neofascists) with no chance of joining the government. Governing coalitions therefore had to be built from among the remaining 60 percent, which was extremely heterogeneous, though always dominated by the DC.

Since the opposition could not win, it had no chance of calling sitting governments to account for their behavior. Intense political competition therefore took place within governing coalitions, as parties jockeyed for marginal advantages over their coalition partners, or as rivals dueled within the same party. Serious reforms became even less likely, because the resistance of just a few key figures within the coalition could bring the government's support below 50 percent or precipitate crises and cabinet reshuffles that consumed weeks or even months.

The end of the old party system has not produced the hoped-for breakthrough. There has, to be sure, finally been true alternation in office between government and opposition. And governments no longer fall with such alarming frequency. It is early, however, to announce the dawn of a new era of stability in Italian politics. A new party system has emerged, but it remains numerically fragmented and ideologically diverse (Chapter 19). Governing coalitions may fly apart on short notice, and several have. Electoral reform and the resulting personalization of prime ministerial candidates has helped overcome one shortcoming of the old system, but only one coalition—Berlusconi's second government—lasted a full legislative term, and even it experienced a cabinet reshuffle because of internal divisions.

The Prime Minister's Powers. The Italian prime minister is one of the weaker heads of government in Western Europe, only partly by design. When the dominant party is united, or when the governing coalition has an uncontested leader, the prime minister's power is enhanced. When coalitions prove to be less cohesive, prime ministers, no matter how dynamic or charismatic, are undermined. Consider Silvio Berlusconi, whose forceful personality surely did not change between 1994 and 2001. But while his first government lasted barely six months, his second—a coalition almost identical to the first—broke all records, lasting 1,409 days.[1] The second time around, Berlusconi made firm promises to his coalition partners, and extracted their firm commitment to stick with him in exchange.

By the 1980s, the growing crisis of the parties finally permitted some strengthening of the prime minister's role vis-à-vis the cabinet, subjecting ministers to more control. In the late 1990s, Prodi and D'Alema implemented far-reaching administrative reforms. An economic "superministry" was created, combining the previously divided Budget and Treasury Ministries (Ciampi was the first incumbent), and budgetary procedures were restructured and modernized.[2] Other ministries were combined, and more coordination was established.

Italian cabinets have been politically cumbersome and physically ungainly. In the early 1990s, it appeared as though cabinets were going to become more streamlined: the number of ministers and junior ministers (undersecretaries) was reduced. But as the solidity of governing coalitions started to erode, and as the parties have reasserted themselves, ministers and undersecretaries have expanded again, rivaling and sometimes surpassing First Republic figures.[3] This practice guarantees the representation of diverse interests and the distribution of patronage and influence, but it obviously undermines coherent policymaking.

The idea of giving more power to the prime minister, or the president, used to be dismissed out of hand with solemn reminders about Mussolini. Since the late 1990s, with the memory of Mussolini fading and the chronic problem of cabinet instability becoming all too apparent, new proposals to increase executive power have continually been put forward. Part of the left remains adamantly opposed to any such exercise, but most of the center-left now favors at least some strengthening of the prime minister's powers. The right has generally favored a stronger executive, but its proposals have varied widely, ranging from a semi-presidential system similar to that of France to a much stronger prime minister with a reduced role for the president of the republic.

President of the Republic: A Sometimes Controversial Office

The president is the head of state and representative of national unity. Presidents are elected by secret ballot in a joint session of both chambers of Parliament, with an additional sixty representatives from the regions. On the first three ballots, a two-thirds majority is required; from the fourth, a simple majority suffices. The term of office is seven years. The constitution does not forbid reelection, but no one has served more than one term. One reason is that, with very few exceptions, presidents have tended to be quite elderly.

The president's powers include designating a prime minister and using a suspensive veto, which can send a law back to Parliament unsigned with a note explaining the president's reservations. A simple majority vote can override vetoes, in which case the president must sign the bill. Presidents use this veto sparingly, but often to great effect. Since governments are inevitably multiparty coalitions, the reservations of the head of state are usually enough to sway at least some members of the coalition. The president also chairs the Supreme Defense Council and the Supreme Council of the Judiciary (Consiglio Superiore della Magistratura, CSM). These are supposed to be honorific titles, but with sometimes-stormy relations between politicians and the judiciary, this latter role can often be politically charged. The designation of a prime minister was once the president's most important power, for there were often several plausible contenders for the role. When the party system went into crisis in the 1990s, prime ministers were chosen from outside the parties in an even clearer assertion of presidential prerogative. For reasons outlined above, this discretion effectively disappeared as new electoral systems produced pre-established coalitions with clear leaders.

The visibility and importance of the office became pronounced in the course of *Tangentopoli* and the collapse of the governing parties. Because almost all significant power rests in Parliament, and therefore the parties, a crisis of authority inevitably resulted when their legitimacy crumbled. The resulting power vacuum created considerable freedom to maneuver in other branches of government. Into this vacuum stepped not only the president but the judiciary as well.[4]

The most dramatic developments occurred during the term of Oscar Luigi Scalfaro, a Christian Democrat who exercised unprecedented discretionary powers between 1992 and 1999. In 1992, he informed Prime Minister Amato that politicians under a judicial cloud, no matter how strongly supported by their parties, would be unacceptable as members of cabinet. In 1993, he chose Italy's first nonpolitical prime minister (Carlo Azeglio Ciampi) to lead the country to general elections, and he then played an active role in choosing members of Ciampi's cabinet of specialists.[5] Finally, and most important, he resisted a furious campaign by the center-right in 1994 to call elections when Berlusconi's first government collapsed. A more cautious president might well have immediately dissolved Parliament, but Scalfaro feared that elections in such rapid succession would further delegitimize Parliament.

With more clear electoral outcomes, the president has less opportunity to steer events than he had in the early 1990s. Scalfaro was succeeded by Ciampi in 1999, whose term was less controversial than that of his predecessor. There were, however, occasions when Ciampi criticized Berlusconi directly and indirectly, weighed in on governmental deliberations, and vetoed controversial laws on telecommunications reform and immunity from prosecution. In 2006, Ciampi was succeeded by Giorgio Napolitano, a highly respected former Communist.

Historically, the center-right wished to reinforce the powers of the presidency, along the lines of the French Fifth Republic's semipresidentialism. This changed under Berlusconi's second term in office, and, with the left's traditional hostility to strong executive power, any variation of presidentialism is probably a dead letter for the foreseeable future.

Bureaucracy and Civil Service

Few institutions enjoy much respect in Italy, but the bureaucracy is especially reviled. Centralized and inflexible traditions, outmoded recruitment practices, low pay, ironclad job security, and practically every other shortcoming known to complex organizations are all combined in Italy's public administration. Italy's administrative system hardly ends with the formal ministerial bureaucracies and the career civil servants who staff them, however. Its most unique aspects are found in the state-owned firms, holding companies, autonomous agencies and enterprises, and special institutions that still saturate the country, despite the pace of reforms since the 1990s.

This sprawling structure is highly politicized *and* extraordinarily fragmented; it is also the key to understanding much of the political system's paralysis. This bureaucracy evolved and expanded when the DC overwhelmingly dominated its coalition partners, and therefore claimed most key ministries for itself while installing its own people in the top positions in the bureaucracy and state-controlled economic institutions. The system was fragmented from the beginning, not only because of (limited) power sharing among coalition partners but even more because the DC itself was divided internally. This huge spoils system provided independent power bases within the ruling party. Forty-five uninterrupted years at the center of the system, at least thirty-five of which were spent carving it up, created a dynamic that did not end with the collapse of the DC and PSI.

The Regular Public Administration.   In terms of the number of people it employs, the Italian bureaucracy is not out of line with the rest of Western Europe.[6] The real problem lies in the way ministries—and to some extent the entire legal culture undergirding the Italian state—are organized. They seem designed to maximize inefficiency and demoralization through the ranks: they are overcentralized and rule bound; promotion disregards merit and rewards seniority and political connections; and the pay and working conditions are terrible. Especially at lower levels, absenteeism is widespread, second jobs are more the rule than the exception, and service is arrogantly delivered, appallingly slow, and hampered by manipulation and corruption.

The republic inherited a bureaucracy staffed with Fascist appointees, and it took nearly a full generation to be rid of the old guard. Meanwhile, those who rose through the ranks during the First Republic were highly sensitive to the ruling parties' wishes. The system became even more rule-conscious as unionization spread through the lower ranks, giving workers a new awareness of their rights. Reforms in the 1980s addressed some problems, against stiff internal resistance. One sensitive observer says these reforms were "ingested" and integrated into the system's old structures and processes.[7] As with so many other important changes in Italy, *Tangentopoli* created the conditions for more rationalization and streamlining than had previously been possible, though the results have been mixed.[8]

The system is reinforced by its formalism: entrance examinations stress abstract concepts and knowledge of legal minutiae rather than technical skills. This helps account for the high proportion of southerners at all levels of the civil service. The lack of opportunities in the Mezzogiorno, along with the high enrollment of southerners in legal and philosophical faculties in the universities, makes the south a prime recruiting ground for public employment. The high proportion of southerners in the bureaucracy, in turn, feeds Northern League stereotypes that the state panders to the south.

Despite all the legal-rational trappings, the civil service, with a few exceptions, is highly fragmented and shot through with influence and patronage. A tradition of autonomous, centralized little empires was reinforced after World War II, as ministries were "colonized" by the ruling parties, often by one or two power groups within the DC.

This colonization made the bureaucracy an effective patronage machine but a much less satisfactory mechanism for the delivery of services. The most significant reform was a 2001 revision of the constitution by the center-left, which decentralized power down to the regional and subregional levels of government. As responsibilities for such vital functions as education, health care, and public safety, with their huge staffs and large budgets, are passed down to lower levels of the state, such decentralization has profound implications for the bureaucracy (see the discussion of local government below).

Public and Semipublic Institutions: State Enterprises and Autonomous Agencies

Italy's public agencies have counterparts nearly everywhere in the advanced capitalist world, although Italian agencies are astonishingly numerous. Their number ranges anywhere from forty thousand to over fifty thousand, depending on how one counts.[9] State monopolies in Italy may historically have covered a few unusual sectors (salt and bananas come to mind), and some public corporations may have slightly different structures elsewhere, but the state-run, nonstock corporation is a stranger to few modern capitalist societies. In Italy, key industries of this type, such as railroads and telephone and telegraph services, date back to the turn of the twentieth century.

Health, pension, social security, and welfare agencies and institutions are also often nationalized, although in most advanced societies many of these are under direct ministerial control. In Italy, however, they evolved as autonomous agencies, parallel to Catholic and other charitable institutions. They are organized under the Ministry of Labor and Welfare, but the major institutions control the investment of their own funds, which amount to billions of euros. They operate under strict guidelines, but their potential leverage over the economy is immense. The largest agency is the Social Security Institute (Istituto Nazionale di Previdenza Sociale, INPS). For at least twenty years there have been halting steps toward reorganizing and making the entire range of welfare agencies under INPS more efficient. This process has been resisted fiercely by thousands of local mini-agencies representing a variety of special interests.

All Western societies contain abundant examples of the political use of state services, but Italy stands out in the degree to which the control of agencies, along with the allocation of payments, became flagrant instruments of political patronage. Italy is also unique in the degree to which political parties have been the agents (and beneficiaries) of such practices.[10]

The extent and variety of public ownership of industry has made Italy unique among West European democracies. The Institute for Industrial Reconstruction (IRI) was not disbanded or its holdings privatized at war's end; its role in the economy steadily expanded, and other holding companies, most notably the National Hydrocarbons Agency, or ENI (Ente Nazionale Idrocarburi), an energy conglomerate, and EFIM (Ente Partecipazioni e Finanziamento Industriale Manifatturiera), covering state-owned industries in the south, were also created. The increasing use of the holding companies for partisan ends at the expense of efficiency, along with unrelenting pressure from the European Union (EU), finally resulted in the formal dissolution of IRI in 2000.

These extensive resources played an active role in Italy's reconstruction and in laying the groundwork for the Economic Miracle. From admirable beginnings, narrow partisanship and the rampant distribution of positions to key power groups' constituencies soon broke out. Influential jobs were doled out in proportion to parties' (or factions') political leverage—a phenomenon the Italians call *lottizzazione*. This created a system in which purely political, or extremely shortsighted, criteria governed decisions. Only with the collapse of the old party system and the establishment of more rigorous technical governments under Amato, Ciampi, and Dini in the 1990s was privatization undertaken in serious and sustained fashion. Even then, it was often ferociously opposed, and sometimes sabotaged, by entrenched interests inside the public firms as well as by powerful banking and industrial interests in the private sector that were in no rush to see the economy become too competitive.

Other State Institutions

With a centralized model copied largely from France, the Italian state reaches everywhere into society. We limit ourselves here to two areas of great importance for all democracies, and of particular significance for Italy: the use of force and the role of the judiciary.

The Military and the Police

Under the *Statuto albertino*, the military swore allegiance to the king, so that Victor Emmanuel III had the authority to order the arrest of Mussolini in 1943, and to have a legally constituted government negotiate an eventual alliance with the Allies. In the republic,

the armed forces primarily served to provide young men from different areas of the country with a sense of national identity. All males over eighteen had to serve eighteen months, and southerners were commonly posted in the north, and vice versa. By the 1990s, exemptions became increasingly easy to obtain, and the draft was entirely abolished in 2005.[11] The military is now supposed to be fully voluntary and much smaller in size, characterized by the sort of professionalism required in a modern, high-tech army.

The line between the military and the police is not always sharp in Italy: the term "forces of order" can refer to both the police and the military. The Carabinieri, for example, are a national police force trained and organized as a branch of the military, and historically they were staffed at the lower ranks with draftees. The regular police, in contrast, are responsible to the Ministry of the Interior.

The intensity of cold war polarization in Italy—above all the presence of the largest Communist party in the Western world—and the extensive social movements that have marked Italian politics ever since the 1960s meant that the postwar period was marked by encounters that were often violent and frequently lethal. The Italian military had several quick response battalions of shock troops stationed around the country, which were notorious for intervening in labor disputes. Through the 1950s and into the 1960s, the police or military regularly fired on demonstrating peasants or workers. In the 1960s and 1970s, deadly force decreased significantly and was almost always limited to demonstrating students or youth; the most recent case was in antiglobalization protests in Genoa in 2001, where the forces of order shot one demonstrator to death, and physically assaulted dozens of others.

The Judiciary

No institution played a more controversial role in the transition to Italy's so-called Second Republic than the judiciary. Like the rest of the political system, the judiciary was often exposed to blatant political manipulation. The fight against organized crime and political corruption was often hampered when investigations got too close to centers of political power. Since 1992, however, corruption scandals showed how effective judicial investigators could be when not held back. The corruption scandals turned prosecutors into national heroes, but they also sowed the seeds of bitter political resentment, reinforcing trends toward an increasingly politicized judiciary and raising troubling questions about the role of the courts in a modern democracy. Here, as elsewhere, Italy's institutional framework is far from consolidated.

Article 104 of the constitution affirms the judiciary's independence, and provides for a Superior Council of the Judiciary to guarantee that independence. Another departure from continental tradition was the introduction of judicial review, with the stipulation that a Constitutional Court would be the final arbiter of a law's constitutionality (Article 134). These innovations were reactions to fascism's abuses, but the DC stalled their implementation as long as it could.

The Constitutional Court, finally established in 1956, has fifteen members, appointed on a rotating basis to nine-year nonrenewable terms. A third of its members are named by Parliament, a third by the president of the republic, and the remaining third by the highest courts in the country. It can review cases only on appeal. It cannot, in other words, rule on the constitutionality of a law after it has been passed but before it is promulgated, as in France, nor can it be directly petitioned, as in Germany. But the appeals procedure has proven to be a powerful tool in addressing legislative paralysis. On numerous occasions, the Court has forced parliamentary action by striking down obsolete and regressive laws—for example, those regulating police powers and criminal procedures, or those governing family law and the role of women—that dated to the Fascist era. Faced with a legislative vacuum in the absence of the old laws, Parliament enacted far-reaching, modernizing reforms.

In the early postwar period, the highest-ranking judges were mostly Fascist appointees. Many never accepted the principle of judicial review and often ignored the Constitutional Court's rulings. They delayed the evolution of the legal and judicial system until, by the end of the 1970s, they had finally faded from the scene. The reason the previous system of justice had remained intact through the late 1950s was nakedly political. During the height of the cold war, the government aimed to marginalize the left and weaken it in every possible way. A Fascist penal code simplified that task.

'A LIVELLA

The major parties' perceived involvement in *Tangentopoli* **(1993). The executioner is the period's leading prosecutor, Antonio Di Pietro, who eventually entered politics himself.**
Source: © Giorgio Forattini, from *Mascalzonate: Il Meglio di Forattini a Colori*, courtesy Giorgio Forattini.

Because the 1931 code was intended to outlaw all political activity, it was easy to use the legal system to obstruct and harass the labor movement.

Pressures from above and below finally forced the system to change. The Constitutional Court's activism and relative independence have made it one of the more respected institutions in the country. This is less true of the higher levels of the regular criminal courts: investigations take blatantly false and politically motivated paths for years, powerful judges shift the venues of investigations to sabotage them, decisions are rendered for extremely obscure motives, and so on.

Formally, the judicial branch is insulated from direct political interference by the Superior Council of the Judiciary, which was finally instituted in 1959. This is a twenty-four-member body, two-thirds of whom are directly elected by members of the judiciary, further reinforcing its independence. Parliament chooses the remaining third from practicing lawyers and legal academics. In a clear effort to rein in the autonomy of the judiciary, the center-right weakened the Superior Council in 2002, doing everything it could to diffuse and fragment the way the judges choose their own representatives.[12]

The judiciary is governed by civil service rules (such as tenure and de facto automatic promotion based on seniority) in a setting that can be highly politicized. Since the 1970s, judges have engaged in job actions and, more rarely, strikes. The Superior Council has witnessed highly politicized disputes that break along classic left-right lines, but also more narrow, corporate struggles in which the judiciary as a body tries to assert its rights or prerogatives against anything perceived as outside interference.

Its willingness to organize and promote itself aggressively has strengthened the judiciary's already great power, raising serious questions about its insulation from the political process.[13] The bureaucracy of the Ministry of Justice is, notoriously, the creature of the judges, who are legally entitled to its top positions. Judges lobby external agencies with little concern for what would be considered a conflict of interest in other countries. They are also entitled to stand for political office and participate in arbitration panels or other semipublic agencies. These privileges—or abuses—have generated efforts over the years to cut down their power, which then further politicizes their role.

Delayed Reform. Textbooks written thirty-five years ago wondered how the Italian judicial system had survived into the 1970s, and matters have become much worse since then.[14] Judges themselves evoke contradictory public responses. There is great public sympathy for prosecuting magistrates, who sometimes literally risk their lives when they exercise the duties of office. In the late 1970s and early 1980s, they were targeted by left-wing terrorists; since then, threats and murders have been carried out by the mafia. At the same time, the arbitrary workings of the regular courts are legendary. Wrongful prosecutions, endless delays, and damaging leaks to the press without the possibility of response by the accused have ruined many reputations.

A new penal code was introduced in 1989, which mixes aspects of two different legal systems—not always coherently. Still, it is an improvement over the old (Fascist) code, in which, for instance, the accused was not informed of charges or evidence until a trial date was set. Pretrial investigations and trial deliberations are now far more open, but the new system takes even more time for evidence gathering and discovery than the old. (Well-heeled defendants—Berlusconi is a prime example—drag cases out until the statute of limitations expires.)

Public prosecutors are part of the judiciary in Italy and exercise more police powers than elsewhere in the West, where they are under the control of the executive branch. Aggressive prosecutorial techniques, combined with some magistrates' penchant for self-promotion and leaks to the press, created instant popular heroes in the 1990s, but also convinced some that the prosecutors had their own agenda. The worst abuses give pause to sober observers on all points of the political spectrum. Berlusconi's complaints about judicial abuses of power are self-serving, but they resonate among people who are not necessarily his political allies. At the same time, his obvious self-interest cast a shadow over his government's efforts to reform the judiciary—even when some proposals were quite reasonable.[15]

This is a pity, for improvements are long overdue. Cases are chronically backlogged, the machinery grinds slowly, and the intolerable becomes the norm. Those unfortunate enough to be jailed for minor offenses regularly serve the maximum sentence before coming to trial. An incredible 60 percent of Italy's prison population is awaiting trial, a situation regularly denounced by the European Court of Human Rights. Lawyers stall their clients' cases, knowing that amnesties are issued every few years to clear the docket. When sentences finally are handed down, they are often so lengthy and obscure that even experts have trouble deciphering them. And the judicial bureaucracy remains as rule-bound and labyrinthine as any in the Italian system. In a country that produces a sarcastic remark for almost every occasion, few are as telling as, "Italy is the cradle of the law and the grave of justice."

Local Government

There are three levels of subnational government in Italy: *comuni* (the Italian term for all municipalities, towns, and cities), provinces, and regions. As political entities, the *comuni* were by far the most important into the 1980s, and they remain the liveliest sites of local politics in the country. In administrative terms, however, the province was historically the major subdivision of the country, linked directly by the prefect, a member of the national bureaucracy, to the Ministry of the Interior in Rome and run at times like colonial offices. The idea of abolishing the provinces used to be considered in discussions of streamlining Italy's governing structures, but their number has actually increased in recent years. The regions had no formal status until the formation of the republic, and only the special regions had any significant powers until the 1970s. With the transfer of increasing power their way, regions have come to occupy the most important place in subnational politics.

The Comuni

There are roughly eight thousand *comuni* in Italy. Their relatively large size means that towns are generally populous enough to reproduce most of the parties, and the partisan conflict, found at the national level. In 1993, a new electoral law for towns with populations greater than fifteen thousand maintained list voting but introduced a separate, more important ballot for individual mayoral candidates.* Mayors are now directly elected, rather than being chosen by party leaders after the votes are counted. If no candidate obtains an absolute majority on the first ballot, a runoff is held between the two candidates who got the most votes. High voter turnout in general elections (around 80 percent) is nearly matched in local elections, which occur every five years. Mayors may only serve two full terms.

The new electoral system, which was introduced just as the old party system was imploding, helped rejuvenate local politics in Italy. Introduction of a property tax in 1994 provided the *comuni* with considerable financial autonomy. Big-city mayors now

enjoy high visibility and legitimacy because they can claim a clear popular mandate. Some have vaulted onto the national political stage. Other prominent politicians have been "parachuted" into big cities to give themselves more visibility.

The Regions and Italy's Emerging Federal Structure

The constitution provides for two types of regions. Five special regions received significant autonomy almost immediately. These include Sardinia, Sicily, and three areas on the northern border of the country with strong French, Germanic, and Slavic cultural characteristics. Various powers were supposed to devolve to the fifteen ordinary regions, but Parliament did not pass the relevant enabling legislation until 1970.

The PCI's strength in the red zones, where it regularly obtained more than 40 percent of the vote, explains why the DC dragged its heels in devolving power to the regions, thus depriving the opposition of an important political lever. This was not the only instance of constitutional sabotage by the DC, but it was the most nakedly partisan in motivation.

Like the larger city governments, regional councils vary in size according to population. They are elected for five-year terms, and, as has happened at every level of Italian political life in the 1990s, a new electoral system, different from all the others, is now in place. Influenced by the mayors' experience, a constitutional amendment passed in 2000 provides for the direct election of regional presidents in a single ballot. Alliances are constructed by party lists around individuals, with each list declaring its support of one or another candidate for regional president. Alliances are important, for only 80 percent of the seats are distributed proportionally to the lists. The remaining 20 percent serve as a premium to "top up" the winner's share, thus guaranteeing a working majority—generally a minimum of 55 to 60 percent of the seats. Winning majorities are "blocked" for two years—that is, alliances must be honored, or new elections are called. This arrangement avoids coalitions of convenience that would divide the victor's premium and then immediately dissolve, with each party keeping the additional seats for itself.

---

*For towns with fewer than fifteen thousand inhabitants, the list receiving the most votes, even a relative majority, receives two-thirds of the seats. The remaining third is divided proportionally among all other lists.

Rome's centralizing tendencies have been dramatically eroded in recent years. Several laws passed in 1997 and 1998 extensively overhauled the central government's relations with local government. Even more significant developments have taken place since 2001. In that year, the center-left, almost as its last act in office, passed a constitutional amendment enacting a semifederalist reform, which was then upheld by a popular referendum.* The center-right passed the most ambitious decentralizing reforms of all in 2005, devolving considerable powers to the regions.[16] But these changes were nullified when they were rejected by another constitutional referendum in 2006.

The current arrangement tries to maintain national unity and not aggravate the already large gap between north and south.[17] But it does formally create principles of federalism in the Italian constitution, including the explicit designation of some areas of legislation as exclusively the province of the regions, along with the principle of *subsidiarity*—that is, the idea that powers not explicitly reserved for the central state belong to its subnational units.

Evidence that the regions have become rooted in Italy is that they tend to reproduce the country's historical cleavages in their own operations. In a famous, and controversial, study, political scientist Robert Putnam argues that by almost all relevant measures—from how efficiently they deliver services to whether they even manage to spend the funds earmarked for their use—southern regions lag behind the rest of the country, while the red regions of the center and the industrialized areas of the north show the most initiative.[18] It is hard to argue with the evidence (although critics take issue with Putnam's explanation for north-south differences, which he traces all the way back to the Middle Ages). Efforts to put the 1997–1998 reforms into practice once again saw the north and center in the lead, with the south well in arrears. Yet some recent developments suggest that the situation in the south might not be quite as irreversible as Putnam sometimes seems to suggest. For instance, the Campania region, and its capital city, Naples, have made notable progress since the mid-1990s.

---

*All previous referenda in Italy, save for the 1946 vote that abolished the monarchy, were of the abrogative variety (see Chapter 19).

The European Dimension

As is the case for every member nation of the EU, it has become increasingly difficult to understand the functioning of many of Italy's political institutions in isolation from those of the EU. To cite just one example from the discussion of federalism immediately above: when the center-left revised the constitution, it made explicit reference to EU guidelines in rewriting Article 118. The new rules state that the central government has the right to determine whether regional legislation falls within EU legal guidelines; if it feels these are being violated, it can immediately refer the matter to the Constitutional Court.[19]

Even more revealing were Italy's efforts through the 1990s to enter the Economic and Monetary Union (EMU), and then to remain a member in good standing. This required modification not only of the country's policymaking processes, but of many of its structures as well. To ensure compliance with EU directives, the Department for the Coordination of Community Policies was established and given ministerial status. The same pressures led to the deregulation of financial markets, the abolition of the Ministry of State Holdings early in the 1990s, and, perhaps more subtly, the creation of the Treasury and Budget superministry later in the decade. These actions reflected the need to streamline and modernize economic decision making, but once EU standards had become imperative, such streamlining could not be avoided.

Nevertheless, as we saw in Chapter 17, not everything that has changed in Italy is a result of the *vincolo esterno*, the external constraint imposed by the EU. Internal factors played at least as significant a role in shaping Italy's recent evolution as did external ones. This is true of the governing of the economy, and it is even more true with regard to institutional changes.

The Policymaking Process

Postwar politics in Italy were indelibly marked by the intrusion of the country's parties into every nook and cranny of social, political, and economic life. This phenomenon was so pervasive that the Italian political system was described as a *partitocrazia* ("party-ocracy").

Its negative impact on the policymaking process is evident in everything from the sheer number of governments that Italy has had to endure to the tortured, fragmented, and conflict-riddled itinerary of so much of the legislation that successive governments have tried to shepherd through Parliament.

Since the 1980s, some things have changed in Italy, although only under great internal and external pressure. Nevertheless, even if they only did so under duress, Italy's governors proved that it is possible to streamline executive operations and executive-parliamentary relations, and to act decisively in areas of vital concern to the economy by producing budgets that many observers would have believed impossible a few years earlier.

These innovations were introduced thanks to several factors. One was a somewhat stronger and more assertive executive, made possible by the parties' crisis. Another was the decision to combine previously fragmented ministries into an economic "superministry" and start its life under the leadership of a figure as prestigious as Carlo Ciampi, the former governor of the Bank of Italy. Cautious senior civil servants in the old economic departments were bypassed in the new decision-making process, which passed the initiative to technocrats from the Bank of Italy and the Treasury, as well as to academic economists from the Finance Ministry and various think tanks.[20] Improved control by the executive over financial policy was duly noted by Berlusconi, who kept the same structures in place during his own time in office.

Perhaps the Italian system responds only to extraordinary pressure, but the past fifteen years show that not all pressure to change has to be generated externally. It may have taken the political earthquake of *Tangentopoli* and the collapse of the old party system, but these triggered an effort to overhaul the country's entire political practice. Recall that much of the attention to institutional reform grows out of a desire to see Italy become a "normal country." Repeated electoral reforms, various schemes to strengthen the executive, and many other proposals reflect a widely shared desire to simplify the party system and to create a bipolar alternation in power between government and opposition. Some goals have been realized, but with mixed results.

Berlusconi's victory in 2001, for example, marked the first time a coalition achieved solid majorities in both chambers—the conditions for the sort of majority rule that reformers had long hoped for. But although his second government broke the longevity record, its legislative achievements were rather modest.[21] Part of the explanation lies in the considerable energy spent on laws meant to ease Berlusconi's legal problems at the expense of more serious legislation. But his government's most ambitious initiative—an ambitious set of constitutional reforms—was rejected by the 2006 referendum.

As we have seen throughout this chapter—and indeed throughout the entire discussion of Italy—events since the 1990s have witnessed important changes, even though the fragmentation and polarization that dogged the First Republic persists and obviously compromises any complete transition to radically renovated institutional arrangements or practices. As long as such profound divisions persist, it is hard to be optimistic that truly significant departures in the policy realm will emerge in the near or even medium term.

Notes

[1] Massimo Giannini, "Le illusioni dello sconfitto," *La Repubblica*, April 21, 2005, p. 1.

[2] David Felsen, "Changes to the Italian Budgetary Regime: The Reforms of Law No. 94/1997," in David Hine and Salvatore Vassallo, eds., *Italian Politics: The Return of Politics* (Oxford: Berghahn Books, 2000), pp. 157–173.

[3] Silvio Buzzanca, "I ministeri sono aumentati e il centrosinistra insorge," *La Repubblica*, June 12, 2001, p. 4.

[4] Enzo Balboni, "President of the Republic, Judges and the Superior Council of the Judiciary," in Stephen Hellman and Gianfranco Pasquino, eds., *Italian Politics: A Review*, vol. 7 (London: Pinter, 1992), pp. 49–67.

[5] Gianfranco Pasquino and Salvatore Vassallo, "The Government of Carlo Azeglio Ciampi," in Carol Mershon and Gianfranco Pasquino, eds., *Italian Politics: Ending the First Republic* (Boulder, Colo.: Westview Press, 1995), pp. 55–73.

[6] David Hine, *Governing Italy: The Politics of Bargained Pluralism* (Oxford: Clarendon Press, 1993), esp. pp. 232, 237.

[7] Paul Furlong, *Modern Italy: Representation and Reform* (London: Routledge, 1994), pp. 87–88.

[8] Martin J. Bull and James L. Newell, *Italian Politics: Adjustment Under Duress* (Cambridge: Polity Press, 2005), p. 150.

[9] For the higher figure, see Furlong, *Modern Italy*, p. 88; for the lower number, see Hine, *Governing Italy*, p. 229.

[10] Maurizio Ferrera, "Il mercato politico-assistenziale," in Ugo Ascoli and Raimondo Catanzaro, eds., *La società italiana degli anni ottanta* (Bari: Laterza, 1988), pp. 327–328.

[11]Claudia Fusani, "Addio alla leva obbligatoria," *La Repubblica,* July 30, 2004, p. 12.

[12]David Nelken, "Berlusconi e i giudici: Legittimi sospetti?" in Jean Blondel and Paolo Segatti, eds., *Politica in Italia: Edizione 2003* (Bologna: Il Mulino, 2003), pp. 143–145.

[13]Giuseppe Di Federico, "La crisi del sistema giudiziario e la questione della responsabilità civile dei magistrati," in Piergiorgio Corbetta and Robert Leonardi, eds., *Politica in Italia: Edizione 88* (Bologna: Il Mulino, 1988), esp. pp. 108–113.

[14]P. A. Allum, *Italy: Republic Without Government?* (New York: Norton, 1973), p. 184; Raphael Zariski, *Italy: The Politics of Uneven Development* (Hinsdale, Ill.: Dryden Press, 1972), chap. 9, esp. p. 319.

[15]Patrizia Pederzoli, "The Reform of the Judiciary," in Carlo Guarnieri and James L. Newell, eds., *Italian Politics: Quo Vadis?* (New York: Berghahn Books, 2005), pp. 157–158.

[16]For an overview, see Salvatore Vassallo, "The Constitutional Reforms of the Center-Right," in Guarnieri and Newell, eds., *Italian Politics: Quo Vadis?*, pp. 117–135.

[17]This discussion draws on Anna Cento Bull, "Verso uno stato federale? Proposte alternative per la revisione costituzionale," in Paolo Bellucci and Martin Bull, eds., *Politica in Italia: Edizione 2002* (Bologna: Il Mulino, 2002), pp. 205–223.

[18]Robert Putnam, *Making Democracy Work* (Princeton, N.J.: Princeton University Press, 1993).

[19]Cento Bull, "Verso uno stato federale?" p. 207

[20]Claudio M. Radaelli, "Networks of Expertise and Policy Change in Italy," *South European Politics and Society* 3 (Autumn 1998): esp. pp. 4–18.

[21]Giliberto Capano and Marco Giuliani, "Il parlamento italiano tra logica di governo e logica istituzionale: Molto fumo per quale arrosto?" in Blondel and Segatti, *Politica in Italia: Edizione 2003*, pp. 174–182.

CHAPTER 19

Representation and Participation

An antifascist constitution left the Italian Parliament much stronger than its counterparts in the rest of Western Europe. Italy's parties benefited from this balance of political power and have continued to reinforce it, despite immense changes since the 1990s. We will also see that popular mobilization and protest have been in abundant supply for half a century and show no sign of abating.

The Legislature

By design, and because of political dynamics since World War II, Parliament is the overwhelming center of power in the Italian political system.

Parliament's Powers and Anomalies

Italy's Parliament votes governments into and out of office and has wide latitude in passing laws. In joint session, it elects (and may impeach) the president of the republic; it chooses a third of the members of the Constitutional Court and of the Superior Council of the Judiciary; and it may amend the constitution. There are two constitutional limits on parliamentary abuses of power. One is judicial review. The other is the abrogative referendum, permitting the nullification of all or part of some laws by popular vote.

Laws are made in a fashion similar to other parliamentary systems, although the executive has less control over the legislative agenda than elsewhere. Laws can be proposed either by the government or by private members, and Italy distinguishes itself in not limiting the number of private-member bills, although in recent years there has been a big drop in private-member bills that become laws.[1] Government bills usually originate in ministries, but in contrast to a country like France, with its activist state tradition (and competent top civil servants), this historically meant that innovation-shy bureaucrats passed along proposals dictated by the groups that incessantly lobby them. Only since the 1990s has a more expert corps of policymakers made its presence felt, at least in matters of finance and the economy.

Proposals then pass to the committee that corresponds to the relevant ministry, where many such proposals simply die. A number follow the "normal" legislative itinerary, familiar to students of parliamentary politics: after being picked apart and/or amended, bills are reported out of committee and submitted to Parliament. But in Italy more bills are passed in committee than on the floor of Parliament. The bills that do get to the floor are debated in two stages. First, a general motion for approval is presented, and the broad principles of the law are discussed. Then, specific articles are discussed in detail. At this stage amendments can be presented. (A classic obstructionist tactic is to present hundreds of microscopically different amendments.) This process is identical in each chamber, and bills must pass, in identical form, in both chambers.

Some rules seem designed to slow down operations and maximize potential mischief. The most unusual are worth brief examination.

Pure Bicameralism. The Chamber and the Senate, with roughly 950 total members, have *identical* powers. This clumsy arrangement was produced by differences between the Christian Democrats (DC) and the left in the Constituent Assembly. Neither side got what it wanted, and they could only agree on something with no apparent virtues. No standing committee exists to reconcile different versions of the same law; each chamber must pass identical versions of a bill. Stalling or sabotage is most evident when controversial legislation is at stake (such as abortion in the late 1970s, or conflict of interest in the late 1990s). Yet when the will exists, party leaders quickly come to terms. Pure bicameralism is an absurd impediment in a system that already has enough problems.

Committees That Legislate. As in other legislatures, standing committees can amend proposals beyond recognition or kill them by refusing to refer them to the floor of the Chamber or Senate. But committees can also pass proposals on most subjects directly into law under conditions that are far less open to scrutiny than on the floor of Parliament. In these circumstances, committees meet with deliberative powers (*in sede deliberante*). The cabinet, one-fifth of the committee's members, or a tenth of the members of the Chamber can demand that a bill be brought to the floor and voted up or down without debate. This option is exercised only with regard to controversial laws. In this way, Parliament's standing committees often become miniature legislatures, which explains Italy's prolific legislative production. Over a thousand laws, most addressing minor matters, are passed in a five-year legislature, and three-quarters of these are passed *in sede deliberante*. Yet even this figure represents a huge drop compared with the past.[2]

The Secret Ballot.   A secret ballot was originally required for all votes in the Chamber of Deputies. Although not strictly required in the Senate, secret ballots are used there as well, when requested (as is often the case). The 1848 *Statuto albertino* devised this as a way to control party leaders, but its effect is to keep citizens from knowing how their representatives vote. Secret ballots are licenses to sabotage one's own party or coalition. Italians call this "sniping," and it has undermined many governments. Since the late 1980s, spending and revenue bills require open votes, and only constitutional amendments, electoral regulations, and questions of personal morality and family law are now subject to secret balloting. Nonetheless, secret ballots can still disrupt Parliament.

Representative Principles and the Electoral System

Adults over eighteen are automatically registered to vote for the Chamber of Deputies. Citizens twenty-five or older vote for senators. Both chambers are completely renewed in general elections. Parliament sits for a maximum of five years; the average legislature has lasted just under four years. Senators must be at least forty years old, and deputies twenty-one. Through 1992, elections were held under a nearly unrestricted form of proportional representation (PR), especially for the 630-seat Chamber, where 1.5 percent of the vote usually guaranteed seats to a party. Under PR, voters select a party list, and seats are then assigned in proportion to each party's vote.

In 1993, riding the tide of *Tangentopoli*, reformers hoped to eliminate PR, reduce the number of parties, and force representatives to be more responsive to their constituents. They also sought to produce a bipolar party system. It might be unrealistic to expect Italy's fragmented party system to shake down to just a few parties, but even two clear clusters or coalitions would be a big improvement. A bipolar party system has in fact resulted, but it remains fragmented.

Electoral System Changes

The 1993 reform produced a system similar to the one that elects the German Bundestag, but the Italian version is more complicated. Three-fourths of the seats in the Chamber of Deputies were allocated to single-member districts; the remaining one-quarter were determined by PR lists. Because the Parliament that passed this law contained sixteen parties, the resulting compromise was inevitable.[3] The prevalence of winner-take-all contests forced parties to form alliances before the elections, and to find presentable candidates throughout the country if they hoped to be successful. (In the past, candidates' success was guaranteed by their placement high on the list, and negotiations over government took place after the results were in.)

Between 1994 and 2001, this mixed system generated a bipolar logic, which in turn produced the desired alternation in power of center-right and center-left coalitions. But in 2005, the center-right brought back PR, with several features designed to encourage large electoral blocs (hence preserving bipolarity). Smaller parties must obtain a minimal vote threshold in order to be awarded seats in Parliament, but the floor is lower for parties that enter pre-electoral alliances. Most importantly, the alliance that receives the most votes is guaranteed a minimum of 55 percent of the seats in the Chamber. The Senate also has a seat bonus, but it is assigned on a regional basis, and hence does not guarantee a governing majority. The 2005 reform also designated a number of seats in each chamber to Italians living overseas, something the far right had long demanded.

These changes reflected desperate efforts by Berlusconi to block an expected center-left victory in 2006, but the institutional tinkering backfired. The center-left won by the narrowest of margins in the Chamber (.07 percent), yet obtained a sixty-six seat majority thanks to the bonus. In the Senate, it actually received a few thousand votes less than the center-right, but the overseas vote gave it a two-seat majority.[4] The center-left is committed to eliminating the present system, so we can expect a new, and presumably highly complicated, electoral system before too long.

Referenda as a Direct Link to the People

In 1946, a referendum abolished the monarchy and made Italy a republic. The 1948 constitution allows for two types of popular referendum. The first (Chapter 18) may be called to ratify a constitutional revision that did not obtain a two-thirds majority in Parliament. This measure has been used twice, in 2001 and 2006. The second is the abrogative referendum; as the name indicates, this challenges all or part of an existing law. Its first use was an unsuccessful attempt in 1974 to abolish the 1970 divorce law. It has been employed fourteen times, on fifty-nine different laws.[5]

An abrogative referendum's sponsors must specify the law, or parts of a law, to be eliminated. This requires half a million valid voters' signatures or identical motions passed by five regional councils. The Constitutional Court then rules on the validity of the challenge. If the referendum is declared admissible, a vote must be held within a prescribed period, with all the costs and disruptions that this implies. Should Parliament amend the targeted legislation before the vote, the referendum is nullified. If a vote is held, and at least half the electorate turns out, the law is either abrogated (a majority votes yes) or it stands.

Some referenda have represented true watersheds. In addition to divorce, one could cite 1981, when abortion was upheld, or 1985, when the CGIL's effort to defend the *scala mobile* was defeated. In 1991 and 1993, referenda forced changes in the electoral system, which speeded the collapse of the old party system. But referenda have been used so indiscriminately that their future is uncertain: the last five efforts were all nullified because of low turnout.

Political Parties and the Evolving Party System

Italy was dominated for two generations by a handful of parties and a distinctive party system. The older parties either no longer exist or have changed dramatically. After fifteen years, the new party system is still consolidating. It is important to understand the current dynamic and the most likely scenarios. Yet ignoring the historical context would render the present system incomprehensible.

The Party System Through the Late 1980s: Christian Democratic Centrality

The starting point is the DC's dominance. For nearly thirty years, some of Western Europe's most turbulent socioeconomic changes barely rippled the surface of the Italian party system. The vote for Christian Democracy wavered less than a single percentage point in five consecutive elections in the 1960s and 1970s (Table 19.1). DC "centrality" refers to two things: its occupation of the center of the political spectrum and the fact that it was the key player in every government of the First Republic. The large left-wing and smaller right-wing opposition parties were ruled out of participation in any government, for they were not considered loyal to the democratic rules of the game. Deep divisions, mirrored by PR, created one of the most complex yet immobile party systems in the democratic world.

In the forty-five years that centrist or center-left coalitions governed Italy, the only mystery was which minor parties would join the DC in power. The center, totally dominated by the DC, held stable at around 40 percent through the 1970s. Three small lay (non-Catholic) parties were the DC's satellites. When the DC's share of the vote dropped well below 40 percent in the 1980s, its reliance on the Socialist Party (PSI) became absolute, a dependency the PSI was quick to exploit.

Although the left was divided between Communists and Socialists, it was dominated by the PCI from 1948 on. Smaller parties—far left, ecological, and civil libertarian—commanded limited support. Counting the PSI as left-wing (a problematic assumption by the 1980s), the left steadily rose to a high of more than 45 percent in the 1970s but slipped to around 40 percent thereafter.

The neofascist MSI (Italian Social Movement) monopolized the extreme right from the 1970s on. This was the real pariah of the party system, because of its fascist past, but also because its commitment to democracy remained questionable into the 1980s.

Table 19.1

Vote Obtained by Italian Parties in General Elections Under Proportional Representation During the "First Republic," 1946–1992 (percentage obtained by each party list in the 1946 Constituent Assembly and in the Chamber of Deputies thereafter)

Party	1946	1948	1953	1953	1963	1968	1972	1976	1979	1983	1987	1992
Far Left[a]	18.9%	—	—	—	—	4.5%	2.8%	1.5%	2.2%	1.5%	1.7%	5.6%
PCI/PDS	[d]	31%[b]	22.6%	22.7%	25.3%	27.0	27.2	34.4	30.4	29.9	26.6	16.1
PSI	20.7	—	12.7	14.3	13.9	14.5[c]	9.6	9.6	9.8	11.4	14.3	14.5
PR	—	—	—	—	—	—	—	1.1	3.5	2.2	2.6	1.2
Greens	—	—	—	—	—	—	—	—	—	—	2.5	3.0
PSDI	[d]	7.1	4.5	4.6	6.1	[d]	5.1	3.4	3.8	4.1	3.0	2.9
PRI	4.4	2.5	1.6	1.4	1.4	2.0	2.9	3.1	3.0	5.1	3.7	4.7
Leagues[e]	—	—	—	—	—	—	—	—	—	—	0.5	8.7
DC	35.2	48.5	40.1	42.4	38.3	39.1	38.7	38.7	38.3	32.9	34.3	29.7
PLI	6.8	3.8	3.0	3.0	7.0	5.8	3.9	1.3	1.9	2.9	2.1	3.0
Far Right[f]	8.1	4.8	12.8	9.0	6.9	5.8	8.7	6.1	5.9	6.8	5.9	5.4
Others	4.4	2.3	2.7	1.4	1.1	1.3	1.1	0.8	1.2	3.2	2.8	3.2
Total	100.0	100.0	100.0	100.0	100.0	100.0	100.0	100.0	100.0	100.0	100.0	100.0

[a] For 1963 and 1968, includes the PSIUP, which split from the PSI; from 1992, includes Rifondazione Comunista, which split from the PCI/DS.

[b] Result of united PCI-PSI list (Democratic Popular Front).

[c] Result of united PSI-PSDI list (United Socialist Party).

[d] Social Democrats were part of the PSI in 1946, split in 1947, then temporarily reunited with them during 1966–1969.

[e] Lombard League until 1992; Northern League thereafter.

[f] Uomo Qualunque and monarchists in 1946; neofascists and monarchists until 1972; MSI (neofascists) until 1992; AN thereafter.

Key: AN = National Alliance; DC = Christian Democracy; MSI = Italian Social Movement; PCI = Italian Communist Party; PDS = Democratic Party of the Left; PLI = Italian Liberal Party; PR = Radical Party (until 1992; Pannella list thereafter); PRI = Italian Republican Party; PSI = Italian Socialist Party; PSDI = Italian Social Democratic Party; PSIUP = Socialist Party of Proletarian Unity.

Sources: For 1946 and 1948, Giuseppe Mammarella, *Italy After Fascism: A Political History, 1943–1965* (Notre Dame, Ind.: University of Notre Dame Press, 1966), pp. 116, 194. Data since the 1953 elections compiled by author from newspapers.

The End of the Old Equilibrium (1989 and Beyond)

A dozen parties held seats at the beginning of the 1980s; by the 1990s their number had reached sixteen. More dramatic, the share of the vote going to lists that had not existed in the early 1980s went from a tenth in 1987, to a quarter in 1992, to nearly half in 1994.

The crumbling old system finally succumbed to the combined onslaught of international and domestic events (the fall of communism, exploding deficits and accumulated debt, and *Tangentopoli*). Finally, the new electoral system, introduced in 1993, made it more difficult for the crisis-riddled DC to occupy the middle of the spectrum.

The old system collapsed with astonishing speed. By 1994, the PSI was all but wiped out. The once mighty DC had lost its left wing, renamed itself, and then lost its right wing. It tried to run as a centrist alternative to the left and right in 1994, and plunged from 30 percent to a mere 11 percent of the vote. Then it split again. The neofascist MSI broadened its appeal for 1994, and began a serious transformation after 1995. Berlusconi leaped to prominence at the head of Forza Italia, which had not even existed five months earlier, and led a center-right alliance dubbed the Freedom Pole to victory.

Berlusconi's victory demonstrated that it was absolutely essential to build broad alliances before elections. The left's defeat convinced the former communist PDS that its only hope of victory lay in a broad center-left alliance, which produced the Ulivo (Olive Tree) alliance for the 1996 elections. Led by Romano Prodi, a Catholic with impressive economic credentials, the Ulivo defeated a badly divided Freedom Pole. But serious divisions weakened the center-left, which was defeated in 2001 by a renamed (House of Freedoms) but essentially identical coalition to the one that won in 1994. In 2006, the center-left, itself now called the Union, won the narrowest of victories.

Despite important changes, the new party system is more fragmented than the old. Differences in style and content separate Berlusconi from his post-Fascist and former Christian Democratic partners, to say nothing of the Northern League. The left is, if anything, just as divided, and it projects an image of constant bickering and maneuvering. Moreover, several old and new political groups, remnants of the former DC and some lay parties of the center, are unhappy with the system's bipolar logic. Uncomfortable in either bloc, they dream of controlling the balance of power from the center, which so recently seemed destined to remain irrelevant.

Christian Democracy and Its Successors

The DC's catch-all, multiclass, composite nature allowed it to be all things to all people. This may have denied Italy a true conservative party, not to mention consistency in economic or social policy, but it was an impressive recipe for raw political success. Its guaranteed governing role kept the DC united, despite deep internal divisions.

DC support rested on four pillars: religion, anticommunism, patronage, and the halo effect that derived from being in power as Italy rapidly developed into a prosperous, advanced capitalist democracy. As most of these factors eroded, and anticommunism disappeared altogether, patronage became increasingly important in holding together disparate constituencies. Slipping strength forced the DC to distribute more spoils to its partners (above all, the PSI). The 1980s saw limits imposed on state spending because of ballooning deficits and the growing national debt, policed by the European Community.

Corruption scandals in the 1990s finally made the DC vulnerable to head-on attack. This was more a political than a judicial vulnerability, for governing parties had weathered past scandals with impunity. But with the alibi of anticommunism finally exhausted, the old political elite could finally be held accountable for its many shortcomings.

The DC fell below 30 percent of the vote in 1992—*before* the most damaging revelations of *Tangentopoli*. Then, once the scandal broke, the DC went into free fall. Already losing ground to the League in the north, it was now being displaced by the MSI in the south. The 1994 name change to the Popular Party (PPI—its original name when founded after World War I) represented an effort to salvage some respectability for this once mighty machine. But it was too late.[6]

The bipolar logic of the new electoral system crushed the PPI between the left and Berlusconi's Pole in 1994. It was most severely punished in the new single-member districts, where it won only four seats (out of 475). Following this debacle, the PPI's right wing joined another ex-DC remnant in Berlusconi's coalition where they eventually formed the Union of Christian Democrats (UDC). The PPI won the right to keep its name after a nasty legal battle and joined the Ulivo. Reflecting the old DC's centrist vocation, most former Christian Democrats have never been entirely comfortable in either of Italy's two dominant electoral blocs.

Between Left and Right: Centrist Parties and Formations

The minor lay parties went into crisis in the 1980s, when Craxi moved the Socialists toward the center, crowding a small political space. Increasing bipolarity after 1994 effectively sealed these parties' fates. Most who allied with Berlusconi joined his party, Forza Italia. Others were among the founders of the Ulivo in 1995 or later joined other left-leaning centrists.

Aside from genuine ideological differences, political grudges and maneuvering for position have hurt the center-left's image. Prodi's followers, furious when he was pushed out of office in 1998, joined with others to form their own party, hoping to strengthen what they called the "centrist leg" of the coalition. This party then spent much of the next two years trying to undermine D'Alema, whom they blamed for allowing Prodi to be dumped. In 2001, Prodi's supporters joined other Catholics and lay centrists to give concrete form to the "centrist leg," creating a new party, Democracy Is Liberty (DL), more commonly known by its symbol, the Daisy (Margherita). In 2001, with 14.5 percent, this new group came close to equaling the DS's total (see Table 19.2). In 2006, the two main parties in the coalition ran together under the Olive Tree symbol and obtained 31.2 percent of the vote, almost exactly their separate 2001 results.

The Left

Italy is unique in the West in having a Communist Party or its successor dominate the left throughout the postwar period. The post-Communists have tried several times to reinvent themselves and revitalize the left, with disappointing results. In 2006, the most ambitious effort to date was launched, aiming to produce a single center-left party out of the Olive Tree coalition.

The Communist Party (PCI)/Democratic Party of the Left (PDS)/Left Democrats (DS). The left continues to be dominated by the heir to the PCI. Despite its evolution before the end of communism and its total transformation since then, the "original sin" of the Left Democrats (Democratici di Sinistra, DS) is something neither opponents nor allies let it forget.

The PCI almost became a governing party in the 1970s, when it reached 34.4 percent of the vote. In 1989, however, when the Berlin Wall fell, its fortunes had been declining for a decade. It then embarked on a radical revision of its name, symbol, and structure. After two years of lacerating divisions and a schism, the PCI formally became the PDS in 1991, adopting an oak tree as its new symbol, relegating the old hammer and sickle to the base of the tree. In 1996, the PDS nosed out Forza Italia as the largest party in the country, although with a mere 21 percent of the vote. In 1998, seeking to expand its base and appeal, it changed its name again, but aside from dropping the hammer and sickle, the DS only managed to absorb some minuscule leftist formations. Later in the same year, its secretary, Massimo D'Alema, replaced Prodi—the first former Communist to lead a Western government. But a cabinet shuffle, not an election, put him in office.

When the Ulivo chose a candidate for prime minister for the 2001 elections, it named the centrist mayor of Rome; his main rival was the ex-Socialist prime minister Giuliano Amato. The DS, reminded by its allies that moderate voters are leery of former Communists, did not put forward a candidate of its own.

An Electoral and Strategic Dilemma. The PCI was in crisis long before communism collapsed in the East. Changes begun in the late 1980s by Secretary-General Achille Occhetto, such as making ecology and feminism central planks in the party's platform, were an effort to make the PCI relevant to younger Italians while defining a new identity.

The PDS's beginnings were not very promising. It rose to just over 20 percent in 1994, but Berlusconi's victory drove home the point that if the left ceded the center of the spectrum to others, it would remain on the losing side of every election. Massimo D'Alema took over the party in 1994, and swiftly moved it even further toward the center. Under a new leader for the 2001 elections, the DS fell back to its historic low point

Table 19.2

Election Results in the "Second Republic": Chamber of Deputies, 1994–2006

List or Bloc	1994 Seats*	1994 Percentage of Vote**	1996 Seats*	1996 Percentage of Vote**	2001 Seats*	2001 Percentage of Vote**	2006 Seats*	2006 Percentage of Vote**
Center-Right[a]	**336**		**246**		**368**		**281**	49.7
Forza Italia	99	21.0	122	20.6	189	29.4	140	23.7
MSI/AN	108	13.4	92	15.7	97	12.0	72	12.3
Ex-DC	29	[b]	30	5.8	41	3.2	39	6.8
Minor Lay Parties	8	3.5	2	1.9	11	1.0	4	2.3
Lega Nord	117	8.4			30	3.9	26	4.6
Lega Nord (alone in 1996)			**59**	10.1				
Pact for Italy (1994)	**4**							
PPI (split in 1995)	33	11.1						
Segni Pact	13	4.6						
Center-Left[c]	**213**		**284**		**242**		**348†**	49.8
PDS/DS	109	20.4	150	21.1	138	16.5	226[d]	31.2
"For Prodi" (1996) Daisy List (2001)	—	—	67	6.8	76	14.5		
Ex-PSI, Lay Parties	14	2.2	32	4.3	[e]		18	2.6
Verdi	11	2.7	14	2.5	18	2.2	15	2.1
Other Leftist Groups	30	3.1	19	4.0	9	1.7	16	2.3
Others	22	4.4						
Rifondazione Comunista (allied in 1994 and 2006)	39	6.0	**35**	8.6	**11**	5.0	41	5.8

Note: From 1994–2001, the electoral system used had 475 single-member constituencies (75% of all seats); the remaining 155 seats were distributed according to the proportion of votes obtained by party lists. In 2006 the system was a proportional list system with a bonus that ensured a 55 percent majority of seats to the largest list. Numbers will not add up to 100 percent or 630 seats because lists and blocs are selective.

*Boldfaced numbers indicate all seats won outright by a bloc or by separate lists.

**Percentage of vote is that obtained by individual lists on the separate proportional ballot from 1994 to 2001. For 2006, there was only a proportional ballot with the exception of 11 very large overseas single-member districts.

†Includes the bonus assigned to the largest allied list.

[a]In 1994, ran as Freedom Pole (north) and Pole of Good Government (center-south); in 1996, ran as Freedom Pole; in 2001 and 2006, ran as House of Freedom.

[b]Did not present a separate list; all seats were won in single-member contests.

[c]In 1994, ran as a leftist alliance called the Progressives; in 1996 and 2001, ran as the Olive Tree; in 2006, ran as the Union.

[d]In 2006, the DS and the Daisy List ran together as the Olive Tree List.

[e]With Daisy List in 2001.

Source: Compiled by the author from various press and Web sources.

(16 percent) and has been plagued with continuous internal squabbling, which further undermines its public image.

Nor did the loss of the most militant factions to Rifondazione Comunista in 1991 solve the identity crisis, which has dragged on for over fifteen years. From the start, those who remained in the party differed fundamentally about its future.[7] Should it remain solidly within the socialist family, albeit moving more toward the center? Or should it conclude that old left-wing identities have become obsolete and that the future lies in turning a broad coalition like the Ulivo into a new political party? The latter view gained strength over the years, and was formally ratified in 2007—against the strong opposition of what remained of the DS's left wing.

Toward the Democratic Party?   Prodi's success as the only leader to defeat Berlusconi (twice) suggested that the center-left's future lay more toward the center than the left. A former left-wing Christian Democrat, Prodi proved the value of technical competence combined with the ability to build bridges to more moderate (and Catholic) electors.

The center-left's victory in 2006 accelerated the belief within its two major components that the time had finally come to take the next logical step and turn an electoral alliance (the Ulivo in 1996 and 2001, the Union in 2006) into a political party. In 2007, both the DS and the Margherita held congresses that committed them to join together in a Democratic Party by the end of the year.[8]

This is a huge gamble, for, even without its left wing, there is much that divides the DS from the Margherita—especially such important issues as the role of the Catholic Church in Italian society—as well as very intense personal rivalries. However desirable a simplification of the party system might be, there is little evidence so far that the different components of the center-left have more success when running under the same label than they do when they compete separately in an electoral alliance.

Smaller Left-Wing Groupings.   Much of what remained of the left wing of the DS announced that it would not join the PD. Instead, it would seek to create a new grouping—tentatively named Democratic Left—out of the various forces on the left side of the spectrum.

This will likely be a loose coalition, for unity on the left has always been elusive.

Ex-Socialists.   No party was more devastated by *Tangentopoli* than the PSI. It barely managed 2 percent of the vote in 1994, after which it disintegrated into squabbling mini-groups. By then, Craxi was a fugitive from justice; he died in exile in Tunisia in 2000. The new leadership of the PSI took the party into the center-left, but most *craxiani* became Berlusconi's partners; some joined Forza Italia, while others formed their own tiny party.

The Far Left.   From the 1960s on, the PCI's increasing moderation drove the most militant leftists outside the party. Even after the mass mobilizations of the Hot Autumn, this space remained restricted, although the small (2 percent) Proletarian Democracy (Democrazia Proletaria, DP) tried to expand its appeal by becoming a vocal exponent of feminism, antinuclearism, and ecology as these themes gained support in Italy.

The 1991 creation of Partito della Rifondazione Comunista (PRC), or the Communist Refoundation Party, altered the nature of the far left. Its roots in the PCI gave the new party 150,000 members, ties to the unions, and considerable mass appeal. But in addition to radicals who left the old PCI, Rifondazione included rigid Stalinist ex-Communists as well. When DP dissolved and joined Rifondazione, the PRC became a grab bag of everyone to the left of the PDS.

Rifondazione has polled between 5 and 9 percent, giving it considerable leverage in Italy's fragmented politics. It faces a delicate balancing act between supporting center-left governments and leading a left-wing opposition that is social (that is, extraparliamentary) as well as political. It underwent internal splits in both 1995 and 1998 as dissidents broke ranks to support the government in power. The second split occurred when the PRC withdrew its external support of Prodi's government, forcing his resignation. Five years of Berlusconi finally convinced Rifondazione's leadership to join the center-left in 2006, and one of the party's rewards was to see its leader named Speaker of the Chamber of Deputies.

The PRC and the former left wing of the DS will dominate any new left-wing grouping that emerges as a counterpoint to the Democratic Party.

Other Small Formations. The Green phenomenon came late to Italy, which meant that many activists had previous political experiences and identities, ranging from the moderate center to the far left. A single group was formed in 1990 but remained quite divided internally. Intensely committed to their own independence, the Greens initially refused to join the Ulivo but eventually supported Prodi and his successors, usually winning the environmental portfolio. Jealous of their autonomy, they most recently refused to participate in the preparations to found the Democratic Party.

Another group whose impact has been greater than its small size is the Radical Party (PR). Its leader, Giacinto (Marco) Pannella, has been among Italy's most flamboyant political figures. He is given to hyperbolic statements and actions such as hunger strikes and was immodest enough to name the group after himself (the Pannella List) when he liquidated the PR in the early 1990s for egotistical reasons.[9]

The PR embraced causes ignored by others: women's rights, civil rights (of a libertarian sort), conscientious objection, and ecology. Starting in the 1970s, it used the referendum more often than any other organization in order to embarrass the major parties. It has also stressed developed countries' responsibilities to the Third World. The Radicals are hard to categorize using standard left-right criteria. Pannella supported Berlusconi in 1994 but brought his party into the center-left by 2001. The Radicals once represented an innovative form of protest politics, but their limited repertoire and changing times have marginalized them.

The Center-Right Freedom Pole/ House of Freedoms

Divisions on the center-right are as great as those on the center-left, but the balance of power within the House of Freedoms gives it more stability than the Ulivo. Berlusconi remains the only plausible candidate to lead this alliance, which casts a shadow over the future. His party is more than twice the size of its next-largest ally, further reinforcing his position, to his partners' frequent chagrin. Squabbling aside, truly profound changes have taken place on the right of the political spectrum in Italy.

Ex-DC Centrists. These are the most moderate members of the coalition, many of whom accept the bipolar logic of the new party system through gritted teeth and would prefer to be part of a centrist "third pole." Several different rump parties have formed, dissolved, and re-formed under one Christian Democratic label or another; in its present incarnation as the UDC (Unione dei Democratici Cristiani, Union of Christian Democrats) it obtained nearly 7 percent of the vote in 2006. They are both social and economic conservatives in Italian terms, but these former Christian Democrats are also embarrassed by their coalition partners. In the 1990s, they had more reservations about the post-Fascists. More recently the League's stridency (and occasional racism) and continuing disagreements with Berlusconi have made the UDC the alliance's most restive member.

The Lega Nord. In 1991, the strongest of various regional leagues, the Lombard League, led by the mercurial Umberto Bossi, brought them all together as the Northern League (Lega Nord). Leagues first appeared in DC strongholds in the northeast, in areas historically hostile to the state and outside intervention. Ilvo Diamanti, an acute observer, notes that the various leagues departed from more traditional bases of identity and representation, such as religion versus secularism, or class, and took other longstanding cleavages (such as north-south, center-periphery, "common folks" versus big government) and gave them fresh expression, altering the political landscape.[10] In the words of another student of the phenomenon, the League turned the southern question into the northern question.[11] The small businesses and industries it represents have been dynamic contributors to Italy's economy. But for the League, they are also the repositories of traditional virtues in a rapidly changing world; they are the expression of family (as opposed to impersonal corporate) values and of deep roots in small communities.

The Lega began as an antitax, anti-big government movement. It presented itself as the defender of honest, hardworking "little people" of the north whose taxes subsidize a bloated Roman bureaucracy and its southern clients, portrayed in stereotyped terms as lazy parasites. The Lega was originally pro-EU, arguing that the virtuous north would be part of a "Europe based on regions." Highly critical of Berlusconi and his post-Fascist ally, Bossi nevertheless led the Lega into the center-right in 1994, effectively guaranteeing its victory in the north—and hence in Italy. But when Bossi saw his grassroots support slipping, he brought down the government after only six months. Bossi then set the Lega on a more radical path. He resuscitated separatist ideas and became highly critical of the European Union, now viewed as the expression of big business, economically and culturally antithetical to northern business-people and workers alike. And while there was still no love lost for southern Italians, the truly menacing "outsiders"[12] were now being identified as the immigrants who threaten Italy's Christian, European identity.

The Lega's high point came in 1996, when, running separately under the mixed electoral system, it gained more votes than any other party in the north; by splitting the center-right vote in single-member districts, it enabled the Ulivo to win. By the end of the 1990s, the Lega's stridency made it easier for Forza Italia to attract the support of business. Moreover, Bossi's "go it alone" stance created tension within his own movement. Activists worried that isolation would condemn the Lega to permanent political isolation.

Pragmatism finally prevailed. Bossi increasingly spoke of devolution rather than separation. His criticism of the Vatican turned into an emphasis on traditional Christian values. With a firm promise from Berlusconi to introduce a federalist reform of the constitution, the League joined the House of Freedoms. Now that the center-right could present a single candidate in northern single-member constituencies, it won nearly three-quarters of these seats in 2001 and was back in power. From his position as minister of institutional reform, Bossi made sure that immigration reform and, of course, devolution were put high on the parliamentary agenda. Bossi was seriously incapacitated by a stroke in 2004 and has been somewhat less visible since then, but he remains the League's unquestioned leader.

The Lega entered the second Berlusconi government in precarious health, which helps explain its provocative behavior. Its support, on a downward trend after 1996, plummeted in 2001 and only recovered slightly in 2006 to 4.6 percent. Absolute numbers can be deceptive, since its support is highly concentrated in the north, but in 1996, it gained over 10 percent of the national vote.

Forza Italia. When Berlusconi burst onto the political scene in late 1993, his party was dubbed the *partito-azienda*, or "Company Party," since its structure and

staff came from his business empire. Forza Italia (FI) was more than a facade, however; skilled advertising executives used their expertise to create a formidable electoral machine. Berlusconi conducted a smooth American-style campaign informed by focus group research and extensive public opinion polling.[13] That someone with so many interests would seek to protect them is evident. That he would vault into Palazzo Chigi (the prime minister's residence) as head of the largest party in the country six months after entering politics is extraordinary. And that in the course of this unprecedented personal triumph he would also help radically reshape Italian politics, not least by bringing the MSI into the democratic fold and hastening its evolution, was yet another triumph for the man known as "Il Cavaliere" (from his honorific title, Knight of Labor). He and his advisors immediately understood that the new electoral law would reward alliance building, and he proved immensely talented at that task.

But Il Cavaliere proved a better campaigner than prime minister, a better empire builder than politician. He also claimed not to understand why people thought it problematic that he owned three of Italy's four private networks and directly or indirectly controlled all three public networks. Berlusconi's obtuseness and insincerity over conflicts of interest undermined his credibility even among his supporters.

Yet he did not simply sulk after being driven into the opposition in 1995. He dramatically reorganized his party, giving it a solid grassroots structure with incentives to ensure participation and a semblance of internal democracy.[14] Externally, he lobbied incessantly for greater legitimacy and was rewarded in 1999 when FI was allowed to join the European Popular Party (Christian Democrats) in the European Parliament. And Forza Italia is now not only Italy's largest party, it is arguably also the best-organized, given the DS's drift and internal divisions.[15]

Berlusconi remains Forza Italia's—and the House of Freedom's—greatest strength as well as its greatest liability. His behavior is always self-serving, and often erratic and unstatesmanlike. His willingness to have Parliament pass laws made to measure for him and his cronies, his insensitivity to the very idea of a conflict of interest, his outbursts against the judiciary, and his seeming indifference to democratic practices all explain why some of his allies would like to see him disappear. Yet he remains the dominant figure on the center-right and the only one capable of keeping it together.

The (Former) Far Right.   Since the postwar republic was explicitly antifascist, formally banning the reconstitution of the Fascist Party,[16] the MSI was the true pariah of the First Republic. It was the direct descendant of the ugliest, pro-Nazi phase of the Fascist Party. It flirted with antidemocratic elements and remained ambiguous about democracy well into the 1980s. As its leadership and original constituency aged, the MSI's appeal centered on anticommunism and a hard line on law and order. It called for state intervention in the economy, considering free-market capitalism to be antisocial. The MSI always championed family values, and despite strong anticlerical strains in the original Fascist movement, this party was pro-life and generally conservative on matters of church doctrine. But because it had been excluded from office throughout the postwar period, it could attack the degeneration of the party system.

The MSI was shaken by the end of communism. Its future appeared bleak as it became clear that proportional representation was on its way out. The new electoral systems required alliances, and who would make common cause with Mussolini's heirs?

The DC's collapse rescued the MSI. Stepping into the vacuum, the party vaulted to prominence in mayoral elections in Rome and Naples in December 1993. Berlusconi gave the neofascists a big boost by declaring that he would willingly vote for them against the left. The MSI lost both runoffs, but it was now a force to be reckoned with. Its telegenic young leader, Gianfranco Fini, scrambled to reassure the public by adopting free-market rhetoric and creating a broad right-wing National Alliance (AN) with the help of a few refugees from the DC and PLI. But everyone knew that the AN was the creature of the MSI.

The postfascists became Italy's third-largest party in 1994, more than doubling their vote (to over 13 percent). The AN became Berlusconi's most faithful ally, and its loyalty was richly rewarded in terms of cabinet seats, undersecretaries, and appointments to myriad patronage positions. After the government's forced resignation, the AN remained unswervingly loyal to Berlusconi.

The MSI's transition to full democratic respectability was incomplete, but from the mid-1990s on, Fini resolutely set the party on a new course.[17] His methods were autocratic, but his content was moderate. Fini embraced liberal democracy, denounced the Fascist regime's racism and anti-Semitism from 1938 on, and even acknowledged the Resistance's contribution to postwar Italian democracy. In 2003, now vice prime minister of Italy, Fini traveled to Israel and renounced fascism as "absolute evil" in a speech that drew even the left's admiration. This break with the past drove some nostalgic leaders (most famously, Alessandra Mussolini) out of the party and marked the AN's definitive move away from the far right. In the same period, Fini also surprised everyone—including Berlusconi—by suggesting that legal immigrants should be allowed to vote in local elections. He also drew closer to ex-Christian Democrats among his coalition partners, expressing growing frustration at Bossi's headline grabbing and Berlusconi's gaffes.

These actions are meant to firmly establish the AN's legitimacy as a moderate member in good standing of the center-right—leaving the far end of the spectrum to the Lega (and the tiny group of nostalgic ex-Fascists who left AN). These maneuvers are also meant to position Fini as the next leader of the coalition should Berlusconi be brought down or otherwise exit the scene. With roughly 12 percent of the vote, AN is the second-largest party in the coalition, albeit only half the size of FI. Yet no matter how statesmanlike or moderate he may appear, Fini and his party are condemned for the foreseeable future to bob along in Berlusconi's wake.

Elections

Because of the changes since 1992, postwar trends as well as the four elections since 1994 have already been discussed here and in preceding chapters. Let us simply recall that the so-called First Republic, under proportional representation, provided almost monotonously predictable electoral results from the 1950s into the 1980s. The largest three parties remained the same, in the same exact order (DC-PCI-PSI), from 1948 to 1992. And then the major governing parties were shattered, while new (or renovated) parties gave rise to a new party system. After no real change of governing formulas for forty-five years and no alternation in power at all, the elections of 1996 and 2001 saw alternation between two rival blocs. Another electoral system in 2006 again saw the ruling coalition replaced by the opposition.

Decades, and in some cases generations, of rooted political traditions do not disappear overnight. The "red" (Marxist) and "white" (Catholic) subcultures, although diminished, continue to be relevant. The PCI disappeared over fifteen years ago, but the red zones remain the areas where the left's support is strongest. Similarly, the white zones of the northeast still choose between contending conservative forces. And religion remains a very strong, if imperfect, indicator of one's placement on the left-right spectrum. The south, with the exception of 2001, has become the most competitive area of the country.[18]

It is also important to remember that alternation between the two electoral blocs has not reflected large swings in the actual vote—on the contrary. Different electoral systems have provided governing majorities in very close, sometimes evenly divided, contests.

From the late 1970s until 2001, voter turnout declined slowly but steadily. Italy used to have one of the highest turnout rates in the world, and it remains high comparatively. Turnout dropped below 90 percent in 1983 and hit a low point (just over 81 percent) in 2001. In 2006 it rose to 83.6 percent.[19]

Political Culture, Citizenship, and Identity

The intertwining of socioeconomic and territorial factors in Italian history makes it difficult to derive useful generalizations from any one of these phenomena considered in isolation.

Social Class, Religion, and Regionalism

Class, religion, and regionalism have had pronounced political dimensions throughout modern Italian history.

As noted above, red and white subcultures linger, although in diluted fashion. These divisions were never equal in strength or geographical distribution. Catholicism has been a more powerful and diffused force in Italy than the various strands of Marxism. Furthermore, the strong subcultures were located in areas that may surprise people unfamiliar with Italian

history and politics. The red areas are not the old northern industrial heartland but the central regions of Emilia-Romagna, Tuscany, and Umbria. The white areas, where religion is most deeply rooted, are found in the northeast, in the Veneto and eastern Lombardy.

Political subcultures in Italy cut across classes more than is appreciated. This is less surprising for white areas, since Catholic social thought rejects class conflict, but even the leftist subculture is broadly based, owing to its agrarian, anticlerical origins. Italian Socialists and Communists were always less obsessed with factory workers than their counterparts elsewhere, such as in France.

Far weaker, until recently, have been all variants of modern bourgeois subcultures, such as secular liberalism and conservatism, which failed to acquire mass bases as they did in most of the rest of the West. These secular forces were stunted by *trasformismo*, repressed by fascism, and then delegated much of their role to the DC after 1945. Their historic political expressions survived and evolved in the form of the minor lay parties of the center, until secularization and the erosion of the major subcultures finally produced a more "laical" political culture.

Ironically, with the decline of the DC, class has become a more solid predictor of political preference. But some of the relationships between class, or closely related indicators such as formal education, and political preference depart from conventional expectations. It is not surprising that the party that draws the greatest share of independent businesspeople's vote is Forza Italia. But the center-right attracts a larger share of private sector wage earners than does the center-left. Wage earners in the public sector, in contrast, opt for parties of the left or center-left much more frequently. And more highly educated voters tend to prefer the center-left to the center-right.[20]

National, Ethnic, and Regional Identity

Fascism appears to have inoculated Italians against nationalism. And the country's history since the Risorgimento has conspired to make Italians the most "European" of all West European publics. They are far more ready to delegate decision making to Brussels, which may reflect the lack of pride they feel in Italian institutions.[21]

Even under fascism, justifications for Italian nationalism often seemed contrived, as when Mussolini spoke of an "Italic" race, or introduced legislation that defined Italians as "Aryan." With the exception of parts of the northeast that are adjacent to predominantly Slavic areas, ethnic identification was not a significant factor in Italian society or politics until the Northern League politicized it. But the Lega was working with the raw material of history: regional identities have been extremely powerful in Italy, reflecting the extraordinary diversity of the various areas that were united in the nineteenth century. And northern disparagement of southerners had racist undertones long before the arrival of Umberto Bossi: epithets for southerners include "Moroccan" and "African."

It is absurd to think of the north-south cleavage in ethnographic terms. Indeed, it is a gross oversimplification to speak of a southern culture or political style. It is the case, however, that the south's dependent development and resulting distorted class and social structures have shaped its political institutions, which, in turn, have shaped public attitudes. These distortions are most evident in the ways they have rendered southern politics especially vulnerable to patronage networks and clientelistic patterns of politics.

Similarly, the League's emergence shows that in periods of rapid change and the undermining of old certainties, local identities can assume increasing importance or can even be invented out of whole cloth ("Padania," which refers to the area around the Po River valley, is the League's imagined heartland).

These new territorial identities have, as noted, occasionally been expressed in ethnic or racial terms. The League has used September 11, 2001, to justify its anti-Islamic discourse, but it can hardly be held responsible for all acts of intolerance against immigrants. Italians love to portray themselves as warm, tolerant people, as befits a country that sent tens of millions of emigrants to other lands. But Italian citizenship laws are quite restrictive. Italy distinguishes between foreigners born in Europe and those born elsewhere, and it sets far more restrictive citizenship requirements for non-Europeans. Only recently has the center-left introduced legislation that would make it somewhat easier for non-Europeans and their children to become citizens.

Gender

As was noted in Chapter 17, discrimination against women in Italy is embedded in welfare state regulations and the labor market everywhere, but especially in the south. Discrimination may have cultural or religious roots, but it was sanctioned by the law for a very long time, and in myriad ways. In the immediate postwar period, women needed their husband's permission to apply for passports. In parts of southern Italy, well into the 1960s, preserving family honor demanded that women marry the "suitors" who had kidnapped and raped them. It took a reform of family law in 1975 to establish parity between both partners in a marriage, or to permit a head of family to be of either sex. Divorce was illegal until 1970, abortion was illegal until 1978, and both these laws were challenged by referenda strongly backed by the Roman Catholic Church.

Many reforms were sped along by the existence of a strong women's movement, whose influence spread with extraordinary rapidity (see below). And it is a sign of just how much the country had changed that both referenda failed by overwhelming margins.

But persistent gaps in employment rates, salaries, and opportunities for promotion demonstrate how very far Italy still has to go. And changes in public consciousness have hardly been accompanied by dramatic changes in many areas of society and politics. For instance, despite repeated solemn promises by the political parties, the current gender breakdown in the Italian parliament remains low, at 17.3 percent female deputies—and this figure represents an immense jump over previous legislatures.[22]

Interests, Social Movements, and Protest

Italian civil society has been more volatile, and more fragmented, than in most Western democracies.

Business Organizations

Because of divided governing coalitions and the factional nature of the DC, interest groups in the First Republic had multiple targets to lobby. Most groups in Italian society divided along left-right lines, but even the group that should have been largely immune to such division nonetheless found ample grounds for disunity along other dimensions.

The Confederation of Italian Industries (Confindustria) represents companies in the private sector. The 1960s and 1970s produced the greatest strains as the old oligopolies, and the very numerous smaller firms (those with fewer than one hundred employees), were usually antilabor, while the dynamic large firms that produced consumer goods favored rapid agreements with the unions. They also supported broader social reforms—not only because they were more enlightened but also because theirs were more labor-intensive industries. They needed society to absorb the costs of improving the conditions under which working people lived; otherwise firms would have to foot the bill alone.

As labor weakened in the 1980s, the worst rifts in the capitalist front began to heal. Confindustria gave a greater voice to some of its historically silenced members; its presidents in the 1990s were chosen from the Association of Young Industrialists and then from the very dynamic small-firm sector. By the early 1990s, as state enterprises were sold off, Confindustria's ranks were expanded. In the course of the 1990s, Confindustria was instrumental in labor relations reforms, but it also became more politically assertive, demanding budgetary rigor, tax reform, and an overhaul of an inefficient bureaucracy and institutions—all in the name of making Italy more responsive to European and international competitive pressures.[23] As discussed in Chapter 17, Confindustria openly supported Berlusconi in 2001, but his government's lack of responsiveness and Italy's continuing economic slide soon saw business again take a more autonomous stance. Although Confindustria would dearly like to see governments take more dramatic economic measures, it realizes that confronting the unions too directly can be counterproductive.[24]

Organized Labor

Throughout the postwar period, organized labor was politically divided, and, as a result of the exclusion of the Communists, no government ever contained all of labor's major representatives. These limitations had a profound effect on every aspect of labor relations and reform legislation in Italy, but they did not always result in crushing defeats for the unions and the working

class. Particularly when the unions were united, they often achieved more (in job security, guaranteed wage increases, and pensions) than did their counterparts in other countries—even those with the relative luxury of Socialist or Social Democratic governments to defend them. The flurry of legislation and contractual guarantees that followed the Hot Autumn of 1969–1970 are clear examples.

The Hot Autumn brought the major confederations—the General Confederation of Italian Labor (CGIL), the Italian Confederation of Workers' Trade Unions (CISL), and the Union of Italian Labor (UIL)—close to reuniting. By the end of the 1970s, however, with renewed tensions between the PCI and PSI, strains developed both among the three confederations and also within the CGIL, where Communists and Socialists coexisted. By the 1980s, the major confederations were again divided and faced declining membership and growing competition from autonomous unions and the Committees of the Base (COBAS).

Chapter 17 discussed the establishment of tripartite consultation among labor, management, and the government in 1993. Not surprisingly, cooperation has been greater under center-left governments. The unions have fought hard to preserve some benefits—above all, pensions—but they are aware of their diminished leverage, and they generally acquiesce in neoliberal reforms when they are allowed some say in the speed and extent of these reforms.[25]

The Church and the Catholic World

No discussion of Italian society and politics can ignore the immense role played by this unique institution. In the immediate postwar period, the church under Pope Pius XII did not hesitate to exercise its influence, often harshly. The church was supposed to stay out of politics, but it did not, making clear that the "political unity of Catholics" (voting for the DC) was essential. Pius XII excommunicated Communist and Socialist party activists at the height of the cold war. And through the 1960s, the DC retained or expanded Fascist-era laws banning material offensive to the church, its moral standards (nudity or suggestiveness in magazines, films, or theater), or its dogma (such as information on contraception as well as the availability of contraceptives).

Blatant interference faded in the more open era brought in by Pope John XXIII and the Second Vatican Council of 1962–1965. The divorce (1974) and abortion (1981) referenda also signaled how much even this most Catholic of societies had changed. By the mid-1980s, sensing the crumbling legitimacy of the political system, the Italian hierarchy of the church increasingly distanced itself from all parties. In 1995, with the DC gone, the pope formally ratified an already established policy: Catholics could have diverse political loyalties.[26]

The Vatican's even-handedness appeared to shift in 2006, when it clearly "tilted" toward the center-right while avoiding singling out any specific parties as favorites. This is not entirely surprising, since Benedict XVI was the Vatican "enforcer" of doctrinal orthodoxy before becoming pope, and he has not hesitated to express strong opinions on numerous issues. When a 2005 referendum tried to repeal a very restrictive law governing medically assisted procreation, stem-cell research, and related issues, the church actively counseled voters to stay at home to guarantee the referendum's failure. Barely a quarter of the electorate bothered to vote, and church leaders quickly claimed this as a great victory.[27] In 2007, in opposition to the center-left's efforts to allow civil unions that would give legal rights to unmarried couples (gay or straight), the church organized a massive "Family Day" demonstration in Rome. The event revealed serious divisions within the governing majority and forced the government to back away from its proposal.

But the church's positions are not uniformly conservative. With the exception of a few intolerant cardinals, it has taken a compassionate approach to immigration, which has softened the tones of public debate and has probably helped produce less harsh legislation on a potentially inflammatory topic.

Social Movements and Protest

Italy has a long history of both organized and spontaneous social movements. What all social movements have in common is that they arise outside, or quickly escape the control of, established parties. *New* social movements—and this justifies the adjective—are distinguished by raising demands that do not easily fit the platforms and identities of the traditional parties, in contrast with, say, peasant or workers' or regional movements in the past.

New movements often became explosive because of Italy's slow, sometimes paralyzed, political processes. Moreover, the major parties blanketed society very effectively; their effort to absorb everything, capturing and channeling social activity in their own organizations, left limited room to develop autonomous interest groups or citizens' movements. This controlling capacity began to break down in the late 1960s and had effectively vanished by the end of the 1980s.

In terms of size and impact on society, the most significant movement in recent times was the workers' activism that began in the 1960s and peaked during the Hot Autumn. Because of the explosive social and political context of the late 1960s, the boundaries between the labor movement and broader social movements effectively disappeared. Spilling out of the factories, workers took up the banners of numerous social reforms, such as housing, transportation, health care, and other social services. The major cities also saw large urban protest movements. Among other things, these movements discredited Christian Democratic rule in the big cities and produced important reforms. The urban movements initially agitated against the severe shortage of affordable housing, which led to spectacular, large-scale occupations of public housing projects. They also focused on services such as schools, health, parks, and day care.

Most recently, following the Ulivo's defeat in 2001, organized labor and a broader grouping of civil society groups staged large, sometimes spectacular demonstrations against various policies of the center-right—openly challenging the left to take more of the initiative itself. The unions, led by the CGIL, demonstrated against proposed pension reforms: some of these demonstrations became more generic antigovernment rallies and attracted millions of protesters. An even more original phenomenon saw enormous crowds of demonstrators join hands around government buildings to protect them symbolically against Berlusconi when he was prime minister. The most notable cases occurred outside the Ministry of Justice and the state-owned broadcast company in protest against his perceived attacks on the judiciary and his control of the media.

Student and Youth Movements. Student and youth movements have taken diverse forms. In the late 1980s, they were sporadic, uncoordinated protests against barely functioning high schools and universities. But in the 1960s, they had a highly ideological leftist character. They often originated around protests against the Vietnam War, which was especially important in radicalizing young Catholics for the first time. These movements peaked in 1967–1968, eventually furnishing activists for the far left as well as for more mainstream parties. They provided critical contributions to factory and urban struggles, and trained militants and future leaders for the traditional left. For example, nearly a quarter of all Communist militants, and over one-third of those who joined the party in the 1970s, had some experience in movements or groups (excluding the unions) prior to joining the PCI.

Autonomous Movements and Terrorism.   A totally different movement appeared in the 1970s on the fringes of the far left. Calling itself "autonomous" from all existing organizations, it was, broadly speaking, antipolitical with a violent extremist fringe. Much smaller than the 1960s movement, it left a significant impression. It attacked all parties, as well as unions and the more privileged sectors of the working class. Even more deliberate, and lethal, violence broke out in the late 1970s, when left-wing terrorist groups such as the Red Brigades and Front Line reached their peak. These groups were never a mass movement, but they attracted diffuse sympathy among disillusioned leftists, especially the young, at least until terrorism escalated from symbolic acts to kneecappings and then hundreds of murders. Former prime minister Aldo Moro was the best-known victim, but others included judges, police, journalists, politicians, and left-wing trade unionists.

Ultimately, the most interesting thing about Italian left-wing terrorism was how long it lasted. In part this reflects the clumsiness and brutality of the Italian forces of order. But as the breadth of support suggests, it also reflects the deeper crisis of Italian institutions and society. Yet, notably, Italy never enacted measures as repressive as those introduced by the West Germans, who faced a less serious threat.

The Women's Movement.   As occurred elsewhere, the feminist movement of the 1960s and 1970s in Italy originated in the extraparliamentary left, which preached egalitarianism but relegated women to subordinate roles. The traditional left was slow to appreciate the strength and depth of the feminist challenge. Feminists within the parties and unions kept up the pressure, however, and events, especially the momentous 1974 referendum on divorce, rapidly converted the unpersuaded. In fairness to the traditional left, the victories on divorce and abortion would never have been so lopsided without the left's full mobilization of its forces. Nor would the dramatic gains represented by the complete rewriting of family law have been possible without the left's active support in Parliament.

The ideas of the women's movement penetrated Italian society with striking speed, at least in the cities. Since the late 1970s, however, the women's movement in Italy, as elsewhere, has fragmented, although there remain umbrella organizations that occasionally mobilize women around specific issues, and certain strands of feminism are very influential in the universities.

Conclusions

The material in this chapter provides a deeper understanding of some of the worst pathologies of postwar Italian democracy, above all the *partitocrazia* that occupied civil society, politicizing many aspects of normal life. This in turn helps us understand the popularity of such different populistic appeals as that of Bossi and the League, on the one hand, and Berlusconi and Forza Italia, on the other. Each, in different ways, takes advantage of a cynicism toward politics and politicians that permeates broad strata of Italian society.

But the material in this chapter also provides a better understanding of the vibrancy of Italian democracy, despite its many flaws. In spite of an often self-serving political class—or perhaps because of the naked cynicism of established parties and politicians—Italy has seen extraordinary levels of social mobilization and various forms of popular pressure from below, as well as aggressive prosecutors and reform-minded politicians who act within existing institutions. These activities, at times independently, on other occasions in more coordinated fashion, helped consolidate and reform Italian democracy. Democracy is, after all, not an end state that one achieves, once and for all, but rather a continuing process, with significant advances, but also with periods of stagnation and backsliding.

Notes

[1] Martin J. Bull and James L. Newell, *Italian Politics: Adjustment Under Duress* (Cambridge: Polity Press, 2005), p. 123.

[2] Paul Furlong, *Modern Italy: Representation and Reform* (London: Routledge, 1994), p. 129.

[3] Richard S. Katz, "The New Electoral Law," in Carol Mershon and Gianfranco Pasquino, eds., *Italian Politics: Ending the First Republic* (Boulder, Colo.: Westview Press, 1995), pp. 93–112.

[4] Daniela Gianetti and Elisabetta De Giorgi, "The 2006 Italian General Elections: Issues, Dimensions, and Policy Positions of Political Parties," *Journal of Modern Italian Studies* 11 (December 2006): 498.

[5] Bull and Newell, *Italian Politics: Adjustment Under Duress*, pp. 134–137, lists every referendum through 2003. In 2005, a four-item referendum on medically assisted procreation was held.

[6] Douglas Wertman, "The Last Year of the Christian Democratic Party," in Mershon and Pasquino, *Italian Politics*, pp. 142–143.

[7] Bruno Mascitelli and Emiliano Zucchi, "Whither the Democratici di Sinistra?" *Journal of Southern Europe and the Balkans* 8 (August 2006): 205–208.

[8] The congresses are documented at the websites of both the DS (http://www.dsonline.it/) and the Margherita (http://www.margheritaonline.it/).

[9] Mark Donovan, "I referendum del 1997: Il troppo stroppia?" in Luciano Bardi and Martin Rhodes, eds., *Politica in Italia: Edizione 98* (Bologna: Il Mulino, 1998), p. 201.

[10] Ilvo Diamanti, "The Northern League: From Regional Party to Party of Government," in Stephen Gundle and Simon Parker, eds., *The New Italian Republic: From the Fall of the Berlin Wall to Berlusconi* (London: Routledge, 1996), p. 113.

[11] Roberto Biorcio, "La Lega nord e la transizione italiana," *Rivista italiana di scienza politica* 29 (April 1999): 56.

[12] See Paul M. Sniderman et al., *The Outsider: Prejudice and Politics in Italy* (Princeton, N.J.: Princeton University Press, 2000).

[13] Renato Mannheimer, "Forza Italia," in Mannheimer, ed., *Milano a Roma: Guida all'Italia elettorale del 1994* (Rome: Donzelli, 1994), p. 40.

[14] Emanuela Poli, *Forza Italia: Strutture, leadership e radicamento territoriale* (Bologna: Il Mulino, 2001), chaps. 3–5.

[15] Gianfranco Pasquino, "A Tale of Two Parties: Forza Italia and the Left," *Journal of Modern Italian Studies* 8 (Summer 2003): 203–207.

[16] Item XII of "Final and Transitional Arrangements" of the Constitution. This was never enforced.

[17] Marco Tarchi, *Dal MSI ad AN* (Bologna: Il Mulino, 1997), p. 146.

[18] John Agnew, "Remaking Italy? Place Configurations and Italian Electoral Politics Under the 'Second Republic,'" *Modern Italy* 12 (February 2007): 27–35.

[19] http://www.parties-and-elections.de/italy.html

[20] ITANES (Italian National Electoral Studies), *Perché ha vinto il centro-destra* (Bologna: Il Mulino, 2001), chap. IV.

[21] Liviana Tossutti, "Between Globalism and Localism, Italian Style," *West European Politics* 25 (July 2002): 52, 68f.

[22] http://www.camera.it/deputatism/248/lista.asp

[23] Liborio Mattina, "Abete's Confindustria: From Alliance with the DC to Multiparty Appeal," in Stephen Hellman and Gianfranco Pasquino, eds., *Italian Politics: A Review*, vol. 8 (London: Pinter, 1993), pp. 153–156.

[24] Giuseppe Berta, "Confindustria Under Montezemolo," in Carlo Guarnieri and James L. Newell, eds., *Italian Politics: Quo Vadis?* (Oxford: Berghahn Books, 2005), pp. 229–230.

[25] Vincent Della Sala, "Maastricht to Modernization: EMU and the Italian Social State," in Andrew Martin and George Ross, eds., *Euros and Europeans: Monetary Integration and the European Model of Society* (New York: Cambridge University Press, 2004), p. 146.

[26] Ilvo Diamanti and Luigi Ceccarini, "Catholics and Politics After the Christian Democrats: The Influential Minority," *Journal of Modern Italian Studies* 12 (March 2007): 45–46.

[27] Chiara Martini, "Il referendum sulla fecondazione assistita," in Grant Amyot and Luca Verzichelli, eds., *Politica in Italia: Edizione 2006* (Bologna: Il Mulino, 2006), pp. 203–224.

CHAPTER 20

Italian Politics in Transition

Postwar Italy became one of the world's richest societies, and its political system, for all its flaws, successfully evolved into a vibrant, open democracy against odds that once seemed formidable. Present difficulties must be viewed against these impressive achievements.

Fifteen years have passed since people started using the expression "Second Republic" to describe where Italy seemed to be going. Such terminology may make the Italian situation appear even more problematic than it is, for it obviously, and intentionally, invokes comparison with the French Fourth and Fifth Republics. Leaving aside the happy fact that, unlike France under the crisis of decolonization, Italy has at no time in the past decade seemed on the verge of civil war, the French transition was guided by a single individual (Charles de Gaulle) who was able to impose a coherent vision on a traumatized nation. In contrast, Italy's transition is uncertain because it has been anything but a guided process: for better and for worse, it is the product of democratic give and take. The actors struggling to redefine Italian politics include those that were pure products of the old system, those that were entirely new, and those that had one foot in each.

Political Challenges and Changing Agendas

Italy has not had to deal with the sorts of shocks and traumas that accompanied French decolonization and German unification. It does, however, have to face several daunting challenges.

Transition—and Continuity— in the Party System

Although events since 1994 have not produced everything reformers hoped for, they have led to changes that were unimaginable just a few years earlier. Successive elections have been won by alternating, opposed political blocs; in 2006 a sitting government was ousted by the opposition for only the second time since World War II. The parties that dominated Italian politics for nearly half a century have undergone profound changes, been reduced to bit players, or disappeared altogether. New electoral systems at all levels have speeded the changes.

But some of the worst aspects of the First Republic remain, suggesting that the Italian transition has stalled,

VOTATECI, E' QUI CHE DOVETE PASSARE IL RESTO DELLA VITA.

"Vote for us, you have to spend the rest of your life here." Italy's governing parties are represented waist-deep in garbage for the 1985 local elections.

Source: © 1985 Giorgio Forattini, from *Forattini Classics, 1985–1990.* Courtesy Giorgio Forattini.

well short of the new era of politics that seemed imminent in the mid-1990s. The party system is more fragmented than ever. The First Republic had between ten and twelve parties in Parliament by the early 1990s. In 2001 and again in 2006, almost everyone sitting in Parliament belonged to one of two broad alliances. But in 2006 the center-right counted five distinct groups, while the center-left had twice that number, even after the closest election in history.

This situation increases the blackmail potential of the tiniest group within each coalition, making it unlikely that a new electoral law—which would be the third since 1992—will improve matters. The smaller groups have managed to entrench themselves, and unless voting behavior changes dramatically, institutional tinkering is not likely to alter the present situation.

Another trend that recalls the *partitocrazia* of the First Republic is a return to bloated cabinets (the better to represent everyone in the coalition). Governments after 1994 seemed to be moving toward more simplification, but things started to change in the late 1990s; Prodi's 2006 government was the largest in history.[1] This bloat further reinforces the impression that political elites have fallen back on old patterns and are increasingly cut off from—and oblivious to—public exasperation with endless maneuvering in Rome.

It remains to be seen whether the formation of a center-left Democratic Party (the DS and Margherita along with a few minor formations) will truly simplify the party system, or merely transfer the current fragmentation under one large umbrella. The move toward unification on the center-left has provoked a countermove by parties to the left of the DS to form a single group of their own, but these smaller formations are, if anything, even less likely to leave behind their specific identities. Berlusconi has also suggested the creation of a single party of the center-right, but this has proven to be a complete nonstarter given the differences within that alliance.

Unresolved Political and Institutional Questions

Berlusconi's return to the opposition renders his conflicts of interest less problematic for Italian democracy than when he occupied the prime minister's office. But as long as he remains the only plausible leader of the center-right, Italian democracy remains anomalous. And that is not the only unresolved question Italy faces.

Berlusconi's Personal Problems and Broader Implications for Italian Politics. Berlusconi has never shown much concern over his conflicts of interest. His victory in several referenda in 1995 that would have limited his broadcasting franchises or regulated commercials on the private networks reinforced his belief that he could sway public opinion when it really mattered. His insensitivity to this problem can be breathtaking; he has said that he "breaks out in hives" whenever the words "conflict of interest" or "equal time" are mentioned. Nothing he did while in office between 2001 and 2006 suggested that he had experienced a change of heart.

In fact, in 2004, Freedom House downgraded Italy from a rating of "Free" to that of "Partly Free" and dropped its world ranking to seventy-fourth overall in its assessment of press freedom, putting Italy in the company of Benin, Peru, and the Philippines. The reasons for the demotion were the conflicts of interest and continued manipulation of and interference in the exercise of press freedoms by the government.[2]

It remains one of the center-left's greatest failures that, while in office between 1996 and 2001, it failed to address the conflict-of-interest issue, in the vain hope of enlisting Berlusconi's support (which failed to materialize) for ambitious constitutional reforms. Not surprisingly, Berlusconi's second term did more

to sidestep the issue than address it, producing a completely toothless set of regulations. With the center-left back in power, new proposals were working their way through Parliament in 2007 as this chapter was being written, but it remains to be seen whether serious legislation will be possible given the very narrow majority in the Senate.

Stalled Constitutional Revision = Stalled Transition? In 1947, the Italian political system appeared permanently fragmented; proportional representation guaranteed fair representation to all parties while making it nearly impossible for one party to obtain an absolute majority in both chambers of Parliament. Thus, the method for revising the constitution—absolute majorities in both chambers must pass identical versions of the proposed change on two occasions at least three months apart (Article 138)—was quite restrictive when written. There would have to be very broad agreement indeed in order to change Italy's institutional framework, and of course no such agreement existed—or was expected.

With the introduction of electoral systems whose goal is to produce stable governing majorities—which do not necessarily mirror popular sentiment—the situation changes. In fact, the elaborate amending formulas of most countries with majoritarian electoral systems reflect concern that it should not be too easy to amend constitutions. Even countries with proportional representation have established more restrictive conditions than Italy for altering their constitutions.*

Article 138 does stipulate that should the amending majority be less than two-thirds of each chamber, a popular referendum may be called to ratify the changes. And this vote—in contrast to that of an abrogative referendum—does not require that half of all eligible voters turn out. As we saw in Chapter 18, such referenda were held in 2001 and again in 2006: the first ratified the Ulivo's semifederalist reforms; the second rejected the center-right's more radical proposals.

There was much to criticize in the center-right's reforms, starting with a version of federalism that, in many eyes, promised to allow the richer north to keep far more of its own money at the expense of the south

---

*Sweden, for instance, requires two separate votes, but an election must occur between votes.

(Berlusconi's concession to the Northern League). But the reforms did at least address some of the Italian system's worst features, such as reducing the number of parliamentarians and eliminating the absurdity of pure bicameralism. Several key reforms are long overdue and may now prove more difficult than ever to realize. These include a smaller Chamber of Deputies (it currently has 630 members) and a conversion of the Senate into some sort of "chamber of the regions" (which would be much reduced from its present 315 members and directly elected but similar in other ways to the German Bundesrat).

Continuity and Change in Italian Society

"The Religious Question" has—thankfully—faded in significance, but the existence of the *Roman* Catholic Church means that this issue will always have special significance in Italy. At the same time, with respect to immigration, Italy's situation is becoming increasingly similar to that of its largest neighbors. Both of these issues deserve closer scrutiny.

Religion and Politics.   It is worth recalling just how profoundly Italy has changed with regard to the role of religion. There was always enormous diversity from region to region, but even the most solidly Catholic areas have been dramatically transformed over the past generation. Ireland may have narrowly approved divorce in a 1995 referendum, but Italy did so massively in 1974. In 1981, almost 70 percent of Italians voted to uphold a liberal abortion law, funded through the national health system. At the same time, religion's imprint is unmistakable. Italian divorce law is extremely restrictive, requiring five years of separation. Italy was the last of the EU 15 to legislate on medically assisted procreation (in 2004), and the law it produced is by far the most restrictive in Western Europe.[3]

As we saw in Chapter 19, an effort to abrogate that restrictive law failed miserably as the Italian church actively, and successfully, campaigned to keep that law on the books. And the Vatican and the Conference of Italian Bishops have been similarly aggressive in pursuing issues that run afoul of official doctrine.

This aggressiveness, combined with the church's clear "tilt" to the right in the 2006 elections, has fed speculation that we are witnessing the dawn of a new era of partisan, polarized political engagement on the part of the church—an era that appeared to have ended with the dissolution of the DC. This concern receives at least partial support from survey research on the 2006 election.[4] Following the great shake-up of the party system in 1994, the Catholic vote had been reasonably widely distributed between the two major blocs, with a slight edge going to the center-right. But in 2006, the division became quite pronounced, with the most observant Catholics almost twice as likely to vote for the center-right as the least religious respondents. The reverse was also the case; agnostics and nonbelievers were almost twice as likely to vote for the center-left.[5]

Does this signal the dawn of a new era? Some caution is in order. First, one election cannot establish a trend, let alone a sea change. Second, although the 2006 results do indicate a more religiously polarized electorate, both coalitions remain quite heterogeneous, and the religious-lay divide cuts through both the center-left and the center-right. Recent developments may indeed turn into a trend if the church feels strongly enough about social and scientific issues. In this regard, it is important to note that Benedict XVI shares the doctrinal conservatism of John Paul II but is far more interested in domestic Italian politics than his predecessor was. At the very least, recent developments suggest that the church will continue to function as a formidable combination of both a social movement and a powerful political lobby.[6]

Immigration.   Compared to the other countries in this text, Italy's immigrant population remains relatively low, at just over 5 percent. But the rapid growth of newcomers from outside Europe has produced dramatic, sometimes disruptive changes. Since the 1980s, a country that had mainly experienced foreigners as middle-class tourists has now encountered large numbers of black or brown field hands, street vendors, domestic laborers, and factory workers in its largest cities and in the smaller centers of the newly industrialized periphery of the north. The most highly visible minorities are North Africans and sub-Saharan Africans, whose presence occasionally generates intolerant reactions. With the growth of immigration has also come the involvement of more marginal elements in drugs, prostitution, and other crimes. The underside of immigration inevitably receives extensive coverage in the sensationalist press, which plays into a growing public sense of insecurity that is related more to crime than to the threat of job loss.[7]

The politicization of immigration varies depending on which coalition is in power in Rome. Almost as soon as the center-left took office, for example, it announced its intention to liberalize Italy's quite restrictive citizenship laws and to roll back the most punitive aspects of a law passed by Berlusconi's government in 2002. But immigration is also an issue the center-left tries to avoid whenever it can, given how easy it is for the right to manipulate anti-immigration themes for its own benefit.

But the center-right in Italy hardly speaks with a single voice on immigration. The Northern League took the lead in politicizing immigration, making antiforeign pronouncements that often spill over into outright racism. The AN, sensitive to its fascist past, has tried to distinguish itself from the Lega's intolerance, while Forza Italia has taken a cautious approach, emphasizing law and order while delegating a more visible role to its allies. Former Christian Democrats within the center right have been a consistent voice for tolerance.

The Economy, State Spending, and Industrial Relations

In 1987, Italy boasted that its Gross Domestic Product had surpassed Great Britain's. After bringing up the rear of the EU 15 for most of the past decade, recent figures for Italy's GDP estimated it at around 80 percent of the UK's.[8] During Berlusconi's last year in office, Italy's enormous national debt, which had been edging downward for over a decade, actually increased.

As we saw in Chapter 17, there are many explanations for Italy's seemingly chronic economic problems, including disproportionately high spending on pensions, and quite low expenditures on research and development and on more active labor market policies such as longer-term training programs. Pension reforms over the past fifteen years have seen expenditures level off at around 15 percent of GDP,[9] but this is still much higher than the EU average, and will rise dramatically as the population ages. Labor market reforms have been limited under the center-left, while under the center-right they were concerned mainly with making it easier to fire workers and introduce more "atypical" (part-time or limited-term) contracts.

Given these realities, it is not surprising that organized labor would have a better working relationship with center-left than with center-right governments. But since the center-left has been more conscientious than the center-right about keeping deficits within bounds, its relations with the unions—particularly the CGIL—are fraught with tension. Quite understandably, the unions resist inroads into existing benefits and stall the implementation of whatever concessions they do make. The center-left has neither the power nor the political will to impose dramatic changes on the unions, while the bargains it strikes with them raise howls of protest from industrialists in Italy and economic watchdogs in Brussels that not enough is being done, and that it is being done too slowly.

On the surface, it is equally unsurprising that Confindustria sided openly with Berlusconi in 2001, for business organizations are expected to lean to the right. But this was actually a departure, for in 1996 Confindustria had favored Prodi, calculating (correctly) that he was the best bet to bring Italy into the EMU. The industrialists quickly grew impatient with what they saw as Prodi's concessions to the unions. They turned to Berlusconi in 2001.

But business then grew disillusioned with Berlusconi, who, mirroring Prodi, had to placate his own coalition partners, at a time when the industrialists wanted economic rigor—plus money for investments and research and development.[10] Nor did many industrialists wish to see relations with the unions become too hostile. Signaling its discomfort with the Berlusconi government's tone and policies, in 2004 Confindustria elected a leader who sought a rapprochement with organized labor. Yet when Prodi took office in 2006, despite conciliatory gestures to business and promises to press on with pension reform, he also indicated that his government would roll back some of Berlusconi's labor market reforms. The tense and unstable equilibrium of recent years is likely to continue.

Italian Politics, Terrorism, and Italy's Relation to the United States

Throughout the postwar period, Italy was both a reliable partner in the North Atlantic Treaty Organization (NATO) and an ardent proponent of European integration. With regard to NATO, DC-led governments showed a willingness to follow the U.S. lead to a degree that was often slavish, reflecting the unwavering support they received from the United States as long as the PCI dominated the opposition. After the cold war ended, Italy remained a dependable, compliant ally of the United States. For example, when NATO controversially waged war against Yugoslavia over Kosovo, Italy actively supported that effort. This support was all the more striking in that it came when Massimo D'Alema, the former Communist, was prime minister.

This history provides a context within which to view Berlusconi's open break with France and Germany in supporting the U.S.-led invasion and occupation of Iraq (Italian public opinion was overwhelmingly opposed). Berlusconi's "tilt" toward the United States, and his willingness to oppose the French and Germans on other issues as well, led to speculation as to whether Italy was fundamentally breaking with past foreign policy and security practices.[11] During the same period, Berlusconi appalled Brussels by going to Russia and endorsing President Putin's "antiterrorist" actions in Chechnya, despite the EU's official condemnation of human rights violations in that region.

After making allowances for Berlusconi's personality quirks, a balanced analysis would conclude that, at most, his policies may have pulled Italy a bit more toward Washington and a bit less toward Brussels, but that no dramatic departures were to be expected in Italian foreign policy. With Prodi's return to office in 2006, not surprisingly given Prodi's previous job as president of the EC, Italy moved back toward a more muiltilateralist, Brussels-oriented set of policies. But these are more subtle shifts than policy reversals. Even on so controversial an issue as Iraq, although Prodi's government pulled Italy's last contingents out of the country, the withdrawal had actually begun months earlier, while Berlusconi was still in office.

The Challenges of European Integration

It is generally acknowledged that the European sword of Damocles hanging over Italy in the 1990s forced successive governments to undertake measures that had previously been avoided if Italy was to avoid the humiliation of exclusion from full partnership in Europe. It would be an oversimplification to argue that all of Italy's recent fiscal virtue (such as it is) and reform initiatives can be laid at the door of Brussels or the Maastricht convergence criteria or, more recently, the Growth and Stability Pact.[12] But there can be no doubt that these external constraints have strongly influenced Italy's policies—and problems—for close to two decades.

Italians used to lead their neighbors in their pro-EU attitudes, but as Italy's economic performance has lagged, less enthusiastic attitudes have emerged, particularly since the introduction of the single currency.[13] On balance, public opinion remains narrowly pro-European, reflecting the impact of an economy that has not fared particularly well since Italy joined the euro zone.

Public opinion also reflects the impact of partisan politics: Romano Prodi was president of the European Commission when Berlusconi's second term began in 2001, and Il Cavaliere was eager to blame Brussels (and his once and future rival) for just about everything.

But Berlusconi was reflecting the resentment of some of his own constituents. Many social groups that support the right fear the uncertainly that deeper European integration will bring—with reason. Moreover, when Prodi had introduced higher taxes and more rigorous enforcement of the tax code, they felt particularly aggrieved.[14] Italy's huge independent stratum of shopkeepers, small businesspeople, professionals, and proprietors of small industrial firms account for an astonishing 35 percent of the workforce. This puts Italy nearly 10 percent ahead of France, which has the next-highest proportion among larger West European nations.[15] And these groups habitually avoid or evade paying their full share of taxes (Chapter 17).

Of course, it is not only the right's constituents who have their doubts about the benefits brought by increasing European integration. Many sectors of organized labor—above all employees from industries threatened by international competition—have been among the most Euroskeptical groups in Western Europe. And all segments of organized labor chafe at the austerity measures (and hence restrictions on pay and benefits) that they see as direct results of Italy's EU membership.

Growing disillusion with Europe has additional political implications for Italy. Italian enthusiasm about European integration was always explained, in part, as a reflection of dissatisfaction with the functioning of their own political system.[16] If the transition to the Second Republic continues to flounder, and Italians become more negative about EU membership, what implications will this have for politics?

Italian Politics in Comparative Perspective

No one would hold Italy up as a model to be emulated, but different aspects of Italian history and politics are by no means exceptional or unique.

Many of the most interesting historical comparisons can be made with Germany, above all concerning late unification as nation-states and the subsequent reliance on an interventionist pattern of industrialization compared to Britain's laissez-faire model. Indeed, late in the nineteenth century, Italy deliberately shifted from a British to a Prussian pattern. Another quite stimulating, if unsettling, series of comparisons with Germany can be made concerning the social and political alliances that dominated both countries through World War I, including their ultimate capitulation in the face of Fascist challenges to democracy. Christian Democracy was a widespread phenomenon in the immediate post–World War II period in Europe, but few countries were as dominated by Christian Democrats as Italy and Germany, even though the sister parties increasingly diverged as time wore on.

Japan provides the only comparison among advanced industrial democracies that were completely dominated by a freely elected single party for two generations. For similar reasons, this comparison brings to light extraordinary levels of corruption, including collusion with organized crime, although the fact that Japan has a much stronger state tradition does represent a significant difference in comparison with Italy.[17] Comparativists who prefer cultural explanations for many political phenomena, including corruption, might want to look to more straightforward *political* explanations such as the length of time a single party spends in power without a genuine opposition, for there are few relevant similarities in Italian and Japanese culture.

France provides the obvious comparison when we examine the postwar domination of the opposition by a Communist Party and a rebellious and divided labor movement. In the French case, this situation lasted until 1981, when a left led by the Socialists won elections. In Italy, the PCI's domination of the opposition lasted until the end of communism itself. The Italian Socialist Party (PSI) was forced to carve out its own space and decided that its fate lay in the center of the political spectrum—a decision that many socialist and social democratic parties were making at the time in southern Europe (for instance, in Portugal, Spain, France, and Greece). This similarity itself invites further analysis. But these other Socialist parties were far stronger than the PSI and were not obliterated by corruption scandals, even though most have in fact been implicated in serious misbehavior. (The susceptibility of Socialist parties to corruption as they abandon their old identity and organizational structures is yet another interesting theme.)

More generally, Italian politics has been dominated for years by classic questions of democratic theory: Which institutions offer the best chance for effective democratic government? What is the trade-off between stable government and the faithful representation of ideological and programmatic differences, between stability and grassroots initiatives like the referendum? Can institutional engineering produce desired results? These issues have not just been debated, they have been fought out in the political arena.

Italy's current situation may be unique. This is not a transition from authoritarianism to democracy, which Italy underwent in 1945, and which other parts of the world have undergone more recently. If the Italian transition is carried forward, it will be from a party-dominated, assembly-style democratic regime, with severe problems of political immobility, to another, ideally more efficient type of democratic regime. This may prove to be the rarest sort of transition of all, for despite the supposed flexibility of democratic institutions, democracies rarely undertake major institutional overhauls. And they simply *never* seem to do so unless forced by massively disruptive and traumatic events such as war, revolution, or national paralysis. It is worth recalling that the French transition from the Fourth to the Fifth Republic occurred as a response to the trauma of decolonization and the Algerian War; *society* threatened to tear itself apart in a crisis that was far more than merely political. The Italian transition is strictly political.

Italy has generally lacked France's flair for political drama, although in its own crafty way it often manages to achieve more than its neighbor—like pension reform in the 1990s, but, even more tellingly, as a comparison of 1968 in France with Italy's Hot Autumn reveals. Will Italy achieve a transition to a Second Republic that is a radical new departure without the trauma that such changes seem to require? Or will it continue to be the country of The Leopard,[18] where everything seems to change so nothing in fact really changes at all?

Notes

[1]At 102, with 25 ministers and 77 undersecretaries. Gianfranco Pasquino, "Introduction. The Italian Political System After the 9–10 April 2006 Elections," *Journal of Modern Italian Studies* 11 (December 2006): 469.

[2]The ranking was downloaded at www.freedomhouse.org/research/pressurvey/allscore2004.pdf.

[3]Chiara Martini, "Il referendum sulla fecondazione assistita," in Grant Amyot and Luca Verzichelli, eds., *Politica in Italia: Edizione 2006* (Bologna: Il Mulino, 2006), pp. 206–207.

[4]Paolo Segatti, "I cattolici al voto, tra valori e politiche dei valori," in ITANES (Italian National Electoral Studies), *Dov'è la vittoria? Il voto del 2006 raccontato dagli italiani* (Bologna: Il Mulino, 2006), esp. pp. 110–113.

[5]Ibid., p. 110.

[6]Ilvo Diamanti and Luigi Ceccarini, "Catholics and Politics After the Christian Democrats: The Influential Minority," *Journal of Modern Italian Studies* 12 (March 2007): 48.

[7]Carl Ipsen, "Immigration and Crime in Contemporary Italy," *Journal of Modern Italian Studies* 4 (Summer 1999): 275.

[8]Anthony Giddens, *Europe in the Global Age* (Oxford: Polity Press, 2007), p. 37.

[9]ISTAT, *L'Italia in cifre, 2005* (available at www.istat.it), p. 25.

[10]Giuseppe Berta, "Confindustria Under Montezemolo," in Carlo Guarnieri and James L. Newell, eds., *Italian Politics: Quo Vadis?* (N.Y.: Berghahn Books, 2005), esp. pp. 227–230.

[11]Vincent Della Sala, "Maastricht to Modernization: EMU and the Italian Social State," in Andrew Martin and George Ross, eds., *Europe and Europeans: Monetary Integration and the European Model of Society* (New York: Cambridge University Press, 2004), pp. 126–149.

[12]Martin J. Bull and James L. Newell, *Italian Politics: Adjustment Under Duress* (Oxford: Polity Press, 2005), pp. 212–214.

[13]Paul Ginsborg, *Italy and its Discontents, 1980–2001* (London: Penguin Books, 2001), pp. 176 and 252.

[14]Ilvo Diamanti and Renato Mannheimer, "Le basi sociali del voto: La frattura che attraversa i ceti medi," in Mario Caciagli and Piergiorgio Corbetta, eds., *Le ragioni dell'elettore: Perché ha vinto il centrodestra nelle elezioni italiane del 2001* (Bologna: Il Mulino, 2002), p. 140.

[15]Bull and Newell, *Italian Politics*, p. 215.

[16]James Walston, "Italian Foreign Policy in the 'Second Republic': Changes of Form and Substance," *Modern Italy* 12 (February 2007): 97–101.

[17]For a comparison of the two countries that starts in the nineteenth century and continues to the end of the twentieth, see Richard J. Samuels, *Machiavelli's Children: Leaders and Their Legacies in Italy and Japan* (Ithaca, N.Y.: Cornell University Press, 2003).

[18]The reference is to Giuseppe Tomasi di Lampedusa's classic novel of the Risorgimento, *Il Gattopardo* (Milan: Feltrinelli, 1966), p. 24. An English-language edition is *The Leopard* (New York: Pantheon, 1960).

Part 5 Bibliography

Bufacchi, Vittorio, and Simon Burgess. *Italy Since 1989: Events and Interpretations*. New York: St. Martin's Press, 1998.

Bull, Anna Cento, and Mark Gilbert. *The Lega Nord and the Northern Question in Italian Politics*. Basingstoke, U.K.: Palgrave, 2001.

Bull, Martin, and Martin Rhodes, eds. *Crisis and Transition in Italian Politics*. London: Frank Cass, 1998.

Bull, Martin J., and James L. Newell. *Italian Politics: Adjustment Under Duress*. Oxford: Polity Press, 2005.

Clark, Martin. *Modern Italy, 1871–1995*. 2nd ed. London: Longman, 1996.

Cozza, Maurizio, and Luca Verzichelli. *Political Institutions in Italy*. Oxford: Oxford University Press, 2007.

Ferraresi, Franco. *Threats to Democracy: The Radical Right in Italy After the War*. Princeton, N.J.: Princeton University Press, 1996.

Gilbert, Mark. *The Italian Revolution: The End of Democracy, Italian Style?* Boulder, Colo.: Westview Press, 1995.

Ginsborg, Paul. *A History of Contemporary Italy: Society and Politics, 1943–1988*. London: Penguin, 1990.

————. *Italy and Its Discontents, 1980–2001*. London: Penguin, 2001.

Gundle, Stephen, and Simon Parker, eds. *The New Italian Republic: From the Fall of the Berlin Wall to Berlusconi*. London: Macmillan, 1996.

Hellman, Judith Adler. *Journeys Among Women: Feminism in Five Italian Cities*. New York: Oxford University Press, 1987.

Hellman, Stephen. *Italian Communism in Transition: The Rise and Fall of the Historic Compromise in Turin, 1975–1980*. New York: Oxford University Press, 1988.

Italian Politics: A Review. London: Frances Pinter, 1986–1993; Boulder, Colo.: Westview Press, 1993–1998; London: Berghahn Books, 1999–.

Journal of Modern Italian Studies. London: Routledge, 1995–.

Locke, Richard. *Remaking the Italian Economy*. Ithaca, N.Y.: Cornell University Press, 1995.

Lumley, Robert. *States of Emergency: Cultures of Revolt in Italy from 1968 to 1978*. London: Verso, 1990.

Lyttleton, Adrian. *The Seizure of Power: Fascism in Italy, 1919–1929*. London: Weidenfeld and Nicolson, 1973.

McCarthy, Patrick. *The Crisis of the Italian State: From the Origins of the Cold War to the Fall of Berlusconi*. New York: St. Martin's Press, 1995.

Modern Italy (Journal of the Association for the Study of Modern Italy). London: Routledge, 1998–.

Procacci, Giuliano. *History of the Italian People*. Hammondsworth, England: Penguin Books, 1973.

Putnam, Robert. *Making Democracy Work: Civic Traditions in Modern Italy*. Princeton, N.J.: Princeton University Press, 1993.

Samuels, Richard J. *Machiavelli's Children: Leaders and Their Legacies in Italy and Japan*. Ithaca, N.Y.: Cornell University Press, 2003.

Stille, Alexander. *The Sack of Rome*. New York: Penguin, 2006.

Tarrow, Sidney. *Democracy and Disorder: Protest and Politics in Italy, 1965–1975*. Oxford: Clarendon Press, 1989.

Woolf, S. J., ed. *The Rebirth of Italy, 1943–1950*. New York: Humanities Press, 1972.

Websites

ISTAT, Italy's National Statistical Institute:
www.istat.it/english/
Current as well as historical series of social and economic data.

Istituto Carlo Cattaneo:
www.cattaneo.org/
Excellent archives of social and political data, often in historical series. In Italian.

The Italian press agency's English-language site:
http://www.ansa.it/site/notizie/awnplus/english/english.html

Italian Studies Web, Western European Studies Section:
http://wess.lib.byu.edu/index.php/Italian_Studies_Web

PART 6

Russia in Transition

Joan DeBardeleben

CHAPTER 21

The Making of the Modern Russian State

Politics in Action

Russian President Vladimir Putin stirred up a diplomatic storm with his speech at the Forty-third Munich Conference on Energy Security on February 10, 2007. A particular target of Putin's comments was U.S. plans to deploy a missile defense system in Central Europe. In response, Putin posed the question: "Who needs the next step of what would be, in this case, an inevitable arms race? I deeply doubt that Europeans themselves do." Putin also expressed concern about the continuing expansion of NATO in Russia's immediate neighborhood: "It represents a serious provocation that reduces the level of mutual trust. And we have the right to ask: against whom is this expansion intended?"[1] The speech involved an explicit attack on what Putin depicted as a unipolar international system. He indicated that "one state and, of course, first and foremost the United States, has overstepped its national borders in every way." But at another level, Putin was addressing European leaders, suggesting that they were not taking an assertive enough stand against American dominance. Putin noted that the GDP of Brazil, Russia, India, and China (combined) is greater than that of the EU. "And according to experts this gap will only increase in the future." He also asserted that neither NATO nor the EU should seek authority to justify the use of military force, a decision that, in his view, could only legitimately be taken by the United Nations. At the same time Putin gave Russia credit for the collapse of the Berlin Wall: "the fall of the Berlin Wall was possible thanks to a historic choice—one that was also made by our people, the people of Russia—a choice in favor of democracy, freedom, openness and a sincere partnership with all the members of the big European family."

The European reaction to Putin's speech was mixed. In attempting to take advantage of anti-American sentiment in Europe, Putin may have overplayed his hand. European leaders were already wary of changes in Russia that seemed to undermine the democratic gains of the 1990s, even if they sympathized with some of Putin's concerns about a "unipolar" world. Following Putin's speech, discussion of a possible new cold war began to circulate in policy circles in both the United States and Europe, and all of this followed shortly after the disappointment of the November 2006 Russian-EU summit in Helsinki, at which negotiation of a new agreement between the two parties was scuttled by Polish objections to Russia's embargo of meat imports from Poland. Nervousness over Europe's energy dependence on Russia had followed Russia's withholding of energy supplies from the Druzhba Pipeline through Belarus, affecting Poland and Germany. Chancellor Angela Merkel responded: "It is not acceptable when there are no consultations about such moves."[2] Observers were also well aware that the upcoming electoral cycle in Russia, including legislative elections (for the State Duma) in December 2007 and presidential elections in March 2008, while likely to result in continuity rather than change, would probably mean the replacement of Putin by a new Russian president. Although both Putin and his predecessor, Boris Yeltsin, had repeatedly declared Russia's European identity and "European choice," in early 2007 the meaning of that choice, and how it related to Russia's policy toward the United States, was more ambiguous than it had ever been in the postcommunist period.

Geographic Setting

In December 1991, the Soviet Union ceased to exist. Each of the fifteen newly independent states that emerged in early 1992 began the process of forming a new political entity. This section focuses on the Russian Federation, the most important of these fifteen successor states. With a population of 142.8 million,[3] Russia is the largest European country in population and in size. In territory, it is the largest country in the world, spanning ten time zones.

Russia underwent rapid industrialization and urbanization in the Soviet period; only 18 percent of the population lived in urban areas in 1917; 73 percent do now. Despite its vast expanses, less than 8 percent of Russia's land is arable, while 45 percent is forested. Russia is rich in natural resources, which are generally concentrated in the vast regions of western Siberia and the Russian north, far from Moscow, the Russian capital. Russia's wealth includes deposits of oil, natural gas, mineral resources (including gold and diamonds), and extensive forestland. Oil and natural gas exports are now the main sources of Russia's economic wealth and trade potential.

Before the Communists took power in 1917, the Russian empire extended east to the Pacific, south to the

Russian Federation, March 2008

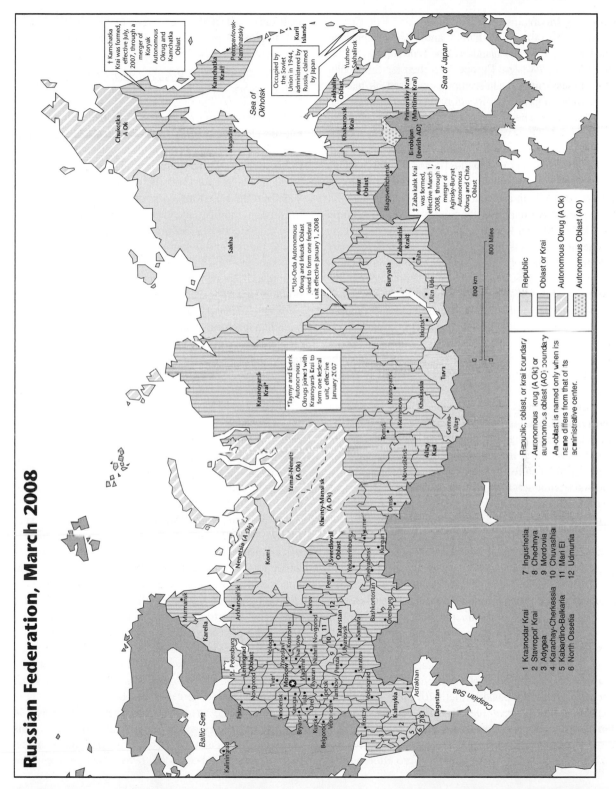

Caucasus Mountains and the Muslim areas of Central Asia, north to the Arctic Circle, and west into present-day Ukraine, eastern Poland, and the Baltic states. Unlike the empires of Western Europe, with their far-flung colonial possessions, Russia's empire bordered its historic core. In its unprotected location spanning Europe and Asia, Russia had been repeatedly invaded and challenged for centuries. This exposure to outside intrusion encouraged an expansionist mentality among the leadership; some historians argue that this factor, combined with Russia's harsh climate, encouraged Russian rulers to craft a centralizing and autocratic state.[4]

With the formation of the Soviet Union after World War I, the Russian Republic continued to form the core of the new multiethnic state. Russia's ethnic diversity and geographic scope have always made it a hard country to govern. Russia has also, on and off, faced pockets of instability and regional warfare on several of its borders, most notably in the Central Asian countries of Tajikistan and Afghanistan and in the countries of Georgia and Azerbaijan on Russia's southern border. Since Russia became an independent state in 1991, the country's western neighbors have included Ukraine, Belarus, and several EU member states (Finland and those that joined in May 2004—Estonia, Latvia, Lithuania, and Poland). Some observers have described Russia as Eurasian, reflecting the impact of both Asian and European cultural influences. Indeed, Russia is located at a critical juncture between Europe, the Islamic world, and Asia. Although this position creates opportunities, it also means that Russia's influence with other countries is not undisputed.

Critical Junctures

Russian development in the twentieth century has seen several periods of dramatic political change, sometimes marked by violence and prolonged uncertainty. Like the rest of Europe, Russia suffered through two world wars, but in addition the country experienced a major revolutionary transformation in 1917, radical socioeconomic upheaval in the 1920s and 1930s, and a painful and still incomplete transition after the collapse of the Soviet communist system in 1991. Not only the nature of the political system, but also the size and boundaries of the country were altered more

than once. All of these changes present a fascinating but perplexing process of political development.

The Decline of the Russian Tsarist State (Late 1800s to 1917)

Until the revolution of 1917, Russia had taken a separate developmental path from Western Europe, which may account for the different political outcomes in the twentieth century. In Russia, social classes were able to wield much less autonomous power in relation to the state, and the state took on a much more extensive role in furthering industrialization. Certain cultural patterns, such as collectivism (an emphasis on group over individual rights), and a continuing close link between the Russian Orthodox Church and the tsarist state, also differentiated Russia from Western Europe. Finally, the political leadership had suffered repeated setbacks in the international sphere in the late nineteenth and early twentieth centuries, partly because Russia's domestic structures were too weak to support a successful foreign policy. Foreign debacles in turn sparked domestic unrest; for example, Russia's involvement in World War I became the final catalyst for the fall of the tsarist regime.

Before 1917 Russia was ruled through an autocratic system headed by the tsar—the Russian monarch and emperor. The historian Richard Pipes explains that tsarist Russia had a patrimonial state, that is, a state that not only ruled the country but also owned the land.[5] The economic and agricultural system tied the majority of the population (peasants) to the nobles (through serfdom), the state, or the church, whose land they worked. In 1861 Tsar Alexander II emancipated the serfs as a part of his efforts to modernize Russia and make it militarily competitive with the West. Although they were now made legal persons, the emancipated peasants were still obligated to pay redemption fees to the state for forty-nine years to gain ownership of the land. Not until 1907, with the Stolypin reforms, were redemption payments abolished and measures taken to replace the peasant commune with private cultivation. Peter Stolypin, president of the tsar's Council of Ministers, hoped that a more truly independent and prosperous peasantry would soon take on the attributes of the petite bourgeoisie in the countryside. However World War I interrupted this process in 1914, and the regime was so severely shaken by the international crisis that revolutionary forces were

Critical Junctures in Soviet and Russian Political Development

1917	The Bolshevik seizure of power
1918–1921	Civil war and war communism
1921–1928	New Economic Policy
1929	Stalin consolidates power
1929–1953	Stalin in power
1929–1938	Collectivization and purges
1941–1945	Nazi Germany invades Soviet Union; "Great Patriotic War"
1953	Death of Stalin
1953–1955	Leadership change after Stalin's death
1956–1964	The Khrushchev era and de-Stalinization
1965–1982	The Brezhnev era and bureaucratic consolidation
1982–1985	Leadership change after Brezhnev's death
1985–1991	The Gorbachev era and *perestroika*
1991	Popular election of Boris Yeltsin as president of Russia (June); collapse of the USSR and formation of fifteen independent states (December); establishment of the Russian Federation as an independent state
1992	Market reforms launched in Russia (January)
1993	Adoption of the new Russian constitution by referendum; first (multiparty) parliamentary elections in the Russian Federation (December)
1995	Second parliamentary elections in the Russian Federation; Communists win the most seats (December)
1996	The first presidential elections under the new Russian constitution; Yeltsin is reelected
1998	Financial crisis and devaluation of the ruble
1999	Third parliamentary elections in the Russian Federation; Unity Party gains strong support, as does Communist Party; resignation of Yeltsin as president (December)
2000	Election of Vladimir Putin as president of Russia
2003	Fourth parliamentary elections in the Russian Federation; strong win for United Russia Party (December)
2004	Reelection of Vladimir Putin as president of Russia (March); September hostage taking of school children and bloody conflict to free hostages in Beslan, southern Russia; Putin announces new centralizing measures

able to topple it in 1917, before Stolypin's blueprint had a chance to be tested.

Might Russia have followed a path similar to that of Western Europe had World War I not intervened? This is a question that cannot be answered definitively, but there was no substantial bourgeoisie or entrepreneurial class to provide a political foundation for constitutional government and political liberalism, as had developed in most Western European countries. The key impetus

for industrialization came from the Russian state and from injections of foreign capital (especially French, English, German, and Belgian), in the form of joint-stock companies and foreign debt incurred by the tsarist government. The dominant role of state and foreign capital was accompanied by the emergence of large factories alongside small, private workshops. Trade unions were illegal until 1906, and even then their activities were carefully controlled. Worker discontent grew, alongside that of liberal intellectuals, students, and, later, peasants, in the wake of the defeats in the Russo-Japanese war and continued tsarist repression. This discontent culminated in the revolution of 1905, which involved widespread strikes in the cities and rural uprisings. The tsarist regime was able to maintain control, however, through repression and a measure of economic reforms, until its collapse in 1917.

The Bolshevik Revolution and the Establishment of Soviet Power (1917–1929)

The Russian revolutionary movement of the nineteenth century had its roots in certain elements of the nobility, many of whom were strongly influenced by European schools of thought, such as German Idealism and the French enlightenment. Initially the revolutionaries were not Marxists. In the 1840s to the 1880s they were populists, united by their faith in the Russian peasantry and seeing in the peasant commune (the *mir*) an indigenous base for building socialism. As the intrusion of foreign capital and Western values seemed increasingly inevitable, many revolutionaries turned to Marxism. The Marxist approach was attractive for several reasons: it gave an important role to the intelligentsia; it proclaimed the inevitability and desirability of social change and industrialization; and it affirmed the role of science and education, endeavors appreciated by many members of the intelligentsia who objected to Russia's backwardness. In embracing Marxism, some Russian intellectuals also expressed their ambivalence toward Western culture. Although the West was seen in many ways as more progressive and advanced than Russian society, with its backward and oppressive institutions, these intellectuals were repelled by the inhumane factory conditions that Western capitalism had spawned. They emphasized Russia's potential, since a socialist revolution might allow Russia to become an example for Western Europe.

The Marxist party, the Russian Social Democratic Labor Party (RSDLP), formed in 1898, had to make some adaptations of Marx's ideas to apply to Russian conditions. Russia's working class was small, and capitalism was only beginning to push out feudal relations in the countryside. Although there were disagreements within the RSDLP about how to respond, one section of the

party, the Bolsheviks, under the leadership of Vladimir Lenin, ultimately seemed to find a formula for success.

In 1917, at the height of World War I, two revolutions broke out in Russia. The March revolution threw out the tsar (Nicholas II) and installed a moderate provisional government. In November, the Bolsheviks, led by Vladimir Lenin, overthrew that government. This second revolution marked a major turning point in Russian history. Instead of trying to imitate West European patterns, the Bolsheviks applied a dramatically different blueprint for economic, social, and political development; and which they hoped workers in Europe would follow suit.

The Bolsheviks believed that their revolution reflected the political interests of a particular social class, the proletariat (working class). Most of the revolutionary leaders, however, were not themselves workers but were from a more educated and privileged stratum, commonly referred to as the intelligentsia. But in 1917, the Bolsheviks' slogan, "Land, Peace, and Bread," appealed to both the working class and the discontented peasantry, which made up over 80 percent of Russia's population.

The Bolsheviks formed a tightly organized political party based on their own understanding of democracy. Their strategy was founded on the notions of democratic centralism and vanguardism, concepts that differed significantly from Western European ideas of liberal democracy. Democratic centralism mandated a hierarchical party structure in which leaders were elected from below, with freedom of discussion until a decision was taken, but once a decision had been made strict discipline was required in implementing party policy. Over time, the centralizing elements of democratic centralism took precedence over the democratic elements, as the party tried to insulate itself first from informants of the tsarist forces and later from both real and imagined threats to the new regime. The concept of a vanguard party governed the Bolsheviks' (and later the Communist Party's) relations with broader social forces. Party leaders claimed that they understood the interests of the working people better than the people did themselves. Over time, this philosophy came to rationalize virtually all actions of the Communist Party and the state it dominated. Neither democratic centralism nor vanguardism emphasized democratic procedures or accountability of the leaders to the public. Rather, these concepts focused on achieving a "correct" political outcome that would reflect the "true" interests of the working class, as defined by the leaders of the Communist Party.

Once in power, the Bolsheviks formed a new government, which in 1922 brought the formation of the first Communist Party state, the Union of Soviet Socialist Republics (USSR), henceforth referred to as the Soviet Union. In the early years, the Bolsheviks felt compelled to take extraordinary measures to ensure the survival of the regime. The initial challenge was an extended civil war (1918–1921) for control of the countryside and outlying regions. The Bolsheviks introduced war communism to ensure the supply of materials necessary for the war effort. The state took control of key economic sectors and forcibly requisitioned grain from the peasants. Political controls also increased: the *Cheka*, the security arm of the regime, was strengthened, and restrictions were placed on other political groups, including other socialist parties. By 1921, the leadership had recognized the political costs of war communism: the peasants resented the forced requisitioning of grain, and the policy blocked economic initiative. In an effort to accommodate the peasantry, the New Economic Policy (NEP) was introduced in 1921 and lasted until 1928. State control over the economy was loosened so that private enterprise and trade could revive. The state, however, retained control of large-scale industry and experimented with state control of the arts and culture.

Gradually, throughout the 1920s, the authoritarian strains of Bolshevik thinking eclipsed the democratic elements. Lacking a democratic tradition and bolstered by the vanguard ideology of the party, the Bolshevik leaders engaged in internecine struggles following Lenin's death in 1924. These conflicts culminated in the rise of Joseph Stalin and the demotion or exile of prominent party figures such as Leon Trotsky and Nikolai Bukharin. By 1929, all open opposition, even within the party itself, had been silenced. Sacrifices of democratic procedure were justified in the name of protecting class interests.

The Bolshevik revolution also initiated a period of international isolation for the new state. To fulfill their promise to bring peace, the new rulers had to cede important chunks of territory to Germany under the Brest-Litovsk Treaty (1918). Only the defeat of Germany by Russia's former allies (the United States, Britain, and France) reversed some of these concessions. However, these countries were hardly pleased with internal developments in Russia. Not only did the Bolshevik revolution bring expropriation of foreign holdings and Russia's withdrawal from the Allied war effort, it also represented the first successful challenge to the capitalist order. As a result, the former allies sent material aid and troops to oppose the new Bolshevik government during the civil war.

Lenin had hoped that successful working-class revolutions in Germany and other Western countries would bolster the fledgling Soviet regime and bring it tangible aid. When this did not occur, the Soviet leaders had to rely on their country's own resources to build a viable economic structure. In 1924, Stalin developed the idea of building "socialism in one country." This policy defined Soviet state interests as synonymous with the promotion of socialism, suggesting that socialism could be built in Russia even without successful revolutions in other countries. The policy simultaneously set the Soviet Union on a course of economic isolation from the larger world of states. To survive in such isolation, the new Soviet state pursued rapid industrialization and increased political control.

The Stalin Revolution (1929–1953)

From 1929 until Stalin's death in 1953, the Soviet Union faced another critical juncture. During this time, Stalin consolidated his power as Soviet leader by establishing the basic characteristics of the Soviet regime that substantially endured until the collapse of the Communist system in 1991.

The Stalin revolution brought changes to virtually every aspect of Soviet life. The result was an interconnected system of economic, political, and ideological power. The state became the engine for rapid economic development, with state ownership and control of virtually all economic assets (land, factories, housing, and stores). By 1935, over 90 percent of agricultural land had been taken from the peasants and transformed into state or collective farms. This collectivization campaign was justified as a means of preventing the emergence of a new capitalist class in the countryside, but it actually targeted the peasantry as a whole, leading to widespread famine and the death of millions. Survivors who resisted were arrested or exiled to Siberia. In the industrial sector, a program of rapid industrialization favored heavy industries (steel mills, hydroelectric dams, machine building); production of consumer goods was neglected. Economic control was exercised through a complex system of central economic planning, in which the state planning committee (Gosplan) set production targets for every enterprise in the country; many economists consider that, by its nature, such a centralized planning system would be bound to engender inefficiencies. The industrialization campaign was accompanied by social upheaval. People were uprooted from their traditional lives in the countryside and catapulted into the rhythm of urban industrial life. Media censorship and state control of the arts strangled creativity as well as political opposition. The party/state became the authoritative source of truth; anyone deviating from the authorized interpretation could be charged with treason.

In the early 1920s, the Communist Party was the only political party permitted to function, and by the early 1930s, open opposition or dissent within the party itself had been eliminated. Gradually, the party became subject to the personal whims of Stalin and his secret police. Party bodies ceased to meet on a regular basis and no longer made important political decisions. Party ranks were periodically cleansed of potential opponents, and previous party leaders as well as citizens from many other walks of life were violently purged (arrested, sentenced to labor camps, and sometimes executed). Overall, an estimated 5 percent of the Soviet population was arrested at one point or another under the Stalinist system, usually for no apparent cause. The arbitrary and unpredictable terror of the 1930s left a legacy of fear. Only among trusted friends and family members did people dare to express their true views. Forms of resistance, when they occurred, were evasive rather than active: peasants killed their livestock to avoid giving it over to collective farms, laborers worked inefficiently, and absenteeism was high.

Isolation of Soviet citizens from interaction with the outside world was a key tool of Stalinist control. Foreign news broadcasts were jammed, travel abroad was highly restricted, and contacts with foreigners brought citizens under suspicion. The economy was isolated from interaction with the international economic system. Although this policy shielded the Soviet economy from the effects of the Great Depression of the 1930s, which shook the capitalist world, the policy also allowed an inefficient

system of production to survive in the USSR. Protected from foreign competition, the economy failed to keep up with the rapid pace of economic and technological transformation in the West.

In 1941, Nazi Germany invaded the Soviet Union, and Stalin had little choice but to join the Allied powers. Wartime casualties were high, approximately 27 million people, including 19 million civilians. Even today wartime sacrifices and losses are frequently recalled, since World War II had such a profound impact on the outlook of an entire generation of Soviet citizens. Soviet propaganda dubbed it the Great Patriotic War, evoking images of Russian nationalism rather than of socialist internationalism; the sacrifices and heroism of the war period remained a powerful symbol of Soviet pride and unity even after the collapse of Communist power. The war period was marked by support for traditional family values and a greater tolerance for religious institutions, whose support Stalin sought for the war effort. Among the social corollaries of the war effort were a declining birthrate and a long-lasting gender imbalance as a result of high wartime casualties among men. The war also affected certain minority ethnic groups that were accused of collaborating with the enemy and were deported to areas farther east in the USSR. These included Germans, Crimean Tatars, and peoples of the northern Caucasus regions such as the Chechens, Ingush, and Karachai-Balkar. Their later rehabilitation and resettlement brought renewed disruption, contributing to the ethnic conflicts of the post-Soviet period.

The Soviet Union was a major force in the defeat of the Axis powers in Europe. After the war, the other Allied powers allowed the Soviet Union to absorb new territories into the USSR itself (these became the Soviet republics of Latvia, Lithuania, Estonia, Moldavia, and portions of western Ukraine), and they implicitly granted the USSR free rein to shape the postwar governments and economies in eastern Germany, Poland, Hungary, Czechoslovakia, Yugoslavia, Bulgaria, and Romania. Western offers to include parts of the region in the Marshall Plan were rejected under pressure from the USSR. With Soviet support, local Communist parties gained control of all of these countries; only in Yugoslavia were indigenous Communist forces sufficiently strong to gain power largely on their own and were later able to assert their independence from Moscow.

Following World War II, the most prominent features of Soviet communism were largely replicated in those areas newly integrated into the USSR and in the countries of Eastern Europe. The Soviet Union tried to isolate its satellites in Eastern Europe from the West and to tighten their economic and political integration with the USSR. The Council for Mutual Economic Assistance (CMEA) and the Warsaw Treaty Organization (a military alliance) were formed for this purpose. With its developed industrial economy, its military stature bolstered in World War II, and its growing sphere of regional control, the USSR emerged as a global superpower. But the enlarged Soviet bloc still remained insulated from the larger world of states. Some countries within the Soviet bloc, however, had strong historic links to Western Europe (especially Czechoslovakia, Poland, and Hungary), and in these areas, domestic resistance to Soviet dominance forced alterations or deviations from the Soviet model. For example, in Poland, collectivization of agriculture was never successfully implemented, and Hungary's New Economic Mechanism (introduced in 1968) involved bringing some market elements into the economy. Over time, the countries of Central and Eastern Europe served not only as geographic buffers to direct Western influence on the USSR but also as conduits for such influence. In the more Westernized Baltic republics of the USSR itself, the population firmly resisted assimilation to Soviet rule and eventually spearheaded the disintegration of the Soviet Union in the late 1980s.

Attempts at De-Stalinization (1953–1985)

Stalin's death in 1953 triggered a critical juncture in Soviet politics. Even the Soviet elite realized that Stalin's system of terror could be sustained only at great cost to the development of the country. The terror destroyed initiative and participation, and the unpredictability of Stalinist rule inhibited rational formulation of policy. From Stalin's death until the mid-1980s, the USSR saw a regularization and stabilization of Soviet politics. Terror abated, but political controls remained in place, and efforts to isolate Soviet citizens from foreign influences continued. At the same time, the 1960s and early 1970s were a period of relative affluence. Economic growth, while moderate compared to the 1930s, was used to a much greater extent to provide the population with a more comfortable lifestyle.

Nikita Khrushchev, who succeeded Stalin as the party leader from 1955 until his removal in 1964, embarked on a bold policy of de-Stalinization. Although his specific policies were only minimally successful, he initiated a thaw in political and cultural life, an approach that planted the seeds that ultimately undermined the Stalinist system. Khrushchev rejected terror as an instrument of political control and revived the Communist Party as a vital political institution able to exercise political, economic, and cultural authority. The secret police (KGB) was subordinated to party control, and party meetings resumed on a regular basis. However, internal party structures remained highly centralized, and elections were uncontested. In the cultural sphere, Khrushchev allowed sporadic liberalization, with the publication in the official media of some literature critical of the Stalinist system, such as Aleksandr Solzhenitsyn's *One Day in the Life of Ivan Denisovich*, a description of life in the Stalininst labor camps.

Leonid Brezhnev, Khrushchev's successor, who headed the party from October 1964 until his death in 1982, partially reversed the de-Stalinization efforts of the 1950s and early 1960s. Controls tightened once more in the cultural sphere. People who expressed dissenting views (members of the so-called dissident movement) through underground publishing or publication abroad were harassed, arrested, or exiled. However, unlike in the Stalinist period, the political repression was predictable: people knew when they were transgressing permitted limits of criticism. The Brezhnev regime could be described as primarily bureaucratic and conservative, seeking to maintain existing power structures rather than to introduce new ones.

From the late 1970s onward, an aging political leadership was increasingly ineffective as it attempted to address the mounting problems facing Soviet society. Economic growth rates declined, and improvements in the standard of living were minimal. Many consumer goods were still in short supply, and quality was often mediocre. As the economy stagnated, opportunities for upward career mobility declined. To maintain the Soviet Union's superpower status and competitive position in the arms race, resources were diverted to the military sector, which gutted the capacity of the consumer and agricultural spheres to satisfy popular expectations. Russia's rich natural wealth was squandered, and costs soared for exploiting new resource deposits (mostly in

Siberia). High pollution levels lowered the quality of life and health in terms of morbidity and declining male life expectancy. At the same time, liberalization in some Eastern European states and the telecommunications revolution made it increasingly difficult to shield the population from exposure to Western lifestyles and ideas. Among a certain critical portion of the population, aspirations were rising just as the capacity of the system to fulfill them was declining. In this context the next critical transition occurred.

Perestroika *and* Glasnost *(1985–1991)*

Mikhail Gorbachev took office as a Communist Party leader in March 1985 at the relatively young age of fifty-three. He hoped to reform the system in order to spur economic growth and political renewal, but without undermining Communist Party rule or its basic ideological precepts. Four important concepts formed the basis of Gorbachev's reform program: *perestroika, glasnost, demokratizatsiia,* and "New Thinking." *Perestroika* (restructuring) involved decentralization and rationalization of economic structures to enable individual enterprises to increase efficiency and take initiative. The central planning system was to be reformed, but not abolished. To counteract the resistance of entrenched central bureaucracies, Gorbachev enlisted the support of the intelligentsia, who benefited from his policy of *glasnost. Glasnost* (openness) involved relaxing controls on public debate, the airing of diverse viewpoints, and the publishing of previously prohibited literature. *Demokratizatsiia* (Gorbachev's conception of democratization) was an effort to increase the responsiveness of political organs to public sentiment, both inside and outside the party, introducing some elements of competitive elections, a law-based state, and freer political expression. Finally, "New Thinking" in foreign policy involved a rethinking of international power in nonmilitary terms. Gorbachev advocated integration of the USSR into the world of states and the global economy, emphasizing the common challenges facing East and West, such as the cost and hazards of the arms race and environmental degradation.[6]

Gorbachev's policies triggered a fundamental change in the relationship between state and society in the USSR. Citizens pursued their interests and beliefs through a variety of newly created organizations at the national and local levels. These included ethnonationalist movements, environmental groups, groups for the rehabilitation of Stalinist victims, charitable groups, new or reformed professional organizations, political clubs, and many others. The very existence of these groups implicitly challenged the Communist Party's monopoly of power. By March 1990, pressures from inside and outside the party forced the Supreme Soviet (the Soviet parliament) to rescind Article 6 of the Soviet constitution, which provided the basis for single-party rule. Embryonic political parties challenged the Communist Party's monopoly of political control. In the spring of 1989, the first contested elections since the 1920s were held for positions in the Soviet parliament, although those elections did not permit competition between political parties. These national elections were followed by elections at the republic and local levels in 1990, which, in some cases, put leaders in power who pushed for increased republic and regional autonomy.

The most divisive issues facing Gorbachev were economic policy and demands for autonomy by many of the constituent republics. Only 50.8 percent of the Soviet population was ethnically Russian in 1989. In several of the fourteen non-Russian republics that made up the USSR, popular front organizations formed. First in the three Baltic republics (Latvia, Lithuania, and Estonia) and then in other union republics (particularly Ukraine, Georgia, Armenia, Moldova [formerly Moldavia], and Russia itself), demands for national autonomy and, in some cases, for secession from the USSR were put forth. Gorbachev's efforts to bring consensus on a new federal system for the fifteen union republics failed, as popular support and the self-interests of elites took on an irreversible momentum, resulting in "separatism mania."

Gorbachev's economic policies failed as well. They involved half-measures that sent contradictory messages to enterprise directors, producing a drop in output and undermining established patterns that had kept the Soviet economy functioning, albeit inefficiently. The economic decline reinforced demands by union republics for economic autonomy. To protect themselves, regions and union republics began to restrict exports to other regions, despite planning mandates. Separatism mania was accompanied by "the war of laws," as regional officials openly defied central directives. In response, Gorbachev issued numerous decrees; their number increased as their efficacy declined.

Gorbachev achieved his greatest success in foreign policy. Just as his domestic support was plummeting in late 1990 and early 1991, he was awarded the Nobel Peace Prize, reflecting his esteemed international stature. Under the guidance of his New Thinking, the military buildup in the USSR was halted, important arms control agreements were ratified, and many controls on international contacts were lifted. In 1989, Gorbachev refused to prop up unpopular communist governments in the East European countries. First in Hungary and Poland, then in the German Democratic Republic (East Germany) and Czechoslovakia, pressure from below pushed the communist parties out of power, and a process of democratization and market reform ensued. Politicians in both East and West declared that the cold war was over. But, to Gorbachev's dismay, the liberation of Eastern Europe fed the process of disintegration in the Soviet Union itself.

Collapse of the USSR and the Emergence of the Russian Federation (1991 to the Present)

On August 19, 1991, a coalition of conservative figures attempted a coup d'état, temporarily removing Gorbachev from the leadership post to stop the reform initiative and to prevent the collapse of the USSR. The failed coup was the death knell of the Soviet system. While Gorbachev was held captive at his summer house (*dacha*), Boris Yeltsin, the popularly elected president of the Russian Republic, climbed atop a tank loyal to the reform leadership and rallied opposition to the attempted coup. Yeltsin declared himself the true champion of democratic values and Russian national interest. The Soviet Union collapsed at the end of 1991 when Yeltsin joined the leaders of Ukraine and Belorussia (later renamed Belarus) to declare the formation of a loosely structured entity, called the Commonwealth of Independent States, to replace the Soviet Union. In December 1991, the Russian Federation stepped out as an independent country in the world of states. Its independent status (along with that of the other fourteen former union republics of the

USSR) was quickly recognized by the major world powers.

Yeltsin proclaimed his commitment to Western-style democracy and market economic reform, marking a radical turn from the Soviet past. However, that program was controversial and proved hard to implement. The market reform produced severe and unpopular economic repercussions as it disrupted traditional economic patterns. The Russian parliament, elected in 1990, mirrored popular skepticism as it hesitated to embrace the radical reform project. The executive and legislative branches of the government failed to reach consensus on the nature of a new Russian constitution; the result was a bloody showdown in October 1993, after Yeltsin disbanded what he considered to be an obstructive parliament and laid siege to its premises, the Russian White House. The president mandated new elections and a constitutional referendum in December 1993. The constitution, adopted by a narrow margin of voters, put in place a set of institutions marked by a powerful president and a relatively weak parliament.

Yeltsin's economic reform program, while fundamentally altering economic relations, failed to produce an effective market economy; a major financial crisis in August and September 1998 was the culmination of this failed reform process. The financial crisis triggered a political one. In 1999, Yeltsin nominated a surprise candidate to the post of prime minister of Russia. Vladimir Putin, a little-known figure from St. Petersburg, was a former KGB operative in East Germany. His political advance was swift, and the rise in his popularity was equally meteoric. In December 1999, Yeltsin, apparently ill and unable to command the reins of power, resigned as president of the Russian Federation. Elections were announced for March 2000; the result was a resounding victory for Putin, with an even stronger show of support in elections that followed for the federal legislative body, the State Duma (hereafter Duma), in December 2003 and for the presidency in March 2004. Putin's tenure as president benefited from auspicious conditions, as high international gas and oil prices fed tax dollars into the state's coffers. In 1999, the economy experienced its first real growth in over a decade, a trend that has continued into the new millennium.

BORIS NIKOLAEVICH YELTSIN

On February 1, 1931, Boris Yeltsin was born to a working-class family in a village in the Russian province of Sverdlovsk located in the Ural Mountains. Like so many men of his generation who later rose to top Communist Party posts, his education was technical, in the field of construction. His early jobs were as foreman, engineer, supervisor, and finally director of a large construction combine. Yeltsin joined the Communist Party of the Soviet Union in 1961, and in 1968 he took on full-time work in the regional party organization. Over the next ten years he rose to higher positions in Sverdlovsk oblast, first as party secretary for industry and finally as head of the regional party in 1976. In 1981, Yeltsin became a member of the Central Committee of the CPSU and moved onto the national stage.

Because of Yeltsin's reputation as an energetic figure not tainted by corruption, Mikhail Gorbachev drafted Yeltsin into his leadership team in 1985. Yeltsin's first important post in Moscow was as head of the Moscow party organization. Gorbachev also selected Yeltsin to be a nonvoting member of the USSR's top party organ, the Politburo.

Yeltsin soon gained a reputation as an outspoken critic of party privilege. He became a popular figure in Moscow, as he mingled with average Russians on city streets and public transport. In 1987 party conservatives launched an attack on Yeltsin for his outspoken positions; Gorbachev did not come to his defense. Yeltsin was removed from the Politburo and from his post as Moscow party leader in 1988; he was demoted to a position in the construction sector of the Soviet government. At the party conference in June 1988, Yeltsin defended his position in proceedings that were televised across the USSR. Yeltsin's popular support soared as the public saw him single-handedly taking on the party establishment.

Rivalry between Gorbachev and Yeltsin formed a backdrop for the dramatic events that led to the collapse of the Soviet Union in December 1991. Yeltsin represented a radical reform path while Gorbachev supported gradualism. Yeltsin established his political base within the Russian Republic; thus Russia's self-assertion within the USSR was also a way for Yeltsin to secure his own position. Under his guidance on June 8, 1990, the Russian Republic declared sovereignty (not a declaration of independence, but an assertion of the right of the Russian Republic to set its own policy). One month later, Yeltsin resigned his party membership. On June 12, 1991, Yeltsin was elected president of the Russian Republic by direct popular vote, establishing his legitimacy as a spokesman for democratization and Russian independence.

During the attempted coup d'état by party conservatives in August 1991, Yeltsin reinforced his popularity and democratic credentials by taking a firm stand against the plotters while Gorbachev remained captive at his dacha in the Crimea. Yeltsin's defiance gave him a decisive advantage in the competition with Gorbachev and laid the groundwork for the December 1991 dissolution of the USSR engineered by Yeltsin (representing Russia) and the leaders of Ukraine and Belorussia. In an unusual turn of events, the rivalry between Yeltsin and Gorbachev, as well as between their differing approaches to reform, was decided through the disbanding of the country Gorbachev headed.

In 1992, Yeltsin embarked on the difficult task of implementing his radical reform policy in the newly independent Russian Federation. Economic crisis, rising corruption and crime, and a decline of state authority ensued. Yeltsin's popularity plummeted. His reputation as a democratic reformer was marred by his use of force against the Russian parliament in 1993 and in the Chechnya war in 1994–1996. Although Yeltsin's campaign team managed to orchestrate an electoral victory in 1996, Yeltsin's day was past. Plagued by poor health and failed policies, Yeltsin could hope only to serve out his presidential term and groom a successor. He succeeded in the latter, designating Vladimir Putin as acting president upon his own resignation in December 1999. By 2004, however, Yeltsin expressed disillusionment with the direction of Putin's political reforms. In reaction to Putin's move to end the direct election of governors in that year, Yeltsin remarked, "The stifling of freedoms and the rolling back of democratic rights will mean, among other things, that the terrorists will have won."[1] Mixed reviews of Yeltsin's achievements followed his death on April 23, 2007, just as opinions about the approach of his successor were also divided.

---

[1] "Yeltsin fears for Russia freedoms," *BBC News*, September 17, 2004, http://news.bbc.co.uk/2/hi/europe/3663788.stm (accessed May 12, 2005).

Russia after September 11

Following the attacks on the World Trade Center and the Pentagon on September 11, 2001, President Putin expressed solidarity with the American people in their struggle against terrorism. Terrorist attacks in Russia reinforced a sense of common purpose between the two world powers. Unanimity quickly unraveled, however, as Russia withheld its support for the American incursion into Iraq.

Russia itself had suffered a string of terrorist attacks beginning in 1999 that were initially related to the Chechen separatist movement but later with more extensive international ties, creating a sense of insecurity among Russian citizens. Some of the more serious incidents occurred following 9/11. On October 23, 2002, over 700 hostages were held by bomb-laden terrorists in a Moscow theater; at least 120 died, including the hostage-takers. In August 2004, two Russian passenger planes crashed simultaneously, killing at least eighty-nine passengers. Other attacks targeted schools, apartment buildings, and public transport. One of the most serious and galvanizing events was the hostage-taking in Middle School No. 1 in the town of Beslan in southern Russia (population about 34,000) on the first day of the 2004–2005 school year. As parents accompanied children to school, for what is traditionally a festive opening day, terrorist forces with explosives strapped to their bodies herded the children and families into the school gymnasium, for what was to become a 52-hour siege. Not permitting the victims food or water, the hostage takers made demands that were unacceptable to the Russian government: the removal of Russian troops from the neighboring secessionist region, the Republic of Chechnya, and the release of Chechen rebels held by the government. On Friday, September 3, Russian Special Forces heard an explosion inside. Fearing the worst, they stormed the building in an effort to release the victims. Over 300 of the 1,000 hostages, the majority children, were dead.

Following the Beslan tragedy, Putin announced reforms to bring increased central control over selection of regional governors, and a counterterrorism law was proposed that would make it easier to restrict press freedom and civil liberties in the face of alleged terrorist threats. Even as economic growth in Russia had taken a positive turn since 1999, worries about personal and collective security renewed concern about the capacity of the Russian state to safeguard the well-being of its citizens. Many Russians apparently came to the conclusion that democracy is of less importance than ensuring stability and security.

Despite some tensions with the United States, after 9/11 Russia was granted an enhanced status in relationship to organizations such as NATO and the Group of 7 (G-7, a group of leading industrial nations, which became the G-8 with Russia's addition). Still an outsider, as several Central and East European countries joined NATO and the European Union (EU), Russia faced the issue of how to balance its global, European, and Eurasian roles. In his 2005 address to the Federal Assembly, Putin affirmed his conviction that "above all else Russia was, is, and will, of course, be a major European power" and defined as a task to "continue its civilizing mission on the Eurasian continent."[7]

The relationship between U.S. President George W. Bush and Russian President Vladimir Putin reflects moments of tension in the light of Russian objections to the U.S. invasion of Iraq and U.S. criticism of Russian political developments.   *Source:* AP Images.

Russia after the French and Dutch Veto of the European Constitution

As an outsider to the European Union, Russia was not directly affected by the unsuccessful referenda about the European constitution. More important for Russia was the May 2004 enlargement that brought eight former postcommunist countries into the EU. Three of these were former republics of the Soviet Union (Estonia, Latvia, and Lithuania), and in two of these countries (Estonia and Latvia) there remained a large Russian population. Other new EU member states were also part of the former Soviet bloc (the Czech Republic, Hungary, Poland, Slovakia), while Slovenia had been part of communist Yugoslavia. Although the EU's efforts to conclude a constitutional treaty were in large part spurred by the challenges of governing the Union after enlargement, for Russia the challenges posed by the EU's expansion were quite different. Not only did enlargement fundamentally change the basis of Russia's long-term political and economic relationships with these neighboring states, it also created specific tensions relating to new border regimes, as these countries prepared to enter the Schengen group (the set of European countries that, in principle, have open borders with no passport control). In particular, a portion of Russia's own territory, Kaliningrad *oblast*, was separated from the rest of Russia, as land travel to Kaliningrad was possible only by passing through EU member states, either Lithuania or Poland. Thus visas would be needed for land travel under the new Schengen requirements. Following difficult negotiations a facilitated visa regime was agreed upon, but Russia pushed for visa-free travel to the EU as a long-term solution.

As it stands, the inability of the European Union to forge a unified position, particularly on foreign policy issues, gives Russia greater flexibility in negotiating simultaneously with individual Member States and at the EU level. On the other hand Russia looks to Europe as an ally in opposing a "unipolar world." Yet another consideration may be that further EU enlargements, following the accessions of Romania and Bulgaria in January 2007, might be slowed by the constitutional impasse. As the EU faces difficulties "digesting" the 2004 and 2007 enlargements, the bid for membership of countries like Ukraine becomes less realistic. "Enlargement fatigue," a factor potentially contributing to the failure of the constitution, might give Russia breathing space to draw its neighbors back into its orbit of influence.

Themes and Implications

Russian efforts at reform following the collapse of communism in 1991 present a mixed picture. The Russian state has clearly established its status as an influential actor in the international sphere under Vladimir Putin's leadership, and a sustained economic upturn and rich energy resource base seem likely to assure Russia's continued economic influence as well. However, in early 2008, domestic political support remained closely tied to the person of Vladimir Putin even as he approached the end of his term in office. The question remains as to whether this political support can be transferred to his successor, given the weak legitimacy of Russian political institutions and the contested basis of collective identity.

Historical Junctures and Political Themes

Following the collapse of the USSR in 1991, international support for the new reform-oriented government in Russia surged, with the proliferation of aid programs and international financial credits. The honeymoon, however, is now over. In the 1990s Russia's status as a world power waned, and the expansion of Western organizations (NATO, EU) to Russia's western border undermined its sphere of influence in Central and Eastern Europe. Russia's eastern neighbors, except Belarus, looked more to Europe than to Russia as a guidepost for the future. But Russia's economic recovery, the rise of energy prices, and Europe's dependence on imports of Russian natural gas and oil provided an important basis for Russia's renewed international influence. No longer simply a supplicant in its relationship to the West, Russia reasserted its role as a major European power under Putin's leadership. However, Russia's defense of a disputed presidential election outcome during Ukraine's Orange Revolution in November 2004 suggested the primacy of Russian national interest over democratic values. With its "near abroad," Russia has not found an effective manner to establish itself as a respected regional leader.

For nearly a decade after the collapse of the Soviet system, the Russian Federation seemed mired in a downward spiral of economic collapse and political paralysis. By the late 1990s, the Russian public was disillusioned and distrustful of its leaders, and resentment remained over the dismal results of the Western-inspired reform program. In the new millennium, growth rates have, however, seen a process of recovery, budget surpluses have become routine, and the population has shown a marked increase in economic confidence. Questions, however, remain about the depth of the apparent economic recovery. Some experts attribute the economic turnaround to high oil prices rather than to effective government policy; global economic trends could potentially push Russia back into a renewed slump. At the same time, wide disparities in wealth and income, as well as important regional inequalities, continue to plague the system. Although many important policy problems have been addressed, others remain unresolved, including inadequate levels of foreign investment, capital flight, continuing high levels of inequality, the decline in the agricultural sector, and corruption. Furthermore, in 2005 reforms of the welfare system elicited broad public protest, as vulnerable groups feared a collapse of the social safety net they rely on for basic subsistence. The public remains skeptical of many features of a market economic system, which feeds suspicions that public optimism could easily turn sour in the face of a new economic jolt, such as occurred in 1998.

Concerns about the fate of Russian democracy have also become widespread in the West as well as among certain groups inside Russia. On the positive side, the constitution adopted in 1993 has gained a surprising level of public acceptance, even as observers express intensifying concern that key reforms adopted after 2000 may be undermining real political competition. The regime justifies these changes as necessary to ensure state capacity to govern and to secure continuing economic growth, but critics wonder whether the Russian desire for order could lead to an authoritarian outcome. The establishment political party, United Russia, favored by Putin, seemed to be emerging as the dominant political force in the lead up to elections in December 2007 for the Duma. Speculation circulated about whom Putin would promote, and with

what degree of success, as his favored successor in the March 2008 presidential election, or whether, at the last minute, Putin would find a way to stand for a third term himself, despite a constitutional prohibition.

Finally, Russians continue to seek new forms of collective identity. The loss of superpower status, the dominance of Western economic and political models, and the absence of a widely accepted ideology have all contributed to uncertainty about what it means to be Russian and where Russia fits into the world as a whole. Meanwhile, Russia itself suffers from internal divisions. Although overt separatism has been limited to the Republic of Chechnya, differing visions of collective identity have emerged in some of Russia's ethnic republics, particularly in Muslim areas. Other aspects of identity are also being reconsidered. Social class, a linchpin of Soviet ideology, may take on increasing importance in defining group solidarity, as working people seek new organizational forms to assert their rights. Changing gender roles have challenged both men and women to reconsider not only their relationships to one another, but also the impact of these changes on children and community values.

Implications for Comparative Politics

Many countries in the world today are attempting a transition from authoritarian rule to democratic governance. In Russia's case, one of the most important factors affecting this process is the tradition of strong state control. From tsarist times through the Soviet period, and now influencing present developments, is a history of a strong state organized around a central political figure. Russians have come to expect the state to provide a modicum of security and well-being. In addition, the intertwined character of politics, economics, and ideology in the Soviet Union has made democratization and economic reform difficult to realize at the same time. In effect, four transition processes began simultaneously in the early 1990s: democratization, market reform, a redefinition of national identity, and integration into the world economy. Whereas other democratizing countries may have undergone only one or two of these transitions at a time, Russia has tackled all four at once, and this has complicated each aspect of the process. The difficulties of extricating political from economic power are particularly stark. Because the former Communist elites had no private wealth to fall back on, corrupt or illegal methods were sometimes used to maintain former privileges—methods taken over by Russia's new capitalist class. Citizens, confronted with economic decline and an ideological vacuum, have been susceptible to appeals for strong state control, as well as to nationalist appeals. No doubt economic uncertainty has made the Russian public willing to accept strong leadership and limits on political expression that would be resisted in many Western countries. Examining these linkages between political and economic forces in Russia may provide insights for understanding other political settings. The Russian case also offers an opportunity to explore how differing cultural characteristics and diverse economic settings may affect how people understand the meaning of democracy.

Notes

[1] Vladimir Putin, "Speech and the Following Discussion at the Munich Conference on Security Policy," President of Russia Website, February 10, 2007, www.kremlin.ru/eng/speeches/2007/02/10/0138_type82912type82914type82917typc84779_118123.shtml (accessed September 21, 2007).

[2] "Russia Faces Angry EU in Energy Dispute," *Deutsche Welle*, January 9, 2007, www.dw-world.de/dw/article/0,2144,2304963,00.html (accessed September 21, 2007).

[3] Federal State Statistics Service of the Russian Federation, 2006, www.gks.ru/free_doc/2006/b06_13/04-01.htm (accessed September 21, 2007).

[4] Richard Pipes, *Russia Under the Old Regime* (London: Widenfelt & Nicolson, 1974).

[5] Ibid., pp. 22–24.

[6] Mikhail Gorbachev, *Perestroika: New Thinking for Our Country and the World* (New York: Harper, 1987).

[7] Vladimir Putin, "Annual Address to the Federal Assembly of the Russian Federation," President of Russia Website, April 25, 2005, www.kremlin.ru/eng/speeches/2005/04/25/2031_type70029type82912_87086.shtml (accessed September 21, 2007).

CHAPTER 22

Political Economy and Development

The collapse of the Soviet system in late 1991 ushered in a sea change, radically reducing the state's traditionally strong role in economic development and opening the Russian economy to foreign influence. However, the process of market reform that the Russian government pursued after 1991 brought with it a dramatic decline in economic performance as well as fundamental changes in social relationships. To respond, the Russian government struggled to create tools to regulate the new market forces and to manage the effects of global economic influence. Since 1999, after experiencing an unprecedented period of economic depression from 1991 to 1998, Russia has experienced renewed economic growth, but this growth has been built largely on the country's wealth of energy and natural resources. Extreme levels of social inequality and corruption remain, so that the relative costs and benefits of Russia's transition from a state-run economy to some form of quasi-market economy are still contested.

The Postwar Settlement and Beyond

Although it would be inappropriate to speak of a postwar settlement in the Soviet Union comparable to the pattern in Western Europe, we can speak of the emergence of a post-Stalinist settlement that extended from the death of Stalin in 1953 until the decline and collapse of the communist system in 1991. Although the Soviet Union was in no sense a political democracy during this period, this does not mean that the political leadership was indifferent to the needs of the population. In contrast to the Stalinist reliance on ideological indoctrination and terror to maintain state dominance over society, in the post-Stalinist period Khrushchev began a process that reflected greater responsiveness to the needs of the population at large as well as the broader political elite. The next Soviet leader, Leonid Brezhnev, brought further regularization and predictability into the Soviet political sphere so that the post-Stalinist settlement was characterized by a relative calm that some Western experts have dubbed a tacit social contract.[1] This tacit social contract implied not only an unwritten political accord, but also a set of economic and social relationships. According to this idea, in exchange for political compliance, the population enjoyed job security; a

lax work environment; low prices for basic goods, housing, and transport; free social services (medical care, recreational services); and minimal interference in personal life. Wages of the worst-off citizens were increased relative to those of the more educated and better-off portions of the population. The intelligentsia (historically Russia's social conscience and critic) was allowed more freedom for public discussion of issues that were not of crucial importance to the regime. The broader political elite also benefited as the Brezhnev leadership embarked on a policy of stability. Brezhnev made few personnel changes; this policy gained him the political loyalty of an aging elite that lacked the dynamism required to address pressing social and economic problems, such as declining growth rates, low levels of innovation, and poor productivity. In many ways, the post-Stalinist settlement contained the origins of its own decline, which was rooted in part in reduced capacity of the economy to fulfill expectations.

The post-Stalinist settlement was based in a centralized economic planning model that was able to deliver basic necessities to the Soviet population at relatively low cost, a feature that was a fundamental support for the tacit social contract. Under the Soviet command economy, land, factories, and all other important economic assets belonged to the state. Short- and long-term economic plans defined production goals, but these were frequently too ambitious to meet. Prices were controlled by the state; only in the peasant markets and the illegal black market did prices fluctuate in response to conditions of shortage or surplus. Evaluation of enterprises was not based on profit indicators, but primarily on meeting production quotas; therefore production decisions were not sensitive to price signals. Enterprises had neither the incentive nor the resources to increase production of goods in short supply or to respond to consumer demands. But the state could direct production to important social or economic priority sectors. Although military production was one such priority, others involved meeting essential social needs, as discussed below. Because of the focus on material production, ecological goals were subordinate to production quotas. Large nature-transforming projects (hydroelectric dams, huge factory complexes) were glorified as symbols of Soviet power. Energy intensity was among the highest in the world, and many priority industries (metallurgy, machine building, chemicals, and energy production) were highly polluting.

Another foundation of the post-Stalinist settlement was the relative isolation of economy and society from global influences. In the economic sphere, firms and individuals were not permitted to develop direct links to foreign partners; these were all channeled through the central economic bureaucracy. Such international isolation shielded the economy from recessions and depressions that plagued Western economies, but without foreign competition, the quality of many Russian consumer goods was low by international standards. Economic relations with neighboring countries that were part of the Soviet bloc, such as Poland, Hungary, Czechoslovakia, Bulgaria, and Romania, were conducted within the context of the centrally planned economy on the basis of the Council for Mutual Economic Assistance (CMEA), a kind of Soviet equivalent of the Common Market. Often particular regions in the USSR or countries in the Soviet bloc specialized in production of particular types of goods, which created trade synergies that made the entire economic system interdependent.

In the social sphere, the centralized Soviet system allowed the leadership to establish priorities. Meeting social goals was a clear policy focus, producing some of the most marked achievements of the Soviet system that also contributed to the stability of the post-Stalinist system. Benefits to the population included free health care, low-cost access to essential goods and services, maternity leave (partially paid), child benefits, and disability pensions. Mass education was another social priority of the Soviet regime, taking the form of universal access to primary and secondary schooling—leading to nearly universal literacy in a short period of time. Postsecondary education was free of charge, with state stipends provided to university students.

Guaranteed employment and job security were other core elements of the tacit social contract; only in exceptional cases could an enterprise fire an employee. Participation in the labor market was high: almost all able-bodied adults, both men and women, worked outside the home. Citizens received many social benefits through their place of employment, making the Soviet workplace a social as well as an economic institution. The full-employment policy made unemployment compensation unnecessary. The retirement age was fifty-five for women and sixty for men, although in the early 1980s about one-third of those beyond retirement age continued to work. Modest pensions were guaranteed by the state, ensuring a stable but minimal standard of living for retirement.

Another feature of the system was the relatively low level of inequality. As a matter of state policy, wage differentials between the best- and worst-paid were lower than in Western countries. This approach seemed in harmony with overriding cultural values, but it reduced the incentive for outstanding achievements and innovation. Because land and factories were state owned, individuals could not accumulate wealth in the form of real estate, stocks, or ownership of factories. Any privileges that did exist were modest by Western standards. Political elites did have access to scarce goods, higher-quality health care, travel, and vacation homes, but these privileges were hidden from public view. An underlying assumption seemed to be that a dismal equality was superior to the tensions and discontent that visible inequality might evoke.

For the intelligentsia, the regime offered increased opportunities for political participation by involving experts in policy debates, frequently calling upon economists, legal scholars, and other experts to provide advice on issues of economic and social policy. Although some members of the intelligentsia complained of inadequate material rewards (because of the regime's relatively egalitarian wage and social policies), incentives for working within the system were reinforced by increased recognition and access to information. By exercising strict control over dissidents (such as in the crackdown in the late 1970s on the Helsinki Watch Group that monitored human rights violations), the Soviet regime also set clear bounds for what was acceptable criticism. Further, contact with the West was discouraged. Travel to Western countries was restricted mainly to scholars, state/Party functionaries, athletes, and artists. Although tourist travel to the Soviet Union from Europe became commonplace, Soviet citizens were discouraged from having sustained contact with Western visitors. In this way, the regime hoped to stem rising expectations that would be difficult to satisfy. At the same time, the official media continued to disseminate information emphasizing unemployment, inflation, and crime in the West, all of them factors that Russia itself would experience once the communist system collapsed.

The post-Stalinist settlement and the tacit social contract on which it was based had a "carrot and stick" character. The repressive apparatus of the state continued to punish those who exceeded permissible bounds of dissent, but methods of control were more predictable and less violent than in the Stalinist period. More and more citizens had grown up under the Soviet system and were accustomed to those patterns of life; older population groups could compare their situation favorably with the past.

The Decline of the Post-Stalinist Settlement

The Brezhnev team's implicit social contract was effective at maintaining social stability for some years, but by the late 1970s a series of interconnected problems reached dramatic proportions just as the aging Brezhnev leadership seemed to have lost even the minimal dynamism it once had. At the root of these problems was a faltering economy. Growth rates, which had been between 6 and 7 percent annually in the 1950s, dipped below 3 percent by the last half of the 1970s and fell even lower in the 1980s. Slower growth meant greater difficulty in satisfying consumer and social expectations. Although Soviet growth may not have been unusually low by Western standards, per capita income was considerably lower than in the West. The arms race placed additional pressure on the Soviet economy. To maintain parity with the United States, the USSR had to devote a considerably larger proportion of its gross national product (GNP) to the military sector. Other factors also complicated economic policy by the late 1970s. Due to the isolation of the Soviet economy, both producers and consumers were denied access to many advances available in Western industrial societies, and Soviet producers were not spurred to make improvements in response to external competitive forces. Soviet economic structures could be effective only if shielded from global economic influences, and they were increasingly rigid, inhibiting innovation and increases in productivity required to support rising social expectations.

Although the Soviet Union was rich in natural resources, by the 1970s the most easily accessible deposits in the western part of the country were approaching depletion. To deal with this, Soviet leaders gave priority to the development of northern Siberia to permit exploitation of oil, natural gas, and precious metals. However, Siberian development proved to be complicated and expensive, due to permafrost conditions, transport distances, and the necessity of paying higher wages to attract workers. As the costs of extracting natural resources increased over time, real economic gains would depend on more effective production techniques and a more efficient workforce—aspects of production that the Soviet model did not encourage. Demographic patterns suggested serious future imbalances in the distribution of labor. In terms of quality of life, environmental quality declined, resulting in increasing health problems for the population. Finally, inadequate technological safeguards and an insufficient regulatory structure led to the disastrous nuclear accident at Chernobyl (in Ukraine) in 1986, which contaminated immense areas of agricultural land in Ukraine and Belorussia (now Belarus), as well as some areas of Russia. For many this disaster symbolized the broad-ranging failures of the Soviet economy to fulfill its ideological promises.

As economic problems mounted, the legitimacy of the system declined. By the early 1980s corruption within Party and state organs had increased, generating cynicism and low morale in the population. Slower expansion of the economy meant decreased opportunities for upward social mobility. Young people had to lower their aspirations and many took jobs below their skill levels. High levels of alcoholism contributed to a decrease in life expectancy for Soviet men, and an increase in infant mortality signaled a crisis in the health care system. Although basic social needs were met in the Soviet Union, production did not match consumer demands, which undermined workers' motivation to increase their labor productivity. Many goods and services, although economically in the reach of every citizen, were in short supply, so queues were a pervasive part of everyday life. The availability of advanced medical equipment was limited, and sometimes under-the-table payments were required to prompt better-quality service. Housing shortages restricted mobility and forced young couples and their children to share small apartments with parents. An irony of the system was that labor in many sectors was in constant short supply, a reflection of the inefficient use of the work force. Labor productivity was low by international standards and work discipline weak: drunkenness and absenteeism were common, further adversely affecting labor productivity. A Soviet saying of the time captured this element of the tacit social contract: "We pretend to work, they pretend to pay us." Although the lax work atmosphere reduced the likelihood and frequency of labor conflicts, it also kept production inefficient.

In this context Mikhail Gorbachev undertook a fundamental rethinking of the post-Stalinist settlement. However, Gorbachev's efforts to reform the economic system were halting and contradictory. The results were declining economic performance, increasing regionalism, and an uncertain economic environment. Only after the collapse of the USSR in 1991 did a concerted effort at fundamental economic change take place within the Russian Federation, marking a definitive end to the post-Stalinist settlement. Establishing a new economic foundation for social consensus would not prove so easy.

State and Economy

The transition from a planned economy based on state ownership to a market system based on private ownership has been a difficult one for Russia, involving a period of steep economic decline, with recovery beginning only in 1999. Determining an effective economic role for the state has been a major challenge for the post-Communist political leadership in Russia.

Economic Management

Principles of economic management radically changed after the collapse of the Soviet Union. In 1992, Boris Yeltsin immediately endorsed radical market reform, sometimes referred to as shock therapy because of the radical rupture it implied for the economy. The changes were to be rapid and thorough, jolting the Russian economy into a new mode of operation. Although shock therapy would inevitably throw large parts of the economy into a downward spin, reformers hoped the recovery would be relatively quick and that citizens would accept short-term economic sacrifices,

including rising unemployment and higher prices, in order to achieve longer-term economic benefits.

Market reform assumed a radically reduced role for the state in economic management. First and foremost this was because privatization put formerly state-owned factories in private hands. In addition, the government encouraged the formation of new small private businesses. Second, government control over most prices was ended; prices were to reflect supply and demand, spurring new private owners to respond to consumer demands and to increase efficiency and quality through exposure to a competitive economic environment. Finally, the economy was opened to international influences, largely removing the state's role as intermediary between Russian firms and foreign partners, suppliers, or markets.

In January 1992, Yeltsin's team removed or loosened price controls on most goods, resulting in high inflation, fuelled by the soft monetary policy of the Central Bank of Russia; the consumer price index increased by about 2,500 percent between December 1991 and December 1992. Money was printed with nothing tangible to back it up. Real wages (after controlling for the effects of inflation), on average, declined by an estimated 50 percent between late 1991 and January 1993. International lenders, most notably the International Monetary Fund (IMF), placed strict conditions on Russian loans in order to try to control inflationary tendencies, but the restrictions on the money supply that these policies implied produced their own problems.[2] By the late 1990s Russia was in the grip of a severe depression, more intense than the Great Depression of the 1930s in the United States and Western Europe. Industrial production was less than half the 1990 level. Basic industrial sectors such as machine building, light industry, construction materials, and wood products were the worst off. The depression fed on itself, as declining capacity in one sector deprived other sectors of buyers or suppliers. Consumer purchasing power dropped with the decline in real wages. Firms were unable to pay their suppliers, were in arrears to their employees, and owed taxes to the government. Even the state was behind in its wage, social benefit, and pension payments. Under these conditions, barter arrangements became common, often involving intertwined linkages of several enterprises or organizations.

Privatization. The government's program of rapid privatization of state enterprises produced other problems. In 1992, a privatization law was passed, and by early 1994, an estimated 80 percent of medium-sized and large state enterprises in designated sectors of the economy had been transformed into joint-stock companies. The most widely adopted method for privatizing state enterprises gave managers and workers of the enterprise (jointly) the right to acquire a controlling packet (51 percent) of enterprise shares at virtually symbolic prices. Each citizen of Russia was issued a privatization voucher with a nominal value of 10,000 rubles (about ten U.S. dollars). This privatization method allowed workers to use these vouchers to acquire shares in the enterprises where they worked. Although seeming to guarantee each citizen a portion of the benefits of the process, the voucher system did not achieve this goal. The value of the vouchers was too small, and the average Russian citizen didn't have the knowledge to use them effectively. This method, dubbed insider privatization, also had some negative consequences. Because workers held shares, managers were reluctant to increase efficiency by firing excess labor, which kept work discipline lax. At the same time, workers could not exercise effective use of their shares because of weak legal protection for shareholders and the weak economic position of many enterprises. Some managers extracted personal profit from enterprise operations rather than investing available funds to improve production. In addition, many managers did not have the necessary skills to restructure enterprise operations effectively, and some resisted badly needed outside investment that might threaten insider ownership. In August 2001, legislation strengthening shareholder rights was signed by the president, but the measure came too late to give the average citizen a say in economic management.

During a second stage of privatization, launched in 1995, firms could sell remaining shares for cash or investment guarantees. However, many enterprises were unattractive to potential Russian or foreign investors because they were white elephants with backward technology that would require massive infusions of capital for restructuring. Some of the more attractive enterprises (in sectors such as oil and gas production, telecommunications, mass communications, and minerals) fell into the hands of developing financial-industrial conglomerates that had acquired their wealth through positions of power or connections in the government. The loans-for-shares program of 1996 was particularly controversial and is credited by some observers with helping to secure the position of Russia's wealthy and powerful business elite by granting favored businessmen control of lucrative enterprises (through control of state shares) in exchange for loans to the cash-strapped Russian government. Private entrepreneurs were actively encouraged by the new Russian leadership to form small start-up businesses, and these new ventures were often the most dynamic. They too, however, faced a number of obstacles, which included confusing regulations, high taxes, lack of capital, and a poor infrastructure (transport, banking, and communications) for doing business. With the breakdown of the Soviet distribution system, trade became the most lucrative arena for new firms. These included thousands of small kiosks on city streets; over time, the most successful ones moved into permanent quarters, alongside a wide range of restaurants, cafes, and entertainment establishments. Although the number of small businesses increased quickly in the early 1990s, they have provided only about 10–15 percent of employment and GNP, compared to over 50 percent in most European countries, and the share does not seem to be increasing.

Privatization in Russia was rapid and thorough, compared to other postcommunist countries, but the results were disappointing. Productivity and efficiency did not increase significantly; unprofitable firms continued to operate; investment was weak; and the benefits of ownership were not widely or fairly distributed. The government continued to subsidize ineffective operations through various means, making most Russian firms uncompetitive and unattractive to potential investors. Reform of agriculture produced even more disappointing results than industrial privatization. Large joint-stock companies and associations of individual households were created on the basis of former state and collective farms. These privatized companies operated inefficiently, and agricultural output declined throughout the 1990s. Foreign food imports (including meat and a whole range of processed goods) also undercut domestic producers, contributing to a downward spiral in agricultural investment and production.

In 2003, a new Land Code took effect, allowing the sale of agricultural land for agricultural purposes, with some restrictions, including the exclusion of foreign buyers.[3]

As privatization failed to bring the promised benefits, renationalization of some enterprises came under discussion. This option was, for the most part, rejected, except in key cases, such as the dominant company involved in the natural gas industry, Gazprom; by 2006, the state owned a controlling share of the company. The pivotal importance of the energy sector for renewed economic growth and as a foreign policy resource made state control of this sector an important political asset.

Obstacles to Successful Market Reform. A key obstacle to the success of the market reform agenda has been the weakness of economic management by state institutions. This may seem ironic, since one of the main ideas underlying market reform was to reduce state control of the economy. Even in established market economies, however, an effective state apparatus is essential to carrying out needed regulatory and law-enforcement functions. Two examples illustrate the point: tax collection and law enforcement. Without an effective tax collection system, the government cannot acquire the revenues needed to pay its own bills on time, to provide essential services to the population, and to ensure a well-functioning economic infrastructure (such as transportation, energy, and public utilities). Likewise, without effective state enforcement, business contracts cannot be upheld, and key regulatory functions, no matter how well designed on paper, cannot be executed. Thus the weakness of important functions such as regulation of the banking sector, of industrial standards, of health and safety, and of labor standards generates economic uncertainty. If government cannot provide these services efficiently, businesses may take matters into their own hands, for example, by hiring private security services, turning to the mafia for protection, or paying bribes. Weak government capacity feeds corruption and criminality, producing risks both to business and to the population at large. In one area, the efficiency of tax collection, the Russian government has made great strides in recent years. However in other areas the Russian state remains weak and often ineffective.

Until 2004, the central state had difficulty exerting its authority in relation to the regions of the Russian Federation, of which there were eighty-nine until December 2005, when the first merger of regions occurred, reducing the level to eighty-five by early 2008. Centralizing reforms partially remedied this situation, but in the process generated other problems, discussed in Chapter 23.

A second obstacle relates to the power of business oligarchs, wealthy individuals who have benefited from the privatization process and often have had significant political influence as well.[4] These new Russian capitalists gained control of important economic assets but often did not reinvest their profits to spur business development; rather, wealth was siphoned off through capital flight, in which money was removed from the country and deposited in foreign accounts or assets. Diverse methods of laundering money to avoid taxes became widespread in the 1990s. Upon becoming president, Putin took measures to rein in the power of the economic oligarchs, making clear that those who attempted to use their financial positions to affect political outcomes would suffer sanctions.

Several attacks on media moguls were the first stage in this process, as business magnates Vladimir Gusinsky and Boris Berezovksy were targeted. Gusinsky's NTV was almost the only TV critic of the Kremlin's military action against the secessionist Republic of Chechnya; Gusinsky also had close ties to President Vladimir Putin's political rival, Moscow mayor Luzhkov. Berezovksy was also a thorn in the Kremlin's side, threatening to broadcast charges on TV-6 alleging government links to 1999 apartment bombings that had been attributed to terrorists. Charges of tax evasion and fraud were brought against both men and were defended as part of the government's campaign to assure proper business practices by business oligarchs. Berezovsky fled to self-imposed exile in the United Kingdom, while Gusinsky fled to Spain.

A controversial new chapter in Putin's battle with the oligarchs opened in October 2003 when Mikhail Khodorkovsky, the chief executive officer and major shareholder of the giant Russian oil company, Yukos, was placed under arrest for fraud and tax evasion. Cited by *Forbes* as Russia's richest man, Khodorkovsky's company was forced to dispose of its major asset, Yuganskneftegas, to pay tax bills presented by the

Russian government. Following a high-profile trial in May 2005, Khodorkovsky was sentenced by a Russian court to nine years in prison on charges of fraud, tax evasion, and embezzlement. Critics of the government charged that the process was motivated and influenced by political considerations and that it marked a step back from democratic reform and due process. Many critics felt the attacks on Khodorkovsky, Gusinsky, and Berezovsky were cases of selective enforcement to rid the president of economically powerful critics. Khodorkovsky had publicly opposed key government initiatives, provided support to opposition political parties, and proposed radical changes in political structures, changes that would have weakened the power of the Russian presidency. The attack on Yukos at least temporarily undermined investor confidence (including foreign investors) among shareholders who feared government pretexts for economic takeovers.

Corruption is another major obstacle to effective economic management. Transparency International, an independent civil society organization devoted to exposing and fighting corruption throughout the world, produces an annual Corruption Perceptions index, based on a compilation of independent surveys. In 2007, Russia received a poor ranking, 2.3 on a 10-point scale, with 10 being the least corrupt.[5] This placed Russia in a tied position of 143 (with three other countries, including Indonesia and Gambia) out of the 180 countries surveyed. This position contrasts sharply with ratings of Western countries; eleven of the EU-15 countries as well as Norway, Switzerland, Iceland, the United States, and Canada placed among the twenty-two countries perceived to have the lowest levels of corruption. Although Putin set the reduction of corruption as a goal early in his first term of office, Russia's 2006 score showed insignificant improvement over the year 2000 (from 2.4 to 2.5 on the 10-point scale). Putin's failure to reduce both the reality and perception of corruption represents a major weakness in his ability to manage the economy.

Various forms of corruption can have different impacts on economic performance. Although petty corruption may help to compensate for inefficiencies in the economic system or in state services, one form of corruption, often referred to as "state capture" (the ability of firms to turn state regulations to their advantage through payoffs to officials), has been a major

impediment to economic development.[6] More generally, low levels of law and order undermine economic growth and the capacity of the state to support good economic performance, especially when combined with rapid democratization.[7] Like corruption, the government's inability to control both ordinary and organized crime is another weakness in economic management.

Economic Recovery. Despite these problems with economic management, since 1999 Russia's economic slide has reversed. Economic growth registered 6.3 percent in 1999 and has remained in positive territory ever since, with 6 to 7 percent growth in GDP since 2003, representing the first years of sustained economic recovery since the Soviet collapse.[8] Other developments have fueled optimism about Russia's economic future. A budget surplus has replaced a deficit, and the foreign debt load has declined from 90 percent of GDP in 1998 to 33.3 percent in 2006.[9] Several factors contributed to the reversal, but most had less to do with government policy than with factors outside the state's control. One factor was a radical devaluation of the ruble after the August 1998 financial crisis. The ruble's devaluation led to a sharp reduction in imports of Western commodities, making Russian producers competitive. Firms could now improve their products, put underused labor back to work, and so increase productivity. The state budget benefited from improved tax revenues; barter declined, as did payment arrears.[10]

A second trigger for the economic upturn was rising international oil and gas prices, making Russian economic success heavily dependent on its natural resources. Tax proceeds from oil and gas revenues also have spilled into government tax coffers, making up as much as 20 to 30 percent of the budget.[11] A Stabilization Fund, created by the Russian government to hold excess income from high oil and gas prices, reached about $64.7 billion in September 2006.[12] The Fund is intended to protect the country from the shock of a possible future decline in energy prices and also to prevent the government from establishing expenditure levels that may not be sustainable. However, critics suggest that the government should be using some of the budget surplus to deal with pressing issues such as shoring up the pension fund or increasing investment in critical infrastructure and industrial capacity of the country.

To be sure, since coming to office Putin has taken some measures to improve the state's ability to manage the economy. After a sluggish first year, an active legislative program emerged in 2001 and 2002. A new Ministry for Economic Development and Trade was charged with developing the underlying concept. One of the first steps involved simplifying the tax system, in order to increase tax compliance and facilitate enforcement. A 13 percent flat income tax was one very visible aspect of the package, and adjustments were made to corporate taxes as well. Other government initiatives included amendments to the corporate governance law to protect shareholders' rights; legislation to control money laundering; provision for the sale of land to both domestic and foreign buyers (in the first instance, commercial and urban land only); a new labor code that tightened conditions for trade union organization; a new system governing the distribution of authority and of tax revenues among the center, the regions, and local organs; a new customs code; pension reform; amendments to the bankruptcy law; and initiatives to reduce subsidization of housing and communal services. Efforts to secure Russia's membership in the World Trade Organization have been another project of the government that has fueled optimism about Russia's trade growth. In 2004, the EU confirmed its support for Russian membership in the World Trade Organization (WTO), and in November 2006 the United States and Russia agreed on a trade pact that overcame another obstacle to Russia's admission. Nonetheless, WTO membership was still on the table in 2007. From 2005 onward, criticism was again emerging that the government was sluggish in pushing forward further reforms, that the economic bubble could burst if energy prices fell, and that the exchange rate for the ruble was again reaching levels that could undermine the competitiveness of domestic production.

Social Policy

The Soviet experience led Russians to expect a broad range of social welfare support from the state, expectations that are hard to realize in a market economy and in the face of declining economic performance. In the 1990s, budget constraints necessitated cutbacks in state welfare programs at a time when there was a growing need for them. Pensions had less and less buying power, and state services proved inadequate to deal with the increasing problems of homelessness and poverty. In line with the new market ideology, some spots in universities were accessible only through payment of tuition while others were free of charge; and although a system of universal health care remained, higher-quality health care became more obviously dependent on ability to pay. Benefits provided through the workplace were cut back, as even viable businesses faced pressures to reduce costs and increase productivity.

Winners and Losers of Economic Reform.   Some groups have benefited from the reform process, while others have suffered sharp declines. Wage rates are highest for highly skilled employees in the natural resource sectors (such as oil and gas), in banking and finance, and for individuals with marketable skills such as knowledge of English or German. At the extreme end, the wealthiest enjoy a standard of living that is luxurious even by Western standards. These people, many of them multimillionaires with Western bank accounts, were able to take advantage of the privatization process to gain positions in lucrative sectors like banking, finance, oil, and gas.

On the other side, in the 1990s, the number of homeless and beggars skyrocketed, especially in large cities like Moscow, a magnet for displaced persons and refugees from the war zones on Russia's perimeter. Furthermore, as a result of low wage levels, the majority of those in poverty were, and continue to be, the working poor. Poverty is highest among rural residents, the unemployed, the less educated, pensioners, and the disabled, but it has declined in recent years. Among the employed, declines in income have affected those without easily marketable skills, including unskilled laborers in low-priority sectors of the economy and people working in areas of public service such as education. Consumer price inflation gradually declined over the 1990s but still had an important impact on incomes; in 1999 the rate of inflation was 86 percent, falling to around 10 percent in 2006.[13]

Unemployment has been lower than expected because many enterprises have kept underemployed staff on their rolls, at low wages or with temporary layoffs. Official estimates are about 9.8 percent in 2000 and between 6 and 9 percent in 2004 to 2006, but actual rates are probably higher.[14] These figures also hide short-term layoffs, workers who are still employed but only sporadically paid, or people who have shifted to partial employment. On the other hand, employment in the shadow economy goes unreported. Levels of unemployment are particularly high in some regions, including republics and regions with high ethnic minority populations. Aboriginal groups in Russia's far north have suffered especially adverse effects as a result of the economic decline. Northern regions depend on the maintenance of a fragile transport and communications system for deliveries of basic necessities such as fuel and food. Social impacts of economic stress have included higher rates of crime, suicide, and mortality; and alcoholism continues to be a significant problem, particularly for males. All of these factors increase the likelihood of dysfunctional family structures, producing a particularly marked impact on children.

With the economic upturn following 1999, large differentials in income and wealth remain, but the portion of the population living below the subsistence level has declined noticeably (from 27.3 percent of the population in 2001 to 15.8 percent in 2005). Overall, since 2000, levels of personal consumption have grown following years of decline, but many individuals (particularly men) work two to three jobs just to make ends meet. Public opinion surveys indicate that between 2003 and 2007 most Russians expected little change in the economic situation of their families in the near future.[15]

Reforms in Social Policy.   A particularly contentious issue, which led to massive street demonstrations in several Russian cities in early 2005, involves changes to social welfare policy. Referred to as the "monetarization of social benefits" (Federal Law 122), the reforms involved cutbacks in the free provision of services (such as public transport and medicine) to groups such as pensioners, veterans, and the disabled and they were replaced by a modest monetary payment, lower than the cost people would have to pay for the services. Subsidies for public utilities and housing were also reduced.

Viewed as part of the liberal reform process, these reforms were intended to increase the role of the market and to reduce the direct financial burden on local governments. Research does indicate that those who had previously received the benefits were often not the most disadvantaged. The reform, in this sense, involved an effort to target state support to the more needy parts of

the population, in line with general efforts to reduce the poverty rate. However, many Russians viewed the changes as a direct reduction in social welfare, a rescinding benefits that had been earned by those who had served the country through years of hardship. Following large-scale demonstrations throughout the country, the government agreed to a modest increase in pensions and to a restoration of transportation subsidies. Although Putin's popularity suffered a temporary decline during this episode, it rebounded quickly. Nonetheless, the issue galvanized popular discontent, providing the political opposition with the opportunity to mobilize popular protests against the government.

In 2005 Putin announced a new program of National Projects intended, to some extent, to redress inadequacies in the social sector and to reverse Russia's decline in population. The Projects focus on four priority areas: health care, education, housing, and agriculture. Some observers interpret them as a modest step back from reliance on market vehicles to address social policy, in line with traditional expectations of citizens about the leading role of the state in social welfare. The National Projects, under the stewardship of First Deputy Prime Minister Dmitry Medvedev, got off to a slow start, however; opinion surveys indicate that most Russians were not impressed by what had been achieved by 2007 and had only modest hopes for the future.[16]

Society and Economy

The changing nature of the Russian economy brought with it transformations in the social structure and attitudes in Russian society. Whereas the Soviet system was built on an ideology emphasizing social equality and collective responsibility, market reforms tend to reward individual initiative with greater economic returns. Thus the nature of social inequality and social expectations is undergoing a process of gradual but radical transformation.

Inequality and Ethnic Minorities

According to the most recent census, carried out in 2002, ethnic Russians make up just under 80 percent of the population, compared to 51 percent of the Soviet population in 1989. The second largest group is the

Tatars (3.8 percent), a group which has its own republic in the Russian Federation and which has an Islamic cultural base. There are several other Islamic groups in Russia, including those (in addition to the Tatars) inhabiting republics around the Volga River (the Bashkirs, 1.2 percent, and the Chuvash, 1.1 percent), and smaller groups in the northern Caucasus region (Chechens, Ingush, Dagestani). Another significant minority group is Ukrainians, a Slavic group close to the Russians ethnically, making up 2 percent of the population but without their own territory within Russia, rather a diaspora from neighboring Ukraine. As these data suggest, there are a large number of smaller population groups in Russia, including aboriginal peoples of the Russian north. In recent years immigration has introduced even further diversity into the Russian population, involving small but rising numbers of Chinese, Vietnamese, and Koreans, as well as larger numbers of people from neighboring former Soviet republics such as Georgia, Armenia, and Azerbaizhan.[17]

Inequality in Russia is to some degree related to ethnicity, but data are not available to document these relationships. Rather, regional differences provide some indication of these patterns. Twenty-one of Russia's federal units are republics, explicitly based on the presence of a minority ethnic group in the region. (See the map in Chapter 21, p. 325.) Therefore regional

differences, while indicative, are not a perfect measure of ethnic inequality, especially since differences within particular regions are also substantial. Using the Human Development Index as a guide, a 2005 World Bank report concludes that "differences across Russian regions are at least as large as differences among a majority of countries in the world. At one end of the spectrum, Moscow is on a par with Portugal and Argentina, while on the other hand Tuva compares with Indonesia and Nicaragua." At the same time, the authors note that Russia's pattern of regional inequality is similar to that of "other large countries with a complex regional structure."[18] The richest regions are large cities in largely Russian ethnic areas (Moscow, St. Petersburg) and those areas rich in natural resources. Poor regions include those in the trans-Caucasus area and other marginalized locations.

Inequality and Women

During the Soviet period, the official ideology of the party advocated gender equality and integration of women into the labor market. This stance was rooted in the belief that economic inequality between the genders and, in particular, economic dependence of women on their husbands, was a primary factor that prevented women from achieving their potential and from making an optimal contribution to society. Soviet women did achieve virtual equality in educational opportunity by the end of the Stalinist period, and by the 1980s 86 percent of Soviet working age women were in the labor force; children were either cared for in public day care facilities or by relatives (usually the grandmother, since the retirement age for women was fifty-five). Despite their relatively high levels of qualification, in the Soviet period women occupied lower-status and lower-paid jobs than men, particularly in sectors such as retail trade, education, health, culture, and administration. An exception was the medical profession, where the majority of physicians were women, but that occupation enjoyed relatively lower status than in the West.

In the Soviet period, demands on Russian working women were heavy due to their triple burden (employee, wife, and mother). In addition poor supplies of consumer goods, lack of laborsaving devices (such as dishwashers and automatic washing machines), and a weak consumer service sector (such as carry-out restaurants and laundries) made these duties time consuming. In

---

Figure 22.1

Immigration into Russia, 1997–2006

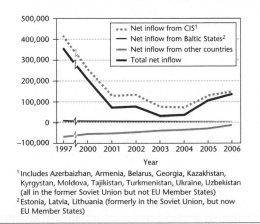

- ···· Net inflow from CIS[1]
- —— Net inflow from Baltic States[2]
- ····· Net inflow from other countries
- —— Total net inflow

[1] Includes Azerbaizhan, Armenia, Belarus, Georgia, Kazakhstan, Kyrgystan, Moldova, Tajikistan, Turkmenistan, Ukraine, Uzbekistan (all in the former Soviet Union but not EU Member States)
[2] Estonia, Latvia, Lithuania (formerly in the Soviet Union, but now EU Member States)

Source: Calculated from data on the website of the Federal State Statistics Service of the Russian Federation, www.gks.ru.

the post-communist period, the service sector has grown dramatically and consumer goods are widely available in stores; however, only a certain portion of the population has the financial resources to take advantage of these facilities. For most Russians, the situation deteriorated in the 1990s; some women and even more men took on two to three jobs to make ends meet. Since 1999, when economic growth was restored, consumption and incomes have begun to rise, giving larger numbers of Russians access to the benefits of a consumer society and reducing the burden of domestic duties on more affluent parts of the population.

In general, women have proven more adaptable to change than men, evidenced in life expectancy rates. Life expectancy for Soviet men fell from sixty-six years in 1966–1967 to under fifty-nine in 2003 (from seventy-four to seventy-two for women), rising only slightly by 2005.[19] Women still carry the bulk of domestic responsibilities, and most women feel compelled to work outside the home to contribute to the family income. Many women take advantage of the permitted three-year maternity leave, which is only partially paid. Employers are sometimes reluctant to hire women of childbearing age, since exercise of maternity leave is often viewed as disruptive in the workplace. Some data suggest, however, that while women are more likely to register with unemployment offices and take longer to find new jobs, levels of actual unemployment are about equal for men and women.[20]

The Generation Gap

Generational change is an important factor in understanding Russia's economic development. Younger Russians are often better equipped to adapt to new economic conditions than their elders. Not only are they more flexible due to their age, but they also have different expectations; whereas those who grew up in the Soviet system became accustomed to a network of social protection and state programs, young people are more oriented toward maximizing self-interest and more likely to appreciate the importance of individual initiative in securing their economic future. Their educational experience has reinforced these skills and attitudes, and they tend to be more supportive of the market transition.

Nonetheless, people may resist changing certain cultural attitudes that are not congruent with a market

economy, and if they do so, these changes will likely take generations. These attitudes include a weak tradition of individual entrepreneurship, a widespread commitment to egalitarian values, and a reliance on relations of personal trust rather than written contracts. Profit, as a measure of success, is less important to many Russians than is support for friends and coworkers; thus, firing redundant workers may be an unpalatable approach. Selection of business partners or recruitment of personnel may be strongly influenced by personal contacts and relationships rather than by merit. The incentive structures of the Soviet period also have been internalized by older population groups, including features that encourage risk avoidance, low productivity, poor punctuality, absenteeism, lack of personal responsibility and initiative, and a preference for security over achievement.[21] However, young people in Russia are gradually being socialized in a new cultural environment, and when offered appropriate incentives, Russian employees tend to operate at high levels of efficiency and, after a period of time, to adopt those work habits that are rewarded by the employing organization.

Some other examples of generational differences in Russia mirror West European patterns. For example, public opinion surveys in 2006–2007 indicate that while 54 percent of respondents between eighteen and twenty-four years of age use the Internet, usage is lower among older age groups, at a level of 15 percent for forty-five to fifty-four-year-olds, and 4 percent for those fifty-five years of age and above.[22] On the other side, the young are more likely than the old to be unemployed in Russia, the highest rates affecting those between twenty and twenty-nine years of age; in 2005 the state statistical agency indicated a rate of 17.9 percent for those in their early twenties and 13 percent for those twenty-five to twenty-nine.[23] Nonetheless, public opinion surveys indicate that younger people are more satisfied than older people with the way the government is handling the economy and are more positive about the situation in the country. Atypical of Western societies, however, is the overall structure of employment income in relation to age. Here younger people who are employed often have an advantage, since their skills are more up-to-date and relevant to current market demands. Pensioners and many older employees in Russia, rather than anticipating "golden years" of comfort, are often at the lowest levels of the income scale.

The Dilemmas of European Integration

An important change since 1991 has been Russia's increasing integration into the global economy, and in this context, Europe has been a particularly important point of reference. Gorbachev permitted joint ventures and reduced barriers to foreign contacts. The Yeltsin and Putin governments have pursued this policy even more aggressively. Over time, restrictions on foreign investment have been loosened and in some sectors lifted entirely, and firms are now allowed to conclude agreements directly with foreign partners. The value of the ruble has been allowed, to some extent, to respond to market conditions. Western investment has gradually increased, and Western governments (with Germany at the top of the list) have made generous commitments of technical and humanitarian assistance. Assistance programs have included training programs to help government officials, individual entrepreneurs, and social organizations adapt to the new challenges of market reform. The World Bank, the International Monetary Fund (IMF), and the EU have also contributed substantial amounts of economic assistance, often in the form of repayable credits. In recent years, with economic revival, Russia is no longer dependent on this assistance; and since 2001, the Russian government has decided to forgo additional IMF credits.

The nature and extent of Russia's future economic integration with Europe may have an important impact on the country's economic performance. Whereas in 1994, Ukraine was Russia's most important trading partner, now EU countries top the list: in 2005 the Netherlands received 10.1 percent of Russian imports, followed by Italy (9.6 percent) and Germany (8.1 percent). Germany provided 13.4 percent of imports in 2004, followed by Ukraine (7.9 percent), China (7.3 percent), and the United States (4.6 percent).[24] In 2006, Russia's foreign trade with countries of the expanded EU (more than 50 percent of the total) far exceeded combined exports to the countries of the Commonwealth of Independent States (CIS).[25] Thus, by now the European Union is Russia's most important trading partner; particularly important is the export of oil and gas resources to Europe. While Europe is dependent on Russia for energy, Russia also depends on Europe as a consumer of this most important export commodity. In 2006, over 65 percent of Russian exports were fuels or energy, whereas only about 6 percent were machinery and equipment, with other resources such as metals and timber making up a large part of the balance.[26] In 2004, the EU confirmed its support for Russian membership in the World Trade Organization (WTO), as observers speculated that a quid pro quo had been reached in exchange for Russian agreement to raise domestic oil prices (since their low level allegedly gives Russian producers an unfair competitive advantage) and to ratify the Kyoto Accord on Climate Change, an important priority of the European Union.

In addition to expanding the proportion of Russia's trade with the EU, Russia and the EU were set to renegotiate the EU-Russia Partnership and Cooperation Agreement (first concluded in 1997) at the EU-Russia summit in 2007; however, Poland, now an EU member state, vetoed the negotiations due to a Russian embargo on meat imports from Poland. Despite such problems, Russia's economic recovery provided increased leverage in the EU-Russian relationship after 1999. For example, Russia demanded designation as a strategic partner of the EU, rejecting inclusion in the EU's European Neighborhood Policy. In 2003 four *Common Spaces* for EU-Russian cooperation were agreed upon (Common Economic Space; Freedom, Security, and Justice; External Security; Research, Education, and Culture), and in 2005 *Roadmaps* for the development were set out. The 2004 EU enlargement brought other changes in the EU-Russian relationship. Russia, after some resistance, agreed to apply the terms of the EU-Russia Partnership and Cooperation Agreement to the new Member States, which brought some changes to trading relationships with those countries. A longer-term issue for Russia resulting from EU enlargement has to do with border regimes. As Estonia, Latvia, Lithuania, and Poland prepare to join the Schengen group, the border controls between these countries and Russia have been tightened. In addition to the human impacts, there are also potential economic effects, as cross-border trade, particularly "shuttle trade" involving small operators who trade goods at favorable prices across the border, are subject to stricter control. Cross-border initiatives of the European Union, such as Euroregions or EUROREG programs, create the opportunity for Russia to develop positive economic linkages with regions in bordering EU countries, as was done with Finnish partners earlier, and in this way to take advantage of EU funding. Meanwhile, Russia pushes for visa-free travel to Europe.

Russia has had problems attracting foreign investment, even in its improved economic circumstances since 1999, but levels have been rising since 2002.[27] Nonetheless, levels of foreign direct investment still remain low compared to other East European countries—less than 4 percent of the per capita level achieved in the Czech Republic and Slovakia, and about a quarter of the Polish level in 2002. In 2006, 55 percent of foreign investment came from the Netherlands, Cyprus, and Luxembourg—countries that have been major recipients of Russian capital flight— suggesting that some of these investment funds may be repatriated Russian capital or profits.[28]

Russia in the Global Economy

With a highly skilled work force and an advanced technological base in certain sectors (especially military sectors), Russia has many of the ingredients necessary to become a competitive and powerful force in the global economy. However, reliance on energy exports to bolster the economy and government tax base poses risk. If the country's industrial capacity is not restored, reliance on natural resource exports will leave Russia vulnerable to global economic fluctuations in supply and demand. At the same time, its wealth in natural resources has given Russia advantages compared to its neighbors. Ultimately, Russia's position in the global economy will depend on the ability of the country's leadership to fashion a viable approach to domestic economic challenges and to facilitate differentiation of the country's export base.

Notes

[1]Peter Hauslohner, "Politics Before Gorbachev: De-Stalinization and the Roots of Reform," in Alexander Dallin and Gail W. Lapidus (eds.), *The Soviet System in Crisis: A Reader of Western and Soviet Views* (Boulder, Colo.: Westview Press, 1991), pp. 37–63.

[2]See, for example, Joseph Stiglitz, *Globalization and Its Discontents* (New York: W. W. Norton & Co., 2002).

[3]Gregory Feifer, "Putin Tries Incremental Rather than Radical Reform in the Countryside," *RFE/RL Russian Political Weekly* 3, no. 8 (February 21, 2003), www.rferl.org/reports/rpw/2003/02/8-210203.asp (accessed September 21, 2007).

[4]Sergei Peregudov, "The Oligarchic Model of Russian Corporatism," in Archie Brown (ed.), *Contemporary Russian Politics:*

A Reader (New York: Oxford University Press, 2001), p. 259.

[5]Transparency International, Annual Report 2006, p. 21; http://www.transparency.org/policyresearch/surveys_indices/cpi/2007 (accessed September 21, 2007).

[6]Joel Hellman and Daniel Kaufmann, "Confronting the Challenge of State Capture in Transition Economies," *Finance and Development* 38, no. 3 (September 2001), www.imf.org/external/pubs/ft/fandd/2001/09/hellman.htm (accessed September 21, 2007).

[7]Victor Polterovich and Vladimir Popov, "Democratization, Quality of Institutions and Economic Growth," manuscript based on a revised version of a paper presented at the GDN Sixth Annual Conference in Dakar, January, 2005, p. 38, www.nes.ru/%7Evpopov/documents/Democracy-2006April.pdf (accessed September 21, 2007).

[8]Economist Intelligence Unit (EIU), *Country Report: Russia* (London: EIU, December, 2006). p. 5; (December 2003), p. 5.

[9]Economist Intelligence Unit (EIU), *Russia: Country Profile 2007*, p. 67; 2002, p. 52.

[10]Jacques Sapir, "Russia's Economic Rebound: Lessons and Future Directions," *Post-Soviet Affairs* 18, no. 1 (January–March 2002): 6.

[11]E. T. Gurvich, "Makroekonomicheskaia otsenka roli rossiiskogo neftegazovogo sektora" (Macroeconomic Evaluation of the Role of the Russian Oil-Gas Sector), *Voprosy ekonomiki* no. 10 (2004).

[12]Novosti Russian News and Information Agency, Sept. 11, 2006; en.rian.ru/business/20060911/53714492.html (accessed September 21, 2007).

[13]Economist Intelligence Unit (EIU), *Country Report: Russia* (December 2006). p. 5; (December 2003), p. 5.

[14]Economist Intelligence Unit (EIU), *Country Report: Russia* (March 2002), p. 13; Federal State Statistics Service, Russian Federation, http://www.gks.ru/free_doc/2007/b07_11/06-01.htm (accessed November 26, 2007).

[15]Levada-Center, *Vestnik obshchestvennogo mnenia* (November–December 2004): 104; and Levada-Center data, www.levada.ru/economic.htmlonlinel (accessed September 21, 2007).

[16]Public Opinion Foundation, "National Projects: Preliminary Results and Prospects," January 18, 2007, bd.english.fom.ru/cat/societas/society_power/nat_project. For the website about the National Projects, see www.rost.ru/ (accessed September 21, 2007).

[17]2002 census of the Russian Federation, www.perepis2002.ru/ct/html/TOM_04_01.htm (accessed September 21, 2007).

[18]World Bank, "Russian Federation Reducing Poverty through Growth and Social Policy Reform," Report No. 28923-RU, (February 24, 2005), pp. 32–33.

[19]Federal State Statistics Service, Russian Federation, http://www.gks.ru/free_doc/2007/b07_11/05-08.htm (accessed November 27, 2007).

[20]Sarah Ashwin and Elaine Bowers, "Do Russian Women Want to Work?" in Mary Buckley, ed., *Post-Soviet Women: From the*

Baltics to Central Asia (Cambridge: Cambridge University Press, 1997), p. 23.

[21] Victor Zaslavsky, "From Redistribution to Marketization: Social and Attitudinal Change in Post-Soviet Russia," in Gail W. Lapidus, ed., *The New Russia: Troubled Transformation* (Boulder, Colo.: Westview Press, 1994), p. 125.

[22] Public Opinion Foundation, "The Internet in Russia: Russia on the Internet," 18th release, Winter 2006–2007, www.bd.english.fom.ru/report/whatsnew/eint0701 (accessed September 21, 2007).

[23] Federal State Statistics Service of the Russian Federation, www.gks.ru/free_doc/2006/b06_13/05-15.htm (accessed September 21, 2007).

[24] Economist Intelligence Unit (EIU), *Country Report: Russia*, (December 2005), p. 5.

[25] Economist Intelligence Unit (EIU), *Russia: Country Profile 2007*, pp. 52–53.

[26] Ibid, pp. 52, 66.

[27] Federal State Statistics Service of the Russian Federation, www.gks.ru/free_doc/2006/b06_13/22-15.htm (accessed September 21, 2007).

[28] Economist Intelligence Unit (EIU), *Russia: Country Profile 2007*, p. 54.

CHAPTER 23

Governance and Policymaking

When Russia became an independent country in December 1991, dramatic changes in state structure and governing processes followed. The new Russian leadership endorsed liberal democratic principles as the basis of its new political institutions, and in April 2005 Putin declared, "[T]he development of Russia as a free and democratic state [is] the main political and ideological goal."[1] Critics, however, are less certain about the development of democracy in Russia, as measures introduced by Putin to strengthen presidential power seem to undermine some of the Russian Federation's founding democratic principles. Disagreement over the status of Russian democracy and its future forms the backdrop for our examination of Russian state structures and policymaking.

Organization of the State

As noted in Chapter 21, ratification of the new Russian constitution in 1993 was a contentious political process that followed a violent confrontation between the president and the parliament. The process culminated in a narrowly successful popular referendum on a document that reflected Yeltsin's own preferences. Nonetheless, public opinion polls suggest that over time the new constitution has acquired broad-based popular legitimacy, even if its interpretation is sometimes hotly contested and many of the institutions that it establishes do not enjoy popular trust (see Figure 23.1).

The document affirms many established principles of liberal democratic governance—competitive elections

Figure 23.1

Level of Trust in Various Institutions in Russia

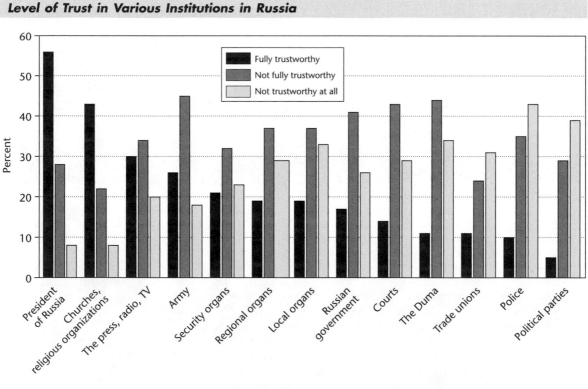

Source: Levada Center, www.levada.ru/press/2004092702.html (accessed April 28, 2005).

within a multiparty context, separation of powers, an independent judiciary, federalism, and protection of individual civil liberties. However, another key feature is the strength of the president's executive power. This feature is both a response to the demands for leadership that are required in a period of radical change and a reflection of Russia's political tradition, which has long been characterized by strong central political authority. Despite the constitutional basis for strong executive power, in practice throughout the 1990s the state demonstrated only a weak capacity to govern. Associated declines in economic performance elicited a countertendency after Putin's election in 2000 in the form of a recentralization of political power.

The constitution also lays the groundwork for institutional conflict between governing structures, conflicts that have not always taken a constructive form. The Russian Federation inherited a complex structure of regional subunits from the Soviet period. Between 1991 and 1993, negotiations between the central government and the various regions led to the establishment of a complicated federal structure with eighty-nine federal units. Some of these subnational governments demanded increased autonomy—even sovereignty—and one, Chechnya, demanded independence, leading to a protracted civil war.

The relationship between organs of the federal government has also been conflictual, particularly during Yeltsin's presidency. The constitution makes the executive dominant but still dependent on the agreement of the legislative branch to realize its programs. Tension between the two branches of government, which are selected in separate electoral processes, was a persistent obstacle to effective governance in the Yeltsin years. The executive itself has two heads (the president and the prime minister), which introduces another area for potential intrastate tension. Relations between the executive and judicial branches were also strained in the Yeltsin years, and the establishment of real judicial independence remains a significant political challenge. Finally, poor salaries and lack of professionalism in the civil service have increased corruption and political influence on decision making. Putin's centralizing measures have tried to address all of these areas of contention, but, some would argue, in so doing they may be undermining the very checks and balances that are supposed to offer protection against re-establishment of authoritarian control.

Many of the difficulties that face the new Russian state are, at least in part, legacies of the Soviet period. Following the collapse of the USSR, the new political leadership tried to wipe the slate clean and start anew. However, some political scientists emphasize the importance of path dependence, that is, the manner in which past experience shapes the choices and options available for change.[2] Some observers see in Putin's

CURRENT CHALLENGES: The Chechnya Crisis

Despite its small size and population (estimated at 600,000 in 1994), the breakaway republic of Chechnya occupies an important position on Russia's southern border. The republic is widely thought to be a safe haven for criminal elements that operate in Russia. In the early 1990s, the Russian leadership feared that Chechnya's attempted secession from the Russian Federation might embolden other republics to pursue a similar course. These concerns motivated Russia to send troops into Chechnya on December 11, 1994, fueling a regional civil war.

The desire for independence has deep roots in Chechnya. Prior to its incorporation into the Russian Empire in 1859 and again after the Bolshevik revolution in 1917, local forces fought to maintain Chechnya's independence. In 1924, Chechnya was made part of the USSR, and in 1934 it was joined with an adjacent region, Ingushetia, to form a single "autonomous republic" within the Soviet Union. During World War II, following an anti-Soviet uprising, Stalin deported hundreds of Chechens to Soviet Central Asia.

(continued)

CURRENT CHALLENGES: The Chechnya Crisis (cont.)

Taking advantage of the ongoing political upheaval in the USSR, in October 1991 the newly elected president of the republic, Dzhokar Dudaev, declared Chechnya's independence from Russia. In 1992, Checheno-Ingushetia was officially recognized by the Russian government as two separate republics. Following the split, Chechen leaders continued to pursue independence, a claim rejected by the Russian government. Intervention by Russian military forces in December 1994 evoked widespread criticism within the Russian Federation and from opposition parties. Some opposed the intervention completely, in favor of a political solution; others were primarily critical of the ineffective manner in which the war effort was carried out. The campaign was poorly organized, and internal dissension within the army and security forces demoralized the troops. Civilians in Chechnya and the surrounding regions suffered at the hands of both sides. In 1995 and 1996, hostage takings by Chechen rebels in the adjacent regions, Stavropol *krai* and the republic of Dagestan, took the conflict beyond Chechnya's borders.

The unpopular war became an important issue in the 1996 presidential campaign and threatened to undermine Yeltsin's already fragile support. In late May 1996, a cease-fire agreement was signed, and in June, Yeltsin decreed the beginning of troop withdrawals. In September 1996, an agreement with the rebels was again signed. The joint declaration put off a decision on Chechnya's status for five years, leaving the issue unresolved.

On January 27, 1997, an election was held for the president of the Republic of Chechnya. Observers generally considered the vote to be fair, with 79 percent of the eligible population participating. In a race involving thirteen candidates, Aslan Maskhadov received 59 percent of the vote. Relative to other leading candidates, Maskhadov was considered to be a moderate. However, he publicly supported Chechnya's independence, and later, after he was removed from power by Moscow, he became a rebel leader and was killed by Russian forces in March 2005.

In 1999, terrorist bombings, attributed to Chechen rebels, occurred in apartment buildings in Moscow and two other Russian cities, causing approximately 300 deaths. The second war against Chechnya was launched as Yeltsin sent nearly 100,000 Russian troops to regain control of the breakaway republic. The troops occupied the Chechen capital Grozny; refugees spilled into surrounding areas and beyond Chechnya's borders. Allegations of human rights violations were made against both Russian troops and Chechen rebels; Western governments and international organizations such as Human Rights Watch demanded that the Russian government comply with international human rights standards. Russian authorities continue to resist external involvement in the situation, maintaining that the Chechnya crisis is a domestic political issue. At the same time, in an effort to gain Western acceptance for Russia's military actions, President Putin has repeatedly emphasized the existence of links between Chechen rebels and international terrorist networks, including Al Qaeda.

Since 1999, Russian authorities have periodically claimed imminent victory in the military struggle. However, Russian forces have proven unable to rout rebels from the mountainous regions of the republic. A string of terrorist attacks by Chechen rebels since 1999, intensifying in 2004 with the Beslan tragedy, placed the problem clearly in the public mind. In March 2003, Russian authorities tried to set Chechnya on a track of normalization by holding a referendum on a new constitution for the republic that would confirm Chechnya's status within the Russian Federation. This symbolic act has not stopped the conflict. In October 2003, Akhmad Kadyrov was elected president of Chechnya with Russian support in a controversial process, only to be killed by Chechen rebels the next year. In March 2005, former Chechen president Aslan Maskhadov was killed by Russian forces; in July 2006 Russian forces announced that they had also killed the more radical insurgent leader Shamil Basayev, who claimed responsibility for the Beslan hostage taking.

Source: Adapted from *Introduction to Comparative Politics*, 3rd ed. Copyright 2004 by Houghton Mifflin Company. Reprinted with permission.

reforms a reversion to practices and patterns that are reminiscent of the Soviet period, namely, centralization of power and obstacles to effective political competition. Other analysts interpret these measures as necessary to solidify rule of law and the state's capacity to govern; both are prerequisites of democratic development. An assessment of this debate requires a bit of background on Soviet political structures.

Before Gorbachev's reforms, top organs of the Communist Party of the Soviet Union (CPSU) dominated the state. The CPSU was a hierarchical structure in which lower party bodies elected delegates to higher party organs, but these elections were uncontested, and top organs determined candidates for lower party posts. The Politburo, the top party organ, was the real decision-making center. A larger body, the Central Committee, represented the broader political elite, including regional party leaders and representatives of various economic sectors. Alongside the CPSU were Soviet state structures that formally resembled Western parliamentary systems but had little decision-making authority. The state bureaucracy had day-to-day responsibility in both the economic and political spheres but operated in subordination to the party's directives. People holding high state positions were appointed through the *nomenklatura* system, a mechanism that allowed the CPSU to fill key posts with politically reliable individuals. The Supreme Soviet, the parliament, was a rubber-stamp body; its members were directly elected by the population, but the single candidate who ran in each district was chosen by higher CPSU organs (but was not necessarily a party member).

In theory, the Soviet state was governed by a constitution (the last one was adopted in 1977). In practice, however, the constitution was of symbolic rather than operational importance since many of its principles were ignored. The constitution provided for legislative, executive, and judicial organs, but separation of powers was considered inapplicable to Soviet society because the CPSU claimed to represent the interests of society as a whole. With the power of appointment firmly under party control, there could be little legislative or judicial independence. When the constitution was violated (as it frequently was), the courts had no independent authority to protect its provisions. The Soviet Union was also designated a federal system; that is, according to the constitution, certain powers were granted to the fifteen union republics (which have since become independent states). However, this was phony federalism, since all aspects of life were overseen by a highly centralized Communist Party. Nonetheless, the various subunits that existed within the Russian Republic (*autonomous republics, krais, oblasts*, and *okrugs*) were carried over into the Russian Federation in an altered form, an example of path dependence.

Gorbachev began a process of radical institutional change through the introduction of competitive elections, increased political pluralism, reduced Communist Party dominance, a revitalized legislative branch of government, and renegotiation of the terms of Soviet federalism. He also tried to bring the constitution into harmony with political reality, and many constitutional amendments were adopted that altered existing political institutions. Taken together, these changes moved the political system haltingly and unevenly in a direction resembling the liberal democratic systems of the West.

Even before the collapse of the USSR, political institutions began to change in the Russian Republic, a constituent unit of the Soviet Union. A new post of president was created, and on June 12, 1991, Boris Yeltsin was elected by direct popular vote as its first incumbent, giving him a base of popular legitimacy. In some ways, the evolution of governance and policymaking in the Russian Federation since 1991 can be seen as a laboratory for engineering democratic governance, somewhat analogous to the experience of Germany and Japan after World War II, but in this case the outcome is still unclear.

The Executive

The 1993 Russian constitution establishes a semi-presidential system, formally resembling the French system but with even stronger executive power (see Figure 23.2). The president, who holds primary power, is the head of state, and the prime minister, appointed by the president but approved by the lower house of the parliament (the State Duma), is the head of government. This dual executive can introduce tensions within the executive branch, as well as between the president and the Duma. As a rule of thumb, the president has overseen foreign policy, relations with the regions, and the organs of state security, while the prime minister has focused attention on the economy and related issues. However, with Yeltsin's continuing health problems in 1998 and 1999, operative power shifted toward the prime minister. Ever since the election of Vladimir Putin in March 2000, however, the primary locus of power has returned to the presidency, with economic powers gradually shifting back into the hands of the prime minister.

The president is elected directly by the population every four years, with a constitutional limit of two consecutive terms. In 1996, the first presidential elections returned Yeltsin to power, despite his waning

Figure 23.2

Political Institutions of the Russian Federation (R.F.), 2007

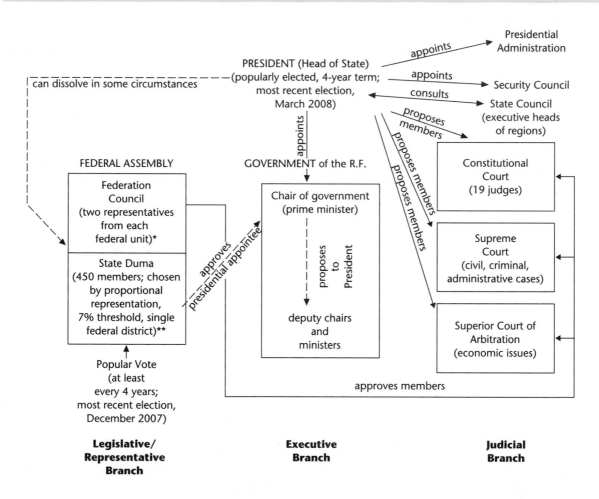

* One representative is appointed by the regional representative body and one by the regional executive. The Federation Council originally had 178 members, but the size will gradually decline as the result of mergers of federal units.
** Effective for the 2007 Duma elections; 2003 elections involved 225 seats chosen by proportional representation with a 5% threshold and 225 seats elected in single-member, winner-takes-all districts.

popularity. In December 1999, Yeltsin resigned from office, making the prime minister, Vladimir Putin, acting president until the March 2000 elections, which he won handily. Putin's 2004 electoral victory was even more stunning (winning 71 percent of the vote, with his closest competitor receiving under 14 percent), but some international observers alleged that media bias raised questions about its genuine democratic character. The constitution excludes a third consecutive term, so throughout 2006 and 2007 speculation was rife about whom Putin might be grooming as a successor to run in the March 2008 elections when his second term of office ended. Putin has pointed out that he could run again after stepping out for one term.

One of the president's most important powers is the authority to issue decrees, which Yeltsin used frequently to address contentious issues such as privatization, salaries of state workers, the running of the economy, and anticrime measures. Presidential decrees have the force of law until formal legislation is passed, but because they can be annulled as quickly as they are approved, they do not command the same respect as actual laws. Although presidential decrees may not violate the constitution or specific legislation passed by the bicameral legislature (the Federal Assembly), they do allow the president to ignore an uncooperative or divided parliament. Yeltsin's decision in 1994, and again in 1999, to launch the offensive in Chechnya, despite strong objections from a broad range of political groups, was not approved by either house of parliament. President Putin has used his power of decree less extensively than Yeltsin did, in part because Putin has managed to forge a more cooperative relationship with the parliament and has been able to resolve many policy debates through the legislative process.

The president has other powers, including the right to call a state of emergency, impose martial law, grant pardons, call referenda, and temporarily suspend actions of other state organs if he deems them to contradict the constitution or federal laws. Some of these actions must be confirmed by other state organs (such as the upper house of the parliament, the Federation Council). The president is commander-in-chief of the armed forces and conducts affairs of state with other nations. Impeachment of the president is a complicated process involving the Duma, the Federation Council, the Supreme Court, and the Constitutional Court. If the president dies in office or becomes incapacitated, the prime minister fills the post until new presidential elections can be held.

An American political scientist, Henry Hale, has dubbed political systems like Russia's *patronal presidentialism.*[3] Such systems (which Hale uses to describe several other Soviet successor states as well) involve strong presidential powers combined with "the exercise of political authority primarily through selective transfers of resources rather than formalized institutional practices, idea-based politics, or generalized exchange as enforced through the established rule of law."[4] In such systems, power is rooted in the leader's own personal authority, which is, in part, maintained through the transfer of benefits in exchange for political loyalty. Although one might expect the importance of patronage or clientelism to decline as democratic transformation strengthens, in the Russian case these dynamics have been reinforced by several recent institutional changes, particularly with respect to Russia's subnational units, described below. In addition to these dynamics, however, the president's authority is maintained by control of an extensive administrative apparatus.

The Prime Minister and Cabinet

The Russian government is headed by the prime minister, flanked by varying numbers of deputy prime ministers. The president's choice of prime minister must be approved by the Duma. During Yeltsin's presidency, six prime ministers held office, the longest being Viktor Chernomyrdin, from December 1992 until March 1998, and the final one being Vladimir Putin, appointed in August 1999. In September 2007 Putin stunned the political elite in Moscow by accepting the resignation of Mikhail Fradkov, who had been prime minister since 2004, less than three months before the Duma election. Putin received easy Duma confirmation of his nominee, Viktor Zubkov. Zubkov, sixty-five years old, was prior to this a relative unknown, head of the Federal Financial Monitoring Service; he had worked with Putin earlier in his career in St. Petersburg, prior to his appointment to the federal tax service in 1993. The change in the government in September 2007 time fed speculation about the upcoming presidential race, as

Zubkov announced he might also run for this post. Until that time, it was presumed that Putin would throw his support either to Sergey Ivanov, who was made First Deputy Prime Minister in a cabinet shuffle on February 15, 2007 (from his post as Defense Minister), or Dmitry Medvedev, who was also First Deputy Prime Minister since November 2005. Medvedev, trained as a lawyer and hailing from Putin's home base of St. Petersburg, was previously head of the presidential administration under Putin and serves as chair of the board of directors of Gazprom. Shortly after Zubkov was appointed, Putin suggested that he might consider being prime minister after his term as president ends.

The prime minister can be removed by the Duma through two repeat votes of no confidence passed within a three-month period. Although the process has been attempted several times in the past decade, usually spearheaded by the Communist Party faction, it has never succeeded. For example, a no-confidence attempt occurred in February 2005, spurred by objections from opposition factions to government changes to the provision of social benefits (see Chapter 22). The attempt received only 112 of the needed 226 votes. On occasion, the president has also had difficulty gaining approval of his nominee for prime minister, most notably following the 1998 financial crisis when three prime ministers were in office over a seventeen-month period. Here, too, the Duma has ultimately been reluctant to defy the president because rejection of the candidate three times can lead to dissolution of the Duma itself. The prime minister has never been a member of the dominant party or coalition in the Duma; thus, principles of party accountability that apply in most West European parliamentary systems are not operative in Russia. Without disciplined parties and with no formal links between parties and the executive branch, the process of gaining Duma acceptance of government proposals depends on the authority of the president and on the particular configuration of power at the moment.

Ministers other than the prime minister do not require parliamentary approval. The prime minister makes recommendations to the president, who appoints these officials. Following the appointment of Zubkov, in September 2007, a cabinet shakeup occurred, but as of this writing it is not clear whether this would involve simply a change in personnel or a change in the structure of government ministries as well. In early

2007, there were sixteen ministries alongside numerous other executive bodies, such as state committees, commissions, and federal services, such as the Federal Security Service and the Tax Inspectorate. Of the sixteen ministries, five are directly under the president's authority. These include Internal Affairs; Foreign Affairs; Civil Defense, Emergency Situations, and Response to Natural Disasters; Defense; and Justice. The remainder work under the guidance of the government (prime minister). Ministers and other agency heads are generally career bureaucrats who have risen through an appropriate ministry, although sometimes more clearly political appointments are made. Many agencies have been reorganized, often more than once. Reorganization of the state's bureaucracy results not only from restructuring of the economy and of state functions; top leaders may also use restructuring to induce political loyalty and place their clients and allies in key positions in the new agencies. For example, Putin has drawn heavily on colleagues with whom he worked earlier in St. Petersburg or in the security establishment, referred to as *siloviki*, in staffing a variety of posts in his administration. With the collapse of the *nomenklatura* system, politicians and government officials look to people they trust to staff their organizations. In an effort to increase the role of merit and the professional character of the civil service, various reforms have been attempted, which will be discussed below.

One change made by Putin when he came into office was the creation of a new Ministry for Economic Development and Trade, headed by German Gref. This ministry took over functions of several previously existing ministries, as did a new Ministry of Industry, Science, and Technology. Observers question whether such reorganizations produce substantive benefits, and some are especially controversial. For example, the State Committee for Environmental Protection was abolished by a May 2000 decree, and its responsibilities were transferred to the Ministry of Natural Resources. The mixing of responsibility for overseeing both use and protection of natural resources in this single agency may be an indicator of the low priority of environmental protection (as compared to resource use). Functions of the State Committee on Northern Affairs were transferred to the Ministry for Economic Development and Trade, a measure that was viewed by some as a downgrading of northern concerns on the government's agenda.

Ministers in the government do not represent political parties; thus Russia does not have a form of cabinet government similar to that of parliamentary systems in Western Europe. Although the government is accountable to the president and to some extent to the Duma, its composition does not reflect the outcome of the Duma elections. The relationship of the prime minister to the president has more to do with personal accountability than with partisan affiliation, since, at least until 2007, the Russian president was not the leader or even a member of any particular party. Thus, an intriguing aspect of Russian governance is that selection of the prime minister, although requiring approval of the Duma, has not been clearly influenced by election outcomes. Despite the fact that the Duma elections in both 1993 and 1996 gave the lion's share of seats in the Duma to the opposition parties, the prime minister, who was associated with a smaller establishment party, was not changed.

The National Bureaucracy

The new Russian state inherited a large bureaucratic apparatus. Despite proclaimed intentions, efforts to downsize the executive bureaucratic apparatus have not succeeded. In fact, since 2000, the size of the federal bureaucracy has increased each year, and those employed in public administration increased by about 33 percent between 1994 and 2005.[5] Nonetheless, the Russian bureaucracy is not excessively large by West European standards. The absence of a civil service system has meant that regularized procedures for selection, promotion, and evaluation of public servants in the federal and regional bureaucracies have not been developed. Rather, the system has features of clientelism where patron-client networks, which were important in the Soviet period, continue to play a key role in the presidential administration and other state organs. These linkages are similar to old-boys' networks in the West (and for top positions, they most often involve men in the Russian case); they underscore the importance of personal career ties between individuals as they rise in bureaucratic or political structures. A study of the Organization for Economic Cooperation and Development (OECD) identifies a "paradox of post-Soviet Russia," that "Russia has a weak state but strong officials."[6]

Alongside the state bureaucracy, the presidential administration serves the president directly. With some 2,000 employees, the presidential administration can duplicate or compete with the formal agencies of the state, even as government ministries report directly to the president.[7] The presidential administration is active in developing proposed legislation and government programs. The current structure of the presidential administration was established by a decree of March 2004. Part of the presidential administration, the State Legal Office, reviews all legislation before the president signs it. The president has also created various advisory bodies that solicit input from important political and economic actors and co-opt them into support for government policies. These organs have no constitutional status and can be abolished at will. The most important are the Security Council and the State Council; their administrative apparatus is part of the presidential administration. Formed in 1992, the Security Council advises the president in areas related to foreign policy and security (broadly conceived) and includes heads of appropriate government bodies (the so-called power ministries such as Defense and the Federal Security Service), the prime minister, and the heads of seven federal districts created in 2000. The State Council was formed in September 2000 as part of Putin's attempt to redefine the role of regional leaders in federal decision making (see below). The State Council, which includes all of the regional heads, has a consultative role, but does not give the regional executives any real power. A smaller presidium, made up of seven of the regional heads selected by the president, meets monthly. Although Putin appointed a prominent business leader, Aleksandr Abramov, as first secretary of the council, the president himself chairs the body and seems to keep a tight rein on its discussion agenda. Topics for discussion at the State Council or its Presidium have a practical focus; for example, in 2007 these included development of the space industry, reform of housing and utilities, and industrial development in Russia.

Both the Russian public and policymakers consider the performance of the state bureaucracy to be of low quality. Public opinion surveys in 2004 and 2005 indicate that 71 percent of the respondents felt that the bureaucracy hampers economic development, and the most important deficiencies cited included corruption and "indifference to people."[8] Efforts to improve the quality of public service include a law on the civil service, adopted in 2004, a presidential decree on the structure of executive bodies (2004), and a resolution, *Concept of Administrative Reform*, adopted by the government in 2005. The civil service reform introduces principles such as competitive appointments, provision of job descriptions and contracts for public servants, conflict of interest regulations, and procedures for dispute resolution. The administrative reform measures, among other things, seek to clarify functions of executive organs and to set standards for providing public services. Obstacles to effective reform of the civil service and administrative practice have produced only slow progress. Among the barriers are the lack of an independent agency to carry out the reform, a lack of transparency in government practices, and a limited body of expertise in this area. For example, the notion of "conflict of interest" (a situation where an official's private interests may interfere with his or her exercise of public duties) is a relatively new one in the Russian administrative environment, since personal contacts have traditionally been an important vehicle for gaining special access or benefits. Established ways of doing things may also engender resistance to practices that link promotion to performance reviews and to the establishment of truly independent regulatory agencies. An OECD report suggests that some gains have been made in reducing bureaucratic interference with business activities.[9] But there is also continuing evidence of selective enforcement, in which sanctions or legal actions are applied differentially, with decisions apparently influenced by political considerations or private interests.

Public and Semipublic Institutions

Although the privatization policies of the 1990s resulted in the transformation of most state enterprises into joint-stock or privatized companies, in limited sectors of the economy partial or complete state ownership has remained fairly intact or even been restored after earlier privatization was carried out. Public or quasi-public ownership may take the form of direct state or municipal ownership of assets, or it may involve majority control of shareholding by state or municipal organs in a "privatized" firm. Economic sectors more likely

to involve public or quasi-public ownership include telecommunications (the nonmobile telephone industry in particular), public transport (railways, municipal transport), the electronic media (television), and the energy sector. A prime example from the energy sector is Gazprom, the natural gas monopoly, where the federal government controls just over 50 percent of the shares. The seizure of assets of Yukos, an oil company previously owned by Khodorkovsky (discussed in Chapter 22), increased government involvement in this part of the energy sector. Another oil company, Sibneft, was purchased in the open market by Gazprom, increasing the share of state ownership in the oil sector to over 30 percent in 2005. Several television stations are publicly owned, either on a national basis (ORT, RTR), by regions, or by municipalities. Many newspapers, some at the regional level, receive financial support from the regional government, and their chief editors may be subject to appointment or approval by local political authorities. Indirect state influence is also realized through the dominant ownership share in many regional TV stations by Gazprom-Media, a subsidiary of the state-controlled natural gas company.

In other areas, such as education and health care, although some private facilities and institutions have emerged in recent years, these services are still primarily provided through so-called budget (tax-supported) agencies. Although some prestigious new private universities, often with Western economic support, have cropped up in major urban areas, Russia's large historic universities remain public institutions. Likewise, a state-run medical care system assures basic care to all citizens, even while private clinics and hospitals are taking on growing importance in servicing the more affluent parts of the population. In the public transport sector, smaller private companies that provide shuttle and bus services have grown up alongside publicly owned transport networks. In general, public or quasi-public agencies offer services to citizens at a lower price, but often also with lower quality.

Significant parts of the social infrastructure remain under public or quasi-public control. In the Soviet period many social services were administered to citizens through their places of employment. These included day care, housing, medical, and vacation facilities, as well as food services and some retail outlets. Between

1991 and the end of the 1990s a process of divestiture resulted in the transfer of most of these assets and responsibilities to other institutions, either to private owners or, often, to municipalities. For example, while many state- or enterprise-owned apartments were turned over to private ownership by their occupants, an important part of the country's housing stock was placed in municipal ownership. Thus local governments play an important role in administering such services to the population. In some cases firms provide financial support to municipal organs to help maintain these services,[10] which work to the benefit of the firm's workforce.

Despite the important role of public and quasi-public institutions in the economy, Russia has not developed effective corporatist (or tripartite) structures, such as exist in many West European countries, to achieve cooperation between the state, business, and labor. Efforts to set up a tripartite commission in the early 1990s failed, both because organizations identified to represent business and labor were not necessarily representative and because they did not have the authority to command the loyalty of their constituents. The government has established various regulatory agencies to oversee important parts of the public infrastructure but these are often ineffective in carrying out their functions. The Russian Central Bank is another state organ that exerts substantial influence over economic policy, through its control of monetary policy, without being directly part of the executive branch. Political authorities, including the president, are responsible for appointing the executive officials in many public and quasi-public institutions, so the link between state authorities and these public sector financial and economic institutions can be quite close.

These examples indicate a continuing close relationship between major economic institutions and the state. For several reasons these ties are likely to remain strong in the coming years. First, Russian tradition, even before Soviet times, involved a more active economic role for the state than is typical of even the most state-led approaches to economic governance in Western Europe, such as in France or the Nordic countries. Second, the bias toward privatization of public services, supported by liberal economic theory that governed market reform in the early 1990s, was largely discredited by the dismal economic experience of that decade. Thus a reversion to a more traditionally active role for

the state has taken hold, and along with it quasi-public and public institutions are making a comeback. As evidence of this trend, the overall share of GDP created in the nonstate sector increased from 5 percent in 1991 to 70 percent in 1997, then fell from 70 percent in 1997–2004 down to 65 percent in 2005–2006.[11]

Other State Institutions

While the executive organs of the government, particularly the presidency, are the most powerful actors in the Russian political system, other institutions also play an important role. Particularly during Putin's terms of office, the security organs took on increasing prominence, while subnational governments were brought under greater control of the central government in Moscow. The independence of the judiciary has increased since Soviet times, but in some cases judicial processes are not completely shielded from the influence of the executive branch.

The Military and Security Organs

Because of Vladimir Putin's career background in the Soviet security agency (the KGB), he has drawn many of his staff from this arena. Thus, while the formal rank of the Federal Security Service (FSB, the successor to the KGB) has not changed, the actual impact of the security establishment has gained importance in the Putin era. This development preceded the events of September 11, 2001, and the importance placed on security concerns reflected, in part, Putin's own personal background; whether this would change after the 2008 presidential race might depend in part on who is elected. Because many Russians are alarmed by the crime rate and terrorist bombings, restrictions on civil liberties have not elicited the popular concern typical of many Western countries. At the same time, there is widespread public cynicism about the honesty of the ordinary police (*militsiia*); many believe that payoffs by the mafia and even by ordinary citizens can buy police cooperation in overlooking crimes or ordinary legal infractions such as traffic tickets.[12] Such suspicions are likely often correct.

The Soviet military once ranked as one of the largest and most powerful forces in the world, second only to that of the United States, and it made the country a superpower. Since the military was represented in the political structures (almost always having at least one representative on the Politburo), political loyalty to the civilian authorities represented a good bargain for the military establishment. The Communist Party controlled military appointments, and although the military did lobby for particular policies and sometimes played a role in Kremlin intrigues, it never usurped political power. During the August 1991 coup attempt, troops remained loyal to Yeltsin and Gorbachev, even though the Minister of Defense was among the coup plotters; there were no orders to fire on Soviet citizens who took to the streets in defense of the government. In October 1993, despite some apparent hesitancy in military circles, military units defended the government's position, this time firing on civilian protesters and shocking the country. It is noteworthy that in not a single postcommunist country has the military intervened to take power, which suggests that communist rule helped to cement the principle of civilian political control, earlier exercised through the Communist Party and now through elected political figures.

In the postcommunist period, the political power and prestige of the military have declined radically. Both Gorbachev and Yeltsin oversaw a reduction in military expenditures, which undermined the privileged position of military interests, bringing a decline in facilities for military personnel and a reduction in conventional and nuclear forces. Plans to downsize the military have been a source of tension between the political leadership and the military establishment, and the Putin government proclaimed its commitment to continue the process. However, in the face of the U.S. proposal to install a missile defense system in Europe, Putin indicated a need for Russia to strengthen its security and military capabilities and threatened to suspend Russia's participation in the Treaty on Conventional Forces in Europe, failing approval of its proposed changes to the agreement to respond to Russia's security concerns. Reports of deteriorating conditions in some Russian nuclear arsenals have also raised international concerns about nuclear security. In addition, the situation of military personnel, from the highest officers to rank-and-file soldiers, has deteriorated dramatically, producing a potential source of political unrest.

As of 2007, the Russian Federation still maintains a system of universal male conscription, but

noncompliance and draftees rejected for health reasons have been persistent problems; a law to permit alternative military service for conscientious objectors took effect in 2004. Although critics of the military service law welcome the concept, they are critical of the restrictive conditions that the law imposes on alternative service. The period of conscription for those drafted after January 1, 2007, was reduced from two years to eighteen months and down to one year in 2008, in line with a gradual shift to a smaller professional military corps.[13]

Alongside the military, various security organizations exist in Russia, including governmental organs such as the Federal Security Service (FSB) and the Ministry of Internal Affairs (which oversees the police, or *militsiia*, including special units). Officials associated with the security sector in Russia are frequently referred to as the *siloviki*, many of whom have career links to Putin; sometimes the *siloviki* are viewed as an informal interest group. High crime rates indicate a low capacity of the state to provide legal security to its citizens. Thus, in addition to state security agencies, there are a range of private security agencies that provide protection to businesses and individuals. A network of intrigue and hidden relationships makes it hard to determine the boundaries of state involvement in the security sector, and the government's inability to enforce laws or to apprehend violators may create an impression of state involvement even where there may have been none. A prominent example is the case of former FSB agent, Alexander Litvinenko, who claimed in 1998 that he was threatened after failing to fulfill an FSB order to kill Boris Berezovsky; in 2000 he took political asylum in the United Kingdom (UK) and continued his outspoken criticism of the Russian government. In November 2006 Litvinenko was fatally poisoned in London with the rare radioactive isotope polonium-210; traces of the material were found in public places elsewhere in the city and on commercial aircraft that had traveled to Moscow, presenting a hazard to the general public. On his deathbed Litvinenko accused the Kremlin of being responsible for his death, although British and Russian investigators subsequently were not able to establish such a link. In May 2007, the UK formally requested extradition of Andrei Lugovoi, an ex-KGB agent, to stand trial for the murder, but the Russian government refused, citing a constitutional prohibition.

The issue sparked tension between the two countries, including expulsion of diplomats on each side. These kinds of incidents generate an atmosphere of insecurity and bizarre linkages reminiscent of cold war–era spy novels.

The Judiciary

Concepts such as judicial independence and the rule of law were poorly understood in both prerevolutionary Russia and the Soviet era. Gorbachev, however, emphasized the importance of constructing a law-based state, judicial independence, and due process. These concepts have been embedded in the new Russian constitution and are accepted both by the public and political elites. However, their implementation has been difficult and not wholly successful.

In Russia, a Constitutional Court was formed in 1991. Its decisions were binding, and in several cases even the president had to bow to its authority. After several controversial decisions that challenged the president's authority, Yeltsin suspended the operations of the court in late 1993. However, the new Russian constitution again provided for a Constitutional Court with the power to adjudicate disputes on the constitutionality of federal and regional laws, as well as on jurisdictional disputes between various political institutions. Justices are nominated by the president and approved by the Federation Council, a procedure that produced a stalemate after the new constitution was adopted, so that the court became functional only in 1995. Among the justices are political figures, lawyers, legal scholars, and judges. Since 1995, the court has established itself as a vehicle for resolving conflicts that relate to the protection of individual rights and conformity of regional laws with constitutional requirements. The court has been cautious in confronting the executive branch, on which it depends to enforce its decisions.

Alongside the Constitutional Court is an extensive system of lower and appellate courts, with the Supreme Court at the pinnacle. These courts hear ordinary civil and criminal cases. In 1995, a system of commercial courts was also formed to hear cases dealing with issues related to privatization, taxes, and other commercial activities. The Federation Council must approve nominees for Supreme Court judgeships, and the constitution also grants the president power to appoint judges at other levels. Measures to shield judges from political pressures include criminal prosecution for attempting to influence a judge, protections from arbitrary dismissal, and improved salaries for judges. The Russian judicial system operates on a civil code system, like most of continental Europe. One innovation in the legal system has been the introduction of jury trials for some types of criminal offenses.

Subnational Government

The collapse of the Soviet Union was precipitated by the demands of some union republics for more autonomy and, then, independence. After the Russian Federation became an independent state, the problem of constructing a viable federal structure resurfaced. The Russian Federation inherited a complex structure of regional subunits from the Soviet period. Between 1991 and 1993, negotiations between the central government and the various regions led to the establishment of a federal structure that included eighty-nine units, which had different historical origins and designations (twenty-one republics, forty-nine *oblasts*, six *krais*, ten autonomous *okrugs*, one autonomous *oblast*, and two cities with federal status, namely, St. Petersburg and Moscow). Discussion of possible mergers of proximate federal units to reduce their number continues; such changes are subject to approval by popular referendum; referenda in relation to five such mergers had been approved by voters between December 2003 and March 2007.[14] Once implemented, these mergers would bring the number of regions down to eighty-three (as of March 1, 2008). For example, through a referendum on April 17, 2005, voters in three Siberian regions approved the merger of the two smaller autonomous *okrugs* into the larger Krasnoyarsk *krai*, effective January 1, 2007.

One of the first issues to arise in the development of Russia's federal system was whether all of the eighty-nine units should have equal status. The republics have viewed themselves as a special category because of their different status in the Soviet period (then called autonomous republics) and the presence of significant minority groups within their borders. They have also been the most assertive in putting forth claims for autonomy or even sovereignty. The most extreme example is

Chechnya, whose demand for independence has led to a protracted civil war. The Russian government's determination to oppose Chechen secession reflects its fear that separatist sentiment could spread. This has not happened, although other republics have declared sovereignty, an ambiguous claim rejected by the Constitutional Court. The ethnic dimension complicates political relations with some of the republics. For example, in Tatarstan, one of the most populous and most assertive of the republics, the titular nationality (the Tatars) forms about half of the population. In the Republic of Sakha (formerly Yakutia), which has valuable diamond reserves, Yakuts form one-third of the population. The republics tend to be in peripheral areas of the Russian Federation, except for Tatarstan and Bashkortostan, which lie in the center of the country. The titular nationalities (Tatars and Bashkirs) in these two republics, as well as in some of the republics of the Caucasus region, are of Islamic cultural background, but Islamic fundamentalism has not been a significant problem in Russia since decades of Soviet socialization seems to have acculturated most parts of the Muslim population to secular, scientific values.

Despite the fact that the constitution grants equal status to all units of the federation, republics have received some special rights, such as declaring a second state language (in addition to Russian) and adopting their own constitutions. From 1994 to 1998, forty-six individual treaties were signed, first between the federal government and several of Russia's republics and then with other units of the federation. These documents were not supposed to contradict the federal constitution, but some provisions actually did. These treaties outlined the jurisdiction of each level of government and granted special privileges, including special rights in relation to natural resource revenues and division of tax revenue—often to the benefit of the ethnic republics. This ad hoc approach produced a system of asymmetrical federalism, giving different regions varying privileges. The result was an escalation of regional demands and a drop in the perceived fairness of central policy.

It is no wonder that following the March 2000 election Putin gave special priority to the establishment of a uniform system of federal-regional relations, governed by standard legal principles. He immediately took several steps to realize this objective, first by harmonizing regional laws and republic constitutions with federal legislation and federal constitutional provisions. Another new measure gave the president the power, pending approval by a court, to remove a governor and disband a regional legislature if they engage in anticonstitutional activity. In 2002, the Constitutional Court upheld the measure, but with many restrictions on its use. Another contentious issue was the 2002 deadline for rescinding the special bilateral treaties that Yeltsin had concluded. Although several regions resisted giving up privileges that the treaties afforded, all but a handful have been annulled. Among remaining treaties is the one with Tatarstan; negotiations about its amendment to satisfy federal and republic demands resulted in a new draft treaty that would have granted Tatarstan some continued autonomy in economic policy, tax powers in the oil industry, and assurances that the Tatar president would be someone who speaks the national language. However, the Federation Council refused to approve the treaty in February 2007, with the head of the body describing it as a potentially dangerous precedent for other regions.[15]

Other reforms to the federal system introduced by Putin in 2000 were even stronger measures to strengthen what he has called the "power vertical". This concept involves the strengthening of an integrated structure of executive power from the top (presidential) level down through to the local level. Critics have questioned whether the idea is actually consistent with federal principles. A first step in this direction was the creation of seven federal districts on top of the existing federal units. Although not designed to replace regional governments, the districts were intended to oversee the work of federal offices operating in these regions and to ensure compliance with federal laws and the constitution. Putin's appointees to head these new federal districts included several individuals (all male) with backgrounds in the security services, reinforcing concerns that the federal districts could become a powerful instrument of central control. In practice, however, the federal districts have been less intrusive in the affairs of the regions than many feared.

A second set of changes to create the power vertical has involved the position of regional executives themselves (that is, the governors of the regions and presidents of the republics, hereafter also referred to as governors). In the Yeltsin period, there was extensive political conflict over the method of selecting governors: initially, they were appointed by the president, but Yeltsin finally agreed to their popular election, which gave them greater legitimacy and independence from Moscow. Beginning in 1996, the governors, along with the heads of each regional legislative body, also sat as members of the Federation Council, the upper house of the Russian parliament. This arrangement gave the regional executives a direct voice in national legislative discussions and a presence in Moscow, but it divided their attention between their executive responsibilities in their home regions and their duties in Moscow. In 2001, Putin gained approval for a revision to the composition of the Federation Council; regional executives were, as of January 2002, no longer members of the Federation Council. Rather, one regional representative is appointed by the regional executive and the other by the regional legislature. Some governors resisted this change, seeing it as an assault on their power (they also lost the legal immunity that goes along with being a member of parliament). Putin made concessions to make the change more palatable, for example, giving governors the right to recall their representatives. The State Council was formed to try to assure the regional executives that they would retain some role in the federal policymaking arena, even after losing their seats in the Federation Council.

The implementation of these changes has been accompanied by the exercise of soft power mechanisms, namely, the strengthening of patron-client relations between central authorities and the governors and presidents of republics. A striking feature of this reform process has been the minimal protest that has issued from governors themselves, even as their power and independence have been progressively undermined. In the belief that cooperation would yield more benefits, no doubt some governors were hesitant to take an opposing stance that might alienate the powerful president. Thus, in addition to formal changes, some observers have noted the capacity of federal authorities, particularly the president, to use administrative pressure to gain acquiescence, if not compliance, in pursuing a particular reform design. This use of administrative pressure reinforces a personalistic and clientelistic system of political power.

After the Beslan hostage taking in September 2004, Putin identified corruption and ineffective leadership at the regional level as culprits in allowing terrorists to carry out the devastating school hostage taking. Accordingly, he proposed an additional reform that created a decisive element of central control over regional politics. Approved by the State Duma in December 2004, the change eliminated popular election of governors and put their selection in the hands of the president, with approval by the regional legislature. Like the system for approval of the prime minister, if the regional legislature refuses the president's nomination three times, the president may disband the regional legislative body and call for new elections. Since governors and republic presidents are therefore dependent on the goodwill of the president for appointment and reappointment, a self-perpetuating political process has taken on a formal character, which has led some observers to declare the death of Russian federalism. Recent elections of regional legislatures have consolidated the pro-Putin forces, in the form of victories for the dominant United Russia party in all but exceptional cases.

Fiscal federalism (the process of distribution of tax revenues among the various levels of government) has been another problematic area in center-regional relations. Although the Soviet state pursued a considerable degree of regional equalization, regional differences have increased in the Russian Federation. The Putin government has accepted the principle of regional equalization and has tried to create a more regularized system for determining the distribution of revenues, taking account of both the regional tax base and differences in the needs of various regions (for instance, northern regions require higher expenditures to maintain basic services). An additional area requiring attention is the role and powers of local governments. A new law on local self-government, adopted in 2003, elicited praise for more clearly defining the jurisdictions of the various levels of government, and criticism for increasing the dependence of local officials on regional authorities.

The European Dimension

European integration has had only a minimal effect on internal governance patterns in Russia. Although Russian leaders express verbal support for Western principles of democracy and human rights, European leaders have been critical of recent changes that centralize political authority, a process they see as moving Russia away from democratic principles. While Russia has become more integrated with Europe economically, Russia does not aspire to EU membership and thus is under no compulsion to adopt elements of EU policies, standards, or practices, unless they accord with Russian national interests.

Throughout the 1990s a certain imbalance in resources and power characterized the relationship between the EU and the Russian Federation, evidenced by the fact that many of Russia's former allies sought and later achieved EU membership, which effectively limited Russia's sphere of influence on its eastern border. In this context, the European Union and Western governments applied the principle of conditionality to aid programs for Russia: Russian recipients, whether the government or nongovernmental partners, were required to fulfill certain conditions, often related to democratization, human rights, and market reform, in order to be granted economic or technical assistance. Under Putin's leadership, Russia has rejected conditionality as a principle governing the EU-Russian relationship and has insisted on a "strategic partnership" based on bargaining, negotiation, and the pursuit of mutual self-interest. In response to Russia's objections, the EU designated Russia as a "strategic partner," placing the country in a separate category from the EU's other eastern neighbors (such as Ukraine, Moldova, and Belarus).

Nonetheless, Russia continues to have access to apply for EU funds to promote joint initiatives with European partners, including border regions in neighboring EU Member States. For example, programs associated with the EU's "European Neighborhood and Partnership Instrument" are designed to "markedly improve cross-border cooperation with countries along the EU's external land and maritime borders, thus giving substance to our aim of avoiding new dividing lines."[16] Such cross-border initiatives could potentially encourage political leaders in Russia's border regions to seek greater autonomy from the Russian central government in pursuing such partnerships. However it seems unlikely that any of these programs and partnerships will be strong enough to change fundamental political relationships inside the Russian Federation.

Meanwhile, a variety of international and European training and assistance programs continue to function in Russia to impart Western skills and standards to officials and civil society actors at all levels. The impact of these types of programs, as well as increased travel by Russians to European destinations for business or pleasure, will undoubtedly have a gradual yet profound effect on Russia's future.

The Policymaking Process

Policymaking occurs through both formal and informal mechanisms. The Russian constitution lays the ground rules for the adoption of legislation, which is one formal mechanism of policymaking. Although the federal government proposes most legislation, regional legislatures, the president and his administration, individual deputies, and some judicial bodies may also do so. Various organizations may be involved in drafting legislation, including the presidential administration, the parliamentary staff, and a special office within the federal government that is responsible for drafting economic legislation. Often, expert consultants or a special commission are also involved in the process, as well as bodies such as the Security Council. In August 2000, the president formed the Entrepreneurship Council to solicit input from the business elite; meetings were also held with the Russian Union of Industrialists and Entrepreneurs regarding issues that relate to economic and social policy affecting the business sector. Whereas in the Yeltsin years only 35 to 40 percent of legislation was based on initiatives issuing from the executive branch, the proportion rose to 60 percent in the first half of 2001.[17]

In order for a bill to become law, it must be approved by both houses of the parliament in three readings and signed by the president. If the president vetoes the bill, it must be passed again in the same wording by a two-thirds majority of both houses of parliament in order to override the veto. Budgetary proposals can be put forth only by the government, and, in the Yeltsin years, they elicited sharp controversy in the parliament since proposed budget reductions affected key interests and groups, such as regional and local governments, other state agencies, the military, trade unions, enterprise directors, state employees, and pensioners. With a more favorable budgetary situation and a more compliant parliament, these measures were less contentious in the Putin presidency. Many policy proclamations are made through presidential or governmental decrees, without formal consultation with the legislative branch. This decision-making process is much less visible and may involve closed-door bargaining rather than an open process of debate and consultation.

Informal groupings also have an important indirect impact on policymaking, which was very evident in the Yeltsin years. A prominent example was lobbying by oligarchs and industrialists, representing the managerial interests of some of Russia's large privatized industries. Business magnates, as well as Russia's largest banks, were able to exert behind-the-scenes influence to gain benefits, including a share in the privatization of lucrative firms in sectors such as oil, media, and transport. Putin tried to reduce the direct political influence of this increasingly wealthy economic elite, both through the measures described above against the oligarchs and also by formalizing business input through bodies such as the Entrepreneurship Council. However, less powerful or less well-organized interests are generally excluded from the policy process. In almost all cases, participation in policymaking does not extend to representatives of more broadly based citizens' groups.

Notes

[1]Vladimir Putin, "Annual Address to the Federal Assembly of the Russian Federation," website of the President of Russia, April 25, 2005. www.kremlin.ru/eng/speeches/2005/04/25/2031_type 70029type82912_87086.shtml (accessed September 22, 2007).

[2]For an example of path-dependent analysis, see David Stark and Laszlo Bruszt, *Postsocialist Pathways: Transforming Politics and Property in East Central Europe* (Cambridge and New York: Cambridge University Press, 1998).

[3]Henry E. Hale, "Regime-Cycles, Democracy, Autocracy, and Revolution in Post-Soviet Eurasia," *World Politics* 58 (2005): 134.

[4]Ibid., p. 138.

[5]William Tompson, "From 'Clientelism' to a 'Client-centered Orientation'? The Challenge of Public Administration Reform in Russia," *Organization for Economic Cooperation and Development*, Economics Department Working papers, no. 536, January 15, 2007, p. 9, www.olis.oecd.org/olis/2006doc.nsf/linkto/eco-wkp(2006)64 (accessed September 22, 2007).

[6]Ibid., p. 7, citing an earlier OECD document.

[7]Thomas Remington, *Politics in Russia,* 2nd ed. (New York: Longman, 2001), pp. 53–54.

[8]Cited in Tompson, p. 11, based on surveys by the Institute of Sociology of the Russian Academy of Sciences and the Public Opinion Foundation.

[9]Tompson, op cit.

[10]Pertti Haaparanta, Tuuli Juurikkala, Olga Lazareva, Jukka Pirttilä, Laura Solanko, and Ekaterina Zhuravskaya, "Firms and Public Service Provision in Russia" (working paper), *Center for Economic and Financial Research*, www.cefir.ru/papers/WP41 .pdf (accessed September 22, 2007).

[11]EBRD Transition Report, 2006. I am grateful to Vladimir Popov for this reference.

[12]Remington, *Politics in Russia,* pp. 53–54.

[13]"More than 133,000 men to be conscripted in spring 2007 decree," Novosti (Russian News and Information Agency), March 29, 2007, http://en.rian.ru/russia/20070329/62813437 .html (accessed September 22, 2007).

[14]These included: the merger of Komi-Permyak autonomous *okrug* with Perm oblast into Perm *krai* (referenda December 7, 2003; merger of Taimyr and Evenk autonomous *okrugs* into Krasnoyarsk *krai* (referenda April 17, 2005, effective January 1, 2007); merger of Koryk autonomous *oblast* with Kamchatka *oblast* to form Kamchatka *krai* (referenda October 23, 2005, effective July 1, 2007); merger of Ust-Ordinsk Buryat autonomous *okrug* with Irkutsk *oblast* to form Irkustk *oblast* (referenda April 16, 2006, effective January 1, 2008); and merger of Aginsk-Buryat autonomous *okrug* with Chita *oblast* to form Zabaikalsk *krai* (referenda March 11, 2007, effective March 1, 2008). Referenda results available from www.vybory. izbirkom.ru/region/izbirkom (accessed September 23, 2007).

[15]"Senators Block Moscow-Kazan Power-Sharing Treaty," Radio Free Europe/Radio Liberty, February 22, 2007, www.rferl.org/featuresarticle/2007/02/135aa370-f83a-4390-964d-bea497 b99659.html (accessed September 22, 2007).

[16]"European Neighbourhood Policy: Funding," http://ec.europa. eu/world/enp/funding_en.htm (accessed September 22, 2007).

[17]Economist Intelligence Unit (EIU), *Country Report: Russia* (September 2001), p. 13.

CHAPTER 24

Representation and Participation

Gorbachev's policies in the 1980s brought dramatic changes in the relationship between state and society, as *glasnost* sparked new public and private initiatives. Most restrictions on the formation of social organizations were lifted, and a large number of independent groups appeared. Hopes rose that these trends might indicate the emergence of civil society, an autonomous sphere of social life that could influence the state without being dependent on it. However, just a few years later, only a small stratum of Russian society was actively engaged; the demands of everyday life as well as cynicism about politicians and state institutions led many people to withdraw into the private domain and to endorse strong political leadership that would ensure stability and continued economic growth. With only minor fluctuations, Putin's approval rating stabilized at 65 to 70 percent after his election in 2000, while trust in public institutions remained low and the public's ability to affect policy seemed questionable. Watching street activism spill over into institutional instability in neighboring Ukraine during and after the Orange Revolution in November 2004, Russian authorities may have seen public apathy as an important pillar of social stability in Russia. To avoid upsetting the delicate social balance that existed, in 2006 and 2007 several laws were passed in an effort to check social forces that could nurture social division, without suppressing all forms of constructive civic engagement. These measures included better oversight of foreign organizations, support for pro-system youth groups, and marginalization of illegal immigrants.

Among the potential sources of social instability in 2007 was the uncertainty surrounding the upcoming electoral cycle. As Putin's second, and, according to constitutional provision, last term of office approached its end in March 2008, uncertainty about who would succeed him introduced a worrying element for Russia's political elite. Since public support was heavily focused on Putin's person, rather than on Russia's institutions or values, replacement of Putin by someone equally popular might be hard to achieve.

Uncertainty as to whether, at the last moment, Putin would change his mind and support a constitutional revision that would permit him a third term, whether he would attempt to anoint a favored successor, or whether he would encourage an electoral race between two establishment candidates fueled speculation in 2007;

evidence of a division within the elite was muted, but in 2007 some prominent political figures were speaking out in strong terms about the increasing dangers of an authoritarian outcome in Russia.

In such a situation various potential leaders or factions of the elite might consider mobilizing the masses (the public) to affect the outcome, whether this be through electoral campaigns (possibly including media manipulation and fraud), through street protests, or through other methods. In 2007 regional elites were no doubt keeping a watchful eye on Moscow, trying to position themselves so as to land on the winning side of the Putin succession.

Meanwhile, occurrences across the border in Ukraine in April 2007 evoked concern in Moscow. The Ukrainian president and parliament were deadlocked over whether President Yushchenko could dissolve the parliament and call new elections; the conflict threatened to spill into Kiev's streets. The Ukrainian events demonstrated the risks involved in allowing uncertainty among the elites to nurture mass discord. Historically, Soviet leaders have had a kind of elite pact or an informal agreement not to mobilize the public in support of one or another elite faction or leader in situations of potential social instability. (The events of the 1920s are instructive. When Leon Trotsky, a prominent Marxist leader, was expelled from the party's leadership, he did not take his cause to the streets, because his loyalty to the larger Bolshevik cause was greater than his desire to win the factional battle.) Whether the tradition of elite solidarity still governs the behavior of the current Russian leadership is uncertain; in the absence of any unified ideological commitment, an elite split in the face of an unclear succession could result in some leaders attempting to mobilize the public on their side, beyond the framework of normal electoral competition. Russian leaders no doubt worried about his possibility, as they peered over their border with Ukraine. And although public mobilization might be seen as an indicator of an active civil society, it could just as well create a crisis that would set Russia back on a more authoritarian path.

The Legislature

The Russian legislature, the Federal Assembly, came into being after the parliamentary elections of December 12, 1993, when the referendum ratifying the new Russian constitution was also approved. The upper house, the Federation Council, represents Russia's constituent federal units. The lower house, the Duma, has 450 members and involves direct popular election of candidates and parties. This body was named after the short-lived assembly that was formed by the tsar following the revolution of 1905 and thus emphasizes continuity with the Russian (rather than the Soviet) tradition. The first Federal Assembly elected in the post-communist period served only a two-year term. Subsequent elections to the Duma have occurred every four years, in 1995, 1999, 2003, and 2007. As noted in Chapter 23, in some special circumstances, earlier elections can be called.

Within the Duma, factions unite deputies from the same or allied parties. The Duma also has a number of standing committees. Up until 2001, committee chairships were distributed among the most important factions of the Duma; however, in 2005 all twenty-nine heads came from the dominant United Russia faction, with just six committees having first deputy chairs from other party factions.[1] The Duma elects its own speaker (or chair); since July 2003 this has been Boris Gryzlov, head of the United Russia Party. After the 1995 and 1999 elections, the speaker of the Duma came from the Communist Party, which had the highest electoral showing in those votes.

Deputies do not reflect the demographic characteristics of the population at large as closely as they did in the Communist period. For example, in 1984, 33 percent of the members of the Supreme Soviet were women;[2] in 2005, they constituted less than 10 percent of the Duma. Women head four committees, two in the traditionally "female" areas of health and women/family/children. (The other two areas are nationalities and the North/Far East.[3]) In 2000, manual workers made up less than 1 percent of Duma deputies, in contrast to 35 percent in the 1985 Supreme Soviet.[4] It is important, however, to remember that the implicit demographic quotas that the CPSU enforced in the Soviet period were primarily symbolic since the Supreme Soviet was largely powerless. On the other hand, the underrepresentation of women and workers in the present Duma indicates the extent to which Russian politics is primarily the domain of male elites.

The upper house of the Federal Assembly, the Federation Council, has two members from each of Russia's federal regions and republics, but the method of selection has varied over time. A new procedure,

phased in between 2000 and 2002, involves appointment of one representative by the regional executive and the other by the regional legislature, whereas from 1995 until that time, the elected governor/president of each region and the regional legislative head were themselves members. Since 2000, the Federation Council has gradually become quite a compliant organ, although formally it plays a role in approval of federal laws and in some cases takes up examination of particular legislative issues.[5] Many prominent businessmen are among the appointees, and in some cases the posts may be granted in exchange for political loyalty, which raises doubts about whether the body adequately represents interests of the regions. Party factions do not play a significant role in the Federation Council. Deputies to the Federation Council, as well as to the Duma, are granted immunity from criminal prosecution.

The constitution grants parliament powers in the legislative and budgetary areas, but these powers can be exercised effectively only if parliament operates with a high degree of unity. In practice, the president can often override the parliament through mechanisms such as the veto of legislation. To override the veto, two-thirds of the members of the Federal Assembly must support the original wording of the bill. Each house of parliament has the authority to confirm certain presidential appointees, in addition to the prime minister. For example, the Duma confirms the chair of the Central Bank of Russia, and the Federation Council confirms judges of higher courts. The Federation Council must also approve presidential decrees relating to martial law and state emergencies, as well as deploying troops abroad.[6] In some cases, failure to approve the president's nominees has produced stalemate or prevented certain offices from functioning for a period of time.

Conflict between the president and the legislative branch was frequent in the 1990s. Following electoral rebuffs in the 1993 and 1995 parliamentary elections, Yeltsin confronted a parliament that obstructed many of his proposed policies, but the parliament had neither the power nor the unity to offer a constructive alternative. Following the 1999 elections, the situation was somewhat less conflictual, and from 2003 to 2007 the Duma cooperated with the president, since about two-thirds of the deputies were tied to the United Russia faction, closest to the president, even though this party won only 49 percent of the seats in the previous election (2003).[7] However, with conflict over the monetarization of social benefits (discussed in Chapter 22), cracks marred the unity of the United Russia faction.

Society's ability to affect particular policy decisions through the legislative process is minimal. First, the blocs and parties in the parliament are isolated from the public at large and suffer low levels of popular respect. Many of the mechanisms that link parties and parliaments to citizens in Western democracies do not exist in Russia: interest associations to lobby the parliament are weak, and the internal decision-making structures of parties are generally elite-dominated.

Political Parties and the Party System

One of the most important political changes following the collapse of communism was the shift from a single-party to a multiparty system. In the USSR, the CPSU not only dominated state organs but also oversaw all social institutions, such as the mass media, trade unions, youth groups, educational institutions, and professional associations. It defined the official ideology for the country, set the parameters for state censorship, and, through the *nomenklatura* system, ensured that loyal supporters occupied all important offices. Approximately 10 percent of adults in the Soviet Union were party members, but there were no effective mechanisms to ensure that the party leadership was accountable to its members. Because the CPSU did not have to compete for political office, it was a party of a special kind, whose authority could not be openly questioned.

National competitive elections were held for the first time in the USSR in 1989, but new political parties were not formal participants in Russian elections until 1993. Since then, a confusing array of political organizations has run candidates in elections. A new law on political parties went into effect in July 2001, which tightened the conditions for forming and registering parties. Following additional changes that are effective for the 2007 Duma elections, parties must have at least 50,000 members, with branches of at least 500 members in at least half of the regions of Russia. In early 2007, twenty-five registered parties[8] met these conditions. Only organizations that are registered as political parties are now permitted to run candidates. Although critics have portrayed these

changes as artificially reducing voter choice, defenders argue that they will help to bring order to a chaotic and fragmented party system.

Russian political parties have some peculiarities when compared to their Western counterparts. In the 1990s, many parties formed around a prominent individual. The Yabloko party, for example, was named from the first letters of its founders' names, forming the Russian word for "apple." Duma ballots have listed not only the names of the blocs and parties but also their leaders.[9] Most Russian parties do not have a firm social base or stable constituency. Many Russians are hesitant to join a political party, perhaps because of unhappy experiences with the CPSU, and others simply distrust politics and politicians. Furthermore, other than the Communist Party of the Russian Federation (KPRF), Russian parties are young, so deeply rooted political identifications have not had time to develop. Finally, many citizens do not have a clear conception of their own interests or of how parties might represent them. In this context, image making is as important as programmatic positions, so parties appeal to transient voter sentiments. Nonetheless, party membership has grown in recent years. As the situation in the country stabilizes, the interests of particular groups (for example, blue-collar workers, business entrepreneurs, or groups based on age, gender, or region) may take a more central role in the formation of parties.

Despite the personalistic nature of party politics, some key cleavages help to explain the political spectrum. A major cleavage relates to economic policy. Nearly all parties have voiced support for the market transition to replace the centralized Soviet economy. However, communist/socialist groupings have been more muted in their support and have argued for a continued state role in providing social protection and benefits for vulnerable parts of the population. The liberal/reform groupings, on the other hand, have advocated more rapid market reform, including privatization, free prices, and limited government spending. The now dominant United Russia Party charts a middle ground, appealing to voters from a wide ideological spectrum and supporting market reform, but in a less radical form than the more strongly liberal reformist groups would prefer. Another dividing line relates to national identity. The nationalist/patriotic parties emphasize the defense of Russian interests over Westernization. They strongly criticize the expansion of NATO into countries neighboring Russia; they favor a strong military establishment, protection from foreign economic influence, and reconstitution of some former Soviet republics into a larger federation. Liberal/reform parties, on the other hand, advocate integration of Russia into the global market and the adoption of Western economic and political principles—positions that go along with their general support for radical market reform. Again, the United Russia Party has articulated an intriguing combination of these viewpoints, identifying Europe as the primary identity point for Russia, but at the same time insisting on Russia's role as a regional power, pursuing its own unique path to democratization and market reform.

Despite Russia's ethnic diversity, ethnic and regional parties have not had a significant effect on the national scene and only a minimal one in particular regions. Recent amendments to the party law make it even more difficult than previously for regional parties to emerge. Similarly, religion, although an important source of personal meaning for many Russians, has not emerged as a significant basis for political identity among ethnic Russians, who primarily adhere to the Russian Orthodox strain of Christianity. Nonetheless, in recent years, rising expressions of Russian nationalism and ethnic intolerance have erupted, particularly in relation to the primarily Muslim Chechens.

Russian political parties do not fit neatly on a left-right spectrum. Nationalist sentiments crosscut economic ideologies, producing the following party tendencies:

- The traditional left, critical of market reform and often mildly nationalistic
- Liberal/reform forces, supporting assertive Western-type market reform and political norms
- Centrist "parties of power," representing the political elite
- Nationalist/patriotic forces, primarily concerned with identity issues and national self-assertion

The most important parties in all four groupings, when not in power, have acted throughout as a loyal opposition; that is, they have not challenged the structure of the political system but have chosen to work within it. A distinctive feature of the party system in the prelude to the 2007 Duma election was the dominance of one party, United Russia. Some observers speculated that the formation of a second centrist party, A Just Russia, had the blessing of the Kremlin in order to give the impression that real competition existed in a situation where various informal mechanisms of power were increasingly marginalizing opposition political parties.

The Russian Left: The Communist Party of the Russian Federation (KPRF)

Consistently represented in the Duma since 1993, the KPRF was by far the strongest parliamentary party after the 1995 elections, winning over one-third of the seats in the Duma. Although it maintained strong electoral performance, the KPRF's relative position was weakened after the 1999 election because the Unity Party (the predecessor of the United Russia party) gained almost an equal number of votes and seats. As indicated in Table 24.1, in the 2003 elections, United Russia's support dropped by about one-half, to 12.6 percent of the party list vote (compared to 24.3 percent in 1999 and 22.3 percent in 1995). In May 2005, only 10.4 percent of deputies were in the KPRF faction, compared to about 25 percent after the 1999 election and close to 35 percent after the 1995 election.[10] The KPRF, the clearest successor of the old CPSU, appears to be a party in decline. In the December 2007 elections for the state Duma, the party won 11.6 percent of the votes (between 12 and 13 percent of seats in the Duma), making it the second largest group in the legislature, but far behind the dominant United Russia party, which won approximately 70 percent of the seats. The KPRF's popular vote represented a decline of only 1 percent from 2003.

In addition to its socialist economic approach, Russian nationalism is a prominent undertone in the party program. The party defines its goals as being democracy, justice, equality, patriotism and internationalism, a combination of civic rights and duties, and socialist renewal. The KPRF opposes the private sale of agricultural land but accepts substantial elements of the market reform package, favoring a combination of state and private ownership. Primary among the party's concerns are the social costs of the reform process. Thus, it has supported state subsidies for industry to ensure timely payment of wages and to prevent bankruptcies. The party's detractors see its leaders as opportunistic rather than as true democrats, but others point out that in the late 1990s communist governors in some of Russia's regions acted pragmatically rather than ideologically (indeed many "converted" to the

United Russia Party in later years). The party has operated within the constitutional framework in pursuing its political goals.

Support for the party is especially strong among older Russians, the economically disadvantaged, and rural residents. The party is no longer credible as a vanguard organization representing the working class. Instead, it appears to represent those who have adapted less successfully to the radical and uncertain changes that have occurred since the collapse of the Communist

state, as well as some individuals who remain committed to socialist ideals. Although one might expect Russia to offer fertile ground for social democratic sentiments like those that have been successful in the Scandinavian countries, the KPRF has not capitalized on these sentiments, nor has it made room for a new social democratic party that could be more successful. Its principal failures have been an inability to adapt its public position to attract significant numbers of new adherents, particularly among the young, as well as the

Table 24.1

Top Parties in the State Duma Elections[a]

Party or Bloc[b]	Percent of 1995 Party List Vote[c]	Percent of 1999 Party List Vote[c]	Percent of 2003 Party List Vote[c]	Percent of Duma Seats 2003[d]	Percent of 2007 Party List Vote[e]	Percent of Duma Seats Based on 2007 Vote[e]	Comments	Party Leader
Centrist/Establishment								
United Russia	—	(23.3)	37.6	49.3	64.3	70.0	Formed as Unity Party in 1999, then merged with Fatherland, All-Russia to form United Russia	Boris Gryzlov, party chair, but Vladimir Putin to head the party list on the ballot (2007)
A Just Russia	—	—	—	—	7.7	8.4	Formed in 2006 from three political parties: Party of Life, Rodina, and the Russian Party of Pensioners	Sergey Mironov
Fatherland, All-Russia	—	13.3	—	—	—	—	Merged into United Russia in 2001	Yuri Luzhkov, Evgenii Primakov (1999)
Our Home Is Russia	10.1	1.2	—	—	—	—	Chernomyrdin, was prime minister, 1992–1998	Viktor Chernomyrdin (1995, 1999)
Liberal/Reform								
Union of Rightist Forces	(3.9)	8.5	4.0	0.7	1.0	0	Russia's Choice (1993), Russia's Democratic Choice/United Democrats (1995)	Nikita Belykh
Yabloko	6.9	5.9	4.3	0.9	1.6	0	Opposition liberal/reform party	Grigoriy Yavlinsky

Table 24.1

Top Parties in the State Duma Elections[a] (cont.)

Party or Bloc[b]	Percent of 1995 Party List Vote[c]	Percent of 1999 Party List Vote[c]	Percent of 2003 Party List Vote[c]	Percent of Duma Seats 2003[d]	Percent of 2007 Party List Vote[e]	Percent of Duma Seats Based on 2007 Vote[e]	Comments	Party Leader
Communist/Socialist								
Communist Party of the Russian Federation	22.3	24.3	12.6	11.6	11.6	12.7		Gennady Zyuganov
Nationalist/Patriotic								
Liberal Democratic Party of Russia	11.2	6.0	11.5	8.0	8.1	8.9	In 1999 participated in elections as Bloc Zhirinovsky	Vladimir Zhirinovsky
Rodina (Motherland Bloc)	—	—	9.0	8.2	—	—	Left/center nationalist party; merged into A Just Russia	Dmitry Rogozin, Sergey Glaziev (2003)

[a]As of 2008, blocs of parties were not permitted to stand in elections.

[b]Figures may not add to 100 percent or to the total number of deputies in the State Duma because smaller parties and independents are excluded. Table includes only parties winning at least 4.0 percent of the national party list vote in one of the three elections (but not all such parties).

[c]Percentage of the total popular vote the party or bloc received on the proportional representation portion of the ballot in the year indicated. A dash indicates that the party or bloc was not included on that ballot or did not win a significant portion of the vote. Numbers in parentheses are votes for predecessor parties, similar to the one running in 2007.

[d]The sum of seats won in the proportional representation (party list) vote and the single-member district vote. Number of deputies in the faction changed over time following the elections.

[e]In 2007 all of the seats are to be allocated according to the party list (proportional representation) ballot for parties receiving at least 7 percent of that vote; the single-member district vote was discontinued. The final distribution of seats in the Duma is an estimate at the time of printing, based on results reported by the Russian Electoral Commission, December 3, 2007.

Source: Revised from DeBardeleben, Joan, "Russia" in *Introduction to Comparative Politics*. Copyright 2004 by Houghton Mifflin Company. Reprinted with permission; and for the 2003 figures, *The Economist. Country Briefings: Russia*. http://www.economist.com, April 25, 2005.

absence of a charismatic and attractive political leader. The party also failed to assert its legitimate claim to leadership in the government after its strong showing in the 1995 election, thus sacrificing its reputation as an effective parliamentary opposition force. For this reason, part of the blame for the weakness of an effective loyal opposition may lie at the door of the KPRF.

Rodina (Motherland), a party that is hard to classify, was registered in 2002. Although we include it in the left category, it might legitimately also be considered a nationalist formation. Led by Dmitry Rogozin and Sergey Glaziev, this relative newcomer received 9 percent of the party-list vote in 2003 and initially constituted about 9 percent of the deputies in its Duma faction after that election. In informed Russian circles, the party's creation is considered to have been fostered by the Kremlin, in an effort to divert support from the more threatening KPRF. In January 2005 some Rodina

Duma deputies embarked on a highly visible hunger strike to protest the effects of the government's monetarization of social benefits. Glaziev subsequently apparently fell out of favor with the Kremlin,[11] and the party joined with two others to form another Kremlin-sanctioned party, A Just Russia, in 2006 (discussed below).

Centrist Parties: United Russia and A Just Russia (the Upstart)

Since 2003, one political party, United Russia, has achieved political dominance at both the national and regional levels. Although neither formal leader nor member of this party, Putin's name stood at the head of United Russia's electoral list in the 2007 Duma elections, and the party has provided loyal support for the system of presidential power that was erected under his leadership.

United Russia's predecessor, the Unity Party, rose to prominence together with Vladimir Putin in the elections of 1999 and 2000. In 2001, the Unity Party joined with a potential establishment rival, Fatherland/All-Russia, and later took the name United Russia in 2004. Although Putin is not formally head of the party, United Russia is clearly a vehicle for cementing his political power. The party enjoyed a meteoric rise, finishing a close second runner to the KPRF in the 1999 Duma elections. In this first electoral foray, the party won 23.3 percent of the party-list vote and seventy-three seats in the Duma; this increased to 37.6 percent of the party list in 2003 and just over 64 percent in 2007. In 2005, through the merger of Unity with other parties and attraction of other deputies, 67 percent of Duma deputies had joined the United Russia faction, to climb higher after the 2007 elections.

Previous centrist formations, despite their close association with the government and regional political elites, had failed to develop a base of popular support. What explains United Russia's success? An important factor is the association with Putin, but the party has also built an effective political machine that generates persuasive incentives for regional elites. Even some governors not in the party agreed to appear on the party's Duma electoral list in 2003. The party has a rather poorly defined program, which emphasizes the uniqueness of the Russian approach (as distinct from Western models), an appeal to values of order and law, and a continued commitment to moderate reform. Its official website[12] indicates that the party is more focused on prominent people than on ideas, which justifies its designation as a cadre party, in contrast to the KPRF, for example, which is clearly of the programmatic party type. United Russia is, at the same time, truly a "party of power," focused on winning to its side prominent and powerful people who will then use their influence to further bolster the party's support. By 2005, United Russia had, through a combination of carrots and sticks, brought sixty-four regional executives (governors and heads of republics) into the fold, along with increased influence in regional legislatures.[13] Combined with increasingly centralized control within the party, the result is a powerful political machine reinforced by the president's power over gubernatorial appointments.

United Russia has drawn electoral support from every other part of the political spectrum, making the party a catchall electoral organization. In 2007 no other party was able to pose a real challenge to United Russia's dominance. Particular concerns centered on the ability of the state to apply selective enforcement of complex legislation governing the electoral process and the registration of political parties in such as way as to disadvantage or even disqualify potentially attractive competitors. These concerns were reinforced by the experience in some of the elections for regional legislatures in 2006 and 2007. For example, in March 2007 the Yabloko party, a liberal democratic party that has gained at least some representation in the Duma in every federal election since 1993, was disqualified from running in the regional electoral contest in St. Petersburg *oblast* due to a contested failure to comply with the law regarding party registration.

Another new centrist "establishment" party, A Just Russia, was founded in 2006, based on an amalgam of three small parties (Rodina, Party of Life, and the Party of Pensioners). The party was formed by Putin loyalist Sergey Mironov, chair of Russia's upper legislative body, the Federation Council. Like Rodina, this party is considered by many observers to represent an effort to demonstrate the competitive nature of Russia's electoral system, while undermining opposition parties that could pose a real threat to United Russia. Although formed just a year earlier, the party had a highly developed website by 2007, indicating a considerable resource base. More specifically the party espouses support for social protection measures and a reduction in economic inequality, placing it to the left of United Russia on the political spectrum and offering a political magnet for dissatisfied supporters of the Communist Party.[14] Understandably, Communist Party leaders view such socialist proclamations with a jaundiced eye, suspecting that, like Rodina, the party is a Kremlin prop.

Mironov's loyalty to Putin was evidenced by his suggestion in March 2007 that the constitution should be amended to allow Putin to run for a third term, and his support for extending the presidential term of office to seven years. Even if it is a creation of the Kremlin, A Just Russia caused a political squall when it defeated United Russia in regional legislative elections in the southern region of Stavropol in March 2007, an unexpected outcome that suggested that the party could take on a life of its own. Some observers thought it possible that the party might pick up significant support from regional elites who were low on the totem pole in the United Russia hierarchy. In fact, the party won somewhat under 8 percent of the vote in the 2007 legislative elections, placing it just above the 7-percent threshold required for Duma representation. It seems unlikely that A Just Russia will become a major political force, given the loyalty of its leadership to Putin. Nonetheless, the experience with A Just Russia suggests that the Kremlin cannot necessarily foresee the consequences of supporting the formation of a second "establishment" party. What the party's formation does demonstrate is that the Kremlin cannot necessarily foresee the consequences of supporting the formation of this second "establishment" party.

As noted, other attempts to form centrist parties have been markedly less successful than United Russia, so it is possible that A Just Russia will have the same fate. Fatherland, which joined with Unity to form United Russia, was also a party of established political elites. Founded in 1998, the prominence of the party's leader, Yuri Luzhkov, mayor of Moscow, was more important than its platform. Although associated with Moscow, a capital city whose privileges are both envied and resented in the regions, Luzhkov's success in modernizing the city gave him the image

of an effective leader. The party joined with another centrist grouping, All-Russia, headed by the relatively popular former foreign minister and short-time prime minister, Evgenii Primakov, in 1999. Fatherland/All-Russia won a respectable 13.3 percent in the 1999 Duma party-list vote, bringing the total centrist vote (with Unity) up to 36.6 percent. It was widely expected that Primakov would run for president in March 2000, but presumably due to Putin's overwhelming popularity, he too climbed on the Unity bandwagon.

Liberal/Reform Parties

More than any other part of the political spectrum, the liberal/reform parties have found it hard to build a stable and unified electoral base. Many Russians held aspects of the liberal program, such as privatization and shock therapy, responsible for Russia's economic decline. Leaders from this grouping, such as Yegor Gaidar, who was acting first prime minister under Yeltsin, and Anatoly Chubais, who oversaw Yeltsin's privatization plan, even now have low ratings with the population. Another liberal reformer, the economist Grigory Yavlinsky, who has consistently taken a critical stance toward the government's policies, enjoys a more loyal following, particularly among intellectuals. Until 1999 his party, Yabloko, enjoyed the most success among these parties.[15] Four parties or blocs running on a pro–market reform plank won seats in the Duma in the 1993 elections, and several liberal/reform parties split the vote in 1995, which reduced their representation in the Duma. On November 21, 1998, the brutal murder by contract killers of the liberal/reform politician and Duma member Galina Starovoitova (one of Russia's most prominent female politicians) resulted in renewed efforts to form a united political bloc in the form of the Union of Rightist Forces (URF).[16] In 1999, the URF received only 8.5 percent of the party-list vote, while Yabloko, with its more critical stance toward the government, ran separately, pulling in just 5.9 percent. In 2003, for the first time, neither Yabloko nor the URF reached the 5 percent cutoff; thus, the liberal/reform parties were not represented in the Duma at all from 2004–2008. Based on results of regional elections in early 2007, political observers anticipated that SPS might make an adequate comeback to be represented in the next Duma. In the 2007 elections, support for both parties fell to below 2 percent, eliminating them from the Duma. The parties alleged unfair electoral practices as part of the explanation.

These groups espouse a commitment to traditional liberal values, such as a limited economic role for the state, support for free-market principles, and the protection of individual rights and liberties. Although this philosophy provided the impetus for Yeltsin's original reform agenda, his refusal to associate himself with any political party deprived these groups of a strong organizational resource. The unpopularity of Yeltsin's reform approach also undermined support for its ideological soulmates. Although liberal/reform figures are often referred to as the "democrats" because of their Westernizing approach, many Russians associate them with Russia's economic and national decline. Support for liberal/reform parties generally is stronger among the young, the more highly educated, urban dwellers, and the well-off. Thus, ironically, those with the best prospects for succeeding in the new market economy have been among the least successful in constructing an effective political party.

Nationalist/Patriotic Parties

To the surprise of many observers, the Liberal Democratic Party of Russia (LDPR), headed by Vladimir Zhirinovsky, got the strongest support on the party ballot in 1993, winning almost 23 percent of the vote; this declined to 11 percent in 1995 and 6 percent in 1999, but rebounded to 11.5 percent in 2003, down to 8.2 percent in 2007, placing it third behind the Communist Party. Neither liberal nor particularly democratic in its platform, the party might more properly be characterized as nationalist and populist. Its populism is based on Zhirinovsky's personal charismatic appeal. Some Russians say, "He speaks our language," while others radically oppose his provocative style and nationalist rhetoric. In his speeches, Zhirinovsky openly appeals to the anti-Western sentiments that emerged in the wake of Russia's decline from superpower status and the government's perceived groveling for Western economic aid. The party has supported revival of an expanded Russian state to include Ukraine, Belarus, and possibly other neighboring areas. Concern with the breakdown of law

and order seems to rank high among its priorities. However, despite Zhirinovsky's radical demeanor, he has often supported the government on key issues, most notably the war in Chechnya. Zhirinovsky's support has been especially strong among working-class men and military personnel. Other parties and leaders have taken up a softer version of the patriotic theme, so the resurgence of support for the LDPR in 2003 suggests that nationalist sentiment in Russia is increasing, not declining. More radical groups, such as the National Bolsheviks,[17] which combines nationalist and left-wing revolutionary ideology, have also sought influence outside the electoral process, enduring periodic raids or restrictions from the government.

Elections

In the postcommunist period, elections seemed to be a constant phenomenon in Russia, partly because presidential, legislative, and regional/local elections are generally held on separate occasions. The initial euphoria with the competitive electoral structure has been replaced by voter fatigue, although turnout in federal elections remains respectable, generally between 60 and 70 percent, but down to 56 percent in the 2003 Duma election and 63 percent in the 2007 election. In regional and local contests, participation rates have at times fallen below the required minimum participation rate to make the vote valid (a requirement since eliminated), necessitating repeat balloting. National elections receive extensive media coverage, and campaign activities begin as much as a year in advance. Elections are now big business, involving extensive use of polling firms and public relations experts. Up until 2003, national elections were generally considered to be reasonably fair and free, but international observers expressed serious concerns about the conduct of the 2003 vote and the campaign that preceded it; even more serious violations were raised in regard to the 2007 election.[18]

Up through 2003, the electoral system for selecting the Duma resembled the German system, combining proportional representation with winner-take-all districts. Half of the 450 deputies were selected on the basis of nationwide party lists, with any party gaining 5 percent of the national vote entitled to a proportional share of these 225 seats. Voters were given the explicit option of voting against all candidates or parties. In the 2003 Duma election, 4.7 percent of voters chose this option. The remaining 225 deputies in the current Duma were elected in single-member plurality districts; these races usually involved local notables, although many winning candidates associated themselves with particular parties. Some independent candidates joined party factions once they were in the Duma; in 2005, the Duma had twenty-one independent deputies. The final balance of forces in the parliament after the 2003 election was determined by the combined result of the party-list vote and the single-member district votes, but not made proportional to the results on the party-list vote, as in Germany. Until 1999, despite the electoral rebuffs in 1993 and 1995, Yeltsin did not install a prime minister reflecting party strength in the Duma. In 1999 and 2003, parliamentary elections offered qualified support for the government.

In 2005, changes to the electoral law were approved, which took effect for the 2007 Duma election. These involve abolition of the single-member districts, subsuming selection of all 450 deputies on the party-list ballot into one national proportional representation district, with a minimum threshold for representation of each party raised to 7 percent. Parties are required to include regional representatives on their lists from across the country. For those parties above the 7 percent threshold, choice of deputies from the list must reflect strength of the vote in the various regions. In addition, according to the 2001 law on political parties, in order to participate in the election a party must have affiliates in more than half of the regions of Russia, with a certain number of registered members in these regions. Therefore, parties with a strong political base in one or several regions, comparable to the Christian Democratic Union in Germany or the Bloc Quebecois in Canada, would be represented in the national parliament only if they had organizations of the requisite size in half of the regions in the country and gained 7 percent of the national vote. Under the new party legislation, the number of successful parties is likely to decline, and parties will probably be more dependent on national party machines. Thus the law is likely to have a strongly centralizing character, as well as making political parties more central to the electoral process.

While the new requirements may simplify choices before the electorate, they may also limit options available to the voter, particularly in combination with 2006 national legislation that removed the "against all" option from the ballot. These changes, plus allegations of interference with nomination and party registration processes, may reduce the effectiveness of elections as vehicles of popular control. Since 1999, opposition parties have experienced a sharp decline in electoral success, with the rapid ascent of United Russia. One reason is genuine popular support for Putin, as well as the failure of the opposition parties to develop appealing programs or field attractive candidates. However, other factors also play a role. Media coverage has favored the party of power and the president. Administrative control measures and selective enforcement have delimited the scope of acceptable political opposition, particularly when this has involved potential elite support for challengers, the example of Khodorkovsky being a case in point. In addition, the carrot-and-stick method has wooed regional elites, producing a bandwagon effect, which has been reinforced by the abolition of gubernatorial elections. Dependent on the president's nomination for reappointment, regional leaders have a further incentive to join the United Russia team. Finally, potential opposition forces have been co-opted through party mergers and through formation of fellow-traveler parties (such as the Rodina party before the 2003 election and A Just Russia party since 2006).

Results of presidential elections have not mirrored parliamentary election outcomes, and Russia has yet to experience a real transfer of power from one political grouping to another, which some scholars consider a first step in consolidating democratic governance. Although the KPRF topped the list in the 1995 Duma elections, the party's leader, Gennady Zyuganov, was not able to defeat Yeltsin in the presidential election of 1996. Zyuganov did even more poorly against Putin in the 2000 vote; even in areas of traditional support (the so-called Red Belt in central European Russia), Putin generally outscored him. In 2003, Zyuganov did not run. Under the Russian constitution, presidential elections are held every four years. If no candidate receives a majority of the votes in the first round, a runoff election is held between the two top contenders. Although the 1995 election went to a second round (Yeltsin won 35 percent in the first and 54 percent in the second round against Zyuganov), in 2000 Putin won handily, with nearly 53 percent of the vote against ten other candidates in the first round, and in 2004, he got an even stronger 71 percent in the first round.

Indications that opposition forces were restricted in their ability to participate in the 2007 elections included a Supreme Court decision in March 2007 to deregister the Liberal Party, disputing the party's records on member registration. The head of the party, long-time political activist Vladimir Ryzhkov, stated, "This is part of the Kremlin's policy of suppressing the opposition. It's being done to prevent opposition parties from taking part in elections."[19] Observers in both the West and within Russia wondered whether the electoral contests would offer a free choice to Russian voters, or whether a United Russia victory was a foregone conclusion.

Political Culture, Citizenship, and Identity

Political culture can be a source of great continuity in the face of radical upheavals in the social and political spheres. Attitudes toward government that prevailed in the tsarist period seem to have endured with remarkable tenacity. These include acceptance of a tradition of personalistic authority, highly centralized leadership, and a desire for an authoritative source of truth. The Soviet regime embodied these and other traditional Russian values, such as egalitarianism and collectivism; at the same time, the Soviet development model glorified science, technology, industrialization, and urbanization—values that it superimposed on the traditional way of life of the largely rural population. When communism collapsed, Soviet ideology was discredited, and the government embraced political and economic values from the West. Many citizens and intellectuals are skeptical of this "imported" culture, partly because it conflicts with other traditional civic values such as egalitarianism, collectivism, and a broad scope for state activity. A crisis of identity resulted for both elites and average citizens, and the current government priorities collide with some traditional values even while they appeal to others.

One way to study political culture is to examine evidence from public opinion surveys, which suggest that there is considerable support in Russia for liberal democratic values, such as an independent judiciary, a free press, basic civil liberties, and competitive elections. Colton and McFaul conclude from survey results that "a significant portion of the Russian population acquiesces in the abstract idea of democracy without necessarily looking to the West for guidance."[20] The authors find that Russians are divided on the proper balance between defense of individual rights and the maintenance of order; other experts conclude that Russians' desire for a strong state and strong leaders does not imply support for authoritarian government.[21] On the other hand, democratic values may not be deeply enough entrenched to provide a safeguard against authoritarian rule.

In the Soviet period, the mass media, the educational system, and a variety of other social institutions played a key role in propagating the party's political values. Now, students are presented with a wider range of views, and the print media represent a broad spectrum of political opinion, but the electronic media increasingly reflect the government position. The electronic media are particularly susceptible to political pressure, because of the costs and limited availability of the technology needed to run television stations. Unequal media access, in favor of the pro-presidential forces, was criticized by international observers of the 2003 and 2004 federal elections. Financial interests and mafia attacks on investigative journalists have inhibited press freedom. The print media is considerably more diverse than TV, but on occasion political and economic pressure is used by national and regional governments to limit the publication of highly critical viewpoints. Another obstacle to the creation of a responsible and critical press are violent attacks, including murders, of journalists who exposure corruption or who are outspoken in their criticism of established interests.

Social Class

Social class identity was a major theme in the Soviet period. The Bolshevik revolution was justified in the name of the working class, and the Communist Party of the Soviet Union claimed to be a working-class party that had transformed the Soviet Union into a society free of class conflict, representing the interests of all of the working people. However, many dissidents and average citizens perceived an "us-them" relationship with the political elite in Soviet times, which some dissident intellectuals conceptualized in terms of class conflict between the party leadership and the mass of the Soviet population. Because social class was a major part of the discredited Soviet ideology, in the postcommunist period many Russians have been skeptical of claims made by politicians to represent the working class, thus most postcommunist parties and politicians have not invoked this terminology. Even the Communist Party of the Russian Federation, in its party program, does not explicitly identify itself as a working-class party; characterizing itself as "true to the interests of working people," the KPRF "sees its task as being to join social-class and national-liberatory movements into a unified mass opposition movement and to give it a conscious and purposeful character."[22]

The notion of a middle class is a more attractive reference point for many Russians. Russian sociologists identify the growth of a middle class as an as-yet elusive but potentially stabilizing social dynamic. This concept of a middle class is rooted in Western sociological theory rather in a Marxist orientation, and denotes a society where the bulk of the population enjoys a comfortable standard of living and provides support for a stable political order. The appeal of a middle-class society, which Russia admittedly has not achieved, suggests a focus on consumerism and individual achievement, rather than on class solidarity and political struggle. At the same time, many Russians remain uncomfortable with the extreme individualism that characterizes Western middle-class society; they retain a more collectivist cultural orientation, although the focus for their collectivist sentiments is the circle of family, friends, and work colleagues rather than a social class.

Nonetheless, labor solidarity has played an important role in some sectors of the Russian economy. The official trade unions established under Soviet rule have survived under the title of Federation of Independent Trade Unions (FITU). However, FITU has lost the confidence of large parts of the workforce. In some sectors, such as the coal industry, new independent trade unions have formed, mainly at the local level. Labor actions have become an important form of social protest through spontaneous strikes, transport blockages, and even hunger strikes. In the mid- to late

1990s, the main grievance was late payment of wages, and strikes were most prevalent among coal miners, in the transportation sector, and in the public service. In 1998, coal miners in Siberia blocked railway arteries to protest late wage payments. Later that year, teachers from various regions of the country participated in protest actions against wage delays; in the city of Ulyanovsk, a hunger strike led to the death of one teacher. The use of such nontraditional forms of protest is a radical and desperate attempt to gain the attention of domestic and international authorities. Immediate concessions are often offered in response to such protests, but the underlying problems are rarely addressed. The number of organizations affected by actual labor strikes spiked in 1995, declined, then rose again in 2004–2005. However, according to data from the Federal State Statistics Service of the Russian government, the length of time each worker spent on strike was relatively short in 2004–2005, so apparently these strikes often took the form of one-day protest actions rather than extensive labor disputes that may be more typical of countries with collective bargaining traditions. This suggests that working-class organizations are only weakly oriented toward sustained collective action or able to support it. Although class conflict as a focus of social organization is momentarily in abeyance, it may well generate more pronounced collective identities later in this century.

Citizenship, National Identity, Race, and Ethnicity

Russia is a multiethnic state. Therefore one important aspect of the search for identity relates to what it means to be Russian. The distinction between ethnic identity and civil identity is an important one. The Russian language itself has two distinct words for "Russian": *russkii*, which refers to an ethnicity, and *Rossiiskii*, which has a civic meaning and includes people of various ethnic backgrounds who are Russian citizens. The name of the country, Rossiiskaia Federatsiia, invokes the latter sense. Thus there is an official recognition that being a Russian citizen need not imply Russian ethnicity. This situation contrasts with some countries in Western Europe where national identity is more clearly associated with a particular ethnic or national group. This issue is also affected by the large number of ethnic

Russians who live in other parts of the former Soviet Union; some have returned to Russia, but others remain abroad, and their status has been a sore point in relations between Russia and the governments of neighboring countries, particularly Estonia and Latvia.

In recent years there are increasing concerns about the rise of an exclusionary form of Russian nationalism among certain parts of the population. This phenomenon has appeared in the rise of fringe nationalist parties, extremist nationalist youth movements, and intermittent attacks on visible minorities. Muslim groups from Russia's southern regions have been the target of ethnic stereotyping. In addition, refugee flows from some of the war-torn regions of the Transcaucasus (Georgia, Azerbaijan, and neighboring regions of southern Russia such as Chechnya and Ingushetia) have heightened national tensions. Individuals from some of these regions play an important role in Russia's trade sector and are viewed by many Russians as speculators and crooks. Recent terrorist attacks have heightened prejudices, particularly against Chechens. Official state policy, although explicitly opposing these extreme nationalist tendencies, may, in some case, have implicitly fed them. For example, in the face of tensions between Russia and neighboring Georgia, an embargo was placed on imports to Russia, and people of Georgian ethnicity were expelled from public markets and Georgian children from public schools on the grounds that many were in the country illegally. Legislation effective April 1, 2007, banned noncitizens without proper residence documents and work permits from Russia's numerous outdoor markets, a measure that was more generally threatening to visible minorities and that greatly reduced the number of vendors. At various times, in the name of fighting domestic terrorist threats, individuals of Chechen background have been detained and expelled from Russian cities. However, Russian leaders have also made efforts to channel nationalist sentiments in a more benign direction. In 2005, an extreme nationalist group, the National Bolsheviks, was banned by a Russian court on technical grounds; although the decision was overturned by a higher court, the organization is not allowed to run in elections.

A somewhat controversial phenomenon is the youth group, Nashi (Ours), formed in 2005. Although claiming to oppose fascism in Russia, some observers consider the group itself to nurture intolerance and fascist sentiments. The colloquial term *nashi* (ours) evokes an "us-them" dichotomy, and members of the group express anti-Western sentiments. In 2006 the British Ambassador to Russia was reported to have suffered harassment by Nashi supporters after attending a conference convened by opposition liberals earlier in the year.[23] Among Nashi's goals are to educate youth in Russian history and values and to form volunteer groups to help maintain law and order. The group is openly supportive of Putin, seeing him as a defender of Russia's national sovereignty. Although most observers see Nashi as enjoying Kremlin support (Putin has met several times with Nashi activists), others speculate that the Kremlin may be concerned about the potentially divisive nature of some of Nashi's actions.

Religion has long played a role in shaping Russian identity. Today, the Russian Orthodox Church appeals to many citizens who are looking for a replacement for the discredited values of the Communist system. A controversial law passed in 1997 made it harder for new religious groups to organize themselves; the law was directed primarily, however, at Western proselytizers. Human rights advocates and foreign observers protested strongly, again raising questions about the depth of Russia's commitment to liberal democratic values.

Gender

Attitudes toward gender relations in Russia reflect traditional family values. It is generally assumed that women will carry primary responsibility for child care and a certain standard of "femininity" is expected of women both inside and outside the workplace. Currently, women in families with adequate financial resources more often choose to stay home with children than was previously the case, but this still remains the exception rather than the norm, and many families cannot afford to consider this option. Fathers play a relatively small role in child raising; many women still rely on grandparents to help out. The birthrate in Russia fell from 16.6 births per 1,000 people in 1985 to a rate of 10.4 in 2006, while the death rate was 15.2.[24] The decline in population has been tempered by the immigration of ethnic Russians from other former Soviet republics. Although declining birthrates often accompany economic modernization and characterize many West European societies as well, in Russia this phenomenon is less the result of a positive choice than due to daily hardships, future uncertainty, a declining standard of living, and continued housing shortages. In May 2006 Putin announced a doubling of monthly child support payments and a large monetary bonus for women having a second child to boost the birthrate. Public opinion surveys indicate that most Russians believe a higher standard of living, including better housing and jobs, would encourage larger families.[25] At the same time, policymakers are concerned that population decline will hinder economic recovery.

Feminism is not popular in Russia, since many women consider it inconsistent with traditional notions of femininity or with accepted social roles for women. Even so, a number of civil society organizations have grown up in Russia to represent the interests of women; some of them advocate traditional policies to provide better social supports for mothers and families, while others challenge traditional gender roles and definitions. Changing cultural norms affect gender relations in other ways as well. A permissive cultural environment, propagated in advertising and through the mass media, represents women more frequently as sex objects. Advertising also reinforces commercialized images of female beauty that may not correspond to cultural expectations or to healthy lifestyles. In the face of unemployment and the breakdown in traditional social linkages, increasing numbers of young women have turned to prostitution to make a living; HIV/AIDS rates are also increasing at a rapid rate, fuelled by prostitution, low levels of information, and the rise of drug trafficking related to Russia's more permeable eastern border with countries like Afghanistan.

Interests, Social Movements, and Protest

Since the collapse of the USSR, numerous political and social organizations have sprung up in every region of Russia, representing the interests of groups such as children, veterans, women, environmental advocates, pensioners, and the disabled. Other groups are professional unions, sports clubs, trade unions, and cultural organizations. Many such organizations grew out of Soviet-era associations, such as the trade unions and nature protection societies, but now they can mobilize more openly and spawn new independent offshoots or competitors. Important societal groups include the Committee of Soldiers' Mothers of Russia, the Socio-Ecological Union, the "Chernobyl" Union, and the Society of Veterans. The most successful interest associations have been those formed by better-off elements of society (such as new business entrepreneurs), officials, or, until recently, groups receiving funding from international or foreign agencies. Most locally based interest associations have small staffs and, in addition to foreign funding, rely for support on local government, contracts for work carried out, and commercial activities. Dependence on Western aid can divert nongovernmental organizations' (NGOs') agendas from concerns of their constituents to priorities of their foreign sponsors.

Many observers saw such blossoming activism as the foundation for a fledgling civil society that would nurture the new democratic institutions established since 1991. However, there have been many obstacles to realizing this potential. Organizations generally must register with local authorities, and some develop such close relationships with the local administration as to undermine their independence. In January 2006 Putin signed legislation amending laws on public associations and noncommercial organizations. These controversial changes, protested widely by Western governments, placed new grounds for denying registration to such organizations, established new reporting requirements (particularly for organizations receiving funds from foreign sources), and increased government supervisory functions. Special requirements are placed on foreign noncommercial nongovernmental organizations operating in Russia; accordingly, several foreign organizations, such as Amnesty International and Human Rights Watch, were forced to temporarily suspend activities while seeking to comply with the new requirements. The new measures were justified as necessary to respond to external terrorist threats, but many commentators see them as an effort to reduce the likelihood that civil society activists with external contacts might foment unrest similar to what happened in Ukraine in 2004 or in Georgia in 2005.

With popular activism on the rise in neighboring countries, observers wondered whether it could have a contagion effect in Russia. Between November 2003 and March 2005, three post-Soviet countries experienced largely nonviolent upheavals, which threw out establishment figures. In each case, a color or flower was adopted as a symbol for the opposition, and the events came to be associated with that symbol. The popular protests followed fraudulent elections; elections were effective in bringing change, but not in the expected way, through the ballot box, but rather by exposing corruption in the system. In two cases (Ukraine and Georgia), repeat elections were held following a court ruling, reversing the original outcome. Foreign support for the protest groups was a point of hot discussion. In fact, in commenting on the Ukrainian protests, the Russia press depicted this as a case of external intervention in the domestic affairs of Ukraine because of foreign financial support for the protestors camped out in Kiev.

November 2003: Georgia

Georgia's Rose Revolution saw public protests against rigged parliamentary elections; the court declared them invalid. New presidential and parliamentary elections in early 2004 replaced Eduard Shevardnadze, the longtime incumbent, with opposition figure Mikheil Saakashvilli. Support from the Open Society Foundation, funded by George Soros, was alleged by critics to have played a pivotal role in activating opposition forces.

November 2004: Ukraine

Ukraine's Orange Revolution followed the fraudulent presidential runoff election of November 21, 2004, when Viktor Yanukovich was declared to have defeated Viktor Yushchenko. Following a court ruling, repeat elections made Yushchenko the winner. An east-west regional split was an important factor in the contest, with Yushchenko favoring more asser-tive efforts for integration with the EU, while Viktor Yanukovich followers were more inclined to close relations with Russia. Russia provided aid to Yanukovich and objected to the repeat vote, while Western organizations assisted Yushchenko supporters. (Orange was the color of Yushchenko's party.)

March 2005: Kyrgyzstan

Kyrgyzstan's Tulip Revolution occurred after parliamentary elections in February 2005. This resulted in the ouster of incumbent president Askar Akayev one month later, who fled the country to Kazakhstan and Moscow in the face of the protests, which included minor violence. Akayev finally resigned in early April with new elections scheduled for July.

Could Russia experience its own color or flower revolution? Analysts disagree, and they also argue over what color or symbol it would take if it did occur. Many observers emphasize that "Russia isn't Ukraine." Reasons for reaching that conclusion vary. Defenders of the system emphasize the broad popular support for Vladimir Putin. Critics point to the more subtle methods of achieving popular compliance in Russia, so that a fraudulent election of the Ukrainian variety would be unnecessary to keep incumbents in power; others cite the absence of checks and balances to permit a redressing of undemocratic outcomes.[1] Yegor Gaidar argues that in countries like Ukraine, democracy, nationalism, and European values are associated with one another, while Russia suffers from a "postimperial syndrome" that makes it hard for westernizing democrats to link to nationalist sentiments.[2]

What color might a Russian revolution be? Gaidar implies it would be red, but not communist red, rather bloody red: the problem is that, unlike the situation in Ukraine, "it is impossible to unite nationalists and democrats in street politics without the possibility of a dangerous, violent development occurring." Another idea is that any popular "revolution" in Russia might soon turn gray, since it would be controlled by the gray suits in Moscow.

---

[1]Masha Lipman, "How Russia Is Not Ukraine: The Closing of Russian Civil Society," Policy Outlook Carnegie Endowment for International Peace, January 2005.

[2]"The Economic and Political Situation in Eurasia: Why Russia Is Not Ukraine," Policy Outlook Carnegie Endowment for International Peace, April 21, 2005, http://www.carnegieendowment.org/events/index.cfm?fa=eventDetail&id=770. Summary on website prepared by Alina Tourkova, Junior Fellow with the Russian and Eurasian Program at the Carnegie Endowment for International Peace.

The government has attempted to channel public activism through official forums, such as the Civic Forum, an unprecedented all-Russian congress of nongovernmental organization activists held in November 2001 in Moscow. Organized with government support, the event elicited both enthusiasm and skepticism among activists in NGOs. Although pleased with the official recognition given to civil society organizations, some activists viewed the event as mainly a public relations effort to indicate the government's openness to social input. A newer initiative is the Public Chamber, created in 2005 by legislation proposed by the president. Based on voluntary participation by presidential appointees and representatives recommended by national and regional societal organizations, the organization is presented as a mechanism for public consultation and input, as well as a vehicle for creating public support for government policy. It appears to reflect a corporatist approach that might serve to co-opt public activists from more disruptive forms of self-expression. In 2001, at the Civic Forum, then prime minister Mikhail Kasyanov, later turned critic, referred to an age-old Russian malady— the "lack of connectedness and communication between the authorities and society."[26] The question remains whether these government-sponsored organizations and events will really address this problem or whether they are only a reflection of the Kremlin's efforts to co-opt potential opposition and maintain firm control.

A variety of mass-based political organizations protest the current political direction of the government, but in 2007 the authorities tried to restrict public demonstrations and protests. An alternative political grouping, The Other Russia, unites a wide range of prominent political critics,[27] while advocating liberal democratic values and human rights. The group held an alternative conference in July 2006 to draw attention to threats to Russian democracy; the Dissenters' Marches that they organized in Moscow and St. Petersburg in mid-April 2007 proceeded according to plan, despite a ban by local authorities, resulting in the detention of the group's leaders, including Gary Kasparov, the world chess champion. Other movements, such as the Movement Against Illegal Immigration,[28] lie on the other end of the political spectrum, organizing protests such as a public action called "Moscow—a Russian

city" in April 2007. As these examples indicate, public protests span the political spectrum and can come into conflict not only with the authorities but also with one another.

At the time of this writing, one cannot say that civil society has really formed in Russia. Whatever forms of collective identity have emerged, social forces do not easily find avenues to exert constructive and organized influence on state activity. As Russian citizens awaken to political awareness, they seem to sway between activism and apathy, and the political system wavers along a path between fledgling democratic innovations and renewed authoritarianism. Only the future will tell.

Notes

[1]Compiled by the author from the website of the State Duma, www.duma.gov.ru. See the section on "Sostav i struktura GD/ Komitet i kommissii GD" (accessed September 22, 2007).

[2]David Lane, *State and Politics in the USSR* (Oxford: Blackwell, 1985), pp. 184–185.

[3]Compiled by the author in 2007 from the website of the State Duma, www.duma.gov.ru. See the section on "Sostav i struktura GD/ Komitet i kommissii GD."

[4]Thomas Remington, *Politics in Russia*, 2nd ed. (New York: Longman, 2001), p. 102.

[5]See the Constitution of the Russian Federation, Articles 105 and 106, www.constitution.ru/en/10003000-06.htm (accessed September 22, 2007).

[6]Ibid., Article 102.

[7]Compiled by the author from the website of the State Duma, www.duma.gov.ru. See the section on "Sostav i struktura GD/ Deputatskie obedineniia."

[8]For a listing of registered parties, see the website of the Federal Electoral Commission of the Russian Federation, www.cikrf.ru/ cikrf/politparty/ (accessed September 22, 2007).

[9]For a copy of the 1999 ballot, see Remington, *Politics in Russia*, pp. 182–183.

[10]These numbers also include seats won in single-member districts.

[11]"Russian Opposition Figure Withdraws from Politics," *Radio Free Liberty/Radio Europe*, March 9, 2007; www.rferl.org/features article/2007/3/B46A4478-75CD-4F81-BF40-AEED20F77E0C. html (accessed September 22, 2007).

[12]www.edinros.ru/index.html (accessed September 22, 2007).

[13]Darrell Slider, "'United Russia' and Russia's Governors: The Path to a One-Party System," paper presented by the American Association for the Advancement of Slavic Studies National Convention, Washington, D.C., November 17, 2006.

[14]See the party website at www.spravedlivo.ru, in particular, the party platform (accessed September 22, 2007).

[15]See the Yabloko website, in English, at www.eng.yabloko.ru (accessed September 22, 2007).

[16]See the official website of the SPS at www.sps.ru (accessed September 22, 2007).

[17]See the official website of the National Bolsheviks at www.nbp-info.ru (accessed September 22, 2007).

[18]Office for Democratic Institutions and Human Rights, "Russian Federation: Elections to the State Duma 7 December 2003, OSCE/ODIHR Election Observation Mission Report" (Warsaw, January 27, 2004), unpan1.un.org/intradoc/groups/public/documents/UNTC/UNPAN016105.pdf (accessed September 22, 2007).

[19]Luke Harding, "Supreme Court Ban on Liberal Party Wipes Out Opposition to Putin," *The Guardian*, March 24, 2007, www.guardian.co.uk/russia/article/0,2041825,00.html (accessed September 22, 2007).

[20]Timothy J. Colton and Michael McFaul, "Are Russians Undemocratic," *Post-Soviet Affairs* 18 (April–June 2002): 102.

[21]William M. Reisinger, Arthur H. Miller, Vicki L. Hesli, and Kristen Hill Maher, "Political Values in Russia, Ukraine, and Lithuania: Sources and Implications," *British Journal of Political Science* 24 (1994): 183–223.

[22]Programme of the Communist Party of the Russian Federation, in Russian, translation by the author, www.cprf.ru/party/program/ (accessed September 22, 2007).

[23]Adrian Blomfield, "Envoy Demands Kremlin Calls Off Its Youth Gang," *The Telegraph*, December 13, 2006; www.telegraph.co.uk/global/main.jhtml?xml=/global/2006/12/13/wrussia13.xml (accessed September 22, 2007).

[24]For data for recent years see Federal State Statistics Service of the Russian Federation, http://www.gks.ru/free_doc/2007/b07_11/05-05.htm (accessed September 22, 2007).

[25]Public Opinion Foundation, "The Birthrate in Russia: Views and Forecast," March 22, 2007, bd.english.fom.ru/report/whatsnew/ed071222 (accessed September 22, 2007).

[26]Paraphrased by Oksana Alekseyev, "Premier Performance," *Kommersant*, November 23, 2001, excerpted and translated in *The Current Digest of the Post-Soviet Press*, December 19, 2001.

[27]See the website of The Other Russia at www.theotherrussia.ru/eng/ (accessed September 22, 2007).

[28]See the Movement Against Illegal Immigration's official website at www.dpni.org (accessed September 22, 2007).

CHAPTER 25

Russian Politics in Transition

In April 2005, in his annual political address to the Federal Assembly, Putin made a dramatic admission: "Above all, we should acknowledge that the collapse of the Soviet Union was a major geopolitical disaster of the century. As for the Russian nation, it became a genuine drama."[1] At about the same time, in several cities throughout Russia, local officials decided to erect new monuments to Joseph Stalin to commemorate the sixtieth anniversary of the end of World War II in Europe, a move that Putin neither approved nor obstructed. President George W. Bush, in visiting Latvia before his arrival in Moscow to celebrate the events, also evoked images of the past, referring to the Soviet Union's unlawful annexation and occupation of the Baltic States after World War II.[2] A Kremlin spokesperson vehemently denied this depiction of postwar events. The verbal sparring was followed by the two apparently congenial leaders in Moscow honoring the veterans who brought the defeat of Nazism. These events vividly demonstrate the interdependence of Russia and the West, but at the same time the continuing ambivalence and tension in the relationship. The Soviet past continues to haunt and obscure not only Russia's path forward, but also relations with neighbors and potential allies.

Another episode in these complex relationships occurred surrounding events in Ukraine in November 2004. Russia charged that Western actors had fomented public discontent with the Ukrainian presidential election, leading to the division and disruption of the Orange Revolution. This perspective was consistent with the long-standing Russian view that Ukraine's historic and close ties with Russia should not be subverted by the allure of the West (in this case European integration). In this case, the European Union stepped forward to play an important role in mediating the Ukrainian crisis, in particular through the involvement of Javier Solana, the EU High Representative for Common Foreign and Security Policy. The EU had an interest in facilitating an outcome that would further Ukraine's progress toward democratic governance while avoiding a geopolitical clash between Russia and the West.

Political Challenges and Changing Agendas

Russia's future path continues to remain unclear. Will the country move in a "two steps forward, one step backward" progression to a more democratic political

system? Or does the freewheeling atmosphere and political relaxation in the 1990s more likely recall the temporary liberalization that occurred in the 1920s or the short-lived thaw of the Khrushchev period? In 2008 this issue was still hotly contested. American experts have tended to be more pessimistic, while views from within Russia are divided. Many European leaders take a realistic view, considering that Russia is an important neighbor whose interests and values require understanding, at a minimum, and in many cases accommodation.

In the 1990s Russia's status as a world power waned, and the expansion of Western organizations (NATO, EU) to Russia's western border undermined its sphere of influence in Central and Eastern Europe. Russia's eastern neighbors, except for Belarus, looked more to Europe than to Russia as a guidepost for the future. But Russia's economic recovery, the rise of energy prices, and Europe's dependence on imports of Russian natural gas and oil provide an important basis for Russia's renewed international influence. No longer simply a supplicant in its relationship to the West, Russia reasserted itself as a major European power under Putin's leadership. September 11 also provided a new impetus for Russia's claim to be a key link in the antiterrorist chain, alongside the United States. Ironically, however, the war on terrorism has expanded American influence into Russia's traditional sphere of influence as U.S. bases or NATO actions were established in post-Soviet Central Asia (in Uzbekistan and Kyrgyzstan, and in neighboring Afghanistan), creating the potential for new tensions between Russia and the United States.

In the international sphere, Russia's flirtation with Westernization in the early 1990s produced ambiguous results, including severe recession, social dislocation, and dependence on the West for economic aid. Russia's protests against unpalatable international developments, such as NATO expansion, the Desert Fox operation against Iraq in December 1998, and NATO's bombing of Yugoslavia in 1999, revealed Moscow's underlying resentment against Western dominance, as well as the country's relative powerlessness to affect global developments. With a weakened military structure and economy, Russia could do little more than issue verbal protests.

The upturn in the Russian economy that began in 1999 may have been a watershed in the struggle to overcome the transitional recession that plagued Russia from the late 1980s onward. At the same time, severe disparities in income and wealth remain, meaning that a restoration of economic growth may not bring an improved standard of living for large numbers of Russian citizens, particularly the elderly, children, the disabled, and those living in poorer northern regions. Questions also remain about whether income from oil and gas exports will feed the investment needs of other sectors of the economy, or whether they will be appropriated by a privileged elite. Making the economy attractive to foreign investors will require a continued development of the banking sector, legal institutions to ensure enforcement of contracts, and controls on crime and corruption. Although the 1998 devaluation of the ruble brought decreased reliance on Western imports (as they become too expensive), the so-called Dutch disease, in which heavy reliance on export income pushes the value of the currency up, now threatens again to undermine prospects for domestic producers. The Russian economy is no longer shielded from foreign and international influences, and so reverberations in international markets and foreign economies can have a direct impact on the Russian economy. Perhaps the greatest economic challenge facing the Putin administration is establishing policies to ensure a greater diversity of Russia's economic base, which will require reaching a new social accommodation that will bring a stable environment for investment and confidence among Russia's own economic elite as well as among foreign investors. At the same time, the Russian leadership still struggles to find appropriate vehicles for limiting the influence of powerful economic forces on policymaking without undermining political pluralism.

Russia's attempted democratization has been marred by limits on political opposition forces, by corruption, the power of big money, and the limited accountability of its leaders. The political structures put in place by the 1993 constitution have not produced the strong and effective government most Russians desire, nor have these measures permitted ordinary people to feel that their interests are being attended to. Opinion surveys indicate that Russians consider government performance less than satisfactory across a wide range of policy areas, such as crime control, dealing with unemployment, social security, and health care.[3] The continuing disjuncture between high personal support for the president and a continuing lack of confidence in the ability of political central institutions to address the country's problems effectively suggests that the legitimacy of the system is still on thin ice. The more positive working relationship between the executive and legislative branches that emerged under Putin's leadership, as well as efforts to regularize relations between the center and regions, provides prospects for improved institutional performance, but the reduction of vehicles for popular input and heavy-handed efforts to control political opposition already show signs of producing poor policy choices that may elicit public protests and reinforce public cynicism about the motives of politicians and the trustworthiness of institutions.

It is difficult to conceive that the freedoms that have been exercised since 1986 could be easily withdrawn. Russians value the personal freedom they have gained since the collapse of communism. Expanding contacts with the West have made increasingly broad circles aware of the benefits of civic participation, even if the Russian system does not yet realize these potentials. Yet a reversion to a more centralized and predictable set of political practices might, on a conscious or unconscious level, seem familiar and therefore comfortable for many Russians. If security and stability can be combined with rising prosperity, then many Russians appear to be ready to sacrifice democratic rights in exchange for economic improvement and political stability, particularly if personal freedoms are retained.

Despite changes in social consciousness, the formation of new political identities remains unfinished business. In the Soviet period, the state-imposed homogeneity of interests and political repression hindered diverse interest associations from forming. Now, other obstacles prevail. Most people are still preoccupied by the struggle to make ends meet or to increase personal welfare; they have little time or energy to forge new forms of collective action to address underlying problems. Under such circumstances, the appeal to nationalism and other basic sentiments can be powerful. Indications of this are already evident in the fact that political parties with nationalist messages seem to be doing better than liberal forces. The weakness of Russian intermediary organizations (interest groups, political parties, or associations) means that politicians can more easily appeal directly to emotions because people are not members of groups that help them evaluate the politicians' claims. These conditions are fertile ground for authoritarian outcomes, which the government itself might use to keep the public compliant. Still, the high level of education and increasing exposure to international media may work in the opposite direction. Russians are ambivalent and divided on whether Russian culture is also European and many Russians say that they feel themselves to be "Europeans."[4] Nonetheless the desire to have contact with and travel to Europe is widespread; exposure to alternative political systems and cultures may make people more critical of their own political system and look for opportunities to change it. Russia remains in what seems to be an extended period of transition. Radical upheavals have been frequent over the past century—a source of some solace to Russians, as they see their current conditions in continuity rather than in contrast to the past. In the early 1990s, Russians frequently hoped for "normal conditions," that is, an escape from the shortages, insecurity, and political controls of the past. As the new situation becomes familiar, *normality* has been redefined in terms that are less glowing than those conceived in the late 1980s. Russians seem to have a capability to adapt to change and uncertainty that North Americans find at once alluring, puzzling, and disturbing.

Russian Politics, Terrorism, and Russia's Relation to the United States

Over the past several years the threat of terrorism has been a reality for Russians. But unlike the terrorist threat facing the United States, attacks in Russia initially had indigenous roots in the separatist region of Chechnya. Terrorism became a tool of Chechen militants in the face of Russian military efforts to defeat separatist forces. Over time linkages between Russian terrorist groups and international Islamic fundamentalist organizations have become increasingly important, offering an opportunity for Russian cooperation with Western countries in responding to this threat. But unlike the situation facing the United States, the terrorist threat is not seen only as a challenge from outside the country but also as a potential threat to the very integrity of Russia itself. According to Putin, the battle against the terrorist threat is "truly a fight for the unity of the country."[5]

Terrorism has augmented already present social anxieties in Russia that had their roots in the instability and unpredictability characterizing the postcommunist period. In several terrorist incidents female suicide bombers, the so-called black widows of fallen Chechen militants, played a visible role, revealing the deep social rift that had opened in this multiethnic country. Because Russia is a multiethnic state with several Muslim population groups, Russian authorities have had to be careful not to give antiterrorist rhetoric an anti-Muslim tone. As President Putin noted in 2004, "it is clear that to . . . vent anger towards terrorists against people of different beliefs or ethnicities is absolutely unacceptable, and in a country with such a diversity of religions and ethnicities it is completely destructive."[6] Furthermore, he emphasized that it is a goal of terrorists themselves to undermine Russian unity not only by pushing for Chechen separatism, but also by driving a wedge of distrust and hostility between diverse ethnic and religious groups.

It has been difficult for Russian authorities to isolate terrorist elements because of the indigenous roots of the grievances that initially triggered the attacks. Ethnic profiling has, in fact, tainted both government actions and popular sentiments. Individuals with a south Caucasian appearance have felt themselves subject to various forms of harassment, including complaints of arbitrary identity checks, planting of drugs and weapons, and obstruction of registration for residence permits.[7] On the other hand, more recently the Russian government has attempted to undermine the terrorist appeal in Chechnya and surrounding areas by offering a general amnesty for former rebels who have never been convicted of crimes and have agreed to lay down their arms. In terms of policy, recent amendments to a 1998 antiterrorism law place restrictions on the media in disseminating information that might hinder or prevent counterterrorist measures, which some critics view as potentially placing restrictions on freedom of speech. Efforts to combat terrorism have become increasingly centralized since the Beslan crisis. In 2006, the FSB (the Federal Security Service, successor to the KGB) was granted the main coordinating role in the form of a "National Antiterrorist Committee." Beslan also led to a broadened legal definition of terrorism that critics felt could be used to ban antigovernment meetings or demonstrations. On a popular level, terrorism has reinforced the power of nationalist appeals.

Alongside these domestic political issues, terrorism has affected Russia's foreign relations in a variety of ways. On the positive side, this common threat created a potential for cooperation and shared interests between Russia, the United States, and major European countries. Even before 9/11, the West's recognition that Russia's involvement was crucial to finding a diplomatic solution to the Kosovo crisis in 1999 marked a turning point, heralding a new period of increased cooperation between Russia and the Western world. Following 9/11, evidence of warmer relations included the formation of a NATO-Russia Council in May 2002, marking an era of closer cooperation in areas such as control of international terrorism, arms control, nonproliferation, and crisis management.[8] The next month, at the 2002 G-8 summit meeting in Kanaskis, Canada, it was announced that Russia would assume the presidency of the organization in 2006 and host the annual summit meeting.[9] As a further sign of the positive trend in United States–Russia relations, in May 2002 Presidents Bush and Putin agreed to a treaty involving further reductions in the nuclear arsenals of the two countries.

Despite these steps, tensions began to emerge after 2002. Not only did nongovernmental organizations such as Human Rights Watch charge Russia with acts of violence against the Chechen civilian population, as well as instances of arbitrary arrests and sexual attacks on women,[10] but in 2004 and 2005, American officials openly criticized Putin's centralizing moves as antidemocratic. European leaders echoed these sentiments, but in softer tones. Figures in American business circles viewed the attack on Khodorkovsky as interference in business operations, producing inhibitions to investments in the crucial energy sector. Europeans were disturbed by interruption in Russian energy supplies to Europe, caused by Russia's unilateral decision to cut off oil supplies to Europe due to a conflict with Belarus over the latter's alleged siphoning of oil from the pipeline traversing Belarusan territory. German Chancellor Angela Merkel responded sharply: "It is not acceptable if there is no consultation on such issues. That destroys confidence, and this is no basis for smoothly building up a constructive relationship."[11]

Other tensions between Russia and the United States were a direct result of the strategy adopted by the American government in responding to 9/11. Russia's previous troubles in Afghanistan made Russian authorities reticent in criticizing NATO actions against the Taliban there, but the establishment of American bases in neighboring countries, which Russian considered

part of its traditional sphere of influence, reinforced Russian concerns about expanding American influence. The American incursion into Iraq in March 2003 met with strong Russian disapproval, following disappointment with the American withdrawal from the Anti-Ballistic Missile Treaty. The expansion of NATO and American influence into neighboring Georgia induced Russia to undertake an embargo on trade with Georgia and raised relations between Georgia and Russia to an unprecedented high level of tension. These issues culminated in Putin's speech in Munich in February 2007, after which American officials attempted to mend fences by inviting Russia to participate in the establishment of the antimissile initiative in Central Europe. Russian diplomats reacted with skepticism about U.S. motives. The Russians accused the Americans of trying to foment a split between European countries, while the United States viewed Russian reactions as an effort to feed transatlantic and intra-European tensions.

A critical element of Russia's relations with both the United States and its West European neighbors rests with Russia's rich endowment of oil and natural gas. The source of about 10 percent of the world's oil production and the country most richly endowed with natural gas (about a third of the world's total reserves), Russia has been dubbed by some as a "new energy superpower." The United States began an "energy dialogue" with Russia in 2002, as the United States hoped to increase energy imports from Russia to diversify its international energy dependence. At the Bush-Putin meeting in Bratislava in February 2005, this was again reaffirmed as a bilateral priority, along with efforts to counter terrorism, facilitate space cooperation, and assure Russia's WTO accession.[12] The energy dialogue had been initiated between the EU and Russia even earlier, in 2000, with a goal of increased integration of EU-Russian energy markets and assurances of energy security for the EU.[13] Europeans urged Russia to sign the Energy Charter, which would regulate economic aspects of energy relations, but Russia refused, as a result of differing policies governing transit and investment. Russia's policy of applying world market prices to its closest neighbors (Ukraine, Belarus) would seem consistent with Western market principles, but in practice it has generated new problems. Europeans feared they might be victims of international disputes playing out in the former Soviet bloc, in part, as a result of these price adjustments. Although the United States was not directly affected by these disputes, they fed preconceptions in the United States about the unreliability of Russia as a business partner.

The Challenges of European Integration

Western and Russian public opinion surveys suggest a continuing values gap between Europe and Russia over the meaning and importance of such key ideas as democracy, human rights, and market reform.[14] Although most Russians support these notions in an abstract sense, their understanding of them has been shaped by a distinctly different political tradition and particular set of political experiences. Efforts to define democracy in a distinctively Russian way have also been taken up by the political elite, for example, the articulation in 2006 of a notion of "sovereign democracy" by Vladislav Surkov, a deputy head of Putin's presidential administration.[15] To many Russians today, democracy's reputation was marred by its association with the economic decline and political unpredictability of the 1990s; according to this perspective, democracy, while an admirable value in the abstract, may be less important than political stability and a reasonable standard of living. Although the concept of democracy has a distinct appeal in the region (partly because it has been associated with Western affluence), to much of the population it means, above all, personal freedom and, to some extent, rule of law, rather than support for notions of political accountability or the civic role of the citizen. Likewise, although human rights such as freedom to travel, free expression, and the right to worship are widely supported by Russians, tolerance for minority rights may be less well understood, particularly in an environment where Russian national identity has suffered humiliation in the face both of Russia's decline from superpower status and of instability related to the war in Chechnya; mobilization of anti-Semitic and nationalist sentiments is also an important trigger for xenophobic sentiments. And although the benefits of a market economy, namely, the availability of consumer goods and the right to pursue individual economic interests, are attractive, the withdrawal of the state from traditional areas of social provision is widely criticized in Russia.

European leaders, on the other hand, promote political values as an important objective of EU and national foreign policies, seeing Europe as a normative actor in spreading progressive European values. So while Europe seeks to Europeanize Russia, many Russians resent the assumption of moral superiority that underlies this objective and they feel compelled to defend the legitimacy of Russian traditions and interests. Although certain aspects of the European project are embraced in Russia, such as the benefits of greater economic integration and the promotion of science, technology, and education, at a more fundamental level, many Russians see their country as part of both Europe and Asia. The extreme version of this viewpoint, which has been taken up by Russian nationalists such as Alexander Dugin, poses a fundamental conflict between Westernizing views and Russia's distinctive Eurasian character. In a more general sense, the question might be asked whether the patrimonial and collectivist thrust of Russian culture is really compatible with Western economic and political ideas. At the same time, Russian authorities continue to affirm Russia's European identity and to support closer European ties in multiple forms, including visa-free travel, access for Russian firms to European markets, and an encouragement of European investment in Russia.

Russian Politics in Comparative Perspective

The way in which politics, economics, and ideology were intertwined in the Soviet period has profoundly affected the nature of political change in all of the former Soviet states and generally has made the democratization process more difficult. Unlike developing countries that are currently experiencing democratization and economic transformation, Russia is a highly industrialized country with a skilled and educated work force. Although this offers advantages, the high level of development is associated with a host of problems: a heavily damaged natural environment, obsolescent industries, entrenched bureaucratic structures, a nuclear arsenal that must be monitored and controlled, and a public that expects the state to provide a stable system of social welfare. Unlike modernizing elites in the developing world, Russian leaders must first deconstruct existing modern structures before constructing new ones. For example, inefficient or highly polluting factories need to be closed or radically renovated, the military-industrial complex has to be cut back or converted to other uses, and the state must accustom the public to more modest expectations about the ability of the state to provide the array of social benefits that the Soviet system offered. These problems make it difficult for the state to manage the domestic and international challenges it confronts.

How is Russia faring compared to some of the other postcommunist systems that have faced many of these same challenges? The nations of Central and Eastern Europe and of the former Soviet Union were all subjected to a similar system of economic, political, and ideological power during the period of communist rule. Some were under communist rule for shorter periods of time (in particular, those countries that joined the EU in 2004 and 2007), but most parts of the former Soviet Union shared with Russia more than seven decades of communist rule. Despite the efforts of the Soviet leadership to establish conformity throughout the region, national differences did emerge. The countries of Central Europe and the three Baltic states had closer historical ties and greater cultural exposure to Western Europe; ideas of liberalism, private property, and individualism were less foreign to citizens in countries such as Czechoslovakia, East Germany, and Hungary than in regions farther east, including Russia. The Roman Catholic Church in Poland provided a focal point for national identity, and Poland's historical antipathy to Russia produced a stronger resistance to the imposition of the Soviet model than in other Slavic countries of the region. Such cultural, geopolitical, and historical differences affected the shape that communist rule took in the various countries, but they also created a greater receptivity to European integration and to adopting the EU's norms and practices in Central Europe.

Within the Soviet Union, too, there was considerable variation among the union republics that became independent states in 1991. The Baltic republics of Latvia, Lithuania, and Estonia have followed the path of the Central and East European countries outside of the USSR; they strove to meet EU accession criteria and became members of the EU in May 2004. At the other extreme, the Central Asian republics retained aspects of traditional Muslim culture, preserved the extended family structure, and, even within the structure of the Communist Party, maintained a greater prominence for links rooted in the clan system indigenous to the region.

Given the diversity of nations that were subject to the communist system, it is not surprising that paths of extrication from communist rule should also vary widely. A rule of thumb, simple as it seems, is that the farther east one goes in the postcommunist world, the more difficult and prolonged the transition period has been. This is partly because the more westerly countries of Central Europe that were outside the USSR (Poland, Hungary, Czech Republic, Slovakia), as well as the Baltic states, faced the realistic prospect of EU accession and thus had a strong motivation to embark on fundamental reform to meet the EU's conditions. Also, these countries were under communist rule for a shorter period of time. Although political and economic liberalization generally follows this West-East axis, an exception is Belarus, which has liberalized less than Russia.

In terms of economic performance, postcommunist countries that liberalized the least, such as Uzbekistan and Belarus, suffered less severe recessions in the 1990s because state institutions remained more fully intact. However, these less-reformed economies may face painful adjustments in the future. Because Russia possesses rich deposits of natural resources (including energy resources), it has been able to cope with the ruptured economic ties that resulted from the collapse of the Soviet Union better than some of the less-well-endowed states. In addition, Ukraine and particularly Belarus are still suffering from the severe economic and health effects of the 1986 accident at the Chernobyl nuclear power plant, and the Central Asian states confront the disastrous effects of Soviet-imposed emphasis on cotton production and associated environmental degradation. Russia (along with Ukraine) has been the focal point of international economic assistance because of its size, its large nuclear arsenal, and its geopolitical importance. Although this aid has been insufficient to make the government's overall reform program successful, other parts of the former Soviet Union (with the likely exception of the Baltic States) have received even less international assistance, despite their weaker economic position.

Progression along the various dimensions of transition is uneven across postcommunist countries, and Russia seems now to be progressing economically, while regressing politically, with nationalism on the rise and aspirations to the status of a regional and global super-power resurfacing. In the political sphere, virtually all of the postcommunist states claim to pursue some form of democratization, but in some cases, this is more in name than in practice, particularly in Central Asia. Belarus has a distinctively authoritarian government. In all of the postcommunist states, the attempt to construct democratic political institutions has been characterized by repeated political crises, weak representation of popular interests, executive-legislative conflict, faltering efforts at constitutional revision, and corruption. These features are more marked in the countries farther east.

Although Russian politics has been highly contentious and the government has operated at very low levels of efficacy and legitimacy for most of the past decade, with the exception of the Chechnya conflict Russia has escaped major domestic violence and civil war, unlike parts of the former Yugoslavia, Armenia, Azerbaijan, Georgia, Moldova, and the Central Asian state of Tajikistan. For all their problems, Russian politicians have conducted themselves in a relatively civil manner, and neither Yeltsin nor Putin has appealed to exclusivist definitions of Russian identity. Citizenship rights for all ethnic groups have been maintained, and state-sponsored racism is largely absent. However, as noted in Chapter 24, worrisome signs have appeared that xenophobia and ethnic intolerance may be inadvertently fed by some government policies that are intended to deal with illegal immigrations or perceived threats from abroad. These policies may lead to marginalization of ethnic minorities and therefore could potentially undermine Russia's already fragile social structure.

Russia will undoubtedly continue to be a key regional force in Europe and Asia. Its vast geographic expanse, rich resource base, large and highly skilled population, and the legacy of Soviet rule will ensure this. Yet its former allies in Central Europe, as well as the Baltic states, are gradually drifting into the orbit of Western Europe economically and politically. Following the 2004 and 2007 enlargements of the EU, Russia's most important Western neighbor, Ukraine, has made clear its aspiration to EU membership, while Russia has not. Although Ukraine is divided internally over its future course, the European dream is an increasingly important reference point. Russian leaders seem to appreciate the isolation this could imply,

but they seem unwilling to adopt certain crucial aspects of Western political practice. Over the past few years, while Russia has resisted a unipolar world order dominated by the United States and while Russia's leaders have shown a desire and willingness to identify themselves as a European country, Russia has an ambivalent relationship to accepting crucial norms that would underlie an effective and enduring partnership.

Will Russia find a place for itself in the world of states that meets the expectations of its educated and sophisticated population? Nearly a decade into the new millennium, prospects are still unclear. One thing is certain: Russia will continue to be an important international force, both regionally and globally. If Russia's experiment produces a stable outcome that benefits the majority of the population, then it may offer a path of quasi-democratic development that could serve as a model for countries farther east. If authoritarian tendencies take hold in Russia, then incipient democracies elsewhere in the region may also take a further backward step.

Notes

[1]Vladimir Putin, President of Russia website, www.kremlin.ru/eng/speeches/2005/04/25/2031_type70029_87086.shtml.

[2]Elisabeth Bumille, "Bush, Arriving in Baltics, Steps into Argument with Russia," *New York Times*, May 7, 2005.

[3]Based on a survey carried out by the author in conjunction with Russian partners headed by Viktor Khitrov and the Institute of Sociology of the Russian Academy of Sciences. The research was conducted by regional partners in Stavropol *krai*, Nizhnegorodskaia *oblast*, and Orlov *oblast* in 1998 and 2000, and in the same locations in 2004.

[4]See the survey results from December 2006 published by the Levada Centre, "Problemy demokratii v Rossii," odnomernye tablitsy, http://www.levada.ru/aktpro.html (accessed September 22, 2007).

[5]Vladimir Putin, "Speech at a Meeting of the Presidential Council for Coordination with Religious Organisations," President of Russia website, September 29, 2004, www.kremlin.ru/eng/speeches/2004/09/29/1946_type82913_77365.shtml (accessed September 22, 2007).

[6]Ibid.

[7]Human Rights Watch Briefing Paper, "On the Situation of Ethnic Chechens in Moscow," February 24, 2003, www.hrw.org/backgrounder/eca/russia032003.htm (accessed September 22, 2007).

[8]NATO Press Release, "NATO-Russia Relations: A New Quality," May 28, 2002, www.nato.int/docu/basictxt/b020528e .htm (accessed September 22, 2007).

[9]For background on the G-8, see the Canadian government site, "G8 Background," www.g8.gc.ca/background-en.asp (accessed September 22, 2007).

[10]Human Rights Watch, "Russia: Visiting Leaders Should Be Firm on Rights," May 7, 2005, hrw.org/english/docs/2005/05/07/ russia10586.htm (accessed September 22, 2007).

[11]Peter Finn, "Germany's Merkel Assails Russia Over Cutoff of Oil," *The Washington Post*, January 10, 2007, www.washingtonpost. com/wp-dyn/content/article/2007/01/09/AR2007010900749.htm (accessed September 22, 2007).

[12]White House Press Release, "U.S.-Russia Joint Fact Sheet: Bratislava Initiatives," February 24, 2005, www.whitehouse.gov/ news/releases/2005/02/20050224-7.html (accessed September 22, 2007).

[13]European Commission, "EU–Russia Energy Dialogue, Fifth Progress Report," November 2004, ec.europa.eu/energy/russia/ joint_progress/doc/progress5_en.pdf (accessed September 22, 2007).

[14]S. White, M. Light, and I. McAllister, "Russia and the West: Is There a Values Gap?" *International Politics* 42 (2005): 314– 333; and results of a recent survey undertaken by the Europe– Russia Centre (Brussels) and the Levada-Center (Moscow) on February 14, 2007, "Russian Perceptions of European Values," www.levada.ru/press/2007021501.html.

[15]Vladislav Surkov, "Paragraty pro suverennyiu demokratiiu," November 11, 2006, website of United Russia, http://www .edinros.ru/news.html?id=116746 (accessed September 22, 2007).

Part 6 Bibliography

Aslund, Anders. *Building Capitalism: The Transformation of the Former Soviet Bloc*. Cambridge, UK, and New York: Cambridge University Press, 2002.

Bialer, Seweryn, ed. *Politics, Society, and Nationality Under Gorbachev*. Boulder: Westview, 1989.

Black, J. L. *Vladimir Putin and the New World Order: Looking East, Looking West?* Lanham, Md.: Rowman and Littlefield, 2004.

Blasi, R. Joseph, Maya Kroumova, and Douglas Kruse. *Kremlin Capitalism: The Privatization of the Russian Economy*. Ithaca, N.Y.: Cornell University Press, 1997.

Brown, Archie, and Jack Gray. *Political Culture and Political Change in Communist States*. New York: Holmes & Meier Publishers, 1979.

Colton, Timothy J. *Transitional Citizens: Voters and What Influences Them in the New Russia*. Cambridge: Harvard University Press, 2000.

DeBardeleben, Joan, ed. *Soft or Hard Borders: Managing the Divide in an Enlarged Europe*. Aldershot, UK: Ashgate, 2005.

Eckstein, Harry, Frederic J. Fleron, Jr., Erik P. Hoffman, and William M. Reisinger. *Can Democracy Take Root in Russia? Explorations in State-Society Relations*. Lanham, Md.: Rowman & Littlefield, 1998.

Evans, Jr., Alfred B., Laura A. Henry, and Lisa McIntosh Sundstrom, eds. *Russian Civil Society*. Armonk, N.Y.: M.E. Sharpe, 2006.

Fish, M. Steven. *Democracy Derailed in Russia: The Failure of Open Politics*. Cambridge/New York: Cambridge University Press, 2005.

Freeland, Chrystia. *Sale of the Century: Russia's Wild Ride from Communism to Capitalism*. New York: Doubleday, 2000.

Getty, J. Arch. *Origins of the Great Purges: The Soviet Communist Party Reconsidered*. Cambridge: Cambridge University Press, 1985.

Hale, Henry E. "Regime Cycles: Democracy, Autocracy, and Revolution in Post-Soviet Eurasia." *World Politics* 58 (October 2005): 133–165.

Hoffman, David E. *The Oligarchs: Wealth and Power in the New Russia*. New York: Public Affairs Press, 2002.

Hough, Jerry, and Merle Fainsod. *How the Soviet Union Is Governed*. Cambridge: Harvard University Press, 1979.

Humphrey, Caroline. *The Unmaking of Soviet Life: Everyday Economics after Socialism*. Ithaca, N.Y.: Cornell University Press, 2002.

Kolsto, Pål, and Helge Blakkisrud, eds. *Nation-Building and Common Values in Russia*. Lanham, Md.: Rowman & Littlefield Publishers, 2004.

Ledeneva, Alena V. *How Russia Really Works: The Informal Practices That Shaped Post-Soviet Politics and Business*. Ithaca, N.Y.: Cornell University Press, 2006.

Lewin, Moshe. *The Gorbachev Phenomenon: A Historical Interpretation*. Berkeley: University of California Press, 1991.

Levgold, Robert, ed. *Russian Foreign Policy in the Twenty-First Century and the Shadow of the Past*. New York: Columbia University Press, 2007.

Motyl, Alexander J., Blair A. Ruble, and Lilia Shevtsova, eds. *Russia's Engagement with the West: Transformation and Integration in the Twenty-First Century*. Armonk, N.Y.: M. E. Sharpe, 2005.

Pipes, Richard. *Russia Under the Old Regime*. New York: Scribner, 1974.

Oates, Sarah. *Television, Democracy and Elections in Russia*. London/New York: Routledge, 2006.

Reddaway, Robert, and Robert Orttung, eds. *The Dynamics of Russian Politics: Putin's Reform of Federal-Regional Relations*. 2 vols. Rowman & Littlefield, 2004 (volume 1); 2005 (volume 2).

Remington, Thomas F. *Politics in Russia*. 3rd ed. Boston: Pearson Education, 2004.

Robinson, Neil, ed. *Institutions and Political Change in Russia.* Houndsmill, Basingstoke, UK: Macmillan; New York: St. Martin's Press, 2000.

Sakwa, Richard. *Putin: Russia's Choice.* London/New York: Pearson Longman, 2006.

Shevtsova, Lilia. *Putin's Russia.* Rev. ed. Moscow: Carnegie Institute, 2005.

Solomon, Peter H., Jr., and Todd S. Fogelson. *Courts and Transition in Russia: The Challenge of Judicial Reform.* Boulder, Colo.: Westview Press, 2000.

Stoner-Weiss, Kathryn. *Resisting the State: Reform and Retrenchment in Post-Soviet Russia.* Cambridge/New York: Cambridge University Press, 2006.

Tolz, Vera. *Russia.* London: Arnold; New York: Oxford University Press, 2001.

Weigle, Marcia A. *Russia's Liberal Project: State-Society Relations in the Transition from Communism.* University Park: Pennsylvania State University Press, 2000.

Wilson, Andrew. *Virtual Politics: Faking Democracy in the Post-Soviet World.* New Haven: Yale University Press, 2005.

Websites

The Carnegie Moscow Center:
www.carnegie.ru/en/

Center for Russian and East European Studies, University of Pittsburgh:
www.ucis.pitt.edu/reesweb/

Itar-TASS News Agency:
www.itar-tass.com/eng/

Johnson's Russia List:
www.cdi.org/russia/johnson/default.cfm

Radio Free Europe/Radio Liberty:
www.rferl.org/newsline/

Moscow News Weekly:
www.mnweekly.ru/

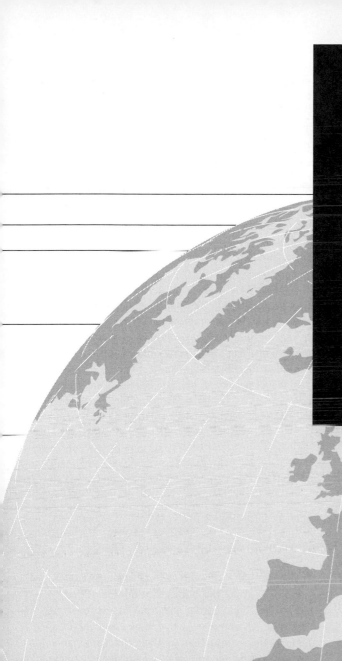

PART 7

East-Central Europe in Transition

David Ost

CHAPTER 26

The Making of Modern East-Central Europe

Politics in Action

A few snapshots from the land that used to be Czechoslovakia provide a wonderful picture of the complex and fascinating events that have been shaping East-Central Europe in recent years.

Late 1989. Commentators around the world speak of the dawning of a new age of freedom and democracy, symbolized first by the fall of the Berlin Wall on November 9 and then by the "Velvet Revolution" unfolding immediately afterward in Czechoslovakia. It is in Prague that the sense of promise and hope is most evident. Velvet is smooth, soft, and friendly, more an aesthetic concept than a political one. And that is what makes the term so appropriate. The strikes that brought down the government, in fact, were begun by actors who announced that they would use the stage to press for political freedom. Within days, first students and then the majority of workers had joined in. The protesters demanded civic rights: freedom of the press and association, an end to the Communist Party's monopoly on power, a truly representative political system. Workers and intellectuals, urbanites and farmers, Czechs and Slovaks, liberals and conservatives—all came together behind the program of the new opposition. With a huge general strike showing the unity of the population and the Soviet Union no longer ready to intervene, the government was powerless to resist. By the end of December, the veteran playwright and dissident Vaclav Havel, only recently released from jail, is named the new president of Czechoslovakia. The country enters the new year and new decade filled with hope, united behind a new leader who promises tolerance for all and a velvet-smooth transition to a just, democratic, and prosperous new system.

Mid-1992. The Velvet Revolution is ripping apart. Civic Forum, the political organization that led the Revolution, has broken into pieces, and the new voices speak the language not of tolerance but of blame. Slovakia's leaders blame the Czechs for Slovak problems and say they want to secede. Leading Czech politicians say a divorce is fine with them. They, in turn, blame "Communists" for continuing Czech problems, even though no communists are in power. Those who remain loyal to the original goals of freedom and

tolerance warn against this new politics of witch-hunt and resentment. But this group is decisively beaten in the 1992 elections. Vaclav Havel resigns from the presidency as the country prepares to split apart. The revolution seems to have taken off its velvet gloves.

Early 1994. Despite all the tensions of the past year, the breakup of the country goes smoothly. It is a velvet divorce, with the two sides agreeing amicably on dividing territory and property. Vaclav Havel is elected president of the new Czech Republic. Optimism reigns as the new country's first parliamentary elections are held.

2007. After nearly two decades of independence, the Czech Republic is still somewhat unsure of its new identity. In the late 1990s, economic growth slowed, unemployment rose, and a series of corruption scandals exploded the myth that everything was all right. President Havel stepped down, and Euro-skeptic Vaclav Klaus was elected by parliament in his place. The country joined the North Atlantic Treaty Organization (NATO) in 1999, although without great public support, and was critical of NATO actions in Kosovo. It joined the European Union (EU) in 2004, but President Klaus led the fight against the EU's draft constitution. Although the government supported the U.S. war in Iraq, the people were largely opposed. The Czech Republic has indeed "reentered the West," but many citizens seem not quite so happy to be there.

These snapshots show the hopes and fears of the new East-Central Europe: the hopes that nonviolent revolution is possible, that border questions can be resolved amicably, that economic growth can benefit everyone; and the fears that nationalism will win out against unification, that no postcommunist economy can escape economic crisis, and that integration into the West creates as many problems as it solves.

The worst part of the postcommunist transformation is definitely over. Although the first years after 1989 saw economic declines greater than during the Great Depression in the West, most countries in the region began growing by 1996. Poland's gross domestic product (GDP) exceeded 1989 levels in 1997, and Hungary followed soon after. All of the countries have now had several multiparty elections, and basic freedoms are guaranteed everywhere. There is greater inequality than before, but also real political democracy. But not all the questions are resolved, and this is what makes the region so fascinating. Having freed itself from dependence on the Soviet Union, how will it react to its new dependence on the EU? Can the many young people who lost job opportunities because of the economic crisis find their way? Or will they leave the country seeking better opportunities? Or turn to right-wing extremism? In 2006, Polish politics took an extremist turn, as representatives of far-right parties entered the government. Democracy may prevail, but what kind of democracy? These are the questions we will be exploring in this chapter.

Geographic Setting

Until 1989, East-Central Europe meant the countries between West Germany and the Soviet Union that were ruled by Communist parties. It thus had an ideological as well as a geographic referent: Prague, now the capital of the Czech Republic, was considered to be in "the East" while Vienna, although located east of Prague, was in "the West." By this definition, the region encompassed East Germany, Poland, Czechoslovakia, Hungary, Yugoslavia, Romania, Bulgaria, and Albania. After 1989, East Germany disappeared, Czechoslovakia split in two, and Yugoslavia divided six ways (into Bosnia, Croatia, Macedonia, Montenegro, Serbia, and Slovenia). Six more countries arose west of Russia after the collapse of the Soviet Union: Estonia, Latvia, Lithuania, Belarus, Ukraine, and Moldova. Altogether, that adds up to nineteen, four more than the number of countries in the EU in 2003. The chapter switches back between calling the region East-Central Europe and just East Europe; the meaning is the same.

The terrain in this region is quite diverse, becoming steeper and more rugged the farther south you go. It ranges from the flat plains of Poland in the north to the rugged hills, valleys, and mountains in the former Yugoslavia. The flat plains of Poland ("*pole*" means "fields") have enabled strong armies to occupy the country with ease, while the sprawling mountains of the former Yugoslavia help explain why no single army (or even the former Yugoslav state) was ever able to conquer it fully, leaving many different ethnic groups

to coexist in the area. As the accompanying maps show, all of these countries are rather small. Poland is the largest in terms of population and territory, with a population of nearly 38.5 million (plus several million Poles living in diaspora) and a territory of over 300,000 square kilometers (about the size of New Mexico). Slovenia is the smallest, with a territory of just over 20,000 square kilometers (slightly smaller than New Jersey) and a population of 2 million. Hungary has 10 million people in 93,000 square kilometers (just smaller than Indiana), while the Czech Republic has 10.2 million people and 78,000 square kilometers (just smaller than South Carolina). In the former Yugoslavia, Serbia and Montenegro is the largest of the successor countries, with 102,000 square kilometers (about the size of Kentucky) and 10.8 million people (although only 700,000 in Montenegro). Croatia and Bosnia each have about half as much space and populations of 4.5 million people. See Table 26.1 for full population figures.

Table 26.1

How Many Live Where?

Country	Population (millions, est., 2007)
Albania	3.6
Bosnia and Herzegovina	4.6
Bulgaria	7.3
Croatia	4.5
Czech Republic	10.2
Estonia	1.3
Hungary	10.0
Latvia	2.3
Lithuania	3.6
Macedonia	2.1
Moldova	4.3
Montenegro	0.7
Poland	38.5
Romania	22.3
Serbia	10.2
Slovakia	5.4
Slovenia	2.0

Source: CIA World Factbook; www.cia.gov/library/publications/the-world-factbook/index.html.

Eastern and
Central Europe

0   200 Miles

0   200 Kilometers

NORWAY

SWEDEN

FINLAND

ESTONIA

LATVIA

North
Sea

DENMARK

LITHUANIA

RUSSIA

NETHERLANDS

Baltic Sea

•Gdansk

•Szczecin

BELARUS

BELGIUM

GERMANY

Warsaw
✪

Vistula

LUXEMBOURG

POLAND

FRANCE

Prague ✪

CZECH REP.

Danube

SLOVAKIA

UKRAINE

SWITZERLAND

AUSTRIA

✪ Bratislava

SLOVENIA

✪ Budapest

MOLDOVA

Ljubljana•

HUNGARY

•Zagreb

ROMANIA

CROATIA

Bihac•

BOSNIA-

Belgrade
✪

Bucharest
✪

ITALY

Adriatic Sea

HERZEGOVINA
Sarajevo•

SERBIA
and
MONTENEGRO

Danube

Black Sea

Corsica

BULGARIA

Kosovo

✪ Sofia

Sardinia

MACEDONIA

Tirana ✪

ALBANIA

TURKEY

GREECE

Aegean Sea

SYRIA

Mediterranean Sea

Crete

CYPRUS

TUNISIA

LEBANON

Critical Junctures

Although each country has its own unique history, the communist and postcommunist experiences of all mean they have had many features in common. This chapter focuses on the three countries that make up the political and geographic heart of East-Central Europe: Poland, Hungary, and the Czech Republic. These three not only have the largest economies in the region but also, historically, the most active citizenry. All of them had uprisings that were crucial to the breakup of the communist system, and all developed innovative transformation plans afterwards. They were the first of the Eastern European countries to be invited into NATO, and today they are the leading Eastern countries in the enlarged European Union. We will also refer frequently to the Yugoslav experience—the only one of the Eastern European countries to break down into war. Looking at all these countries helps put into perspective the developments of the entire postcommunist world: we see first the history of underdevelopment, the legacy of (west) European colonialism, reasons for the embrace of communism, and then the different ways countries exited from communism, some peacefully and others collapsing into civil war. They provide insights that will surely prove valuable in the years ahead as we see what develops in countries such as China, Cuba, or North Korea.

We can identify seven critical periods in the shaping of modern East Central Europe: the long era of subordination to neighboring powers, the attainment of independence after World War I, the introduction of communism after World War II, the collapse of communism in 1989, the process of European integration in the late 1990s, the aftermath of September 11, and the period after the apparent collapse of the European Constitution in 2005.

Underdevelopment and Subordination (Fifteenth Century to World War I)

During the martial law period in Poland in 1982, the title of a popular protest song was "Let Poland Be Poland." Some Poles, however, thought that such a notion was precisely the problem. "Let Poland be Sweden," they said, "Let Poland be England! Let us be anything but Poland!"

What the naysayers chiefly had in mind was Poland's location: between Russia and Germany, countries that have always dominated it. The theme of wanting to be some other country, however, is a recurring refrain in Eastern Europe. And it points to three central problems: domination by other states, a multiplicity of nationalities on the territory of one state, and a long history of economic backwardness.

The roots of Eastern European underdevelopment go back to the rise of capitalism in the West. Most of East Europe began turning to the West for its manufactured goods as early as the fifteenth century, and this early dependency had serious consequences.[1] Until the nineteenth century, no part of Eastern Europe except the Czech lands was able to make much progress in industrialization. Without the economic base on which to build viable states, East European nations fell under the influence, and frequently the outright occupation, of stronger neighbors all around: Prussia in the west, Russia to the east, and the Hapsburg and Ottoman empires in the south. The period of state formation in Western Europe therefore was a period of state erosion in Eastern Europe.

Poland, for example, was the largest country in Europe in the fifteenth century. It began to decline when its powerful landowners joined together to clip the powers of the monarchy. By the seventeenth century, the Polish king had lost the right to raise taxes, create an army, dismiss officials, or enact laws without the landowners' explicit consent. Neighboring states were not under similar constraints, and the result was devastating: beginning in 1772, Russia, Prussia, and Austria simply began carving up the country among themselves. By 1795, Poland had ceased to exist as a state. It would regain its independence only in 1918.

Although Poland's encounter with the world of strong states was perhaps most dramatic, the other Eastern European countries also suffered from being small countries in a region of large states. Hungary, for example, was conquered by the Turkish Ottoman Empire in 1526, and by Austria 150 years later, before carving out semi-independence in 1867. The Czechs came under the control of the Austrian empire in 1620, although, unlike the other conquered nations, they were able to turn this to their economic advantage, becoming a nation of prosperous bourgeois producers. They sought independence only when the Austrian

Critical Junctures in East-Central Europe's Political Development

1772	Partition of Poland by Russia, Prussia, and Austria begins.
1795	Completion of partition of Poland.
1867	Hungary wins limited autonomy as Austrian (Hapsburg) empire becomes Austro-Hungarian Empire.
1914–1917	World War I.
1918	Poland and Czechoslovakia become independent.
1938	Munich Agreement, in which Britain and France allow Nazi Germany to seize much of Czechoslovakia, is signed.
1939	Germany invades Poland; Britain and France declare war on Germany. World War II begins.
1945	Soviet Red Army liberates East Europe from Nazi rule and introduces communist government.
1953	Stalin dies.
1956	Uprisings against Stalinist rule in Hungary and Poland.
1968	"Prague Spring" in Czechoslovakia, suppressed by Soviet Union; major student protests in Poland, repressed by domestic authorities.
1970	Polish shipworkers strike and are repressed by government; this leads to change in country's leadership.
1980	Rise of Solidarity movement in Poland.
1981	Repression of Solidarity and declaration of martial law.
1985	Gorbachev comes to power in Soviet Union.
1989	Collapse of communism in East Europe.
1990	Lech Walesa, leader of Solidarity is elected president of Poland.
1991–1995	War rips apart former Yugoslavia.
1993	Czechoslovakia splits into two countries.
1993	First parliamentary victory by former communists in postcommunist East-Central Europe (in Poland).
1998	European Union commitment, in principle, to induct Eastern European countries into the EU.
1999	Poland, Hungary, and the Czech Republic join NATO; soon after, NATO begins bombing of Serbia on behalf of Kosovo (a territory in Serbia in which ethnic Albanians were being persecuted).
2003	American invasion of Iraq is supported by most Eastern European countries. Poland sends 2,400 troops (the fourth largest contingent after the U.S., U.K., and Italy), and commands small occupation zone in south-central Iraq.
2004	Poland, Hungary, and the Czech Republic, along with Slovakia, Slovenia, Estonia, Latvia, and Lithuania join the European Union. Bulgaria, Estonia, Latvia, Lithuania, Romania, Slovakia, and Slovenia join NATO.
2007	Bulgaria and Romania join the European Union.

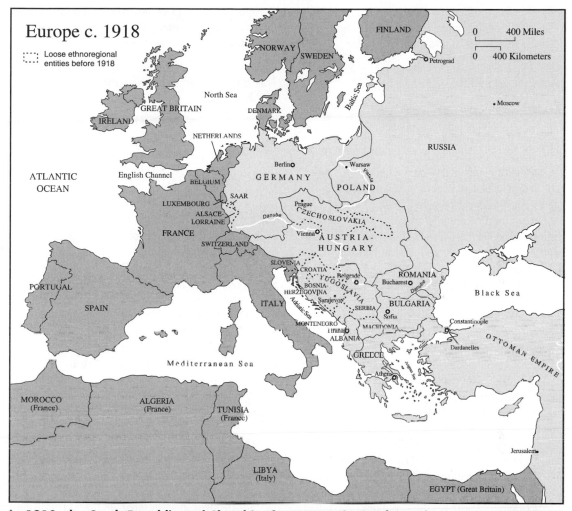

Europe c. 1918

Loose ethnoregional
entities before 1918

In 1918, the Czech Republic and Slovakia, former provinces of Austria-Hungary, united to
form Czechoslovakia; and Serbia, Croatia, Bosnia-Herzegovina, Slovenia, Montenegro, and
Macedonia united to form Yugoslavia. The dotted lines on the map show the borders of
each former entity. Poland's border with Russia was in dispute during this period.

Empire collapsed, and, together with the neighboring agrarian Slovaks, they formed their own state in 1918.

Yugoslavia followed the most complex path to statehood. Long dominated by the Ottoman Empire, large parts of it were then conquered by the Austrians. Serbia finally fought its way to independence in 1878, and then, with the collapse of rival powers after World War I, took the neighboring republics under its wing to form an independent Yugoslavia in 1918. Although linguistically similar, the new country was religiously very diverse, with

Roman Catholicism, Orthodox Christianity, and Islam (represented by Croatia, Serbia, and Bosnia, respectively) all figuring prominently. These political, economic, and religious differences laid the groundwork for conflicts that would emerge many times, most recently in the wars of the 1990s.

Careful readers may have noticed that Poland, Czechoslovakia, and Yugoslavia all gained independence in 1918. Why then? Because the four empires that had previously dominated the region—Austria,

Germany, Russia, and Turkey—all crumbled as a result of World War I. Maintaining independence, however, proved to be almost as hard as achieving it.

Independence (1918–1939)

The key problem for Eastern Europe after World War I was how to build stable states, given the multiplicity of nations. Several million Hungarians, for example, lived outside Hungary's borders. Millions of Germans lived far from Germany's borders. Poland had a large Ukrainian minority and also had Europe's largest Jewish population. (Jews constituted 11 percent of Poland's total population, but up to 40 percent or more of the population of its cities.) All other East-Central European states also had large Jewish minorities, and several had significant Roma, or Gypsy, populations as well.

The western powers that directed the emergence of the new Eastern Europe after World War I wished to create states that were ethnically homogeneous. With so many nationalities living in such close proximity, however, the goal was impossible to achieve. Instead, each country was left with a hodgepodge of nationalities, all of which (except for Jews and Roma) had their "own" states nearby. The result was the rise of an aggressive, antidemocratic, so-called "integralist," nationalism, in which each country's "official" nation trampled on the rights of minorities within.

Ethnic antagonisms, along with poverty and economic and social dislocation, made it exceedingly difficult to build liberal democracy. Instead these antagonisms led directly to World War II, in which millions were killed, tens of millions terrorized, and the region's economies were almost totally destroyed.[2] It is no wonder that by 1945, most East-Central Europeans considered the interwar years to be one giant failure and that many turned to the Left for hope.

The communists, who had rejected the status quo before the war and represented the victorious power afterward, reaped the benefits of the growing desire for a total break with the past. To many, communism seemed to be a solution to the two problems that had plagued the region for generations: economic underdevelopment and a weak state. After all, communism had already seemed to solve these problems in the Soviet Union. And so it was not simply the Red Army of the USSR that brought socialism to East-Central

Europe. After years of poverty, dictatorship, national rivalries, and war, many East-Central Europeans were ready for it themselves.

The Beginnings of Communism (1945–1949)

East Europeans hoped that the Red Army's expulsion of the Nazis meant that the region had finally become free of foreign domination. Instead, the outside world bore down on them again, this time in the form of the Soviet Union. Stalin's Red Army occupied East-Central Europe as it expelled the Nazis during its march to Berlin in 1944–1945. Hoping to make sure the region would never again become hostile territory, Stalin sought to create a buffer zone between the Soviet Union and the West by imposing Soviet-style socialism on the countries his armies occupied. Trying to squelch variation, he insisted on a carbon-copy socialism for everyone. Each country was ruled by the Politburo of the national Communist Party. The judiciary was dominated by the party, and so was the civil service. The party exercised control through the nomenklatura principle, meaning that it chose the people not only for nominally elected offices but also for key positions in the national bureaucracy, local government, industry, trade unions, educational institutions, and most other public organizations.

Millions of people supported the communist program in the 1940s. Young people were particularly attracted to the new system, for communism offered them something grandiose to believe in: the struggle to industrialize the country and build a great new world.[3] It also offered plenty of good new jobs. Indeed, for young people from peasant and working-class backgrounds, the Stalinist years were a time of improbable social mobility. In contrast to the unemployment lines of the past, the party had jobs to offer in industry, agriculture, the media, schools, the bureaucracy— anywhere one wanted. Many workers quickly rose to positions of higher authority, since the chief qualification for advancement was only that the applicant be committed to communism. Indeed, formal education often hindered one's chances for success, for it was considered a sign of a bourgeois background.

At the same time, the Stalinist years were a time of almost incomprehensible brutality. People were punished for their pasts, arrested for their private views, detained for telling jokes,[4] and even deported to Siberia without trial. Some defended these policies, saying that each country was engaged in a revolution and that enemies were lurking everywhere. But as the list of enemies kept getting longer and as police control embraced more and more of society, people turned increasingly against communism, seeing it as a betrayal of their hopes for a better world. They then began the long struggle for democracy.

The Rebirth of Democracy (1956–1989)

Although no dissenting voices were tolerated during the peak Stalinist years beginning in 1949, that changed soon after Stalin's death in 1953. New voices began to be heard. Critics known as "revisionists" argued that Stalinism was an aberration of true socialism and that socialism meant what the young Karl Marx himself had thought it meant: democracy for all. What began as a trickle turned into a torrent after the Twentieth Congress of the Soviet Communist Party in February 1956, when Soviet leader Nikita Khrushchev denounced Stalin as a tyrant and called for a return to "true Leninism." Khrushchev's speech seemed almost an invitation to East Europe to make changes. And within months, protests inspired and led by the democratic socialist revisionists gripped both Poland and Hungary. Soon, the party leaders whom Stalin had earlier purged returned to power: Imre Nagy in Hungary and Wladyslaw Gomułka in Poland. But when Nagy declared Hungary's intention to withdraw from the Warsaw Pact (the communist states' military alliance), the Soviets responded by sending in the Red Army. After many days of fierce fighting and thousands of casualties, the Soviets ousted Nagy and installed János Kádár as the new leader. In Poland, Gomułka understood the lesson and managed to defuse popular protests and to reestablish party control.[5]

Nevertheless, 1956 changed East Europe forever. Despite having repressed popular rebellions, neither Kádár nor Gomułka ever tried to reestablish the total control of the state over society that was the hallmark of Stalinist totalitarianism. Indeed, both countries soon experimented with economic reform and gradually allowed critics of the party (including, in Poland, the Catholic Church) to take part in public life. In Yugoslavia, meanwhile, democratic socialist ideology made even further progress. After the country was denounced by Stalin, who feared the independence of its dynamic leader, Josip Broz Tito, the Yugoslav Communist Party adopted a different, nonstatist type of socialism, based on regional autonomy and self-management by workers.

As elsewhere in the world, 1968 shook up East Europe. First came the so-called Prague Spring, the democratic movement in Czechoslovakia. It began as a program for economic reform. The Stalinist economic program, which was first developed in the Soviet Union as a crash industrialization program for poor peasant countries, had been particularly unsuitable for Czechoslovakia, with its strong industrial infrastructure and well-educated urban population. In 1962, it became the first communist country to record a decline in industrial output. Economists proposed reforms aimed at increasing managerial responsibility and promoting greater individual incentive. But inevitably, in this country with strong democratic traditions, the call for greater economic freedom became a call for political freedom as well. When Alexander Dubcek became head of the party in January 1968, Communist Party reformers promulgated a program of thoroughgoing democratic reform, declaring that freedom of speech was indispensable to a modern economy and arguing that authority should derive from knowledge and expertise rather than party affiliation.[6] By spring, Czechoslovakia had become a wide-open society, with censorship abolished and everyone speaking out on everything.

The Soviets grew alarmed. Although the democratic changes had been set in motion by the Communist Party, they seemed to make the party irrelevant, something the Soviets viewed as a threat to their security. In August 1968, Soviets sent troops to crush this democratic socialist experiment, thrusting the country into a long, gloomy period of political repression that would end only in 1989.

Poland's 1968 began over cultural issues, after officials closed a theatrical production of a nineteenth-century Polish play—because of its allegedly anti-Soviet character. Students reacted with a wave of protests, attacking government repression and demanding freedom of speech. The government responded by arresting student leaders, organizing goon squads of workers to beat up demonstrators, and launching a vast anti-intellectual and anti-Semitic campaign. Why anti-Semitism? Not because of any "Jewish problem" in Poland—there were only a small number of Jews still living in the country, as most had been wiped out by Hitler—but to root out the liberal intelligentsia, to whom anti-Semitism was anathema. Two years later, it was workers who led protests, particularly shipyard workers, who took to the streets in Gdańsk and Szczecin to protest price increases and to demand independent trade unions. Party authorities decided to "defend socialism" by shooting down dozens.

The new democratic oppositionists thus drew from 1968 the lesson that political change in East Europe would not come from above. They now set out to force it from below through the promotion of a wide variety of independent social activities. The goal was to get people to do things—anything—just as long as they did it on their own, with no official mediation. Writing, printing, or reading an independent newsletter; organizing, publicizing, or attending an independent lecture series or discussion group: these were among the main forms of opposition activity. This was the time of the *samizdat* press (uncensored and self-published periodicals) and of "flying universities" (unofficial classes meeting in different homes for each session). Such activity was considered the most important kind of political opposition possible. As conceptualized at this time, the aim of political opposition was not to take control of the state but to *democratize society*. If people felt and acted like free citizens, the opposition believed, then they would become free citizens. Eventually the state would have to follow along.

The East European opposition thus rediscovered the concept of *civil society*: the idea that politics meant not just government but the whole sphere of daily social interactions. People began fighting not so much for free elections and parliamentary democracy, which seemed far removed and perhaps beside the point, but for the right to have some social space free from the state. Writers wanted space to write about what they were interested in; students wanted space to study what and how they wanted to study; workers wanted space to form their own trade unions.

A number of brilliant writers and theoreticians emerged in East-Central Europe in the 1970s to give voice to these new aspirations; among them were Vaclav Havel in Czechoslovakia, Adam Michnik in Poland, and George Konrad in Hungary.[7] Organizations soon emerged, too, seeking to promote new civic activities and build an independent civil society. The most important and influential of these organizations was the Workers' Defense Committee, known by its Polish initials KOR. Formed by oppositionist intellectuals in Poland in 1977 to defend workers persecuted for going on strike the year before, KOR soon began sponsoring civic initiatives throughout the country, such as *samizdat* publications, lecture series, trade union organizing, and even some charitable work, often together with the Catholic Church. Combined with the independent workers' movement, KOR's activity helped bring about the remarkable Solidarity movement that spelled the beginning of the end of communism in East-Central Europe.

Polish workers had their own traditions, too. In 1970, shipyard workers had struck for the right to form independent trade unions. Ten years later, they went on strike again. In the new environment of civic activism, intellectuals from all over the country flocked to their aid, helping them print pamphlets and negotiate with the government. The strike ended with the signing of the Gdańsk Accord on August 31, 1980, which resulted in the formation of the "independent self-governing trade union Solidarity" headed by a thirty-seven-year-old electrician named Lęch Wałęsa. It signified the beginning of the end of the state socialist system.[8]

In the next sixteen months Poland was the site of a unique democratic revolution. Without making any attempt to seize state power, workers in Poland acted as if they were already citizens of a free and democratic state. Solidarity was perhaps the most democratic trade union that ever existed. All leadership meetings were attended by journalists, who published detailed accounts in the union press, carefully documenting who had said what. Although the union did push for wage increases, its main goal was simply to exist—to make sure the state respected the rights of social groups to organize on their own. Long years of political repression had convinced workers that political freedom was the most important goal of all.

Solidarity was threatening to the Communist system, not because it demanded political power—in fact, it did not—but just because it existed. Communism was based on central planning. The party made all public decisions and coordinated all public activities. Yet it could not do such things when millions of people gave their allegiance to an independent trade union that the party could not control. And so on December 13, 1981, the Polish authorities declared martial law and banned Solidarity. For the next seven years, the party tried to patch back together a system that had come apart at the seams. As it turned out, the system could not be mended.

The Collapse of Communism (1989–1991)

In a breathtaking few months in 1989, communist rule collapsed in one country after another in East-Central Europe. While most readers have probably heard of the fall of the Berlin Wall, which took place in November 1989, the real end to the communist era happened not in Germany but in Poland, and was a direct result of the Solidarity movement.

The turning point came in the summer of 1988 when workers in several factories went on strike against economic reforms and for the legalization of Solidarity once again. Seeing that there was no other way to restore calm and achieve economic reform, the Polish leadership, with the support of new Soviet leader Mikhail Gorbachev, agreed to talk with the banned Solidarity leadership. The strikes ended at once, and in February 1989 Solidarity and the party entered into negotiations that ended two months later. Solidarity had become legal again, and Poland was preparing for its first real elections in fifty years. The June elections saw the Communist party defeated thoroughly. Solidarity had succeeded in peacefully winning society away from its leaders, and Poland became the first East European country since World War II to have a noncommunist government.

After Poland, communist power fell swiftly elsewhere in the region: first in Hungary, then East Germany—with the fall of the Berlin Wall on November 9—then in Czechoslovakia, and soon after in Romania and Bulgaria.[9] The culmination came in August 1991 with the end of Communist Party rule in Russia itself.

How to explain these historic events? Perhaps the best theory proposes an explanation that is rooted in the dynamics of modernization. According to this view, put forth by Moshe Lewin with respect to events in Russia, the region at the start of the communist period was both economically and socially underdeveloped, which led many people to support a strong state that would take control in order to improve lives. Then, when economic and educational levels did in fact improve, people sought more responsibility for their own lives and no longer believed they needed the state to set the rules. Soon even the party elite stopped believing that its rule was necessary for progress, thus setting the stage for their relinquishing of power. In the end, one could say, the system failed because it succeeded: the communist political system was no longer appropriate to the socioeconomic world the communists had built.[10]

The Road to European Integration

Having shed its communist identity, East Europe now wanted to "rejoin" the West, in particular by entering the European Union. In order to do so, the new governments had to undertake a vast reform of their economic and political institutions. This meant not just making them democratic but making them conform to the rules and expectations that prevailed in the EU, which was done by passing through their parliaments the panoply of EU laws known as the *acquis communautaire*, the large body of legal obligations that bind the member states together.

In the early 1990s, the EU set up loose association agreements with Eastern European countries and began various aid and education programs. Most EU countries soon allowed visa-free travel to Eastern European citizens. Formal negotiations for full membership began only in 1998. In 2004, eight Eastern European countries entered the EU: Poland, Hungary, the Czech Republic, Slovakia, Slovenia, and Estonia, Latvia, and Lithuania. In 2007, Bulgaria and Romania also became full members.

If entering the EU signified economic integration with the West, entry into NATO represented the security side of integration. The incorporation of the region into NATO began sooner than the EU process and proceeded much quicker. As a U.S.-dominated military bloc rather than a complex economic and political union of independent states, NATO demands relatively little of its members besides the subordination of their armies. Although Russia, as well as some antimilitarists in Europe and the United States, called on

NATO to disband now that the Cold War had ended, most of East Europe sought a NATO guarantee against potential future Russian interference. Given this, plus the fact that American and European elites wanted to make sure the United States stayed involved in European affairs, NATO decided not to disband but to enlarge. Poland, Hungary, and the Czech Republic—East-Central Europe's new elite—became full members of NATO in March 1999. Five years later, in 2004, Bulgaria, Romania, Slovakia, Slovenia, Estonia, Latvia, and Lithuania were admitted as well.

East Central Europe after September 11

The hijacked planes smashing into the World Trade Center and the Pentagon in September 2001 had dramatic repercussions for East-Central Europe. In particular, it was the U.S. response to those events that simultaneously strengthened the region's relations with the United States and hurt its ties to West Europe.

East Europeans reacted to the news of the day with the same horror, disbelief, and outpouring of sympathy for America as everyone else in Europe. Their support for U.S. military action in Afghanistan, whose government had been working closely with Al Qaeda, was also shared with the rest of Europe. Things changed, however, when the United States began preparing for an unprovoked invasion and occupation of Iraq. France and Germany opposed American plans, calling for the continuation of sanctions instead, but the United States dug in its heels.

The question for East-Central Europe was which ally to choose. In the end, it sided with the United States. Poland sent 2,400 troops to Iraq and agreed to lead an occupation zone. Bulgaria, Hungary, Romania, Latvia, Slovakia, and Lithuania sent smaller contingents. Why did the east take the position it did? It was a combination of choice and necessity. Poland, for example, has a long pro-American history and has tried to stake out a role as the United States' most loyal Eastern ally. Many Eastern European citizens, meanwhile, sympathized intrinsically with the idea of getting rid of a dictator, and believed—erroneously, as it turned out—that the United States really knew how to successfully bring peace and democracy to Iraq. Yet the governments also felt that they had no choice. The United States was simply too powerful to alienate.

NATO's newest members and those still hoping to get in felt that public support of the United States was obligatory, even at the risk of alienating the EU. And these actions did indeed alienate much of the EU. French president Jacques Chirac treated East Europe's support for the United States as tantamount to betrayal. The EU's newest soon-to-be members, he said, "missed a great opportunity to shut up." U.S. Defense Secretary Donald Rumsfeld, meanwhile, praised them as harbingers of a "new Europe," in contrast to the "old" one in the west. September 11 thus both exposed and created new divides in the world of states that East-Central Europe would have to learn to navigate: divides between Europe and the United States over how to exercise power in the world, and divides within the new European Union itself.

East-Central Europe after the French and Dutch Veto of the European Constitution

The French and Dutch rejection of the European Constitution came as a shock to the newest EU members. For the larger and stronger countries, particularly Poland and the Czech Republic, however, it was a pleasant shock. That is because these countries believed that the constitution would help build up a so-called "core" Europe dominated by France and Germany, but consign Easterners second-class citizenship. Poles objected both to the proposed new voting procedures for the European Commission, which limited Poland's influence, and also to the constitution's lack of reference to the singular importance of Christianity in European history. Politicians in the Czech Republic criticized the constitution for allegedly being too centralist. To put it simply, few in the east mourned the apparent demise of the European Constitution.

Opinion in the region is divided, however, on what should happen now. Some say this is a good opportunity for the Eastern countries to exert influence in devising a new constitution, while others think it's best to do nothing and let the constitution die. Either way, the French and Dutch voters may have done the new members a favor: they showed them that they were not the only ones with reservations about the constitution, they weakened the notion of a western "core" able to dominate the EU, and they laid the grounds for a more legitimate and widely-accepted political union in the future.

Themes and Implications

A traveler in Eastern Europe is often told of an old jinx wished upon one's enemies: "May you live in interesting times!" Perhaps unfortunately for them, Eastern Europeans have always lived in interesting times. The region has been at the center of all the late, great "isms:" imperialism, nationalism, fascism, communism, democratization, and now global capitalism. Eastern Europe has gone from a neglected backwater to a harbinger of change. We can learn a great deal about the challenges faced by countries throughout the world by studying this region closely.

Historical Junctures and Political Themes

Perhaps nowhere else in Europe is the link between this book's first two themes, "world of states" and "governing the economy," clearer than in the countries of the east. For example, by entering the postcommunist era with a large foreign debt, East-Central Europe needed aid from the west to get its economies going. The west did offer help, but demanded in return that the region open up its economies to foreign products and investment. Because of the imbalance of power, however, West Europe did not reciprocate: it kept its markets closed to many products in which the east had a comparative advantage. The pre-enlargement European Union then insisted that Eastern countries adapt to western economic rules and standards, thus making it difficult for the east to continue its social welfare obligations to its citizens. How countries are able to govern their economies thus depends considerably on their location in a world of states.

Just as this book's first two key themes are so closely related in East-Central Europe, so too are its last two themes: the democratic idea and the politics of collective identity. The ruling communist parties were never able to instill a strong procommunist identity among the people. They succeeded in making people dependent on the state but not in making them feel grateful to it. On the contrary, since state control was so all-embracing, it became common for people to think of the state as the enemy. People with a complaint about anything could plausibly blame the state rather than some other social group or themselves.

In 1989, this antidictatorial collective identity came to the fore. People saw themselves now as "citizens" fighting for "democracy" against an oppressive state. To be a democratic citizen meant to have a voice in public life. People did not organize in 1989 as workers or intellectuals, urban or rural, men or women, gays or straights. They organized as citizens, united together and demanding democracy for all.

After 1989, democracy also came to mean the effort to build up the different social classes of a capitalist system. In former times in the West, this had led to the generation of powerful class identities, manifested in things like strong trade unions. But class is an identity that has not come easily in postcommunist society. On the contrary, because the Communist Party used the language of class to justify their dictatorship, many people rejected class language after 1989—even though it was only then that classes were being formed! Workers thus found themselves angry over their economic situation, but they were not well organized to defend themselves. Only new elites began to organize themselves as a class, fighting to make sure that public policy serves its interests. In this way, however, many workers have been alienated by the postcommunist system, and a system without the support of working people cannot be very strong or very stable.

East-Central Europe has not seen a great deal of identification along gender lines, either. Women certainly faced a great many problems under communism, owing to poorer educational opportunities and a strong macho culture. (Because of endemic shortages, shopping and cooking were even more of a burden than in the West.) Nevertheless women, like men, tended to see communism, and not gender relations, as the sole enemy.

Just as class differences became more potent in the postcommunist era, so have gender differences. In the early 1990s, when enterprises began to cut back on their work forces, women were the first to be fired. Where good new jobs were to be had, women were increasingly hired on the basis of looks, not qualifications. Such experiences have led to the emergence of a women's movement and new gender identities, but the legacy of the past makes this a slow process.[11]

Far more than along class or gender lines, people in East Europe identify themselves along national lines. That is, we see a clash today between nationalism and internationalism—or, as it is frequently characterized, between nationalism and "Europeanism." The

Europeanist is one who feels part of a new, upwardly mobile, economically productive community, moving collectively into the twenty-first century. Those who tend to feel this way are the budding entrepreneurs, economic professionals, students studying business and foreign languages, and many former dissidents.

The nationalist, on the other hand, feels threatened by the changes. To the nationalist, dependence on the East is being replaced by dependence on the West. Where communism once threatened traditional values, now liberalism, global capitalism, and secularism threaten those same values. The people who embrace this new identity are usually those least able to prosper in the new environment, such as unskilled workers with few contemporary marketable skills or the elderly living in rural areas without much new investment. For these people, postcommunism is not very pleasant, and they have good reason for feeling threatened by "the West" and all that it implies. Rejecting communism and capitalism alike, they find solace in and proclaim the merits of the nation instead. The "nation" is seen as a community of regular people—people just like them. Making policy in the interests of the nation means that state policy should benefit these "regular people" rather than the educated and the "cosmopolitans" who admire the West so much.

Implications for Comparative Politics

Rarely can we see an entire region in such transition as contemporary Eastern Europe, with so many exciting political, economic, and social experiments. Issues of democratization, globalization, privatization, and nationalism appear in this region in a way they appear nowhere else. Although capitalism beckons, the old appeals of communism still tug. While the people are enticed by the opportunities to belong to a single global culture, their national pride and legacies of resistance keep them connected to smaller-scale national and cultural values as well. With the eruptions of ethnic nationalism existing side by side with the desire to join the EU, we see the tensions that political scientist Benjamin Barber has described as "jihad vs. McWorld"—the former referring to the desire to hold onto the local styles and traditions that "McWorld," or the push for global market uniformity, tends to sweep away.

As the postcommunist transformation recedes into the past, Eastern Europe comes increasingly to resemble the west. For example, today it faces the problem, quite common in the west, of how to maintain its relatively high social welfare expenditures in the face of limited state budgets. East European countries will face considerable pressure in coming years to lower those budgets even more in order to enter the Euro zone (adopting the Euro as their currency). Other countries face similar pressures from globalization. This change in political economy affects party politics, too. For what has changed in comparative politics in today's age of globalization is that there often appears to be little choice in the kind of economic policies states pursue. When this happens, parties compete not by favoring capitalism or socialism, as often happened in the past. Rather, the divide is often between liberals and populists: between those who focus on defending individual rights, minority rights, and rule of law, versus those articulating an exclusionary nationalist or religious politics in order to win the votes of those who seek some kind of alternative. Recent election results in both Western and Eastern Europe, such as in Poland in 2005, suggest that right-wing populist parties may be gaining the upper hand.

So these are, indeed, interesting times. Political scientists, sociologists, economists, and anthropologists have unprecedented opportunities for understanding the dynamics of social change through looking at the particulars of East-Central Europe. That is what we will do in the chapters ahead.

Notes

[1] For an account of Eastern European states and nations in the premodern era, see Perry Anderson, *Lineages of the Absolutist State* (London: Verso, 1974).

[2] See Joseph Rothschild, *Return to Diversity: A Political History of East Central Europe Since World War II* (New York: Oxford University Press, 1989), chap. 2.

[3] For a wonderful account of why Czech and Slovak intellectuals chose to join the Communist party, see Antonin Liehm, *The Politics of Culture* (New York: Grove Press, 1968).

[4] See Milan Kundera's novel *The Joke* (New York: Harper and Row, 1982).

[5] For an account of Eastern European protests up to 1980, see Chris Harman, *Class Struggles in Eastern Europe, 1945–1983* (London: Bookmarks, 1988).

[6]For two inside accounts of the rise of Czechoslovak reform communism, see Alexander Dubcek, *Hope Dies Fast* (New York: Kodansha International, 1993), and Zdenek Mlynár, *Nightfrost in Prague* (New York: Karz, 1980).

[7]Vaclav Havel, *The Power of the Powerless* (Armonk, N.Y.: M. E. Sharpe, 1985); Adam Michnik, *Letters from Prison* (Berkeley and Los Angeles: University of California Press, 1986); George Konrad, *Antipolitics* (San Diego: Harcourt Brace Jovanovich, 1984).

[8]On the Solidarity experience, from its early roots in the pre-war period to the fall of the Communist government, see David Ost, *Solidarity and the Politics of Anti-Politics* (Philadelphia: Temple University Press, 1990).

[9]See Timothy Garton Ash, *The Magic Lantern* (New York: Random House, 1990).

[10]See Moshe Lewin, *The Gorbachev Phenomenon* (Berkeley: University of California Press, 1994).

[11]On gender issues in early postcommunism, see Nanette Funk and Magda Mueller, eds., *Gender Politics and Post-Communism* (New York: Routledge, 1993).

CHAPTER 27

Political Economy and Development

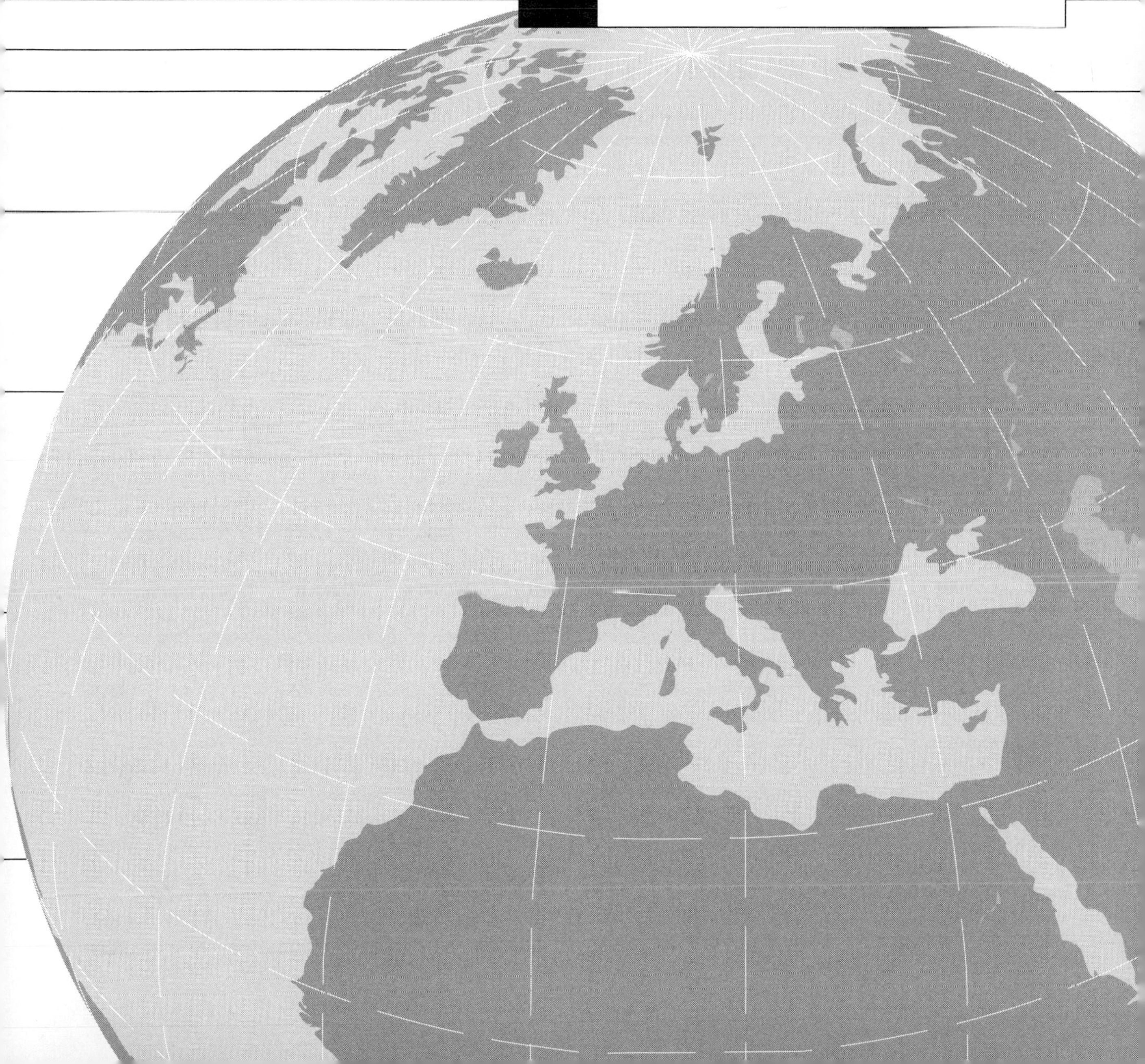

We hear a great deal now about communism having been an economic failure. But in 1945, it was capitalism that was synonymous with failure for many East Europeans. The term evoked memories of mass unemployment, economic depression, vast social inequalities, uncontrollable greed, and war. The reason that communism was able to win support, or at least grudging acceptance, from much of the population was that it promised something else: hope.

The "Peculiar Settlement" and Beyond

After World War II, most West European countries embarked on an economic program that entailed enhanced state intervention, expansion of social welfare programs, and state-sponsored mediation between labor and business. This came to be known as the "postwar settlement." In East Europe, the economic changes went much deeper, and so we call it a *peculiar settlement*.

Immediately after the war, the new communist authorities promised a planned economy with jobs for all, social mobility for society's poorest, stable prices, and general economic progress. To make good on this program, the new regimes would rely not on "outdated" market forces but on a massive use of state power. In Europe at the time, there was nothing unusual about increasing the role of the state. Capitalist governments in Western Europe were doing the same thing. In the East, however, government sought not just to regulate the economy and promote cooperation between labor and capital, but to take over the economy completely so that the state could plan everything. Total planning required complete ownership of factories, workshops, retail stores, and farms. Constructing a planned economy—or, as it was often called, a command economy—therefore meant nationalizing all private property used for production and building a huge bureaucratic apparatus to administer all this property.

In West Europe, governments worked to mediate the relationship between capital and labor. Both groups retained their autonomy (and capital retained its property), but they were persuaded to moderate their antagonisms. In East-Central Europe, the state abolished the relationship between capital and labor and essentially substituted itself for both groups. Factories and businesses were taken over by the state, and trade unions were turned into arms of the state. (Individuals did, of course, maintain ownership of their personal possessions.) For a number of reasons, this approach never led to the levels of prosperity in the West, but it did provide for social peace and regular growth.

For the first two decades of communist rule, the arrangement essentially worked. The protests that did arise concerned only the political aspects of the arrangement. Beginning around 1968, however, not only the political side but the entire settlement began to break down. The moves toward economic reform showed that signs of a new political economy were emerging in East-Central Europe as indelibly as they did in the West.

The Rise of the "Peculiar Settlement"

By 1949, the Stalinist transformation had largely been accomplished: the state had effectively eliminated private property in the manufacturing and service sectors, with farming only slightly behind. From then on, the entire economy was to be managed by state-run institutions.

The state accomplished several undeniably beneficial achievements. By concentrating resources, it built up heavy industry very quickly. It eliminated unemployment by bringing millions into the work force, including peasants from the countryside and women, who now entered the labor market at rates only slightly lower than men. Having obtained a job, moreover, a person had it for as long as he or she wished, since a job was considered a right, not a privilege. The state kept prices on most essential goods at a low and affordable level, one of the reasons people often had to stand in long lines. And it facilitated vast social mobility. Hundreds of thousands of youths, unskilled workers, and illiterate peasants found that they suddenly had a future, if only they joined the party (see Table 27.1). In Hungary, 60,000 workers were made enterprise managers during the 1949–1953 period alone.

On Soviet insistence, East Europe carried out its new policies without help from the rest of the world. The West offered Marshall Plan aid, but the offer was rejected. The West's response was to impose a boycott: no trade, no loans, and no exchange of technology. That symbolized relations between East and West until the détente of the late 1960s.

Table 27.1

Communism Brings Mobility in Eastern Europe

	Agricultural Workforce (percentage)	
	1960	1980
Albania	71	62
Bulgaria	73	24
Czechoslovakia	38	13
East Germany	24	10
Hungary	49	24
Poland	56	26
Romania	74	30
Yugoslavia	70	33

Note: Because of the way these data were collected, the figures slightly underestimate the shift away from agriculture.

Source: Joni Lovenduski and Jean Woodall, *Politics and Society in Eastern Europe* (Bloomington: Indiana University Press, 1987), p. 130.

Failure and Demise

By the 1960s, the economies of East-Central Europe were plagued by shortages, budget deficits, and lack of imagination to deal with the challenges. Employment guarantees remained, but workers often had little to do. Moreover, opportunities for social mobility had declined dramatically. Workers and peasants, whose predecessors had been able to move up rapidly in the initial postwar years, now found that their careers were blocked by those who had advanced in the past and who now constituted a new elite that tried to pass on privileges to their children. These children, meanwhile, sought better and more creative jobs to match their levels of education, but the system, stuck in its old ways, could not generate such new opportunities.

The irony is that the economic problems of the system were a sign not of communism's failure but of its success. Communist leaders had wanted to build up big industrial economies. Having done so, they did not know what to do next. Party authorities, in accord with the plan, had built up an economy that was very successful at producing large volumes of standardized goods and very unsuccessful at producing specialized goods for particular markets. Quantity, not quality, was

key. The entire economic system came to resemble a giant enterprise, where decisions are made by a few at the top and executed by the majority at the bottom. The goods were produced, but initiative and imagination were smothered—fatal flaws in the high-tech global economy that was just emerging. As Daniel Chirot put it, by the 1970s this region had created

> the world's most advanced late nineteenth-century economy, the world's biggest and best, most inflexible rust belt. It is as if Andrew Carnegie had taken over the entire United States, forced it into becoming a giant copy of U.S. Steel, and the executives of the same U.S. Steel had continued to run the country into the 1970s and 1980s![1]

Eastern Europe needed reform, but how could government take away the things people expected from the system without jeopardizing the unwritten social contract on which it depended? According to that contract, the state provided jobs and a steadily increasing standard of living in return for political quiescence, or the acceptance of an unelected government. If they were going to change their political economy, would they have to change the political system, too? Events such as the Prague Spring of 1968—the reform movement in Czechoslovakia—suggested that they would.

The Prague Spring itself should be understood as a first attempt to abandon the peculiar communist postwar settlement. The main proponents of reform were self-proclaimed economic reformers who felt that the party needed to let managers run businesses on a more market-oriented basis, without constant instructions from the bureaucratic center. Thus, the Prague Spring tolerated and even encouraged political freedom as a kind of quid pro quo, offered to civil society in return for giving up the social contract protections provided by the regime. The Soviets invaded the country before tensions in this reform model could be worked through. But the word was out: the peculiar settlement would have to be revised.

Hungary was the next to try to do so. In 1968, it introduced the "new economic mechanism" that reduced the role of the ministries and made individual enterprises more responsible for their own affairs. Unlike in Czechoslovakia, however, political reforms were not part of the bargain. That is one of the reasons the reforms soon ran into trouble: different groups expressed their objections within the party, and the leadership backed off its radical plans so as not to promote political discontent.

In 1970, Poland too felt that it needed to moderate the peculiar settlement and reduce the extensive subsidies that were leading to chronic budget deficits. But instead of trying to reduce waste and make management more efficient, as the Czechs and Hungarians had tried to do, the Poles attempted to solve their problems by challenging the workers head on. When Polish leader Gomułka suddenly announced a dramatic rise in food prices, shipyard workers in the port cities of Gdańsk and Szczecin responded with massive strikes. Gomułka suppressed the strikes immediately, leaving dozens dead. The price hikes were rescinded, but the economic problems persisted, and workers remained mobilized. The experience demonstrated that the peculiar settlement could not be broken on one side only. Painful economic reform might be tolerated only if political reform went along with it. Since neither East-Central Europe's governments nor the Soviet Union seemed ready for political reform, the crisis began to seem irresolvable.

Just as despair began to mount, a temporary solution was found. It was devised by Edward Gierek, who replaced Gomułka as party leader in Poland soon after the 1970 massacres. We can sum up Gierek's strategy as, "Let the West pay for it!" The countries would turn to the West for the investment funds to help develop their stagnant economies and satisfy the appetites of their hungry consumers. The West was willing to make loans to help finance its official enemy for three reasons. First, East Europe was a good investment. Capitalist bankers paradoxically thought it safer to lend money to poor Communist countries than to poor capitalist countries, because in the former the political system was stable and labor was under firm control. Second, détente's temporary easing of the cold war, beginning in the late 1960s, made it politically possible to trade with Eastern Europe. Finally, the price hikes by the Organization of Petroleum Exporting Countries (OPEC) and the subsequent oil crisis made it economically possible to do so, as banks now held billions of so-called petrodollars (used to purchase oil at the new prices), which they needed to loan out. The West needed a market for capital just when the East needed a source.

So for a few years in the 1970s, Poles lived rather well. But by the end of the decade, the country was deep in debt, with spiraling interest payments making the future look bleak. Poland's entry into the global economy had failed. It had fallen into a debt trap similar to the kind that had been crippling the Third World.

By 1980, it had become clear that East-Central Europe's attempt to borrow its way out of the crisis had failed. The crisis of the peculiar settlement now became even greater than before; not only was the economy in even more serious trouble, but popular anger had been stirred up by the continuing lack of political freedom and, perhaps even more, by the sudden disappearance of the consumer goods that people were getting used to.

By 1989, the peculiar settlement had collapsed completely. One by one, East European countries turned to a democratic market economy. The region's peculiar postwar settlement gave way to a rapidly emerging new political economy.

State and Economy

The fall of communism can thus be traced in part to the woes that befell East-Central Europe when it sought reintegration into the global economy. Once a society seeks to play on capitalist turf, it is difficult to play only halfway. The situation is different today. After communism fell, East-Central Europe moved decisively toward the creation of a full market economy and eagerly sought integration into the global economy. Although still shaped by its communist legacies, its problems increasingly resemble those of western market economies.

Economic Management

In 1990, Poland adopted a series of measures known collectively as *shock therapy*. Most of the measures were soon adopted by other governments in the region. The aim was to bring about a quick transition to a capitalist economy run by private owners, without the communist-era guarantee of employment for all.

Shock therapy was intended to take the state out of the business of managing the economy and allow the market to make most of the decisions that state planners used to make. This meant disbanding the planning ministries and granting firms autonomy. Companies stopped being told what to produce, whom to produce for, or what prices to charge for their products. The end of price controls led to soaring inflation. The end of subsidies led to plummeting demand. In 1990 alone, industrial output in Poland declined an astonishing 25.4 percent, followed by another 16 percent drop in 1991. In the communist era, even loss-producing firms were kept alive by the state, since companies served more as job-providers than as profit-makers. Now a firm that did not make a profit had to make adjustments, or else it went bankrupt. With jobs no longer guaranteed, the old social contract quickly disappeared.

In the new arrangement, competitive firms and sectors were to be created by taking the state out of the business of management, opening domestic firms to foreign competition, and empowering a new wealthy class to replace the state as the managing elites. The main tool used to establish this new arrangement was privatization.[2] The aim was to create a new class of property owners with a personal interest in maintaining and developing the economy.

There were two kinds of privatization processes in Eastern Europe, usually referred to as small and large. *Small privatization* was concerned with the retail sector, particularly small shops like groceries, bakeries, or repair shops. This sector was privatized relatively quickly, sometimes by selling the shops to the highest bidder, more often by leasing them to those who worked there. Because there was not a great deal of money (or power) at stake, this process proved not to be very politically contentious. The real conflicts came with *large privatization*, which was concerned with the ownership transfer of the large state enterprises with their large labor force, enormous capital stock, and huge markets.

In Hungary, large privatization began during the communist era, led not by budding new capitalists but by old communist managers. They would get together to set up a new firm, transfer assets to the new entity, and thereby become new capitalist entrepreneurs. After 1990, the postcommunist government cracked down on this practice, but made it much easier for foreign capital to buy up domestic firms. As a result, large privatization in Hungary was very much an elite affair. In Poland and Czechoslovakia, where previous opportunities were more limited, governments made special efforts at least to appear to include more people in the privatization process.

In Czechoslovakia, aside from the sale of some major plants to western buyers, the government decided to privatize industry through a voucher system. In 1992, all citizens were allowed to purchase, at a nominal price, a booklet of stock shares, called points, which they could then invest in a company of their choice. By involving ordinary people in the privatization process, the government hoped to break the ethos of dependence on the state fostered by the old regime and to teach citizens the concepts of risk, profit, and ownership. By making people co-owners, the government hoped individuals would feel they had a stake in the entire process of marketization.

There were two problems with the Czech solution. First, voucher privatization proved not to be so inclusive after all. Within a short period of time, investment funds and banks that were still run largely by the state quickly bought out most of the citizens' vouchers. Formal popular ownership, in other words, was a cover for continuing state control. Second, this lack of real private ownership reduced the pressure on firms to restructure. As a result, Czech firms avoided painful restructuring in the early 1990s, only to have to do so in the latter part of the decade, just when neighboring economies were starting to benefit from changes they had made earlier.

Poland began privatization with a law in July 1990 that spelled out several possible paths and set up a ministry of property transformation to oversee the process. Over the next three years, Poland experimented with various privatization strategies. First, it began selling firms on the open market. But there were not enough buyers, and the government usually ended up with majority ownership anyway. Then it began selling firms to single western buyers, such as a food processing plant to Gerber or a chemical plant to Procter & Gamble. This practice, however, drew stiff opposition. Critics charged that the best firms were being sold at a fraction of their real value, in return for kickbacks or to ingratiate the authorities with the West. Since no one knew what these firms were "really" worth (because their accounting books were based on the artificial prices of the old system), it was impossible to verify these charges. The fierce criticism, however, required the government to take more care before selling firms to foreigners. All East-Central European countries have had to deal with similar complaints.

Seeking to win popular support, Poland in 1995 introduced a plan known as *general privatization*, in which ownership of several hundred state-owned companies was transferred to private investment firms in which individual citizens could buy shares. Whereas in the Czech plan a buyer purchases shares of the company itself, the Polish plan offered people shares of investment firms that were given ownership of various companies. The Poles chose this indirect method because they felt that good management was just as important as privatization. By the end of the 1990s, however, this plan too had run into serious problems, largely because of the poor quality of the firms selected for privatization and the limited capital at the disposal of the investment firms.

In the end, the most common method of privatization in Poland has been to sell or lease firms to their employees. This method was particularly popular with workers, who thereby became formal co-owners of the firm. However, since managers usually put up most of the money, and therefore received most of the shares, workers usually did not get more influence or more money.

This de facto exclusion of labor has been a problem in all the privatization methods. In the original 1990 laws, the government sought to win labor support by reserving a small percentage of shares for the workforce at special prices. But the shares proved unaffordable to many workers even at discount prices, so a 1996 law gave the workforce 15 percent of the shares of a privatized firm for free. Workers therefore got more money, but not necessarily more influence. Privatization in Poland has always been an elite-run affair, despite the powerful role played by the Solidarity trade union.

Finally, there are the many experiences of *bandit privatization*. Not a precise concept, the term refers to the illegal, semilegal, underhanded, nepotistic, coerced, and just plain criminal ways in which government elites have passed on property to themselves or their friends. All countries have had their share of these. Even Czech privatization, so admired by the West in the early 1990s, turned out by the late 1990s to have harbored bastions of corruption in which allies of the ruling Civic Democratic Party gained fortunes by plundering state wealth. One of the worst epidemics of bandit privatization occurred in Croatia, whose president, Franjo Tudjman, tried to put virtually the entire economy in the hands of a few dozen loyal families. One friend of the president was able to "buy" 157 companies with no money of his own.[3] Only after the president's death in 1999 and new elections in 2000 was the public able to learn all this. EU membership or, in the case of Croatia, EU "association agreements," has helped greatly with making corporate sales more transparent.

Social Policy

Over the past decade, Eastern European governments have radically changed their welfare-state profiles. In place of the communist-era tradition of cradle-to-grave services for everyone, the new policy, as elsewhere in Europe, is to provide assistance selectively, to those whom the market economy quite clearly leaves behind.

In the communist era, the main social welfare benefit was provided for all: a guaranteed job. That is definitively over. Table 27.2 shows the rapid increase of unemployment throughout the region. The appearance of unemployment in East-Central Europe has meant the appearance of unemployment insurance, though not on very generous terms. The general pattern is a fixed payment for a set period of time, followed by possible help from a general public assistance fund. In Poland, for example, laid-off workers receive 36 percent of the average national wage for twelve months. If after a year they are still unemployed, they become eligible for public assistance for the indigent (which, at 28 percent of the average wage, still leaves the recipient impoverished), as well as one-time-only payments to help buy clothing or pay rent. Active labor market policies such as retraining and public works have also been common ways of fighting unemployment, particularly in the Czech Republic.

Free health care was another key benefit of the old system. Its scope and quality were deteriorating even before 1989 and have only gotten worse since then. Governments tried to reform the health care sector by imposing hard budget constraints on hospitals and clinics, and encouraging better-off individuals to purchase private health insurance. Private doctors now operate everywhere in the region, leading to a situation in which the wealthier people have access to care that the poor do not. Whereas political connections were the ticket to better health care in the past, now

Table 27.2

Unemployment in the Postcommunist Era

	Registered Unemployment (percentage of labor force)							
	1990	1992	1994	1996	1998	2000	2002	2004
Bulgaria	1.8	15.5	12.8	12.5	12.2	17.9	16.3	12.2
Czech Republic	0.7	5.5	3.2	3.5	7.5	8.8	7.3	8.8
Hungary	1.7	12.0	10.9	10.5	9.1	8.9	5.6	5.9
Poland	6.5	13.6	16.0	13.2	10.4	15.1	19.8	18.2
Romania	1.3	10.0	10.9	6.6	10.3	10.5	6.1	6.0
Serbia and Montenegro	—	—	23.9	26.1	27.2	26.6	26.0	26.0
Slovakia	1.6	5.5	14.8	12.8	15.6	17.9	18.7	18.0
Ukraine	—	—	0.3	1.5	4.3	4.2	3.8	3.5

Notes: 1992 figures for the Czech Republic and Slovakia are for Czechoslovakia as a whole. Beginning in 2000, figures for Serbia and Montenegro do not include Kosovo.

Source: Economic Survey of Europe (New York: United Nations, various editions from 1995 to 2005).

money makes the difference. In most countries health care is still nominally free, but a great many procedures, operations, and medicines were, in fact, available only when citizens pay.

Higher education has been reformed in a similar way. Tuition in the high-profile state universities remains free for those who pass the tough entrance exams, but student aid has been reduced substantially, and the imposition of fees is now widespread. State universities now also admit students who do not pass the entrance exam but who do pay their own fees. Private universities have mushroomed throughout the region, and they help fill the gap. Since 1989, the number of university students has increased substantially in East-Central Europe, but the increase has been almost entirely in the paid sector.

Throughout Europe reforming old-age pensions was one of the key issues in the 1990s. In Hungary, Poland, the Czech Republic, and Slovakia, between 1989 and 1996, economic depression led to the loss of some 5 million jobs. With millions of near-retirement-age workers who were allowed early retirement and young people who had not been hired in the first place, the imbalance between wage earners and retirees grew considerably, jeopardizing the entire pension system. In 1997, Hungary and Poland followed an international trend and adopted

a new system. Future retirees will no longer be guaranteed a set pension. Instead, younger workers today must pay part of their social security contributions into a private investment fund. Their retirement benefits will be based largely on market performance.

Even with the social security net, poverty remains high. In Hungary and Poland, two of the more prosperous countries, over 20 percent of the population lives below the official poverty level. Income inequality has risen dramatically throughout the region since 1989: for example, by 18 percent in the Czech Republic, 19 percent in Hungary, 28 percent in Poland, and 38 percent in Slovakia.[4]

Who gained and who lost in the new Eastern Europe? Right after 1989, those who were young and had higher education fared best. Today many of the young have lost out. Because the elderly vote more, pensions have stayed relatively high, while job training programs for youth have declined, leading hundreds of thousands to look for work in Western Europe. Men have had advantages, as a backlash set in against women in the workplace. Perhaps those who have suffered most are middle-aged workers with little formal education. Education, class, and gender are paying higher returns in the postcommunist era than they ever did in the past.

Society and Economy

Noneconomic factors are as important as economic ones for understanding a nation's politics. Are the people of East-Central Europe attached to democracy as a value? Which do they consider more important: individual rights or the rights of the nation? What about the rights of minorities? Do East Europeans believe in capitalism as a legitimate and desirable economic system? Do they believe in the separation of church and state? What do they think is the proper role for women in public life? Answers to these questions reveal a great deal about how social and political life in East-Central Europe will develop.

Inequality and Ethnic Minorities

The people of East-Central Europe have had a curious relationship with national minorities. Because virtually the entire region was under foreign jurisdiction less than a century ago, people have a sense that they can all be considered minorities. The Czech writer Milan Kundera once wrote that to be a Central European is to be aware that nationhood is not eternal; one's own nation can potentially disappear.[5] But although such a history makes people sensitive to the problems of minorities, it also makes them committed to solidifying their *own* national identity whenever they have the chance. And it is this that has created problems for minority rights in the region.

Most of East-Central Europe's nationalities first had the chance to consolidate their nationhood only after World War I. When the occupying powers collapsed, former minorities suddenly came to power, trying to build a state (government, administration, and military) to serve the interests of their newly dominant national group. The problem, however, was that members of other nationalities automatically became second-class citizens. The national enmities this created contributed to tearing the new states apart internally long before the Nazis came along to finish the job.

As an internationalist party committed to the famous line from *The Communist Manifesto*, "the working class has no nationality," the communists were seen by many as the answer to the minority problems of the past. And indeed, in places like Yugoslavia, the communists succeeded in reducing the fierce ethnic conflicts of the past.

Elsewhere, however, it was the war itself that transformed minority politics. By 1945, most of the region's Jews had been killed and Germans expelled. In Poland, new borders placed Ukrainians and Lithuanians in the Soviet Union instead. In officially multiethnic countries like Czechoslovakia and Yugoslavia, the government continually preached unity, although material inequalities among the nationalities certainly existed.

Minority problems reemerged in the postcommunist era, particularly in the three countries (Czechoslovakia, Yugoslavia, and the Soviet Union) that broke up into multiple states. Elsewhere, the most prominent minority populations are Hungarians in Romania and Slovakia (about 10 percent), Turks in Bulgaria (9 percent), and a large Roma population in Hungary and Slovakia. In recent years, growing prosperity and membership in the European Union have made these countries popular for new groups of immigrants. In Poland, for example, there are tens of thousands of Ukrainians doing occasional labor, and as many Vietnamese who sell Chinese goods in the open-air markets. Although the reemergence of minorities brings a cultural richness that many citizens appreciate, it creates tensions too, especially in the hands of right-wing politicians willing to play on local fears that immigrants are "taking our jobs." This xenophobic lament is untrue—immigration in fact creates more jobs—but it still plays a significant political role, not just in the east but in all of Europe.

Inequality and Women

Another critical noneconomic factor that shapes Eastern European politics today is the role of gender. In contrast to the feminism that has transformed western politics, however, the phenomenon here can best be seen as what Peggy Watson calls *masculinism*—the policy of using power to boost men's chances in the world by cutting back the chances for women.[6] It is a peculiar kind of reaction against communism, for one of the things communism did was to bring women en masse into the work force. Since 1989, however, men have argued that jobs are more important for them than for women, since their role is to support a family (although, in fact, many women are also heads of households). Many married women initially supported this position, but low wages for men and the isolation of staying at home have driven most to try to return to the workplace. They are, however, finding it harder to do so. A common complaint of women today is that they are too often hired on the basis of looks, not qualifications, and that job opportunities plummet markedly for women over fifty. There has, in other words, been a return to old patriarchal stereotypes and old moral and Christian norms throughout the region. As a 2006 United Nations report puts it, "East European women were forced out of the labor force in unprecedented numbers [in the 1990s], exactly at the time when their western counterparts started to take up paid employment in earnest."[7] Interestingly, that means women's employment rates are now about the same in East and West Europe, but the point is that opportunities in the east were declining just as they began to improve in the west. These changing attitudes about gender represent one more way in which noneconomic factors are shaping postcommunist politics.

The loss of jobs for women has had more dire consequences as well, leading to a boom in prostitution throughout the region and beyond. Police in Western Europe report an alarming rise in the number of Eastern European women being exported to the West to work as prostitutes. Typically the cash-poor woman, with declining opportunities at home, is recruited by a dashing man who promises her a fancy "hostess" job in a chic West European establishment. This international trafficking of women, sparked by the region's economic crisis as well as by a high external "demand" for white-skinned prostitutes (of which Eastern Europe has, since 1989, become the world's largest supplier), now counts as one of the biggest and most nefarious of postcommunist "growth industries."[8]

The Generation Gap

Generational differences tend to be greatest at the moment of grand systemic change. And so while young people gravitated disproportionately to communism in the late 1940s, they also gravitated heavily to capitalist democracy in 1989. Just as in earlier times, the new system offered them enormous new possibilities, for if communists did not trust older workers after 1949, capitalists did not trust them after 1989. This does not mean that all young people have benefited. Education, after all, is the chief determinant of success, and highly educated middle-aged people have been more likely to prosper than poorly educated youth. Still, young people

believed they would do better, and they had more opportunities to get the training necessary for the new economy. The new system also gave them the chance to travel abroad, an opportunity they had long been denied. The early twenty-first century still sees many older citizens of the region nostalgic for the security of the past, but young people for the most part never look back.

Culturally, the generation gap is not so great, since most of Eastern Europe had its own 1960s. With the postwar generation embracing rock music and the sexual revolution, just as in the West, young people have not had to fight many battles to participate in an increasingly universal youth culture.[9] On issues like feminism and homosexuality, however, people in their twenties are far more open than others. Unlike in the West, where feminist organizations tend to be led by middle-aged women who came of age in the 1970s, those in the East are run mostly by women aged twenty-five to forty, who became active only in the 1990s. And the fact that gay and lesbian issues can now be discussed openly is a direct result of the changed attitudes of young people. That doesn't mean tolerance prevails. Gay bars do exist in the big cities throughout the area, but homophobia is still prevalent through mainstream East European culture. In Poland, shrill antigay rhetoric helped a right-wing party win the 2005 elections, just as the campaign against gay marriage helped the Republicans in the United States the year before. Still, youth are less likely to be susceptible to such appeals than their elders are. Perhaps the major generational difference today is that young people are highly skeptical of politics. Having come of age after 1989, they are tired of hearing about the "heroes" who "overthrew" communism, and they believe that many of the new leaders are just as corrupt as the old ones ever were. There are few young people in political parties and even fewer in trade unions. Where they do become involved, they tend to work through nongovernmental organizations and new social movements. When the World Bank held its first meeting in a former communist country, in Prague in September 2000, the demonstrations against it were led by activists in their twenties. Nevertheless, political activism remains quite low among East-Central European youth as a whole. They still want to enjoy the freedoms they have rather than struggle for more.

The Dilemmas of European Integration

For Eastern Europe, the year 2004 was the culmination of a dream that until 1989 had seemed unachievable. Poland, Hungary, the Czech Republic, Slovakia, Slovenia, and the three Baltic republics of Estonia, Latvia, and Lithuania became full members of the European Union. Three years later, Bulgaria and Romania also joined. European integration had proceeded at a pace that would have seemed completely unimaginable not so long ago.

The political benefits of EU membership were clear. It signaled membership in an elite transnational institution that was committed to political stability and liberal democracy. For the smaller and historically vulnerable countries of the east, it meant that the stronger countries of the west "had their back." But what were the economic benefits? Here there was a great deal of debate. There certainly seemed to be a lot of negatives. Entry meant opening up all borders to tariff-free trade, and many Easterners feared that their countries could not compete. Could a Polish or Czech machine tool industry survive when facing direct competition with powerful German engineering, which could use the EU's open borders to take over Eastern markets? The east had comparative advantage in food production, due to lower costs, but the old EU was relatively protectionist about food. Moreover, it gave costly subsidies to its own farmers under the Common Agricultural Policy (CAP) program, and although it would extend the program to Eastern farmers upon membership, the subsidies would be much lower than western levels, at least until 2013. As for livestock farmers, the strict, wide-ranging EU regulatory norms seemed to mean that many small producers, who could not meet them, would have to close. Just prior to formal membership, for example, only 150 of Poland's food manufacturers had received licenses to export to the EU. Exactly ten times that many had already been denied.

So while urban inhabitants of East-Central Europe tended to be upbeat about the prospects of joining the EU, rural citizens were worried. They worried even about whether foreigners were going to buy all their land. A standing EU principle allows any EU citizen to buy land in any EU country. Given the disparities in earnings and in accumulated wealth, Eastern European farmers— and parliaments—naturally feared that Westerners could easily outbid Easterners, and that, after all the years of resisting Russia, they'd end up literally selling out to other foreigners instead.

Finally, Easterners were piqued about the limited amount of structural funds they received from the west. For while the EU is supposed to make the state and the economy more efficient, that takes money, and the new members received significantly less structural adjustment funds from the EU budget than previous new entrants had received, despite having many more rules to follow and a tougher environment in which to compete.

Of course, the east got something for following the EU's rules. Already in 1990, the EU began providing funds and technical assistance for economic restructuring and privatization, environmental awareness and protection, student exchanges, and the promotion of "social partnership" in labor relations. In 1991, the EU created the European Bank for Reconstruction and Development, to offer loans for infrastructure projects like highways and pollution controls. Western countries also granted significant debt reduction for Eastern Europe, thus giving it access to new sources of capital. Although some of the assistance came with a high dose of condescension, with western "specialists" raking in high fees often benefiting them more than the countries they were supposed to help,[10] it did help prepare countries for the realities of a market economy. Still, many feared that things would get worse, not better, upon full membership.

How has reality compared to expectations and worries? Reality is better. Many skilled workshops have been modernized and revitalized with funds from western investors, and this, combined with cheaper wages than in the west, has boosted their exports and earnings. Other westerners have started new workplaces in the east, finding the lower wages and good skills available there to be a successful combination. So while the Eastern economies are no longer run entirely by citizens of those countries, many workplaces have been saved, and others created, by the inflow of western capital. Some locals still protest against the big foreign presence—banks in most of the countries in the region are almost 100 percent foreign-owned, and even some economists say this is dangerous in the long-term—but for the most part, people now accept the trade-off.

The agricultural situation also looks better than it did upon entry. Eastern farmers are not getting the same subsidies under CAP as western farmers, but they weren't getting *any* CAP funds before membership, so many small farmers experience the subsidies as a windfall. Larger farmers, meanwhile, find that they can market goods at costs cheaper than western rivals, and have benefited in that way. As for westerners buying up the land, this proved to be one area where the new members were able to put restrictions on the old. They came to agreement in 2004 on a provision by which free western access to eastern real estate would not kick in for seven years, until 2011.

The west's concession on land allowed it to get something in return. Many western laborers feared the cheap competition from eastern workers who would now be able to travel freely. So in return for no free real estate market for westerners in the east, it was agreed that there would be no free labor market for easterners in the west, also for seven years. This came as a blow to easterners who had hoped precisely for this freedom to work in the west. But there was a catch: individual western countries were free to waive the provision and allow eastern EU citizens access to their labor markets right away. Ireland, the United Kingdom, and Sweden did so at once. (In 2006, Spain, Portugal, and Finland followed suit.) The result was that hundreds of thousands of mostly young Eastern Europeans traveled west for work, for the most part with considerable success. There are estimates that up to a million Poles have left to work in Ireland and the UK. And indeed, it is now almost impossible to visit a café in London and not find a Pole as one of the wait staff. Low-cost airlines, meanwhile, now serve cities throughout the east, even in small towns that barely had an airport in the past. Citizens from Rzeszow in southeastern Poland can now fly to London for cheaper than it costs to take the train to Warsaw. This has allowed Easterners to travel more readily, and that has helped the local economy too: whereas past generations of émigrés rarely went back to the east, this new generation travels home often, many bringing back their western earnings to build houses or start businesses in the east. The easy travel and work opportunities have completely transformed rural life in Eastern Europe, although sometimes in bad ways: since Romania joined the EU in 2007, for example, some small towns have lost *all* their young adults to the west. When that happens, the local community always ends up worse off.

Finally, although the east received much lower levels of funding for structural transformation than previous EU entrants, the situation has changed since the countries actually joined the EU. Poland, the east's largest country, received the most structural funds of any EU country in 2007. Actual membership, in other words, is much better for the east than mere candidate membership. Once they have full voting rights and are full-fledged members, their interests are taken far more into account.

East-Central Europe in the Global Economy

Small states cannot shape their environment as large ones can. They must exist in a world where political and economic rule making are dominated by those large states. From 1945 to 1989, East-Central Europe worked closely with the Soviet Union. In the early years, the Soviet Union exercised clear economic control over the region. Since 1989, East-Central Europe has turned decisively to the west. In 1988, the region sent 27.2 percent of its exports to the former Soviet Union and 38.7 percent to developed market economies. Ten years later, the respective figures were 7.5 percent and 71.6 percent. Since 2004, when most of the region entered the European Union, that trend has been even greater. In recent years, Polish exports to the EU have increased about 20 percent per year. Nevertheless, other aspects of globalization have hurt the region. When the United States imposed sanctions on Iraq in 1991, and then invaded the country in 2003, it deprived the Eastern countries of the good business relationships they had with that country. Western pressure to cut back on arms production has also hurt.

Much capital has entered East-Central Europe as a result of direct foreign investment, chiefly from Western Europe. This international investment created new managerial jobs and helped modernize many factories. By the mid-1990s, it began to generate criticism too, as people saw that multinational corporations change their employment plans and investment strategies with remarkable speed. Although some called for safeguards against such policies, incorporation into the European Union has meant that nothing can be done about it.

Clearly, the most important recent economic development for the region has been its entry into the EU.

Although preparations for joining were painful, since West Europe demanded that the east open its markets to western goods without returning the favor, things have been better since. Besides investment in manufacturing, the west has begun outsourcing white-collar work to the east, such as bookkeeping, data-crunching, and accounting. As a *New York Times* article recently put it, "The United States may turn to India to fill many of its call-center jobs and the like. But West Europe is turning more frequently these days to its own backyard, transforming a few urban centers of the former Communist bloc into the Bangalores of Europe."[11] On the other hand, EU membership has enabled East European companies to profit as well. Some have proven quite capable of adapting to global conditions. In 2006, the Polish oil company Orlen bought out a Lithuanian oil company for $2.5 billion, the largest single purchase yet made by an East-Central European company.

Still, the next big hurdle for the Eastern economies will be entry into the euro zone. For unlike with previous EU members, those admitted in 2004 and 2007 were required to eventually join the euro zone as a condition for entry. Since this will mean further cutting budgets and subsidies, it is creating new fears about the loss of industry and the further decline of social safety networks. In Hungary, it has already led to a severe political crisis: government attempts to bring the budget in line in order to meet euro criteria led to massive cutbacks in 2006 and 2007, with hospitals and schools being closed and basic services curtailed. Although unemployment elsewhere in the region fell, in Hungary it has increased. This has led to a series of violent antigovernment demonstrations and increased tensions. So far, only Slovenia has joined the euro zone, in 2007.

In sum, integration in the global economy has brought possibilities for growth and expansion, but also a set of new problems. The biggest problem, of course, was the post-1989 economic depression, the largest in peacetime since the 1930s. As Tables 27.3 and 27.4 show, Poland did not exceed its 1989 GDP level until 1996, while most other countries had to wait until 2000. By the beginning of the new century, life was starting to get better for most East-Central Europeans. But this is not true for Bulgaria or Romania or the former Yugoslavia (with the exception of Slovenia). If we look at one classic indicator, life expectancy, we see in Figure 27.1 that the situation for the region is mixed. By the late 1990s, people in the Czech Republic could expect to live about three and a half years more than they did in the communist era, while those in Bulgaria lived about two years less. EU entry will likely improve things for the region. Although the ten new EU members had an average of 14.1 percent unemployment rate in 2004, compared to 8.0 percent for the previous EU-15, they also had a dynamic 5.1 percent growth rate, compared to the EU-15's sluggish 2.3 percent.

Today, East-Central Europe has definitively reentered the global economy, though in a divided way.

Table 27.3

Transformation by Numbers I: Real GDP, 1989–2001 (1989 = 100)

	1990	1992	1994	1996	1998	2000	2001
Bulgaria	90.9	77.2	77.5	72.2	70.9	76.4	79.5
Czech Republic	98.8	86.9	88.9	98.2	96.4	100.0	103.3
Hungary	96.5	82.4	84.4	86.8	95.1	104.3	108.2
Poland	88.4	84.4	92.1	104.5	117.1	126.7	128.0
Romania	94.4	75.0	79.2	88.2	78.8	79.3	83.5
Serbia and Montenegro	92.1	58.7	41.7	46.8	51.5	45.1	47.9
Slovakia	97.5	78.0	79.0	89.0	97.7	101.2	104.5
Ukraine	96.4	79.3	52.4	41.4	39.4	41.6	45.4

Note: Beginning in 2000, figures for Serbia and Montenegro do not include Kosovo.

Source: Economic Survey of Europe (New York: United Nations, 2002).

Table 27.4

Transformation by Numbers II: Change in GDP from Previous Year (percentage)

	2002	2003	2004
Bulgaria	4.9	4.5	4.6
Czech Republic	1.5	3.2	4.4
Hungary	3.5	2.9	4.2
Poland	1.4	3.8	5.3
Romania	5.1	5.2	8.3
Serbia and Montenegro	3.8	2.1	8.0
Slovakia	4.6	4.5	5.5
Ukraine	7.0	15.8	12.5

Source: *Economic Survey of Europe* (New York: United Nations, 2005).

Figure 27.1

Changes in life expectancy for the region are mixed, roughly reflecting changes in basic economic conditions in the different countries.

Life Expectancy 1987–1997
(change in years)

Country	Life expectancy 1997
Czech Republic	73.9
Slovenia	74.7
Slovakia	72.7
Poland	72.7
Hungary	70.6
Yugoslavia	72.1
Georgia	72.6
Croatia	72.5
Estonia	70.1
Romania	69.0
Albania	71.7
Bulgaria	70.7
Russia	66.9
Ukraine	67.4
EU average:	77.1

While the elite countries of Poland, Hungary, and the Czech Republic are poised to become full, albeit weak, players in the EU, the southeastern countries of Bulgaria, Romania, and most of former Yugoslav republics are still treated more as paupers than as players.

Notes

[1] Daniel Chirot, "What Happened in Eastern Europe in 1989?" in Daniel Chirot, ed., *The Crisis of Leninism and the Decline of the Left* (Seattle: University of Washington Press, 1991), pp. 5–6.

[2] For an overview, see Roman Frydman, Andrzej Rapaczynski, and John S. Earle, *The Privatization Process in Central Europe* (Budapest: Central European University Press, 1993). For a critical account, see David Stark and Laszlo Bruszt, *Post-Socialist Pathways: Transforming Politics and Property in East-Central Europe* (Cambridge: Cambridge University Press, 1998).

[3] Tim Judah, "Croatia Reborn," *New York Review of Books*, August 10, 2000.

[4] Janusz Kornai, "The Great Transformation of Central and Eastern Europe: Success and Disappointment," presidential address of the International Economic Association, February 2006, www .iea-world.com/address.doc.

[5] Milan Kundera, "What Is Central Europe?" abridged version available in Gale Stokes, ed., *From Stalinism to Pluralism* (New York: Oxford University Press, 1991).

[6] See Peggy Watson, "The Rise of Masculinism in Eastern Europe," *New Left Review*, no. 198 (March–April 1993): 71–82.

[7] United Nations Development Fund for Women (UNIFEM, "The Story Behind the Numbers: Women and Employment in Central and Eastern Europe and the Western Commonwealth of Independent States," March 2006, www.unifem.org/attachments/ products/StoryBehindTheNumbers_eng.pdf.

[8] To follow developments on international trafficking and Eastern Europe, see and subscribe to "Stop-Traffic," www.stop-traffic.org.

[9] On the lure of early rock and roll in Eastern Europe, see the wonderful Hungarian film *Time Stands Still* (directed by Peter Gothar, 1981). Interestingly, recreational drug use never caught on in the East as in the West, both because of supply problems (tight border controls dissuaded potential smugglers, and low Eastern pay levels meant it was hardly worth the effort) and because of demand problems (alcohol has always been the drug of choice).

[10] For a powerful critique of Western aid programs to Eastern Europe, see Janine Wedel, *Collision and Collusion: The Strange Case of Western Aid to Eastern Europe, 1989–1998* (New York: St. Martin's Press, 1998).

[11] John Tagliabue, "The Eastern Bloc of Outsourcing," *New York Times*, April 19, 2007.

CHAPTER 28

Governance and Policymaking

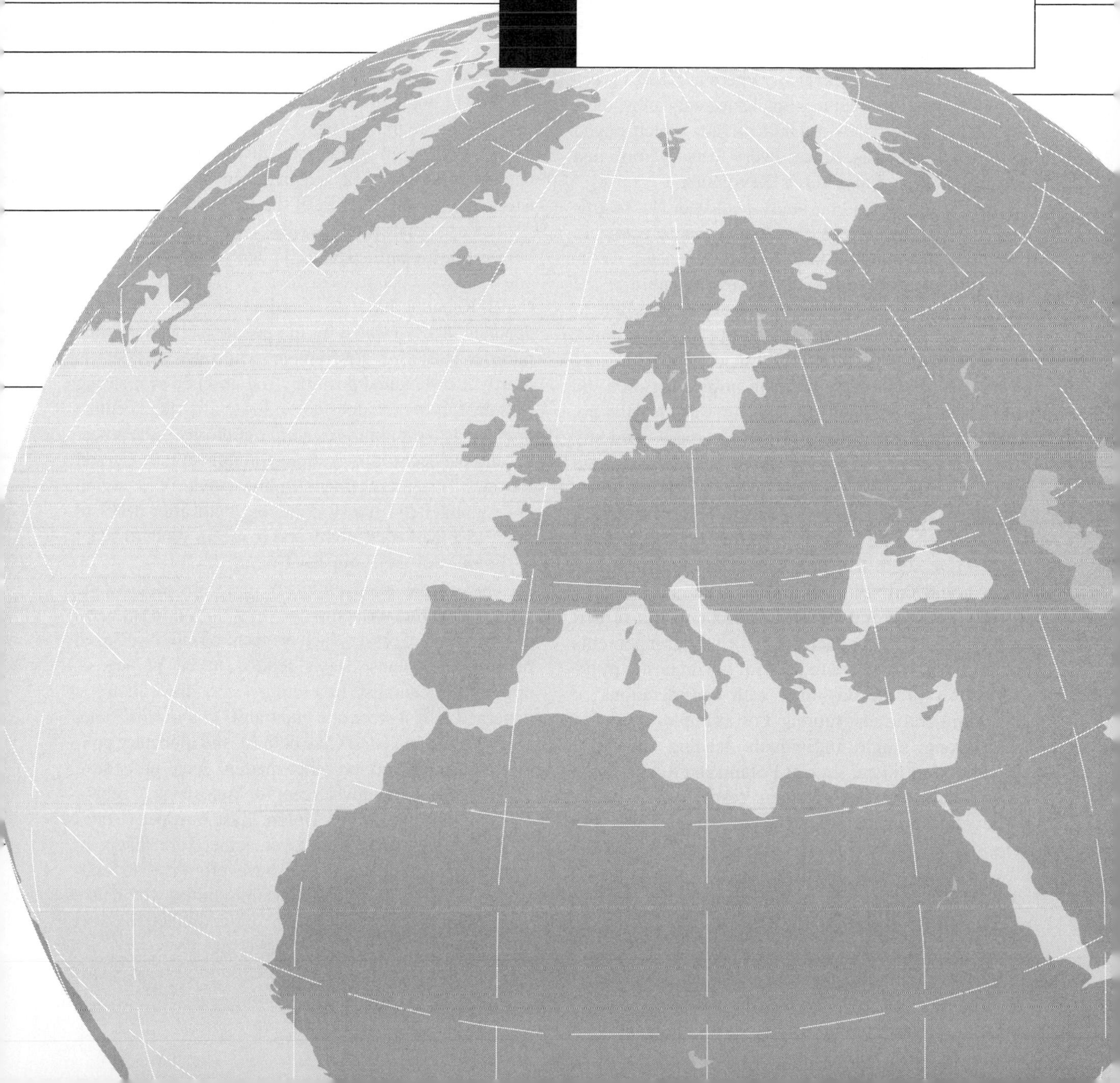

It was one thing to overthrow Communist Party rule. It was something very different to construct a new system to take its place.

The paradox of the East European revolutions of 1989 was that the next day, all the old state officials, save a few at the very top, went to work in the same way and in the same place as before. The police, the mayors, the journalists, the military officers, and the functionaries in the ministries all stayed in place when the Communist Party lost power. There was no violent revolutionary upheaval anywhere in East Europe; even in Romania, street fighting lasted only a few days and did not concern the old bureaucracy, which stayed at its posts. In this sense, every country, not just Czechoslovakia, had a Velvet Revolution.

This institutional continuity could not last indefinitely. When the former dissidents came to power in 1989, one of their first tasks was to recreate government. This meant rethinking the very structure of the state, creating institutions that were appropriate to the kind of democracies the creators hoped to build. The new leaders had to create new ways of exercising power, devise rules for the relationships between the president and parliament, the executive and legislature, citizens and the state, parties and the state. Suddenly institutions were important. All the issues of state building—issues that students in the west tend to see as matters settled long ago—had to be confronted as if for the very first time.

It might seem that politicians, in conditions like these, could calmly look around, take stock of the world's political institutions, and choose those that worked best. But in fact the political arrangements that emerged had more to do with the domestic political battles of the day than with considerations of ideal democratic institutions. For example, countries with strong single individuals leading the fight against communism, such as Poland and Russia (with Lech Wałęsa and Boris Yeltsin, respectively), began to develop presidential systems; those where the struggle was more diffuse, such as Hungary and the former Czechoslovakia, produced parliamentary systems. The rule seems to be applicable to the drafting of constitutions in all countries at all times: the pull of the present is at least as powerful as the lure of the future.

Organization of the State

Contrary to what many Americans believe, there are various types of democratic systems. The U.S. system, in fact, with its popularly elected president as the indisputable political leader, responsible for forming a government, naming a cabinet, and shaping the legislative agenda, is rather unusual. Most democratic systems are parliamentary systems, in which a single house of parliament is responsible for electing the country's political leader, who then rules in close cooperation with parliament and can be removed by parliament at any time. Some countries, like France, have a semipresidential system, in which executive power is divided between a popularly elected president and a prime minister enjoying the support of the legislature.

In East-Central Europe, the clear preference so far has been for a parliamentary system, not a presidential one. Like most countries in the region, Hungary and the Czech Republic have strict parliamentary systems: the deputies, freely elected by the people, choose a prime minister to form a government, while the president is mostly a ceremonial position. The absence of a strong president, however, does not indicate a weak executive branch. On the contrary, executive authority—the power to carry out decisions—is strong throughout East-Central Europe. This arrangement fit the needs of a region undergoing rapid transformations, both after 1989 to move to a market economy and in recent years to adapt to the rules of the European Union.

One of the main criticisms made by democratic activists was that the communist system had led to overcentralization of power. Such overcentralization occurred because communist states tended to be unitary as opposed to federalist. In a *unitary state*, the country is governed as if it were one giant unit. In a *federal state*, only overarching affairs like defense and monetary policies are centralized; on other matters, local units have considerable autonomy. Except for Yugoslavia, Czechoslovakia, and the Soviet Union, East European states were all unitary. One might assume, therefore, that postcommunist politicians would have promoted federalism, in which local regions and communities would take vast responsibility for their own affairs. In fact, that was not the case. Postcommunist governments were so set on making sure that their economic reform plans embraced the entire country that they were reluctant to yield power to local regions. Decision making in Eastern Europe thus remains highly centralized, although the European Union has pushed for more power to be devolved to local levels.

The Executive

Relations between the legislature and the executive have not been highly contentious. The legislatures have generally been supportive of a strong executive office, both because they agree that rapid decisions are necessary in the chaotic postcommunist environment and because a strong executive is the usual European way.

In most East-Central European countries, the prime minister is the chief executive officer, and the president largely a figurehead elected by parliament. Only in Poland is the president elected by the people and given significant authority. This was because of the influence of Lech Wałęsa, the leader of the Solidarity trade union that brought down the old regime, who insisted on a nationwide, popular presidential election in 1990 in order to get rid of the previous communist president and to consolidate his own power. The constitution of 1997 formally enshrined Poland's peculiar semipresidential system, in which power is distributed between the president and prime minister. This arrangement is a bit confusing (even for Poles), since it means that there are basically two executive branches, with the prime minister the more powerful.

Poland's prime minister is responsible for the day-to-day workings of the government, such as drafting a budget or calling out the police. He or she can be ousted only if the government loses a parliamentary vote of confidence. As in Germany, Poland's system calls for a constructive vote of no confidence, meaning that the parliament must propose an alternative government at the same time that it votes down the current one. In 2000, for example, the prime minister lost his parliamentary majority during midterm, but because parliament could not agree on a successor, he stayed on as head of a minority government.

As for the presidency, much depends on the individual in power. Lech Wałęsa was a very active president,

while his successor, Aleksander Kwaśniewski (1995–2005) exercised power in a more restrained way. In 2005, Poles elected the conservative Lech Kaczyński as president. But with his twin brother, Jarosław, serving as prime minister, President Kaczyński has so far played down his own role. Whether this will lead to a further weakening of the presidency remains to be seen. In short, however, the president in Poland is weaker than his counterparts in the United States or France, but stronger than elsewhere in East Europe except in Russia and the former Yugoslavia.

The weakest presidency in Eastern Europe is in the Czech Republic, owing largely to the behavior of its initial occupant, Vaclav Havel. The Czech president does not even have the power to propose legislation. Elected by parliament, not the public, the president can veto laws passed by the legislature, but the legislature can override by a simple majority. Since this is the same number needed to pass the law in the first place, such a veto only forces parliament to look at the legislation a second time. The president can dissolve parliament and call for new elections, but only if the lower house either votes out the prime minister or is incapable of passing legislation for more than three months. That has not yet happened. The current Czech president, Vaclav Klaus, elected in 2003, has tried to make the presidency stronger, but the constitution passed under his predecessor has thwarted his ambitions.

Cabinet Government

In addition to the president or prime minister, the executive branch of government consists of the cabinet and the ongoing bureaucracy charged with implementing policy. Cabinet ministers in Eastern European countries, as in most other European democracies, are nominated by the prime minister and approved or rejected by parliament. Once approved, they are largely free to pursue policy implementation in their areas of responsibility. Confrontations with parliament are rare, since parliaments tend not to keep close tabs on cabinet ministers. This, of course, follows from the nature of the parliamentary system, in which—unlike in the United States—the executive and the legislative branches are always in the hands of the same party or coalition.

In the first years after the fall of the old regimes in 1989, the Finance Ministry was the most important one. Because the economic reforms were so painful, not even prime ministers wanted to take responsibility for them. So they agreed to create powerful finance ministries and let those ministries run the show—and take the blame. In Poland, Hungary, and Czechoslovakia, finance ministers ran economic policy virtually as their own private fiefdoms, with neither the prime minister nor president doing much of anything to interfere.

In recent years, as these countries have made the economic transition and entered the European Union, the ministries of internal affairs and of justice tend to be the most important ones. These two are responsible for the police, intelligence, domestic security, and the courts and prisons. Their importance has increased not so much because of post-9/11 threats of terrorism—although dealing with that is certainly one of their priorities—but because of the rise of civic protests, and because political parties have increasingly promoted law-and-order policies as a way of making people feel more secure in insecure times.

A major problem facing the executive bureaucracy as a whole is the absence of strict ethical rules, which has led to frequent accusations of conflict of interest. Ministers and their underlings, for example, still sometimes sit on boards of directors of companies that they deal with in an official capacity. This leads to popular perceptions of wrongdoing and to negative opinion about government. EU rules have changed matters somewhat, but more on paper than in practice.

Bureaucracy and Civil Service

Below the rank of cabinet minister and vice minister, we enter the ranks of the civil service bureaucracy. The term *bureaucracy* often carries with it a negative connotation, implying cronyism and routine decision making, but a well-functioning bureaucracy is a vital part of sound government. The classic definition was offered in the early twentieth century by the great German social scientist Max Weber (1864–1920), for whom the ideal type of bureaucracy is the group of neutral, well-trained civil servants who administer state policy continuously regardless of which party or government is in office. In the years since the fall of communism, one of East-Central Europe's main goals has been the construction of just such a bureaucracy. To try to achieve this goal, the new regimes have first had to attack the old system of state service known as *nomenklatura*. In that arrangement, the Communist Party chose people for key positions in the state and economy on the basis of political criteria and loyalty to party leadership. Although the *nomenklatura* system abated over the years as increasing numbers of professionals were trained, it remained a continual source of friction between the Communist state and society, a reminder that high qualifications and good work were not always enough for someone to get ahead.

The postcommunist system is supposed to be based on merit. People are supposed to obtain positions in the bureaucracies because of training or hard work. And for the most part it has worked this way. Many people who could not advance in the past for political reasons have been able to make careers in the postcommunist political, economic, and cultural spheres. The European Union (EU) added its own pressure: all countries hoping to join had to pass a civil service law as a precondition for consideration. Expertise, efficiency, and political neutrality are stressed as the ethos of the new public servant.

Transforming bureaucracies, however, is a slow process. In the first postcommunist years, attempts at change did not seem to be working out the way they should. On the contrary, bureaucrats from the past were holding onto their positions or even moving ahead. The old system was gone, but the same people who had made it in the old system were making it in the new one. For people at the top levels of the old bureaucracy, such as bankers and diplomats, perseverance was sometimes facilitated by complex personal ties, which created room for blackmail and corruption. For civil servants lower down in the hierarchy, however, the reason for their perseverance was simply their experience and better training. They may have received that experience and training for the wrong reasons, but if the new system was to be based on qualifications, these people had them.

Peggy Simpson, an American journalist living in Poland, told a story that illustrates this scenario well. In one small town in the mid-1990s, a newly elected mayor, hoping to weed out purely political appointees and to put together a staff of competent officials, ordered new civil service exams for the old staff and anyone else who wanted to take them. When the results came in, the old personnel had the best grades. The "democratic" bureaucracy thus came to look almost identical to the "Communist" bureaucracy, despite the abolition of *nomenklatura*. The old elite was managing to become the new elite.

Public and Semipublic Institutions

East-Central Europe emerged from the Communist system in 1989 with tens of thousands of state-owned enterprises (SOEs). Under the old system, and particularly in the early communist years, the chief goal of SOEs was not to make a profit, and not even to make goods, but to help ensure social and political stability. State factories and enterprises "solved" the unemployment problem by providing jobs for all. They tackled housing problems by building apartment complexes for their employees. Trade unions at the work sites arranged vacations for employees and summer camps for their children, and often they distributed scarce food and appliances to their members. Besides producing goods, by acting much like social welfare agencies in the West, SOEs were a crucial part of the entire political system.

Since 1989, the nature of Eastern Europe's state-owned enterprises has changed dramatically. In the first place, each country has embarked on a program of privatization. But even those enterprises that remain state owned have been fundamentally transformed: They are charged with making a profit and threatened with closure if they cannot perform. Consequently, most of them are no longer the social providers they were in the past. They have sold their housing units, closed their vacation bureaus, and stopped procuring scarce consumer goods for employees. Most important, they no longer guarantee citizens a job.

When enterprises become privately owned and individually managed, the role of regulatory agencies becomes increasingly important. At least it should be. In East-Central Europe, however, the reaction against communist-era state control led to widespread neglect of working conditions and on-the-job safety. Governments were so anxious to promote private business that they offered not only tax breaks but virtual immunity from regulations. Safety rules, overtime provisions,

guaranteed vacations, and other benefits have been violated with impunity, especially in small, private firms. The situation is somewhat better in larger firms with a higher profile and in state firms where unions are still active. Even there, however, official accounts regularly report routine violations and lax regulation.

Willful neglect is not the only cause. Insufficient budgetary funds are also a key problem, and regulatory agencies tend to be at the bottom of the receiving line. This neglect extends to pollution control agencies. Although East Europe has made some strides in fighting pollution, such as installing filters on smokestacks in the giant factories, agencies do not actively combat the dumping of toxic wastes or the lesser but steady polluting practices of small private firms.

One reason there is little money in the coffers for regulatory agencies is that tax collection does not yet operate efficiently. Under the communist system, governments got their funds simply by taking the revenues earned by the country's enterprises. The need for separate, elaborate taxation policies appeared only with the privatization of the postcommunist era. Within a few years, most countries in the region introduced a progressive personal income tax, levied through deductions and a year-end reckoning (as in the United States), as well as a host of disparate corporate taxes. The problem is collection. Due to both abuse of the prevalent tax breaks for business and inadequate and underfunded collection agencies, millions of dollars in revenues are lost each year to unpaid taxes. More efficient collection depends on having more efficient bureaucracies, which in turn depends on more state revenues. Poor tax collection is likely to persist for some years to come, as long as governments continue to see the promotion of business activity as the number-one policy goal and turn a blind eye to the private sector's willful tax evasion.

Other State Institutions

In the communist era, East European citizens had frequent complaints about the police and the judicial system and objected to the lack of true self-government. Since 1989, these institutions have all undergone thoroughgoing reform, although not always producing the most desirable results.

The Military and the Police

Most nondemocratic countries in the late twentieth century had strong and independent militaries. This was true for Latin America, which had a succession of military dictatorships, and even for China, where the military has sometimes played a more important role than the Communist Party. It was not the case in East Europe, however. From 1945 until 1989, the military played a subordinate role in the system. In fact, it was doubly subordinate—first to the Communist Party and then to the Soviet Union.[1] The region's militaries are still subordinate today—both to the country's elected officials and to NATO strategic command.

Because the military was not directly involved in government, and because almost all males at one time served, it remained a popular institution during the communist period. Even in Poland, when the military declared martial law in 1981, most people recognized that it was simply doing the bidding of the party. This lingering support helped the military redefine its role in the postcommunist era. Since 1989, it has been repackaged as a symbol of independence, an institution that has served the nation loyally and will continue to do so in the future. In this way, the military has helped to legitimate the new systems by linking them to the precommunist past.

Since the mid-1990s, the military has undergone yet another transformation by becoming part of NATO. To a large extent, this has meant that the previous subordination to the Soviet Union has been exchanged for a similar one to the United States. Officers now study in American schools, their soldiers train with American troops, and plans are tailored to NATO interests. Membership does, however, ensure that the military does not become too independent, since civilian control over the army is an enshrined NATO principle. Only in the former Yugoslavia did the military become a dominant player in recent years, as a result of the war that tore the country apart between 1991 and 1999. Since then, its role has declined, but it will still be some time before the successor states are considered for NATO membership.

Far more than the military, it was the police that was the feared institution during the communist era. Too often an unchecked power with vast secret networks and large numbers of citizen collaborators who were frequently blackmailed into service, the police penetrated most aspects of everyday life. This was particularly true during the Stalinist years of 1948–1953, although even in the late stages of the communist period, citizens needed police approval for things such as obtaining a passport to travel abroad.

Reforming the police was the first order of business of the postcommunist period. New governments gave orders, effective immediately, instructing the police to desist from arresting political activists and to allow basic democratic rights. Comprehensive internal reform, however, came more slowly. Although some police officials were fired for their previous activities, most, even those engaged in active persecution of the opposition, were judged to have merely been following orders. These were given new training and allowed to stay on the force. Retention rates were even higher among the top espionage forces, whose services were largely retained, with orders to redeploy those services against other enemies. In 2007, the Polish government under the Kaczyński brothers started purging former communist functionaries from the intelligence services. Although popular among some voters, the policy led to complaints that Polish intelligence capabilities were being compromised.

Today most citizens have a very different view of the police from what they had in the past and no longer see them as a feared enemy. On the other hand, not everything has changed. When protesters from around the world came to Prague in 2000 to protest against the International Monetary Fund (IMF), Czech police arrested and held incommunicado thousands of people, denying them food and the right to an attorney, and beating many detainees. In 2005 in Poland, the police beat up participants of a gay rights march in Poznan. Just as in the west, East Europe's police increasingly justify their new use of force by citing threats of terrorism.

The Judiciary

Constitutionally, as well as in public opinion and popular expectations, the judiciary in East-Central Europe is the least powerful of the branches of government—more likely to accept the decisions of the executive and legislature than to challenge them. This relative weakness is rooted in two factors: basic continental European traditions, in which the judiciary has always been weaker than in the Anglo-American model, and the experiences of the communist era, when the courts too often acted as the arm of the Communist Party. East Europeans do not seem to want an activist judiciary. The constitutional courts are the major exception. Charged with assessing the constitutionality of laws, such courts now exist in all Eastern European countries, and are becoming stronger.

Citizens do, however, want a well-functioning judiciary, and it is here that there are the most complaints. Charges of corruption, nepotism, and incompetence are rampant. Basic cases wait months or even years to be heard. As a result, there has begun to be a turn to a more harsh judicial system. In response to crime, which is not very large but is highly publicized by tabloid media, many politicians now promote a "lock 'em up and throw away the key" approach, leading to increased arrests and higher rates of imprisonment. This in turn leads critics to complain of new attacks on civil liberties. Outside of the domestic courts, however, citizens of the region, because they are now also citizens of the European Union, can appeal national decisions to the European Court of Human Rights in Strasbourg.

A particularly troublesome issue for the judiciary has been the question of lustration, or the purging from public office of citizens who served as collaborators with the communist-era security police. In early postcommunist Czechoslovakia, a harsh lustration law resulted in the disbarring of many people from public positions, but the problem is that many of them were totally innocent. The most famous was the case of Jan Kavan, who had been one of Czechoslovakia's most important antigovernment activists after the Soviet invasion of 1968. Acclaimed as a hero after 1989, Kavan was easily elected to the new parliament in 1990. Then one day in 1991, the lustration commission announced that Kavan had been an informer for the secret police. Kavan vehemently denied this, but although he could neither learn the exact charges against him nor see the evidence, he had to leave parliament in disgrace.[2] It took five years before Kavan was officially cleared of all charges. Two years after that, he became the Czech Republic's foreign minister.

Poland may now follow in the early Czech Republic's footsteps. In 2007, it adopted a harsh lustration law, requiring government members at all levels, as well as all school teachers, college professors, journalists,

and heads of private corporations to sign a sworn statement about whether they ever collaborated, to be checked by officials in the Institute for Public Memory. Critics pointed out that the old secret police sometimes named people as informants even when they weren't, meaning that thousands of people would likely be disgraced and thrown out of their jobs without having done anything wrong. As it happens, Poland's Constitutional Court ruled the law unconstitutional, but it is likely to return in a similar form in the next year or two.

Subnational Government

East-Central Europe does not have a tradition of strong independent local self-government. When it was occupied by foreign powers, those powers usually governed from the center. During the first years of independence after World War I, the new governments dreamed up grand developmental schemes that could be implemented only by a strong central state.

The communist system also concentrated power in the center, although in many ways it was actually quite congenial to local interests. For example, since investment decisions were made with political stability rather than profits in mind, the central government distributed resources widely. During the communist period, small cities unlikely to lure investment funds in a private economy had new factories literally thrust on them. And since local authorities were rewarded according to how well they administered their areas, they had a strong interest in forcefully representing local needs to higher authorities. Higher authorities, meanwhile, wanted stability, and so kept doling out funds for wasteful factories and expansive cultural activities. Small towns therefore had clout for two reasons: they were run by party activists trying to make a career for themselves, and the government put money into projects just to keep people employed rather than to make a profit.

The transition to a market economy has changed this rather congenial arrangement. The new central governments needed to reduce expenditures and cut subsidies in an effort to balance their budgets and please foreign lenders and potential investors. The first way they did so was by dramatically cutting aid to local communities. In Poland, for example, soon after the first free local elections in May 1990, the central government shifted to local governments the responsibility for funding day care centers, nurseries, cultural institutions, and local utilities. The problem was that the local communities could not support these services. Many towns did not even have regular revenues, because the large enterprises in their areas were closing down and because tax collecting, where it existed at all, was so irregular. As former Solidarity officials took over local power, they had to make the kinds of tough budget decisions no politician wants to make. In two cities in 1994, former Solidarity activists who had become elected officials were fighting for their political lives because they had to close a few sparsely used day care centers. "I didn't fight against communism in order to do this," they both said. Inevitably, in the 1994 local elections, they were both branded as "antichildren" politicians and were defeated.

Local governments faced similar problems throughout Eastern Europe. In addition, besides fighting with the central government, local officials also began to fight one another. The first free local elections in Hungary in 1990, for example, produced situations in which new parties won a majority in local councils while former Communists from the ruling party won election as mayors. Instead of trying to manage this outcome, quite common in democracies, the local councils in about one hundred small towns and villages made use of loopholes to prevent the mayors from taking office. Such activities came back to haunt the noncommunist politicians in the form of accusations that they were obstructing stable government and contributed to the later electoral triumphs of the ex-communists.

One of the reasons local affairs often became chaotic after 1989 was the absence of political parties at the local level. The forty-five-year monopoly of power by the Communist Party meant that when communist rule collapsed, no organized parties were ready to coordinate power anew. The new parties of the anticommunist opposition were initially based in large urban centers, without much organization elsewhere. Although that has begun to change in recent years, local politics is still poorly developed in this respect.

It would be wrong, however, to concentrate on the negative features of postcommunist local politics. For the other side of the coin is that local areas are now free to govern themselves. The central party apparatus used to appoint mayors and the city council, but now they are elected by the citizens. These democratically elected leaders can make decisions about the town that reflect their own interests rather than the interests of planners in Warsaw or Prague or Budapest. Small cities may no longer have friends in the capital who are always willing to throw money their way, but at least they are free to devise their own solutions to the problems they face. For a great many people, that is the most important feature of all.

The European Dimension

Even before entering the European Union, the preparations for doing so affected East European politics and governance in numerous ways. First of all, their parliaments had to spend most of their time passing the EU's rules and laws. The collection of those rules, called the *acquis communautaire*, runs a gargantuan eighty-thousand pages, and East Europe's parliamentarians (or at least their assistants who actually write the legislation) became familiar with a great many of them.

Right from the start, then, we have here the same theme of *power disparity* that we saw when discussing economic aspects of integration in the previous chapter. Until 2004, Eastern Europe's parliaments were busy passing laws they had had no say in implementing. Even more, because the previous EU had been so lukewarm about admitting the new members, and so many at one time, they monitored the accession process extremely closely—much too closely for East Europeans who resented such intrusive supervision and the implications it carried. This was more than the familiar "democratic deficit" criticized so often in the west: the problem here was not just that citizens played little role in making EU policy but that entire governments were treated as little more than supplicants, forced to pass the bills their overseers asked them to pass.

Scholars trying to characterize the nature of the relationship between the old EU and the Eastern applicants resorted to unflattering analogies: missionary-savage or priest-penitent.[3] In the first version, the old EU plays the role of "civilizer," even colonizer, pushing the witless "natives" to do what's in their best interest, which they do not know themselves. The second version is just a softer variation: the all-knowing "priest," privy to the knowledge of the divine, coaxes the naïve subject in the matters of the truth, administering sanctions when necessary but offering forgiveness when possible. These may be harsh characterizations, but the fact is that until 2004, virtually all the adaptations were made by one side only.

The EU enforced even stricter requirements than it had during previous enlargements and announced that monitoring would continue after full membership as well. Even more, on some issues such as guaranteeing minority rights, the new countries were "asked to meet standards the EU-15 have never set for themselves."[4]

There remains much disagreement on why there was such relatively shabby treatment of the new entrants. Some say it was because the previous fifteen members didn't really want the latest round of enlargement. With the end of the cold war, Europe seemed poised to become an independent force on its own, a new type of political and even moral community. The western members had been working on reconciliation with each other for so long and had made considerable progress. The entry of so many new members, with very different historical experiences, filled with resentments to foreign powers seemed to many in the west as a step backwards. In fact, to protect against the east "dragging them backwards," France and Germany started talking about the creation of a "core Europe," based on the original EU members and specifically on France and Germany. This reluctance about the east came through in the way it related to the east in the period before membership.

So while many in the EU *business* elite supported enlargement—they liked the prospects of using the cheaper labor available in the east, hoping that this would help them lower labor costs in the west as well—the EU political elite was not so supportive, and did not try to make a strong case for enlargement to their citizens. All in all, there was no missing the power disparity in the European enlargement process. As EU officials liked to say, "The Eastern states are joining us, we're not joining them." And this power disparity clearly derived from the economic disparity: the combined gross domestic product of the ten members admitted in 2004 was only about 4 percent that of the old fifteen members, despite adding about 100 million new people. "This is roughly the weight of Mexico's economy as compared to that of the United States," one article put it.[5] So the west could afford to be somewhat ungracious during the accession process, and particularly because it knew it would be much harder to be so once these countries became full members.

Despite this inequality, East European citizens overwhelmingly approved entry into the EU. Each country held a national referendum on membership, and as Table 28.1 shows, people voted strongly in the affirmative. At the time, however, they were not so excited about doing so, as is shown by the relatively low voter turnout, given the historical significance of the outcome. For example, not even 50 percent of Hungarians bothered to vote.

Since 2004, however, things have changed. Popular opinion in the region is much more favorable to

Table 28.1

EU Accession Referendum Results

Country	Date	Yes (percentage)	No (percentage)	Votes Cast (percentage)
Czech Republic	June 13–14, 2003	**77.33**	22.67	55.18
Estonia	September 14, 2003	**66.92**	33.08	64.02
Hungary	April 12, 2003	**83.76**	16.24	45.59
Latvia	September 20, 2003	**67.00**	32.30	72.53
Lithuania	May 10–11, 2003	**91.04**	8.96	63.30
Poland	June 8, 2003	**77.45**	22.55	58.85
Slovakia	May 16–17, 2003	**93.71**	6.29	52.15
Slovenia	March 23, 2003	**89.61**	10.39	60.23

Source: PriceWaterhouseCoopers; www.pwcglobal.com/extweb/service.nsf/docid/E987ADD031C18E1A80256D1E004DF2EA.

the EU, largely because membership has proven far more beneficial than people expected. Cheaper labor costs have brought west European investors into the region, creating new jobs. The elimination of trade barriers has led to a boom in exports: in Poland, exports to the European Union have gone up about 20 percent each year since membership. Perhaps even more important to regular citizens has been the elimination of visa requirements to travel, and, in countries such as the United Kingdom, Ireland, and Sweden, the elimination of work restrictions, as well. Hundreds of thousands of Eastern European citizens, particularly young adults, now take advantage of low-cost airlines to travel and work elsewhere in the EU, and their wages earned abroad have helped economic development at home. In 2004, a majority of Poles believed that membership in the EU would be more harmful than beneficial. By 2007, nearly two-thirds said that membership had been more beneficial.

On political issues, the new Eastern members are also beginning to gain increased respect. The richer western countries now need their support to pursue their grander ambitions. In 2003, French president Jacques Chirac threatened that the region's support for the U.S. invasion of Iraq might delay their EU membership. Nothing like this can happen again. Indeed, Poland in particular has been asserting itself ever since 2004, on several occasions even using its veto power to block EU decisions. The new Eastern European entrants will certainly remain weaker players than their veteran western counterparts, but they will no doubt be accorded more respect in the future than they have in the past.

The Policymaking Process

In recent years there have been two dimensions of policymaking decisions in East-Central Europe: those related to the EU and those focused purely on domestic policy. Policymaking for the EU has been something special. Prior to membership, all applicant countries were required to make extensive changes in their laws in order to conform to EU law. Special national commissions met with special EU commissions to review national laws and see where they needed adaptation. National parliaments then made the changes necessary for the EU, in a largely pro forma fashion. Since membership, Eastern European countries do what all European countries do: when the EU issues a directive, the individual countries devise their own laws to meet that directive, explaining to the EU Commission how exactly the new legislation does so. In other words, the countries of the region are no longer under the kind of micromanagement by the west that they were until 2004.

Aside from issues related to EU accession, most law is made by national parliaments or state agencies on behalf of national constituencies. Who has influence over these decisions? In the United States, a crucial informal policymaking role is performed by lobbies, which undertake lavish campaigns promoting the interests of specific organizations or individuals and aimed exclusively at winning over a few legislators or regulators. Who tries to organize decision makers in East-Central Europe?

For a while, the most influential lobby in East-Central Europe was the "lobby of the West," including the international business and financial community (IMF and the World Bank), western governments, and the EU. After 1989, each postcommunist country thought that its best chance for success was to be invited into the west's institutions or to be chosen for investment by a multinational corporation. For this to happen, the country had to win approval from western banks and governments. Each country sought to convince the west that it, more than its neighbor, was the region's most stable and reform-minded country. Consequently, each tried to introduce whatever policies official western advisory teams recommended. This kind of influence extended not just to parliaments but to quasi-governmental organizations such as national tripartite councils, where representatives of business, labor, and the government discuss industrial relations. As one Bulgarian tripartite commission member put it, negotiations in his country were "not tripartite but quadripartite, with the main partner [being] the IMF."

Over time, domestic lobbies have also formed. At first, this meant representatives of the big state firms that were in danger of going bankrupt. The result was that the very largest firms survived longer than others, so that poverty became worst in rural areas. Then, corporate businesses started forming lobbies, as did some trade unions, although the unions still remain much weaker than they do in West European countries. Of course, groups can influence policy in other ways. On health or education issues, for example, parliamentarians try to satisfy the wishes of doctors or teachers not because these groups have formal lobbies but because they have strong organizations that can mobilize supporters (and voters). Similarly, retirees have benefited from the power of their voting bloc.

Other strong pressures on policymakers can come from nationalist groups in the multiethnic countries and from the church. These groups can sometimes influence policymaking far out of proportion to their numbers. In the early 1990s, nationalists came to dominate policy discussion in Yugoslavia in the same way that the military-industrial complex dominated policy debate in the cold war United States and Soviet Union: by exaggerating the threat from the other side and arguing that it is "better to be safe than sorry." As each side began mobilizing against "the other," the "other" mobilized back, thus "proving" to each that the other really was dangerous, and setting in motion the vicious circle that kept tensions going so long. As for the church, particularly in the strongly Catholic countries of Poland, Slovakia, and Croatia, it exerts power through its direct access every Sunday to millions of citizens, and its control of important media outlets. Such resources have given it disproportionate power. Consequently, despite opinion polls showing strong public support for pro-choice policies in all of these countries, it is the Church that sets the tone, and even shapes the law, on abortion policy.

Recently, a new range of nongovernmental organizations have been trying to influence public policy. Working on behalf of civic, environmental, gender, and human rights issues, such organizations are trying to become more influential as policy-shapers in the future. Still, insofar as business has been the major beneficiary of EU accession, business organizations are likely to retain the dominant influence in domestic legislation in the near future.

Notes

[1] A Polish military official who became a CIA informant describes such subordination in Benjamin Weiser, *A Secret Life* (New York: Public Affairs, 2004).

[2] For an excellent discussion of the Kavan case and its implications, see Lawrence Weschler, "The Velvet Purge," *New Yorker*, October 19, 1992, pp. 66–96.

[3] Andras Sajo, "Corruption, Clientelism, and the Future of the Constitutional State in Eastern Europe," *East European Constitutional Review* 6, no. 1 (Winter 1997), and Wade Jacoby, "Priest and Penitent: The European Union as a Force in the Domestic Politics of Eastern Europe," *East European Constitutional Review* 8, nos. 1/2 (Winter–Spring 1999).

[4] Andrew Moravcsik and Milada Anna Vachudova, "National Interests, State Power, and EU Enlargement," *East European Politics and Society* 17, no. 1 (Winter 2003): 46.

[5] Ibid.

CHAPTER 29

Representation and Participation

In this chapter, we are concerned with how East-Central Europe's systems of political representation work and how its citizens can affect what happens in the political sphere. We focus on parliamentary institutions and on the major parties. Then we look at people's attitudes about nationalism and globalism, the role of the media, and the impact of trade unions, the church, and other social organizations.

The Legislature

In the countries of East-Central Europe, as in most other parliamentary systems, the executive branch tends to shape public policy. That means that the policies discussed by the legislature are almost always those designed by the prime minister and cabinet ministries, not by individual congresspeople (as often happens, for example, in the United States). And since the prime minister and cabinet already have parliamentary support (because such support was necessary for the government to be formed in the first place), their proposals are almost always approved. In a parliamentary system, when one party has a majority, there can be no deadlock: the government passes those laws it wants to pass unless there is intense division within the ruling party. When there is no majority party, however, and only a shaky coalition keeps the government in power, then the government either compromises or is removed.

How do bills get passed? In Poland, bills are first considered by the lower house (*Sejm*), which is the dominant body. If passed, the bill goes to the senate for possible revision. The revisions stand unless the Sejm overrides them by a vote of at least one more than 50 percent of its total members. As in the United States, the president can veto a law passed by parliament, which can then overturn the veto with a two-thirds majority. In countries without a senate or a strong presidency, such as the Czech Republic, a majority vote by parliament is final.

Parliaments can be either exciting arenas for passionate, policy-forming debate or boring chambers where deals worked out in the corridors are merely presented for ratification. We see some of each in East-Central Europe. The Polish parliament has probably had the most lively discussions, for several reasons: the relatively large

number of parties in parliament (today there are six, but from 1991 to 1993 there were eighteen); the inability of any party to win a parliamentary majority (meaning there have always been coalition governments, giving smaller parties influence); frequent conflict between the president and parliament; and a high degree of ideological antipathy between competing groups. The Czech and Hungarian legislatures have been calmer, and have frequently seen deals between the two largest parties to keep public debates out of view. Parliamentary debate did become much more strident in Hungary, however, after street riots in 2006, which the opposition Fidesz party largely supported.

People in East-Central Europe have not been very fond of their parliaments. Within a few years of the fall of communist rule, public opinion gave parliament astonishingly low ratings—less than 10 percent public approval in Poland, Hungary, the Czech Republic, and Slovakia. Such ratings reflected a general dissatisfaction with governments that were imposing painful economic changes. They also reflected the fact that many people who were elected to parliament after 1989 did not know how the institution was supposed to work. East European legislatures in the immediate postcommunist period were top-heavy with writers and historians who could speak plenty about what was wrong with communism but did not know much about parliamentary procedure. For all the ridicule directed at communist-era parliamentarians, who never had to stand for free elections, it turned out that they had a much better idea of how parliamentary rules and procedures worked than did the dissidents who succeeded them. The former communist deputies may never have voted a bill down, but they did negotiate with party circles on the inside, in corridors and in committees, to get specific clauses changed or to have their local interests addressed. Indeed, this was one of the main reasons people began to vote the former communist parties back into power: voters appreciated the political professionalism that was lacking among the newcomers.

Parliament was also becoming much less attractive to potential newcomers. Highly skilled professionals are reluctant to run for office because of the low pay. Although higher than the average wage, the pay is substantially less than one can make, say, working in the new private sphere or for a multinational corporation. Parliamentary deputies do not receive many benefits. Low pay and the absence of conflict-of-interest laws have meant that parliamentarians have tried to supplement their income by being consultants and even members of the board of directors of private corporations. (Naturally, news about these connections leads to even lower popularity ratings for parliament.) By the mid-1990s, as a result of all this, many parties had to go searching for people willing to run on their tickets. One candidate agreed to run on the Hungarian Socialist Party ticket in 1994 only because he was assured that he would lose. Unfortunately, the party did so well that he won. He resigned the next day. Parties often end up running people who are not even party members, but just upstanding citizens likely to have popular support or who at least might be able to earn it. This was standard practice in the communist system, too. Sometimes, parties simply run candidates who pay them for a spot on the ballot.

Overall, then, the quality of parliamentary representation has been poor, and its prestige as a profession has plummeted. In a 2007 Polish poll comparing prestige levels of different professions, "politician" scored the second lowest.

Parliament in the new Eastern Europe has also been very much a male organization. Under the old system, women's share in parliament was about 25 to 40 percent. This relatively large number was due to the communist system of "representation," in which the aim was to replicate in parliament the demographics of society. Workers, farmers, enterprise managers, cultural figures, and women all had their formal positions in parliament, even if real power rested with top party officials, almost all of whom were men. In the first free elections after 1989, the share of women parliamentarians dropped dramatically. Some attained real power, such as Hanna Suchocka, who served as Polish prime minister in 1992–1993. Nevertheless, politics became very much a men's affair in East-Central Europe, and despite some improvements still remains one (see Table 29.1).

Political Parties, the Party System, and Elections

Until 1989, all East-Central Europe had a nearly identical kind of system. The government was run by a Communist Party, and that is all there was to it. The

Table 29.1

Women in National Parliaments, 1991 and 2007

1991 (after first postcommunist election)	Percentage
Bulgaria	8.0
Croatia	4.8
Czech Republic	13.0
Hungary	7.3
Poland	9.6
Romania	3.0
Slovakia	12.7
Slovenia	10.0

2007	Percentage
Bulgaria	22.1
Croatia	21.7
Czech Republic	15.5
Hungary	10.4
Poland	20.4
Romania	11.2
Slovakia	20.0
Slovenia	12.2

Some Comparative 2007 Figures	Percentage
Egypt	2.0
France	12.2
Germany	31.6
Italy	17.3
Russia	9.8
Sweden	47.3
United Kingdom	19.7
United States	16.3
Vietnam	27.3

Sources: For 1991: Nanette Funk and Magda Mueller, eds., *Gender Politics and Post-Communism* (New York: Routledge, 1993). For 2007: website of the Inter-Parliamentary Union: www.ipu.org/wmn-e/classif.htm.

party used different names in different countries (Socialist Workers Party in Hungary, United Workers Party in Poland, Communist Party in Czechoslovakia, and League of Communists in Yugoslavia). In some countries, such as Poland and East Germany, other parties were formally permitted to exist, provided they did not oppose the government (that is, provided they did not act like real parties). But these minor differences did little to mask the essential similarity of a single party governing the state and taking responsibility for all policy.

Looking only at the Central European countries of Poland, Hungary, and the Czech Republic, we can divide postcommunist party development into two stages. In the first stage, lasting from 1990 to 1993, parties and politics were dominated by anticommunism. Liberal and conservative parties each claimed to be the most anticommunist, and, except in the Czech Republic, even the ex-communist parties took great pains to prove their reformed status. In the second stage, since 1994, anticommunism was no longer sufficient to attract votes, as Eastern Europeans began reacting to the realities of new capitalism rather than the memory of old communism. Ideological divides remain strong, but politics has become normal in the sense that parties now win or lose because of their record and their campaign strategies, and not just their stated beliefs.

In this section, we examine the main parties and recent election results in the three key Central European countries.

Hungary

Hungary entered 1989 with two strong anticommunist parties that seemed able to divide all the noncommunist vote between them: the Alliance of Free Democrats (AFD) and the Hungarian Democratic Forum (HDF). The AFD was a procapitalist liberal party, formed and led by the liberal intellectuals who had led the country's democratic opposition since the 1970s. The HDF styled itself as a nationalist and populist movement, slightly suspicious of free-market capitalism, and opposing communism less on the grounds that it was hostile to democracy than that it was contrary to the national and religious identities of Hungary. The 1990 elections made HDP the governing party and AFD the main opposition.

A decade later, both parties had become marginalized. The HDF compromised itself by its four years in power, characterized by scandals, economic decline, and governmental incompetence. The AFD, meanwhile, was soon eclipsed by the Hungarian Socialist Party (HSP), the reformed party of the former communists.

Whereas both AFD and HSP supported democracy and a market economy, the Socialists exhibited more social concern than the liberals did and seemed to be more competent as legislators. (Keep in mind that in Europe, unlike the United States, liberalism implies individualism and promarket beliefs, not support for state intervention or strong welfare provisions.) The only surprise in the 1994 elections was the extent of the HSP victory. After winning 8.5 percent of the vote in 1990, it received an astonishing 54.1 percent in 1994. The AFD moved from being the most anticommunist party in 1990 to being the coalition partner with the former communists in 1994. That situation still persists today (see Table 29.2).

After the conservative HDF had become marginalized by the middle of the 1990s, opposition to the liberal-socialist alliance came to be led by Fidesz. This party began as the Alliance of Young Democrats, a youth group to the AFD, but broke from them soon after. While other parties compromised themselves in the early 1990s by political infighting and co-responsibility for a declining economy, Fidesz attracted support with shrewd political analysis, innovative policy proposals, and one of the country's best public speakers in party leader Viktor Orban. When the AFD entered a coalition government with the Socialists and the HDF saw its support evaporate, the right side of the political spectrum suddenly had a huge hole, and Fidesz has been able to fill it. It won a stunning victory in 1998, in alliance with the conservative agrarian Smallholders Party, and soon changed its name to Hungarian Civic Union. But its increasingly belligerent style of politics, along with a late-1990s economic recession, alienated many voters and pushed the pendulum back to the Socialists. In 2002 and again in 2006, the HSP-AFD coalition regained power, while Fidesz-Hungarian Civic Union has emerged as an even more radical right-wing party.

Poland

Polish politics has been more complicated, with parties forming, folding, winning, losing, and transforming themselves regularly. The only party to win seats in every parliament from 1989 to 2007 is the Democratic Left Alliance (DLA), the successor to the former Communist party. Like Hungary's HSP, the DLA grew thanks

Table 29.2

Elections in Hungary

Executive
President: László Sólyom (2005)
Prime Minister: Ferenc Gyurcsány (2004)
The president is elected to a five-year term by the parliament and becomes nonpartisan after the election.

Parliament
The National Assembly has 386 members elected for a four-year term: 176 members in single-seat constituencies, 152 by proportional representation in multiseat constituencies, and 58 members elected to realize proportional representation. A party must win at least 5% of the national vote to form a parliamentary faction.

National Assembly Elections, April 2006

Party	Ideology	Percentage of Vote	Seats	Change from Last Election (Seats)
Hungarian Socialist Party	Social Democratic	43.2	186	+8
Alliance of Free Democrats	Liberal	6.5	18	−2
Fidesz-Hungarian Civic Union	Conservative	42.0	164	—
Hungarian Democratic Forum	Conservative-Christian	5.0	11	−13
Others		2.3	7	+7
Total		**100.0**	**386**	

Source: www.electionworld.org calculations, available at en.wikipedia.org/wiki/Politics_of_Hungary.

to its professionalism, its embrace of the new political and economic system, the incessant quarreling of its opponents, and its mixture of probusiness policies and advocacy on behalf of the poor. It became a kind of catch-all party, winning the votes of different social groups. It first became the governing party (as the leader of a coalition) in 1993, having won 20 percent of the vote. It received 27 percent of the vote in 1997, but served as the opposition to a conservative government. By 2001 it seemed to have become the dominant party, winning over 40 percent of the vote. Then a series of scandals nearly annihilated it. Its electoral support dropped to 11 percent in 2005.

If the long-time prominence and surviving power of the former Communist party has been one big political surprise of Poland's new democratic system, the other has been the instability and fragmentation of the old anticommunist opposition, which had been organized around the Solidarity trade union movement. In the 1980s, Solidarity virtually "owned" Polish hearts and minds. In the first election of 1989—which came

even before the fall of the Berlin Wall in Germany—Solidarity won 99.9 percent of the seats it contested! On the other hand, its very strength constituted its greatest weakness: there were too many different political tendencies inside Solidarity at the time, and once they no longer needed to unite against the old ruling party, they began to split among themselves. Moreover, until 1993 there was a proporational representation system, but no threshold for gaining parliamentary seats, which led to a plethora of political parties. Sixty-seven parties ran for parliament in 1991, and eighteen won at least one seat. After 1993 a 5 percent threshold was introduced, which has reduced the number of parties regularly in parliament to five or six. It has taken a long while for the dust to settle; indeed, it was only after the 2005 election that perhaps it has.

At first, Solidarity split up electorally along liberal and conservative lines—with "liberal" meaning pro-European, pro-globalization, and pro-human rights, and "conservative" meaning more nationalistic, isolationist, and religious. The liberal tendency initially had the upper hand, since most of Solidarity's key figures were associated with it. The problem, however, was that the party took its trade union, working class base for granted. Because the liberals were above all interested in conforming to Western ways, they emphasized the building of a capitalist economy and maintained that workers would have to be the ones to sacrifice the most to bring it about. Workers, of course, knew they had to sacrifice, but they didn't want to be the only ones to do so; after all, it was thanks to them that the old regime had been toppled. But liberals ignored their objections, downplayed their fears, and—even worse for a political party seeking votes—acted as if workers had no alternative. When the economy plummeted in the first years after 1989, on the liberals' watch, and the industrial economy that had kept so much of the country employed disappeared, workers began seeking other parties.

Some went to the former Communists in the DLA, thus reviving their fortunes. But because many Solidarity supporters would not vote for their former enemies, new conservative parties appeared to vie for their votes—so many parties, in fact, that they ended up splitting the Solidarity vote, allowing the DLA to win the 1993 elections. That stunner brought the conservative parties together, under the aegis of the Solidarity trade union, which had become quite conservative itself by this time. (Keep in mind that "conservative" here means nationalistic and religious, not necessarily probusiness; indeed, since these conservatives were opposing liberals who supported capitalism, they spoke often against business and in favor of workers, unlike conservatives in the United States.) The ensuing Solidarity Electoral Action alliance won power in 1997, but its administration proved to be a great failure. It introduced painful and largely incompetent reforms in health, social security, and local government; tolerated widespread corruption; and oversaw the onset of a new economic downturn, with unemployment levels soaring into the high teens, much higher than in the immediate postcommunist depression of 1990.

The 2001 elections brought the return of the DLA to power, but during this time the old Solidarity opposition recreated itself into two different parties, which at the present time seem to be durable. The first is the Law and Justice Party, led by the twin brothers Jarosław and Lech Kaczyński, which brings together

the law-and-order and religious conservatives who used to belong to Solidarity. The other is the Civic Platform, bringing together the free-market liberals and the less religious conservatives.

These two parties decisively won the 2005 parliamentary elections, and in the presidential elections held the same year, Lech Kaczyński of Law and Justice beat out Donald Tusk of Civic Platform. Many expected the two to form a coalition, but Law and Justice had other ideas. Noting that there had been two extremist right-wing parties in parliament since 2001—the Self-Defense party, led by the truculent farmer Andrzej Lepper (a kind of cross between Robin Hood and Mussolini) and the League of Polish Families, a Catholic fundamentalist, xenophobic and even anti-Semitic party—Law and Justice decided to reach out and form a coalition with them. The coalition of Law and Justice, Self-Defense, and League of Polish Families was formed in 2006, and quickly became the most extreme right-wing government not just in East Europe but in all the European Union, with an authoritarian style, dismissive approach to the free press, and a religious fundamentalism manifested in an unusually belligerent campaign against gay rights.

Late News. Just as this book was going to press, the coalition government broke up and, in October 2007, new elections were held. Civic Platform emerged as the big winner, with just over 41 percent of the vote, with Law and Justice coming in second with 32 percent (see Table 29.3). The DLA, running in an alliance with left-leaning liberals from the former Solidarity movement and calling themselves "The Left and the Democrats," gained 13 percent for a third-place finish, and the Polish People's Party, chiefly representing farmers, came in with a surprisingly strong 9 percent of the vote for a fourth-place finish. The two small extremist parties of the right each got less than 2 percent of the vote, not enough to enter parliament, as most of their previous supporters voted for Law and Justice instead. Civic Platform agreed to form a coalition government with the Polish People's Party, and the result is likely to be a somewhat calmer political scene than during Law and Justice's reign. In the end, Law and Justice was seen as too extreme, and its leader, Jaroslaw Kaczyński, as too hot-headed. Voters objected to his incessant habit of picking fights, of

Table 29.3

Elections in Poland

Executive
President: Lech Kaczyński (2005)
Prime Minister: Donald Tusk (2007)
The president is elected to a five-year term in general elections.

Parliament
Parliament has two chambers. The Sejm (lower house) has 460 members elected for a four-year term by proportional representation in multiseat constituencies with a 5 percent threshold (8 percent for coalitions; requirement waived for national minorities). The Senate has 100 members elected for a four-year term in 40 multiseat constituencies.

Summary of the National Assembly (Sejm and Senat) Elections, October 2007

Party	Ideology	Percentage of Vote	Seats in Sejm	Change from Last Election (Seats)	Seats in Senate
Civic Platform	Centrist	41.5	209	+76	60
Law and Justice	Conservative	32.1	166	+11	39
Left and Democrats (formerly Democratic Left Alliance)	Liberal/Social Democratic	13.1	53	−2	—
Polish People's Party	Agrarian	8.9	31	+6	—
Self-Defense of the Republic of Poland	Agrarian conservative	1.5	—	−56	—
League of Polish Families	Christian nationalist	1.3	—	−34	—
Polish Labor Party	Socialist populist	1.0	—	—	—
Women's Party	Gender-based	0.3	—	—	—
German Minority	Minority party	0.2	1	−1	—
Independents	n/a	n/a	n/a	n/a	1
Total*			**460**		**100**

*Turnout = 53.8 percent

Note: Registered voters were 30,615,471. Votes counted were 16,477,734. Valid votes were 16,142,202; invalid votes were 335,532.

Source: www.electionworld.org calculations, available at en.wikipedia.org/wiki/Polish_parliamentary_election,_2007.

calling critics enemies, and of seeing the world in stark terms of good vs. bad, friend vs. foe. Poland's relations with the European Union had deteriorated under Law and Justice, with Prime Minister Kaczyński being particularly anti-German, and Polish citizens who were benefiting from the EU rejected this as well. The new government, with Donald Tusk as prime minister, is likely to work more harmoniously with the EU, though there will still be conflicts. Relations with the United States will remain strong, although Poland may well be withdrawing its troops from Iraq.

In the new parliament, Law and Justice will be the right-wing opposition and the Left and the Democrats the left opposition. While Jaroslaw Kaczyński will maintain control of the former, the leadership of the latter is unclear. The Left and the Democrats did better than many had expected, but it will need new leadership and new ideas before it can become a dominant force again.

4

4550 CHAPTER 29 Representation and Participation

Czech Republic

Politics in the Czech Republic, as in Hungary, is dominated by relatively clear right- and left-leaning parties, known respectively as the Civic Democratic Party (CDP) and the Czech Social Democratic Party (CSDP). The CDP traces its roots to the 1989 Velvet Revolution (although many liberal intellectuals broke away as the party turned increasingly conservative), while the CSDP is a party revived from the era before World War II. Unlike elsewhere in the region, in other words, the main left party is not the old Communist party, chiefly because that party never sought to convert itself into a mainstream organization. The CDP governed in the early 1990s with a program that combined tough-talking neoliberal rhetoric with a softer social democratic practice. It was a winning combination, until a series of corruption scandals and poor economic results led to its decline, and the rise of the CSDP. The Social Democrats squeaked out an electoral victory in 1998, although the closeness of the race and the perceived need to mollify the West nevertheless led the Social Democrats to offer a portion of power to Civic Forum. Voters, however, did not like the power-sharing arrangement, which seemed too close to the monolithic governments of the past. In 2002, the CSPD won a larger victory and governed on its own. Then in 2006, the Civic Democrats regained a slight edge over the Social Democrats. The two parties have been running almost completely neck-and-neck for the past decade (see Table 29.4).

Thus, nearly twenty years after the collapse of the old regime communist system, new party systems have emerged everywhere in East-Central Europe. For the most part, we see the emergence of two dominant parties representing right and left, with "right," as elsewhere in

Table 29.4

Elections in the Czech Republic

Executive
President: Václay Klaus (2003)
Prime Minister: Mirek Topolanek (2006)
The president is elected to a five-year term by the parliament.

Parliament
The Parliament of the Czech Republic has two chambers. The Chamber of Representatives has 200 members, elected for a four-year term by proportional representation with a 5 percent barrier. The Senate has 81 members, elected for a six-year term in single-seat constituencies, in which one-third is renewed every two years.

Chamber of Deputies Elections, June 2006

Party	Ideology	Percentage of Vote	Seats	Change from Last Election (Seats)
Civic Democratic Party	Conservative	35.4	81	+23
Czech Social Democratic Party	Social Democratic	32.3	74	+4
Communist Party of Bohemia and Moravia	Communist	12.8	26	−15
Christian Democratic Union–Czechoslovak People's Party	Christian Democratic	7.2	13	−9
Green Party	Green	6.3	6	+6
Total*			**200**	

*Turnout = 64.5%

Source: www.electionworld.org calculations, available at en.wikipedia.org/wiki/Czech_elections.

Europe, tending to mean pronationalist more than promarket, and "left" referring to market economy with a social conscience.

Political Culture, Citizenship, and Identity

Except for a short period after coming to power in 1945, the region's communist parties did not try to totally replace people's preexisting loyalties. Especially in the last years before 1989, they sought to use people's allegiances to religion, nationality, class, ethnicity, and political ideology for their own purposes. Since 1989, old identities have combined with new ones to create fascinating and unusual concoctions with great implications for the political future.

Social Class

Because of the formally Marxist ideologies of the past, the countries of East Europe have an unusual relationship to class as an identity. In the early days of the old system, class was an almost obligatory identity. Citizens got credits (or demerits) depending on their class background, and anyone who advanced up the social hierarchy had to claim loyalty to the working class, in whose interests the system was said to be run. Over time, a new elite managed to reproduce itself and get its children into good positions, but it did not quite develop a class consciousness of its own. Everything it did was still supposedly done for the working class. The result was that most citizens were unable to think of themselves in terms of class. Since everyone was supposed to be a worker, no explicit class distinctions could arise, despite obvious social and economic inequalities.

This legacy has a strong impact on the postcommunist period. Although the new era is very much about the creation of a class society—building a capitalist system requires creating a capitalist class, as well as a working class that sees itself as subordinate—class has remained an uncertain identity in the new era. After 1989, even labor did not embrace a working-class identity (the very term "working class" was unpopular, because of its association with the old regime) but saw itself instead as trying to become middle class. The changing economy had an impact here,

too. Just as closing down the old industrial factories in favor of small-scale service and white-collar jobs (everything from security guard to computer programmer) led to the erosion of class identities in the West, it has lately been doing the same in the East. This decline of class identity led to minimal labor unrest in the immediate postcommunist period, despite the steep economic decline. But the situation has begun to change in the last decade, as workers have realized that economic inequalities have become more durable, and that the road to the middle class is more complicated than they had thought.

Citizenship and National Identity

Because of their long experience with foreign domination, East Europeans are extremely attached to their national identities. The communist parties themselves recognized this and did their best to use national themes to their own advantage. Postcommunist governments have behaved similarly, emphasizing their links with the precommunist past, sometimes even acting as if the communist period had never existed. A strong national identity can be conducive to political freedom, but not always. In Poland, for example, the Kaczyński government often implied that its opponents are not "real Poles." In the former Yugoslavia, strong national identities led to the country's breakup and to a ruthless war. As the Czech writer Milan Kundera has noted, the people of East-Central Europe live with the ever-present awareness that statehood has been taken away before and can be taken away again. This awareness leads today's rulers, teachers, and writers to emphasize nationalist themes and national triumphs, even at the cost of historical accuracy. This attitude can lead to abuses, as in the way Serbian historians reinvented the past in the 1980s, turning Croatians into devils and Bosnians into Serbs. (The historians argued that Croatia had always taken advantage of Serbia and that Bosnians were really just Serbs who believed in Islam.) Yet the emphasis on nationalist history is also a necessary process of self-recovery after long years of subordination to the Soviet Union. And the globalization of culture that makes MTV or CNBC available in living rooms throughout Eastern Europe also makes national awareness seem necessary to guard against the "over-Westernization" of young people.

The other strong tendency in the region today is globalization, starting with the embrace of the West. East European countries initially focused their post-communist foreign policies on the effort to enter NATO and the European Union. When these efforts succeeded, young people began increasingly to travel to other countries, learn new languages, break free of local national biases, and become ever more cosmopolitan. This tendency to adopt a more international identity sometimes conflicts with the effort to revive the old national identity.

Until recently, virtually the only people seeking to emigrate to Eastern Europe were ethnic nationals who had lived elsewhere, such as Poles in the Soviet Union or Hungarians in Romania. These immigrants were reintegrated without much difficulty. Recently, however, the immigration situation has become more complicated. First, Eastern Europe is increasingly a place for black market labor for citizens of the former Soviet Union, where wages are much lower. Second, the region's political freedom, relative prosperity, and EU membership have made it an attractive European entry point for refugees from the Middle East, Africa, and Asia seeking political asylum.

What are the implications of all this? On the one hand, the situation leads to tensions. Now that they are finally able to partake in the goodies of being in the West, many in Eastern Europe don't want to share. Others, however, recognize that the new refugees are doing the same thing they themselves did not long ago. Like Ukrainians, they too went west and did black market labor, accepting low wages because different price structures made the money worth more back home. Like Africans looking for asylum, they too sought political refuge in the west on the grounds of being persecuted by the communist system, even when that was not technically true. So do East Europeans try to stop immigration now just because the immigrants are now coming to them, or because the immigrants are not all white? Or do they embrace immigration on the grounds of universal human rights? This is the debate today. Those who are more prosperous tend to like illegal immigrant laborers, since they can hire help cheap. Those who are poorer often see them as competitors for jobs. As for giving asylum to refugees, many locals support the idea in the abstract. But tensions arise because refugee centers are usually located in poor communities. This leads to claims by locals that "foreigners" are getting government handouts, "and what about us?" This becomes the grounds on which right-wing parties win support.

But there is a third category of immigrant that is changing the picture completely: entrepreneurs from Vietnam and China. Eastern Europe's growth opportunities have made it a desirable place to do business. There are now thousands of traders who sell the produce of a booming Asia in the open-air markets of Eastern Europe. Inevitably, many end up staying, leading to the emergence of Vietnamese and Chinese minority communities that are likely to become bigger in the future. This sometimes creates tensions. But it also promotes mutual understanding. Recently the Polish theater group "*Gardzienice*" performed in New York, and one of the stars was a Vietnamese teenager who had grown up in Warsaw. These developments are slowly turning the region into the kind of multiethnic community that globalization is promoting everywhere.

Religion and Politics

During the Communist era, religious affiliation was discouraged but by no means forbidden. The first years of communist rule saw the greatest pressure against organized religion, including the arrest of clergy and the closing down of houses of worship. By the 1960s, however, the authorities' chief concern was to keep religion out of public life. Schools taught that religion was an unnecessary and reactionary social construct—a myth by which people helped make sense of a prescientific world. People could and did have their own private religious values, transmitted chiefly by family tradition, but those who wanted to enter the political or economic elite had to keep such beliefs to themselves.

Of course, this general truth disguises various national particularities. Albania tried to suppress religion outright, closing down all churches and mosques. Poland, by the 1980s, had reached the other extreme, with the martial law government conciliating the Catholic Church at every opportunity in an effort to co-opt the church as a substitute for Solidarity. Most of the region, however, stood somewhere in the middle, although favoring tolerance more than proscription.

Religion became more important in the region in the 1980s. The inability to continue the growth rates of earlier times and the increasing self-organization of citizens committed to the expansion of democratic rights were signs of the economic and political crisis of communism, but they also sparked a crisis of identity. Religious feelings grew in this period as a way of holding onto something solid in a world of continuing change. (Only in the highly secular Czech Republic did religion fail to play an important role in recent political and social transformations.)

Because communism has always been officially antireligious, however, religious feelings in the Communist era often reflected a political attitude more than a religious one. As the Polish writer Witold Gombrowicz put it in 1953, "God has become the pistol with which we would like to shoot Marx."[1] People liked what the church stood for, as an institution opposed to communism, but they had little intention of living their lives according to church instructions. This attitude was most apparent in Poland. The overwhelming majority of Poles considered themselves believers in the 1980s. Yet few Poles lived by church precepts regarding contraception, extramarital sex, divorce, or abortion. (Contrary to the reputation of Catholics in each country, it is far more common to find Catholic families with eight or ten children in the United States than in Poland.) In public opinion polls, whereas Polish society gave better than 90 percent support to the Catholic Church in the 1980s, that number had dropped almost in half by the mid-1990s. Findings like these suggest that religious identities are often more an expression of political values than of religious convictions.[2]

Religion has played the greatest political role in the historically Catholic countries of Poland, Slovakia, and Croatia. In each of these countries, Catholicism is intimately associated with national independence. In Poland, the church kept Polish national traditions alive during the long years when Poland was under foreign rule (1795–1918). State and church were also intimately connected in Croatia and Slovakia during brief periods of World War II when each country attained formal independence under the tutelage of the Third Reich. When people were increasingly dissatisfied with communism, therefore, and identified communism as something alien, something Russian, their longing for a return to national traditions translated into a new attachment to Catholicism. Religious affiliation has expanded elsewhere in the region too—especially Orthodoxy in

Serbia and Bulgaria (as well as Ukraine and Russia) and Islam in Bosnia—as people seek new identities in the postcommunist era.

Many observers expected the collapse of communism to mean the rise of religious fundamentalism throughout the region. In fact, this reaction has not occurred. It is true that people needed something else to believe in once communism was officially discredited. But religion and nationalism were not the only contenders for people's hearts and minds. The market was, too. One of the most striking aspects of East-Central Europe in the immediate aftermath of the fall of communism was people's almost naïve faith that the new capitalist system would solve all the problems of the past. People looked to capitalism to do the kinds of things that communism promised but could not achieve, such as making everyone equally wealthy. One of the reasons people did not join together politically on the basis of a religious identity is that they believed the market would solve their problems. Only in the mid-1990s did faith in the market begin to erode. Populations then began voting for left-wing parties. The fact that people voted for the left in Poland and Hungary, rather than for the religious parties that were already available, demonstrates that identity demands based on religion were not yet widespread. But they could still become so in the future. If existing parties prove unable to resolve economic problems and reduce inequalities, fundamentalist groups might succeed in mobilizing people on the basis of religious demands. And when that happens, political democracy is usually the loser. Since identity demands cannot usually be resolved by distributional means, they must be resolved by political means—for example, by establishing an official church and enforcing "religious values" in public life. By compromising on the protection of minority rights, however, such a solution compromises the principles of liberal democracy, too.

Race and Ethnicity

The famed ethnic heterogeneity of Eastern European states disappeared in the most catastrophic of circumstances. After the Nazi genocide of the Jews, the forced migrations of Poles, Ukrainians, and Germans in 1945, and the ethnic cleansing in the former Yugoslavia in the 1990s, it is no surprise that few ethnic minorities are left. Poland, the most ethnically diverse country before World War II, is the most homogeneous today, with some 98 percent of the population consisting of ethnic Poles. In the Czech Republic, 95 percent are Czechs; in Hungary, 90 percent are Hungarians; in Slovakia, 86 percent are Slovaks. The only significant minorities left in the region are Hungarians in Romania and Serbia, Turks in Bulgaria, and Roma everywhere, particularly in Hungary, Slovakia, and Romania, where they make up from 5 to 10 percent of the population of each of those countries. As for racial difference, there is little sense of that anywhere in the region, although some local populations do consider the Roma, or gypsies, to be of a different race. Jews of course used to be seen in racial terms, but not anymore. Hungary is the only country in the region with much of a Jewish presence, almost entirely in Budapest, but they are almost completely assimilated and do not appear, either to themselves or to others, as a minority.

This high degree of homogeneity, combined with the ban on political protest, meant that there was little organizing on the basis of national identity during the communist era. In that period, it was almost always the ruling parties that played the nationalist card. Romania was the master here, using nationalism to buttress its own highly repressive rule. Through several highly publicized conflicts with the Soviet Union, the elite presented itself as the promoter of the Romanian nation, even as it fiercely repressed its own citizens. The Polish communist party also claimed to be guardians of Polish national identity. At various times of political crisis— 1956, 1968, and 1981—the ruling party claimed that its own rule was essential to preserving Polish independence and that the political opposition was putting national sovereignty in question.

Nationalism emerged strongly throughout the region immediately after 1989, mostly in accordance with Mark Twain's old adage about patriotism being the last refuge of scoundrels and fools. It was deployed by elites as a way to protect their own dominance by diverting the blame for political and economic crisis onto someone else. As noted above, however, the region's own incorporation into the global economy is slowly creating a more multiethnic society. The immediate result of these trends is likely to be more, not less, targeting of minorities by ambitious political elites. But over time these developments will probably undercut the appeal of such dividers, and lead, hopefully, to more inclusive societies.

Gender

Gender identities, like class identities, have not come easily to East-Central Europe. It is not that the former communist systems were really nondiscriminatory, as they claimed to be. Although women did have more professional opportunities than in the West (at least until the West began to catch up in the 1970s), they faced the same double burden of job and housework, which was made more difficult by the need to stand in long lines to buy basic goods. Nevertheless, women did not feel subordinate to men. Rather, both men and women felt subordinate to the system. This was especially true in the last decades of communist rule, when opposition movements were already growing. In the struggle against the overarching system, even politicized women did not wish to undercut that unity by talking about gender issues. For example, although women played a key part in the underground Solidarity movement of the 1980s, they never publicized it. It took a fascinating recent book by the American author Shana Penn to shed light on women's crucial role in the movement; even in Poland, it was the translation of that book into Polish that brought this role to public attention.[3]

But just as labor identities begin to grow in the postcommunist era, so too do gender identities. Gender disparities are quite real in terms of educational possibilities, employment rates, and income—all important issues for would-be professional women trying to move up the hierarchy. By the mid-1990s, such conditions contributed to the emergence of a feminist movement in the region. In new journals and e-mail networks, women have begun to mobilize against these conditions. There have been protests over abortion restrictions, fights for better birthing conditions in hospitals, demands for gender studies programs in universities, and efforts to stigmatize as well as criminalize domestic violence. Political parties on the Left have begun to emphasize gender issues to win women's votes. They have a great deal of success when they speak about equal rights in the workplace, which most people support. They speak less, and have less success, however, with reproductive rights, as these are more contentious issues for the populations at large.

As in the West, gender identities have also been encouraged by business. Many daily newspapers have created special weekly women's sections, chiefly to sell advertising. But since these sections also frequently publish feminist pieces, they inevitably help generate a gender identity that can challenge the "masculinism" that has pervaded the region since 1989.

Interests, Social Movements, and Protest

Given the way that the populations of East-Central Europe united so spectacularly in 1989, it was only natural to expect that the new democracies would be marked by a high level of popular participation. The images of the people celebrating the toppling of the Berlin Wall, or congregating in Prague's central square for the declaration of Vaclav Havel as the new president, suggested that postcommunism would be an era of unprecedented popular involvement in politics, as citizens would defend their interests in the new system with the same verve and enthusiasm as they had in 1989.

Things have not worked out that way. Instead of being filled with well-organized social groups fighting for the interests of their members, postcommunist public life has been surprisingly quiescent. Even in the first years when conditions were so tough, few rallies and demonstrations challenged government policies, and hardly any politically motivated strikes broke out. There was not even much lobbying activity by the kinds of nongovernmental organizations that shape so much policy in the West, such as environmental groups, business associations, trade unions, and women's organizations. Citizens just didn't seem to want to be involved, as Marc Howard discovered in his research.[4] As for the activists of 1989, they either went into government themselves, or sat back and gave the new governments the benefit of the doubt, allowing them to undertake the difficult work of transformation.

Let's look at the example of labor. Because of its symbolic prominence in the past, as well as the depth of the postcommunist economic depression, labor was widely expected to be a very active, organized force after 1989. Its failure to do so had much to do with ideology: having rejected socialist ideology because of the experience of communism, workers embraced the ideology of their enemy's enemy and entered the new era as believers in a market economy. Workers in the West, of course, had succeeded not because they let the market function unimpeded, but because they organized trade unions and political parties and thus secured benefits for themselves. East European labor, however, tended to see only the end result. If this is capitalism, they said, we'll take it. And since, as they were told, building capitalism required time, sacrifice, and a strong managerial class, workers after 1989 accepted the decline in living standards as well as the declining power of unions at the workplace.

Since trade unions were disinclined to defend workers' interests, membership plummeted. And with workers still believing in the beneficence of private ownership, the unions that remained were almost all in the old state sector, not the new private one. (This also resulted from the fact that private companies regularly, albeit illegally, fired workers who tried to organize unions.) The situation began to change in the early 2000s. The key factor was time. People began to experience life under "actually-existing capitalism." (East European dissidents used to speak of "actually existing socialism" to underline the point that the communist system they faced was not the "good" kind of communism that was discussed by many of its proponents, and this similar phrase is appropriate today as a way of making clear that real capitalism has little in common with the idealistic descriptions of *its* ideologues.) Gradually, workers learned the lesson Western labor movements had learned much earlier: for wages and working conditions to get better, workers must organize to make them better. Since the turn of the new century, unions have begun organizing again, even in new private firms. Increasingly, they are receiving support from unions abroad, too. The AFL-CIO and Change to Win, the two main union federations in the United States, have been helping train union organizers in several Eastern European countries, while German unions have promoted unionism in Eastern Europe's new heavy manufacturing sector. There is still a long way to go, and union density rates are still far lower than they were in 1989. Nevertheless, this is a new and potentially important development in the building of a democratic civil society in the former communist countries.[5]

Besides labor issues, the region has lately seen increased political mobilization around gender, religious, and environmental issues. Particularly in the Catholic countries, women, as noted, have staged rallies in defense of abortion rights and against domestic violence. They have begun publishing journals and establishing online networks where they can promote their ideas.[6] As for environmental issues, Green parties have arisen everywhere in the region—and in the Czech Republic, in 2006, they finally won seats in parliament. On the whole, the postcommunist world has seen far less protest than many had anticipated.[7] But this is likely to change in the years ahead, as it has for labor, leading to the further democratization of East-Central European societies.

Notes

[1] Witold Gombrowicz, *Diary: Volume One*, translated by Lillian Vallee (Evanston, Ill.: Northwestern University Press, 1988), p. 27.

[2] For an account of the Polish Catholic Church and its role in politics, see Adam Michnik, *The Church and the Left* (Chicago: University of Chicago Press, 1993); and Maryjane Osa, "Resistance, Persistence and Change: The Transformation of the Catholic Church in Poland," *East European Politics and Societies* 3, no. 2 (Spring 1989): 268–299.

[3] Shana Penn, *Solidarity's Secret: The Women Who Defeated Communism in Poland* (Ann Arbor: University of Michigan Press, 2005).

[4] Marc Morje Howard, *The Weakness of Civil Society in Post-Communist Europe* (Ann Arbor: Cambridge University Press, 2002).

[5] On the transformation of labor in postcommunist society, see David Ost, *The Defeat of Solidarity* (Ithaca: Cornell University Press, 2005); and Stephen Crowley and David Ost, eds., *Workers After Workers' States* (Lanham, Md.: Rowman & Littlefield, 2001).

[6] See, for example, the Network of East-West Women, www .neww.org.

[7] For one account explaining why, see Bela Greskovits, *The Political Economy of Protest and Patience* (Budapest: Central European University Press, 1998).

CHAPTER 30

East-Central European Politics in Transition

This final chapter on East-Central Europe looks more closely at the experiences of the former Yugoslavia—from its violent breakup to its emerging renewal. The story is a mixture of tragedy and perfidy, with elements of democratic durability that hold out hope for the future. A snapshot of Bosnia in 1993 shows signs of all three elements.

In the summer and fall of 1993, the embattled republic of Bosnia and its heroic resistance in the capital, Sarajevo, found itself confronted on all sides by forces calling on it to surrender. Serbia, Croatia, and the European Union all urged Bosnia to sign a treaty dividing the republic into three separate ethnoreligious states—one for Orthodox Serbs, one for Catholic Croats, and one for Muslim Bosnians. The war had already been raging when Bosnia voted for independence from Yugoslavia in 1992. Essentially Bosnia had to vote this way, since Croatia and Slovenia had already left the Yugoslav federation, meaning that Serbia would dominate what was left. Poorer Serbs from the Bosnian countryside, frightened by Serbian nationalists into thinking they would be persecuted by Islamic fundamentalism, declared war against the government in Sarajevo, but their actual fighting was directed not against any Bosnian army but against individual Bosnian Muslims who had been their neighbors for years. Led by paramilitary forces, ethnic Serbs drove hundreds of thousands of Muslims from their homes, destroyed mosques and other signs of Muslim culture, and raped Muslim women as a way of terrorizing the community so that it would vacate the land forever. Then the Serbs proclaimed an independent republic of Serbs in Bosnia. Using a similar ruse about the supposed rise of anti-Christian Muslim fanatics, Croatia joined in, urging ethnic Croats to carve out a Croatian Bosnia in the western part of the country. By 1993, archenemies Serbia and Croatia had begun to work together, for the first time since the breakup of Yugoslavia, to expel Muslims and divide Bosnia between the two of them.

There was, however, one problem: the Bosnian side was not simply the Muslim side. While Serbia and Croatia sought to root out all Muslim culture and people from the areas they controlled, the leadership of Bosnia did not respond in kind. The Bosnian president was a Muslim, but the head of the Bosnian parliament was a Serb. Many of the leading officers in the Bosnian army were Croats and Serbs. In Sarajevo, Serbs, Croats, and Muslims saw themselves first as citizens of Bosnia. Bosnia was keeping alive the hope of a multiethnic republic in which different nationalities could live together, just as they had been doing for hundreds of years.[1] By asking Bosnians to surrender, the world was asking them to betray the multiethnic principles that had been at the heart of Bosnia—the same multiethnic principles to which the world so often pays homage.

For as long as they could, the Bosnians held firm. But in that fall of 1993, with their armies unable to hold out and the world demanding surrender, they finally accepted, grudgingly, the principle of division. Even then, many continued to hope the tide might turn—that the war would shift in Bosnia's favor, that the West would finally intervene on behalf of the multiethnic principles it regularly espouses. In the summer of 1995, the tide did turn. It did so, alas, in a way that only made things worse. First, Serbs took over and murdered almost all the male inhabitants of the Eastern Bosnian city of Srebrenica, despite the fact that the United Nations was supposed to be protecting them. Then the Croatian army expelled hundreds of thousands of Serbs from areas around western Bosnia, turning the region into a Croat stronghold. By late 1995, the war had changed population distribution so much that the once unthinkable ethnic partition now seemed all but inevitable. At this point, the United States became involved, directing the North Atlantic Treaty Organization (NATO) to bomb Serb targets. The United States did not push for a just settlement, however, but only for partition. In December 1995, a peace accord was signed in Dayton, Ohio, effectively dividing Bosnia-Herzegovina into three separate regions for the three different nationalities.* When U.S. troops entered Bosnia as "peacekeepers" in early 1996, they were enforcing the ethnic partition that Bosnian democrats had tried so hard to avoid. The nationalist fundamentalists had won.

Three years later, in 1999, the war spread to Kosovo. This southern province is the historic heartland of Serbia, but over the last half-century it has become

---

*Formally, the accord speaks of a Bosnian-Croat federation governing both Muslims and Croats. In reality, the Bosnians and Croats have had their own distinct administrations from the very beginning.

almost completely Albanian. By the time of the war, fewer than 10 percent of the population was Serb, although the province formally belonged to Serbia. Unable to win sufficient autonomy, militant Albanian separatists began organizing an armed campaign, which intensified after a governmental breakdown in neighboring Albania made arms easily available. The armed campaign led to even greater Serb repression, and by 1998 it seemed to many that Kosovo would be the next Bosnia. In early 1999, the United States demanded that Serbia allow NATO troops to monitor Kosovo. When Serbia, unsurprisingly, refused this violation of its sovereignty, NATO began bombing both Serbia and Serb bases in Kosovo. The bombing lasted for six weeks, until Serbia agreed to a UN occupation of Kosovo. The bombing led to a mass exodus of ethnic Albanians. When the UN (though chiefly, as in Bosnia, the United States) occupied the country and Albanians began to return, ethnic Serbs began fleeing. Already by 2000, the province had been ethnically divided even more dramatically than Bosnia had.

There is, alas, no moral in the stories of Bosnia and Kosovo. The experience reminds us that brute force often still triumphs over the grandest dreams. By demonstrating the worst possible outcome of the breakup of communism, however, these scenarios serve as a model of what must be avoided. The only positive development to come out of this was what happened in the former Yugoslav republic of Macedonia. In 2001, groups of ethnic Albanians, upset at their second-class status and encouraged by the West's actions in Kosovo, began an armed conflict against the Macedonian government. Some demanded greater autonomy, while a radical fringe sought to create a "greater Albania" uniting ethnic Albanians throughout the region. When the government responded with aggressive military action of its own, the stage seemed set for another Balkan ethnic war, perhaps even bloodier and wider than those in the past. But in the end, both sides pulled back from the precipice. In August 2001, the rebels and the government signed a peace agreement stipulating that Albanian would be considered an official language in areas where at least 20 percent of the population is ethnic Albanian and that over a thousand Albanians would be hired as policemen, assigned chiefly to ethnically Albanian areas. Constitutional amendments then solidified the arrangement, and it

has held well ever since. The historic deal showed that it is still possible to settle ethnic disputes peacefully, provided coolheaded politicians maintain such a will.

Political Challenges and Changing Agendas

In trying to understand the tragedy of Yugoslavia, we must go back to one of the fundamental issues we have seen all the East-Central European countries struggling to solve: how to build a market economy and political democracy at the same time. This central challenge, which all postcommunist East Europe has faced, was particularly difficult in the former Yugoslavia. Contrary to popular assumptions, the Yugoslav conflict did not resolve solely around nationalism. Rather, elites in Yugoslavia consciously *used* nationalism in order to divert popular anger away from economic problems, which began in the late 1980s when the country embraced a market economy that quickly led to declining living standards. When democracy finally came to Yugoslavia, people were rebelling not just against communism but also against the market reforms that democratic reformers had already introduced to deal with the economic crisis. Local elites won people over with a promise that national independence would bring prosperity.

A few of the new political parties in postcommunist Yugoslavia tried to define themselves on the basis of a commitment to a market economy and universal rights. These parties were committed to building a liberal market democracy throughout the former Yugoslavia. Most of the new parties, however, made nationalism their central theme. They said that it was not so much the economic policies of the government that were to blame for people being in tough straits, but the fact that these policies were being made by the wrong group of people—in particular, the wrong *nationality*. In the 1990 elections, people tended to vote for the party that promised to make things better for their own nationality. When the democratic elections were over, nationalist parties had won. People had chosen a new postcommunist identity. But it was nationalist, not liberal democratic. They had used the ballot to vote for parties that blamed one nationality for the problems facing another. Instead of agreeing that all citizens should be free and endowed with unalienable individual rights, people voted to privilege one nationality over another.

Things became so bad in Yugoslavia because there were so many nationalities sharing relatively little space, and because each nationality had its own political party and political institutions, whose leaders profited from ethnic conflict. These particular conditions did not exist elsewhere in the region, which is why the destruction and violence of the former Yugoslavia have not occurred elsewhere. Nevertheless, the tensions that result from shock therapy marketization programs have brought problems everywhere in East-Central Europe. In the early 1990s, even in more successful countries like Poland and Hungary, extreme right-wing movements almost came to power. And in Poland in 2005, a coalition government that included extremists did come to power, and immediately started conducting McCarthy-like purges and witchhunts against suspected enemies. The introduction of capitalism, in other words, creates social *anger*, and since Eastern European countries do not have the experience of managing economic problems with the kind of Keynesian class compromise we see in Western Europe, that anger has been directed at various *substitute* targets instead, such as members of other ethnic groups.[2]

The most significant and chronic ethnic problem in the region outside of the former Yugoslavia is in the relationship between the dominant ethnic group and the Roma, or Gypsies. Of course, anti-Gypsy hostility is widespread even far from Eastern Europe. (It is so ingrained that millions of Americans use the word *gypped* without being aware they are using an ethnic slur.) But the problems are particularly acute here, where most Roma still live. In many ways, the situation became worse after 1989. In the communist era, governments outlawed Roma nomadic lifestyles, creating the largely unskilled industrial jobs that allowed Roma to earn a living without constant migration. But after 1989, most of those jobs disappeared. Theoretically, Roma were free to be nomadic again. But most no longer know how to survive that way. The result is that Roma now tend to stay in the communities where they live, but are poorer and more discriminated against than before. Paradoxically, the situation is worse in the more developed countries such as Hungary and the Czech Republic, since these

had been more effective in creating the jobs that changed Roma ways in the past, and have been more ruthless in cutting those jobs ever since.

One 1999 event in the Czech Republic symbolized the problem dramatically. In the depressed mining city of Usti nad Labem (Usti on the Labe River), ethnic Czechs as well as Roma were both for the most part unemployed, and tensions became high. As so often happens, however, instead of joining together to fight for improvements, the two groups turned on each other. Czechs started seeing Roma as a threat, and got local officials to erect a physical wall in the city, separating Roma from the rest of the population. National politicians protested, but the local politicians were within their legal rights. Shattering the optimistic image of a New Europe in formation, the new millennium opened with a Roma ghetto in the heart of Europe. The fall of the Berlin Wall did not spell the end of divisions within Europe.

The protests of the national politicians were not only in vain but also somewhat hypocritical. Official Czech policy has been anti-Roma ever since the new state was founded in 1993. The government did its best to prevent Roma from becoming Czech citizens.[3] A 1969 Czechoslovak law had defined all Roma as citizens of Slovakia regardless of where they lived. This did not mean much at the time, since Czechoslovakia was governed as a single country, but it had great significance after the division of the country in 1993. Although citizens were legally entitled to request a new nationality at this time, most Roma residents did not know this. The result was that by 1994, hundreds of thousands of Roma had become foreigners living in the Czech Republic without any legal basis. Policy like this encouraged the racist practices of local officials in Usti.

The attacks on Roma are part of the way that "losers" in the postcommunist transition seek to negotiate their fate. The politics of blame is a powerful part of East Europe's postcommunist reality. It is not only Roma who are targeted. There has been an alarming surge in violence against refugees and foreigners, particularly from Third World countries. Some people, and parties, have sought to blame economic problems not on other nationalities but on former communists, and have called for banning such people from public life today. In Latvia, discrimination against ethnic Russians remains the rule. Many who have lived there virtually their whole lives still cannot get citizenship because they do not speak Latvian. Elsewhere, people blame "corrupt" bankers for today's problems, or the corrupting influence of "western culture." Still others single out "secular humanism" as the problem and propose religious fundamentalism as the answer. As noted, even in Poland, which has been comparatively successful, such extremism became the rule with the government elected in 2005. In all its guises, this politics of blame is perhaps the chief threat to democratic consolidation in East-Central Europe—indeed, in all of Europe. When one group or way of life is blamed for all the ills of the present, the danger is that that group or way of life may be banned in the future, or shut up in a ghetto as in Usti nad Labem.

East-Central European Politics, Terrorism, and East-Central Europe's Relation to the United States

In his first major speech after the events of September 11, 2001, President George W. Bush declared that "every nation in every region now has a decision to make: either you are with us or you are with the terrorists." At that moment, no country in Europe had any trouble deciding where it stood. All had lost citizens in the attack on the World Trade Center. All sympathized with the United States in its moment of tragedy. All had witnessed the catastrophic human costs of inhumane war on their own soil, and all shared with American citizens their outrage that now it had hit the United States, too. Finally, all knew that those who perpetrated such events were opponents of Europe, too, and of everything Europe in this era of unification was trying to do. And so there was little opposition even when the United States responded by bombing Afghanistan, whose leaders had supported and harbored Al Qaeda. After September 11, all of Europe stood united with the United States.

Less than two years later, President Bush told the world that being "with us" meant supporting the planned invasion and occupation of Iraq, too. Here Europe balked. Popular opinion, particularly in Western Europe, turned strongly against the president, and soon against the United States. Iraq, people pointed out, had nothing to do with international terrorism. Bombing, invading, and occupying a country for no clear reason was just wrong, they

felt, and contrary to the principles they had been working for since the end of World War II. Occupying Iraq in particular would be exceedingly difficult, critics claimed, and would likely make the problem of terrorism even greater.

The East European response was quite different. Public opinion there also opposed the war, although not as ardently as in the West. All the governments in the region, however, felt compelled to support President Bush and the war. Indeed, when world pressure against U.S. plans began to grow just before the invasion of Iraq in March 2003, the leaders of thirteen Eastern European countries—Albania, Bulgaria, Croatia, the Czech Republic, Estonia, Hungary, Latvia, Lithuania, Macedonia, Poland, Romania, Slovakia, and Slovenia— signed statements publicly supporting President Bush and promising to participate in the coalition to disarm Saddam Hussein. Some governments in Western Europe had also gone along—most notably Britain, Spain, and Italy—but the unanimity of the East was on a far different order, as the United States itself understood: thus U.S. Defense Secretary Donald Rumsfeld's famous comment praising the good "new" Europe over the allegedly irrelevant "old" Europe.

Behind the East European unanimity lay a mixture of authenticity and coercion. On the one hand, Eastern Europeans had strong moral feelings about the need for decisive action against oppressive regimes. How governments treated their own citizens, they believed, *should* matter to the world. They also felt that since America had stood beside them during the cold war, offering moral support in the fight against dictatorship, they now had a responsibility to do whatever America and its president asked in return.

But as this last point already indicates, East Europeans, unlike their western counterparts, did not yet see themselves as political actors who *could* say no to the United States. And here was the element of coercion: the power imbalance was so vast that East European leaders felt they had no choice but to do what the United States asked. All but three of these countries were still trying to join NATO. The Bush administration, moreover, had made it clear on numerous occasions that it did not look kindly on critics. In these conditions, no East European government felt it could risk what might happen if it declined to offer its support. Still, each East European government worried about the consequences of its choices. As one Hungarian political analysis put it at the time of the U.S. invasion, "Like other Central and Eastern Europe countries, Hungary faces a choice at the worst possible moment in history." Economic interests pushed one way but security concerns and values pushed another. "On the one hand, 60 to 80 percent of the region's economies are integrated into the European Union" compared to "a mere 3–5 percent" connection with the United States. "On the other hand, since the fall of communism, . . . U.S. political will and military might have been essential to resolving all the crises that have beset the Central and Eastern European region." We take the U.S. side here, the analysis concluded, but we must hope that our "fellow EU members will not see [us] as representing the interests of the United States or as weakening EU cohesion."[4]

As noted in Chapter 26, most countries followed up on their support by sending troops to Iraq, but only Poland sent more than a token force. Its 2,400 troops constituted the fourth-largest military contingent in the coalition, after only the United States, Britain, and Italy. (Not surprisingly, the next three largest suppliers of troops came from three countries still hopeful of joining NATO: Bulgaria, Romania, and Ukraine. The first two were in fact admitted the year after the invasion, in 2004.) Poland was trying to set itself up as the Great Britain of the East—in the sense of being America's most dependable ally, regardless of the circumstances.

Yet by 2004 some of this support began to wane. In part, this was due to the same reasons that support began to wane in the United States: with the strong Iraqi resistance, the seemingly endless casualties, the war and occupation simply were not going as planned. East Europeans were also outraged by the evidence of American torture of Iraqi prisoners, and wondered whether they didn't bear complicity in this, too. There were also more prosaic reasons. East Europeans were upset that they had so far received little in return. Their companies, despite having considerable track records for doing business in Iraq, were still waiting for the much-promised supply contracts to be offered to anyone other than Halliburton and other American firms. Poles in particular felt their contributions had been taken for granted. Not only did they not receive contracts, but they complained that their citizens were still denied visa-free access to the United States, unlike

West Europeans. When Polish president Aleksander Kwaśniewski, the United States' closest friend in East-Central Europe, publicly stated in March 2004 that he had been "misled" by America in the run-up to the war, he was indicating that America could not take Poland's unconditional support entirely for granted.[5]

East Europe's close attachment to the United States has cost it some support. Poland, in particular, is regarded suspiciously by many West European policymakers, who sometimes refer to it as America's "Trojan horse" in the EU. Most EU leaders, however, recognize the bind Poland and other countries in the region are in. They too, after all, were in a similar position vis-à-vis the United States just after World War II. It takes time to gain real sovereignty.

Fortunately, there has not been a terrorist attack in East Europe at the time of this writing. With its large contingent of troops in Iraq, Poland felt increasingly vulnerable after the terrorist bombing of the Spanish railroads in March 2004, which killed two hundred people. While certainly not impossible, such plots are less likely in East Europe, where there has been little immigration in recent decades and where there are no established Middle Eastern communities. Still, police forces have become more vigilant lately and also, as in the United States, more repressive, less protective of civil liberties. All public demonstrations are now seen by the police as potential terrorist sites. Migrants and visitors from developing countries, particularly Islamic ones, are subject to increased monitoring.

The Challenges of European Integration

Let's look at two particular kinds of challenges that European integration poses to the countries of East-Central Europe: one facing the countries already in the EU, the other facing the Balkan countries that are still trying to join. The first can be told through the recent example of Slovakia. One of the keys to successful integration into the EU is the attraction of foreign capital. This, obviously, means that Eastern countries must attract western business. As a late addition to the group of countries allowed to join the EU in 2004, Slovakia worked especially hard at doing this. In 2000, it reduced corporate tax rates from 40 percent to 29 percent, and introduced a five-year tax holiday for foreign investors. In 2001, the government committed itself to subsidizing up to 70 percent of the start-up costs of new businesses in certain regions of the country. In 2004, it went even further: jettisoning the advanced industrialized world's long legacy of progressive taxation, according to which those who earn more pay more, Slovakia became the first country in the region to introduce a flat tax, or a single tax rate, for people and businesses alike, of 19 percent. With incentives like this, along with a large package of subsidies designed specifically for the automotive industry, Slovakia beat out its East European rivals and wooed the Hyundai corporation into opening up an automotive plant, following the already large investment of Volkswagen. The total subsidies amounted to over $100,000 per job created. It is as if the government itself agreed to pay the wages of Hyundai's 2,400 Slovak employees for the next eleven years. Workers are comparatively well paid in the foreign-owned automotive industry, earning about twice the national average. Business accepts these wages because they are still about a fifth of what German workers receive for the same work.

If Slovakia thus gets good manufacturing jobs for some of their workers, how is this a "challenge of European integration"? The answer is in how it affects others in the country. For how can the government *pay* for all this largesse offered to business? The flat tax alone cost nearly $600 million in lost revenue. Add in the subsidies offered to the auto companies and it's clear that the budget was in trouble. Slovakia decided to pay for it in an extremely *regressive* way. It levied a high 19 percent sales tax on medicine, added sales tax on basic food, and increased energy prices. It then slashed unemployment benefits in half. In a word, the poor were made to pay the price. The Roma population was particularly hard hit. Indeed, budget-cutting measures like reducing support for families with more than four children were intended specifically to reduce assistance to Roma, who were already facing nearly 50 percent unemployment rates.

The direct result of all this came in February 2004, when food riots erupted in numerous small, mostly Roma-populated towns. There was looting of supermarkets, as well as organized demonstrations against the new policies. The government responded with force: special police as well as military units sealed off Roma communities, clashed with protesters for days, and ultimately defeated the uprising after arresting several hundred people.

Eastern Europeans longed to join the EU because they hoped to reap the benefits of the latter. But as the Slovak example shows, the kinds of business that move operations to Eastern Europe tend to be the kinds that do not need a prosperous citizenry. As Dorothee Bohle and Bela Greskovits put it, "The social model [typical in Western Europe] has not traveled to the East because [the businesses that go there] are usually the least hospitable to a capital-labor accord."[6] Automakers in Slovakia are trying to export their cars, not sell them on the domestic market. "Trickle-down" does not apply here. Business does not mind making the poor bear the cost of its subsidies, and the government itself sees no other way. In the context of a labor movement that is already weak because of the communist experience, the challenge of European integration is thus that the capitalist experience, which incorporation into the EU finally makes real, will only make labor weaker. Instead of Europe becoming one, integration may perpetuate the situation of two different Europes, with the East remaining at the bottom.

There are, of course, tendencies pushing the other way. Many of the young people who traveled from east to west have begun returning, bringing skills and capital with them. Exports from east to west have shot up since entry into the EU, and as firms become more successful, workers become bolder, which leads to higher wages. There is evidence that Eastern Europe is itself becoming more internally differentiated, with both an increasing high-wage sector and an increased low-wage and poverty-line sector. How these disparate tendencies play out in the future will determine much of what happens politically.

The Balkan countries, in the southern part of East-Central Europe, face different kinds of problems. Aside from Slovenia, Bulgaria, and Romania, none of the other countries is slated for entry into the European Union. In 1999, the EU offered so-called Stabilization and Association Agreements to Albania and to the five former Yugoslav states of Bosnia, Croatia, Macedonia, Montenegro, and Serbia. But they are not likely to become full members in this decade, or perhaps even in the next. In this way, yet another divide is taking place within Europe, between those East-Central European countries in the EU and those on the outside.

East-Central European Politics in Comparative Perspective

How can we best study East-Central Europe today? Until just a few years ago, students studied the region as little more than an afterthought to the study of the Soviet Union. Experts on contemporary Soviet society were treated as automatic experts on Eastern Europe as well. Introductory courses on European politics usually did not even mention the region, except as "the other" against which "the West" was pitted.

Today there is a danger of going too far in the opposite direction. With virtually the entire region already in NATO (against Russia's opposition) and most in the EU as well, scholars are beginning to treat the region as the kidnapped partner of the West, which has finally returned home. European politics courses now regularly deal with transitions in East Europe, while saying barely a word about events in Moscow. College students are discovering that a summer trip to Europe demands stops not just in Paris and Rome but in Prague, Budapest, and Kraków too (and maybe even Riga). In other words, little by little, East Europe is being readmitted to the fold, with Russia and Ukraine carved off as "the other." The East-Central Europe that was once viewed as "belonging" to Russia is increasingly seen as the rightful property of Western Europe instead.

The reality is that East-Central Europe can be understood only in its connections to *both* Western Europe and Russia. It is trying to become more a part of the West today, but the very fact that it must try demonstrates that a chasm still remains. The main streets of downtown Budapest may seem like the main streets of downtown Brussels, but Hungary's or Poland's old industrial sectors still experience problems more similar to those facing Russia or China than to the problems facing Belgium or France. We need to understand not only where East Europe hopes to be going, but also where it has been. As we saw in Chapter 26, East-Central Europe was not just "taken over" by communism; numerous internal factors pushed it in that direction. Today, numerous internal factors keep it from simply becoming another part of Western Europe. In some ways, it resembles not the West but the South, not West Europe but South America and Southern Europe. We need to be careful about how we "locate" countries or regions, so as not to fall into ideological

wishful thinking. This book has tried to highlight East-Central Europe's status as a set of countries in between, with inextricable links to both East and West, both liberalism and communism, both communism and capitalism.

One of the ways to look at these contradictory aspects of East-Central Europe is through the discussion of democratization. How can societies be democratized? How can a newly achieved democracy be consolidated? Over the past two decades these questions have been at the center of research in comparative political science. Beginning in the mid-1970s in Latin America and southern Europe, a series of countries that had long been authoritarian or military dictatorships began the transition to democratic forms of government. By the mid-1980s, theorists had speculated about the causes of this transformation, argued about whether the new democratic systems could be consolidated, and suggested how democracy could best be strengthened. Mainstream political scientists, who had considered communism to be unreformable and totalitarian, thought it unimaginable that East Europe would join this new wave of democratization anytime soon.[7] Within a few years, however, journals and conferences worldwide would be devoted to the new study of "comparative democratization," comparing democratic transformations in Latin America and East-Central Europe.

What can such comparisons teach about how to initiate and consolidate democratic political transitions? What are some of the similarities and differences in transitions to democratic government from right-wing dictatorships and from communist systems?

One common element is that democratic change is preceded by a revitalization of civil society. Indeed, the very term *civil society*, referring to the public sphere for civic and political interaction outside of government, has reentered the vocabulary of political science because of the experience of democratic transformations, particularly in East-Central Europe. We can now see that one of the main weaknesses of mainstream political science was its focus on elites. Until recently, political scientists tended to have a very thin notion of citizenship. Citizens were considered insufficiently trained in public affairs and were advised to leave governing to the experts. "Acceptance of leadership," wrote Joseph Schumpeter, the influential economist and democratic theorist of the

1950s, "is the true function of the electorate."[8] In Latin America and particularly in East-Central Europe, however, it was precisely the citizens who refused to accept leadership who made democratization possible. Without Solidarity in Poland or the independent political activists in Hungary, the communist governments would have had no reason to accept political democracy. Recent democratization movements have returned the study of citizens and civil society to the center of political analysis.

At the same time, comparative analysis also illustrates the importance of *conciliation* and *negotiation*. A mobilized and angry citizenry is not enough. The elites who control the guns must be persuaded that giving up power is in their interests too, or at least that it will not lead to their arrest and prosecution. The authorities need a reliable adversary to negotiate with. And that adversary, representing the citizens in their campaign for democracy, must be prepared to make concessions, even ones most citizens believe to be wrong, in order to persuade the authorities to go along.

What kinds of concessions must democratizers offer? First, they should agree to refrain from locking up the ousted dictator, at least right away. In Chile and in Poland, the respective military leaders Pinochet and Jaruzelski were even able to maintain their positions briefly as head of state, after the first free elections. While some former leaders were eventually prosecuted—in Argentina, Bulgaria, and East Germany, for example—the charges and penalties were relatively minor, and all sides understood that the action was more a public relations campaign on the part of the new regime than an attempt to exact vengeance.

Supporters of the old system have also remained relatively free from persecution. Nowhere was democratization accompanied by an immediate purge of the bureaucracy, not even the military and police bureaucracies. The leading officials were retired, usually with generous pensions intact, but rank-and-file officials tended to retain their posts, at least for a while, until new recruits were brought in and the old guard could gracefully be retired.

In Latin America, the need for conciliation of the old elite also meant a favorable attitude to capitalist big business, which had been the main social base of the dictatorships. Here, paths diverge. For in East-Central Europe, there was no capitalist big business. If conciliation is necessary to calm the fears of potential opponents, then in a postcommunist context, conciliation means maintaining policies favorable to the old working class. Few other groups are likely to be quite as dissatisfied by the postcommunist system. Certainly not former party officials: most were gracefully retired, quietly retained, or enabled to move on to lucrative careers in business and banking, fields they tended to know better than the old dissidents did. Far from suffering, this group has largely benefited from the building of a capitalist system. Working people, however, have only lately begun to benefit from the transition, and not even all of them. That is why they represent a real challenge to democratic consolidation and why they must be conciliated.[9] If workers come to experience democracy as privation, they are likely to be susceptible to the appeals of demagogues and authoritarian nationalists. This was true in Latin America, too, but the existence there of a powerful capitalist class, which was afraid to part with dictatorship because of its fear of labor militance, meant that business-friendly policies were more important in the short run than labor-friendly policies. In East-Central Europe, however, labor-friendly policies are more important as a way of consolidating the new system. Not all supporters of democracy, whether in East Europe or the West, seem to understand this, even today.

Although working-class support for authoritarianism in Russia shows the importance of winning labor to democracy there, too, we should note that the situations in Russia and China are actually quite different from that in East-Central Europe. Russian and Chinese authoritarianism has much stronger roots. Unlike in East Europe, communism was experienced as part of the national tradition, not as something imposed from without. Under communism, both countries became superpowers. As a result, there is far more internal support for the old system than we see in East Europe. Thus, in Russia and China, conciliating potential enemies of democracy requires efforts to change the underlying political culture, not just to reach out to those who may lose economically.

All in all, East-Central Europe's governments must undertake the difficult task of adjusting their systems enough to enter the EU and the global capitalist world, while maintaining the support of both regular citizens and foreign elites—of both working people and investors. This does not mean that all policies must be equally acceptable to all social groups. Such consensus is impossible, and attempting to achieve it would be a recipe for stagnation. But governments must see themselves as the representatives of all citizens, and make sure that the interests of all groups are at least sometimes addressed in public policy.

To be successful in today's global climate, market reform and EU integration must serve the interests of the business community, whether domestic or foreign investors or international financial agencies. To these groups, East-Central Europe must show continuing commitment to establishing favorable investment climates, as well as an ability to maintain tight budgets. It must establish tax policies that promote investment while also guaranteeing the state sufficient resources to develop infrastructure and maintain social stability. At the same time, there will be no long-term stability without the support of labor. In the heavily industrial world that East-Central Europe remains, the working class still constitutes the largest potentially organized sector of the population. It is the group that is most affected by systemic transition and the one whose support is crucial if a democratic system is to survive.

Just as the political system must be transformed in a way that is compatible with economic reform, the economy must be transformed in a way that maintains support for political democracy. Economic reform, in other words, must be politically sensitive and socially aware. Citizens must come to feel that economic reforms are working for them, and not just for the new or old elite. Creating this environment requires such things as a privatization program with shares for employees and citizens, anticorruption and antimonopoly measures, and strong regulatory agencies that safeguard safety, health, and environmental standards. Such policies are necessary not just to maintain a decent and growing standard of living for citizens, but for maintaining the stability of a democratic system. Eastern Europeans are well aware that change does not come without sacrifice. Indeed, what has been surprising in the years since the fall of communism is not how many strikes and protests there have been but how few. But if the postcommunist world comes to be perceived as being just as immoral and rotten as the old one, many people may lose all hope whatsoever. Society would then be overcome by a crushing sense of despair, giving rise to social pathologies like increased crime and violence and political pathologies like the emergence of fascist organizations.

In Europe, whether Western or Eastern, no country is fully accepted today unless it is formally a democracy. Whether a country can build a democratic system depends on a number of factors, such as its political culture, the nature and duration of its authoritarian experience, the degree of popular mobilization, the internal economic situation, international pressures, and the country's location in the global economy. In some countries, political mobilization from below plays the crucial role; elsewhere, a skilled negotiating strategy is key. In countries with a relatively homogeneous population, nationalism may attract support for political democracy, while in multiethnic societies with a history of conflict, it may only damage chances for democracy. Where a capitalist class is strong, economic policy must be favorable to capital; where capital is weak and workers have historically been deemed the dominant class, economic policy must be favorable to working people.

Western governments do not press all countries to democratize. If a country has a commodity the West wants to buy and a culture the West does not understand, the West does not care if it is a democracy or a dictatorship. (Kuwait, with an authoritarian government that was able to supply the West with oil, was not compelled to democratize even after the democratic world organized one of the century's greatest military coalitions in its defense in the 1991 Gulf War.) In Europe, however, and particularly in order to get into the EU, countries must be democratic.

But what does this really mean? For there has also been outside pressure on postcommunist countries to restrict civil liberties in the name of fighting terrorism. There is, in the end, no one form of democracy. Democratic countries can have a presidential or a parliamentary system, extensive or limited state intervention, strong or weak local governments, proportional or single-member-district representation, broad or limited social welfare networks. They can allow unfettered capitalist development, or they can empower communities to restrict the privileges of private capital. They can side more with the United States or more with the European Union, and they can choose to define terrorism as a crime or as a declaration of war.

What makes East-Central Europe so exciting today is that we see so many of these democratic forms in action, and so many of the vital questions for the future laid out on the table. From the civic involvement of the Solidarity movement in Poland to the innovative ideas for involving citizens in economic reforms today, from the resistance of Bosnians against ethnic cleansing to the diverse ways the region is responding to the challenges after September 11, East-Central Europe has much to teach the West about democracy.

Of course, whatever the form of democracy, critics can and will always demand more of it. People can always think of reasons and ways to be more involved in making decisions that affect them. Popular pressure for greater democratization is an inescapable feature of the world as a whole, and particularly of what used to be the Communist world. Democracy is, after all, an eternally unfinished project.

Notes

[1] For a majestic account of Bosnia's multiethnic history over the ages, see the great 1945 novel by Bosnian Nobel Prize author Ivo Andric, *The Bridge on the Drina* (Chicago: University of Chicago Press, 1984).

[2] For more on this argument about the connection of anger and politics, see David Ost, *The Defeat of Solidarity: Anger and Politics in Postcommunist Europe* (Ithaca, N.Y.: Cambridge University Press, 2005).

[3] Jirina Siklova and Marta Miklusakova, "Denying Citizenship to the Czech Roma," *East European Constitutional Review* 7, no. 2 (Spring 1998): 58–64. More information on the East European situation is available on the website of the European Roma Rights Center, www.errc.org.

[4] "The Central European Dilemma: America or Europe?" *Budapest Analyses*, May 20, 2003; www.budapestanalyses.hu/ docs/En/Analyses_ Archive/analysys_17_en.html.

[5] For more on changing Polish attitudes to America and the Iraqi invasion, see David Ost, "Letter From Poland," *The Nation*, October 4, 2004; www.thenation.com/doc.mhtml?i=20041004&s=ost.

[6] "Capital, Labor, and the Prospects of the European Social Model in the East," Working Paper No. 58 in the Program on Central and Eastern European Working Papers Series, Harvard University, 2004. Available at www.ces.fas.harvard.edu/publications.

[7] One prominent scholar went so far as virtually to rule out the possibility of democratic change in the Communist bloc. See Samuel P. Huntington, "Will More Countries Become Democratic?" *Political Science Quarterly* 99, no. 2 (1984): 193–218.

[8] Joseph Schumpeter, *Capitalism, Socialism and Democracy*, 3rd ed. (New York: Harper & Row, 1950), p. 273.

[9] For more on the importance of labor for democratic outcomes, see David Ost, *The Defeat of Solidarity*.

Part 7 Bibliography

Ali, Rabia, and Lawrence Lifschultz. *Why Bosnia?* Stony Creek: Pamphleteer's Press, 1993.

Berend, Ivan. *Central and Eastern Europe, 1944–1993: Detour from the Periphery to the Periphery*. Cambridge: Cambridge University Press, 1999.

Bozoki, Andras, ed. *Intellectuals and Politics in Central Europe*. Budapest: Central European University Press, 1999.

Bunce, Valerie. *Subversive Institutions: The Design and the Destruction of Socialism and the State*. Cambridge: Cambridge University Press, 1999.

Burawoy, Michael, and Katherine Verdery, eds. *Uncertain Transition: Ethnographies of Change in the Post-Socialist World*. Lanham, Md.: Rowman & Littlefield, 1999.

Castle, Marjorie, and Ray Taras. *Democracy in Poland*. Boulder, Colo.: Westview Press, 2002.

Chirot, Daniel, ed. *The Crisis of Leninism and the Decline of the Left*. Seattle: University of Washington Press, 1991.

———. *The Origins of Backwardness in Eastern Europe*. Berkeley and Los Angeles: University of California Press, 1989.

Crawford, Beverly, ed. *Markets, States, and Democracy: The Political Economy of Post-Communist Transformation*. Boulder, Colo.: Westview Press, 1995.

Crowley, Stephen, and David Ost, eds. *Workers After Workers' States: Labor and Politics in Eastern Europe After Communism*. Boulder, Colo.: Rowman & Littlefield Press, 2001.

Domanski, Henryk. *On the Verge of Convergence: Social Stratification in Eastern Europe*. Budapest: Central European University Press, 2000.

Dunn, Elizabeth. *Privatizing Poland: Baby Food, Big Business, and the Remaking of the Polish Working Class*. Ithaca, N.Y.: Cornell University Press, 2004.

Einhorn, Barbara. *Cinderella Goes to Market: Citizenship, Gender, and Women's Movements in Central Europe*. London: Verso, 1994.

Ekiert, Grzegorz, and Stephen Hanson, eds. *Capitalism and Democracy in Central and Eastern Europe: Assessing the Legacy of Communist Rule*. Cambridge: Cambridge University Press, 2003.

Eyal, Gil, Ivan Szelenyi, and Eleanor Townsley. *Making Capitalism Without Capitalists: Class Formation and Elite Struggles in Post-Communist Central Europe*. London: Verso, 1998.

Falk, Barbara J. *The Dilemmas of Dissidence in East-Central Europe*. Budapest: Central European University Press, 2003.

Gagnon, Valere P. *The Yugoslav Wars of the 1990s: A Critical Reexamination of Ethnic Conflict*. Ithaca, N.Y.: Cornell University Press, 2005.

Gal, Susan, and Gail Kligman. *The Politics of Gender After Socialism*. Princeton: Princeton University Press, 2000.

Gardawski, Juliusz. *Poland's Industrial Workers on the Return to Democracy and Market Economy*. Warsaw: Friedrich Ebert Foundation, 1996.

Garton Ash, Timothy. *The Magic Lantern*. New York: Random House, 1990.

Gowan, Peter. *The Global Gamble: Washington's Faustian Bid for World Dominance*. London: Verso, 1999.

Greskovits, Bela. *The Political Economy of Protest and Patience: Eastern European and Latin American Transformations Compared*. Budapest: Central European University Press, 1998.

Grzymala-Busse, Anna M. *Redeeming the Communist Past: The Regeneration of Communist Parties in East-Central Europe*. Cambridge: Cambridge University Press, 2002.

Haney, Lynne A. *Inventing the Needy: Gender and the Politics of Welfare in Hungary*. Berkeley and Los Angeles: University of California Press, 2002.

Hardy, Jane, and Al Rainnie. *Restructuring Krakow: Desperately Seeking Capitalism*. London: Mansell, 1996.

Hockenos, Paul. *Free to Hate: The Rise of the Right in Post-Communist Eastern Europe*. New York: Routledge, 1993.

Howard, Marc Morje. *The Weakness of Civil Society in Postcommunist Europe*. Cambridge: Cambridge University Press, 2003.

Innes, Abby. *Czechoslovakia: The Short Goodbye*. New Haven, Conn.: Yale University Press, 2001.

Jowitt, Ken. *New World Disorder: The Leninist Extinction*. Berkeley and Los Angeles: University of California Press, 1992.

Kennedy, Michael D. *Cultural Formations of Postcommunism: Transition, Nation, and War*. Minneapolis: University of Minnesota Press, 2002.

Kenney, Padraic. *A Carnival of Revolution: Central Europe 1989*. Princeton, N.J.: Princeton University Press, 2003.

———. *The Burdens of Freedom: Eastern Europe Since 1999*. London: Zed Books, 2006.

Kubicek, Paul. *Organized Labor in Postcommunist States: From Solidarity to Infirmity*. Pittsburgh: University of Pittsburgh Press, 2004.

Laba, Roma. *The Roots of Solidarity*. Princeton, N.J.: Princeton University Press, 1991.

Meardi, Guglielmo. *Trade Union Activists, East and West*. London: Ashgate, 2000.

Michta, Andrew A. *The Soldier-Citizen: The Political Army After Communism*. New York: Palgrave, 1997.

Offe, Claus. *Varieties of Transition: The Eastern European and East German Experience*. Cambridge: MIT Press, 1997.

Orenstein, Mitchell. *Out of the Red: Building Capitalism and Democracy in Post-Communist Europe*. Ann Arbor: University of Michigan Press, 2000.

Ost, David. *The Defeat of Solidarity: Anger and Politics in Postcommunist Europe*. Ithaca, N.Y.: Cornell University Press, 2005.

———. *Solidarity and the Politics of Anti-Politics*. Philadelphia: Temple University Press, 1990.

Penn, Shana. *Solidarity's Secret: The Women Who Defeated Communism in Poland*. Ann Arbor: University of Michigan Press, 2005.

Pearson, Raymond. *National Minorities in Eastern Europe, 1849–1945*. London: Macmillan, 1983.

Poznanski, Kazimierz. *Poland's Protracted Transition: Institutional Change and Economic Growth, 1970–1994*. Cambridge: Cambridge University Press, 1997.

Ramet, Sabrina. *The Radical Right in Eastern Europe*. State College: Pennsylvania State University Press, 1999.

———. *Balkan Babel: The Disintegration of Yugoslavia from the Death of Tito to the War for Kosovo*. Boulder, Colo.: Westview Press, 1999.

Rothschild, Joseph. *Return to Diversity: A Political History of East Central Europe Since World War II*. New York: Oxford University Press, 1989.

Schopflin, George. *Politics in Eastern Europe*. London: Blackwell, 1993.

Stark, David, and Laszlo Bruszt. *Postsocialist Pathways: Transforming Politics and Property in East Central Europe*. Cambridge: Cambridge University Press, 1998.

Stokes, Gale. *The Walls Came Tumbling Down: The Collapse of Communism in Eastern Europe*. New York: Oxford University Press, 1993.

Szacki, Jerzy. *Liberalism After Communism*. Budapest: Central European University Press, 1995.

Tworzecki, Hubert. *Learning to Choose: Electoral Politics in East-Central Europe*. Stanford: Stanford University Press, 2002.

Vachudova, Milana. *Europe Undivided: Democracy, Leverage, and Integration After Communism*. Oxford: Oxford University Press, 2005.

Verdery, Katherine. *The Vanishing Hectare: Property and Value in Postsocialist Transylvania*. Ithaca, N.Y.: Cornell University Press, 2003.

———. *What Was Socialism, and What Comes Next?* Princeton: Princeton University Press, 1996.

Wedel, Janine. *Collision and Collusion: The Strange Case of Western Aid to Eastern Europe, 1989–1998*. New York: St. Martin's Press, 1998.

Woodward, Susan. *The Balkan Tragedy*. Washington, D.C.: Brookings Institute, 1995.

Websites

European Roma Rights Centre (ERRC):
www.errc.org

Budapest Analyses, periodic analyses of news and events in Hungary and through East-Central Europe:
www.budapestanalyses.hu/docs/Homepage/En/

European Industrial Relations Observatory On-Line, news and analysis on European industrial relations:
www.eurofound.europa.eu/eiro/

European Union, official site:
europa.eu/index_en.htm

Network of East-West Women-Polaska:
www.neww.org.pl/en.php/home/index/0.html

"Transitions Online," an Internet journal covering Central and Eastern Europe:
www.tol.cz

PART 8

The European Union and the Future of European Politics

George Ross

CHAPTER 31

The Making of the European System

On May 9, 1950, in an elegant room in France's Ministry for Foreign Affairs, Foreign Minister Robert Schuman proposed that France and Germany, plus any other democratic nation in Western Europe that wanted to join, establish a "community" to regulate and govern the coal and steel industries across national borders. To someone who knew little of European history the proposal for a European Coal and Steel Community (ECSC) might have seemed dry and technical. But France and Germany had been at war, or preparing for war, for most of the twentieth century, at huge costs to millions of citizens. In 1950 iron and steel were central to national economic success and war-making power. Schuman's first sentences spoke to the deep issues.

> World peace cannot be safeguarded without creative efforts.... The contribution that an organized and vital Europe can bring to civilization is indispensable to the maintenance of peaceful relations.... Europe will not be made all at once, nor.... in a single holistic construction: it will be built by concrete achievements that will create solidarity in facts. To assemble European nations first demands that opposition between France and Germany be eliminated....[1]

Robert Schuman, a devout Christian Democrat, came from Lorraine, a steel-making area that had long been a battleground between France and Germany. His German counterpart, Konrad Adenauer, chancellor of the new German Federal Republic, was also a devout Christian Democrat who had been mayor of Cologne before Hitler put him in Buchenwald prison. France and Germany were quickly joined by Italy, Belgium, the Netherlands, and Luxembourg to begin the long march toward today's European Union.

The primary author of the "Schuman plan" was Jean Monnet, another founding father of the EU. Monnet was a brilliant transnational networker. A young man during World War I, he had helped organize supplies from North America to Britain and France. Then, after serving at the League of Nations, he went into private business with the elite of Wall Street lawyers and bankers who would dominate American foreign policy after World War II. Monnet became the intermediary between President Roosevelt and the French in World War II. When the war ended he designed France's economic planning process and was at the heart of the French operations

associated with the Marshall Plan (a massive economic assistance program by the United States from 1947 to 1952, designed to rebuild Europe and secure the countries of the region as key alliance partners in the emerging cold war). It was in this role that Monnet, never elected to anything, devised the Schuman Plan.

In 1958, with the Treaties of Rome, the ECSC six agreed to create the European Economic Community (EEC) to construct a "common market." By 1995 this creation had become a European Union (EU) of fifteen nations, covering all of Western Europe.* By 2007, the fiftieth birthday of the Rome Treaties, the EU had twenty-seven members, including ten Central and Eastern European Countries who joined after the end of the cold war. What Schuman and Monnet began is today a European-level system of democratic politics that coordinates, complements, and in a few areas supersedes those of its members. Today's EU has helped build a prosperous unified European economy—the single largest trade bloc in a globalizing world. The EU has helped make Europe a major world power, which has emerged as an unquestionable asset to world peace and helped consecrate democracy across the European continent and elsewhere. When on March 25, 2007, Germany's Chancellor Angela Merkel hosted the heads of state and government of all twenty-seven EU members to a glittering fiftieth birthday party for the EU in Berlin, there was much to celebrate. There was also much to worry about and many difficult tasks on the EU's agenda. This chapter will describe the EU's remarkable accomplishments and the daunting challenges for it that lie ahead.

Critical Junctures and European Integration

The EU began as a group of six Western European countries arrayed around Germany and France, traditional enemies who were embarking on an incredible experiment. EU Europe now covers the entire European

---

*The EU was called the EEC (the European Economic Community), from 1957 to 1965; the EC (for European Communities) after a 1965 "Merger Treaty" bringing the EEC, ECSC, and Euratom (the European Atomic Energy Authority—see Chapter 32) under one institutional roof; and the European Union (EU), after the Treaty on European Union was ratified in 1993.

continent east to west from the Atlantic to borders with Belarus, Ukraine, Russia, and Turkey and, from north to south, from the Arctic to the Mediterranean. Norway and Switzerland are not members, although both have deep trading and other ties to the Union. The troubled ex-Yugoslavian states of the Balkans, still regaining their footing after a terrible bout of warfare, are also outside, with the EU deeply involved in peace-keeping and reconstruction throughout the area, and Croatia is already in line to join. Turkey, a large, predominantly Islamic country, is also now in the very early stages of negotiating EU membership. All told, the EU has some 500 million well-educated citizens, producers, and consumers.

European integration has happened in response to step-by-step challenges. It originated in a world of European states that had become unlivable because of recurrent bloody warfare that reached its peak in the first half of the twentieth century. In World War I (1914–1918), millions were killed and maimed. The twenties and thirties saw wild economic instability that fed the antidemocratic political extremism exemplified by Hitler, Stalin, Mussolini, and Franco. World War II followed, costing tens of millions more European lives.

Built in the Cold War to Fine-Tune a "Golden Age"

Europe in 1945 was at a turning point. The war ended the appeal of antidemocratic regimes, with the exception of communist-party states, led by the USSR, which remained an important alternative until the early 1990s. In many countries new political forces came to power bearing democratic ideals and social reform. The United States, Britain, France, and the Soviet Union jointly occupied Germany and reflected about how to prevent anything like Nazism from ever recurring. Economically, however, Europe was prostrate: cities, factories, and transportation networks lay in ruins, and there was no money to reconstruct them.

The cold war was what really prodded Western Europeans toward integration. The USSR and the United States, wartime allies, had quickly become enemies, creating a bipolar standoff that would last over four decades. Initially dependent on the United States financially, through the Marshall Plan, Western Europeans found themselves inoculated by American military

power against old habits of inter-European conflict. One alternative was integration, which was taken up by the original six ECSC countries in 1950 and then in the 1957 Treaties of Rome that established the European Economic Community.

The EU was lucky to begin in a Golden Age of growing prosperity. Smart economic politics and dedicated efforts to catch up with American innovations helped bring mass production and consumerism to Europe. Full employment, once a dream, briefly became a reasonable goal. States redistributed new wealth through expanded social programs (which provided health care, housing, pensions, and other public goods to citizens), often backed by coalitions that brought effective representation to groups that had long been excluded. These postwar settlements underpinned the widespread triumph of representative democracy in Western Europe. In the process, the first stage of the EU (the EEC, or "Common Market") supplemented national economies. Its customs-free area created a larger trading space and allowed national firms to export more. Its Common Agricultural Policy (CAP) stimulated the modernization of agriculture. Finally, the EEC's common external tariff provided a buffer against the international market and the economic power of the United States.

Stagnation and Renewal: The 1970s and 1980s

International economic change in the 1970s ended this happy situation and stalled integration for a decade. EU members—nine after the United Kingdom, Denmark, and Ireland joined in 1973—responded to oil shocks and "stagflation" (a previously unknown combination of high inflation and low growth) in a disarray of different, often contradictory, policies. Some continued pumping up economies to maintain employment, others tried to beat back inflation by controlling the supply of money, and still others, like Britain after 1979, attacked labor organizations to lower wages. In a customs-free area such policy disarray was dangerous, particularly after international exchange-rate fluctuations were stimulated by the end of the U.S.-sponsored Bretton Woods system that had stabilized exchange rates and trade cycles since the 1940s. By the later 1970s the Common Market was threatened, and postwar settlements were under siege. There were some innovations, like the

European Monetary System (EMS), a plan that was established to improve monetary stability through a system of exchange rate policies. But in general "Eurosclerosis," an inability to move forward, was the rule. Golden Age growth disappeared, EU Europe lost competitiveness, and high unemployment returned.

It took until 1985, with globalization on the horizon, for the EU to find new energy. At that point, EU member states agreed to "complete the single market" with a program designed to create a Europe-wide "space without borders" through new market liberalization. The culmination was the 1991 Treaty on European Union (TEU, ratified in 1993) in which EU members agreed to an Economic and Monetary Union (EMU) that would eventually unify European monetary policy, set up a European Central Bank to run it, and introduce a single European currency, the euro. The TEU also proposed a common foreign and security policy and new cooperation in "justice and home affairs." In all this, the EU was deepened and revitalized.

After the Cold War, Facing Globalization

The international setting then changed dramatically again. The end of the cold war and the collapse of the Soviet empire changed the EU's security situation, brought the reunification of Germany, and raised a new issue of integrating ex-communist Eastern European countries. At the same time, globalization and an international economic policy shift to price stability, hastened in Europe by EMU, forced adoption of new outlooks. In these new economic circumstances the single-market program failed to live up to its promises of renewed economic success. Some EU members did well, but others, including the EU's core continental economies, France and Germany, suffered low growth and high unemployment for well over a decade. In the midst of this, the semiskilled manufacturing jobs that had come with postwar prosperity began to decline in the face of automation and movement to lower-cost labor areas elsewhere in the world. Other places, the United States in the lead, were moving towards a new "knowledge economy" in which high-tech innovation was what counted, yet Europe seemed to lag behind.

These changes led many Europeans to turn inward, questioning national governments and the EU alike. The EU had greatly expanded its roles, particularly in

running European economic affairs, and become very important in their everyday lives. Large promises that leaders had made about these new roles bringing new prosperity and security had not been fulfilled, however. In a general atmosphere of growing malaise about democratic politics, Europeans started to feel they had not been adequately consulted about the EU's growth. From the beginning, European integration had often occurred behind the backs of ordinary citizens through technocratic initiatives that sometimes short-circuited national democratic processes. By the millennium many EU citizens had concluded that there was a "democratic deficit," that the EU's institutions lacked transparency and often seemed unaccountable to citizens.

The end of the cold war also upset Europe's security. The TEU proposed the creation of a common EU foreign and security policy and hinted at the eventuality of a European-level defense capability. The Bosnia and Kosovo wars, which eventually required American intervention, underscored European weakness, and prompted small new steps, more in defense matters than in foreign policy. The EU thus began to create a rapid-reaction force and invested in logistic and intelligence support for it. The United States urged caution, fearing that this might disrupt the North Atlantic Treaty Organization (NATO), which the United States largely controlled, and perhaps create the prospect of a European counterweight. The Amsterdam Treaty (1997) created a new high representative for EU foreign policy and established a more efficient way of representing the EU to third parties. But questions remained. How would Europe confront potential new security problems in its own backyard? What would be the division of labor between NATO and Europe?

Figuring out what to do with the ex-communist countries of Central and Eastern Europe (CEECs) was a more immediate question, however. After the end of the cold war the EU quickly sent aid and negotiated freer trade, in the process encouraging CEEC aspirations to EU membership, and by the second half of the 1990s the EU began full incorporation of the CEECs. Admitting a flock of new, largely poor, members meant organizing new economic interdependencies. It also required transferring resources to help the CEECs to modernize and underwriting democracy in places where its roots were fragile. Many Europeans began to wonder where the final borders of Europe might eventually be. Nevertheless, ten new members joined on May 1, 2004 (8 CEECs as well as Cyprus and Malta) and two more (Bulgaria and Romania) followed in January 2007.

Twenty-seven members, plus vastly expanded EU responsibilities, called for serious reform lest the EU's institutional machinery, built for six members in the 1950s, stop working altogether. European summits in the 1990s puzzled about what to do but had difficulty in agreeing. Finally, in 2002 leaders convened a "European Convention" to encourage the widest possible debate. Many complicated questions quickly made their way onto the convention table. What were the EU's ultimate goals? Was it meant to build markets and then stop, as some maintained? No, said others, building markets was a launching pad for broader political unification. Whatever Europe's goals, however, the Convention also had to face outstanding issues of democratic legitimacy. Its product in 2004 was a new "European Constitutional Treaty" that would be submitted for ratification to the EU's members.

Euro-politics had become more significant in large part at the expense of European national politics, which made the EU one of the bigger reasons for the transitions and critical junctures in national politics that other chapters in this volume discuss. Five decades of economic integration significantly constrain the national autonomy of EU members. With the EU probing new policy realms and globalization, shrinking national sovereignty is a reality. The gains of European integration had come at real costs. Neither local nor national actors can do what they used to do, partly

because of Euro-politics. But Euro-politics was itself a multilevel maze, with localities, regions, and national governments spending more and more time networked at European levels. The result has enormously complicated information flows to citizens and has made democratic public life harder to understand and organize. After the French and Dutch refused to ratify the "constitutional treaty" in the 2005 referendums, the problems of Euro-politics, simmering for years, could no longer be ignored.

European integration has been a dramatic success, but times change, and people move on. Can the EU handle the challenges it presently faces? Will European integration be an effective way to cope with globalization? Is it worth undermining the national communities that once provided European peoples with solid identities? Can European institutions and processes be made more democratic? Should the EU, at present a strange political animal that is not a state but that does many state-like things, move to greater federal integration? The following chapters will try to answer these many questions, first exploring the history of European integration in greater detail, next discussing EU institutions and policymaking, and finally considering the challenges that the EU, its member states, and citizens now face.

Notes

[1]First paragraph of the Schuman declaration of May 9, 1950, GR translation, from Joël Boudant and Max Gounelle, *Les grandes dates de l'Europe communautaire* (Paris: Larousse, 1989), pp. 14–15.

CHAPTER 32

Politics and Economics in the Development of the European Union

Immanuel Kant wrote about European integration in 1789. The comte de Saint-Simon speculated about it only slightly later. In 1849, Victor Hugo presided over a Congress of the Friends of Peace that called for a United States of Europe. Would-be conquerors—Napoleon, Hitler, Stalin—each had their own notions of European unity. The bloodbath of World War I prompted more urgent reflections before fascism dramatically closed the debate.

Born in the Cold War

It required massive changes in the international balance of power after 1945 to open the debate again, in particular it took the emergence of the United States as a superpower and a "cold war" structured around U.S.-Soviet confrontation. As victory approached in World War II, the United States, which was concerned with rebuilding the international trading system, promoted the Bretton Woods system, committing to the dollar as a global reserve currency backed by gold and founding the World Bank to fund postwar reconstruction, the International Monetary Fund (IMF) to stabilize the trading system; and the General Agreement on Tariffs and Trade (GATT), to promote freer trade (succeeded by the World Trade Organization, or WTO, in 1994). Through these decisive gestures, the United States demonstrated its willingness to be the trustee of a new international trading system that could reconstruct market economies after the disasters of the Great Depression and Second World War.

One big problem, however, was that before the countries of Western Europe could trade they had to rebuild. However, they had little to trade until they had done so, and no money to rebuild or to pay for what they bought. The American response, which was prompted by fears about European political stability and about building an international market, was the Marshall Plan (1947), which made billions of dollars available to reconstruct European economies, provided only that the Europeans coordinated how to put the money to good use.[1] Well invested, Marshall Plan funds were a solid foundation for modernization along consumerist lines that the United States had already pioneered. These funds also gave governments space to consolidate social reforms that had been instituted in

the wake of the war. Finally, they solidified attachments to the United States.

The outbreak of the cold war coincided with the Marshall Plan. In its Central and Eastern European sphere of influence, the USSR set about establishing "popular democracies," dominated by local Communists who mimicked Soviet ways and were backed by Soviet troops. The geography of Europe—Paris was only a few hundred miles from a million Soviet troops, plus the power of communists in some Western European electorates nourished American fears that a Soviet westward offensive would be difficult to stop.

Cold war rearmament spurred European integration. The United States, which was committed to the most massive peacetime military buildup in its history, persuaded and financed Western European nations to follow. NATO (the North Atlantic Treaty Organization), founded in 1949, stationed American troops and military supplies throughout Europe to block any offensive from the East. Western Europeans and other allies under unified NATO command were expected to contribute to the common defense. NATO formalized the predominance of American military power in Western Europe. As long as the cold war went on, armed conflict among Western Europeans, the scourge of the first half of the twentieth century, was off the agenda. As part of their plans, the Americans also wanted the Germans in NATO, something that involved rehabilitating, rather than punishing, postwar Germany. The German Federal Republic—carved in 1949 from the American, British, and French occupation zones—was one result. The Soviet zone, in turn, became the German Democratic Republic (GDR), and Germany remained divided until 1990. It followed that the new West Germany, now the front line of anti-Soviet defense, would also be rearmed.

These momentous changes occurred during widespread debate about Europe's future. Everyone agreed that Europe should stop having horrific wars, but the poverty of postwar Europe and tightly controlled national economies made large-scale transnational economic integration difficult. Moreover, different ideas about European integration were hard to reconcile. Federalists wanted supranational institutions and a United States of Europe. Intergovernmentalists sought integration arrangements that would preserve national sovereignty. People also disagreed about what should be integrated and how to start. The 1948 customs union of the Netherlands, Belgium, and Luxembourg (Benelux) was an early, successful, although small-scale, success, but failures and dead ends were more common. The most spectacular setback occurred at the 1948 Congress of Europe, where delegates from sixteen European countries debated everything to an impasse. The one result was the Council of Europe, founded in 1949, which created a Court of Justice to help advance human rights in Europe, but achieved little else.

Starting with Coal and Steel

Although Franco-German conflict had been Old Europe's chronic problem, new Europe's first breakthrough was the European Coal and Steel Community (ECSC) in 1950. The French, overrun by the Germans three times in seventy-five years, had hoped to fragment post-Nazi Germany and neutralize its heavy industrial power. The French steel industry in Lorraine needed coking coal, however, and the closest source was the German Ruhr, so negotiations for an International Ruhr Authority began in 1947. It so happened that the high French official working on the problem was Jean Monnet who, when faced with strong American pressure for a new and less punitive French policy on Germany, proposed to integrate the French and German coal and steel industries in the ECSC. The "original six," including Luxembourg, the Netherlands, Belgium, and Italy, signed the treaty in 1951, and the ECSC was officially created in July 1952. The British refused to participate, announcing that "a political federation limited to Western Europe is not compatible with our Commonwealth ties, our obligations as a member of the wider Atlantic alliance, or as a world power."

Monnet was a "functionalist" who reasoned that integration would never work if it depended on resolving everything at once. Success was more likely if it could be built on transnational cooperation on sectoral problems. Given the interdependencies of modern economies, sectoral economic cooperation was likely to spill over into new areas, and coal and steel were good places to begin. The idea dovetailed with cold war imperatives. The United States was exerting enormous pressure to normalize French-German relations. Germany and France both knew that the United States

would eventually impose its own design if the Europeans could not find one of their own. French public opinion might accept arrangements that promised to neutralize threats from Germany's heavy industries. German industrial interests needed open markets and space to grow. Both the French and Germans were also concerned about coal and steel overproduction, and they wanted to find ways to prevent this. At a stroke, Monnet's ECSC could solve a lot of problems. More important, the ECSC's Monnet-designed institutions would become the model for later steps in integration.

After the ECSC deal, the "Monnet method" was quickly proposed for other sectors, most often failing initially. French and Dutch proposals in 1950 for Europeanizing agriculture never got off the ground. A French proposal for a European transport authority was dropped. A multilateral proposal to establish a European Political Community (focused on foreign affairs) was a nonstarter. Then in 1952 came a Monnet-French proposal for a new European Defense Community (EDC) that sought to capitalize on the need to find acceptable ways for the Germans to rearm, a prospect that frightened most non-Germans. But the EDC collapsed in 1954 when the French themselves refused to ratify it in parliament.[2]

A "Common Market"?

The goal of European integration remained alive, however. The Belgian minister of foreign affairs, Paul-Henri Spaak, inspired by the Benelux arrangements, traveled throughout Europe to enlist other leaders to support a new European Economic Community, or Common Market. The conference of Messina, Italy, in June 1955 was the turning point. Led by Spaak and other Benelux politicians, the ECSC six announced their commitment to create Euratom (a European atomic energy agency), work for the harmonization of European social policies, and launch a European Common Market. The two Treaties of Rome in 1957 were the result, officially founding the European Economic Community (EEC) and Euratom. The French supported Euratom, Monnet's proposal, but were less enthusiastic about the Common Market. Their earlier failure with the EDC led them to negotiate an EEC treaty, but only if they received certain safeguards in return. The Germans knew that a Common Market would help the new German economy and give the new

Federal Republic needed legitimacy. They wanted trade liberalization for industrial products first of all, but the French would accept this only in exchange for a common agricultural policy that would give them preferential access to other EEC markets plus entry for tropical products from colonies and ex-colonies. The British, once again, were conspicuous by their absence. Instead the British sponsored a European Free Trade Association (EFTA) in 1959, including the Scandinavian countries, Iceland, Portugal, Switzerland, and Austria, which was designed to be a competitor for the new EEC.

The Preamble to the Rome EEC Treaty promised ". . . ever-closer union among the peoples of Europe." The Common Market would bring staged removal of barriers to internal trade in industrial goods as well as common rules to abolish "obstacles to freedom of movement for persons, services and capital," all nestled behind a common external tariff with a common commercial policy toward third countries. The Treaty's other objectives included common policies for agriculture, transport, procedures for coordinating EEC economic policy and controlling balance of payments disequilibria, plus a "system ensuring that competition in the common Market is not distorted." On specific Common Market matters member states would be obligated to harmonize their legal systems. There were also provisions for a European Social Fund, a European Investment Bank to promote development in less prosperous regions, and association arrangements that provided special access to the Common Market for overseas ex-colonies. With the exception of internal tariff liberalization, the Treaty was a "framework agreement" that announced general goals but left practical substance to be worked out later on a fixed schedule. Finally, where Rome did not explicitly pool sovereignty in the EEC, its member nations retained their full powers.

The EEC's institutions, which were modeled directly on those of the ECSC, were as significant as its purposes. There was, first of all, an appointed European Commission, sited in Brussels, with exclusive power to propose policy and duties to implement and safeguard the treaty. Next there was a Council of Ministers representing each national government, coordinated by a presidency that rotated every six months which voted on Commission proposals and served as the EEC "legislature." A European Parliament (EP), located in Strasbourg, was initially devoid of real power

and composed of members appointed from national parliaments. Finally, there was a European Court of Justice (ECJ), located in Luxembourg, that could adjudicate litigation and decide in those areas—mainly trade related—where the Rome Treaty granted EEC laws precedence over national statutes.

Jean Monnet, the institutional architect of the ECSC and EU, knew from a lifetime of experience, which included the failure of the League of Nations (where he had been Assistant Secretary General), that little would follow from simple and solemn pledges to cooperate by nation states unless the institutional framework for cooperation contained something to hold its member to their pledges. Thus the Commission was meant to be a motor that would push to expand the EEC's mandate over time, work as central strategic planner and activist for integration, and monitor of policy implementation, even if implementation was left mainly to national governments. It was the Council of Ministers that had the last word over Commission proposals, however, deciding according to rules spelled out in the treaty. Initially, most decisions were taken unanimously, but once the Common Market had been established, this was to change to "qualified majority voting" (QMV) in which member state votes were weighed by their size. Thus as time went on, member states could be outvoted on significant matters. The European Parliament was "consulted" (but did not have binding authority), debated an annual report from the Commission, and could, although it never did, dismiss the Commission on a vote of censure. It could also bring legal action against other EEC institutions before the ECJ for "failure to act." Finally, it could pose questions to which the Commission was obliged to respond.

The institutions of the EEC were also an open-ended experiment whose ultimate scope was left to trial, error, and struggle. The Commission's job was to carve space from the member states' sovereign prerogatives, making difficulties with the Council of Ministers inevitable. Moreover, because it was both powerful and appointed, it was open to charges of being an unelected "Brussels bureaucracy." The Council of Ministers itself hid behind an opaque shroud of diplomacy, which made it vulnerable to challenge about lack of transparency. The initial impotence of the European Parliament quickly created momentum for increased power in the name of diminishing the so-called democratic deficit. The

European Court of Justice could make European law through its rulings and the accumulation of jurisprudence since it was charged with ensuring that "in the interpretation and application of this Treaty the law is observed." Taken together, this meant that in a Europe of nations without its "we the people," the new EEC was certain to face issues of legitimacy.

The EEC nonetheless floated happily on buoyant economic conditions in its early years. Emulating the American model of consumerism and mass production with new houses, roads, and schools, Europeans tasted the joys of cars, household appliances, seaside holidays, and television. In the 1960s, the peak boom decade, average growth in EEC member states was an impressive 5 percent annually, and trade inside the EEC grew even faster. Coexistence between the EEC and national dynamism was not always easy, however.

EEC insiders had hoped that integrationist activists in Brussels, particularly in the Commission, would "Europeanize" rapidly, but some national leaders had little taste for this. As the EEC customs union came into being faster than expected, the United States mobilized the GATT in part to avoid a protectionist "fortress Europe." The Common Agricultural Policy (CAP) caused controversy both internally and internationally. When the Commission proposed an economically liberal CAP, it was junked because it threatened French and German agricultural subsidy systems. When this was replaced by a costly scheme of administered price supports for agricultural goods that protected EEC farmers internationally, the Americans again became unhappy. Making deals in other areas was difficult as well, and Commission attempts to promote common transport, regional, and industrial policies were blocked, despite the explicit goals of the Rome Treaty.

President Charles de Gaulle of France became the symbol of member states' insistence on having the last word. When the British decided quickly that they wanted to join the EEC, but with important exemptions that would allow them to continue Commonwealth trading, everyone but the French agreed. De Gaulle was also deeply suspicious of the British-American "special relationship," and in January 1963, after denouncing the UK for seeking to make the EEC into a "free trade area" and a servant of Anglo-American goals, he vetoed the deal. Then de Gaulle turned on the Commission. Charles De

Gaulle was a firm French nationalist and vehement antifederalist who advocated an intergovernmental "Europe of nations." When Walter Hallstein, the first Commission president, proposed a scheme to finance the CAP that would also enhance the Commission's powers, de Gaulle stopped cooperating and, in September 1965 the French withdrew from the Council of Ministers, which paralyzed decision making. This began the "empty chair" episode, and it had important consequences. The treaties had proposed that after January 1966 the Council might begin to decide by qualified majority. To de Gaulle, this meant that "France . . . would be exposed to having its hands forced in almost any economic matter, hence social and often even political." The result, the "Luxembourg Compromise," made unanimity the norm until the 1980s.

De Gaulle spoke for France, but his words reflected deeper realities. The Common Market began at the high point of Europe's postwar boom. During this period, before globalization began eroding states' capacities, each national government developed its own strategies for governing the economy, including welfare states, subsidies for industry, regulated credit, pump priming to stimulate demand—sometimes outright planning. Such profoundly national models set limits on Europeanization, even if European integration supplemented them in important ways, particularly by increasing intra-EEC trade to stimulate additional growth. The common external tariff also provided some protection from the harsh winds of open international trade, which made the EEC both a buffer against the U.S.-coordinated Bretton Woods system and a subsystem within it. In general, the Common Market was a handmaiden to continental Europe's postwar boom, useful in some policy areas, but an unwelcome intrusion in others.

Crisis and Renewal, 1970–1993

De Gaulle resigned in 1969 and then, for a brief period, EU leaders found new energy for the European project. The 1969 Hague Summit set out plans for greater internal market opening, "widening" the EEC to new members, "deepening" it through larger budgetary powers, establishing some foreign policy coordination ("European political cooperation," a set of arrangements for foreign offices to coordinate on foreign policy issues), and reflecting on the Economic and Monetary Union (EMU). Then the EEC expanded from six to nine members in 1973, when the British, Irish, and Danes joined (Norway negotiated its entrance, but the Norwegians voted against it in a referendum). It also began to acquire its own budgetary resources. Earlier it had depended on direct funding from member state budgets, but from this point it acquired direct revenues from agricultural levies, import duties, and a percentage of national value-added taxes—even though the EEC budget remained small. There were also ambitious plans for regional development (through the creation of the European Regional Development Fund—ERDF) and social policy.

Harder times were at hand, however. The enlargement did not go smoothly. The British had paid too high a price to join—contributing too much to finance the CAP and receiving too little in return, and this turned them into chronic complainers. Next the international monetary situation turned bad after the United States, which was threatened by imports and trade deficits, ended the Bretton Woods dollar/gold standard. Henceforth the dollar "floated" against other currencies, leading to fluctuating exchange rates that were often fed by speculation. The new system was treacherous for the multicurrency EEC, making predictions difficult, dampening enthusiasm, slowing trade growth, and tempting governments to use revaluations as trading weapons. For the Common Agricultural Policy, changes in exchange rates led to changing relative prices across the EEC, creating new tensions, forcing CAP administrators repeatedly to realign price supports, and leading EU bureaucrats to invent new, and quite incomprehensible, ways of paying off those who lost from currency shifting.

The worst was yet to come. Member states had to renege on their pledges to reach full economic and monetary union by 1980, largely because of the oil shocks of 1973 and 1979. Dependent on imported oil paid for in U.S. dollars, Europe had to face rising oil prices that fed an already inflationary economic environment. Profits and investment declined, and European industry began to lose competitive advantage. Trying to confront these new problems then revealed a perplexing "stagflation"—simultaneous inflation and sluggish growth. The growth boom stopped in its tracks while unemployment rose,

governments had to cut back state spending on social programs, and public finances became precarious. By the later 1970s the EEC had begun a downward economic spiral.

There were some European responses to these challenges, primarily through informal intergovernmental deals that were done at the summits of heads of state and government that quickly became a new institution, the European Council (integrated into EC treaties in 1987). In 1974 the new European Council proposed direct elections to the European Parliament, which were held for the first time in 1979. The European Parliament also gained some power of the purse through the creation of "own resources" for European institutions, plus the right to reject the EEC budget as a whole. The most significant innovation was the European Monetary System (EMS), which was brokered by the French president Valéry Giscard d'Estaing and the German chancellor Helmut Schmidt in 1978–1979. The EMS was complicated. All EEC members belonged to it, but membership of its inner circle, the Exchange Rate Mechanism (ERM) included only those willing to accept stronger monetary constraints (the British, for example, did not join until 1990) such as keeping the value of their currency within a "narrow band" of reference (± 2.5 percent) to a weighted "basket" of all member currencies. ERM included mechanisms for market intervention to help threatened currencies and methods for revaluing currencies when the need arose.[3] EMS and the ERM would later prove to be a significant link between the EC's 1970s crisis and the renewal of integration.

EMS notwithstanding, in the early 1980s European integration was seriously endangered by the divergent policy responses of member states. Germany, the one success story, restructured its economy in a context of stable prices. In the early 1980s, however, France had a Socialist administration that briefly pursued statist and inflationary policies. Thatcherite neoliberalism in Britain went its own way, while in the United States, Reagan and the Federal Reserve Bank provoked the deepest international recession since the 1930s. Internally, the EEC was paralyzed by budget disputes in which British governments petulantly demanded their money back—the "British check" issue, often preventing anyone from doing anything else. The EEC was still alive, but the body was not stirring much.

Liberalization and Renewal: The "1992" Program

The European Commission came abruptly back to life in the mid-1980s. The comeback was part of a new strategy to reinvigorate market relationships and create a regional economic bloc around a newly opened European market that was designed to confront the threatening international market environment that we now call globalization.

The failure of the French left precipitated the renewal. After his election in 1981, François Mitterrand initially promoted public ownership, state-driven economic planning, new power for unions and workers, an expanded welfare state, and strong economic stimulation. The program rapidly fueled high inflation, trade deficits, and pressures on the franc that led to three devaluations. By the winter of 1982–1983, the French faced a choice between leaving EMS and doing major damage to European integration or finding an entirely different domestic economic strategy. In March 1983 Mitterrand shifted France's domestic policies toward deflation, austerity, and rapid retreat from *dirigisme* (state-led economic steering). This French about-face on economic governance led the policies of major EU members to converge and made new common action conceivable. Mitterrand tied this shift to diplomatic moves toward renewed European integration, beginning with the French presidency of the EU in the first half of 1984, which resolved many of the issues underlying "Europessimism," such as the "British check" problem and barriers to Spanish and Portuguese membership into the EU. Finally, leaders named Jacques Delors, a former French finance minister, to be the new president of the European Commission.

A week after taking office in 1985, Delors asked the European Parliament, "Is it presumptuous to . . . remove all the borders inside Europe from here to 1992 . . . ?" The first step was a Commission White Paper on Completing the Internal Market, quickly labeled the "1992" program, listing nearly three hundred measures to unify the EU's still largely separate national markets into an "area without internal borders in which the free movement of goods, persons, services and capital is ensured." Internal border posts would go, cross-border formalities simplified, common

European product standards developed, and value-added and excise taxation, obstacles to cross-border trade, would be harmonized—all to be done over eight years leading to "1992."

EU leaders then called an "intergovernmental conference" (IGC) to speed implementation of the "1992" program, producing the Single European Act (SEA, ratified in 1987), the first significant modification of the 1957 Rome Treaties. The SEA tied the single-market program to qualified majority voting in most White Paper areas. Henceforth only the most sensitive single-market matters (fiscal policy, border controls, issues concerning the movement of people, and workers' rights) would still require unanimity, meaning that member states might now be outvoted. The SEA then extended the European Parliament's amending power so that the Parliament could henceforth propose amendments, the so-called cooperation procedure. The SEA also expanded the EU's policy areas to include expanded regional development policy ("economic and social cohesion"), research and development, and environmental policy. Finally, it consecrated the European Council and European Political Cooperation (foreign policy coordination) in the treaty and foresaw further monetary integration.

European integration was moving forward again. The "1992" slogan generated public enthusiasm and played shrewdly to broader political realities. The Germans, facing rising unemployment, needed new trade. The French saw "1992" as an indirect way of enhancing their diplomatic power. The British favored liberalization and deregulation in principle. Big business supported the single market. Weaker support from organized labor—the program could threaten jobs and facilitate "social dumping" (companies relocating to areas with lower social overhead costs)—led the Commission to promise new "social dialogue" between Euro-level "social partners." The European Parliament also became a big supporter, partly because it was hungry for more power in the EU institutional setup. The most important source of support for the new policies was good economic luck, however, an upturn in the European economies.

The Delors Commission rapidly sought more change.[4] The EU faced budgetary crisis, largely because CAP expenses were out of control, and it needed new regional development policies, and the Commission ingeniously combined these problems into a "Delors budgetary package" to change the EU budgeting process. Henceforth member states would negotiate multiyear "financial perspectives," that would avoid annual money fights and enhance the Commission's budgeting role. The package proposed CAP reforms to begin "capping" spending and a "reform of the structural funds" involving new European-level commitment to redistribution from richer to poorer members and a doubling of regional development spending.

Proposals for economic and monetary union came next. EMU could reduce transaction costs, prod restructuring of Europe's financial industries, and make intra-European factor costs more transparent. It would also make wages a better reflection of national productivity, bring national budgetary and fiscal policies closer to economic fundamentals, and provide member state governments a good pretext for pushing through needed economic reforms by blaming them on mandates from the EU. In international terms, the EMU's single currency could, in time, become a reserve currency to rival the dollar. Last but not least, EMU would be another giant step for European integration. A committee chaired by Delors in 1988 set out the outlines for EMU—an independent European Central Bank committed to price stability and a gradual three-stage approach to promote economic convergence among potential members. At the Madrid European Council in June 1989 everyone but the United Kingdom approved another intergovernmental conference to put EMU into the treaties.

Globalization and Uncertainty: From Maastricht to Enlargement

By the autumn of 1989, EU Europe's security had been guaranteed by NATO and American power for four decades. Europe had been divided so long that people thought the division was permanent. "Western" Europe was twelve wealthy EU members and a few other countries with the credentials to be EU members (which most would become in 1995). Eastern Europe was "existing socialism," inefficient, oppressive, and walled off by Soviet power. The Berlin Wall came down in November 1989, however, presaging the end of the cold war and the collapse of the Soviet Union. For Europe, 1989 was a moment of huge joy. Thoughtful Europeans

knew, however, that it would inevitably change the EU's map and agenda.

The first big event was German unification, which the European Commission took the lead in welcoming, even though British prime minister Margaret Thatcher and French president François Mitterrand were skeptical. The wisdom of helping Germany to unify seemed self-evident, however: Germany, which was at the heart of Europe, had been the foundation of the EU's past and should be its future. The next step was to find ways to give ex-socialist societies of Central and Eastern Europe help in democratizing and modernizing economically. From 1989 onward, confronting Europe's East-West divisions would weigh heavily on the EU table. The problem was that the table had already been piled heavily with other things. Practically every speech that Jacques Delors had made after 1985 insisted that EU Europe had to choose between economic survival and decline, and that it needed to change or risk being swamped by globalization.[5] Despite the fall of the Berlin Wall the EU had to complete the agenda of the 1980s, and in particular to implement the proposals for a federalized monetary policy and single currency.

The drive for EMU culminated in the year-long intergovernmental conferences that ended in December 1991 in Maastricht, Holland. Dealing on EMU proved relatively easy, since the 1988 Delors Report had proposed a clear program and the unequal balance of power between Germany and France dictated how final differences would be resolved. The Germans, who had been asked to give up the deutschemark, their most important national symbol and the source of European monetary power, insisted that EMU guarantee price stability and national financial responsibility. The British opposed EMU altogether, but were allowed to opt out, joined by the Danes. The Spanish, seeking larger north-south financial transfers, won a Cohesion Fund that applied to the "Club Med" countries (Spain, Greece, Portugal, and Ireland, the last two not "Med" at all). The first Franco-German difference was about "convergence criteria" to oblige aspirants to EMU to align policies prior to being qualified to join, with the final, harsh, terms set out by Germany. Applicants had to lower national budget deficits to 3 percent of GDP, squeeze down longer-term debt (to 60 percent of GDP), sustain low interest and inflation rates, and stabilize their currencies. The timing of EMU phase-in was the second big issue, with the Germans, feeling the economic pinch of unification, insisted on softening the goals of stage 2. The French wanted an "economic government" to set EMU macroeconomic policy, but the Germans refused, insisting instead on a completely independent European Central Bank that would be statutorily committed to price stability. Deciding the date when the new European Central Bank would actually start its work preparing the single currency was the only French victory. This could occur in January 1997 if a majority of states were eligible, but it had to happen on January 1, 1999, no matter how many were ready. This victory may have been what ensured that EMU actually materialized.

Maastricht turned out to be more complicated than the EMU deal, however, because the Belgians had suggested and the Germans insisted on parallel negotiations on "political union," a set of issues including common EU foreign and security policy, greater democratization, more efficient institutions, and more coherence among the EU's monetary, economic, and political activities. These issues brought out predictable, but profound, disagreements between "federalists" and "intergovernmentalists" and about whether there should or should not be more political integration. The proposed "common foreign and security policy" (CFSP) divided the EU's pro-NATO "Atlanticists" (the British, Dutch, and Portuguese) from those—led by the French—who desired more independent European positions and a robust military capability. These differences led to vague language and results that were more declarations of intent than firm positions. Initially CFSP amounted to what already existed—ongoing European Political Cooperation—writ somewhat larger, a declaration that CFSP might bring "the eventual framing of a common defense policy, which might in time lead to a common defense," and pious hopes that Western European Union, at that point an empty military shell, might become the EU's security arm (either as a pillar within NATO, which the Atlanticists wanted, or the core of an autonomous European military, which the French desired). On "justice and home affairs"(JHA)—matters relating to the free circulation of people in the single market—the "Schengen" arrangements for opening borders between some EU states were to be broadened to all, if possible, with a new "Europol" that would coordinate police information and new action on

"Europeanized" crime. Finally, Maastricht set minimal standards for EU citizenship and pointed toward common approaches to immigration and asylum policies. By far the most significant result, however, was "codecision," which gave the European Parliament equal weight to the Council of Ministers on most Community legislation. The Parliament also acquired the right to vote on proposed Commission presidents. Finally, Maastricht proposed two new institutions, a "Committee of the Regions" and an ombudsman, plus a strengthened Court of Auditors.

Negotiating the Maastricht Treaty on European Union (or TEU) revealed deep disagreement about European integration. Federalists and strong integrationists wanted a "tree" in which everything connected to a common trunk (the Community). Intergovernmentalists and reluctant integrators wanted a "Greek temple" of three separate "pillars" connected through a unifying preamble. The temple builders won. This meant that Maastricht's two great leaps forward beyond EMU, the CFSP and JHA, would each be contained in a separate intergovernmental pillar outside the economic "community," where multilateral negotiating between member states would supplant the "Community method" and its "institutional triangle" (Commission, Council, Parliament). The new title of "European Union" (EU) included the entire temple, as illustrated in Figure 32.1. Before TEU, the workings of "community" institutions, involving complicated relationships among the Commission, Council of Ministers, Court of Justice and Parliament, was already difficult for any but experts to decode and quite different from common understandings of national democracy. Two new "pillars" in two new areas central to everyone's understanding of sovereignty that would work in intergovernmental ways would deepen the confusion.

The TEU was meant to intensify integration, but fatigue had set in, particularly at the national level. The GATT Uruguay Round, the first to undertake opening agricultural trade, came to a head just after Maastricht. Without CAP reform the round would have failed, and European business interests wanted more trade liberalization plus agreement on services, intellectual property, and foreign direct investment. With practically everyone against them, European farmers could not resist serious change, and reform began shifting the

Figure 32.1

The Maastricht Temple

Common Pediment
Common Principles and Objectives
Articles A through F of the Maastricht Treaty
Key Actor for Strategy and Coordination: European Council

Pillar	Community Pillar 1	Pillar 2	Pillar 3
Content	• European Community • European Coal and Steel Community • Euratom (Titles II, III, and IV of the Maastricht Treaty)	Common Foreign and Security Policy (CFSP)	Cooperation in matters of justice and internal affairs (policing transnational crime, migration)
Principle of Governance	Community method Commission importance ECJ jurisprudence	Intergovernmental Council importance National jurisprudence	Intergovernmental Council importance National jurisprudence

CAP from price supports for farm products toward "set-asides" that would pay farmers not to produce, moving Europe closer to American methods for subsidizing farmers. To keep farm interests from rebelling, the new CAP was programmed to cost as much as the old. CAP had become an albatross, an expensive, inefficient scheme of redistributing a lot of taxpayer and consumer resources to a small number of aging farmers and big agribusinesses. The beneficiaries were belligerent about keeping the CAP going, however.

Once the Uruguay Round had forced CAP reform, a second multiyear budgetary package had to be negotiated. Intense debate showed that richer countries had lost their taste for increasing the EU budget, one sign among many that the enthusiasm was waning for greater integration of the later 1980s. Ratifying the Maastricht Treaty also exposed a well of public opposition. The Danes, who had always been reluctant political integrators, voted no in early 1992. Success in an Irish referendum (69 percent to 31 percent) provided brief solace. A French referendum in September 1992 barely approved the TEU—51 percent yes, 49 percent no— and saved, but hardly endorsed, Maastricht.

After the Cold War: New Trials

A bad economic downturn began in early 1992, with growth stagnating and unemployment rising to 10 percent in the larger EU economies, a level not seen since the Great Depression. The single-market program was working . . . to push employers to shed labor. Abrupt monetary crisis made things worse. Beginning in the summer of 1992, fluctuations of the German DM, connected to inflationary pressures from German unification, weakened EMS currencies and obliged higher interest rates. Realigning currencies might have ended problems, but no one wanted this in the middle of the French referendum campaign. The result was "Black Wednesday," September 16, 1992, when the British pound sterling left the ERM, followed by the Italian lira. The Spanish and Irish currencies were also eventually devalued, the currencies of Finland, Sweden, and Norway, three EFTA candidates for EU membership, were cut loose from their pegs to EMS, and some countries reintroduced exchange controls. The EMS crisis darkened the sky over EMU. The EMU convergence criteria, within reach for most EU members until the recession, suddenly became a burden in the face of declining tax revenues, increased public spending, and troubled budgets.

The "1992" period ended on January 1, 1993, in a quiet way that spoke volumes. Yeoman work had been done, but the single market was not quite completed, with delays in value-added tax realignment, liberalizing public procurement and the energy sector, reconfiguring financial markets, and transposing Commission legislation into national law. Failure to remove airport passport controls provided tangible evidence that the free movement of people lagged behind. Finally, promises that the single market would bring back vitality to the European economy had manifestly not been redeemed.

The Delors Commission tried to mobilize member states again in 1993 with a new White Paper on Growth, Competitiveness, and Employment. The paper began by acknowledging that European growth and investment had been shrinking over decades, that the EU's competitive position was worsening, and that there was no easy cure for unemployment. The single market had helped, it argued, but not enough, partly because the rest of the world had also responded intelligently to new globalization. The White Paper asserted that "creating as favorable an environment as possible for company competitiveness" was essential, with particular stress on advanced technology, in which Europe was behind. Member states should also promote flexible small and medium-sized industries and accelerate the building of "trans-European networks" (TENs) in infrastructure (particularly telecommunications) to push Europe toward an "information society," where new comparative advantage would be found. The White Paper also called for reforms to introduce more flexibility into labor markets and welfare states. National employment systems needed to adopt "active labor market policies . . . beginning with commitment to lifelong education."

The new White Paper was prophetic, but, in contrast to 1985, EU members did not have the will to follow its suggestions. Governments had grown tired of high

tension at Euro-level, they faced new domestic economic problems, and their citizens were increasingly skeptical about Europe. The Union also faced another enlargement in 1995 to three new ex-EFTA applicants, Austria, Sweden, and Finland (after the Norwegians rejected membership for the second time). These small, rich, and successful countries fit the EU profile well, but enlargement was disruptive nonetheless. Newcomers always brought their own ideas and had to be fit into the working of EU institutions, making the EU equation more complicated. Finally, the Germans were worried about the reliability of some eventual EMU members, Italy and Spain in particular. The German government's response was to propose a Stability and Growth Pact (SGP, incorporated into the treaty of Amsterdam in 1997) that would keep the EMU convergence targets in force after EMU began.

German concerns were well founded. In the period before final EMU membership was decided, the Italians, with a budget deficit of 7.7 percent and cumulated debt of 124 percent (vs. the target 60 percent) in 1995, looked hopeless, and their efforts at manipulating interest rates on government bonds, privatizing to shift debt off the public ledgers, and other fudging were not reassuring. Spain's 1995 deficit of 6.6 percent led the Commission to threaten suspension of regional development payments, but the 1996 budget was better, and renewed growth brought Spain into line. The French, who were indispensable to EMU, approached convergence with austerity, creative accounting, hyperbole from politicians, and strikes. Even the German government was pressed to propose revaluing the Bundesbank's gold reserves at the last minute, but domestic politics made this impossible. Nonetheless on May 3, 1998, the heads of state and government declared eleven member states eligible for EMU (Greece made twelve in 2000, Slovenia thirteen in 2006). Wim Duisenberg, a Dutchman, became the ECB's first president, with the unhappy French insisting that he be succeeded after four years by Jean-Claude Trichet, a French central banker. EMU thus began, even though many had doubted that it would.

If globalization had begun to challenge the EU economically in the 1990s, the end of the cold war had similar effects on Europe's positions in the world. For four decades the cold war had left little room for autonomous European foreign political and military power. But the successes of European integration after 1985 enhanced the EU's power in the world, particularly in economic matters, and led some to advocate new integration in defense and foreign policy matters. The Maastricht Treaty on European Union brought a new Common Foreign and Security Policy pillar, but as an empty shell that would be filled in later, if member states were willing.

Militarily, the end of the cold war was a shock. The British and Germans stood prepared to confront a Soviet invasion just as the Soviet Union was ceasing to exist. The French, with vast sums invested in an independent deterrent, found themselves with nuclear submarines roaming the seas targeted on newly friendly Central and Eastern European (CEEC) countries. EU member states had to do something to update their security outlooks. Would they do so in a "European" way, within the EU? In 1991, before anyone had time to find answers, armed conflict broke out in Europe for the first time since 1945, when the Yugoslav Federation began to disintegrate. Belgrade, defending the Federation, responded with armed force to declarations of independence by Slovenia and Croatia. Its efforts in Slovenia fizzled immediately, but full-out warfare began in Croatia. The French were pro-Serb and the Germans pro-Croat. There could be no coherent EU response, therefore. When Bosnia-Herzegovina declared independence, the Serbs again sent in the troops. Attempts at EU-UN mediation (including the Vance-Owen Plan of 1993) failed. The EU was humiliated by its inability to do anything useful to curb Serbian brutality and ethnic cleansing. Euro-posturing—solemn statements, high-powered delegations, economic sanctions, attempts at mediation, flattering diplomacy, and other hand-wringing—repeatedly fell short in Croatia and Bosnia, as they would later on in Kosovo. Where Europeans tried to assume peace-keeping roles, they were weak, uncoordinated, and needed NATO help. It took tough American diplomatic brokerage at Dayton to impose a new status quo in Bosnia, and even if Dayton was followed by the hard and dangerous work of European peace keeping on the ground, the humiliation stung.[6] The Americans had the "assets" to present credible threats, allowing them to call the shots in a literal sense, making the Europeans spectators in their own backyard.

EU failure gave rise to new thinking. Between Bosnia and Kosovo, the EU slowly began to move toward some collective foreign policy and defense capability. The evasive wording and impossible decision rules on CFSP in the Maastricht Treaty were changed in the 1997 Amsterdam Treaty to allow "reinforced cooperation" that might circumvent the vetoes that were inherent in Maastricht's unanimity rules. Amsterdam also created a "Mr. CFSP" to serve as the organizing center of EU foreign policy efforts and gave the job to the able Javier Solana, former secretary-general of NATO. It also included the "Petersberg" tasks, first set out in 1992 to define possible new EU military activities, opening the Union to larger humanitarian and rescue intervention, peacekeeping, and the use of force for regional crisis management. In parallel, NATO, reviewing its positions, opened the possibility of a new "European pillar," "Combined Joint Task Forces" ("coalitions of the willing" for crisis management), and a "European Strategic Defense Initiative" (ESDI) which was enshrined in the Amsterdam Treaty. In certain circumstances, NATO might make its assets available to Europeans. However, a NATO subtext was that any new European security aspirations would be kept on a very short leash, as close to NATO as possible, and hence under the close scrutiny of the United States.[7]

Chapter 34 will return to the story of EU Europe's quest for a new place in the world. One important dimension of this story, enlarging the Union to the ex-communist East, began in the 1990s, however. EU enlargement already had a long history. In the 1970s, three new members from EFTA (the United Kingdom, Ireland, and Denmark) joined the original six, in the 1980s. Greece, Spain, and Portugal joined, all recently emerged from harsh authoritarian regimes and in 1995, three rich former-EFTA countries, Austria, Finland, and Sweden, quietly joined, bringing the EU to fifteen members. From this experience the EU had concluded that new applicants should conform to an *acquis communautaire*, the accumulated body of rights and obligations that had come to bind EU member states. The more Europe integrated the more extensive this *acquis* became, eventually stretching into every nook and cranny of lives of potential members, from the organization of markets to operations of companies, courts, and elections. By the new millennium, the codified *acquis* had grown to thirty-two chapters and over 80,000 dense pages.

At the end of the cold war, the Central and Eastern European Countries (CEECS) had little experience with Western-style democracy, market economies, administrative and judicial practices, and many other aspects of life that existing EU members took for granted. Enlarging the EU to the CEECs thus involved imposing Western European standards on them, and making sure the massive reforms that this involved were completed.

The EU started working with the CEECs in the very early 1990s, coordinating and delivering G24 food and humanitarian aid to Poland and Hungary. The PHARE program (a French acronym for *Pologne-Hongrie: Assistance pour la Restructuration des Économies*) which became the EU's major instrument to help all CEECs, eventually extended to infrastructure; help to business, education, training, and research; and funding for environmental protection, including nuclear safety and agricultural restructuring. The EU also quickly helped found a European Bank for Reconstruction and Development (EBRD) to funnel private investment to the CEECs.[8] The carrots and sticks approach was expanded, beginning in 1990, when the Union negotiated conditional "association agreements" (quickly renamed "Europe Agreements"), first with Poland and Hungary, and then with other CEECs, to prepare "a new pattern of relationships in Europe." These agreements included cooperation on foreign policy matters; trade agreements aimed at building a free trade area; and economic, cultural, and financial help; plus the beginnings of aligning EU and CEEC legislation on key market matters (primarily competition rules and intellectual property). The game was reasonably clear. The CEECs had to become ever more like EU members, in exchange for which they would get help, and, if they did the right things, they might ultimately be allowed to join.

The 1993 Copenhagen European Council declared that the EU was willing "conditionally" to accept new memberships provided that applicants met the three basic criteria of stable institutions (defined as guarantees of democracy, the rule of law, human rights, and minority rights), a functioning market economy and capacity to cope with competitive pressures inside the EU, and the ability to adopt the full *acquis communautaire*. In 1994 this was followed up with a detailed "pre-accession strategy" that scheduled regular meetings, began preparations for integrating the CEECs into the single market, and promised new policies on infrastructure, environmental policy, CFSP, justice and home affairs, and other key matters. By this point Poland and Hungary had already applied for membership.

The 1995 Madrid European Council asked the Commission to prepare "opinions" on possible candidates (the first strong step to enlargement) after it had completed a study on the effects of enlargement on the existing EU, proposing finally that full negotiations for membership could begin six months after the Amsterdam IGC ended in 1997. By then ten "associated" candidates, eight CEECs plus Malta and Cyprus, had applied. The Amsterdam Treaty negotiations, in part convened to update EU institutions for the new enlargement, led instead to an inadequate compromise that postponed tough questions to yet another IGC in 2000, demonstrating that member states were unwilling to begin serious change until enlargement was truly at hand. The enlargement process was nonetheless underway. The Commission's important *Agenda 2000*, which had been designed to open discussion on a new financial perspectives package, opined that no CEECs had yet fulfilled the Copenhagen criteria, but that the Czech Republic, Estonia, Hungary, Poland, and Slovenia were within reach, and it recommended opening negotiations with them. The European Council in 1997 then expanded the negotiations to all ten candidates.

The EU's confrontation with issues of economic competitiveness, foreign policy, and enlargement are ongoing events. We will return to them later when we discuss EU policymaking in Chapter 34. Before then, however, we must turn to the all-important, and difficult, matter of understanding European Union institutions.

Notes

[1] See Alan Milward, *The Reconstruction of Western Europe, 1945–1951* (London: Methuen, 1984).

[2] The Americans prevailed, leading in 1954 to the Paris Agreements creating the Western European Union (WEU), admitting the Germans to NATO, and resolving outstanding Franco-German disputes over the Saar. A four-power treaty (France, the United States, the United Kingdom, and Germany) then granted sovereignty to the new German Republic.

[3]Revaluation occurred twenty-six times between 1979 and 1999 (when EMU came into existence).

[4]Delors and his team used the metaphor of "Russian Dolls" when discussing their approach. See George Ross, *Jacques Delors and European Integration* (New York: Oxford University Press, 1995).

[5]Jacques Delors's *Mémoires* (Paris: Plon, 2004) are an essential source on this period.

[6]See Anthony Forster and William Wallace, "Common Foreign and Security Policy," in Helen Wallace, William Wallace, and Mark A. Pollack, *Policy-Making in the European Union,* 5th ed. (Oxford: Oxford University Press, 2005).

[7]See Frank Schimmelfennig, *The EU, NATO, and the Integration of Europe* (Cambridge: Cambridge University Press, 2003).

[8]For a review of enlargement matters, see Ulrich Sedelmeier and Helen Wallace, "Eastern Enlargement: Strategy or Second Thoughts?" in Wallace, Wallace, and Pollack (2005).

CHAPTER 33

The Institutions of the European Union

Europeans founded the Westphalian nation-state system at the end of the Thirty Years War in 1648. The results, over centuries, were strong, powerful states—each with its language, identity, habits, and ways of doing things—who became rivals and often fought one another. Fifty years ago, some of these states decided to work together. Their experiment with interstate cooperation had to begin tentatively, in quite specific areas, while states kept most of their powers and approaches. The institutions for this new, unprecedented, cooperation thus were not to be "statelike," but specially built to govern and manage particular things. Amid all the uncertainty associated with this first fifty years of experimenting, two things are clear. Today's EU is not a state, and it does not seem to be becoming a state. Instead it is a unique and complex system of multilevel governance (MLG) built on cooperation in particular areas.

The Institutional "Triangle" and the "Community Method"

For much of its institutional life, the EU has been primarily the European "community," a triangle of institutions including the European Commission, the Council of (national) Ministers, and the European Parliament. Because the EU was a legal construct, this triangle also operated under the judicial oversight of a European Court of Justice (ECJ). As the EU has matured, new complexities have blurred this portrait. Beginning in the 1970s, regular, official summit meetings of EU heads of state and government, called the European Council, became the EU's longer-term strategic planner and decider of last resort. Then the 1993 Maastricht Treaty on European Union expanded the Union's scope into new areas such as foreign policy, defense and security, criminal justice, and immigration, but because these new areas lay at the core of national sovereignty EU leaders deemed that the somewhat supranational Community institutional "triangle" was not the best place to decide about them, and instead opted for intergovernmental "pillars." The contemporary EU is thus largely a "Community" but also, in certain critical areas, an arena for multilateral negotiation.

The European Commission

The Rome treaties gave the European Commission (EC) three major prerogatives: it has exclusive legal rights to propose Community legislation in the form of regulations, directives, and recommendations (laws binding on all members in the same terms, laws that have to be transposed into the language of national legal codes, plus "soft law" of a suggestive but non-binding nature). It also supervises the implementation of Community policy to ensure that member states transpose EU law into national statutes and carry it out. Finally, it is the "guardian" of the EU treaties, seeing to the observation of EU law and, if need be, bringing member states and private bodies before the ECJ to oblige them to abide by the law. The Commission also acquired an important additional role, as representative of the EU internationally, particularly on all-important trade issues, and a fifth, de facto, role as a collective of activists to think about and agitate for the future of European integration. The Commission is one of EU Europe's most original institutional creations. Intergovernmental cooperation, at the EU's heart, is difficult because national governments have interests that are hard to reconcile. The Commission's job is to devise and propose projects that reflect the common interest.

The Commission, which can only initiate proposals where the EU treaties explicitly allow it to, has a few policy competencies where it behaves a bit like a federal government (although it is very much *not* a government). It alone administers EU competition (antitrust) policies, policing state subsidies to industry, monopoly market power, and mergers. The Commission administers the Common Agricultural Policy (CAP), but member states decide on key policy lines. It also proposes rules for and administers the European single market and manages, and to some extent designs, spending plans to help the EU's poorer regions to develop. It has acquired important roles in European environmental policy, and has a significant role in designing European-level research and development programs. It draws up the basic EU budget, although its proposals are almost always rewritten by member states. Internationally, besides representing the Union in trade matters and in some international organizations, it manages substantial foreign aid and assistance programs and supervises EU diplomatic delegations in over 100 countries.

Commissioners are appointed by member state governments for five-year terms that coincide with the electoral life of the European Parliament. Until 2005 the Commission had two members from each large member state (Germany, France, Italy, the United Kingdom, and Spain) and one each for smaller ones. The 2004–2007 enlargement to ten CEECs, Malta, and Cyprus left only one Commissioner to each member, a total of twenty-seven, too many for the actual number of important Commission jobs. The Commission has a president, nominated by the European Council, who must also be approved by the Parliament, and several vice-presidents who oversee clusters of activities. For some time the European Parliament has had the right to scrutinize the qualifications of each proposed new commissioner, and although it cannot block appointment of specific commissioners, it may withhold approval of the entire Commission, a strong sanction that it has never used.

The group of commissioners works together in a "college,"—a concept foreign to ordinary political bodies—a collective in which each commissioner, whatever his or her tasks, participates in all key decisions equally with all the others. The Commission president has few of the powers of appointment, policy direction, and arbitration of a prime minister. The president's influence, which can be considerable, however, comes mainly from "presiding" over the Commission and planning its agenda, aided by the Commission's general secretariat and legal services. The president also assigns each commissioner a portfolio of precise tasks before he or she enters office (see Table 33.1 for the present Commission), involving political supervision over one or several of the Commission's "services" (General Directorates or DGs). Commissioners do not have independent "ministerial" powers over their services, however, and their supervisory tasks are undertaken in accordance with programmatic lines to which the entire Commission has agreed. Finally, Commissioners are all required to swear "to be completely independent in the performance of their duties [and to] neither seek nor take instructions from any government or from any other body" (Article 157 EEC).

The Commission meets every Wednesday, three times a month in Brussels and once in Strasbourg, France (while at the European Parliament's monthly plenary sessions). It usually takes off the month of August, when governments—and almost everything except vacation resorts—shut down across Europe. The Commission decides matters after a careful collective debate to which each commissioner is expected to contribute knowledgeably, the heart of the college method. Ministers in classic governments are subordinate to prime ministers who ultimately decide, and they are specialists who argue briefs related mainly to their ministry, participating in other areas only as informed spectators. In contrast, Commissioners, as members of the college, participate in all decisions, and their influence depends on doing so effectively. The goal of collegiality is to produce consensus—in theory the Commission stands as one person behind all of its different positions—and it votes only when no consensus can be reached.

Collegial organization necessitates lots of legwork to bring Commissioners up to speed on multiple, complex issues. Commissioners are thus assisted by "cabinets," or personal staffs, composed of a half-dozen ambitious civil servants who work on the entire range of issues on the Commission floor and also with services that are pertinent to the commissioner's portfolio. The cabinet system, borrowed from French and Belgian practices, is controversial because it inserts a layer of operators between commissioners and their administrative services, even though it is difficult to see how the Commission could function as a college without it.

Despite a reputation as an unstoppable "Brussels bureaucracy," the Commission administration is small, around 24,000 people (roughly the size of the staff of a mid-sized European city); only a minority are real "Eurocrats," A-grade officers. National distribution of A-level posts is carefully observed, with some jobs regularly allocated to nationals of particular countries. Each major Commission service is headed by a general director, ranked "A-1," the Commission's highest administrative post. A-level Commission jobs are often more interesting than most national civil service jobs, very well paid (A-1 jobs are now around $250,000 yearly), exempt from national taxes (although the EU

Table 33.1

The Barroso Commission, 2005–2009: Commissioners and Portfolios

Name (country)	Portfolio
Jose Manuel Barroso (Portugal)	President
Margot Wallström (Sweden)	Vice-President, Institutional Relations and Communication Strategy
Günter Verheugen (Germany)	Vice-President, Enterprise and Industry
Jacques Barrot (France)	Vice-President, Transport and Energy
Siim Kallas (Estonia)	Vice-President, Administrative Affairs, Audit, Anti-Fraud
Franco Frattini (Italy)	Vice-President, Justice, Freedom, and Security
Viviane Reding (Luxembourg)	Information Society and Media
Stavros Dimas (Greece)	Environment
Joaquin Almunia (Spain)	Economic and Monetary Affairs
Danita Hübner (Poland)	Regional Policy
Joe Borg (Malta)	Fisheries, Maritime Affairs
Dalia Grybauskaité (Lithuania)	Financial Programming and Budget
Janez Potočnik (Slovenia)	Science and Technology
Jän Figel (Slovakia)	Educational, Training, Culture, Youth
Markos Kyprianou (Cyprus)	Health
Olli Rehn (Sweden)	Enlargement
Louis Michel (Belgium)	Development, Humanitarian Aid
Läsló Kovács (Hungary)	Taxation, Customs Union
Neelie Kroes (Netherlands)	Competition
Mariann Fischer Boel (Denmark)	Agriculture, Rural Development
Benito Ferraro-Waldner (Austria)	External Relations, European Neighborhood Policy
Charlie McCreevy (Ireland)	Internal Market and Services
Vladimir Spidla (Czech Republic)	Employment, Social Affairs, Equal Opportunities
Peter Mandelson (United Kingdom)	Trade
Andris Pielbalgs (Latvia)	Energy
Maglena Kuneva (Bulgaria)	Consumer Protection
Leonard Orban (Romania)	Multilingualism

itself taxes them—lightly), and with numerous perks. A-levels are recruited primarily through an annual European-wide competition that winnows thousands of well-prepared applicants down to the chosen few. Because official Commission documents must be translated into all (23, as of 2007) official languages and official meetings must have simultaneous translation (although working meetings use only English, French, and German) thousands of translators and interpreters are required.[1] The remaining staff are in clerical and other support services, including thousands of jobs for Belgian locals who are paid well above rates in the local labor market.

The Commission's most important job is to design policy proposals and get them passed. It rarely proposes from scratch, however. In most cases it must translate the desires of others, particularly EU member state governments, plus the requirements of international agreements.[2] The Commission thus spends much of its time sounding out politicians, national ministries, and other Euro-level institutions for openings to act. The Commission is also the object of intense lobbying from a wide range of interest groups. Finally, the actual implementation of most Community measures is left to the administrations of member states, monitored by the Commission.

The Commission's primary mission is to advance European integration, and it is usually a hotbed of commitment, hard work, and energy. The EU's founders were aware that simply designating a few areas for inter-governmental cooperation and assigning a few officials to the tasks would have failed because governments would not go far before disagreeing. Creating the Commission, giving it the power of proposing, and encouraging its "collective international intellectual" role was meant as an institutional prod to goad member states to make collective commitments that they would then feel obliged to honor. It is not surprising, therefore, that the Commission has had good moments when it has led Europe toward greater integration and bad periods when governments have refused to be so led. It has historically been most important when key member states—often France and Germany—agreed upon the desirability of greater integration and encouraged the initiatives of a strong Commission president, with the presidency of Jacques Delors from 1985–1994 the most important example. And when key member states have wanted a weak Commission, they have deliberately appointed a weak Commission president—the Luxembourg prime minister Jacques Santer who succeeded Jacques Delors in 1995, for example.

In addition, since 2005, member states have agreed to appoint as Commission president someone, preferably a former prime minister, who shares the political leanings of the most recently-elected European Parliament. The center-right former Portuguese prime minister José Manuel Barroso, president from 2005, thus reflected the results of the 2005 EP elections. The Commission's future is likely to be different from its past, however. Enlargement has obliged change and institutional reconfiguration. With twenty-seven members as of 2007, traditional methods have been suspended. There are not enough significant jobs to spread around, and the large, heterogeneous group makes "collegial" functioning difficult. After 2014, the Commission will have one-third fewer members than the number of member states and Commission membership will be shared over time by a system of rotation. The consequences for the Commission and

the Community Method more broadly are difficult to foresee.

The Council of Ministers

The original EU system was relatively simple. Where the EU could act legally, the Commission proposed and the Council of (national) Ministers disposed as the EU's only real legislator. The European Parliament was "consulted"—it could analyze and comment on proposals, but it lacked real power—while the European Court of Justice reviewed proceedings with an eye to their conformity to the EU's various treaties. In the 1980s things started to change, however. The Single European Act allowed the Parliament to propose amendments, and then the Maastricht Treaty introduced "codecision," which made the Council and Parliament both legislators on Community issues. As if things were not confusing enough, however, Maastricht also introduced the two new intergovernmental "pillars" for CFSP and "justice and home affairs." Both pillars fell almost completely outside the Community (the Commission's proposing role was not in effect, and it played only a small role).

The Council's decision rules add even more complexity. The Rome Treaty foresaw three different voting systems—unanimity, qualified majority voting (QMV, a technique of weighting the voting power of different members according to their relative size), and simple majority—depending on the issue. Difficulties with France in the 1960s then narrowed things to unanimity on anything important for two decades. The SEA (1987) opened up QMV for almost everything in the "1992" program for completing the single market. The Maastricht, Amsterdam, and 2001 Nice Treaties extended QMV, but not to all matters. Under the Nice Treaty weighting system currently in force, member states with the largest populations have 27–29 votes, medium-sized countries have 7–14 votes, and the small countries 3 or 4 votes, with at least 255 out of 345 required for passage. The 2004 Constitutional Treaty proposed replacing this arrangement with a "double majority" formula that would reflect both national votes and population (giving the larger states slightly more influence), such that QMV would involve a 55 percent majority of member states representing 65 percent of the population, while a "blocking minority" needed four member states representing 35 percent.

The Council of Ministers is where member states, the EU's fundamental actors, express their national preferences. The "Council" is composed of ministers empowered by their governments to deal with European issues. Its most important job is passing European laws. It also concludes international agreements for the EU, approves the EU budget (with the Parliament), and decides issues in the intergovernmental CFSP and justice and home affairs pillars. This is a lot, and in practice there are nine different Councils, organized around large functional areas, whose membership varies according to the issues discussed. The sheer number of official Council meetings, over a hundred per year, means that the Council is more or less permanently in session.

The Council is assisted by the Committee of Permanent Representatives, or COREPER (the French acronym). "Permanent representatives" are member state ambassadors to the EU and their deputies, who do much of the preliminary work of shaping Council decisions, refining and vetting matters for the Council (much as *cabinet*s do for the Commission). The ambassadors are usually EU veterans with mastery of EU lore, networks, and methods. COREPER, along with other EU institutions including the Commission, relies on preliminary sorting by 150–200 working committees that are governed by the rules of "comitology" and involving thousands of national civil servants and experts. It also coordinates a number of high-level functional committees, including the Political Committee (with member state and Commission foreign policy "political directors") that prepares the work of CFSP, a special Agriculture Committee, a committee for justice and home affairs matters, and the COPS committee that works on security policy.

The deliberations of the Council of Ministers have always occurred behind closed doors, with only carefully edited results announced to the public. Except through leaks, the public never finds out what debates took place, what alternatives were considered and rejected, and what positions different countries actually took. Minutes are not circulated, even in summary form. Worries about Europe's legitimacy have led to only cosmetic efforts to make the proceedings more open to the public, and a few television broadcasts show parts of Council proceedings, and announcements of votes on certain matters are sometimes released to the media (although the Council usually works on consensus rather than voting). Inside knowledge also remains limited because much of the Council's work is done in bilateral and multilateral discussions before things come close to decision.

The Council is organized by a presidency that rotates among member states every six months and oversees Council-Commission relationships. The presidency's Foreign Minister serves as acting head.[3] Because the powers of the European Parliament have expanded through codecision, the presidency now also coordinates Council-Parliament interactions, including the "conciliation committees" where codecision plays itself out. The presidency submits the Council's annual program to the Parliament. In addition, it prepares and presides over European Council summits. Finally, the presidency speaks for the EU externally on foreign policy matters (excepting trade). The development of CFSP and JHA has broadened the presidency's foreign policy role while establishing a new place for "Mr. Common Foreign and Security Policy" who is also officially the Council's Secretary-General. For foreign policy activity, the acting presidency is aided by the previous and next presidency, the so-called troika.

The member state that holds the presidency thus can play an important role as power broker, coalition builder, and program initiator among member states. French and German presidencies in the 1980s were critical in regenerating momentum for integration, for example, while British presidencies, in contrast, have often brought caution, as befits cautious British outlooks on European integration. Smaller states can have "big" presidents as well—tiny Luxembourg, for example, presided over the most difficult negotiations for the Single European Act and the Maastricht Treaty; Belgium, with its strong pro-integrationist sentiments, promoted the Convention that led to the 2004 Constitutional Treaty; and the Portuguese presidency in 2000 proposed the Lisbon Agenda, the heart of the EU's economic strategy in the new century. The Council presidency has not always been the most effective of EU institutions, however. Discontinuities in leadership, poor national preparation, lack of resources, and occasional ineptitude can disrupt the flow of business. For these reasons the 2004 Constitutional Treaty foresaw replacing it by an appointed European Council president for a two-and-one-half-year (once renewable) term.

The Council of Ministers relies on a 2,000-strong secretariat (but only several hundred A-level administrators), with a staff for the secretary-general, legal services, and seven general directorates. The Council secretary-general, now Javier Solana, and his assistant, who focuses on EU domestic matters, are very important persons. The Council secretariat provides continuity for the rotating Council presidency and translates all EU actions into all official languages—hence the importance of "legal linguists" who are experts in legal translation.

The European Council is an über–Council of Ministers, which came into being in 1974 to institutionalize summit meetings of EU heads of state and government and which the Maastricht TEU Treaty officially named as the body to settle important outstanding issues and strategize the EU's future. It usually meets twice during each six-month Council presidency, and is prepared by the sitting Council presidency with the help of the Council secretariat. European Council meetings are exclusive, with attendance restricted to heads of state or governments and one other minister (usually the foreign minister), the Council secretary-general, plus the Commission president and secretary-general. This relative intimacy is meant to promote open discussion on an agenda that has been narrowed to the most important outstanding matters. But during any actual European Council, which is brief—usually two days— legions of civil servants with cell phones provide proposals, wording, and comment when needed. Negotiating begins with a declaration from the president of the European Parliament, who then leaves, after which issue after issue is discussed, with easy ones resolved quickly and harder ones saved until later. A working lunch after the second session separates the leaders, who start confronting the most difficult problems, from the foreign ministers who expedite the rest. The matters that remain after this provide intense work during the last few hours. The final report—the so-called Presidency Conclusions— provides a running record of basic EU decisions, intentions, and goals that will structure programs for other institutions. The importance of the European Council is clear from a partial list of its recent conclusions (see Table 33.2).

The European Parliament: 750 Characters in Search of an Author?

The balance of power among different EU "triangle" institutions has varied. The Delors years were notable for exceptional Commission leadership. From the aftermath of the Maastricht Treaty to the present, however, the balance of EU power has tipped toward intergovernmental bodies, primarily at the expense of the Commission. The main reason is that European integration has moved into areas like foreign policy, defense, immigration, policing, internal security, and enlargement that lie very close to the heart of national sovereignty. The agendas of the EU's intergovernmental institutions— the Council of Ministers and the European Council— have become more complicated and weighty. One result has been increased difficulty in resolving problems with decisions passed upward to the European Council, now the EU's default decision maker. In other words the more the Council of Ministers dodges bullets, the more bullets the European Council must bite. As intergovernmental approaches have gained ground, however, something else has happened. The European Parliament, the only directly elected supranational parliament on our planet, has also become more important.

The European Parliament (EP) lives a vagabond existence between Strasbourg, France, where it holds its plenary sessions, and Brussels, where it meets in groups and committees (with staff offices in Luxembourg). Originally it was the successor of the ECSC assembly, composed of unelected and powerless members appointed by member state governments.[4] Since 1979 the Parliament has been directly elected (Table 33.3 shows the allocation of seats among member states prior to and after the 2004 enlargement). Candidates to the EP run on national party tickets and then, once elected, their national political groups join European-level party coalitions. The Socialists, in the transnational Party of European Socialists, and the Christian Democrats, in the European Peoples' Party (EPP), have long been the two largest groups, with the Liberals and Greens next, but much smaller.[5] Until 1999 the Socialists were stronger, but the balance has shifted to the EPP in the new century. This Socialist–Christian Democrat center of gravity reflects that of continental European party politics.

Election campaigning is by far the most important act in the political life of any nation, encouraging debate

Table 33.2

Major Conclusions of Recent European Councils

European Council	Product(s)
Fontainebleau, 1984	Solved "British check" issue; expansion to Spain and Portugal unlocked; appointment of Jacques Delors
Milan, 1985	Approved "1992" White Paper; decided intergovernmental conference to modify treaty leading to SEA
Brussels, 1987	Adopted first Delors budgetary package (reform of structural funds)
Madrid, 1989	Accepted Delors report on EMU
Dublin, 1990	Decided German reunification within the EU
Maastricht, 1991	Maastricht Treaty
Edinburgh, 1992	Adopted second Delors budgetary package; decided to negotiate enlargement to four European Free Trade Association countries
Brussels, 1993	Discussed White Paper on Growth, Competitiveness, and Employment
Essen, 1994	Began discussing enlargement to CEECS
Dublin, 1996	Proposed EMU Stability and Growth Pact
Amsterdam, 1997	Amsterdam Treaty
Helsinki, 1999	Adopted "Headline Goal" for European rapid-reaction force by 2003
Berlin, 1999	Approved Agenda 2000 budgetary package to facilitate enlargement
Lisbon, 2000	Lisbon Strategy on competitiveness and knowledge society
Nice, 2000	Nice Treaty
Laeken, 2001	Called for the European Convention
Brussels, 2003	Ten countries signed treaty to join EU on May 1, 2004
Brussels, 2004	Reached agreement on new Constitutional Treaty derived from Convention
Brussels, 2005	New budgetary package for 2007–2013
Brussels, 2007	Discussed proposals on energy, the environment, and global warming

between aspiring leaders and voters about desirable options for future policies, raising levels of political education and consciousness, and reinforcing national solidarities and identity. It had always been hoped that direct elections to the European Parliament, which are now held every five years using a nationally-designed system of proportional representation (the system was supposed to be uniform across the Union, but this has not yet happened) would do the same for EU level politics. It was hoped that such elections would enhance public knowledge about European integration and reinforce the legitimacy of EU institutions. To this point, however, elections to the EP have usually been second-order national elections, treated by national politicians more as important indicators of the relative strength of national political parties than as important events with consequences for the EU. As a result, when European issues are discussed during Euro-parliamentary campaigns, they tend to be proxies for national political conflicts and concerns. This may distance the Parliament and European issues from voters and is undoubtedly one reason why electoral turnout for EP elections has been lower than for national elections, and declining. Sixty-five percent of eligible voters turned out for the first direct elections to the EP in 1979, while only 45.6 percent turned out for those in 2004.

The Parliament elects its president and executive bureau for two-and-one-half-year terms, with the presidency usually alternating between a Socialist and a Christian Democrat (in 2007 the president was a German Christian Democrat). The president presides over parliamentary sessions, participates in periodic interinstitutional discussions with Commission and Council counterparts, and addresses member state

Table 33.3

European Parliament, Seats per Country as of Nice Treaty, 2001* (alphabetical order according to country's name in its own language)							
Country	Seats 1999–2004	2004–2007	2007	Country	Seats 1999–2004	2004–2007	2007
Belgium	25	24	24	Lithuania	—	13	13
Bulgaria	—	—	18	Luxembourg	6	6	6
Cyprus	—	6	6	Malta	—	5	5
Czech Republic	—	24	24	Netherlands	31	27	27
Denmark	16	14	14	Austria	21	18	18
Germany	99	99	99	Poland	—	54	54
Greece	25	24	24	Portugal	25	24	24
Spain	64	54	54	Romania	—	—	36
Estonia	—	6	6	Slovakia	—	14	14
France	87	78	78	Slovenia	—	7	7
Hungary	—	24	24	Finland	16	14	14
Ireland	15	13	13	Sweden	22	19	19
Italy	87	78	78	United Kingdom	87	78	78
Latvia	—	9	9	TOTAL	626	732	786

*The 2004 Constitutional Treaty, when implemented, will cap the size of Parliament at 750.

leaders at European Council summits. However, the bulk of Parliament's hard work is done by seventeen permanent committees which produce detailed, thoughtful reports in their functional areas.[6] The central place of committees has also made them the target for an enormous army of lobbyists.

Increased power for the European Parliament is among the most important recent changes to the EU political system. Originally the Parliament was "consulted" about legislation proposed by the Commission that the Council would decide, after considering Parliament's opinion. This odd situation created a parliamentary lobby for correcting the Community's "democratic deficit."[7] When the Parliament acquired deliberative powers over the Community's annual budget in the 1970s, it first entered indirectly into important policy areas. The Parliament also discovered that it could delay decisions, using the vague time limits for delivering its consultative opinions. The real shift began in 1987, however, when the SEA instituted a "cooperation procedure" for most single-market legislation, allowing Parliament to propose amendments. Maastricht,

Amsterdam, Nice 2001, and Brussels 2004 then brought the invention and refinement of "codecision." Although these different powers still officially coexist, codecision is now the most important legislative process.

"Codecision" is to be taken literally. The Parliament and the Council "codecide" on Commission proposals as if they were two separate legislative houses. The process for doing so, which was set out at Maastricht, was exceedingly complex, however, creating as many as twenty-two different ways to make decisions, which in turn led to clarifications in the Amsterdam Treaty (see Table 33.4). Parliament and the Council each read and discuss Commission proposals twice. If they do not then agree, the proposal goes to a "conciliation committee" of equal numbers from the Council and Parliament. If and when the committee agrees, the measure goes back to Council and Parliament for a "third reading."

Parliament also possesses "assenting" power on Council proposals about applications from prospective new members, international treaties, EMU arrangements, multiyear programs of regional funds, and its

Table 33.4

Overview of Codecision Process

First Reading

1. Commission proposes ▶
    - Parliament gives its initial "opinion" and amendments.
    - If the Council approves Parliament's opinion, measure passes.
    - If not, the Council prepares a "Common Position" to submit to Parliament (which has three months to respond).

Second Reading

2a. If Parliament approves Council's Common Position, or does not respond in three months, the measure passes

or

2b. If Parliament rejects the Council's Common Position by an absolute majority of members, the measure is rejected

or

2c. If Parliament proposes amendments to the Common Position by an absolute majority of members and the Commission states its opinions on them and the Council then approves these amendments (unanimously on those rejected by the Commission), the measure is passed.

If 2c, then

Third Reading

3. Conciliation committee (half from Council, half from Parliament) is convened to seek agreed-upon joint text (six weeks time limit) ▶
    - The measure passes if joint text agreed by the Council and the Parliament.

or

    - If the Conciliation Committee does not agree on a joint text within the six-week time limit, the measure fails.

own electoral procedures. Maastricht also allowed Parliament to call temporary committees of inquiry, receive petitions, and name an EU ombudsman to whom citizens could bring complaints. In addition, the Rome Treaty gave Parliament the right to bring the Commission and Council before the ECJ for "failure to act" in areas where the treaty obliged them to, and later it also acquired the right to sue if the Council infringed on its powers. In the budget area, the Parliament must approve the Commission's annual budget proposal and "discharge" completed budget years (which it has sometimes refused to do). Finally, Parliament has long had the power to vote out the Commission, which it threatened to use for the first time in 1999, leading to crisis and the resignation of the entire Commission.[8] Maastricht enhanced Parliament's oversight of the Commission, giving it the power to approve the appointment of new Commissions as a whole and to be consulted about new Commission presidents (with the 2004 Constitutional Treaty proposing to transform "consultation about" to "election of" the president, although only after Council recommendation of a name).

The most striking aspect of the European Parliament's history is its steady acquisition of more power, clearly related to the EU's chronic problems of political legitimacy. As time went on, European leaders, applying rough-and-ready standards of democratic responsibility and participation, judged it unacceptable that decisions of major importance to citizens should be proposed by an unelected Commission and decided through multilateral diplomatic negotiations by the Council of Ministers. Transforming an appointed Assembly without real power into today's "codecider" was the major way they chose to confront this dilemma. They reasoned that in a Union that is composed of national parliamentary democracies it was logical to approach the issue by progressively endowing a European Parliament with real power.

The results of increased EP power and influence have been positive in many ways. One recent example is found in the Parliament's recent politicking on the Commission's REACH proposal, a controversial program that obliges manufacturers to list and announce potential dangers of 30,000 common chemical substances. The proposal touched complicated issues of health and the environment, called for new ways of certifying and publicizing chemical products, and through its implications frightened an EU chemicals industry with one-third of the world market. The

Parliament drew upon scientific knowledge, environmental activism, and experience with industrial lobbying to bargain hard with different party groups, the Commission, and the Council. Navigation through thousands of amendments and intense work led in 2007 to very progressive environmental protection legislation. A different example might be the Parliament's work on the recent "Services Directive" to extend the single market into services (which now make up 70 percent of EU economic activity). The original Commission proposal, which had been prepared in haste, caused uproar because it appeared to threaten public services and local regulations throughout the EU. The Parliament brokered a compromise resolution that excluded public utilities and national "public good" services like health care and education from liberalization, eliminated the original proposal's "country of origin" principle, while also facilitating freedom of movement and more flexible administrative procedures for transborder providers of many private services.

Growing parliamentary influence is good for European integration, and in time it may lessen indifference and hostility to EU institutions. The EU's legitimacy problems run deep, however, as demonstrated clearly in public lack of interest, lack of knowledge about EU issues, and general dissatisfaction. The absence of a substantial Euro-level political culture among European citizens—excepting, of course, elite groups—is an important cause. The reasons for this absence are complex. The European Parliament as it stands has no right of legislative initiative. Although it deals with proposals from the Commission with intelligence and thoroughness, it can only react to them. In addition, parliaments are most effective when their deliberations connect with the pursuit of specific political platforms, as happens nationally when they deliberate proposals from elected governments. Some form of Euro-level government and opposition structure would give Euro-parliamentary debate a clarity that it now lacks and promote genuine Euro-level parties and coalitions that could bring European issues to European citizens without being obscured by mediation through national politics. Such developments are not yet on the agenda, however.

Intergovernmental Incursions into the "Community Method"

The 1993 Maastricht Treaty on European Union (TEU) clarified and changed Community and Commission prerogatives, by adding some new areas of competence, and also included a clause on "subsidiarity" that decreed that the Commission and Community should act only where objectives could not be achieved by the member states themselves. In addition, economic and social cohesion and environmental policy became "fundamental missions." In legal terms this means that all EU policy areas had to integrate commitment to both of these key missions (at Amsterdam in 1997 equal opportunities for women and men were given the same status). Most importantly, the Maastricht TEU also excluded important new EU areas from Community-institutional triangle processes altogether. The new CFSP and Justice and Home Affairs "pillars" were explicitly intergovernmental, where decisions would be made exclusively by the Council of Ministers and the Commission would play only a minor role. The Amsterdam Treaty, four years later, proclaimed the goal of "establishing an area of freedom, security, and justice" and transferring it into the Community framework within five years, but this has not been achieved.

These arrangements, which the 2004 Constitutional Treaty proposed to phase out, have meant that decisions about most EU cooperation in foreign and defense policy and policing, judicial cooperation, and immigration issues have been made in intergovernmental ways, without the involvement of either the Commission or the European Parliament. Intergovernmental approaches mean unanimous decision making in key issues, implying ponderous movement at best, when stalemate does not preclude movement altogether. Disagreement persists about the wisdom of these "pillar" arrangements, but it is clear that they make understanding EU institutions and processes all the more difficult. And they are already challenging enough.

The European Court of Justice

European integration is ultimately a legal construct. European law is based in the many treaties that member states have signed in the course of fifty years.

EU Legislation and administration follow from this "treaty base," and it bears repetition that the EU cannot act without the legal foundation in the treaties. European law is only part of the laws of European Union member states, but where it exists, it is superior to, and supersedes, member state law.[9] The European Court of Justice (ECJ), born in the ECSC, has been the major actor in making this happen, and its case rulings have provided the EU's sinews and ligaments. The ECJ, "supreme" in EU legal matters, has no jurisdiction over national law when it is unrelated to EU treaties.

The Court, which sits in Luxembourg, is presently composed of twenty-seven justices (one from each member state) and nine advocates-general. Each justice is named for a six-year term, and half the Court is renewed every three years. The justices elect their president for a three-year term. The advocates-general review cases and provide legal opinion to the judges but do not rule on fundamental legal matters. The Court can sit in plenary sessions when it wishes, but must do so when dealing with matters brought before it by a Community institution or member state. Otherwise, it subdivides its work into "chambers" (of three and five judges each), any one of which may refer matters to the full Court. The ECJ's decisions are binding on member states and their citizens. The huge workload of the Court led to the establishment of a Tribunal of First Instance (composed of fifteen judges, again with six-year terms) by the SEA that consecrated the 1992 single-market initiative, primarily to decide complex matters of fact in litigation brought by individuals and companies (for example, actions for damages or actions by Community staff against institutions).

Decisions concerning questions of law (and not of fact) can be appealed from this court to the full ECJ. Cases get to the ECJ in many ways and in many cases—nearly 7,000 in 2005. The most significant route is the "preliminary ruling" procedure in which a national court, presented with a case that may involve European law (in particular whether a national statute conforms to EU law), forwards it to the ECJ for advice which, when given, usually settles the case in question. Next, in "annulment proceedings," anyone, whether a European institution, government, or individual, can ask the court to rule on the legality of European legislation and other measures. A third path involves the Commission or a member state asking the ECJ to decide if a member state has failed to fulfill its EU legal obligations ("treaty infringement proceeding"). Member states, other EU institutions, or individuals may also bring cases against a particular institution for "failure to act" when it ought to have done so under EU treaties. Cases for damages against Community institutions may be considered as well. Member states and EU institutions may also ask for rulings on the compatibility of international agreements with EU law.

As might be expected, recourse to the ECJ has increased greatly with the growing salience of European integration, and its rulings have become central in the evolution of European integration. Table 33.5 lists some significant ECJ cases.[10]

Other Institutions?

The EU has several other significant institutions, most of them recently created. The most significant, those constituting Economic and Monetary Union (the European Central Bank, in particular), those of Justice and Home Affairs (JHA) "second pillar," and the CFSP "third pillar" will be discussed more fully in our next chapter. In Brussels there are two "advisory committees": an Economic and Social Committee with delegates from business, labor, and other professions, and a Committee of the Regions with representatives from the EU's regions that review and submit opinions on pending EU legislation and, informally, are very useful places for organized interests to network and connect with the Commission, Council, and Parliament. There is also an official Court of Auditors and a European Investment Bank that mobilizes investment loans for regional planning and development purposes. Finally, there are now twenty-three "community agencies" scattered across the member states (each member state has a claim) working on informational and regulatory matters of all kinds, from fish stocks to plant variety, health and safety at work to disease prevention and control, the environment, food safety, railways, and many others.

Table 33.5

Significant Decisions of the European Court of Justice

Decision	Importance
Van Gend and Loos, 1963	Ruled that the Community constituted a new legal order of international law derived from the willing limitations of sovereignty by member states whose subjects were member states and their nationals.
Costa v. ENE, 1964	Central in establishing the supremacy of EU law itself.
Van Duyn v. Home Office, 1974	Gave individuals the same right to take employment in another member state as nationals of that state, a landmark ruling about the free movement of people.
Defrenne v. Sabena, 1976	Based upon Article 119 of the Rome Treaty, which enjoined equal treatment of men and women in employment, the case opened up the EU to a wide range of social policy initiatives and further rulings with major consequences in attenuating gender discrimination in EU labor markets.
Vereniging Bond van Adverteerders v. the Netherlands State, 1988	Obliged member states to open up national telecommunications services to competition, an important step in the liberalization of service provision.
Cassis de Dijon, 1979	Perhaps the most famous of the Court's recent cases, it decreed that member states must base their acceptance of EU goods from other member states on the principle of mutual recognition, thus assuming that all member states have reasonable product standards. This ruling, which allowed the EU to avoid unending negotiations to harmonize product standards, was of huge significance to the single-market program.

Notes

[1]For a long time French was predominant, partly because the Commission was designed and built by the French and the Belgians. Since the mid-1990s, however, English has made advances. German is rarely used.

[2]On average only 5–10 percent are from the Commission's own initiatives. The rest are linked to international agreements; follow direct requests from the Council and/or member states; are used to modify existing texts or needed because of ECJ decisions; result from implementing general framework programs (research and development, for example); are obligatory under the treaty (setting agricultural prices, among other things); or originate from requests from firms, particularly concerning trade practices.

[3]Rotation was alphabetical by country when the EU was smaller. For some time, however, it has rotated in a more planned way so that smaller and larger states alternate.

[4]On the Parliament see David Judge and David Earnshaw, *The European Parliament* (London: Palgrave MacMillan, 2003).

[5]Other, smaller, groups include, in order of strength, the Liberals, the Greens, the European Democratic Alliance, the European Right, Left Unity (Communists), and the Rainbow Group. There are also a few unaffiliated members.

[6]For a revealing ethnographic view of the Parliament see Marc Abelès, "Political Anthropology of a Transnational Institution: The European Parliament," in *French Politics and Society* 11, no. 1.

[7]See Shirley Williams, "Sovereignty and Accountability in the European Community," in Robert Keohane and Stanley Hoffmann, *The New European Community* (Boulder: Westview, 1991).

[8]The Parliament had an epiphany in 1999. During the Santer Commission period there was parliamentary restlessness about the Commission's sloppy work, cronyism, and even corruption. Matters came to a head in later 1998 about the "discharge" of the 1996 budget. A successful censure vote might have occurred had the two major party groups agreed on what to do, but in a gesture of reconciliation, and perhaps relief, the Commission agreed on an expert committee to investigate the charges. The

committee's March 1999 report was a crushing indictment of the Commission, noting that ". . . it is becoming difficult to find anyone [in the Commission] who has even the slightest sense of responsibility." The Parliament then looked set to pass a censure vote. Instead, the Commission resigned as a bloc.

[9]Klaus-Dieter Borchardt, *The ABC of Community Law* (Luxembourg: European Commission, 2000), provides a solid introduction to the EU's legal order.

[10]Another effort to give Europeans a sense that there was more to European integration than economics came when Maastricht introduced "European citizenship." All citizens of member states became citizens of the EU with the right to move about and live in any member state (subject to exceptions, mainly concerning work). European Union citizens living outside their own country can vote and be elected in municipal elections in their country of residence and in elections to the European Parliament. Every EU citizen is entitled to full diplomatic protection from any member state embassy and consulate. EU citizens also acquired rights to petition the European Parliament and a new ombudsman/mediator. These clauses clearly bore the potential for elaboration and expansion in new legislation and litigation.

CHAPTER 34

The EU and Its Policies

Reflecting on EU policies begins by recognizing that the EU is not a state, but rather part of a unique new system of European multilevel governance. The EU itself thus works only in those areas where its members have agreed to cooperate. In many of these areas, the EU assists its members by providing common rules to facilitate cooperative action. But even when the EU makes policy itself it is usually networked with other jurisdictions, whether transnational, national, regional, or local, and depends on them for implementation. The EU has grown because EU policy cooperation in one area has sometimes spilled over, leading to cooperation in other areas, as Jean Monnet had hoped. The EU's member states ultimately decide what the Union does, and for half a century they have constantly had to ask themselves "what ought we to do, what can we do, together?"

Building the European Economy: The "Community Method"

The most important single thing the EU has done is to integrate many national markets into one. Its first step, after the Rome Treaties, was to build the "common market," a customs-free area surrounded by a common tariff within which manufactured goods could move freely and where, in addition, there was a common agricultural policy. These achievements were of great historic importance, but they faltered in the crisis of the 1970s. A common market existed in principle, but many practical problems needed resolving before it could really work. People could not circulate freely across borders. Trucks were stalled for hours at customs posts while their drivers filed endless forms. Professionals had difficulty working in counties other than their own. Markets for services remained staunchly national even as service employment grew ever more important. Sales taxes discouraged trade. The public sectors in EU member states bought their equipment and supplies in resolutely "patriotic" ways. Moreover, when economic times became tougher, EU members invented new nontariff barriers to trade, usually restrictive product norms and standards.

One European Market?

The program to "complete the single-market" and create a "space without borders" revived, and probably saved, European integration. The Delors Commission's 1985

White Paper created a new agenda for European policy-making, new economic integration and ultimately, more EU political integration. Backed strongly by European big business, the program was fundamentally liberalizing and deregulating—what scholars have called "negative integration"—to free up national markets, promote new trading between and within EU member states and, ultimately, to create one European market—in practice, not only in theory. Markets need to be framed by rules, however, and the single-market program also involved "re-regulation" on a European level—"positive integration." Uniform standards and norms were necessary, for example. Rules about competition, environmental policy, and some forms of taxation were part of the package. The EU was growing to include poorer countries, and the EU needed new regional development policies so that they too could benefit from the single market. Finally, the "four freedoms" of movement (goods, services, capital, and people) would bring the end of border posts and controls.

The White Paper proposed 300-odd legislative measures to be completed by 1992, making the EU a legislator comparable to that of any of its member states. Under the guidance of a commissioner for the internal market, the whole Commission had to draft specific proposals that involved strategizing and consultation with interests, committees, national-level administrations, the Committee of Permanent Representatives (COREPER), and other Council bodies. Prepared texts then had to be negotiated with Council and Parliament. Thus practically all of the European Commission's different services had to work overtime to feed the "institutional triangle" with new single-market proposals. The European Parliament, which had been endowed by the SEA with amending powers, eagerly followed, and the Council of Ministers went to work deciding by new qualified majority procedures. Member states then had to "transpose" the new rules into national legal codes. Often the results nourished local disobedience, which the Commission then had to monitor—there were 1,500 "infringement" proceedings per year in the early twenty-first century. They were usually brought to the European Court of Justice (ECJ), whose docket was swamped.

One of the more daunting tasks was harmonizing technical standards and norms for consumer and worker safety. Whenever this had been tried before, multilateral negotiations bogged down and often failed. The single-market program thus proposed a different approach to break the logjam: "mutual recognition" rather than harmonizing negotiations. This new approach was based on the ECJ's *Cassis de Dijon* ruling that allowed goods legally marketed in any single member state to circulate freely throughout the EU as long as minimum standards were upheld. The "1992" program also introduced a "new approach" to regulatory legislation in which directives set out minimal standards for a range of similar products or processes. When it came to food supplies, for example, public health standards specified additives, labeling, and food hygiene. The "1992" program also led to some deregulation in insurance, telecommunications, international transport, and audiovisual transmission. Last but not least, sales taxes had to be harmonized to prevent different levels and types of national taxes from distorting competition within the single market.

After 1992, events slowed down, although by the turn of the twenty-first century some 1,500 single-market measures had been enacted. A more leisurely pace was important because EU governments and their citizens needed time to adjust. Much remained to be done, however, and methods for doing it had to change after Maastricht introduced "codecision." Moreover, what remained was harder for members to agree on, particularly in liberalizing the service sector. Services involved nearly 70 percent of European economic activity in the early twenty-first century and opening service markets often threatened established interests and fomented resistance. The Union nonetheless forged ahead, changing intellectual property laws, harmonizing taxation on savings, liberalizing public procurement, opening up telecoms, electricity, and gas provision to greater competition, and making it easier for service businesses to set up in other countries. Beginning in 1999, the Commission also proposed a major action plan for financial services that contained forty-two different measures to harmonize rules and open markets in securities, banking, and insurance.

The most spectacular illustration of the political difficulties of liberating services happened after the Commission drafted its framework "services directive" in 2004. The draft included a "country of origin" proviso that service providers would fall under the legal rules of the country from which they came. This played a major role in leading the French to refuse ratification of the Constitutional Treaty in May 2005, most notably by implanting in French minds a fictitious "Polish plumber" who would lead hordes of foreigners to take jobs from the French. The European Parliament removed the country of origin principle before the directive eventually passed.

Opening up service markets remains a contentious frontier, in particular for those services provided by governments. From the beginning of the EU it was recognized that public services in health, education, public transportation, post offices, and utilities were different from grocery stores and restaurants, and the Rome Treaty exempted "services of general economic interest" from market liberalization. By the new century the nature of service markets had changed, however, and such a blanket exemption was no longer adequate. National monopolies in postal services had been successfully challenged economically by private package delivery firms like FedEx and UPS, for example, and it was clear that pricing and access restrictions for what had once been "natural monopoly" areas (airlines, electricity, gas, and telecoms) could be powerful barriers to trade and provide indirect subsidies to domestic firms. One can envisage challenges to the public nature of health care and education in the future, for example. And as market realities change, the organization of public sectors and tens of thousands of jobs will be challenged, feeding more national anxiety about the EU.

In general, much of the single market has been built, but some difficult construction sites remain. Finishing them will be a heavily politicized process, and at every large step of the way, the job is sure to separate those (usually on the center-right) who insist on a market-driven economy and those on the center-left who insist that state regulation is needed to ensure equity and fairness. In addition, the EU's enlargement to twenty-seven members in 2004–2007 created another single-market frontier. In order to join, new member states had to agree to implement the EU's vast *acquis communautaire* that included all existing market rules and regulations. It was naïve to expect that agreements on paper would translate easily into practice in countries with little experience as liberal market societies. Encouragement, monitoring, and tough political vigilance will be needed well into the near future.

The European Commission calculated in 2002 that the single market had increased EU GDP by 1.8 percent, created 2.5 million more jobs, increased exports and imports, lowered utility prices, and enhanced consumer choice.[1] Corporations have become more European, global, bigger, and powerful. Yet beyond liberalizing the services and doing more to help small business, two things on everyone's scoreboard, the single market has had remarkably small effects on European consumer habits, which remain domestically oriented, and fewer than 2 percent of Europeans actually work in another country. There may be a big European market and many successful Euro-level companies, but national cultures still ride high.[2]

Competition Policy: A Level Playing Field and Honest Players

There would be little point in opening up the European market if companies and countries could then use their power to limit competition within it. The Rome Treaty thus declared that measures should be taken so that "competition in the internal market is not distorted." It granted the European Commission exclusive responsibility for enforcing competition rules, one of the Commission's rare federal competencies. The Commission's competition policy rulings are not submitted for Council approval or reviewed by the European Parliament, but subject only to ECJ review.

The Commission has traditionally done most of Europe's antitrust detection and enforcement on its own, leaving only relatively small cases to national authorities. Anticompetitive firm behaviors—cartels, trusts, and monopolies—are outlawed when they are judged to be against European interests, with the Commission reviewing all cases above a certain minimum size. It also reviews all state aid to firms (subsidies, grants, special tax advantages, and so forth) to assess whether it could create unfair market advantage. Beginning in 1989, the Commission also acquired oversight and control over mergers.[3] When it finds violations, the Commission can impose substantial penalties. Finally, more recently it has played a key role in deregulating public utilities.

The Commission's antitrust powers are both negative—preventing illegal behaviors—and positive—regulating and authorizing. Its DG Competition does the work with a staff of lawyers and economists who monitor company conditions, devour the business press, and observe market developments. "DG Comp" can request information from firms and carry out investigations, including "dawn raids" on offices to obtain company documents. In the mergers area, because mergers in other parts of the world may have market-limiting effects in Europe, the Commission has international scope, making it arguably the most powerful competition authority in the world. Commission investigations of potential antitrust violations often end informally because the threat of Commission action leads to negotiations and redefined plans. But when informal dealing fails, the Commission may levy quite substantial fines—French state-owned companies like Renault and Pechiney, the Belgian chemical giant Solvay, and the Swiss-Swedish packaging company Tetrapak were all fined heavily in the early 1990s, for example. Recently the Commission fined four major elevator manufacturers—two EU, one Swiss, and one American—1.5 billion euros for price fixing. And it has also ruled against Microsoft's practice of "bundling" software programs together in Windows, initially fining it 500 million euros (which Microsoft appealed to the ECJ), later fining Microsoft an even larger amount for noncompliance.

The procedures for merger control involve proactive economic and legal judgments about the possible restraints of trade if a merger occurred. The number of merger cases considered has increased each year, creating clearer procedures and jurisprudence. Perhaps the most spectacular case occurred in 2001, when the Commission blocked an avionics merger between General Electric and Honeywell, even after U.S. authorities had already approved. More often mergers go through after company plans are reformulated to meet the DG Comp's concerns, as, for instance, in 1997 when the Commission obliged Boeing Aircraft to reconfigure parts of its planned merger with MacDonnell-Douglas. DG Comp, which has reviewed several thousands of proposed mergers since 1989, has disallowed only a handful (around twenty).

The problem of state aid to companies is difficult because industries, companies, jobs, and votes are at stake. The Commission has the power to allow certain state subsidies, for example, for projects like well-defined one-off industrial restructuring in industries hit hard by recessions or by world market shifts like shipbuilding, steel, and textiles. It has also allowed subsidies for large projects that might enhance the European market, like the English Channel tunnel, and to shore up regions hit by natural disasters. Still, some member state governments have abiding traditions of state-centered industrial policy, notwithstanding the single market. In airlines, for example, heavily subsidized national carriers have run up against Commission efforts to deregulate the EU airline market.

EU competition policy is in constant evolution. National as well as corporate players push back and insist on the right to use traditional policy instruments, such as subsidies, to promote social cohesion, economic growth, and job creation. ECJ review has also been important, and the Court has slapped down DG Comp on occasion when it has done its work badly. Recently the Commission decided to decentralize competition policy matters below a certain threshold of importance to member state competition authorities, with DG Comp supervising their work. Finally, as the Microsoft and GE-Honeywell cases, among others, show, EU competition policies can have a major effect on how antitrust matters are decided globally, and this is likely to continue.

One Money and One Market: The Euro and EMU

The policy story of the Economic and Monetary Union (EMU) is brief, since EMU only began in 1999 and actual public circulation of the euro only in 2002, but its importance cannot be overestimated. For business, the advantage of having a single currency means more transparent costs and economic indicators. For ordinary Europeans and foreign tourists money no longer has to be exchanged every time a border is crossed. Most important, however, the single market that the EU has built would have been hard-pressed to get through the fluctuations among national currencies that might have happened since 1998 had EMU and the euro not existed.

How does EMU work? Its core, and very federal, institutions include a European Central Bank (ECB) with a president—presently Jean-Claude Trichet, former governor of the Bank of France—and an executive board, sitting at the center of a broader European

System of Central Banks run by a board of governors of the now-thirteen members of EMU (originally eleven in 1999, Greece and Slovenia having joined since). The ECB, located in Frankfurt, Germany, with its large staff of economists and other specialists, is completely independent of political influence, following the Maastricht Treaty, and is required to prioritize the pursuit of price stability in its policies. Price stability, defined as an inflation rate of 2 percent a year or less, is tracked by targeting the money supply and inflation levels, and is achieved primarily through adjusting EMU-wide interest rates. The central banks of EMU member countries, themselves independent of political influence since Maastricht, implement ECB policies.

The coming of EMU on January 1, 1999, and the introduction of euro notes and coins three years later, in January 2002, went very smoothly. The resumption of economic growth in 1998–1999 helped the ECB and allowed it to pursue for a time a monetary policy that dispelled widespread anxiety that its statutory dedication to price stability might nip new growth in the bud. The major initial criticism of the ECB was that it had problems communicating, causing some confusion in financial markets. The new euro fluctuated quite a bit, however. In January 1999 it was valued at $1.18, and by autumn 2000, it had fallen over 25 percent. This slide underlined the relationship of the ECB to the issue of international exchange-rate management. A stable international monetary environment was in everyone's interest, but producing such an environment was only partly up to the ECB. This was further underlined by the devaluation of the U.S. dollar that began in 2002 and saw the euro rising to over $1.40 by 2007, dampening the EU's exports. This devaluation, which began with the collapse of the U.S. dot-com boom, helped bring a return of recession and high unemployment to Europe's core continental economies. And as it happened, the ECB, detecting inflation, hardened its interest rate stance, making it difficult for member states to use countercyclical measures.

The ECB made its philosophy clear quickly. Its job was to do monetary policy and watch out for signs of inflation. If some European countries got into economic difficulty, this was their own fault, most likely caused by selfish market actors and imprudent governments. And if countries were consistently not doing well, they needed to make "structural reform." This usually meant introducing tough neoliberal policies, which could weaken the protections that workers enjoyed and involve cutbacks in welfare state programs such as pensions, unemployment benefits, or housing subsidies.

Criticism of this philosophy—and the welfare retrenchment that it implied—did not target the ECB directly, however. Instead it zeroed in on the 1997 Stability and Growth Pact (SGP) that bound EMU members to the original Maastricht "convergence criteria," particularly the taboo on budgetary deficits of more than 3 percent. More than half of EMU members fell afoul of this after 2000 and by 2005 six member states, including Italy, France, and Germany, were in violation, many for several years in a row. The Commission, whose job it was to monitor the pact, repeatedly invoked "excessive deficit" warnings, but this did not prevent Romano Prodi, then Commission president, from calling the 3 percent requirement "stupid." EMU's "one size fits all" monetary policy also proved troublesome. Initially, ECB policies worked well for France and Germany, for example, because they needed new growth, but also simultaneously heated up the smaller economies of Ireland and Portugal, obliging their governments to adjust painfully. This happened again, but in reverse, to France and Germany in 2003–2004, with greater effect on broader European economic health, as relatively high interest rates inhibited government policies and private investment. EMU clearly needed fine-tuning. Thus after a flurry of criticism and excessive deficit procedures, the Stability and Growth Pact was reformed in 2005 to give members more room to confront the ups and downs of the business cycle, in particular allowing them to discount the current budgetary costs of future-oriented policies like research and restructuring. In difficult circumstances EMU members thus could exceed the annual 3 percent deficit, but they were also enjoined to lower deficits when things went better. That the SGP was reconfigured because bigger continental member states had basically refused to cooperate when the going got rough did not pass unnoticed, however, particularly among smaller EU members.

Problems with ECB policies and the original Stability and Growth Pact were not the entire story. The EMU "federalized" monetary policy for the EU member states who joined—and everyone, including the new members, was required to join eventually, once they were qualified, except those with explicit opt-outs (the UK, Denmark, and Sweden). However, EMU members retained prerogatives over their own macroeconomic policy decisions—most taxing and spending—and this created a situation fraught with pitfalls. Among the—worst, but very real—possible outcomes were national beggar-thy-neighbor strategies that manipulated tax and spending programs to gain competitive advantage over other EMU members. The "Eurogroup" of EMU members that works within the Council of Finance Ministers (ECFIN) has tried to promote coherence—each member is obliged to produce three-year projections that are integrated into public "broad economic policy guidelines" to which actual performance can be compared—but little has really obliged member states to harmonize macroeconomic policies. Since these policies can win or lose elections and are a critical aspect of domestic politics, they will inevitably vary greatly. This situation is certain to mean that the "policy mix" between the federalized monetary policies of the ECB and decentralized macroeconomic policies at the national level will often be unsatisfactory, to the likely detriment of European stability, growth, and competitiveness.[4]

The Common Agricultural Policy: A Very Different Single Market

The Rome Treaty proposed a Common Market in agricultural as well as manufactured products. The Common Agricultural Policy was the result.[5] The CAP remains the single largest item in the EU budget—42 percent in 2005—and it is managed by the Commission. The CAP was originally a system of price supports that kept Community prices for agricultural goods higher than they might otherwise have been and, quite as important, above those on the world market. The CAP helped modernize European agriculture, but the system encouraged farmers to overproduce. Surpluses then had to be stored at great expense and, eventually, dumped internationally below their production costs, bringing down the global price levels. Other major producers, including the United States and Australia, were incensed about this, even if they themselves often indulged in similar practices. The CAP also encouraged farmers to overuse chemical fertilizers, pollute, and damage water tables. Such developments fed reflection about reform, but by the later 1960s farmers had built powerful groups that protected the CAP and its budget in their interests.

The CAP made DG Agriculture the largest administrative unit in Brussels. Its technocrats measured carrots, administered milk quotas, rented storage barns, and sold surplus goods on the world market. Because highly regulated markets tempted fraud, DG Agriculture also had to police farmers to ensure that they actually produced what they claimed. The DG spent and tried to account for vast amounts of money, projected how much more would be needed, and when it proposed prices and regulations was lobbied by agriculture ministers and hard-nosed farmers' organizations who mobilized sheep and cows in the streets of Brussels. Each product area had its own management committee, and the entire system was tracked by the COREPER committee on agriculture. Implementation was left largely to member states, however, closely monitored and audited by the Commission.

The CAP has always been redistributive, shifting income from taxpayers and consumers to farmers and money from country to country, with some member states getting more than others (some poorer countries along with much wealthier Denmark and France). The price support system and subsidized dumping on the international market also created transfers. EU export subsidies had become the CAP's single largest spending category by the 1990s.[6] Finally, there were additional transfers simultaneously to inefficient agricultural regions and to very efficient producers, like French wheat farmers, who hid politically behind laggard colleagues. Today 80 percent of CAP money goes to 20 percent of farmers.

Acrimonious negotiations to reform the CAP started not long after the CAP itself, particularly because member states like Britain and the Netherlands disliked subsidizing phantom Italian tobacco growers, Bavarian hop farmers who drove Mercedes cars, French beet-sugar conglomerates, and prosperous Danes. The deeper problem, however, was that without reform the costs of the CAP were likely to grow larger and larger at the expense of other EU and national activities, eventually to the point of discrediting European integration altogether. Reform began seriously with the first Delors budgetary package of 1988, which established quotas on milk

production, stabilizers to reduce subsidies automatically with the threat of overly high levels of production, and multiyear budget projections to flatten future budget growth. More serious reform came, however, when the CAP became a barrier to completing the GATT Uruguay Round in the early 1990s. The Commission was then able to use threats from GATT partners to constrain farmers to reduce guaranteed price levels and shift the CAP toward land set-asides —"deficiency payments"— and away from price supports. Farmers were paid upfront and this made the CAP budget more transparent, but because buying farmers off was part of the politics of reform the new approach did not save much money.

"Set asides" have since accelerated. The Commission's *Agenda 2000* proposals, to prepare enlargement to the CEECs, plus new reforms proposed by Agriculture Commissioner Franz Fischler in 2002–2003, have largely shifted CAP spending to "rural development" rather than direct price supports, while European prices have fallen relative to world prices. CAP spending to sustain farmers' income is being "decoupled" from traditional market-distorting price supports. One result is that dumping has lessened, if not quite enough to satisfy farm producers in other parts of the world.

The CAP's future remains a battlefield, however. Every time EU member states negotiate multiyear budget deals—now called "financial perspectives"—spending on the CAP is a central issue. Fitting the CAP to Eastern European agriculture was a new challenge for the deal struck at Berlin in 1999. Making new member states, particularly Poland and its plethora of small farmers, full participants in the CAP would have expanded the budget more than anyone wanted. Thus the Poles and others were given transition periods before full CAP participation. A "mid-term" review in 2002–2003 saw the French arrayed against almost everybody but nonetheless able to beat back new budgetary change with the help of the Germans. In the tough negotiations about the EU's 2007–2013 package, the CAP, which was defended tooth and nail by the French, again became part of a complex negotiating end-game. No one won much, but the CAP budget lost least. The practice of paying off farm interests for every CAP reform continued, and if the amounts stopped growing, they at least stayed at a more or less steady state. "Decoupling" CAP subsidies from price supports and shifting spending to rural development left the CAP budget vulnerable after 2013, however. Farmers were a dwindling, and often aging, part of everyone's population, excepting perhaps that of Poland. With French ex-president Jacques Chirac, the CAP budget's champion, finally retired in 2007, the CAP saga could well have come to an end, with some kind of "renationalizing" of subsidies for rural development in the offing.

This would be a positive conclusion, since the international community has long been in conflict with the CAP. The new dispute mechanisms of the World Trade Organization (WTO), for example, immediately clogged up with complaints about the EU's banana regime, hormone-fed meat, and genetically modified agricultural products, which the EU is reluctant to accept, and unfair trade practice suits from bigger "southern" agricultural producers like Australia and Brazil and poorer countries. At time of writing, the WTO DOHA round that began in 2001 was close to foundering in large part because of deadlocks regarding EU agricultural policy.

Regional Development Programs: Solidarity in the Single Market

Regional development funding through the "structural funds" is the EU's other large budgetary item, an expression of solidarity between better-off and less developed regions. There was slight bowing to regional development in the Rome Treaty, mainly to pay off the Italians with their underdeveloped south. But after the EU's first enlargement (in 1973 to the UK, Denmark, and Ireland), a European Regional Development Fund (ERDF) was founded. Enlargement in the 1980s to poorer countries (Greece in 1981, Spain and Portugal in 1986) prompted more energetic efforts, however. The Single European Act established "economic and social cohesion" as a new common policy and "reform of the structural funds" in 1988 sought to focus three different existing funds—the ERDF, the European Social Fund, and the basic agricultural budget (EAGGF)—on regional development. Perhaps more important, financing was doubled over five years, with another doubling in the 1990s. The 1999 budget deal then faced the task of preaccession help for the CEECs by creating a special "Instrument for Structural Policies for Preaccession." Annual spending on the structural funds is now around $50 billion.

EU regional development prioritizes specific development objectives and promotes "partnership" between the Commission, which vets the projects and administers the program, and national, regional, and local levels. The priorities developed in the later 1980s were to assist underdeveloped "objective 1" regions (with the biggest pot of money), help restructure deindustrialized regions, enhance skills and combat long-term and youth unemployment, and aid rural areas. The partnership principle meant that EU funds were to complement, rather than replace, national funding, with national governments obliged to come up with matching funds. The money was provided to coherent multiannual, multitask, and multiregional programs rather than to uncoordinated individual national projects. Prior to 1999 Greece, Ireland, Portugal, Corsica, Sardinia, Sicily, southern Italy, all of Eastern Germany except Berlin, and most of Spain were Objective 1 areas, where income was 75 percent or less of EU average, received two-thirds of the funding. The Maastricht Treaty also added a "cohesion fund" to compensate Greece, Ireland, Portugal, and Spain for participation in the EU's environmental and transport policies.

After the Amsterdam Treaty (1997) prospective enlargement to the CEECs started to reshape regional development policies. The Commission's *Agenda 2000*, a document prepared for discussion on new multiyear "financial perspectives," proposed that structural fund spending should remain at the same relative level—0.46 percent of Community GDP—through 2006, but with 20 percent set aside for pre- and postaccession help to new EU members. EU15 member states refused to raise the budget at that point, however, meaning that money going east had to be taken away from existing western recipients. The Commission thus proposed lowering the portion of the EU15 population receiving funding and cutting the number of priority objectives. The EU15 "cohesion" areas whose living standards had risen above the cutoff point—75 percent of EU average GDP—tried to block many of these changes, with the result that richer EU15 members won funding for pet projects in their own underdeveloped and declining areas. The Berlin 1999 deal thus protected funding for prospective new members but at a reduced level, while Commission control over the process weakened. In 2005 around 65 percent of total funding went to projects in the ten new member states.

The cumulative effects of EU regional development programs are hard to calculate. It is clear, however, that if amounts going to any particular country have been small in absolute terms, they have often provided substantial additions to local investment. Some countries have been spectacularly successful—Ireland, an economic backwater when EU help first arrived, now has the second highest per capita income level in the Union, while some other recipients, like Spain, have also done well. Quite as important, the funds have also provided incentives to EU15 member states to avoid "races to the bottom" through development strategies based on cheap labor and minimalist social policies. One bonus has been that regional levels of government have developed stakes in European integration. Finally, to the degree that increased purchasing power in poorer areas is used to buy goods and services from the rest of the EU, regional development funding has been good for richer donor states.

The structural funds have also provided incentives for administrative reform, a process that has been of great importance for the CEECs. The CEECs, with incomes less than 40 percent of EU average, need the money, even if it may take time before some of them have the capacity to absorb it productively. The emphasis on funding infrastructural improvement in roads, railroads, energy provision, airports, ports, and similar projects brings rapid returns. But the biggest payoff, proven by experiences in Spain, Portugal, and Greece, countries, like the CEECs, that are emerging from illiberal and authoritarian regimes, is that EU regional development can help consolidate good administrative practices, the rule of law, and democracy. If it does the same for the CEECs it will be well worth the cost.

The EU's Quest for Competitiveness: Confronting Globalization

EU policies to promote competitiveness stretch back to the European Coal and Steel Community (ECSC), which had strong powers over producers. More than once the ECSC declared a "manifest crisis" to force structural changes in the industries. The EU since then has often been involved in reconfiguring troubled industries and regions—shipbuilding and textiles, for example. And it has often provided financial aid, retraining programs, temporary trade protection, and voluntary trade restriction agreements with foreign producers. Many of these actions were bailouts or programs to ease the pain of deindustrialization, but by the 1990s regional development funds had taken over the job of aiding rustbelt areas, while EU focus turned toward investment in high-end innovation.

For its first half-century the EU's main activity has been building an open European market, which it understood as the best way to bring Europe to the economic cutting edge. This has never been an easy job, however, demanding deregulating, harmonizing, standardizing, redistributing, networking, monitoring, litigating, and many other things. Today EU Europe is the largest single market in the world—500 million people, prosperous, democratic, at peace, creative and, more generally, a global model for regions in need of new ideas. This has not been enough to push EU Europe to the top of the global economic competitiveness league, however. Fifty years ago Europe was behind the United States, with the EU a catch up tool. By the 1980s the United States had again jumped ahead, particularly in high tech areas, and Japan and the Asian Tigers had become new competitors with distinctive comparative advantages. Without the single-market program and EMU, Europe would have fallen far behind, but these did not prove sufficient to prevent the United States from moving forward again in the 1990s, propelled by information technology while China, India and other low-cost newcomers gobbled up markets in the manufacturing areas where Europe had earlier specialized. Today's issue is the vulnerability of the European economy, including its most up-to-date sectors, to global competition. What can the EU do, beyond market building, to accelerate new modernization and gain a competitive edge? Key areas like research and technological development (R&D) and industrial policy remain primarily national, with each member state deciding its own policies. The EU can provide incentives and forums for new cooperation, however. In the early 1980s, the EU, prodded by Commission activism and business lobbyists, began funding high-tech R&D, particularly with the *Esprit* program for transnational research cooperation among electronics companies. The *Esprit* experience illustrated the problems and paradoxes of promoting European-level "industrial policy," however. Liberals believed that the EU should only act on broad market frameworks while those who favored state-led approaches preferred targeting particular economic sectors. The Information Society DG that administered *Esprit* was thus often accused of French-style statist planning and of being in the pockets of the big companies.

Such disagreements are now in the past, however. The SEA included a clause that allowed the EU to assume some—small—responsibility for Euro-level science policy, and the Maastricht Treaty allowed more EU activity in research and technological development to complement efforts by member states. The 2000 Lisbon Summit was more ambitious, however, calling for the creation of a "European Research Area," and in 2003 EU leaders agreed to raise spending on R&D—primarily national, but also EU-level—to 3 percent of GDP by 2010 (a target that will not be met). The flagship vehicles for EU R&D since the 1980s have been multiyear research "framework programs" drawn up by the Commission and then approved by the Council. Here, as in a range of other policy areas where member states retain autonomy, the EU must work with, rather than substitute for, national policies. The EU can try to seduce national practices in directions that it may think are likely to have higher payoffs, usually by European subsidies, but it has little authority to oblige member states to do anything different from what they want to do on their own. EU policies thus must try to promote greater cooperation and, if possible, convergence, among member states around general European goals.

The main goals of the research framework programs have been to stimulate scientific and technological innovation while providing incentives to create a genuinely European scientific and technological space out of the existing fragmentation of knowledge and research communities. The Sixth Framework Program (2002–2006, with a seventh now beginning) had a—relatively small—budget of 17.5 billion euros to create "a frontier free zone in which scientific resources can be used more efficiently to create more jobs and to make Europe more competitive."[7] Predictably, the effort has been hindered by national rivalries and the relatively low level of EU funding, but there have been successes. EU-promoted cross-border communication, mobility, and collaboration among scientists and researchers have already begun to pay off in terms of greater European focus and coherence, and the EU has

also invested wisely in research issues of immediate trans-European importance—environmental research and health and food safety, for example. There have also been major European "industrial policy" innovations in mobile phones, space technologies, and satellites that have "Europeanized" standards and helped security policy and air transport, among others. Still, European spending on research and development, both public and private, is relatively low compared with competitor areas, and continues to suffer from national fragmentation of effort.

The EU's worries about declining competitiveness found new focus at the Lisbon summit in 2000. The Lisbon agenda, now the EU's flagship economic platform, sought nothing less than to make EU Europe the world's most advanced "knowledge economy" by 2010, by which point the EU was also to have restored full employment and preserved Europe's "social model"—welfare states and labor market policies—through reform. The Lisbon program went well beyond research and development to include upgrading "citizen competence" through education and training for new skills, new infrastructure, and environmental policies for sustainable development.

Results of the Lisbon program have been mixed. Liberalizing services through the "services directive" was one centerpiece, but national resistance to the 2004 Commission proposal watered down the directive. Financial services liberalization, programmed before Lisbon, is incomplete, particularly in retail banking. Proposals to liberate energy markets have foundered because national energy monopolies disapprove. Brussels has moved on chemicals regulation (REACH), climate change (Kyoto), and talked a great deal about lightening its regulatory hand, but what the Commission has been able to do has been severely limited by member state indifference and resistance. This is because the biggest part of Lisbon policymaking lay within national jurisdictions, involving programs that could be decided only by national governments.

Convergence on the Lisbon goals depended on voluntary coordination of member state actions. To stimulate this, Lisbon architects proposed an "Open Method of Coordination" (OMC). OMC involved setting general European goals (without EU legal compulsion), encouraging member states to hold regular and open national discussions about achieving them, identifying the best practices emerging from these discussions, building up statistical and other indicators of progress, and, finally, publicizing successes and failures—naming and shaming—from Brussels. The hope was that repetition of OMC exercises, which came to cover a wide range of policy areas, would change national behaviors to converge around desirable goals. OMC, in other words, was a new technique for Brussels to push the Lisbon agenda through soft law and exhortation because it lacked hard tools.

The ambitions of the Lisbon strategy are so great that it may never really be possible to evaluate its success. Parts of Lisbon would have been done anyway, while others will never be done. As 2010 approaches it is clear that there is much reform going on, but not enough. Lisbon quickly became all things to all people. The center-left, from which Lisbon originally came, saw it as prodding necessary reconfiguration of the gentle labor markets and humane welfare state programs it prized. The center-right, on the other hand, saw it as an elaborate décor behind which to push neoliberal structural reform. When indicators showed that the strategy was falling short in 2004–2005, the center-right Barroso Commission refocused on structural reform and liberalization, leading to some retreat from the OMC and reassignment of responsibilities to member states. Each country now prepares an annual plan, and the European Commission then evaluates the results. This allows member states to pick and choose what they want to do, given national social and political situations.

Shared Policy Areas

The Lisbon story illustrates the mixed nature of the EU as a system for making public policy. In some areas the EU has strong, "vertical" powers that directly shape national policies. In others it has more limited, "horizontal" power to set examples, provide seed money, and cajole, while national policymaking, often zealously protected, remains central. The precise division of labor between member states and the EU is determined by EU treaties. After the EU's scope grew greatly in the 1980s and 1990s, many members determined to resist any new encroachments, reflected in the concept of "subsidiarity" written into Maastricht and refined thereafter, in accordance with which the making of

public policy belongs at the lowest effective jurisdiction. Where the public interest is best served by EU-level policy, there the Union should act. In other areas it must abstain.

Social policy illustrates the "subsidiarity" issue. It is an area where the EU has some influence to exhort countries to follow EU initiatives, but little direct power. "Social models"—particularly welfare state and employment policy arrangements—were essential building blocks for rebuilding national democracies after World War II, and they quickly became one of the central issue areas of national politics. The Treaty of Rome narrowly limited the EU to matters of labor market mobility within the common market, some occupational training, and equal opportunities for men and women (Article 119), and it created a European Social Fund with the vague purposes of making "the employment of workers easier, increasing their geographical and occupational mobility within the Community." In general, however, the EU has coexisted with as wide a variety of social policy regimes as it has had members.

The list of areas where the EU has social policy powers is short. "Equal opportunities" for women and men in the labor force is one—for odd reasons: in 1958 French textile bosses bargained hard to protect themselves against lower-paid German textile workers. EU Europe has since developed very progressive programs for advancing women's rights. The 1985 White Paper on Completing the Single Market then added workplace health and safety out of fear that health and safety "social dumping" might be used as a source of comparative advantage by poorer countries. By the mid-1990s a body of European-level health and safety regulation was on the books. The SEA also included a new Article 118B stating that "the Commission shall endeavor to develop the dialogue between management and labor at European level, which could, if the two sides consider it desirable, lead to relations based on agreement," elaborated into a "Social Chapter" at Maastricht. Under this, when the Commission desired to propose social policy action, it could first ask the "social partners" to negotiate, and, if the negotiations succeeded, their results could become EU legislation, leading to several new social policy directives, including those on working time, consultative European Works Councils (EWCs), parental leave, and regulating "atypical work" (part-time and short-term contracts).

By the later 1990s member states had lost enthusiasm for legislating in social policy areas, however, and the EU social policy path shifted to decentralized "soft" procedures and the open method of coordination (OMC). The 1997 Amsterdam Treaty included new employment policy clauses that gave the EU limited prerogatives to "contribute to a high level of employment by encouraging cooperation between member states." The European Employment Strategy (EES) that followed sought to promote coordination toward common goals, leaving each member state to choose its own approaches. The EES used a range of European economic policy goals and social policy instruments and utilized techniques of management by objectives, creating and using new statistical bases, setting targets, benchmarking best practices, and reviewing achievements comparatively. By 2007 there were signs that the European Employment Strategy and the open coordination offensive were helping, but despite this extension of "soft" activity, the EU's direct influence over social policy remains very limited. Core welfare state programs and employment regulation are national tasks that will not be part of any conceivable future EU mandate, yet few European issues are more important, or politically volatile, than social policy.

Environmental policy is another important shared area conditioned by subsidiarity. The EU and the Commission's DG Environment have had multiyear action programs for thirty years, which the Council and Parliament approve (a sixth program is currently in effect), and EU treaties now set out general principles of environmental protection policy. Environmental programs have promoted codes of conduct, particularly through "green labels" on products. There has been legislation about water and air pollution, noise, waste disposal, protection of biodiversity, and transporting dangerous substances. Environmental impact assessments are now compulsory for all projects above a certain size. And although it began behind the United States on such issues, the EU now has higher standards in most areas.

By the 1990s, certain member states, like the United Kingdom, had begun to resent EU "meddling" in environmental matters. Others, like Spain, which received the new cohesion fund at Maastricht partly in compensation for implementing high EU environmental standards, objected to the high costs of compliance. Environmental policy thus became a favorite target for arguments about subsidiarity, and new guidelines were developed to ensure that the right level of government tackled the correct level of problems. Unlike social policy, however, certain key environmental problems cannot be remedied effectively by national governments and are better addressed transnationally, while serious variations in national environmental standards could easily become barriers to trade.

Strong environmental policy has thus become an important EU fact, for numerous reasons—Europe's dense population, long industrial history, high levels of economic development, vulnerability to resource shortages (particularly energy), and the strength of Green politics and ideas in recent domestic European politics. Moreover, the EU has become an international leader in environmental issues and sustainable development on the global scene, and taking leads in environmental matters in international diplomacy is now an important dimension of EU foreign policy. In its complicated dealings with Russia, the EU was a central player in bringing the Kyoto Protocol into legal operation. The EU's cap-and-trade greenhouse gas limiting scheme is the world's most advanced. Most recently, deepened concern about climate change led the European Commission to set out a new, and very ambitious, program to limit European emission of greenhouse gases and energy consumption, and to encourage technological innovation to pursue sustainable development.[8] This program, if it succeeds, should help launch the successor to the Kyoto Protocol and cement the EU's position as world leader on environmental issues.

Pillars of Sovereignty?
Intergovernmental Europe

The EU's scope has grown substantially, and with this its new policy areas have encroached on core areas of national sovereignty which member states are reluctant to turn over to the "community method." At Maastricht they thus decided that for two of these new areas, "Justice and Home Affairs," and foreign and security policy, they would create two new intergovernmental pillars.

THE EU BUDGET: A Significance Test?

In 2006, EU member states decided on the EU's 2007–2013 "financial perspectives." Appropriations for 2007 are around 126 billion euros (1.1 percent of EU Gross National Income) and will increase only slightly through 2013. Revenues come from a VAT tax levy on member states (15 percent), customs and other duties (15 percent), and a tax on member state GNI (69 percent). 2007 appropriations divide as follows:

Spending Category	Billion Euros
Sustainable Growth, total	54.9
Sustainable Growth: R&D, innovation, energy, transport	9.4
Sustainable Growth: regional policy	45.5
Natural Resources (agriculture, rural development)	56.3
Freedom, Security, Justice (JHA)	0.6
Citizenship (culture, public health, consumer protection)	0.6
EU as a global player (CFSP, aid, development cooperation)	6.8
Administration	6.9

What do these numbers mean?

1. The EU budget grew rapidly in the 1980s and 1990s, has stabilized, and remains small compared to national budgets (now 44.5% on average of GNI). Beware, however! Many EU policies also involve large expenditures out of national budgets.
2. The wording of budgetary categories has changed. "Sustainable development" used to be the "structural funds," for example, and

"natural resources" used to be the CAP. These two items still make up 80% of the EU budget (36% for regional development, 44+% for agriculture).
3. Since the later 1990s member states have been keeping the EU on a tight budgetary leash. The EU budget is not shrinking, because European GNI is growing, but member states prefer to keep money at home than give it to the EU.
4. The number of "net contributors" to the EU budget, who give more to the EU than they receive back, has increased so that practically all the EU15 countries are now "net contributors" and only poorer countries "net beneficiaries."
5. Practically all net contributors, thinking that the others have a better deal, are thus eager to cut their relative contributions. This means that budget dealings are now high-stakes games.
6. The EU budgetary process has two steps. The first is the intergovernmental "grand rendezvous" every five years to agree on multiyear term financial perspectives.
7. The second is a discussion beginning with a draft yearly budget from the Commission submitted to Council and Parliament, who usually produce a revised draft in December. If Parliament rejects the budget, a system of "provisional twelfths" comes on line—monthly expenditures limited to one-twelfth of the previous year's total. Then when the budgetary year is over, the Parliament must "discharge" (approve) it. It was a discharge debate in 1998 that led to the resignation of the Santer Commission in 1999.

Justice and Home Affairs

Justice and Home Affairs (JHA) came onto the EU agenda when separate but urgent law and order problems came together in the 1980s. The Rome Treaty had proclaimed that free movement of people was an important goal, but the early EU had failed to deal with visas, passports, and customs controls at national borders. Despite resistance from some countries, the EU began taking these tasks on in the 1980s. Predictably, as EU borders opened more, organized crime (drugs, trafficking in human beings, money laundering, and terrorism, among other unpleasant activities) Europeanized at the same time as legitimate business, meaning that without new cooperation between member states mobile crime and terrorism would gain a step on national authorities. Next, serious commitment to free movement of people meant that anyone inside the EU could move freely across borders, but individual member states would be in the dark about who might be wandering around their territories unless there was new cross-border cooperation on matters such as external border controls, visas, identification, asylum policies, and other requirements for entry, plus enhanced patrolling of external borders. With anxiety about immigration and immigrants rising everywhere, these problems demanded more than symbolic action. Finally, freedom of movement within the EU, in the absence of more legal cooperation, would leave perfectly respectable EU citizens confronted by a bewildering array of national regulations about civil law, making it difficult for them to know whether their rights would be respected.

None of these problems was a surprise. Initially ad hoc groups of member states formed organizations to confront them, like the Trevi Group on terrorism and the Pompidou Group on drugs, both from the 1970s. However, it was the Schengen Group in the 1980s—originally France, Germany, and the Benelux (with the Schengen *acquis* later incorporated in EU treaties)—that actually began to remove internal border crossings and reflect on the consequences. These organizations, which were often based on separate treaties, were relatively uncoordinated, however, and the need to bring them together was the major factor leading to the JHA pillar at Maastricht. A second reason was Germany's concern about its constitutionally constrained but very permissive asylum rules, which brought record levels of new asylum seekers at the end of the cold war.

The Maastricht Treaty bundled these areas into a "second pillar" whose intergovernmentalism cut out the Commission and Parliament, leaving Justice and Home Affairs ministers to make decisions unanimously. Business was prepared by COREPER and the K4 Committee plus three steering groups (Immmigration and Asylum, Police and Customs Cooperation, Judicial Cooperation on Civil and Criminal Matters) that brought together national experts and practitioners, who were all assisted by Council Directorates-General. Activities

slowly emerged. Europol, for police cooperation among EU member states that gathered, pooled, and circulated intelligence and information, and was well underway even before its members could agree on its rules and regulations. Databases about the Schengen area, customs, asylum-seeking, and stolen property also built up.

Intergovernmentalism proved unwieldy and slow in these areas. National interests and habits were zealously guarded, differences were great, and secrecy was *de rigueur*. Eventually, the Treaty of Amsterdam (followed by the Nice Treaty) agreed to "communitarize" certain JHA areas by 2004, shifting them from intergovernmentalist policymaking back to the "Community Method" and qualified-majority voting. The chosen areas were visas, asylum, and immigration, along with "judicial cooperation in civil matters having cross-border implications" and related specific issues including common procedures at EU external borders and common practices for asylum seekers. Highly sensitive matters of police and judicial cooperation would remain intergovernmental, however.[9] "Communitarization" of these areas proved easier said than done, and progress has been much slower than the original timetable planned.

What began with decentralized efforts to cope with the implications of the EU's opening internal borders and continued under JHA has recently been relabeled an "area of freedom, security, and justice for all." The rhetorical change shifts emphasis from mysterious intergovernmental activities toward rights for EU citizens and legal visitors (along with growing harshness for aspirant and illegal immigrants, part of the general shift in national political focus toward labeling immigration policy a question of "security"). One centerpiece of the new language was the Maastricht Treaty on European Union (TEU) provision on European citizenship that automatically made citizens of EU member states into EU citizens, with rights of movement, residence, voting in European elections, and diplomatic protection abroad. Another was the Charter of Fundamental Rights proposed by the Nice Treaty and included in the 2004 Constitutional Treaty. More generally, JHA proposed new policy harmonization through "mutual recognition," better transnational "readability" of national policies, and more international cooperation on civil law matters like divorce and alimony, child visitation, and financial problems like debt and bankruptcy. There has also been movement toward common EU asylum policies. External border controls, policies on legal immigration, and the general control of immigration lie within EU sights, but progress has been very slow.

Where the police, interior ministers, and criminal law predominate, it is difficult to know what is actually happening, because policymaking remains behind closed doors and actors behave secretively. Nonetheless, we know that there are now a number of monitoring and information agencies functioning across the Union on matters such as drugs, discrimination, and fraud, a European Police College, a European Police Chiefs Task Force, and Eurojust, an organization of senior justice officials to facilitate cross-border prosecutions. In addition, in 2004, a common European arrest warrant superseded complicated national extradition proceedings. Europol's antiterrorist coverage and budget had already grown prior to 9/11, but both grew substantially more thereafter. In the EU, as elsewhere, this sphere is also shrouded in mystery, punctuated only when attacks occur, as in Madrid in 2004 and London in 2005. But there have been few complaints about lack of European cooperation and inefficiency from the American side, even from an American administration that does not hesitate to dress down anyone it judges negatively. This may mean that the Europeans, who, after all, had a very long history with terrorism before 9/11, are doing a good job.

Common Foreign and Security Policy

Jacques Delors, in the Maastricht years, repeatedly, and rhetorically, asked whether the EU would remain a "big Switzerland," an economic giant and a security dwarf. The question is still pertinent. The Maastricht Treaty created another intergovernmental pillar for the new Common Foreign and Security Policy (CFSP) that it—vaguely—envisaged would eventually develop. CFSP is about high EU power politics and military matters. Has the new CFSP led the EU to become a serious international security player? To anticipate, the answer is complicated, but boils down to "no, not yet." Before reaching this conclusion, however, it is important to stress that CFSP is only *part* of EU foreign policy and the most recent and least developed part at that. There are other matters that need discussing first because

they came first—and because they remain closer to the heart of the EU mission.

"Soft" EU Foreign Policy Real Successes?

Having a consistent trade policy toward the outside world was always part of the common, then single, market and By 2004, the EU had become tremendously important in international trade, with 7 percent of the world's population, 30.7 percent of its gross product (more than the United States at 28.3 percent), and 17.7 percent of global trade (equal to the United States), the largest and most open trading zone on the planet.[10] The system of global trade governance, an archipelago of the World Trade Organization (WTO), the IMF, World Bank, the Bank for International Settlements, the G7, and the confusing tangle of international standard and norm-setting organizations affiliated with the UN, is arguably as important to world stability and security as the military balance of power. Deciding EU trade policy is an intergovernmental matter, but one that member states have agreed should be focused on a general mandate administered by the Commission and carried out by the International Trade Commissioner and DG Trade. The EU trade commissioner has become an important world figure who bargains in forums like the WTO and deals with specific regional blocs and states. He is also in regular give-and-take with the Council and Parliament.

Over time, the areas covered by EU international multilateral trade negotiations have expanded—from industrial goods to agriculture, services, and intellectual property rights, for example, in the GATT Uruguay Round, with the EU often in the lead (excepting on agriculture). The EU has also traditionally given privileged trade positions to "ACP countries" (African, Caribbean, Pacific) whose trading relationships with Europe are regulated separately (the ACP countries are exempt from EU customs).[11] Trade openness to ACP countries, extended more recently to most of the world's poorer countries (free trade in "anything but arms"), has helped make the EU more open to developing countries than other rich parts of the world (again, despite agriculture).

Controversies about globalization mean that trade policy processes will structure world events in years to come. As the dimensions of trade under the WTO's mandate grow, for example, matters that used to remain outside trade talks, such as health, environmental, and labor standards, are now on the table, often because the EU has insisted on placing them there. Private diplomacy by large economic interests and the emergence of a lively international civil society composed of protest groups and nongovernmental organizations—first attracting attention at the 1999 Seattle WTO ministerial meetings—are also now facts of life. In all this, the EU has had new openings to act creatively. For example, together with the United States the EU engineered the beginning of the Doha Round, the first WTO multilateral trade session. Doha has since revealed the complexities of a rapidly changing economic world. Protests and pressure continue, but problems lie even deeper. Bringing the poorest of developing societies into the trade game without exploiting them is delicate, since their meager comparative advantages lie largely in agriculture where northern and EU trade protectors are loath to give away anything, and there are disagreements about services, environmental, and labor standards. With new areas of the world, particularly China and India, developing very rapidly due to low labor costs, there are major new threats to established northern interests. The collapse of the Doha Round ministerial talks in Cancún in 2003 demonstrated these processes at work. International trade will continue to be a bumpy road for the EU—and for everyone else, meaning that trade diplomacy will remain a central element in EU foreign policy.

International environmental politics is another EU "soft" foreign policy area. As noted earlier, the coincidence between fears that national environmental policies could be barriers to trade and growing environmental concern in many EU member states has led to new EU roles in environmental guidance and regulation along with qualified majority voting on the bulk of environmental matters.[12] Momentum spilled quickly over into EU international activities, in part because EU leaders were seeking new foreign policy issues where the EU could take a global lead. The biggest splash so far has been the Kyoto Protocol on global warming. The EU accepted the tough Kyoto targets without blinking, and EU diplomacy then linked Russian WTO candidacy to ratification of Kyoto to bring the protocol into effect in 2005. To back this up the EU set up a European emissions trading scheme.

Global leadership on environmental policy is not the same thing as bombs and battle groups, but it is foreign policy nonetheless.

The expansion of the EU itself might be seen as yet another "soft," but very significant, form of foreign policy.[13] To begin with, six very important neighbors, including France and Germany, stopped attacking one another when they decided to cooperate in the 1950s. The club they formed proved attractive to neighbors, and after several enlargements it is evident that the prospect of joining the EU has pushed more and more of these neighbors to democratize, commit to the rule of law, and cooperate for the continental greater good. The mechanisms are simple. If neighbors want in, they have to pay the entry fee of conforming to the *acquis communautaire*. In exchange there are immediate benefits, profitable trade agreements, and financial assistance, plus longer-term payoffs like regional development funding and participation in EU decision making.

The EU does not advertise enlargement as part of its "foreign policy," but the democratizing effects of EU enlargement have been stunning nonetheless. Three formerly authoritarian countries—Greece, Spain, and Portugal—were the huge successes in the 1980s, and the formula shows every sign of working as well for the formerly communist CEECs in the early twenty-first century. The EU has more recently elaborated its approach to offer partial benefits—trade access and assistance—to its "near neighbors" to the east (Turkey, an applicant for membership, the Ukraine, and others). Last but far from least, the EU, through the so-called Barcelona process, has pursued policies, backed by considerable funding, to promote freer markets and reform all around the Mediterranean (including help for infrastructure for Palestine, which has unfortunately been destroyed in recent warfare), an enlightened effort to help this volatile part of its neighborhood find greater prosperity and stability.

Finally, EU humanitarian and development aid are also important "soft" dimensions of the EU's positioning in the world. The EU has been in the development aid business from the beginning, because its founding coincided with the end of European colonialism, and ex-colonial powers, France in particular, felt an obligation toward their former territories (and, simultaneously, sought to maintain some control over them after independence). In time, with the coming of new attitudes and EU members, the EU's aid position has expanded and changed. Beyond special trade agreements between the EU and poor countries, there is now a European Development Fund directed to the ACP countries, special regional aid programs directed to the poorest countries, a cluster of humanitarian aid programs often used to co-finance worthy NGO activities in poorer parts of the world, and the very sophisticated operations of ECHO (the Commission's Directorate-General for Humanitarian Aid) for areas hit by natural disasters, population displacement, and conflicts. The EU (the Union and its member states taken together) gives 50 percent of all public development aid, making it the world's leader. All told, EU member states give 0.34 of their GDP to development aid, below the UN's 0.7 goal but well ahead of the United States and other world regions. EU aid is more and more problem-targeted and conditional. It seeks out infrastructure projects (transportation, water supply, schools, health care), following contemporary canons of sustainable development. It also tries to leverage its aid into better administration and governance in recipient countries.

"Hard" Foreign Policy: The CFSP

Global summits, bombs, and battle groups are nonetheless fundamental elements in foreign policy, and in these areas the story of Maastricht's intergovernmental Common Foreign and Security Policy is central. In these areas of high politics everyone knew that achieving commonality would be difficult, and not only because intergovernmentalism guaranteed slow progress and lowest common denominator compromises. This was because European nations, especially the old imperial powers, had long-standing different perspectives on basic international relations problems that would not easily change. The French were "Gaullist," for example, and had for decades sought to make Europe more independent from American power. The British, in direct contrast, cherished their "special relationship" with the Americans. The Germans, self-effacing in high international politics by historical necessity, needed a prominent EU to stand behind internationally, and this involved trying to conciliate France, the United Kingdom, and the United States without giving up

anything essential. Smaller EU countries might be more flexible, but they were always worried about domination by bigger ones. More recent EU members were special cases. Some, like Ireland, Sweden, and Austria, had neutral pasts. Others, like many CEECs, were pro-American because of what the United States had stood for in the cold war and because the United States had astutely "nailed down" CEEC NATO membership while the EU-15 dithered in uncertain post-cold war conditions.

The term "common foreign policy" ought not thus be misunderstood to mean a *single* European policy. Indeed, EU foreign and security policy was not meant to replace what member states did, as was made amply clear in the EU's incoherent misadventures in the ex-Yugoslavia in the early 1990s. The CFSP had to begin with lesser ambitions, and the most obvious place to start was in security and defense, perhaps around the 1992 "Petersberg tasks" of humanitarian intervention, peacekeeping, and funding combat-ready, properly equipped European forces for regional crisis management. European experts thus argued that the first major challenge for the EU was building rapid-response capacities, and the 1997 Amsterdam Treaty incorporated the "European Security and Defense Identity" (ESDI) proposals allowed under the Petersberg tasks, presumably through closer ties between the EU and a renewed Western European Union (WEU).[14] Amsterdam also set up a policy planning operation in the Council of Ministers.

Not much real progress could occur until EU member states had reviewed their cold war defense positions, however. In 1995 the French ended conscription to form a professional army and rejoin parts of the NATO planning apparatus. It took an unexpected initiative by Tony Blair to make things more concrete, however. After taking office in 1997, New Labour did a defense review, leading Blair to declare in fall 1998 that the European defense situation was "unacceptable" and marked by "weakness and confusion." That December, Blair and Chirac met in St. Malo and issued a "Joint Declaration on European Defense" that advocated giving the "Union . . . the capacity for autonomous action, backed up by credible military forces, the means to decide to use them, and a readiness to do so." EU determination was strongly reinforced by what happened in Kosovo, where the United States called, and fired, most of

NATO's shots. Indeed, in Kosovo some European planes could not fly at night, others could not fly at all, European codes were intercepted, while European troops were ill-equipped, dependent on Americans for intelligence, airlift capacity, command, and communications. As earlier in Bosnia, after American firepower won the battles, Europeans were then assigned cleanup, policing, and aiding duties. The one bright spot was that the Germans, earlier determined not to be involved in things military, had began to participate.

Kosovo led to new decisions. In December 1999 the Helsinki European Council announced "headline goals" for 2003 of a rapid-reaction force of fifty to sixty thousand soldiers, "capable of the full range of Petersberg tasks," deployable within sixty days, that could carry on for a full year (implying triple the number of troops), to be supported by 400 warplanes and 100 ships. The Council of Ministers also began new mechanisms to plan and control forces, including a Council of Ministers Politics and Security Committee, an EU Military Committee (the military chiefs of staff of all EU members), and an EU general staff of 150 officers to prepare Petersberg task scenarios. Uniformed soldiers thus entered the Council building in Brussels for the first time ever.

The Helsinki European Council underlined EU "determination to develop an autonomous capacity to take decisions and, where NATO as a whole is not engaged, to launch and conduct EU-led military operations in response to international crises." This implied that on-again, off-again discussions of linking the WEU closely with the EU were over. The WEU's treaty was not renewed, and the EU then directly took on new, if limited, military duties. The Helsinki goals were revised in 2003 in a new European Security Strategy. Henceforth the target was fifteen battalion-sized battle groups that could be mobilized, with tactical support, in five days, and then be able to operate for thirty days on the ground. The EU thus appeared set on building a new defense identity, although it was in no way a "European army," but rather a coordinated commitment of soldiers and military supplies from member states for particular kinds of missions.

Increasing levels of European defense spending were clearly needed to make a difference, however. In times of budgetary stringency the money was hard to find. More coordination and integration of theEuropean defense industry was also a necessity, but this threatened vested interests and jobs, making it difficult to achieve. The number of ready battalions is now close to full operational capacity, however, and there has been new investment in high-tech fighter planes, smarter weapons, new airlift capacity (the Airbus A400), and new satellites. Moreover, since 2003 the EU has been involved in at least fifteen missions on three different continents. In 2003 the EU took over policing from the UN in Bosnia and Herzegovina (7,000 troops) and then took over militarily from NATO in Macedonia. It also began moving "out of area" for the first time, usually in small contingents of a few hundred men, their equipment, and support. The EU thus recently ended an operation in East Timor; *Operation Artemis*, a 1,500-troop emergency mission to the Democratic Republic of Congo helped calm a troubled region in 2003; Operation EUFOR RD Congo then calmed Kinshasa during the 2006 elections; and the EU is preparing for new, and dangerous, duties in post-NATO Kosovo as soon as international agreement on its status can be reached.

Despite these changes, it remained unclear what the EU's new security capacities were really meant to do. Drawing the lessons of Yugoslavia, were they to "intimidate Milosevic" (the nationalist Serbian leader indicted for war crimes) and other such unpleasant elements in conflicts near the EU, or were they to combine military and nonmilitary dimensions of crisis-management whenever and wherever needed, as the Congo mission implied? And despite strenuous EU denials, were they ultimately the first steps toward a larger EU power footprint in the world? Everything indicated that the EU had no intention of trying to become a superpower, for better or worse. But the Union had military ambitions, particularly in the crisis management realm. Was this a positive compromise allowing the EU to act on the economic matters to achieve what Europeans wanted most, prosperity?

Whatever EU Europe's ultimate goals, its tentative initiatives in defense and security have inevitably spilled over into its relations with the United States. As a French journalist noted, Americans and Europeans "indulge in incompatible dreams. The U.S. wants to be number one, while minimizing the cost to the lives of its soldiers or to its economy. Europeans want to keep the U.S. as the ultimate insurance policy as they evolve towards a common identity."[15] The neoconservative

American Robert Kagan put it another way, claiming that in the security realm Americans were from Mars, Europeans from Venus, by necessity out of weakness.[16] The meanings of these incompatibilities became clearer after the terrorist attacks of September 11, 2001, on the World Trade Center and the Pentagon.

Europeans unanimously expressed massive support and sympathy for Americans after September 11 and bent over backwards to assist U.S. intelligence services to beef up European counterterrorism dispositions. EU member states also supported the U.S.-led expedition to Afghanistan, where, when asked, they assumed their NATO duties, boots on the ground. New global challenges were obliging EU members to look beyond the immediate European environment, however, and here the deep disagreements they had among themselves re-emerged, particularly about Iraq. Europeans knew that the Saddam Hussein regime was repressive, corrupt, and dangerous. Not everyone agreed that this justified preemptive military action, however, and, more generally, the Pentagon's strategy justifying preemptive war did not sit easily.

The Americans, for good reasons, had trouble persuading Europeans that the Iraqis possessed weapons of mass destruction (WMDs) in violation of United Nations resolutions. And when the United States decided to invade Iraq, whatever Europeans thought, those who believed strongly in multilateralism were deeply offended. German chancellor Schröder won reelection in autumn 2002 by opposing U.S. war plans, French president Chirac agreed with Schröder, and they both courted Russia's Putin to their side. Up to the last minute, the British, who had supported U.S. plans from the beginning, hoped for a UN resolution to justify war. The United States was halfheartedly willing to wait for such a new UN resolution, but the French vetoed it in no uncertain terms. A "coalition of the willing" then invaded Iraq, including EU members Spain, Italy, several CEEC then-applicant members, and the UK, despite strident opposition from the French, Germans, and others, plus massive public opinion opposition everywhere in the EU. Discomfort intensified when the United States generated public letters in favor of the war from European governments, including many CEEC accession candidates to the EU, while Donald Rumsfeld praised the "new" Europe and denounced the "old." As the Iraq war became a geopolitically dangerous quagmire,

however, European support evaporated almost completely, even in the UK, where Tony Blair's brilliant political career was terminally damaged.[17]

The EU's "big Switzerland" situation has never been as simple as a dichotomy between a muscular America and a weakling EU. The EU foreign policy story goes well beyond security matters, while in foreign policy terms the EU is far from devoid of international clout, even if its resources are most often of the "softer power" variety. A heavyweight in global trade, global environmental policy, and sustainable development, a significant agent for democratization, and a major player in the international exchange rate regime is difficult to overlook internationally. Moreover, the otherwise troubled 1990s have produced effective EU approaches to humanitarian aid and crisis management, another important, if often overlooked, addition to the Union's foreign policy toolbox. Nonetheless, by any smart bomb and big battalion measures, the EU is a relatively absent player. Whether this will change, and how, in a perilous world that seems destined to become "multipolar" in the future, either despite, or because of, the United States, is unforeseeable.

Notes

[1] See European Commission, *The Internal Market: Ten Years Without Frontiers* (Luxembourg: European Commission, 2002).

[2] Charlemagne, "Singling Out the Market," *The Economist*, February 23, 2007, www.economist.com/world/europe/display story.cfm?story_id=8746366

[3] For a discussion, see European Commission, *Competition Policy in Europe* (Luxembourg: European Commission, 2002), and Paul Craig and Grainne de Burca, *EU Law: Text, Cases, and Materials* (Oxford: Oxford University Press, 2002), chaps. 15–21.

[4] EMU and the euro are on the agendas of the new EU members from the 2004–2007 enlargement. EMU is part of the *acquis communautaire*, and each new member state is obliged to align with and eventually join EMU and is carefully watched for signs that it is doing what is necessary. Transition periods are likely to be quite long, however.

[5] Space is too limited to discuss the common fisheries policy, devoted to conservation and doling out national quotas and areas to the fishing industry.

[6] Elmar Rieger, "The Common Agricultural Policy: Politics Against Markets," in Wallace, Wallace, and Pollack, *Policymaking in the European Union.* 5th ed. (New York: Oxford University Press, 2005).

[7]European Commission, *Looking Beyond Tomorrow: Scientific Research in the European Union* (Luxembourg: European Commission, 2004), p. 6.

[8]Andrea Lenschow, "Environmental Policy," in Wallace, Wallace, and Pollack.

[9]Sandra Lavenex and William Wallace, "Justice and Home Affairs," in Wallace, Wallace, and Pollack.

[10]The numbers come from Pierre Defraigne, "L'Europe et la gouvernance économique mondiale," in IFRI, *Ramses 2007* (Paris: Dunod, 2007), p. 61.

[11]It is these arrangements that fell afoul of the United States, leading to the WTO banana disputes.

[12]Lenschow, "Environmental Policy," in Wallace, Wallace, and Pollack.

[13]A judicious assessment of EU foreign policy is in Chris Patten, *Not Quite the Diplomat* (London: Penguin, 2005).

[14]The WEU was founded in the 1940s and consecrated in the Paris agreements of 1954 that finalized NATO arrangements. It was meant as a politico-military organization of Western European states that would exist alongside NATO, but it never amounted to much. WEU was trotted out briefly after Maastricht as a possible military vessel for CFSP purposes. Its meager organizational capacities were eventually annexed by the EU.

[15]Dominique Moisi, "What Transatlantic Future?" in Werner Weidenfeld, ed., *Creating Partnership: The Future of Transatlantic Relations* (Gutersloh: Bertelsmann Foundation, 1997), p. 99.

[16]Robert Kagan, *Of Paradise and Power: America and Europe in the New World Order* (New York: Knopf, 2003). For a very different EU view, see Robert Cooper, *The Breaking of Nations: Order and Chaos in the Twenty-First Century* (London: Atlantic Books, 2003).

[17]Chris Patten, EU Commissioner for Foreign Relations during 9/11 and the Iraq war years, provides lucid commentary on all this in *Not Quite the Diplomat*.

CHAPTER 35

Euro-Politics in Transition

European integration has succeeded beyond its founders' dreams. The European Union now touches the lives of EU citizens in innumerable and irreversible ways. Starting with six members, the EU now has twenty-seven, and the Union covers the European map. Despite current economic problems, EU Europe is prosperous, with public and social services that are the envy of the world. EU Europe is also an increasingly important and respected global force.

European integration is far from concluded, however, and events in the first years of the twenty-first century indicate that EU Europe is at a crossroads. For the EU's first decades, advocates asserted that integration was a good in itself. This argument was convincing as long as Europeans had memories of the "European civil wars" that had decimated populations and landscapes in the first half of the twentieth century. However, most of today's Europeans were born into a prosperous modernity where the EU is more a fact of life than a moral imperative. When it turned fifty in 2007, therefore, the EU was judged less as an aspiration and moral duty, and more on its own terms, for what it had achieved—and what it could in the future deliver to its vast constituencies. The birthday found Europeans puzzled and unable to avoid really hard questions: What had the EU already done, and was this what we wanted? Where is the EU going, and do we really want to go there? What is the EU for, and why do we need it?

Obscure Problems of a Non-State: Institutions

In December 1991, the Maastricht negotiators decided that they had not quite finished their job of institutional design. And so they proposed another Intergovernmental Conference (IGC) to take up where they had left off. They did not know it, but they were beginning fifteen years of unending, uncertain, and difficult-to-follow high-level negotiations that would end in crisis.

The Maastricht follow-up produced the 1997 Treaty of Amsterdam, which tinkered usefully with CFSP and JHA, and agreed on a new clause to achieve a "high level of employment" that founded the European Employment Strategy. But between Maastricht and Amsterdam the EU had already added three new members (Austria, Sweden, and Finland) and had made

commitments to add twelve more (ten CEECs plus Cyprus and Malta). For the EU, an enlargement of this size implied serious institutional adjustments, for otherwise decision-making capacities would deteriorate. Too many commissioners (and twenty-seven was too many) would undercut collegial methods. Seats in the European Parliament had to be redistributed, but how and on what grounds? In addition, the Council of Ministers had always used a *tour de table* procedure in which each minister had an allotted time to present his government's positions. The more EU members the more unwieldy Council proceedings would be, slowing an already slow process to a crawl. Finally, enlargement involved changing the votes of member states in qualified majorities in ways that were bound to reopen festering issues—small versus large states, how many votes and according to what criteria, and what combination of small countries and large countries could form a blocking minority.

The Amsterdam negotiators put things off to yet another IGC. The Nice negotiations in 2000 were chaotic. Nice projected changes in the composition of the Commission: there would be one Commissioner per member after 2005 and, once the EU reached twenty-seven members, Commission size would be reduced, membership rotated, and not everyone would always have a Commissioner. If the goal was to disempower the Commission, as it was for some member states, this practically guaranteed success. Nice also decided on the membership of a postenlargement Parliament, which would also be too large, probably at the expense of effectiveness. Most important, after bitter struggle between smaller and larger members, Nice decided to reweight qualified majority voting to reflect a "dual majority" that took a country's population into account, but this decision was marred by a last-minute deal that made Spain and Poland more powerful than they should have been. Nice also proposed a new European Charter of Fundamental Rights, with unclear legal status. The negotiations were mean-spirited, and few were happy with the results, especially the Irish, who rejected the Nice Treaty in a 2002 referendum. Last, but not least, Nice proposed yet another IGC in 2004.

In the fall of 2000 the Belgian presidency called a "European convention" of "the main parties involved in the debate on the future of the Union."[1] The convention, to report prior to the 2004 IGC, was to resolve the institutional issues posed by enlargement, propose ways to make the EU a force for stability in world affairs, and bring citizens closer to European goals and institutions. The convention was designed deliberately to get outside the "Brussels beltway" by soliciting suggestions, contributions, and commentaries from anyone who cared to participate, whether individual citizens, NGOs, "social partners," or national politicians. Thousands of NGOs, interest groups, think tanks, and citizens wrote in and anyone could read what they had written on the convention website. The official convention members, who then summarized what they had heard, debated the issues, and produced proposals, were delegates from national parliaments, the European Parliament, national governments, and the Commission.

The convention's president was Valéry Giscard d'Estaing, a former president of France. To Giscard, the term *convention* had the French connotation of a constituent assembly to prepare a constitution, something the president underlined with persistent references to Thomas Jefferson, "Philadelphia 1776," and the U.S. constitutional experience. This rhetoric of "constitutionalization" was probably a mistake. The convention's mandate was limited, its results had to satisfy divided member states, and the solemn grandiosity of constitution writing was likely to raise expectations among fervent "Europeans," on the one hand, and alert skeptics that something dangerous was up on the other.

Giscard suggested that the convention should first "listen" to what Europeans had to say, then break into working groups to focus on big issues, and finally prepare recommendations for the 2004 IGC.[2] The convention was an extraordinary moment in European integration. Populated by politicians rather than diplomats, it was public, open, sometimes loud, and a prize location for complicated strategies, plots, and confrontations. A "draft constitutional treaty" appeared in June 2003. Its preamble, composed by Giscard, began by citing Thucydides in the original Greek and then described Europe as "a continent that has brought forth civilization," whose inhabitants "gradually developed the values underlying humanism: equality of persons, freedom, respect for reason." The text continued to note that Europeans desired prosperity, culture, democracy, and peace, and that the EU would be "united in its

diversity" in a "special area of human hope." Although there had been a big push to have the preamble recognize God and Europe's Christian roots by an alliance including the Vatican, the Poles, Bavarian Christian Democrats, and the Christian right, God and Christianity were eventually edited out.

Giscard aspired to produce a document that any intelligent secondary schoolchild could read. Here he definitely failed. Constructing a single treaty to provide a constitutional base for the EU that also consolidated and clarified fifty years of European integration made this an impossible dream. The final "constitutional treaty" was nearly 300 pages long and, in parts, dense and legalistic. Nonetheless, its most significant proposals would have made the EU more intelligible and effective. The new treaty would have subsumed all earlier treaties to become the single legal basis for Union action, necessitating in its Part III a long, complex reworking of fifty years of EU treaty-making. A permanent president of the European Council would be elected for two and a half years and renewable to replace the rotating presidency and ensure greater continuity. There would also be an EU foreign minister, combining the jobs of "Mr. CFSP" and the external affairs Commissioner, who would also be in charge of a new EU diplomatic service. Qualified majority council voting and codecision would become the rule, unanimity the exception, and QMV would be based on a "double majority" (a majority of states, representing 60 percent of population, for passage). The treaty proposed eventually ending "pillars" by subsuming JHA and CFSP under the "Community Method." It also prescribed the—smaller—number of Commissioners and MEPs after enlargement, carefully defined "subsidiarity," provided an "exit clause" for leaving the EU, and established rules for suspending members who violated basic principles. It included an edited version of the Charter of Fundamental Rights from Nice. Finally, it added a very few new policy prerogatives for the EU.

The draft treaty went to a new IGC—of member-state diplomats—in the summer of 2003. There it very nearly died in a dispute over the number of QMV votes to be given to Spain and Poland. The convention had inherited from the Nice Treaty a situation in which in the two countries had QMV voting power only slightly less than the EU's largest states, which meant that together with an additional small country they could form a "blocking minority." The draft treaty proposed to change this, but Spain and Poland refused to allow it, contributing to the failure to agree at the end of 2003. Negotiations continued, however, and when Spanish elections in March 2004, after the Madrid train bombings, elected a more flexible Socialist government, a deal followed in June incorporating almost all of the convention's proposals.[3]

International treaties have to be ratified, and several EU countries (Ireland, Denmark, Ireland, Luxembourg, Portugal, Poland, the Czech Republic, Spain, the United Kingdom, and the Netherlands) were committed to ratifying the new constitutional treaty by referendum. In France the president had a choice between parliamentary and referendum ratification, and Jacques Chirac chose the latter. Thus in the space of a few days in springtime 2005 both the French and the Dutch voted no, plunging the EU into confusion and crisis. The French vote was 55 to 45 percent against, and the Dutch even more decisive at 61.5 to 38.5 percent.

Referendums are blunt political instruments. Voters often don't answer the questions they are directly asked and instead respond to other, often unrelated, concerns. The EU's postreferendum survey of France concluded that the "reasons why people voted 'no' . . . are based chiefly on national and/or social themes which take precedence over European considerations."[4] The Dutch rejection was a bit more EU-centered, involving Dutch fears about losing influence in an enlarged EU, but 21 percent of voters were also worried about the Dutch economic situation, and 65 percent thought, erroneously, that rejection might "allow for a renegotiation of the Constitution in order to place greater emphasis on the more social aspects."[5] The French and the Dutch were unhappy with their lives and their governments and used referendums to say this. Still, debate on the Constitutional Treaty in both countries had been thorough, and made it clear that voters had little affection for the EU.

A Perfect Storm?

The issues were broader, however, and EU leaders had been forewarned about them. Opinion polls had documented growing disenchantment with the EU for some years. Even people favorable to Europe in the abstract were negative about European policies. Many people cared little and were minimally informed, despite the EU's frenzied activities. As already noted, turnout at elections to the European Parliament in June 2004 had been the worst ever. Euro-skeptic lists had flourished in Poland, Slovakia, the Czech Republic, Sweden, the Netherlands, the United Kingdom, and Austria. National campaigns for the EP were confused, the media paid little attention to them, and when ordinary voters actually thought about the EU, rather than national matters, they were often dissatisfied. The EU was facing a perfect storm in which a number of different negative trends combined to produce a serious crisis.

The first trend was economic. Europe had been economically transformed, in part by European integration, and Europeans in general were vastly better off as a result. But tangible payoffs of integration to citizens had been in decline since the 1990s. It would be wrong to claim that the single market, EMU, and other changes had failed, for without them EU members might have had even more problems. Still, there were serious difficulties. Table 35.1 depicts some key economic trends.

These numbers show big relative gains for the United States over the EU. They also show some EU member states doing better than others. Finally, at the time of the referendums, big continental EU countries, the economic core of the EU, were doing worse than most. Economic problems were undoubtedly among the more important factors in the referendum defeats. The French had faced serious growth and unemployment problems for fifteen years prior to 2005, excepting during the 1998–2001 dot-com boom, and they had good reasons to be anxious about job security and social programs. The Dutch had reformed in the 1990s and then done well, but their very open economy, sensitive to trends in its larger continental neighbors, was in a downturn during the referendum year. Since practically everything that the EU had undertaken since the 1980s—the single market, EMU, the Lisbon strategy—had been sold as necessary to help Europe keep up economically, it was easy for the French, Dutch, and others to conclude that the EU had not delivered.

Behind this lay even more difficult problems. According to Barry Eichengreen, an eminent American economist, Europe faced a deep economic dilemma.[6]

Table 35.1

Growth and Unemployment Rates

	GDP Growth percent			Unemployment percent	
	1995–2002	2003–2004	2004–2005	1995	2005
France	2.1	2.3	1.2	11.6	10.0
Germany	1.4	1.6	1.0	8.2	11.2
Italy	1.3	1.1	0.0	7.8	11.7
Netherlands	2.3	1.7	1.1	7.1	5.2
Spain	3.6	3.1	3.4	23.2	9.2
Sweden	2.7	3.7	2.7	9.2	7.8
United Kingdom	2.8	3.1	1.8	8.6	4.6
EU-15	2.2	2.3	1.5	8.3	10.8
United States	**3.3**	**4.2**	**3.2**	**5.6**	**5.2**

Source: OECD in Figures, 2006–2007 edition.

Postwar Europe's rapid growth was based on catching up with American mass production consumer capitalism. But while Europe was succeeding famously at this "extensive development," the American economy turned to "intensive development" based on constant innovation. "Intensive development" requires flexible labor markets, more agile firms, educational systems that produce new human capital and skills, more mobility, less state intervention, and more research and development. Some EU countries were better prepared than others, but problems and resistance built up in continental EU societies. The wide-ranging reforms that were needed would upset established interests and take time. When impetus for such reform comes from the EU, the EU can be blamed for the discomfort that follows.

Globalization was another factor contributing to the EU's stormy weather. Globalization threatens entire European manufacturing product markets, as new competition from developing economies occurs simultaneously with outsourcing by European companies. Globalized financial markets also constrain government policies. European elites have been deeply concerned about globalization for some time, often arguing, "we need to change fast or we will be in deep trouble." When such preaching can be tied to the EU, the EU can easily be seen as a promoter of harsh globalization rather than as something useful to help Europeans survive it. Preaching about threats of globalization

has also been politically confusing because it has come in heated debate between neoliberals for whom the only solution is complete Americanization and others who seek to preserve Europe's social model through reform.

The myths and realities of enlargement made the storm more ferocious. EU and national elites did a poor job of explaining enlargement to citizens, perhaps because enlargement was so urgent and its complexities so numerous. One result has been that enlargement intensified worries about globalization, particularly since CEECs became choice locations for outsourcing by EU-15 companies. Enlargement also intensified widespread concerns about immigration, a free gift to those trafficking in xenophobia. The scarecrow role that the "Polish plumber" played in French referendum debates was emblematic of this. The French and Dutch referendum campaign also came as the EU opened membership talks with Turkey.[7] The prospect of Turkish EU membership stimulated visions of vast numbers of Turks, mostly Islamic, rushing to the richer parts of Europe looking for jobs. A second fear, shared by elites, was that the size of Turkey's population—if admitted it would become the largest EU member state—would make EU institutions even more unworkable than they had become with new CEEC members. The third fear was that the EU might never stop enlarging. Turkey was already beyond the borders of what most people understood to be Europe. Some

Balkan countries like Croatia were already scheduled for membership, and others, once they learned to behave, had claims. What about the Ukraine, Belarus, Moldova, Georgia, Armenia? And why not North Africa? Where did EU Europe end, or, perhaps, would EU Europe end? What would an EU of fifty members look like?

Finally, the constitutional debate underlined chronic problems people had of making sense of how the EU worked. It was common to talk of an EU "democratic deficit," even if it could be argued that EU institutions met reasonable standards for democracy. At its core, the EU was a "community of democracies" in which democratically elected governments of member states cooperated to set agendas and vote on proposals, and then stood accountable to their electorates for results. The EU had a second source of democratic legitimacy in the democratically elected European Parliament. The European Commission, with its power of initiative, was an odd part of the picture, but it, too, was heavily constrained by member state governments. Finally, there were some EU-level institutions that decided important things "undemocratically"—that is, to which power has been delegated with limited checks and balances, as in competition and monetary policy—but it was not unusual to find similar delegations in national democratic governments.[8] Democratic deficit or not, however, the EU had serious legitimacy problems.

Above all, EU institutions had deep problems of "readability." EU citizens were accustomed to the legends, structures, cultures, and politics of home countries, which had first claim on their loyalties and identities. As political science students know, sophisticated citizens who master what goes on in their own democracies are relatively rare, despite intense socialization, powerful media, and long years of practice. Adding another layer of institutions at EU level and quickly expecting the bulk of citizens to understand and identify with them may be overoptimistic. Moreover, EU institutions do not resemble those at national level, as our own struggle through the EU's thicket has shown. The EU is not a state, and, despite federalist hopes, is unlikely to become one. Yet sometimes it does things that states do and shares in doing things that states used to do all by themselves. And whenever the EU does these things, it may also have an indirect impact on areas where citizens still expect their state to be able to act on its own. In addition, the EU does not look like a state. The Commission is mysterious except to the rare few who understand that it was designed a half century ago to prevent any strong member state from running the EU show and to ensure that member states will honor the commitments to cooperate they have made. Citizens know about the Council of Ministers but are given little information about how it does what it does. The Parliament, which travels incessantly between Strasbourg and Brussels at a cost of $300 million annually, doesn't look like a real parliament—there is no government and opposition, its members don't argue for or against a clear program, its decisions are technical, and they seem to come from all over the place. On top of this there is no EU "we the people," but rather twenty-seven different peoples with different histories, cultures, and languages. These things in themselves are bound to place the EU far away from most of its citizens.

In fact, "real" European politics happens largely in national arenas. Except among elites, there exists little European political culture. National parliamentary discussions rarely place European issues squarely before the public. Elections to the European Parliament remain tightly linked to national political debates. With notable exceptions—Denmark, for example, which constitutionally obliges its national parliament to debate European issues weekly and to submit key Euro-level legal matters to national referenda—national parties and interest groups have barely begun to embrace European matters. The gap between the thickness of national democratic deliberative practices and their thinness at the European level is clear, and its consequences are profound.

In Europe, as elsewhere, the nature of national democracy has also been changing rapidly, adding new uncertainty to the EU's perfect storm. Economic shifts, changes in citizen preferences, the shape of social structures and social problems, new technologies for doing politics, the reconfiguration of political parties, the scope of markets, the increased role of lobbies, and a host of other factors have made national democratic political lives themselves less "readable." Citizen expectations of government developed for an earlier era are now less realistic, politicians have more difficulty responding to citizens, and, in turn, citizens have less trust in politicians.

The EU bears only a small responsibility for this, but it receives a large part of the blame. In part, this is because national politicians have learned to play the EU for their own domestic gains. National governments are the real center of EU decisions. Their leaders eagerly claim credit for such decisions when the results help get more national support. They are just as likely to blame the EU when the opposite is true. This is enhanced by the fact that there are no real "European" media. Virtually everything about the EU is interpreted by national newspapers and audiovisual networks focusing on national audiences and national concerns. The EU, in addition, is a convenient place to make decisions of longer-term importance—big reforms like EMU, for example—that could not be made nationally given the shorter time horizons that govern national political arenas, in which politicians must always keep their eyes on impending elections. Euro-politics has thus become a prized way for politicians to circumvent the blockages and veto points of national politics. The largest EU achievements since the 1980s—the single market, EMU, and enlargement to the CEECs—fall into this category. When the costs and consequences of such EU decisions later hit home, often after the politicians who made them have left power, EU Europe is left to blame.

Futures?

Perfect storms can give way to calm, sunny weather, but they may cause massive damage nonetheless. The EU's institutional crisis caused by failure to ratify the Constitutional Treaty has been hard to overcome. After a long period for reflection, the 2007 German presidency under Chancellor Angela Merkel proposed changing the text to make it shorter, clearer, and less ambitious. The result was a new draft which included most specific components of the Constitutional Treaty—the European Council President, a "High Representative" for foreign affairs, double majority voting in the Council of Ministers and a reduction in the number of Commissioners from twenty-seven to eighteen to begin in 2014, more codecision, to a Charter of Fundamental Rights (with the UK opting-out of its constraints)—but which abandoned constitutional pretensions and amended the 2001 Nice Treaty. The

hope was that quick intergovernmental negotiations would allow the new "reform treaty" to be ratified in time for the 2009 elections to the European Parliament. The result of these negotiations might then have to face referendums in some countries, with some prospects for failure, but the French, Dutch, English, and others clearly hoped to avoid this. There has also been a tentative economic upturn on the continent, but no one knows whether it will be strong enough to allay anxieties about unemployment. Moreover, EU Europe's transition to "intensive" economic development is fraught with difficulties that may take years to resolve. In the meantime the effects of globalization on EU Europe show few signs of slowing. The EU and its citizens may need years to digest enlargement to the CEECs, while the uncertain prospect of new enlargements will weigh heavily. Finally, fifty years have created quasi-permanent EU institutions, and for a long time to come EU citizens will have difficulty "reading" and identifying them. The EU may be stuck in a mid-life crisis.

Like many fifty-year-olds, however, the EU is also in the prime of life.[9] EU Europe has garnered a vast number of new responsibilities in recent decades, and its machinery is working well, by and large. The single market is a constant struggle, as are all such single markets, but it is moving forward and having positive effects for European economic efficiency. Debate continues to swirl around the policies of the European Central Bank, but the technical success of EMU and the euro have been remarkable, both are now irreversible, and the euro now accounts for 25 percent of global currency reserves. The biggest enlargement in EU history, despite creaking and groaning, is a triumph and a huge victory for democracy. The EU will acquire more members—from Balkan CEECs in particular—in years to come. Freedom of movement within the EU has taken off, and Europeans are beginning to know other Europeans much better. "Justice and Home Affairs," an important policy grab-bag to track and regulate this mobility, is moving forward. EU member states, in particular the big ones, may remain divided about "high" foreign policy issues, as Iraq has demonstrated, but the EU has nonetheless learned to do many things internationally and plays an active and indispensable global role. EU institutions may often be misunderstood, and are much too slow-footed, but they continue to produce results. The constitutional treaty crisis has brought home, even to EU idealists, that the EU is not a federal state in becoming, but rather a unique form of interstate cooperation to be understood and cherished as such, and this clarity may eventually calm spirits. Above all, the cooperation that began on a very limited scale five decades ago is now so extensive that few dimensions of European life are not touched by it. It is also evident that there is no way to reverse it since the costs of turning back now vastly outweigh any conceivable benefits.

The most important question concerns how much further the EU will go, and it is unanswerable. Imagine, however, a European Union that is able to make the transition to "intensive development" successfully and to forge forward with new economic growth based on knowledge, research, and renewed human capital. And then think of a Europe that has also found ways to reform its social model so that it can continue to limit inequality, educate children and adults to maximize their talents and opportunities, redesign solidarity among citizens to share the risks of child poverty, job loss, illness, and old age, while providing a full range of high quality public goods and services. Imagine again an EU that has faced climate change and energy shortages successfully and, in the process, has led the rest of the globe in the same direction. Reflect on an EU that has learned to play on a multipolar world stage not as a military superpower, but to limit conflict, engage wisely in innovative peace making, help troubled areas establish order, invest intelligently in developing areas to help end extreme poverty, and engage in effective humanitarian intervention. These things, and others, may not happen. But the very fact that they are plausible speaks eloquently to the EU's achievements, mid-life crisis and all.

Notes

[1]I have drawn on Peter Norman's narrative of the convention, *The Accidental Constitution* (Brussels: Eurocomment, 2003), for much of what follows. For the best book on the place of the convention and constitutional treaty in EU history, see Jean-Claude Piris, *The Constitution for Europe: A Legal Analysis* (Cambridge: Cambridge University Press, 2006).

[2]At this point, when real choices were in the offing, a number of foreign ministers joined the convention to make sure that governmental desires were heard clearly.

[3]The key was a compromise on QMV. The convention had proposed a dual majority system set at 50 percent of member states, representing 60 percent of the population. The final deal became 55–65. Since this implied that France, Germany, and the United Kingdom, were they to agree, would constitute a blocking minority (by virtue of their combined population), a new requirement was added that at least four countries had to agree to block. The Spanish and Polish gave up their Nice advantages in exchange for a procedure that granted a group of countries representing three-quarters of a blocking minority the ability to delay a decision in the hope that a broader consensus might be achieved. The convention's proposal on the Commission was also changed. The current composition of the Commission of one member per member state would continue until 2014, after which the size of the Commission would drop to a number equivalent to two-thirds of member states, chosen by a system of equal rotation. The United Kingdom maintained redlines against QMV in taxation, social policy, and CFSP, while the introduction of QMV for the Union's budget packages was postponed.

[4]Flash Eurobarometer, *The European Constitution: Post-Referendum Survey in France* (Brussels: European Commission, June 2005), p. 17.

[5]Flash Eurobarometer, *The European Constitution: Post-Referendum Survey in the Netherlands* (Brussels: European Commission, June 2005).

[6]Barry Eichengreen, *The European Economy Since 1945* (Princeton: Princeton University Press, 2007).

[7]Turkey applied for EU membership in the 1960s, but nothing much happened until it was declared an "official candidate" for membership in 1999, largely out of foreign policy concerns. The European Council in December 2004 then set a date in the fall of 2005 for the opening of official negotiations, which everyone anticipated would take a very long time.

[8]For one argument see Andrew Moravscik "In Defence of the 'Democratic Deficit': Reassessing Legitimacy in the European Union," *Journal of Common Market Studies* 40, no. 4 (2002).

[9]See "Fit at 50? A Special Report on the European Union," *The Economist*, March 17, 2007.

Part 8 Bibliography

Borchardt, Klaus-Dieter. *The ABC of Community Law*. Luxembourg: European Commission, 2000.

Craig, Paul, and Grainne de Burca. *EU Law: Text, Cases, and Material*, 3rd ed. Oxford: Oxford University Press, 2002.

De Grauwe, Paul. *Economics of Monetary Union*, 5th ed. Oxford: Oxford University Press, 2007.

Delors, Jacques. *Mémoires*. Paris: Plon, 2004.

Dinan, Desmond. *Ever Closer Union*, 3rd ed. Boulder: Lynne Rienner, 2005.

Eichengreen, Barry. *The European Economy Since 1945*. Princeton: Princeton University Press, 2007.

Getz, Klaus, and Simon Hix, eds. *Europeanised Politics: European Integration and National Political Systems*. London: Frank Cass, 2001.

Hix, Simon. *The Political System of the European Union*, 2nd ed. Basingstoke, England: Macmillan, 2005.

Judge, David, and David Earnshaw. *The European Parliament*. London: Palgrave-Macmillan, 2003.

Kagan, Robert. *Of Paradise and Power: America and Europe in the New World Order*. New York: Knopf, 2003.

Lamy, Pascal, and Jean Pisani-Ferry. *The Europe We Want*. London: Arch Press, 2002.

Magnette, Paul. *What Is the European Union?* Basingstoke: Macmillan-Palgrave, 2005.

Martin, Andrew, and George Ross, eds. *Euros and Europeans: EMU and the European Model of Society*. Cambridge: Cambridge University Press, 2004.

Moravcsik, Andrew. *The Choice for Europe: Social Purpose and State Power from Messina to Maastricht*. Ithaca, N.Y.: Cornell University Press, 1998.

Neal, Larry. *The Economics of the European Union and the Economics of Europe*. New York: Cambridge University Press, 2007.

Norman, Peter. *The Accidental Constitution: The Story of the European Convention*. Brussels: Eurocomment, 2003.

Patten, Chris. *Not Quite the Diplomat*. London: Penguin, 2005.

Piris, Jean-Claude. *The Constitution for Europe: A Legal Analysis*. Cambridge: Cambridge University Press, 2006.

Rosamond, Ben. *Theories of European Integration*. Basingstoke: Palgrave, 2000.

Ross, George. *Jacques Delors and European Integration*. Cambridge, England: Polity, 1995.

Scharpf, Fritz. *Governing in Europe: Effective and Democratic*. Oxford: Oxford University Press, 1999.

Schimmelfenig, Frank. *The EU, NATO, and the Integration of Europe*. Cambridge: Cambridge University Press, 2003.

Tsoukalis, Loukas. *What Kind of Europe?* Oxford: Oxford University Press, 2003.

Wallace, Helen, William Wallace, and Mark Pollack. *Policymaking in the European Union*, 5th ed. New York: Oxford University Press, 2005.

Weiler, J. H. H. *The Constitution of Europe*. Cambridge: Cambridge University Press, 1999.

Journals

Agence Europe

Economist

European Union Politics

European Voice

EUSA Newsletter

Financial Times

Journal of Common Market Studies

Journal of European Integration

West European Politics

Websites

Delegation of the European Commission to the USA: **www.eurunion.org**

European Union, official site: **www.europa.eu**

European Union Studies Association (EUSA): **www.eustudies.org**

Think Tanks

Centre for European Policy Studies (Brussels): **www.ceps.be**

Centre for European Reform (London): **www.cer.org.uk**

The Federal Trust (London): **www.fedtrust.co.uk**

Institut d'Études Européennes de l'Université Libre de Bruxelles (Brussels); includes many documents in English: **www.ulb.ac.be/facs/iee**

Max Planck Institute for the Study of Societies (Germany): **www.mpi-fg-koeln.mpg.de**

Notre Europe (Paris); includes many documents in English: **www.notre-europe.eu/en/**

PART 9

EU Europe: Variations on a Theme

Mark Kesselman

Joel Krieger

Conclusion

The title of this book—*European Politics in Transition*—was chosen when the first edition was published. Each time we revise it, we question whether the time has come to change the book's title. After all, how long can a transition last? But each time we have decided that the extent and importance of current changes warrant retaining the title. This edition is no exception. Indeed, the few years since the publication of the last edition have been chock-full of important developments whose cumulative importance more than justifies the word "transition."

As the country sections have analyzed, every country included in *European Politics in Transition* has experienced important developments in the past several years. When we take a step back from describing individual countries in this Conclusion and view Europe from a comparative perspective, we can discern three critical junctures in the recent past. Although one cannot assign precise dates to when the junctures began—and none of the three has ended—their importance amply justifies the claim that European politics has been experiencing an extraordinarily significant transition. We analyze the three junctures by reference to a question related to each one.

Where (and When) Will Europe End?

The question posed in this subsection involves four issues: geographic, cultural, political, and temporal. The first issue relates to the definition of Europe's geographic boundaries. It has become so important recently because it concerns the hot-button topic of Turkey's eligibility for membership in the European Union (EU). Whether Turkey qualifies to become a member in part hinges on the judgment of the present member states whether Turkey is European. And this in turn depends on demarcating the geographic boundaries of Europe. (As we shall see below, the judgment also depends on defining what it *means* to be European.)

For many years after World War II, the cold war complicated any answers to the question of Europe's boundaries because there were in effect two Europes, separated by what British prime minister Winston Churchill called, at the very outset of the cold war in 1947 (soon after he left office), an iron curtain. Churchill meant that there was a firm border that separated the Soviet Union and its allies in East-Central Europe from the industrialized democracies of Western Europe. The border was always to some extent artificial and even misleading. As the chapter on East-Central Europe points out, Prague, the capital of communist Czechoslovakia (presumably, therefore, in Eastern Europe), was further west than Vienna, the capital of Austria, in "Western" Europe. But, however arbitrary the geographic boundary, the iron curtain deeply divided Europe into two for over four decades.

Within Western Europe, as described in the section on the European Union (EU), an increasing number of countries became more and more closely integrated in the European Union. If the question had been asked in 1989, "where does (Western) Europe end?" the answer would have been quite clear: at the old cold war borders separating Germany from Poland and the Czech Republic or Austria from Hungary or Italy from Slovenia—the frontiers of the easternmost countries bordering the Soviet bloc.

However, 1989 was the year that the two Europes moved closer together. As the section on East-Central Europe describes, in 1989 the Velvet Revolution in Czechoslovakia, the victory of the Solidarity Movement in Poland, and the crumbling of the Berlin Wall in the German Democratic Republic all contributed to making the iron curtain history. These developments also laid the groundwork for enlarging the EU to twenty-seven members in 2007. Transition indeed.

Europe has thus come a long way since World War II. But, to repeat our earlier question, where does it end? Are there fixed geographic borders that are cast in stone marking the edge of the European continent and therefore the geographic limit to the EU? Good question—to which dramatically different answers have been given!

Turkey's application for membership in the EU has provoked the debate. We will devote some attention to the issue of Turkish membership in the Conclusion because it highlights several fascinating and important dimensions of where Europe ends.

A simple answer to the question of where Europe ends—but an answer that only begins the conversation—is that Turkey is at the same time both European and non-European, since it is located in Europe and Asia.

The European portion of Turkey ends at Istanbul, the Bosporus Strait (also known as the Istanbul Strait) that connects Europe and Asia. The Asian portion of Turkey begins at this point. Is Turkey primarily European—and, therefore, potentially eligible for membership in the EU? And if it is, what are the potential implications for EU membership of Russia: that immensely more powerful country that straddles the European/Asian divide?

Whether Turkey is "really" European depends only partly on geography. Indeed, for many passionate participants on both sides of the debate, the geographic issue is of secondary importance. What really counts for them is the second meaning of the question of where Europe ends: what makes up Europe's cultural and ideological identity?

This issue is theoretical, not geographic. It can be rephrased as: "what does a country have to do to be European?" Is Turkey European in this cultural sense? Even less than the issue of geographic boundaries, the meaning of European identity is not self-evident. Many conservative participants claim that the core of European identity is its Christian heritage. There is plausible empirical evidence in defense of this claim. The vast majority of European citizens are of Christian background. But there are powerful objections to the claim that Christianity lies at the core of European identity. First, although exact figures are hard to come by and vary a lot by country, a significant proportion of Europeans are *not* Christian: they are Muslim, Jewish, Hindu, and atheist. Further, many self-identified Christians in Europe do not regard their Christian affiliation as the most important element of their identity. This would certainly include the very large number of Christians who are not religiously observant. (Indeed, only a minority of Christians in Europe attend church regularly, defined as two or more times a month.) Finally, most countries in the EU proclaim the importance of secularism, that is, maintaining a separation of church and state, and thus not defining national identity on the basis of religion. Since most countries reject making religion of any kind a key element in defining the national political community, why should matters be different at the EU level?

During the convention that negotiated a draft treaty for a European Constitution, there was heated debate about whether the preamble should refer to Europe as sharing a Christian heritage. It was prudently decided not to do so.

And yet there is no denying that Turkey's accession to membership in the EU would in practice involve a substantial challenge to Europe's identity. Turkey would be the first EU member in which the overwhelming majority of citizens are Muslim. Although Turkey has a secular constitution, this fact does not offset the fact that, at one stroke, 70 million Muslims would be added to the EU's 300 million citizens. It might be noted that EU enlargement to include Turkey might prove very beneficial by making for a more culturally diverse and rich EU. If the EU could emerge more unified from the challenge, this might well help the EU's member states deal with their own challenges of political identity that have been provoked by the increasing scale of Muslim populations in European countries.

Turkey's application for membership raised another significant issue regarding the meaning of European identity: its relation to democracy. The EU takes great pride in being a bastion of democracy. A key requirement for countries applying for EU membership is that they demonstrate a high level of democratic practice. Yet as we will see in surveying the third critical juncture, the precise extent and meaning of democracy is in flux. Turkey's application starkly highlighted this issue. Turkey is a functioning democracy. Ever since a military regime was replaced in 1983 by a civilian regime, Turkey has been a parliamentary democracy with a system of competitive parties and honest elections. However, the Turkish government has also gravely violated democratic procedures and human rights in some key respects. For example, it has tortured and murdered militant members of the Kurdish minority community. It has prosecuted writers and intellectuals who have defended the Kurds and criticized the government. And the government has refused to accept responsibility for genocide against Armenians after World War I despite the fact that responsible international commissions and historians have provided irrefutable evidence that the Turkish army massacred one million Armenians. Yet it is a crime in Turkey even to make this allegation.

That Turkish democracy is imperfect is beyond question. But defenders of Turkey's application for EU membership contend that opposing Turkey's application for membership on these grounds is a smokescreen. They charge that what really motivates opponents is not a high regard for democracy but a low regard for Islam. That is, they claim that the reason opponents consider Turkey to be insufficiently European is not because of its democratic failings but because of its Muslim identity.

In addition to issues involving the geographic and cultural boundaries of Europe, a third—political—issue is related to the question of where Europe ends. This involves the desirable jurisdiction, design, and powers of EU institutions, that is, the question of the appropriate political architecture of the EU. It was this question that stymied ratification of the draft EU constitution in 2005. The stalemate reached over the draft European Constitution provides abundant evidence that there is no end to the debate over where EU political institutions and power should end, as well as the desirable balance between the powers of EU and national political institutions. In 2007, European heads of state agreed on reviving momentum for European integration by negotiating a scaled-back draft treaty. If implemented, the treaty will reduce the bickering over voting rights and promote a more robust EU. But it will certainly not end the debate about where the powers of organized Europe, that is, the EU, should end.

The controversy over Turkish membership, as well as the debate on the EU draft constitution, point to a fourth meaning of the question of where Europe will end: a temporal dimension. When (if ever) will the struggle end to define Europe's geographic borders, cultural identity, and political organization? Judging from the entire history of the EU, there is a simple answer to this question: not in the foreseeable future! Nor is this surprising. As we have seen, the struggle to define Europe involves the most far-reaching questions about European cultural and political life. Struggles around these questions are never fully resolved, not even in the apparently most stable countries (recall the discussion in the British section about the relationship of the geographic entities that comprise the United Kingdom). Little wonder that the transition in European politics will go on for some time!

Nor is the question of where Europe ends the only critical juncture in present-day Europe.

What Is the Meaning and Future of the Third Way?

Several country sections of this book have described how Western Europe experienced a golden era of economic growth and rising standards of living for several decades following the Second World War. (The focus in this discussion is on Western Europe.) This enviable situation resulted from a confluence of many factors: energies were focused on rebuilding Europe's war-torn economies and meeting pent-up demand that had been throttled during World War II. Europe was the beneficiary of Marshall Plan assistance and U.S. military protection. Europe further benefited from adopting technological advances developed in the United States. In many countries, a political alliance of modernizing business groups and labor unions further contributed to the growth spurt.

The political center of gravity in the postwar years was on the center-left. Socialist or social democratic parties were the natural vehicles for organizing a political alliance that not only sought economic growth but did so by relying on extensive state intervention. (Although France was ruled by a variety of political coalitions in the Fourth Republic, which does not conform to the political recipe just mentioned, the planning apparatus described in the French country section was a prototype of state direction.) Social democratic parties were the natural vehicles for managing West Europe's economies at this time for another reason as well. They had a natural affinity for using Keynesian economics to shape economic policy. Why? Because a pillar of Keynesian economics was the principle that growth could be promoted by a generous measure of economic redistribution toward the less affluent, which could be accomplished by state social spending and progressive taxation. Center-right parties, including the Conservative Party in Britain, the Gaullist party in France, and the Christian Democratic parties of Germany and Italy, joined this consensus during the golden era. But the center-left parties were the innovators. (The real trail-blazers were the social democratic parties of the Scandinavian countries—Sweden, Denmark, and Norway.)

The slowdown in economic growth beginning in the 1970s left all political coalitions in disarray. For several years, the old Keynesian formulae were applied

What Is the Meaning and Future of the Third Way?

What Is the Meaning and Future of the Third Way? **539**

in a situation for which they were not appropriate. The result was only to compound the disease. ("Stagflation" was the term coined at the time to describe the situation combining the worst of both worlds of stagnation and inflation.)

Into this world in disarray strode the Iron Lady, British prime minister Margaret Thatcher, in 1979. (She was soon joined by her good friend across the Atlantic, Ronald Reagan.) Thatcher proposed a simple solution to deal with the dismal situation of British (and, by extension, Western European) economic problems: FREE THE MARKETS! As the British section has described, she set about with great determination and ultimate success to attack the obstacles to the free functioning of commodity, financial, and labor markets. The attack involved monetarist economic policy, privatization of state assets, pruning social programs, a frontal assault on the power of organized labor, and a slash-and-burn approach to the layers of state regulation that had developed during the golden era of state intervention. In brief, Thatcher's social and economic policies represented a giant pendulum swing away from Keynesianism.

Across the English Channel, Thatcher's approach was watched with a mixture of scorn and admiration. Scorn because of the pain that it inflicted on British citizens, especially the less fortunate. Grudging admiration for her bold new approach, especially when it began to bear fruit when economic growth revived in Britain in the 1980s.

However, West European governments began to emulate Britain's economic orientation in earnest only after 1997, when Tony Blair and Gordon Brown successfully reshaped Thatcher's economic policies in a more humane fashion through their New Labour policies. As described in the British section, the Third Way both enthusiastically embraces market forces and sponsors vigorous policy interventions designed to enable markets to work their magic. The policies involve pain for those who are now forced to rely on their own efforts to get ahead rather than being dependent on what was disdainfully called the "nanny state," as in the past. But the Third Way of New Labour differs in important respects from Thatcher's single-minded neoliberal approach, in which job seekers were left to sink or swim on their own. It should be emphasized that it differs significantly as well from Old Labour,

that is, the traditional social democratic approach pursued in Britain and many West European countries that relied on the state both to steer the economy and to provide for citizens' welfare. New Labour programs include job training and comprehensive programs to reduce social exclusion to assist those making the difficult transition from welfare to work—and to spur innovation and enhanced competitiveness.

The Third Way thus claims to synthesize the best of market efficiency and social equity. For the past decade, it has been the clear-cut winner on the menu of economic policy orientations available in West Europe. The best evidence of its success was that Britain soared from the bottom of the West European economic growth league tables in the 1980s to the top in the first decade of the twenty-first century. As the social analyst Ralf Dahrendorf noted, in a remark quoted in the Introduction, the result has been that "the Third Way debate has become the only game in town—the only hint at new directions for Europe's politics in a confused multitude of trends and ideas."[1]

There are two important indications of the Third Way's influence outside Britain. First, a new crop of political leaders has taken office in recent years whose economic approach mirrored that of Tony Blair and Gordon Brown. They include Angela Merkel in Germany, Romani Prodi in Italy, and Nicolas Sarkozy in France. Their economic programs were not identical to that of Blair and Brown, partly because the configuration of economic and political forces in their respective countries is different. However, for the Third Way to be the only game in town, it is not essential that the precisely identical program be applied everywhere. Just as with Keynesianism, variations on a central theme are not only possible but essential if the program is to be effective in the specific context of each country. In thinking about the economic orientation of governments described in the country studies of this book, we invite students to consider the degree to which the Third Way has become the name of the game of economic governance in Europe.

The second evidence of Third Way success is at the EU level. To a considerable extent, the EU's economic policy direction has been more influenced by the Third Way than by other any economic model. The EU has increasingly developed market-friendly policies in the sphere of economic regulation at the same time that it has taken halting steps toward policy interventions in the social sphere, such as to promote gender equality. The Lisbon strategy, implemented by the EU in 2001—and still a focus of its economic and social strategy—has Third Way stamped all over it. In emphasizing the need for reduced government regulation and investment in people and education to spur innovation and competitiveness and combat social exclusion, it is a classic statement of Third Way policymaking.

The Third Way has helped propel Britain back to the ranks of a world-class economy. And Europe has also reversed a period of decline in the competition among regions of the world.

At the same time, the Third Way is not without flaws. In every country that has applied the Third Way model in the past decade, economic inequalities have increased. Third Way policies offer a helping hand to the less educated in their quest to adapt to stern labor market demands. But the help provided may not be adequate for them to meet the challenge. Perhaps, given the competition spurred by globalization, inequalities would increase in any event, and many would fall further behind as the global economy accelerates. Yet redistribution to promote economic equality, a goal high on the agenda of the center-left in the postwar period, is nowhere in evidence nowadays. Further, privatization does not necessarily improve the quality or reduce the price of services that were previously offered by the state. It remains an open question to what extent the Third Way model has increased the quality of life of citizens living in societies where the model has been implemented.

A final question is the future of the Third Way. An answer heavily depends on whether it will continue to promote economic growth in Britain and the EU. And there is no way to predict the outcome. In today's globalized world, if there is one constant, it is that nothing is constant! Note, for example, the enormous gains of some recent newcomers, notably China and India, who are crowding European companies out of European and global markets.

Rather than attempt to predict the future trajectory of the Third Way, which will heavily depend on how the economies of the European countries and the EU fare, it is preferable to analyze further implications of the two critical junctures we have already analyzed.

How will they shape a third critical juncture: the extent and character of democracy in Europe?

What Is the Extent and Meaning of Democracy in Europe?

The third critical juncture that contributes to the transition occurring in European politics concerns the extent and meaning of democracy. By extent, we mean, as we did in the discussion above of where Europe ends, both the geographic extent and substantive content of democracy. In the relatively short time since the 1990s, the geographic reach of democracy in Europe has considerably increased. Virtually every East-Central European country formerly under Soviet domination, as well as Russia itself, has undergone varying forms of democratic transitions and has thereby made a substantial contribution to what the political scientist Samuel Huntington called the third (and latest) wave of democratization in the world.[2]

It is indisputable, then, that there has been an enormous geographic extension of democracy—a *quantitative* increase in democracy. Has the greater extent of democracy been matched by an increase in the *quality* of democracy? On this score, the consensus crumbles.

One can point to two pieces of evidence on the affirmative side. First, some progress has been made in reducing the democratic deficit of the EU. Granted, the size of the deficit was enormous and remains far too large (as will be discussed below). But, as the EU section described, the elected body of the EU, the EU Parliament, has gained significant power of initiative, control, and codecision in recent years. Further, member-state parliaments have gained the right to be consulted about EU directives. It is probable that additional measures, for example, the possibility for citizens to sponsor initiatives that might become the focus of EU regulations, may further extend the participatory and representative aspects of EU decision making.

Within the countries surveyed in this book, there is also strong evidence that the quality of democracy is high. In many countries, democratic elections have permitted citizens to "throw the rascals out" and elect alternative coalitions to power. Courts have functioned not only to sanction private citizens who violate laws but to hold corrupt politicians to account. Parliaments in some states have enacted reforms to narrow the gender gap and increase the political representation of women. Social movements have organized to press demands that they judge are not being adequately expressed in parliament and heard by their government. In brief, judged by the check list of procedures to define democracy that was enumerated in the Introduction, democracy in Europe is generally alive and well.

And yet . . . is all for the best in the best of all possible worlds?—to paraphrase the words of Voltaire and Leibniz, which are often invoked as a warning to guard against undue complacency! To begin with, the case for skepticism about the direction of European democracy, the democratic deficit of the EU, continues to be all too present. For most European citizens, the EU is a quite opaque, distant set of institutions. It may be inevitable, in an association numbering 300 million citizens, that citizens cannot participate directly and feel closely connected to governing institutions. Whether inevitable or not, that is the present situation in Europe—and an important reason for the French and Dutch no votes in 2005.

The same argument has been used to explain why citizens in many European countries (and beyond) are discontented with their governments, as reflected in high rates of abstentions in elections, electoral swings, frequent political alternation, and public opinion polls that document citizens' low regard for their political leaders. (Things are far worse in Russia, where under the presidency of Vladimir Putin there was a strong tendency toward governmental abuse of power.)

A frequently heard claim is that the possibility for democracy is limited because political issues are complex and governments are inevitably far removed from citizens in countries with sizeable populations. This assertion amounts to an indirect defense of the democratic deficit and we believe that the argument is deeply flawed. If EU institutions are distant and opaque, and if national political institutions often are too, this is partly a matter of choice, not necessity. It reflects a failure to establish mechanisms in which citizens could participate more fully to formulate and debate EU policy options. Often, EU and national government officials act as if they considered that democracy is too important to be entrusted to the people!

And this leads to a more demanding standard to judge European democracy, one that goes beyond the requirement that governments respect democratic procedures. It sets the bar higher by evaluating the *outcome* of these procedures. We cannot do justice here to this immensely interesting and important issue. Once again, we invite students to consider the question. One way to start is to compile a list of what you consider the most important issues that should be addressed by policy makers. It might include unemployment, adequate and affordable medical care, environmental protection, confronting climate change, equality, the quality of urban and rural life, rising standards of living—to name a few. Next, assess the extent to which existing governments (at the national and EU level) have confronted and been effective in addressing the issues. When you complete the exercise, you will probably decide that the glass is neither completely full nor completely empty. But is the level closer to the top or the bottom, and why?

Final Thoughts

Any one of the critical junctures described above would warrant retaining "transition" in the title of this book. Taken together, these three junctures comprise among the most momentous changes that have occurred in European politics since the end of World War II. Where, then, is the present transition in European politics headed? An anecdote from another time and place can sharpen the question.

The debates held at the Constitutional Convention in Philadelphia in 1787 that was convened to write a Constitution for the new republic were secret. However, the delegate James Madison took detailed notes of what was said. He records that, during the months in which the debates took place, delegates continually wondered what one member thought who did not actively participate in the Convention: the elderly and revered figure Benjamin Franklin. On the last day of the proceedings, after the Convention had reached agreement on the text of the new Constitution, Franklin asked to be recognized. All eyes were riveted on him. Franklin observed that, during the debates, he often noticed, carved into the back of the chair used by George Washington, the presiding officer of the Convention, a sun low on the horizon. Franklin confessed to his fellow delegates that he frequently wondered during the passionate debates whether the sun was rising or falling. Now that the Convention had reached agreement on the new Constitution, Franklin reported with satisfaction his complete confidence that the sun in question (symbolic, of course, of the newly created Union) was a *rising* sun.[3]

We wish that we could be as confident about Europe's future, both the future of individual countries and the future of the EU, as Franklin was about the future of the United States. What we can report is that Europe has extraordinary resources to meet the challenges of today's infinitely complicated, daunting— and sometimes exhilarating—world. May it use them wisely!

Notes

[1] Ralf Dahrendorf, "The Third Way and Liberty: An Authoritarian Streak in Europe's New Center," *Foreign Affairs* 78, no. 5 (September–October 1999): 13.

[2] Samuel P. Huntington, *The Third Wave of Democracy: Democratization in the Late Twentieth Century* (Tulsa: University of Oklahoma Press, 1991).

[3] U.S. Congressional Records, Max Farrand, *The Records of the Federal Convention of 1787,* vol. 2, debate of September 17, 1787, accessed at http://memory.loc.gov/ammem/amlaw/lwfr.html, on November 9, 2007.

INDEX